THE
NORTON
SAMPLER

EIGHTH EDITION

ALSO BY THOMAS COOLEY

❖

Back to the Lake:
A Reader for Writers

The Norton Guide to Writing

Adventures of Huckleberry Finn,
A Norton Critical Edition

The Ivory Leg in the Ebony Cabinet:
Madness, Race, and Gender in Victorian America

Educated Lives:
The Rise of Modern Autobiography in America

THE
NORTON
SAMPLER

Short Essays for Composition

EIGHTH EDITION

THOMAS COOLEY

THE OHIO STATE UNIVERSITY

W. W. NORTON & COMPANY
New York ❖ *London*

W. W. Norton & Company has been independent since its founding in 1923, when William Warder Norton and Mary D. Herter Norton first published lectures delivered at the People's Institute, the adult education division of New York City's Cooper Union. The firm soon expanded its program beyond the Institute, publishing books by celebrated academics from America and abroad. By mid-century, the two major pillars of Norton's publishing program—trade books and college texts—were firmly established. In the 1950s, the Norton family transferred control of the company to its employees, and today—with a staff of four hundred and a comparable number of trade, college, and professional titles published each year—W. W. Norton & Company stands as the largest and oldest publishing house owned wholly by its employees.

Editor: Marilyn Moller
Associate Editor: Elizabeth Mullaney
Managing Editor, College: Marian Johnson
Project Editor: Melissa Atkin
Electronic Media Editor: Cliff Landesman
Editorial Assistant: Tenyia Lee
Marketing Manager: Lib Triplett
Production Manager: Ashley Polikoff
Photo Editor: Nelson Colón
Permissions Manager: Megan Jackson
Permissions Clearing: Bethany Salminen
Design Director: Rubina Yeh
Designer: JoAnn Metsch
Composition: Westchester
Manufacturing: R. R. Donnelley

Library of Congress Cataloging-in-Publication Data.
978-0-393-91946-2 (pbk.)

W. W. Norton & Company, Inc., 500 Fifth Avenue, New York, NY 10110-0017
wwnorton.com

W. W. Norton & Company Ltd., Castle House, 75/76 Wells Street, London W1T 3QT
1 2 3 4 5 6 7 8 9 0

CONTENTS

THEMATIC CONTENTS **XVII**

PREFACE **XXVII**

CHAPTER 1: READING AS A WRITER 1

. . . .

Two Essays on Writing: Annie Dillard and the Moth

Annie Dillard ❖ **From** *Holy the Firm* **3**

How many of you, I asked the people in my class, which of you want to give your lives and be writers?

Annie Dillard ❖ **How I Wrote the Moth Essay—and Why** **8**

I realized that the burning moth was a dandy visual focus for all my recent thoughts about an empty, dedicated life. Perhaps I'd try to write a short narrative about it.

Identifying Common Patterns / How Annie Dillard Uses Common Patterns / Learning from the Essays in this Book / Some Strategies for Reading

CHAPTER 2: THE WRITING PROCESS 24

. . . .

Planning / Generating Ideas / Organizing and Drafting / Revising / Editing and Proofreading

CHAPTER 3: WRITING PARAGRAPHS 42

. . . .

Supporting the Main Point / Developing Paragraphs / Introductory Paragraphs / Concluding Paragraphs

CHAPTER 4: DESCRIPTION 59

A BRIEF GUIDE TO WRITING A DESCRIPTION 63

Everyday Description / A Missing Cat Flyer 71

*Grace Welte ❖ **Bracken County, Northern Kentucky** 72

With each turn of the wheel, there is a hollow metal clink . . . clink . . . clink, all in harmony with the wheel and married perfectly to the speed of the tractor.

Paul Crenshaw ❖ **Storm Country** 79

Sometimes it will stop raining when the funnel falls. Sometimes the wind stops and the trees go still and the air settles on you as everything goes quiet.

Brian Doyle ❖ **Joyas Voladoras** 85

Each one visits a thousand flowers a day. They can dive at sixty miles an hour. They can fly backward. They can fly more than five hundred miles without pausing to rest. But when they rest they come close to death. . . .

Cherokee Paul McDonald ❖ **A View from the Bridge** 90

"He's mostly silver, but the silver is somehow made up of *all* the colors, if you know what I mean." I stopped. "Do you know what I mean by colors?"

Alice Steinbach ❖ **The Miss Dennis School of Writing** 96

Miss Dennis always wore a variation of one outfit—a dark-colored, flared woolen skirt, a tailored white blouse and a cardigan sweater, usually black, thrown over her shoulders and held together by a little pearl chain.

　　Can you see her? I can. And the image of her makes me smile. Still.

Ann Hodgman ❖ **No Wonder They Call Me a Bitch** 106

As alarming as the Gaines-burgers were, their soy meal began to seem like an old friend when the time came to try some *canned* dog foods.

E. B. White ❖ **Once More to the Lake** 114

I felt the same damp moss covering the worms in the bait can, and saw the dragonfly alight on the tip of my rod. . . . It was the arrival of this fly that convinced me beyond any doubt that everything was as it had always been, that the years were a mirage and that there had been no years.

*Annotated Example

CHAPTER 5: NARRATIVE   123

. . . .

A BRIEF GUIDE TO WRITING A NARRATIVE   126

Everyday Narrative / A Book Cover   134

*Carrie Barker ❖ **But Two Negatives Equal a Positive**   135

"I can't believe I figured out you were pregnant before you did," he said. "What kind of woman are you?" He was teasing, but I failed to see humor in the situation.

Barbara Kingsolver ❖ **In Case You Ever Want to Go Home Again**   143

I took liberties with history. I wrote long, florid inscriptions referring to our great friendship of days gone by. I wrote slowly. I made those guys wait in line *a long time*.

Thomas Beller ❖ **The Ashen Guy**   149

At first glance he looked like a snowman, except instead of snow he was covered in gray, asbestos-colored ash. . . . A small plume of dust drifted off the top of his head as he walked, echoing the larger plume of smoke drifting off of One World Trade behind him.

Heidi Julavits ❖ **Turning Japanese**   155

As the months pass, I remain miserably uncertain about all things but one: I would kill for a trashy American sweet. I do not miss cheese or pasta or even my friends, but I do miss, with a maddening intensity, that blast of sugar that only a glazed cruller can provide.

Yiyun Li ❖ **Orange Crush**   161

Even my mother had an empty Tang bottle with a snug orange nylon net over it, a present from one of her fellow schoolteachers. She carried it from the office to the classroom and back again as if our family had also consumed a full bottle.

Mary Mebane ❖ **The Back of the Bus**   167

Most Americans have never had to live with terror. I had had to live with it all my life—the psychological terror of segregation, in which there was a special set of laws governing your movements. You violated them at your peril. . . .

Lynda Barry ❖ **The Sanctuary of School**   177

I was with my teacher, and in a while I was going to sit at my desk, with my crayons and pencils and books and classmates all around me, and for the next six hours I was going to enjoy a thoroughly secure, warm and stable world. It was a world I absolutely relied on. Without it, I don't know where I would have gone that morning.

CHAPTER 6: EXAMPLE   184

A BRIEF GUIDE TO WRITING AN ESSAY BASED ON EXAMPLES   187

Everyday Example / A Lighted Billboard   193

*Monica Wunderlich ❖ **My Technologically Challenged Life**   194

In my house, technology does not exist, at least not for my parents. In fact it was 1995 when my father finally had to part with his beloved rotary phone. . . .

The Onion ❖ **All Seven Deadly Sins Committed at Church Bake Sale**   200

In total, 347 individual acts of sin were committed at the bake sale, with nearly every attendee committing at least one of the seven deadly sins as outlined by Gregory the Great in the Fifth Century.

Janet Wu ❖ **Homeward Bound**   206

My grandmother has bound feet. Cruelly tethered since her birth, they are like bonsai trees, miniature versions of what should have been.

Alex Horton ❖ **Metal Memorials**   211

Occasionally my bracelet spurs conversations with friends and co-workers who did not know I was in the army or deployed to Iraq. I still don't feel completely comfortable answering their questions but I'm always happy to talk about the name on my wrist. His name was Brian Chevalier, but we called him Chevy.

Richard Lederer ❖ **English Is a Crazy Language**   216

Sometimes you have to believe that all English speakers should be committed to an asylum for the verbally insane. In what other language do people drive in a parkway and park in a driveway? . . . In what other language can your nose run and your feet smell?

Joanna Weiss ❖ **Happy Meals and Old Spice Guy**   222

Ad agencies do assiduous research into what people already want; "Old Spice Guy" came about because Procter & Gamble understood that women buy most of their husbands' body wash, and presumably want it to smell manly.

David Sedaris ❖ **Laugh, Kookaburra**   227

This was not a real stove but a symbolic one, used to prove a point at a management seminar she'd once attended. "One burner represents your family, one is your friends, the third is your health, and the fourth is your work."

CHAPTER 7: CLASSIFICATION 238

. . . .

A BRIEF GUIDE TO WRITING A CLASSIFICATION ESSAY 240

Everyday Classification / Drunk or Buzzed? 246

*Eric A. Watts ❖ The Color of Success 247**

"Hitting the books," expressing oneself articulately, and, at times, displaying more than a modest amount of intelligence—these traits were derided as "acting white."

Amy Tan ❖ Mother Tongue 253

I spend a great deal of my time thinking about the power of language—the way it can evoke an emotion, a visual image, a complex idea, or a simple truth. Language is the tool of my trade. And I use them all—all the Englishes I grew up with.

Jack Hitt ❖ The Dollar-Store Economy 262

In the basement of American capitalism, you can see the invisible hand at work, except it's not invisible. It's actually your hand.

Warren Buffett ❖ Stop Coddling the Super-Rich 274

I checked with my mega-rich friends to learn what pain they were expecting. They, too, were left untouched.

David Brooks ❖ Harmony and the Dream 279

The world can be divided in many ways—rich and poor, democratic and authoritarian—but one of the most striking is the divide between the societies with an individualist mentality and the ones with a collectivist mentality.

Robert Lustig et al. ❖ The Toxic Truth about Sugar 284

Passive smoking and drunk-driving fatalities provided strong arguments for tobacco and alcohol control, respectively. The long-term economic, health-care, and human costs of metabolic syndrome place sugar overconsumption in the same category.

CHAPTER 8: PROCESS ANALYSIS 292

. . . .

A BRIEF GUIDE TO WRITING A PROCESS ANALYSIS 297

Everyday Process Analysis / How to Draw Cartoons 304

*Jessica Walden ❖ **Chasing Loons** 305

If for some reason you cannot see your loon, you may catch its long mournful wail. . . . The sound echoes from shore to shore and surrounds you in your canoe. The loon is there, somewhere. You can hear it.

Jon Katz ❖ **How Boys Become Men** 316

No. A chicken would probably have had the sense to get out of the way. This boy was already well on the road to becoming a *man,* having learned one of the central ethics of his gender: Experience pain rather than show fear.

Allegra Goodman ❖ **So, You Want to Be a Writer? Here's How.** 322

To begin, don't write about yourself. I'm not saying you're uninteresting. I realize that your life has been so crazy no one could make this stuff up. But if you want to be a writer, start by writing about other people.

Jeffrey Skinner ❖ **Some Stepping-Stones to Writing a Poem** 327

I really don't know of a better, more specific description of the odd and intuitive way poems may be made. In one compressed paragraph (well, now two) we see clearly how the associative process moves in many directions at once in the poet's brain. . . .

Philip Weiss ❖ **How to Get Out of a Locked Trunk** 333

Every culture comes up with tests of a person's ability to get out of a sticky situation. . . . When they slam the [car] trunk, though, you're helpless unless someone finds you. You would think that such a common worry should have a ready fix, and that the secret of getting out of a locked trunk is something we should all know about.

Adam Penenberg and Marc Barry ❖ **The Pizza Plot** 342

After doing some initial Internet research, Barry bought a $10 prepaid phone card from a nearby grocery so his calls couldn't be traced. He set up bogus voice-mail and fax-forwarding lines with a company called American Voice Mail.

CHAPTER 9: COMPARISON AND CONTRAST 353

A BRIEF GUIDE TO WRITING A COMPARISON-AND-CONTRAST
ESSAY 356

Everyday Comparison / A Coffee Mug 363

*Dan Treadway ❖ **Football vs. Asian Studies** 364

Football is the most popular spectator sport in the state of Texas without rival. . . . Vietnamese is the third-most-spoken language in the state of Texas behind English and Spanish.

Jeff Jacoby ❖ **Watching Oprah from Behind the Veil** 368

She is a self-made billionaire, with worldwide interests that range from television to publishing to education. They are forbidden to get a job without the permission of a male "guardian," and the overwhelming majority of them are unemployed.

Bruce Catton ❖ **Grant and Lee: A Study in Contrasts** 373

No part of either man's life became him more than the part he played in this brief meeting in the McLean house at Appomattox. Their behavior there put all succeeding generations of Americans in their debt. Two great Americans, Grant and Lee—very different, yet under everything very much alike.

Pico Iyer ❖ **Chapels** 382

We've always needed chapels, however confused or contradictory we may be in the way we define our religious affiliations; we've always had to have quietness and stillness to undertake our journeys into battle, or just the tumult of the world.

Gary Soto ❖ **Like Mexicans** 390

But the woman I married was not Mexican but Japanese. It was a surprise to me. For years, I went about wide-eyed in my search for the brown girl in a white dress at a dance.

Deborah Tannen ❖ **Gender in the Classroom** 397

Male students are more likely to be comfortable attacking the readings and might find the inclusion of personal anecdotes irrelevant and "soft." Women are more likely to resist discussion they perceive as hostile, and who are most likely to offer personal anecdotes.

Roger Cohen ❖ **The Meaning of Life** 406

The monkeys are part of a protracted experiment in aging being conducted by a University of Wisconsin team. Canto gets a restricted diet with 30 percent fewer calories than usual while Owen gets to eat whatever the heck he pleases.

CHAPTER 10: DEFINITION 412

. . . .

A BRIEF GUIDE TO WRITING A DEFINITION ESSAY 415

Everyday Definition / Social Media Explained 421

*Lawrence Collerd ❖ **City of Big Shoulders** 422

At this point I get off the train to transfer to another line; this is the hub, the Loop, the center.

Dave Barry ❖ **Guys vs. Men** 427

And what, exactly, do I mean by "guys"? I don't know. I haven't thought that much about it. One of the major characteristics of guyhood is that we guys don't spend a lot of time pondering our deep innermost feelings. There is a serious question in my mind about whether guys actually *have* deep innermost feelings unless you count, for example, loyalty to the Detroit Tigers. . . .

Tanya Maria Barrientos ❖ **Se Habla Español** 436

The Spanish language was supposedly the glue that held the new Latino community together. But in my case it was what kept me apart. . . . I wanted to call myself Latina, to finally take pride, but it felt like a lie. So I set out to learn the language that people assumed I already knew.

Geeta Kothari ❖ **If You Are What You Eat, Then What Am I?** 442

I want to eat what the kids at school eat: bologna, hot dogs, salami—foods my parents find repugnant because they contain pork and meat byproducts, crushed bone and hair glued together by chemicals and fat. . . . Indians, of course, do not eat such things.

Erin McKean ❖ **Redefining Definition** 449

But the traditional dictionary definition, although it bears all the trappings of authority, is in fact a highly stylized, overly compressed, and often tentative stab at capturing the consensus on what a particular word "means."

Jack Horner ❖ **The Extraordinary Characteristics of Dyslexia** 454

But what most non-dyslexics don't know about us, besides the fact that we simply process information differently, is that our early failures often give us an important edge as we grow older.

Mike Rose ❖ **Blue-Collar Brilliance** 459

I couldn't have put it in words when I was growing up, but what I observed in my mother's restaurant defined the world of adults, a place where competence was synonymous with physical work.

CHAPTER 11: CAUSE AND EFFECT 471

. . . .

A BRIEF GUIDE TO WRITING A CAUSE-AND-EFFECT ESSAY 474

Everyday Cause and Effect / A Poster 481

*Elisa Gonzales ❖ **Family History 482**
It is true, though, that I have always feared my father. . . .

Tim Wendel ❖ **King, Kennedy, and the Power of Words 487**
After King's assassination, riots broke out in more than 100 U.S. cities—the worst destruction since the Civil War. But neither Memphis nor Indianapolis experienced that kind of damage.

Marissa Nuñez ❖ **Climbing the Golden Arches 493**
Working at McDonald's has taught me a lot. . . . I'd like to have my own business someday, and working at McDonald's is what showed me I could do that.

Henry Louis Gates Jr. ❖ **A Giant Step 499**
"Pauline," he said to my mother, his voice kindly but amused, "there's not a thing wrong with that child. The problem's psychosomatic. Your son's an overachiever."

Myriam Marquez ❖ **Why and When We Speak Spanish in Public 506**
Let me explain why we haven't adopted English as our official family language.

Ann Hood ❖ **Long Beautiful Hair 510**
That should have been the end of my hair saga. Goal achieved; move on to the next thing. But life is not so simple.

CHAPTER 12: ARGUMENT 517

. . . .

A BRIEF GUIDE TO WRITING AN ARGUMENT 520

Everyday Argument / T-Shirt on a Stick 533

*Liz Addison ❖ **Two Years Are Better Than Four** 534

I believe the community college system to be one of America's uniquely great institutions.

Johnson C. Montgomery ❖ **The Island of Plenty** 539

The United States should remain an island of plenty in a sea of hunger. The future of mankind is at stake. We are not responsible for the rest of humanity.

Mark D. White and Robert Arp ❖ **Should Batman Kill the Joker?** 545

But if we say that Batman should kill the Joker, doesn't that imply that we should torture terror suspects if there's a chance of getting information that could save innocent lives?

Arianna Huffington ❖ **Empathy** 550

In fact, in this time of economic hardship, political instability, and rapid technological change, empathy is the one quality we most need if we're going to flourish in the twenty-first century.

Mind and Media: Is *Google* Making Us Stupid? 558

Steven Pinker ❖ **Mind Over Mass Media** 559

Far from making us stupid, these technologies are the only things that will keep us smart.

Nicholas Carr ❖ **Hal and Me** 563

For some people, the very idea of reading a book has come to seem old-fashioned, maybe even a little silly—like sewing your own shirts or butchering your own meat.

Andrea Lunsford ❖ **Our Semi-Literate Youth? Not So Fast** 570

As one who has spent the last 30-plus years studying the writing of college students, I see a different picture. For those who think Google is making us stupid and Facebook is frying our brains, let me sketch that picture in briefly.

Moneyball: Are College Sports Worth the Price? 577

Michael Rosenberg ❖ **Let Stars Get Paid 578**

College athletes cannot be paid. Every American knows this. The concept is as entrenched in our bloodstreams as cholesterol. We have accepted it for so long . . . that we don't even remember the reasons anymore.

Joe Posnanski ❖ **College Athletes Should Not Be Paid 584**

Maybe they can have the players wear a little patch on their shoulders with the name of the booster who gave the player the money to come to the school. That touchdown was scored by Tommy Tutone and brought to you by Bob's Trucking.

Laura Pappano ❖ **How Big-Time Sports Ate College Life 591**

"It's not something I usually admit to, that I applied to Ohio State 60 percent for the sports. But the more I do tell that to people, they'll say it's a big reason why they came, too."

CHAPTER 13: CLASSIC ESSAYS AND SPEECHES   602

. . . .

Thomas Jefferson ❖ **The Declaration of Independence**   606

We hold these truths to be self-evident, that all men are created equal, that they are endowed by their Creator with certain unalienable Rights, that among these are Life, Liberty and the pursuit of Happiness.

Jonathan Swift ❖ **A Modest Proposal**   612

I have been assured by a very knowing American of my acquaintance in London, that a young healthy child well nursed is at a year old a most delicious, nourishing, and wholesome food, whether stewed, roasted, baked, or boiled. . . .

Abraham Lincoln ❖ **Second Inaugural Address**   623

Both parties deprecated war, but one of them would *make* war rather than let the nation survive, and the other would *accept* war rather than let it perish, and the war came.

Sojourner Truth ❖ **Ain't I a Woman?**   627

If my cup won't hold but a pint, and yours holds a quart, wouldn't you be mean not to let me have my little half measure full?

Virginia Woolf ❖ **The Death of the Moth**   630

It was as if someone had taken a tiny bead of pure life and decking it as lightly as possible with down and feathers, had set it dancing and zigzagging to show us the true nature of life.

Martin Luther King Jr. ❖ **I Have a Dream**   634

We have also come to this hallowed spot to remind America of the fierce urgency of Now. This is no time to engage in the luxury of cooling off or to take the tranquilizing drug of gradualism. Now is the time to make real the promises of democracy.

APPENDIX: USING SOURCES IN YOUR WRITING   641
PERMISSIONS ACKNOWLEGMENTS   681
GLOSSARY / INDEX   690

THEMATIC CONTENTS

CULTURES AND ETHNICITIES

Tanya Maria Barrientos ❖ *Se Habla Español* **436**

David Brooks ❖ *Harmony and the Dream* **279**

Henry Louis Gates Jr. ❖ *A Giant Step* **499**

Pico Iyer ❖ *Chapels* **382**

Jeff Jacoby ❖ *Watching Oprah from Behind the Veil* **368**

Heidi Julavits ❖ *Turning Japanese* **155**

Jon Katz ❖ *How Boys Become Men* **316**

Martin Luther King Jr. ❖ *I Have a Dream* **634**

Geeta Kothari ❖ *If You Are What You Eat, Then What Am I?* **442**

Yiyun Li ❖ *Orange Crush* **161**

Myriam Marquez ❖ *Why and When We Speak Spanish in Public* **506**

Mary Mebane ❖ *The Back of the Bus* **167**

Joe Posnanski ❖ *College Athletes Should Not Be Paid* **584**

Mike Rose ❖ *Blue-Collar Brilliance* **459**

Gary Soto ❖ *Like Mexicans* **390**

Amy Tan ❖ *Mother Tongue* **253**

Dan Treadway ❖ *Football vs. Asian Studies* **364**

Sojourner Truth ❖ *Ain't I a Woman?* **627**

Eric A. Watts ❖ *The Color of Success* **247**

Janet Wu ❖ *Homeward Bound* **206**

GENDER

Carrie Barker ❖ *But Two Negatives Equal a Positive* **135**

Dave Barry ❖ *Guys vs. Men* **427**

Ann Hood ❖ *Long Beautiful Hair* **510**

Jeff Jacoby ❖ *Watching Oprah from Behind the Veil* **368**

Jon Katz ❖ *How Boys Become Men* **316**

Marissa Nuñez ❖ *Climbing the Golden Arches* **493**

Deborah Tannen ❖ *Gender in the Classroom* **397**

Sojourner Truth ❖ *Ain't I a Woman?* **627**

Philip Weiss ❖ *How to Get Out of a Locked Trunk* **333**

HISTORY

Bruce Catton ❖ *Grant and Lee: A Study in Contrasts* **373**

Lawrence Collerd ❖ *City of Big Shoulders* **422**

Alex Horton ❖ *Metal Memorials* **211**

Thomas Jefferson ❖ *The Declaration of Independence* **606**

Martin Luther King Jr. ❖ *I Have a Dream* **634**

Abraham Lincoln ❖ *Second Inaugural Address* **623**

Mary Mebane ❖ *The Back of the Bus* **167**

Jonathan Swift ❖ *A Modest Proposal* **612**

Sojourner Truth ❖ *Ain't I a Woman?* **627**

Tim Wendel ❖ *King, Kennedy, and the Power of Words* **487**

Mark D. White and Robert Arp ❖ *Should Batman Kill the Joker?* **545**

Janet Wu ❖ *Homeward Bound* **206**

HOME AND FAMILY

Carrie Barker ❖ *But Two Negatives Equal a Positive* **135**

Tanja Maria Barrientos ❖ *Se Habla Español* **436**

Lynda Barry ❖ *The Sanctuary of School* **177**

Lawrence Collerd ❖ *City of Big Shoulders* **422**

Paul Crenshaw ❖ *Storm Country* **79**

Henry Louis Gates Jr. ❖ *A Giant Step* **499**

Elisa Gonzales ❖ *Family History* **482**

Ann Hood ❖ *Long Beautiful Hair* **510**

Pico Iyer ❖ *Chapels* **382**

Barbara Kingsolver ❖ *In Case You Ever Want to Go Home Again* **143**

Geeta Kothari ❖ *If You Are What You Eat, Then What Am I?* **442**

Yiyun Li ❖ *Orange Crush* **161**

Myriam Marquez ❖ *Why and When We Speak Spanish in Public* **506**

Mike Rose ❖ *Blue-Collar Brilliance* **459**

David Sedaris ❖ *Laugh, Kookaburra* **227**

Gary Soto ❖ *Like Mexicans* **390**

Amy Tan ❖ *Mother Tongue* **253**

Grace Welte ❖ *Bracken County, Northern Kentucky* **72**

E. B. White ❖ *Once More to the Lake* **114**

Janet Wu ❖ *Homeward Bound* **206**

Monica Wunderlich ❖ *My Technologically Challenged Life* **194**

HUMOR AND SATIRE

Dave Barry ❖ *Guys vs. Men* **427**

Roger Cohen ❖ *The Meaning of Life* **406**

Ann Hodgman ❖ *No Wonder They Call Me a Bitch* **106**

Barbara Kingsolver ❖ *In Case You Ever Want to Go Home Again* **143**

Richard Lederer ❖ *English Is a Crazy Language* **216**

The Onion ❖ *All Seven Deadly Sins Committed at Church Bake Sale* **200**

Adam Penenberg and Marc Barry ❖ *The Pizza Plot* **342**

David Sedaris ❖ *Laugh, Kookaburra* **227**

Jonathan Swift ❖ *A Modest Proposal* **612**

Monica Wunderlich ❖ *My Technologically Challenged Life* **194**

LANGUAGE AND IDENTITY

Tanya Maria Barrientos ❖ *Se Habla Español* **436**

Barbara Kingsolver ❖ *In Case You Ever Want to Go Home Again* **143**

Geeta Kothari ❖ *If You Are What You Eat, Then What Am I?* **442**

Richard Lederer ❖ *English Is a Crazy Language* **216**

Myriam Marquez ❖ *Why and When We Speak Spanish in Public* **506**

Erin McKean ❖ *Redefining Definition* **449**

Amy Tan ❖ *Mother Tongue* **253**

Deborah Tannen ❖ *Gender in the Classroom* **397**

LIFE AND DEATH

Thomas Beller ❖ *The Ashen Guy* **149**

Roger Cohen ❖ *The Meaning of Life* **406**

Annie Dillard ❖ *From* Holy the Firm **3**

Brian Doyle ❖ *Joyas Voladoras* **85**

Ann Hood ❖ *Long Beautiful Hair* **510**

Alex Horton ❖ *Metal Memorials* **211**

Jessica Walden ❖ *Chasing Loons* **305**

E. B. White ❖ *Once More to the Lake* **114**

Mark D. White and Robert Arp ❖ *Should Batman Kill the Joker?* **545**

Virginia Woolf ❖ *The Death of the Moth* **630**

MEDIA

David Brooks ❖ *Harmony and the Dream* **279**

Nicholas Carr ❖ *Hal and Me* **563**

Jeff Jacoby ❖ *Watching Oprah from Behind the Veil* **368**

Yiyun Li ❖ *Orange Crush* **161**

Andrea Lunsford ❖ *Our Semi-Literate Youth? Not So Fast* **570**

Erin McKean ❖ *Redefining Definition* **449**

Steven Pinker ❖ *Mind Over Mass Media* **559**

Joanna Weiss ❖ *Happy Meals and Old Spice Guy* **222**

Mark D. White and Robert Arp ❖ *Should Batman Kill the Joker?* **545**

MEMORIES OF YOUTH

Lynda Barry ❖ *The Sanctuary of School* **177**

Roger Cohen ❖ *The Meaning of Life* **406**

Lawrence Collerd ❖ *City of Big Shoulders* **422**

Paul Crenshaw ❖ *Storm Country* **79**

Henry Louis Gates Jr. ❖ *A Giant Step* **499**

Elisa Gonzales ❖ *Family History* **482**

Ann Hood ❖ *Long Beautiful Hair* **510**

Jon Katz ❖ *How Boys Become Men* **316**

Barbara Kingsolver ❖ *In Case You Ever Want to Go Home Again* **143**

Geeta Kothari ❖ *If You Are What You Eat, Then What Am I?* **442**

Yiyun Li ❖ *Orange Crush* **161**

Mary Mebane ❖ *The Back of the Bus* **167**

Mike Rose ❖ *Blue-Collar Brilliance* **459**

David Sedaris ❖ *Laugh, Kookaburra* **227**

Gary Soto ❖ *Like Mexicans* **390**

Alice Steinbach ❖ *The Miss Dennis School of Writing* **96**

Grace Welte ❖ *Bracken County, Northern Kentucky* **72**

E. B. White ❖ *Once More to the Lake* **114**

Janet Wu ❖ *Homeward Bound* **206**

MORALITY AND ETHICS

Carrie Barker ❖ *But Two Negatives Equal a Positive* **135**

Warren Buffett ❖ *Stop Coddling the Super-Rich* **274**

Arianna Huffington ❖ *Empathy* **550**

Martin Luther King Jr. ❖ *I Have a Dream* **634**

Robert Lustig et al. ❖ *The Toxic Truth about Sugar* 284

Johnson C. Montgomery ❖ *The Island of Plenty* 539

Adam Penenberg and Marc Barry ❖ *The Pizza Plot* 342

Michael Rosenberg ❖ *Let Stars Get Paid* 578

Jonathan Swift ❖ *A Modest Proposal* 612

Jessica Walden ❖ *Chasing Loons* 305

Tim Wendel ❖ *King, Kennedy, and the Power of Words* 487

Mark D. White and Robert Arp ❖ *Should Batman Kill the Joker?* 545

NATURE AND THE ENVIRONMENT

Paul Crenshaw ❖ *Storm Country* 79

Annie Dillard ❖ *From* Holy the Firm 3

Annie Dillard ❖ *How I Wrote the Moth Essay—and Why* 8

Brian Doyle ❖ *Joyas Voladoras* 85

Cherokee Paul McDonald ❖ *A View from the Bridge* 90

Johnson C. Montgomery ❖ *The Island of Plenty* 539

David Sedaris ❖ *Laugh, Kookaburra* 227

Jessica Walden ❖ *Chasing Loons* 305

E. B. White ❖ *Once More to the Lake* 114

Virginia Woolf ❖ *The Death of the Moth* 630

OVERCOMING HARDSHIP AND DISABILITY

Lynda Barry ❖ *The Sanctuary of School* 177

Henry Louis Gates Jr. ❖ *A Giant Step* 499

Elisa Gonzales ❖ *Family History* 482

Ann Hood ❖ *Long Beautiful Hair* 510

Jack Horner ❖ *The Extraordinary Characteristics of Dyslexia* 454

Jeff Jacoby ❖ *Watching Oprah from Behind the Veil* 368

Martin Luther King Jr. ❖ *I Have a Dream* 634

Cherokee Paul McDonald ❖ *A View from the Bridge* **90**

Marissa Nuñez ❖ *Climbing the Golden Arches* **493**

Mike Rose ❖ *Blue-Collar Brilliance* **459**

Monica Wunderlich ❖ *My Technologically Challenged Life* **194**

PUBLIC POLICY

Lynda Barry ❖ *The Sanctuary of School* **177**

David Brooks ❖ *Harmony and the Dream* **279**

Warren Buffett ❖ *Stop Coddling the Super-Rich* **274**

Alex Horton ❖ *Metal Memorials* **211**

Arianna Huffington ❖ *Empathy* **550**

Thomas Jefferson ❖ *The Declaration of Independence* **606**

Martin Luther King Jr. ❖ *I Have a Dream* **634**

Abraham Lincoln ❖ *Second Inaugural Address* **623**

Robert Lustig et al. ❖ *The Toxic Truth about Sugar* **284**

Johnson C. Montgomery ❖ *The Island of Plenty* **539**

Laura Pappano ❖ *How Big-Time Sports Ate College Life* **591**

Jonathan Swift ❖ *A Modest Proposal* **612**

Sojourner Truth ❖ *Ain't I a Woman?* **627**

Tim Wendel ❖ *King, Kennedy, and the Power of Words* **487**

Mark D. White and Robert Arp ❖ *Should Batman Kill the Joker?* **545**

SCIENCE AND TECHNOLOGY

Nicholas Carr ❖ *Hal and Me* **563**

Brian Doyle ❖ *Joyas Voladoras* **85**

Roger Cohen ❖ *The Meaning of Life* **406**

Andrea Lunsford ❖ *Our Semi-Literate Youth? Not So Fast* **570**

Robert Lustig et al. ❖ *The Toxic Truth about Sugar* **284**

Adam Penenberg and Marc Barry ❖ *The Pizza Plot* **342**

Steven Pinker ❖ *Mind Over Mass Media* **559**

Jessica Walden ❖ *Chasing Loons* **305**

Monica Wunderlich ❖ *My Technologically Challenged Life* **194**

SCHOOL AND EDUCATION

Liz Addison ❖ *Two Years Are Better than Four* **534**

Tanya Maria Barrientos ❖ *Se Habla Español* **436**

Lynda Barry ❖ *The Sanctuary of School* **177**

Nicholas Carr ❖ *Hal and Me* **563**

Annie Dillard ❖ *How I Wrote the Moth Essay—and Why* **8**

Allegra Goodman ❖ *So, You Want to Be a Writer? Here's How.* **322**

Jack Horner ❖ *The Extraordinary Characteristics of Dyslexia* **454**

Jon Katz ❖ *How Boys Become Men* **316**

Andrea Lunsford ❖ *Our Semi-Literate Youth? Not So Fast* **570**

Marissa Nuñez ❖ *Climbing the Golden Arches* **493**

Laura Pappano ❖ *How Big-Time Sports Ate College Life* **591**

Joe Posnanski ❖ *College Athletes Should Not Be Paid* **584**

Jeffrey Skinner ❖ *Some Stepping-Stones to Writing Poetry* **327**

Alice Steinbach ❖ *The Miss Dennis School of Writing* **96**

Deborah Tannen ❖ *Gender in the Classroom* **397**

Dan Treadway ❖ *Football vs. Asian Studies* **364**

Jessica Walden ❖ *Chasing Loons* **305**

Eric A. Watts ❖ *The Color of Success* **247**

SOCIOLOGY AND ANTHROPOLOGY

David Brooks ❖ *Harmony and the Dream* **279**

Jack Hitt ❖ *The Dollar-Store Economy* **262**

Jeff Jacoby ❖ *Watching Oprah from Behind the Veil* **368**

Mike Rose ❖ *Blue-Collar Brilliance* **459**

Deborah Tannen ❖ *Gender in the Classroom* **397**

Joanna Weiss ❖ *Happy Meals and Old Spice Guy* **222**
Philip Weiss ❖ *How to Get Out of a Locked Trunk* **333**

SPORTS AND LEISURE

Dave Barry ❖ *Guys vs. Men* **427**
Lawrence Collerd ❖ *City of Big Shoulders* **422**
Jack Hitt ❖ *The Dollar-Store Economy* **262**
Ann Hodgman ❖ *No Wonder They Call Me a Bitch* **106**
Pico Iyer ❖ *Chapels* **382**
Cherokee Paul McDonald ❖ *A View from the Bridge* **90**
Laura Pappano ❖ *How Big-Time Sports Ate College Life* **591**
Joe Posnanski ❖ *College Athletes Should Not Get Paid* **584**
Michael Rosenberg ❖ *Let Stars Get Paid* **578**
David Sedaris ❖ *Laugh, Kookaburra* **227**
Dan Treadway ❖ *Football vs. Asian Studies* **364**
Jessica Walden ❖ *Chasing Loons* **305**
Joanna Weiss ❖ *Happy Meals and Old Spice Guy* **222**
E. B. White ❖ *Once More to the Lake* **114**

STUDENT WRITING

Liz Addison ❖ *Two Years Are Better than Four* **534**
Carrie Barker ❖ *But Two Negatives Equal a Positive* **135**
Lawrence Collerd ❖ *City of Big Shoulders* **422**
Elisa Gonzales ❖ *Family History* **482**
Marissa Nuñez ❖ *Climbing the Golden Arches* **493**
Dan Treadway ❖ *Football vs. Asian Studies* **364**
Jessica Walden ❖ *Chasing Loons* **305**
Eric A. Watts ❖ *The Color of Success* **247**
Grace Welte ❖ *Bracken County, Northern Kentucky* **72**
Monica Wunderlich ❖ *My Technologically Challenged Life* **194**

WRITERS AND WRITING

Annie Dillard ❖ *from* Holy the Firm **3**

Annie Dillard ❖ *How I Wrote the Moth Essay—and Why* **8**

Allegra Goodman ❖ *So, You Want to Be a Writer? Here's How.* **322**

Barbara Kingsolver ❖ *In Case You Ever Want to Go Home Again* **143**

Richard Lederer ❖ *English Is a Crazy Language* **216**

Erin McKean ❖ *Redefining Definition* **449**

Jeffrey Skinner ❖ *Some Stepping-Stones to Writing Poetry* **327**

Alice Steinbach ❖ *The Miss Dennis School of Writing* **96**

Tim Wendel ❖ *King, Kennedy, and the Power of Words* **487**

Virginia Woolf ❖ *The Death of the Moth* **630**

PREFACE

The Norton Sampler is a collection of short essays for composition students illustrating the basic rhetorical patterns of description, narration, example, classification, process analysis, comparison and contrast, definition, cause and effect, and argument.

Like the cloth samplers of colonial America that young people made in order to practice their stitches—and their ABCs—*The Norton Sampler* assumes that writing is a practical art that can be learned by studying and applying these basic, familiar patterns. Each chapter of readings focuses on a single pattern and includes five or so essays organized primarily around that pattern. Each reading is followed by a host of study questions and writing prompts.

Most of the model essays in the *Sampler* are only a few pages long, and even the longest can be easily read in one sitting. The essays are not only short but complete. I have found over the years that even classic essays are often reprinted with unacknowledged changes—yet as teachers, we cannot credibly ask students to study beginnings, middles, and endings or the shape of an argument if those forms and shapes are not the work of the author. Thus I have taken pains to include complete essays, or, in a few cases (indicated in the headnotes), complete chapters of books or sections of longer articles.

Though the chapters and essays in *The Norton Sampler* can be taken up in any order, the first chapter introduces the four basic modes of writing—description, narration, exposition, and argument—and includes two essays by Annie Dillard that show the processes that one writer typically goes through in order to capture her ideas on paper. One of these essays, "How I Wrote the Moth Essay—and Why," was specially commissioned for the *Sampler*. This chapter also shows students how to read and analyze a text, including the selections in this book, with an eye to using the various modes in their own writing.

Next come a chapter on the writing process and a brand new chapter on writing paragraphs. The rest of the book takes up the modes of writing in greater detail. Chapters 4 and 5 are devoted, respectively, to the basic techniques of description and narration. These are followed by six chapters of exposition, ranging from the simpler techniques of exemplification and classification to the more complex strategies of process analysis, comparison, definition, and cause and effect. Then there is an extended chapter on argument, followed by a chapter of classic essays that demonstrate how the modes work in combination. Finally comes an appendix on research and documentation, and a glossary/index.

HIGHLIGHTS

- **Great readings by a wide variety of fine writers.** There are 71 readings in all—more than in any earlier edition—with 35 titles new to this edition. All selections cover topics that should spur students' interests, from such recent pieces as Andrea Lunsford's account of how social media make students better writers and Warren Buffett's essay on taxing the super-rich, to old favorites by E. B. White and Sojourner Truth.

- **Everyday examples** that show how the patterns taught in this book play an important role across media—from book covers and billboards to cartoons and missing cat posters.

- **More student writing.** Essays by gifted student writers are now included in each chapter of readings, and those essays are **annotated** to show how they illustrate the principles discussed in the chapter.

- **A new chapter on writing paragraphs,** with an in-depth discussion of topic sentences, transitions, and parallel structures—and how to use the modes to develop coherent paragraphs, including introductory and concluding paragraphs.

- **New navigation features** make the book especially easy to use. Notes in the margins explicitly link the readings with writing instructions, and a combined glossary/index provides full definitions of key terms and concepts, serving as an easy reference point for students.

- **Help for students whose primary language is not English,** including glosses for unfamiliar terms and cultural allusions, templates to help students get started writing, and grammar tips.

- **Updated coverage of argument,** with two *new* clusters of readings on current issues: the effects of recent technologies upon the human mind and the all-pervading influence of big-time sports on college life.

ACKNOWLEDGEMENTS

There are three people above all whom I want to thank for their work and support on this new edition of *The Norton Sampler*: my wife Barbara Cooley, a gifted technical writer, editor, and blogger; Marilyn Moller, editor extraordinaire, who continues to shape an entire generation of composition texts, including this one; and my project editor at Norton, Melissa Atkin, who got the book out in good time and good form. Then there is Barry Wade, original editor of the *Sampler*; Julia Reidhead and Rebecca Homiski, constant supporters of the book; and all the other people at Norton who have made possible this and earlier editions, including managing editor Marian Johnson, who has generously attended to matters both great and small; Lib Triplett and Ashley Cain, who helped spread the word about the book; Bethany Salminen, who cleared the permissions; Nelson Colón, who researched the photos; Elizabeth Mullaney, who was my hands-on editor; and Tenyia Lee, who helped keep us all on track —and more. I'm also grateful to Michal Brody for her excellent work on the instructor's notes and quizzes and to JoAnn Metsch for her superb design.

I am also indebted to Richard Bullock of Wright State University for allowing me to draw from his research and experience in the research appendix, and to Gerald Graff and Cathy Birkenstein, whose work inspired the writing templates in this book.

Among the teachers and composition experts across the country who reviewed this edition in progress and gave me advice on the selections and pedagogy, I wish especially to thank Matthew Allen, Purdue University; Mary

Baken, Webster University; Britt Benshetler, Northwest Vista College; Shannon Blair, Central Piedmont Community College; Matthew Bodie, St. Petersburg College; Linda A. Cohen, Bridgewater State University; Kate Cottle, Wilmington University; Linda Jensen Darling, University of California–Los Angeles; Ashley Dawson, College of Staten Island/CUNY; Kathleen D. Driscoll, Bristol Community College; Nancy England, University of Texas–Arlington; Janice Fioravante, The College of Staten Island; Lisa Fitzgerald, Long Beach City College; Kenneth E. Harrison, Jr., Webster University; P. C. Hironymous, Glendale College; Cheryl Hunter, NHTI, Concord's Community College; Renee Iweriebor, Hostos Community College; Ray P. Linville, Sandhills Community College; Crystal Manboard, Northwest Vista College; Amanda Menking, Blinn College; Amy Miller, University of Louisville; Christine Pipitone-Herron, Raritan Valley Community College; Jennifer A. Turner, The Citadel; Julie Vega, Sul Ross State University; Courtney Huse Wika, Black Hills State University; Tamara Wilson, Flagler College; Andrena Zawinski, Laney College; Melinda Zepeda, Northwest Vista College.

Many thanks, too, to my colleagues in composition at Ohio State over the years, including the late Edward P. J. Corbett, who influenced a generation of scholars and teachers of writing; to Roy Rosenstein of the American University of Paris; and to Ron and Elizabeth Beckman of Syracuse University.

Thomas Cooley

THE
NORTON
SAMPLER

〰〰〰〰〰〰〰〰〰〰

EIGHTH EDITION

CHAPTER ONE

READING
AS A WRITER

✦✧✦✧✦✧✦✧✦✧✦✧✦✧✦✧✦✧✦✧✦✧✦✧✦✧✦✧✦✧✦✧✦

Writing is a little like sewing or weaving. The end product is a written text that must be constructed thread by thread using certain basic patterns and strategies that good writers follow all the time in their work. In fact, the root meaning of *text*, like *textile,* is something *woven*—a fabric of words.

As with any practical art, we learn to write by writing. Many of the fundamental patterns and strategies of writing that we all must master if we're to construct tightly woven texts of our own, however, we learn in part by reading the work of other writers. Thus we'll be reading the essays throughout this book *as writers*, with an eye for what we can learn from them about writing. Coolly and systematically (but maybe with a little passion), we'll pay close attention to how the pieces fit together—and how we can use those same techniques in our own work.

In this chapter, we'll start by focusing on two essays by the Pulitzer Prize-winning writer Annie Dillard. The first essay, from *Holy the Firm* (1977), originally appeared in *Harper's* under the title "The Death of a Moth." The second essay, which Dillard wrote expressly for *The Norton Sampler,* is entitled "How I Wrote the Moth Essay—and Why." According to Dillard, these two texts are "the most personal" ones she's ever written. Taken together, they offer her inspired (and inspiring) answer to a question that all writers face: "How do you go from nothing to something? How do you face the blank page without fainting dead away?"

Feel faint? See Chapter 2 for detailed answers to such vexing questions about the writing process.

❧ 1 ❧

TWO ESSAYS ON WRITING:
ANNIE DILLARD AND THE MOTH

Annie Dillard (b. 1945) grew up in Pittsburgh, the daughter of well-to-do parents, whose literate life at home she describes in *An American Childhood* (1987). In her master's thesis at Hollins College, Dillard focused on Walden Pond as a link "between heaven and earth" in the work of Henry David Thoreau, to whom she has often been compared for her meditative essays on nature and spirit. Two of those meditations are reprinted here. The first essay, from *Holy the Firm* (1977), originally appeared in *Harper's* under the title "The Death of a Moth," immediately inviting comparison with Virginia Woolf's classic essay, "The Death of the Moth." Like Woolf's, Dillard's piece is not really about insects, but about writing; and it is the end product of a rigorous process of composition that Dillard herself describes in the second selection, "How I Wrote the Moth Essay—and Why." As part of that process, Dillard applied her skills as a reader to her own writing by rigorously reading and revising her early drafts. "Revising is a breeze," says Dillard, "if you know what you're doing—if you can look at your text coldly, analytically, manipulatively. Since I've studied texts, I know what I'm doing when I revise" (15).

ANNIE DILLARD

FROM HOLY THE FIRM

I live on northern Puget Sound, in Washington State, alone. I have a gold cat, who sleeps on my legs, named Small. In the morning I joke to her blank face, Do you remember last night? Do you remember? I throw her out before breakfast, so I can eat.

There is a spider, too, in the bathroom, with whom I keep a sort of company. Her little outfit always reminds me of a certain moth I helped to kill. The spider herself is of uncertain lineage, bulbous at the abdomen and drab. Her six-inch mess of a web works, works somehow, works miraculously, to keep her alive and me amazed. The web itself is in a corner behind the toilet, connecting tile wall to tile wall and floor, in a place where there is, I would have thought, scant traffic. Yet under the web are sixteen or so corpses she has tossed to the floor.

The corpses appear to be mostly sow bugs, those little armadillo creatures who live to travel flat out in houses, and die round. There is also a new shred of earwig, three old spider skins crinkled and clenched, and two moth bodies, wingless and huge and empty, moth bodies I drop to my knees to see.

Today the earwig shines darkly and gleams, what there is of him: a dorsal curve of thorax and abdomen, and a smooth pair of cerci[1] by which I knew his

---

1. Plural of cercus, the posterior "feeler" of an insect.

name. Next week, if the other bodies are any indication, he will be shrunken and gray, webbed to the floor with dust. The sow bugs beside him are hollow and empty of color, fragile, a breath away from brittle fluff. The spider skins lie on their sides, translucent and ragged, their legs drying in knots. And the moths, the empty moths, stagger against each other, headless, in a confusion of arching strips of chitin like peeling varnish, like a jumble of buttresses for cathedral domes, like nothing resembling moths, so that I should hesitate to call them moths, except that I have had some experience with the figure Moth reduced to a nub.

Two summers ago I was camping alone in the Blue Ridge Mountains in Virginia. I had hauled myself and gear up there to read, among other things, James Ramsey Ullman's *The Day on Fire*, a novel about Rimbaud that had made me want to be a writer when I was sixteen;[2] I was hoping it would do it again. So I read, lost, every day sitting under a tree by my tent, while warblers swung in the leaves overhead and bristle worms trailed their inches over the twiggy dirt at my feet; and I read every night by candlelight, while barred owls called in the forest and pale moths massed round my head in the clearing, where my light made a ring. 5

Page 21 gives some specific suggestions for responding to your reading.

Moths kept flying into the candle. They would hiss and recoil, lost upside down in the shadows among my cooking pans. Or they would singe their wings and fall, and their hot wings, as if melted, would stick to the first thing they touched—a pan, a lid, a spoon—so that the snagged moths could flutter only in tiny arcs, unable to struggle free. These I could release by a quick flip with a stick; in the morning I would find my cooking stuff gilded with torn flecks of moth wings, triangles of shiny dust here and there on the aluminum. So I read, and boiled water, and replenished candles, and read on. 6

One night a moth flew into the candle, was caught, burnt dry, and held. I must have been staring at the candle, or maybe I looked up when a shadow crossed my page; at any rate, I saw it all. A golden female moth, a biggish one with 7

2. French poet Arthur Rimbaud (1854–1891) himself began writing at age sixteen and produced his major work before he was twenty. Ullman's novel was published in 1958.

OPPOSITE: *Page from the first draft of the essay from* Holy the Firm.

Jan B.

Kindling

Two summers ago I ~~last camped~~ was camping alone in the Blue Ridge mountains in Virginia. I had hauled myself and gear up there to read, among other things, ~~on piece~~ James Ramsey Ullman's ~~novel~~ The Day on Fire, a novel that ~~had~~ ~~don't remember~~ made ~~a writer~~ ~~grace~~ want to be a writer when I was sixteen; I was hoping it would do it again. So I read ~~all~~ every day sitting under a tree by my tent, ~~pausing to eat~~ four or five times and ~~walk once or twice, and I read~~ ~~all~~ every night while warblers ~~swung~~ sang in the leaves overhead and bristleworms trailed their inches over the twiggy ~~ground~~ dirt at my ~~(side)~~ ~~feet~~ feet, and I read every night by candlelight, while ~~the~~ the barred owls called in the forest and pale ~~moon~~ ~~now no when my light made toward me, where my light~~ ~~moths~~ moths massed in the clearing. ~~I made~~ ~~the woods.~~ made a ~~head,~~ ring.

The ~~moths flew on~~ Moths kept flying into the candle. They would hiss a~~nd~~ ~~spatter~~ and recoil, lost upside down in the darkness ~~shadows~~ among my cooking pans. Or they would singe their wings and fall, and their ~~hot~~ ~~burnt~~ wings would stick, as if melted, to whatever they the first thing touched, a pan, a lid, a spoon, so that the ~~moths~~ singed moths could struggle only in tiny arcs, unable to ~~free~~ flutter free. These I could release ~~with~~ by a quick flip ~~by~~ with a stick; in the morning I would find my cooking stuff embossed with torn flecks of moth wings, little triangles of shiny dust here and there on the aluminum. So I read, and boiled water, and replenished candles, and read on.

      One night to female ~~one moth~~ flew into the candle, was caught, burned dry and held ~~and burned so fast~~ sizzled, drop-ped ~~and some~~ more into the wet wax, stuck, flamed and fried in a second. Her wings burnt right off ~~and~~ disappeared ~~in~~ a thin, foul smoke, her legs ~~crackled~~ spattered and curled, her head ~~jerked~~ ~~crackled and jerked~~ (like small arms fire)

      ~~He~~ ~~fanned wings~~ I must have been staring at the candle, or maybe I looked up when a shadow crossed my page; at any rate, I saw ~~the white thing.~~ it all.

Jan 2

a two-inch wingspan, flapped into the fire, dropped her abdomen into the wet wax, stuck, flamed, frazzled and fried in a second. Her moving wings ignited like tissue paper, enlarging the circle of light in the clearing and creating out of the darkness the sudden blue sleeves of my sweater, the green leaves of jewel-weed by my side, the ragged red trunk of a pine. At once the light contracted again and the moth's wings vanished in a fine, foul smoke. At the same time her six legs clawed, curled, blackened, and ceased, disappearing utterly. And her head jerked in spasms, making a spattering noise; her antennae crisped and burned away and her heaving mouth parts crackled like pistol fire. When it was all over, her head was, so far as I could determine, gone, gone the long way of her wings and legs. Had she been new, or old? Had she mated and laid her eggs, had she done her work? All that was left was the glowing horn shell of her abdomen and thorax—a fraying, partially collapsed gold tube jammed upright in the candle's round pool.

And then this moth-essence, this spectacular skeleton, began to act as a wick. 8
She kept burning. The wax rose in the moth's body from her soaking abdomen to her thorax to the jagged hole where her head should be, and widened into flame, a saffron-yellow flame that robed her to the ground like any immolating monk. That candle had two wicks, two flames of identical height, side by side. The moth's head was fire. She burned for two hours, until I blew her out.

She burned for two hours without changing, without bending or leaning— 9
only glowing within, like a building fire glimpsed through silhouetted walls, like a hollow saint, like a flame-faced virgin gone to God, while I read by her light, kindled, while Rimbaud in Paris burnt out his brains in a thousand poems, while night pooled wetly at my feet.

And that is why I believe those hollow crisps on the bathroom floor are 10
moths. I think I know moths, and fragments of moths, and chips and tatters of utterly empty moths, in any state. How many of you, I asked the people in my class, which of you want to give your lives and be writers? I was trembling from coffee, or cigarettes, or the closeness of faces all around me. (Is this what we live for? I thought; is this the only final beauty: the color of any skin in any light, and living, human eyes?) All hands rose to the question. (You, Nick? Will you?

Margaret? Randy? Why do I want them to mean it?) And then I tried to tell them what the choice must mean: you can't be anything else. You must go at your life with a broadax. . . . They had no idea what I was saying. (I have two hands, don't I? And all this energy, for as long as I can remember. I'll do it in the evenings, after skiing, or on the way home from the bank, or after the children are asleep. . . .) They thought I was raving again. It's just as well.

I have three candles here on the table which I disentangle from the plants and light when visitors come. Small usually avoids them, although once she came too close and her tail caught fire; I rubbed it out before she noticed. The flames move light over everyone's skin, draw light to the surface of the faces of my friends. When the people leave I never blow the candles out, and after I'm asleep they flame and burn.

11

FOR DISCUSSION AND WRITING

1. What is Annie Dillard referring to when she says, "I'll do it in the evenings, after skiing, or on the way home from the bank" (10)? Explain.

2. Dillard appears to be drawing an ANALOGY between the burning moth and the writer. What does her use of this figure of speech imply about the nature of the writer's calling as Dillard sees it? Point to specific details in the text.

3. What would you say to George, the student who posted the following on bookcritics.org: "I need to know the significance of the butterfly in Annie Dillard's 'Death of a Moth.' This essay made absolutely no sense to me so I really need some help."

4. Recall a visit you made to a place where you felt especially close to the natural environment—the wilderness, a city park, or the beach, for example. Make a list of the physical details—objects, sounds, smells, tastes, colors, textures—that you remember most vividly from that experience.

5. Using your list of details as a basis, write a few paragraphs describing the place you visited and telling what you did there. Be sure to explain why this particular experience made you feel especially close to the natural world.

ANNIE DILLARD

HOW I WROTE THE
MOTH ESSAY—AND WHY

It was November 1975. I was living alone, as described, on an island in Puget   1
Sound, near the Canadian border. I was thirty years old. I thought about
myself a lot (for someone thirty years old), because I couldn't figure out what I
was doing there. What was my life about? Why was I living alone, when I am
gregarious? Would I ever meet someone, or should I reconcile myself to all this
solitude? I disliked celibacy; I dreaded childlessness. I couldn't even think of anything to write. I was examining every event for possible meaning.

I was then in full flight from success, from the recent fuss over a book of   2
prose I'd published the previous year called *Pilgrim at Tinker Creek*. There were
offers from editors, publishers, and Hollywood and network producers. They
tempted me with world travel, film and TV work, big bucks. I was there to turn
from literary and commercial success and to rededicate myself to art and to
God. That's how I justified my loneliness to myself. It was a feeble justification
and I knew it, because you certainly don't need to live alone either to write or to
pray. Actually I was there because I had picked the place from an atlas, and I
was alone because I hadn't yet met my husband.

My reading and teaching fed my thoughts. I was reading Simone Weil,   3
First and Last Notebooks. Simone Weil was a twentieth-century French intellectual, born Jewish, who wrote some of the most interesting Christian theology

I've ever read. She was brilliant, but a little nuts; her doctrines were harsh. "Literally," she wrote, "it is total purity or death." This sort of fanaticism attracted and appalled me. Weil had deliberately starved herself to death to call attention to the plight of French workers. I was taking extensive notes on Weil.

In the classroom I was teaching poetry writing, exhorting myself (in the guise of exhorting my students), and convincing myself by my own rhetoric: commit yourself to a useless art! In art alone is meaning! In sacrifice alone is meaning! These, then, were issues for me at that time: dedication, purity, sacrifice. 4

Early that November morning I noticed the hollow insects on the bathroom floor. I got down on my hands and knees to examine them and recognized some as empty moth bodies. I recognized them, of course, only because I'd seen an empty moth body already—two years before, when I'd camped alone and had watched a flying moth get stuck in a candle and burn. 5

Walking back to my desk, where I had been answering letters, I realized that the burning moth was a dandy visual focus for all my recent thoughts about an empty, dedicated life. Perhaps I'd try to write a short narrative about it. 6

I went to my pile of journals, hoping I'd taken some nice, specific notes about the moth in the candle. What I found disappointed me at first: that night I'd written a long description of owl sounds, and only an annoyed aside about bugs flying into the candle. But the next night, after pages of self-indulgent drivel, I'd written a fuller description, a description of the moth which got stuck in candle wax. 7

The journal entry had some details I could use (bristleworms on the ground, burnt moths' wings sticking to pans), some phrases (her body acted as a wick, the candle had 2 flames, the moth burned until I blew it out), and, especially, some verbs (hiss, recoil, stick, spatter, jerked, crackled). 8

Even in the journals, the moth was female. (From childhood reading I'd learned to distinguish moths by sex.) And, there in the journal, was a crucial detail: on that camping trip, I'd been reading about Rimbaud. Arthur Rimbaud—the French symbolist poet, a romantic, hotheaded figure who attracted me enormously when I was sixteen—had been young and 9 self-destructive. When *he* was sixteen, he ran away from home to Paris, led a dissolute life, shot his male lover (the poet Verlaine), drank absinthe which damaged his brain, deranged his senses with drunkenness and sleeplessness, and wrote mad vivid poetry which altered the course of Western literature. When he was in his twenties, he turned his back to the Western world and vanished into Abyssinia[1] as a gunrunner.

With my old journal beside me, I took up my current journal and scribbled and doodled my way through an account of my present life and the remembered moth. It went extraordinarily well; it was not typical. It seemed very much "given"—given, I think, because I'd asked, because I'd been looking so hard and so long for connections, meanings. The connections were all there, and seemed solid enough: I saw a moth burnt and on fire; I was reading Rimbaud hoping to rededicate myself to writing (this one bald statement of motive was unavoidable); I live alone. So the writer is like the moth, and like a religious contemplative: emptying himself so he can be a channel for his work. Of course you can reinforce connections with language: the bathroom moths are like a jumble of buttresses for cathedral domes; the female moth is like an immolating monk, like a hollow saint, a flame-faced virgin gone to God; Rimbaud burnt out his brains with poetry while night pooled wetly at my feet.   10

I liked the piece enough to rewrite it. I took out a couple of paragraphs— one about why I didn't have a dog, another that ran on about the bathroom spider. This is the kind of absurdity you fall into when you write about anything, let alone about yourself. You're so pleased and grateful to be writing at all, especially at the beginning, that you babble. Often you don't know where the work is going, so you can't tell what's irrelevant.   11

It doesn't hurt much to babble in a first draft, so long as you have the sense to cut out irrelevancies later. If you are used to analyzing texts, you will be able to formulate a clear statement of what your draft turned out to be about. Then you make a list of what you've already written, paragraph by paragraph, and see what doesn't fit and cut it out. (All this requires is nerves of steel and lots of   12

1. Historic, Arabic-derived name for Ethiopia, a country in eastern Africa.

coffee.) Most of the time you'll have to add to the beginning, ensuring that it gives a fair idea of what the point might be, or at least what is about to happen. (Suspense is for mystery writers. The most inept writing has an inadvertent element of suspense: the reader constantly asks himself, where on earth is this going?) Usually I end up throwing away the beginning: the first part of a poem, the first few pages of an essay, the first scene of a story, even the first few chapters of a book. It's not holy writ. The paragraphs and sentences are tesserae—tiles for a mosaic. Just because you have a bunch of tiles in your lap doesn't mean your mosaic will be better if you use them all. In this atypical case, however, there were very few extraneous passages. The focus was tight, probably because I'd been so single-minded before I wrote it.

I added stuff, too, to strengthen and clarify the point. I added some speculation about the burning moth: had she mated and laid her eggs, had she done her work? Near the end I added a passage about writing class: which of you want to give your lives and become writers? 13

Ultimately I sent it to *Harper's* magazine, which published it. The early drafts, and the *Harper's* version, had a different ending, a kind of punch line that was a series of interlocking statements: 14

> I don't mind living alone. I like eating alone and reading. I don't mind sleeping alone. The only time I mind being alone is when something is funny; then, when I am laughing at something funny, I wish someone were around. Sometimes I think it is pretty funny that I sleep alone.

I took this ending out of the book version, which is the version you have. I took it out because the tone was too snappy, too clever; it reduced everything to celibacy, which was really a side issue; it made the reader forget the moth; and it called too much attention to the narrator. The new ending was milder. It referred back to the main body of the text.

Revising is a breeze if you know what you're doing—if you can look at your text coldly, analytically, manipulatively. Since I've studied texts, I know what I'm doing when I revise. The hard part is devising the wretched thing in 15 the first place. How do you go from nothing to something? How do you face the blank page without fainting dead away?

To start a narrative, you need a batch of things. Not feelings, not opinions, not sentiments, not judgments, not arguments, but specific objects and events: a cat, a spider web, a mess of insect skeletons, a candle, a book about Rimbaud, a burning moth. I try to give the reader a story, or at least a scene (the flimsiest narrative occasion will serve), and something to look at. I try not to hang on the reader's arm and bore him with my life story, my fancy self-indulgent writing, or my opinions. He is my guest; I try to entertain him. Or he'll throw my pages across the room and turn on the television.

I try to say what I mean and not "hide the hidden meaning." "Clarity is the sovereign courtesy of the writer," said J. Henri Fabre, the great French entomologist, "I do my best to achieve it." Actually, it took me about ten years to learn to write clearly. When I was in my twenties, I was more interested in showing off.

What do you do with these things? You juggle them. You toss them around. To begin, you don't need a well-defined point. You don't need "something to say"—that will just lead you to reiterating clichés. You need bits of the world to toss around. You start anywhere, and join the bits into a pattern by your writing about them. Later you can throw out the ones that don't fit.

I like to start by describing something, by ticking off the five senses. Later I go back to the beginning and locate the reader in time and space. I've found that if I take pains to be precise about *things*, feelings will take care of themselves. If you try to force a reader's feelings through dramatic writing ("writhe," "ecstasy," "scream"), you make a fool of yourself, like someone at a party trying too hard to be liked.

How to describe things is covered in Chapter 4.

I have piles of materials in my journals—mostly information in the form of notes on my reading, and to a lesser extent, notes on things I'd seen and heard during the day. I began the journals five or six years after college, finding myself highly trained for taking notes and for little else. Now I have thirty-some journal volumes, all indexed. If I want to write about arctic exploration,

16

17

18

19

20

OPPOSITE: *Dillard's first encounter with the moth: a page from her journal, 1974.*

in there were quickly, too.

The rip on thigh seam is 10" long. Oh, dear jeans.

Last night moths kept flying into the candle. They would hiss & spatter & recoil, lost upside down & flopping in the shadows among the pans on the table. Or — and this happened often, & again tonight — they'd burn their wings, & then their wings would stick to the next thing they'd touch — the edge of a pan, a lid.... these I could free with a quick flip with a spoon or something.

Some, of course, burnt badly & couldn't get away. One moth flew in the near candle. Her wings burnt right off, her legs & head crackled and jerked. Her body was stuck upright in the wax; it must have been dry. Moths are dry. Because it acted as a wick; without burning itself, it drew up wax from the pool, and gave off a steady flame for two hours, until I blew ~~the candle~~ it out. That one candle had two flames. Brightened up my whole evening.

I was screaming to them last night. I got upset, & it was in my voice. Wonder what the neighbors thought: no! don't do it! please — no! So tonight I read in the lodge. After the B & O, I read upstairs on the couch.

Talked to Steve, at Contes w/ KK; talked to Richard twice, at noon, & now.

I don't know what those firm segmented multi-legged invertebrates are, but they're all over the place up here. Bristleworms? they're hard on the outside, chitinous I guess. Anyway. One on the path today was on its side, struggling. A big spider of the harvestman sort, but w/ a big grey body, was all over it doing I know not what, & so was a fly.

say, or star chemistry, or monasticism, I can find masses of pertinent data under that topic. And if I browse I can often find images from other fields that may fit into what I'm writing, if only as metaphor or simile. It's terrific having all these materials handy. It saves and makes available all those years of reading. Otherwise, I'd forget everything, and life wouldn't accumulate, but merely pass.

The moth essay I wrote that November day was an "odd" piece—"freighted with heavy-handed symbolism," as I described it to myself just after I wrote it. The reader must be startled to watch this apparently calm, matter-of-fact account of the writer's life and times turn before his eyes into a mess of symbols whose real subject matter is their own relationship. I hoped the reader wouldn't feel he'd been had. I tried to ensure that the actual, historical moth wouldn't vanish into idea, but would stay physically present.   21

A week after I wrote the first draft I considered making it part of the book (*Holy the Firm*) I had been starting. It seemed to fit the book's themes. (Actually, I spent the next fifteen months fitting the book to *its* themes.) In order to clarify my thinking I jotted down some notes: 22

> moth in candle:
>
> the poet—   materials of world, of bare earth at feet, sucked up, transformed, subsumed to spirit, to air, to light
>
> the mystic— not through reason
>   but through emptiness
>
> the martyr—virgin, sacrifice, death with meaning.

I prefaced these notes with the comical word "Hothead."

    It had been sheer good luck that the different aspects of the historical truth fit together so nicely. It had actually been on that particular solo camping trip that I'd read the Rimbaud novel. If it hadn't been, I wouldn't have hesitated to fiddle with the facts. I fiddled   23

How to make an informal outline is explained on p. 31.

with one fact, for sure: I foully slandered my black cat, Small, by saying she was "gold"—to match the book's moth and little blonde burnt girl. I actually had a gold cat at that time, named Kindling. I figured no one would believe it. It was too much. In the book, as in real life, the cat was spayed.

This is the most personal piece I've ever written—the essay itself, and these notes on it. I don't recommend, or even approve, writing personally. It can lead to dreadful writing. The danger is that you'll get lost in the contemplation of your wonderful self. You'll include things for the lousy reason that they actually happened, or that you feel strongly about them; you'll forget to ensure that the *reader* feels anything whatever. You may hold the popular view that art is self-expression, or a way of understanding the self—in which case the artist need do nothing more than babble uncontrolledly about the self and then congratulate himself that, in addition to all his other wonderfully interesting attributes, he is also an artist. I don't (evidently) hold this view. So I think that this moth piece is a risky one to read: it seems to enforce these romantic and giddy notions of art and the artist. But I trust you can keep your heads. 24

FOR DISCUSSION AND WRITING

. . . .

1. Why is Annie Dillard generally opposed to "writing personally" (24)? What dangers and pitfalls in particular does she think the writer of a personal narrative should try to avoid?

2. Dillard advises the aspiring writer to "look at your text coldly, analytically, manipulatively" (15). Why does she give this advice? How does the writer, in her view, acquire the ability to do such close, analytical reading?

3. How, according to Dillard, should a writer use DESCRIPTION to support what a piece of writing has to say, particularly any "well defined point" the writer might want to make (18)? Point to specific details in her text that show how Dillard herself uses this particular mode of writing.

4. The "hard part" about writing, Dillard says, is getting started in the first place, going "from nothing to something" on the blank page (15). What does a writer need "to start a narrative," according to Dillard (16)? How, and how well, does this essay illustrate what she says about the early stages of the writing process?

5. Write an essay explaining how you usually write. Include such information as where and when and under what conditions you work best, the supplies and materials you use, and the processes you go through, including your reading and research.

IDENTIFYING COMMON PATTERNS

Like writing, reading is an active process. Even when you take a thriller to the woods or beach and read just for fun, your brain is busily at work translating the words on the page into mental images and ideas. It's even busier when you read to see what a text has to offer you as a writer, as Annie Dillard did the night the moth flew into her campfire. Let's now consider some of the patterns we'll be looking for as we explore the texts in this book.

Suppose you went on a camping trip in the mountains. After settling in and doing a little fishing and hiking, you text the following messages to a friend back home:

- nce hr bt bggy

- ptchd tnt, lnchd cnoe, cght 2 bass

- fsh bggr thn last yr

- grt hkng, u shld cm

These four text messages—and they're still *texts*, whether composed with a pencil or on a smartphone—are examples, however brief, of four traditional *modes* of writing: description, narration, exposition, and argument. These basic patterns of writing can be defined as follows:

- DESCRIPTION* appeals to the reader's senses. Descriptive writing tells what something looks, feels, sounds, smells, or tastes like ("nice here but buggy"). Patterns and methods of description are discussed in Chapter 4.

- NARRATION is storytelling. Narrative writing focuses on events; it tells what happened ("pitched tent, launched canoe, caught two bass"). Patterns and methods of narration are discussed in Chapter 5.

- EXPOSITION is informative writing ("the fish are bigger this year than they were last year"). Exposition explains by giving EXAMPLES (Chapter 6); by CLASSIFYING (Chapter 7); by analyzing a PROCESS (Chapter 8); by COMPARING AND CONTRASTING, (Chapter 9); by DEFINING (Chapter 10); and by analyzing CAUSES AND EFFECTS (Chapter 11). Exposition is the form of writing you are likely to use most often. Examinations, research papers, job applications, sales reports, insurance claims—in fact, almost every scrap of practical writing you do over a lifetime, including your last will and testament—will require expository skills.

- ARGUMENT is persuasive writing. It makes a claim and offers evidence that the writer hopes will be sufficient to convince the reader to accept that claim—and perhaps even to act on it ("the hiking is good here; you should come"). Patterns, methods, and strategies of argument are discussed in detail in Chapter 12.

Now let's go back to the Dillard essays and see what they can teach us about these basic patterns of writing. If we can grasp how Dillard uses these common patterns to create such fine pieces of work, we'll be well on our way to adapting these same patterns in our own writing.

---

*Words printed in SMALL CAPITALS are defined in the Glossary/Index.

HOW ANNIE DILLARD USES
COMMON PATTERNS

Let's look now at the various patterns that Annie Dillard uses in her two essays, starting with the one about the death of the moth.

The parts of Dillard's essay that focus on events—particularly those that took place on the night the moth flew into the flames and "frazzled and fried"—are in the NARRATIVE mode (7). Here the writer is using common strategies and techniques of storytelling, for example by constructing a PLOT that involves conflict, climax, and resolution. In fact, the basic framework of Dillard's essay is that of a narrative, much like those you'll read in Chapter 5.

In addition to telling a story, Dillard also weaves in a detailed DESCRIPTION of the scene. In particular, she describes the physical campsite (with its mundane pots and pans and other gear) and the striking figure of the burning moth whose wings "ignited like tissue paper, enlarging the circle of light in the clearing and creating out of the darkness the sudden blue sleeves of my sweater, the green leaves of jewelweed by my side, the ragged red trunk of a pine" (7). Here Dillard is using common techniques of descriptive writing (discussed in Chapter 4) that are both SUBJECTIVE (the moth as symbol) and more scientifically OBJECTIVE (the moth as a garden variety insect with a thorax and "two-inch wingspan.")

Why is Dillard so scrupulously describing the death of a mere moth? Instead of expressing some strange bug fetish, Dillard's essay is making a highly personal statement about reading for inspiration and about the nature of what writers do. The focal point of Dillard's description is the burning moth itself, but the underlying purpose of her essay is to draw a COMPARISON between the burning moth and the writer. Comparison is discussed in Chapter 9.

The point of Dillard's comparison is to explain what being a writer means to her. What it means, in short, is devotion and sacrifice. This is why the moth is drawn to the flame that consumes it "like a hollow saint" (9). This a Romantic view of the writer, inspired not only by Dillard's reading of the French Romantic poet Arthur Rimbaud, but also by her immersion in the work of the American writers Henry David Thoreau and Ralph Waldo Emerson, who typically read the natural world for signs of the divine.

But why is Dillard making such a point about writing in the first place? In addition to narrating, describing, and comparing, it would seem that Dillard is also constructing an ARGUMENT (Chapter 12). The purpose of that argument—by a writer who is also a committed teacher of writing—is to inspire her students to take up the torch: "How many of you, I asked the people in my class, which of you want to give your lives and be writers?" (10).

See p. 524 on how to state your point.

When you construct a text, you may have reason to weave together several patterns, as Dillard does in her first essay. Sometimes, however, you'll find that one particular mode of writing fits your purpose or topic best or will be most likely to reach your audience, and then you might use that pattern to organize an entire piece of writing.

This is the case with Dillard's second essay, "How I Wrote the Moth Essay—and Why." The piece includes traces of several patterns; but it is written, by and large, to explain a process. Dillard's stated purpose in this second essay is to explain how and why she wrote the first essay. Thus the dominant pattern she uses is PROCESS ANALYSIS, the strategy discussed in Chapter 8.

In addition to explaining, step by step, how she wrote a particular essay comparing an inspired writer (dedicated to her task) with a moth drawn to a flame, Dillard is also analyzing a larger process for us here: the process of writing itself. As she explains it, the process Dillard went through in order to compose her essay is essentially the same process we all go through when we write: finding a subject to write about and taking notes on it; mulling the subject over for a while and writing out a draft; revising that draft "analytically"; and, finally, editing and proofreading what we've written to make a finished version. (We'll examine all these activities in detail in the next chapter, "The Writing Process.")

See p. 24 on how writing is a recursive process.

LEARNING FROM THE ESSAYS IN THIS BOOK

Throughout this book, you'll be learning how writers of all stripes follow certain fundamental patterns and use many other common strategies and techniques in their writing, as Annie Dillard does in her moth essays, and as you will in all the writing that you do. Like a spider weaving its web, however, every writer, including you, uses these familiar patterns and techniques in his or her own distinctive ways. As you'll soon see by studying the essays in the *Sampler*, the exact patterns you choose will vary with your purposes and audiences.

To help you recognize these patterns and techniques and think about how you might use them in your own writing, most of the essays in this book are followed by a complete set of study questions and writing prompts. These questions and prompts approach the readings in the following ways:

- FOR DISCUSSION. These questions are intended to help you look at the text as an exchange of ideas between a writer and a reader, prompting you to read in order to understand what the text is saying—and to discover your own views on the subject under discussion. In other words, these are questions that will help you think about what the author is saying and then to consider what you think, and why.

- STRATEGIES AND STRUCTURES. These questions will help you to recognize and understand how the text is constructed—to think about what patterns and techniques the authors have used to organize their ideas and present them to an audience, and to imagine how you might use them in your own writing.

- WORDS AND FIGURES OF SPEECH. These questions focus on the language and style of the text. They're designed to help you think about both the literal and figurative meanings of specific words and phrases.

- FOR WRITING. These are prompts that will help you get started, in some cases by suggesting topics to write about, and in other instances, by asking questions to help you respond to whatever the author of the reading has said.

SOME STRATEGIES FOR READING

When you read any text, you generally engage in several activities: previewing, reading closely and critically, and responding. Let's take a look at each of these.

Previewing a Text

Before you plunge into a text, take a few moments to survey the territory. Try to get a sense of where the text is going and what you want to focus on. Here are some tips for previewing the readings in this book:

- *Look at the headnote* to learn about the author and the original context— the time, place, and circumstances in which the text was written and published.

- *Think about the title.* What does it reveal about the topic and TONE of the text? Are you expecting a serious argument? An essay that pokes fun at its subject? Something else? Clearly the title of Annie Dillard's *Holy the Firm*, for instance, evokes the world of the spirit (*holy*). Might the other half, *firm*, suggest something about nature, as in *firm* ground?

- *Skim the text for an overview,* noting headings, boldfaced words, lists, and so on.

- *Skim the introduction and conclusion.* What insights do they give you into the purpose and message of the text?

- *Think about your own purpose for reading.* Do you want to obtain information, confirm a fact or opinion, fulfill an assignment? How will your purpose affect what you focus on?

Reading Closely and Critically

Reading a text closely and critically is a little like investigating a crime scene. You look for certain clues; you ask certain questions. Your objective is to determine, as precisely and accurately as you can, both what the text has to say and how it says it. Your primary clues, therefore, are in the text itself—the actual words on the page.

If you've previewed the text, you already have some idea of what it's about. Now is the time to examine it closely. So pull out your pencil and highlighter, and annotate the text as you go along—jot down questions or comments in the margins, underline important points, circle key words, and mark places you may want to come back to. Here are some questions to ask yourself as you read:

- **What is the writer's main point?** Is it clearly stated in a thesis? If so, where? If the main point is not stated directly, is it clearly implied? This is a key question to ask, for example, about Annie Dillard's essay on the death of the moth; otherwise, we are likely to misread it as an essay about insects when it is really about writing.

- **What is the writer's primary purpose?** To provide information? Sell a product or service? Argue a point of view? Make us laugh? Tell a story? What's motivated the author to write—is he or she responding to something others have said?

- **Who is the intended audience?** Readers who are familiar with the topic? Those who know little about it? People inclined to agree—or disagree? How can you tell?

- **What is the tone of the text?** Serious? Informal? Inspirational? Strident?

- **How and where does the writer support the main point?** Look for specific details, facts, examples, expert testimony, or other kinds of evidence.

- **Is the evidence sufficient?** Or does it fail to convince you? Are sources clearly identified so that you can tell where the material is coming from?

- **Has the writer fairly represented—and responded to—other points of view?** Has any crucial perspective been left out?

- **What is the larger historical and cultural context?** Who is the author? When was the text written? What other ideas or events does it reflect?

Responding to What You Read

After you have read and reread a text closely, think about and respond to it in writing. Here are a few tips for doing so:

- **Summarize what you've read in your own words.** If you can write a brief, accurate summary of the main point, you probably have a good grasp of what you've read.

- **Think about and record your own reactions.** Where are you most inclined to accept the writer's ideas? Least inclined? Aren't sure? Indicate specific passages in the text where you think the writer's ideas are particularly well presented, whether you agree with those ideas or not.

- **Consider what you've learned about writing.** Note any techniques that you might want to try in your own writing, such as a particularly tight introduction, cogent use of examples, apt choice of words, or striking application of visuals. With Dillard's moth essay, for instance, a key lesson might be learned from how she uses physical details, such as the image of the burning moth, to suggest abstract ideas.

CHAPTER TWO

THE WRITING
PROCESS

◇◇

U NLIKE flying from Seattle to Hawaii, writing is not a linear process. We plan, we draft, we revise; we plan, we draft, we revise again. In addition, we tend to skip around as we write, perhaps going back and completely rewriting what we've already written before plunging in again. This chapter is about the various stages of the writing process that you will typically go through in order to get from a blank page or screen to a final draft.

PLANNING

Before you plunge headlong into any writing assignment, think about the nature of the assignment, the length and scope of the text you're supposed to write, and your PURPOSE* and AUDIENCE. To help budget your time, also keep in mind two things in particular: (1) *When the assignment is due.* As soon as you get an assignment, jot down the deadline. And remember that it's hard to write a good paper if you begin the night before it's due. (2) *What kind of research the assignment will require.* For many college papers, the research may take longer than the actual writing. Think about how much and what kind of research you will need to do, and allow plenty of time for it.

*Words printed in SMALL CAPITALS are defined in the Glossary/Index.

Considering Your Purpose and Audience

We write for many reasons: to organize and clarify our thoughts, express our feelings, remember people and events, solve problems, persuade others to act or believe as we think they should. As you think about *why* you're writing, however, you also need to consider *who* your readers are. The following questions will help you think about your intended purpose and audience:

- **What is your reason for writing?** Do you want to tell readers something they may not know? Entertain them? Change their minds?

- **Who is going to read (or hear) what you say?** Your classmates? Your teacher? Readers of a blog? Your supervisor at work?

- **How much does your audience already know about your subject?** If you are writing for a general audience, you may need to provide some background information and explain any terminology that may be unfamiliar to them.

- **What should you keep in mind about the makeup and background of your audience?** Does the gender of your audience matter? How about their age, level of education, occupation, economic status, or religion? Are they likely to be sympathetic or unsympathetic to your position? Once you have sized up your audience, you'll be in a better position to generate ideas and EVIDENCE that will both support what you have to say and appeal to that audience.

Coming Up with a Subject—and Focusing on a Topic

Before you can get very far into the writing process, you will need to come up with a subject and narrow it down to a workable topic. Though we often use the words interchangeably, a *subject*, strictly speaking, is a broad field of inquiry, whereas a *topic* is a specific area within that field. For example, if you are writing a paper on "the health care system in the United States," your teacher will still want to know just what approach you plan to take to that general subject. A good topic focuses in on a specific area of a general subject—such as the *causes* of waste in the health care system, or *why* more Americans need health insurance, or *how* to reform Medicare—that can be adequately covered in the time you have to write about it.

With many writing assignments, you will be given a specific topic, or choice of topics, as part of the assignment. Make sure you understand just what you are being asked to do. Look for key terms like *describe, define, analyze, compare and contrast, evaluate, argue.* Be aware that even short assignments may include more than one of these directives. For example, the same assignment may ask you not only to define Medicare and Medicaid but also to compare the two government programs.

For some assignments, you will have to find a topic, perhaps after meeting with your teacher. Let your instructor know if you're already interested in a particular topic. Ask your instructor for suggestions—and start looking on your own. In each chapter in this book, you'll find ideas for finding a topic and for developing it into an essay by using the basic patterns of writing—DESCRIPTION, NARRATION, EXEMPLIFICATION, CLASSIFICATION, PROCESS ANALYSIS, COMPARISON, DEFINITION, CAUSE AND EFFECT, and ARGUMENT—that good writers use all the time.

GENERATING IDEAS

Once you have a topic to write about, where do you look for ideas? Over the years, writing teachers have developed a number of techniques to help writers generate ideas. All of the following techniques may come in handy at various points in the writing process, not just at the outset.

Freewriting

Simply put pen to paper (or fingers to keyboard) and jot down whatever pops into your head. Here are some tips for freewriting:

1. Write nonstop for five or ten minutes. If nothing comes to mind at first, just write: "Nothing. My mind is blank." Eventually the words *will* come—if you don't stop writing until time runs out.

2. Circle words or ideas that you might want to come back to, but don't stop freewriting. When your time is up, mark any passages that look promising.

3. Freewrite again, starting with something you marked in the previous session. Do this over and over and over again until you find an idea you want to explore further.

Keeping Lists

Keeping lists is a good way to generate ideas—and to come up with interesting examples and details. Here are some tips for keeping a list:

- A list can be written anytime and anywhere: on a computer, in a notebook, on a napkin. Always keep a pencil handy.

- If your lists start to get long, group related items into piles, as you would if you were sorting your laundry. Look for relationships not only *within* those piles but *among* them.

Brainstorming

When you brainstorm, you write down words and ideas in one sitting rather than over time. Here are a few tips for brainstorming:

- If you are brainstorming by yourself, start by jotting down a topic at the top of your page or screen. Then write out a list of every idea, comment, or word that comes to mind.

- Brainstorming is often more effective when you do it collaboratively, with everyone throwing out ideas and one person acting as scribe. If you brainstorm with others, make sure everyone contributes—no one person should monopolize the session.

Asking Questions

Journalists and other writers ask *who, what, where, when, why,* and *how* to uncover the basic information for a story. Here is how you might use these questions if you were writing an essay about an argument in a parking lot:

- **Who** was involved in the argument? What should I say about my brother (one of the instigators) and his friends? The police officer who investigated? The witnesses?

- **What** happened? What did the participants say to one another? What did my brother do after he was struck by one of his friends?

- **Where** did the argument occur? How much of the parking lot should I describe? What can I say about it?

- **When** did the argument take place? What time did my brother leave the party, and when did he arrive in the parking lot?

- **Why** did the argument occur? Did it have anything to do with my brother's girlfriend?

- **How** would my brother have reacted if he hadn't been drinking? Should I write about the effects of alcohol on anger management?

Keeping a Journal

As we learned from Annie Dillard in Chapter 1, a personal journal can be a great source of raw material for your writing. Often, what you write in a journal today will help you with a piece of writing months or even years later. Here are some pointers for keeping a journal:

- Write as informally as you like, but jot down your observations as close in time to the event as possible.

- The observations in a journal do not have to deal with momentous events; record your everyday thoughts and experiences.

- Make each journal entry as detailed and specific as possible; don't just write, "The weather was awful" or "I went for a walk." Instead, write, "Rained for an hour, followed by hail the size of mothballs" or "Walked from the wharf to Market St."

Doing Research

Most academic writing—and especially longer assignments—will require at least some research beyond simply thinking about your topic and deciding what you want to emphasize. Finding out *and taking notes* on what has already been said on your topic, particularly by experts in the field, is basic to writing about anything much more complicated than how to tie your shoes. (And even there, you can find whole websites devoted to the subject.)

When you do research and writing in any field, you enter into an ongoing "conversation" with others who have preceded you in that same field of inquiry. Quoting, paraphrasing, or otherwise referring to what they have said is common in academic writing, and you'll find copious information on how to do this in the Appendix ("Using Sources in Your Writing"). Whenever you use someone else's work, of course, you need to document your sources scrupulously and accurately, using a standard form of citation. The Appendix, which uses the style of the Modern Language Association (MLA), will help with this, too.

As with any lively conversation, the purpose of doing research is not only to learn what others are saying but to spark ideas of your own. To keep track of those ideas (and your sources), consider keeping a research journal. It can reside in a section of a personal journal or, even better, in a separate research notebook or file on your computer. Here again, Annie Dillard is a great model. "I have piles of materials in my journals—mostly information in the form of notes on my reading," she says in "How I Wrote the Moth Essay—and Why." "If I want to write about arctic exploration, say, or star chemistry, or monasticism, I can find masses of pertinent data under that topic."

ORGANIZING AND DRAFTING

Once you have an abundance of facts, details, and other raw material, your next job is to organize that material and develop it into a draft. Generally, you will want to report events in chronological order—unless you are tracing the causes of a particular phenomenon or event, in which case you may want to work backward in time. Facts, statistics, personal experience, expert testimony, and other evidence should usually be presented in the order of their relative importance to your topic. But more than anything else, the order in which you present your ideas on any topic will be determined by exactly what you have to say about it.

Stating Your Point

Before you actually begin writing, think carefully about the main point you want to make—your THESIS. You may find that your thesis changes as you draft, but starting with a thesis in mind will help you identify the ideas and details you want to include—and the order in which you present them to the reader. Often you'll want to state your thesis in a single sentence as a THESIS STATEMENT.

What makes a good thesis statement? First, let's consider what a thesis statement is not. A simple announcement of your topic—"In this paper I will discuss what's wrong with the U.S. health care system"—is not a thesis statement. A good thesis statement not only tells the reader what your topic is, it makes an interesting CLAIM *about* your topic, one that is open to further discussion. That's why statements of fact are not thesis statements, either: "More than forty-five million people in the United States have no health insurance." Facts may support your thesis, but the thesis itself should say something about your topic that requires further discussion. For example: "To fix health care in America, we need to develop a single-payer system of health insurance."

A thesis statement like this at the beginning of your essay clarifies your main point—and it helps to set up the rest of the essay. In this case, the reader might expect a definition of a single-payer insurance system, with an analysis of the effects of adopting such a system, and an argument for why those particular effects will provide the needed fix.

Making an Informal Outline

Making an informal outline can also help you organize and develop your draft. Simply write down your thesis statement, and follow it with the main subpoints you intend to cover. Here is an informal outline that one student in a medical ethics class jotted down as she drafted a paper on the American health care system:

> THESIS: The costs of health care in America can be contained by paying for medical results rather than medical services.
> —what the current fee-for-services system is
> —problems with the system, such as unnecessary tests, high administrative costs
> —how to reform the system
> —how to pay for the new system

Using the Modes

As you draft, consider using the various MODES OF WRITING to help you think of things to say about your topic. For example:

- Use DESCRIPTION (pp. 59–70) to show what some aspect of your topic looks, sounds, feels, smells, or tastes like: "I stood on the steps with my father as he pointed into the distance, where a dark funnel coiled downward from the black clouds, like smoke or wind, taking shape and color."

  —PAUL CRENSHAW, "Storm Country"

- Use NARRATION (pp. 123–33) to tell a story about some aspect of your topic: "I was seven years old the first time I snuck out of the house in the dark."

  —LYNDA BARRY, "The Sanctuary of School"

- Use EXAMPLES (pp. 184–92) to give specific instances of your topic: "Every culture comes up with tests of a person's ability to get out of a sticky situation. The English plant mazes. Tropical resorts market those straw finger-grabbers that tighten their grip the harder you pull on them, and Viennese intellectuals gave us the concept of childhood sexuality—figure it out, or remain neurotic for life."

    —PHILIP WEISS, "How to Get Out of a Locked Trunk"

- Use CLASSIFICATION (pp. 238–45) to divide various aspects of your topic into categories: "If you make money with money, as some of my super-rich friends do, your [tax] percentage may be a bit lower than mine. But if you earn money from a job, your percentage will surely exceed mine—most likely by a lot."

    —WARREN BUFFETT, "Stop Coddling the Super-Rich"

- Use PROCESS ANALYSIS (pp. 292–303) to explain how some aspect of your topic works or is made: "Although the word 'espionage' conjures images of shady characters in overcoats who are hired to steal nuclear secrets, today's corporate spies are decidedly less glamorous. For one, they are hired to find out prosaic things like a company's marketing plan, the state of its R and D or a factory's production capacity. (Valuable, yes, but not sexy.) And instead of fancy gizmos like exploding pens and secret decoder rings, often all they need to get the job done is a telephone."

    —ADAM PENENBERG AND MARC BARRY, "The Pizza Plot"

- Use COMPARISON AND CONTRAST (pp. 353–62) to point out similarities and differences in various aspects of your topic: "The classroom is a different environment for those who feel comfortable putting themselves forward in a group than it is for those who find the prospect of doing so chastening, or even terrifying."

    —DEBORAH TANNEN, "Gender in the Classroom"

- Use DEFINITION (pp. 412–20) to explain what some aspect of your topic is or is not: "Should I explain . . . that I am Guatemalan by birth but *pura gringa* by circumstance?"

    —TANYA MARIA BARRIENTOS, "Se Habla Español"

- Use CAUSE AND EFFECT (pp. 471–80) to explain why some aspect of your topic happened or what effects it might have: "What made the pain abate was my mother's reaction. I'd never, ever heard her talk back to a white person before."

  —HENRY LOUIS GATES JR., "A Giant Step"

- Use ARGUMENT (pp. 517–32) to make and support your thesis: "In fact, in this time of economic hardship, political instability, and rapid technological change, empathy is the one quality we most need if we're going to flourish in the twenty-first century."

  —ARIANNA HUFFINGTON, "Empathy"

Templates for Using the Modes as You Draft

When you draw on the modes to help you develop a draft, you probably won't end up using them all. As with any other kind of writing strategy, go with the ones that work for your particular topic, purpose, and audience. The following templates outline ways to use the modes to get started with almost any topic ("X"). Don't take these as formulas where you just have to fill in the blanks; there are no easy formulas for good writing. However, these templates can help you get started with some of the basic moves you'll need to make as you draft:

> ► X can be described as having the following characteristics: _____, _____, and _____.
>
> ► What has happened to X is _____, _____, and _____.
>
> ► Some examples of X are _____, _____, and _____.
>
> ► X can be divided into the following categories: _____, _____, and _____.
>
> ► The process of X can be broken down into the following steps: _____, _____, and _____.

- X is like Y in that both are _____ and _____; however, X is different from Y in _____ and _____.

- X can be defined as a(n) _____with the following characteristics: _____ and _____

- X was caused by _____and _____; the effects of X are _____ and _____.

- What should be done about X is _____, _____, and _____.

The Parts of a Draft

As you use your outline, thesis statement, and the modes to construct a draft, think of it as having essentially three parts: a beginning, a middle, and an ending. Each of these parts should be shaped with your potential reader in mind.

Your beginning, or *introduction*, is the first thing the reader sees. It should grab—and hold—the reader's attention. The introduction should also tell the reader exactly what you're writing about and, most of the time, should include a clear statement of your thesis. Occasionally, you may want to build up to your thesis statement, but most of the time it's best to state your thesis right off the bat. (For more examples and information about drafting an introduction, see p. 55.)

The middle, or *body*, of your draft may run anywhere from a few paragraphs to many pages. This is the part in which you present your best commentary and evidence in support of your main point. That evidence can include facts and figures, examples, the testimony of experts (usually in the form of citations from sources that you carefully acknowledge), and perhaps your own personal experience. How much evidence will you need?

The amount of evidence you'll need will depend in part on how broad or narrow your thesis is. A broad thesis on how to combat climate change would obviously require more—and more-detailed—evidence than a thesis about the cost of textbooks at a campus bookstore. Ultimately, it is the reader who determines whether or not your evidence is sufficient. So as you draft, ask yourself questions like these about the details you should include:

- *What is the best example I can give to illustrate my main point?* Is one example enough, or should I give several?

- *Of all the facts I could cite, which ones support my thesis best?* What additional facts will the reader expect or need to have?

- *Of everything I've read on my topic, which sources are absolutely indispensable?* What others were particularly clear or authoritative on the issue? How do I cite my sources appropriately? (For more information on using and citing sources, see the Appendix.)

- *Is my personal experience truly relevant to my point?* Or would I be better off staying out of the picture? Or citing someone whose experience or knowledge is even more compelling than mine?

In the ending, or *conclusion*, of your draft, you sum up what you have to say, often by restating the thesis—but with some variation based on the evidence you have just cited. For instance, you can make a recommendation ("more research is needed to show which frequently prescribed medical tests actually work") or explain the larger significance of your topic ("lowering health care costs for individuals will allow more people to be covered without incurring additional outlays"). (For more examples and information about drafting a conclusion, see p. 57.)

Using Visuals

Illustrations such as graphs and charts can be especially effective for presenting or comparing data, and photographs or drawings can help readers "see" things you describe in your written text. For example, if you were writing about the Civil War generals Grant and Lee, you might want to supply your readers with photographs like the ones on pp. 377–78 of the two men in uniform. But remember that visuals should never be mere decoration or clip art. When considering any kind of illustration, here are a few guidelines to follow:

- *Visuals should be relevant to your topic and support your thesis* in some way. In this book, for example, you'll notice that most of the chapters include an illustrated example, such as a sign or cartoon, showing how the mode of writing discussed in that chapter is used in an everyday writing situation.

- *Any visuals should be appropriate for your audience and purpose.* You might add a detailed medical drawing of a lung to an essay on the effects of smoking directed at respiratory specialists—but not to an essay about smoking aimed at a general audience, who wouldn't necessarily need—or want—to see all the details.

- *Refer to any visuals in the text* ("in the diagram below")—and, if necessary, number them so readers can find them ("see fig. 1").

- *Position each visual close to the text it illustrates,* and consider adding a caption explaining the point of the visual.

- *If you use a visual you have not created yourself,* identify the source.

REVISING

Revising is a process of *re-vision,* of looking again at your draft and fixing problems in content, organization, or both. Sometimes revising requires some major surgery: adding new evidence, cutting out paragraphs or entire sections, rewriting the beginning, and so on.

Many writers try to revise far too soon. To avoid this pitfall, put aside your draft for a few hours—or better still, for a few days—before revising. Start by reading your draft yourself, and then try to get someone else to look it over—a classmate, a friend, your aunt. Whoever it is, be sure he or she is aware of your intended audience and purpose. Here's what you and the person with fresh eyes should look for:

- *Title.* Does the title pique the reader's interest and accurately indicate the topic of the essay?

- *Thesis.* What is the main point of the essay? Is it clearly stated in a thesis statement? If not, should it be? Is the thesis sufficiently narrow?

- **Audience.** Is there sufficient background information for the intended readers? Are there clear definitions of terms and concepts they might not know? Will they find the topic interesting?

- **Support.** What evidence supports the thesis? Is the evidence convincing and the reasoning logical? Are more facts or specific details needed?

- **Organization.** Is the draft well organized, with a clear beginning, middle, and ending? Does each paragraph contribute to the main point, or are some paragraphs off topic?

- **Modes of Writing.** What is the main mode the writer uses to develop the essay? For example, is the draft primarily a NARRATIVE? A DESCRIPTION? An ARGUMENT? Should other modes be introduced? For instance, would more EXAMPLES or a COMPARISON be beneficial?

- **Sources.** If there is material from other sources, how are those sources incorporated? Are they quoted? Paraphrased? Summarized? Is source material clearly cited following appropriate guidelines for documentation, so readers know whose words or ideas are being used? Does the source material effectively support the main point? (For tips on using sources and citing them properly, see the Appendix.)

- **Paragraphs.** Does each paragraph focus on one main idea and, often, state it directly in a clear topic sentence? Do your paragraphs vary in structure, or are they too much alike? Should any long or complex paragraphs be broken into two? Should short paragraphs be combined with other paragraphs, or developed more fully? How well does the draft flow from one paragraph to the next? If any paragraph seems to break the flow, should it be cut—or are transitions needed to help the reader follow the text? (For more help with paragraphs, see Chapter 3.)

- **Sentences.** If all of the sentences are about the same length, should some be varied? A short sentence in the midst of long sentences can provide emphasis. On the other hand, too many short sentences in a row can sound choppy. Some of them might be combined.

- *Visuals.* If the draft includes visuals, are they relevant to the topic and thesis? If there are no visuals, would any of the text be easier to understand if accompanied by a diagram or drawing?

After you analyze your own draft carefully and get some advice from another reader, you may decide to make some fairly drastic changes, such as adding more examples, writing a more effective conclusion, or dropping material that doesn't support your thesis. All such moves are typical of the revision process. In fact, it is not unusual to revise your draft more than once to get it to a near-final form. Recall, for instance, all of the revisions that Annie Dillard made in the moth essay, as she recounts in "How I Wrote the Moth Essay—and Why" in Chapter 1. As Dillard puts it, "It doesn't hurt much to babble in a first draft, so long as you have the sense to cut out irrelevancies later."

EDITING AND PROOFREADING

When you finish revising your essay, you've blended all the basic ingredients, but you still need to put the icing on the cake. That is, you need to edit and proofread your final draft before presenting it to the reader.

When you edit, you add finishing touches and correct errors in grammar, sentence structure, punctuation, and word choice. When you proofread, you take care of misspellings, typos, problems with margins and format, and other minor blemishes. Here are some tips that can help you check your drafts for some common errors.

Editing Sentences

Check that each sentence expresses a complete thought. Each sentence should have a subject (someone or something) and a verb performing an action or indicating a state of being. (The Civil War started in 1861.)

Check capitalization and end punctuation. Be sure that each sentence begins with a capital letter and ends with a period, a question mark, or an exclamation point.

Look for sentences that begin with it or there. Often such sentences are vague or boring, and they are usually easy to edit. For example, if you've written "There is a security guard on duty at every entrance," you could edit it to "A security guard is on duty at every entrance."

Check for parallelism. All items in a list or series should have parallel grammatical forms—all nouns (Lincoln, Grant, Lee), all verbs (dedicate, consecrate, hallow), all phrases (of the people, by the people, for the people), and so on.

Editing Words

There, their. Use *there* to refer to place or direction, or to introduce a sentence. (Was he there? There was no evidence.) Use *their* as a possessive. (Their plans fell apart.)

It's, its. Use *it's* to mean "it is." (It's often difficult to apologize.) Use *its* to mean "belonging to it." (Each dog has its own personality.)

Lie, lay. Use *lie* when you mean "recline." (She's lying down because her back hurts.) Use *lay* when you mean "put" or "place." (Lay the blanket on the bed.)

Use concrete words. If some of your terms are too ABSTRACT (Lake Michigan is so amazing and incredible), choose more CONCRETE terms (Lake Michigan is so cold and choppy that swimming in it often seems like swimming in the ocean).

***Avoid filler words like* very, quite, really, and truly.** You could write that "John Updike was truly a very great novelist," but it's stronger to say, "John Updike was a great novelist."

Editing Punctuation

Check for commas after introductory elements in a sentence.

> ▶ After that day, it was as if Miss Dennis and I shared something.
> —ALICE STEINBACH, "The Miss Dennis School of Writing"

Check for commas before **and, but, or, nor, so,** *or* **yet** *in compound sentences.*

▶ Book sales are down, but creative writing enrollments are booming.
—Allegra Goodman, "So, You Want to Be a Writer? Here's How."

Check for commas in a series.

▶ Even when I'm not working, I'm as likely as not to be foraging in the Web's data thickets—reading and writing emails, scanning headlines and blog posts, following *Facebook* updates, watching video streams, downloading music, or just tripping lightly from link to link.
—Nicholas Carr, "Hal and Me"

Put quotation marks at the beginning and end of a quotation.

▶ Finally he said, "Once you get to be thirty, you make your own mistakes."
—Philip Weiss, "How to Get Out of a Locked Trunk"

▶ "Dogs love real beef," the back of the box proclaimed loudly.
—Ann Hodgman, "No Wonder They Call Me a Bitch"

Check your use of apostrophes with possessives. Singular nouns should end in *'s*, whereas plural nouns should end in *s'*. The possessive pronouns *hers, his, its, ours, yours,* and *theirs* should not have apostrophes.

▶ But to me, my mother's English is perfectly clear, perfectly natural.
—Amy Tan, "Mother Tongue"

▶ With these rulings and laws, whites' attitudes towards blacks have also greatly improved.
—Eric A. Watts, "The Color of Success"

▶ The average human being in a country such as ours saw as many images in a day as a Victorian inhaled in a lifetime.
—Pico Iyer, "Chapels: On the Importance of Being Quiet"

Proofreading and Final Formatting

Proofreading is the only stage in the writing process where you are *not* primarily concerned with meaning. Of course you should correct any substantive errors you find, but your main concern is the surface appearance of your text: misspellings, margins that are too narrow or too wide, unindented paragraphs, missing page numbers.

It is a good idea to slow down as you proofread. Use a ruler or piece of paper to guide your eye line by line; or read your entire text backward a sentence at a time; or read it aloud word by word. Use a spellchecker, too, but don't rely on it: a spellchecker doesn't know the difference, for example, between *their* and *there* or *human* and *humane.*

Also check the overall format of your document to make sure it follows any specific instructions that you may have been given. If your instructor does not have particular requirements for formatting, follow these standard guidelines:

Heading and title. Put your name, your instructor's name, the name and number of the course, and the date on separate lines in the upper-left-hand corner of your first page. Center your title on the next line, but do not underline it or put it in quotation marks. Double-space the heading and title.

Typeface and size. Use ten- or twelve-point type in an easy-to-read typeface, such as Times New Roman, Courier, or Palatino.

Spacing and margins. Double-space your document. Leave at least one-inch margins on each side and at the top and bottom of your text.

Paragraph indentation and page numbers. Indent the first line of each paragraph five spaces. Number your pages consecutively, and include your last name with each page number.

CHAPTER THREE

WRITING PARAGRAPHS

◇△◇△◇△◇△◇△◇△◇△◇△◇△◇△◇△◇△◇△◇△◇△◇△◇△◇

THIS chapter is about writing paragraphs. A paragraph is a group of closely related sentences on the same topic. In any piece of writing longer than a few sentences, paragraphs are necessary to indicate when the discussion shifts from one topic to another. Just because a group of sentences is on the same topic, however, doesn't mean they're all closely related. All of the following sentences, for example, are about snakes:

> There are no snakes in Ireland. Ounce for ounce, the most deadly snake in North America is the coral snake. Snakes are our friends; never kill a snake. North America is teeming with snakes, including four poisonous species. Snakes also eat insects.

Although they make statements about the same topic, these sentences do not form a coherent paragraph because they're not closely related to each other: each one snakes off in a different direction. In a coherent paragraph, all the sentences work together to support the main point.

SUPPORTING THE MAIN POINT

Suppose the main point we wanted to make in a paragraph about snakes was that, despite their reputation for evil, snakes should be protected. We could still mention snakes in North America, even the deadly coral snake. We could say that snakes eat insects. But the sentence about snakes in Ireland would have to go. Of course, we could introduce additional facts and figures about snakes and snakebites—so long as we made sure that every statement in our paragraph worked together to support the idea of conservation. For example, we might write:

> Snakes do far more good than harm, so the best thing to do if you encounter a snake is to leave it alone. North America is teeming with snakes, including four poisonous species. (Ounce for ounce, the most deadly snake in North America is the coral snake.) The chances of dying from any variety of snakebite, however, are slim—less than 1:25,000,000 per year in the United States. Snakes, moreover, contribute to a healthy ecosystem. They help to control the rodent population, and they eat insects. (Far more people die each year from the complications of insect bites than from snakebites.) Snakes are our friends and should be protected; never kill a snake.

This is a coherent paragraph because every sentence contributes to the main point, which is that snakes should be protected.

Don't Go Off on a Tangent

Anytime the subject of snakes comes up, it is tempting to recall the legend of Saint Patrick, the patron saint of Ireland who, in the second half of the fifth century, is said to have driven the snakes from the land with his walking stick. Beware, however, of straying too far from the main point of your paragraph, no matter how interesting the digression may be. That is, be careful not to go off on a tangent. The term *tangent*, by the way, comes from geometry and refers to a line that touches a circle at only one point—on the periphery, not the center.

Every sentence in Richard Lederer's essay, p. 216, makes the point that "English Is a Crazy Language."

   And, incidentally, did you know that St. Patrick used a three-leaf clover to explain the Christian doctrine of the Trinity to the Irish people? Which is why shamrocks are associated with St. Patrick's Day. Also, there's another really interesting legend about St. Patrick's walking stick. . . . But we digress.

Topic Sentences

To help you stay on track in a paragraph, state your main point in a TOPIC SEN-
TENCE that identifies your subject (snakes) and makes a clear statement about it
("should be protected"). Most of the time your topic sentence will come at the
beginning, as in this paragraph from an essay about the benefits of working at
McDonald's:

> Working at McDonald's has taught me a lot. The most important
> thing I've learned is that you have to start at the bottom and work your
> way up. I've learned to take this seriously—if you're going to run a
> business, you need to know how to do all the other jobs. I also have
> more patience than ever and have learned how to control my emotions.
> I've learned how to get along with all different kinds of people. I'd like
> to have my own business someday, and working at McDonald's is what
> showed me I could do that.
> —MARISSA NUÑEZ, "Climbing the Golden Arches"

When you put the topic sentence at the beginning of a paragraph like this, every
other sentence in your paragraph should follow from it.

Sometimes you may put your topic sentence at the end of the paragraph.
Then, every other sentence in the paragraph should lead up to the topic sentence.
Consider this example from an essay on hummingbirds that ultimately makes a
statement about all living things:

> Mammals and birds have hearts with four chambers. Reptiles and
> turtles have hearts with three chambers. Fish have hearts with two
> chambers. Insects and mollusks have hearts with one chamber. Worms
> have hearts with one chamber, although they may have as many as
> eleven single-chambered hearts. Unicellular bacteria have no hearts at
> all, but even they have fluid eternally in motion, washing from one side
> of the cell to the other, swirling and whirling. No living being is without
> interior liquid motion. We all churn inside.
> —BRIAN DOYLE, "Joyas Voladoras"

All of the statements in this paragraph are about hearts, or otherwise pertain to the circulation of fluid ("liquid motion") within the body of living creatures. Thus, they all contribute to the topic sentence at the end: "We all churn inside."

Sometimes the main point of a paragraph will be implied from the context, and you won't need to state it explicitly in a topic sentence. This is especially true when you're making a point by telling a story. In both of the following paragraphs from her essay about working at McDonald's, Marissa Nuñez explains how she got the job in the first place:

> Two years ago, while my cousin Susie and I were doing our Christmas shopping on Fourteenth Street, we decided to have lunch at McDonald's.
>
> "Yo, check it out," Susie said. "They're hiring. Let's give it a try." I looked at her and said, "Are you serious?" She gave me this look that made it clear that she was.

Nuñez doesn't have to tell the reader that she is explaining how she came to work for McDonald's because that point is clear. (Also, she later writes that "finally one day the manager came out and said we had the job.")

Topic sentences not only tell your reader what the rest of a paragraph is about; they help, collectively, to tie all your ideas together in support of the main point of your essay. In Nuñez's case, the main point is what she learned about people, business, and herself from working at a fast-food restaurant, as she states clearly at the beginning: "Working at McDonald's has taught me a lot."

To see how topic sentences work collectively to tie an essay together and to support the main point of the essay, read through each paragraph in "Climbing the Golden Arches" (pp. 493–98), and scout out topic sentences like these:

- Before you can officially start working, you have to get trained on every station (7).
- Working at McDonald's does have its down side (11).
- The most obnoxious customer I had came in one day when it was really busy (12).
- Sometimes we make up special events to make the job more fun for everyone (14).

Once you've identified a number of the topic sentences in Nuñez's essay, read back through her entire narrative but skip the topic sentences. The take-away here is that it's still an interesting story; but without the topic sentences, the narrative is less coherent, and the significance of the events is less clear.

Using Parallel Structures

Most of the topic sentence sentences in Nuñez's essay have basically the same grammatical form: Subject + Verb + Phrase. Parallel structures like this are a good way to help readers see the connections between your sentences and your ideas.

Using parallel structures can help you to link ideas within paragraphs as well as between or among them. Brian Doyle used them in his paragraph about hearts and liquid motion: "Reptiles and turtles have hearts with three chambers. Fish have hearts with two chambers. Insects and mollusks have hearts with one chamber." The similarities in form among these sentences tie them together in supporting the topic sentence to come: "We all churn inside."

See how parallel structure is used in "Watching Oprah from Behind the Veil," p. 368.

Parallel structures indicate key elements in a paragraph, or even in an entire essay. They do not, however, tell the reader exactly how those pieces of the puzzle fit together. For this we need transitions.

Using Transitions

Paragraphs are all about connections. The following words and phrases can help you to make TRANSITIONS that clearly connect one statement to another—within a paragraph and also between paragraphs.

- **When describing place or direction:** across, across from, at, along, away, behind, close, down, distant, far, here, in between, in front of, inside, left, near, next to, north, outside, right, south, there, toward, up

- **When narrating events in time:** at the same time, during, frequently, from time to time, in 2007, in the future, now, never, often, meanwhile, occasionally, soon, then, until, when

- **When giving examples:** for example, for instance, in fact, in particular, namely, specifically, that is

- **When comparing:** also, as, in a similar way, in comparison, like, likewise

- **When contrasting:** although, but, by contrast, however, on the contrary, on the other hand

- **When analyzing cause and effect:** as a result, because, because of, consequently, so, then,

- **When using logical reasoning:** accordingly, hence, it follows, therefore, thus, since, so

- **When tracing sequence or continuation:** also, and, after, before, earlier, finally, first, furthermore, in addition, last, later, next

- **When summarizing:** in conclusion, in summary, in the end, consequently, so, therefore, thus, to conclude

Consider how transitional words and phrases like these work together in the following paragraph about a new trend in shopping; the transitions are indicated in **bold**:

> We are awakening to a dollar-store economy. **For years** the dollar store has **not only** made a market out of the leftovers of a global manufacturing system, **but** it has **also** made it appealing—by making it amazingly cheap. **Before** the market meltdown of 2008 **and** the stagnant, jobless recovery that followed, the conventional wisdom about dollar stores—**whether** one of the three big corporate chains (Dollar General, Family Dollar, and Dollar Tree) **or** any of the smaller chains (**like** "99 Cents Only Stores") **or** the world of independents—was that they appeal to only poor people. **And while** it's true that low-wage earners still make up the core of dollar-store customers (42 percent earn $30,000 or less), what has turned this sector into a nearly recession-proof corner of the economy is a new customer base. "What's driving the growth," says James Russo, a vice president with the Nielsen Company, a consumer survey firm, "is affluent households."
>
> —JACK HITT, "The Dollar-Store Economy"

Without transitions, the statements in this paragraph would fall apart like beads on a broken string. Transitions indicate relationships: they help to tie the writer's ideas together—in this case by showing how they are related in time (*for years, before*), by contrast (*not only, but also; whether, or*), and in comparison (*like, and while*).

DEVELOPING PARAGRAPHS

There are many ways—in addition to supporting a topic sentence and using parallel structures and transitions—to develop coherent paragraphs. In fact, all of the basic patterns of writing discussed in this book work just as well for organizing paragraphs as they do for organizing entire essays. Here are some examples, with explanations of how they draw on the various modes of writing.

Describing

A common way of developing a paragraph, especially when you're writing about a physical object or place, is to give a detailed DESCRIPTION (Chapter 4) of your subject. When you describe something, you show the reader how it looks, sounds, feels, smells, or tastes, as in the following description of a tarpon that has just been caught by a blind boy; the point of the paragraph is to help the reader (and the boy) to picture the fish:

> Okay. He has all these big scales, like armor all over his body. They're silver too, and when he moves they sparkle. He has a strong body and a large powerful tail. He has big round eyes, bigger than a quarter, and a lower jaw that sticks out past the upper one, and is very tough. His belly is almost white and his back is a gunmetal gray. When he jumped, he came out of the water about six feet, and his scales caught the sun and flashed it all over the place.
> —CHEROKEE PAUL MCDONALD, "A View from the Bridge"

Descriptions of physical objects are often organized by the configuration of the object. Here the object is a fish, and the writer develops this descriptive paragraph by moving from one part of the fish to another (scales, tail, eyes, jaw, belly, back), ending up with an overall view of the whole tarpon glinting in the sun.

In "Storm Country," p. 79, Paul Crenshaw organizes his description around common weather patterns.

Narrating

One of the oldest and most common ways of developing a paragraph on almost any subject is by narrating a story about it. When you construct a NARRATIVE (Chapter 5), you focus on events: you tell what happened. In the following paragraph, a writer tells what happened on the day she returned to her hometown in Kentucky soon after publishing her first novel:

> In November 1988, bookstoreless though it was, my hometown hosted a big event. Paper banners announced it, and stores closed in honor of it. A crowd assembled in the town's largest public space—the railroad depot. The line went out the door and away down the tracks. At the front of the line they were plunking down $16.95 for copies of a certain book.
>
> —BARBARA KINGSOLVER, "In Case You Ever Want to Go Home Again"

Narratives are organized by time, and they usually present events in chronological order. In this narrative, the time is a particular day in 1988 when the triumphant young author returns to her hometown for a booksigning. The events of the day ("banners announced," "stores closed," "crowd assembled," "line went out the door") are presented in chronological order—all leading up to the climactic event ("plunking down" the money to buy the book) at the end of the paragraph.

Giving Examples

When you use EXAMPLES (Chapter 6) to develop a paragraph, you give specific instances of the point you're making. In the following tongue-in-cheek paragraph, a linguist uses multiple examples to show how "unreliable" the English language can be:

In this unreliable English tongue, greyhounds aren't always grey (or gray); panda bears and koala bears aren't bears (they're marsupials); a woodchuck is a groundhog, which is not a hog; a horned toad is a lizard; glowworms are fireflies, but fireflies are not flies (they're beetles); ladybugs and lightning bugs are also beetles (and to propagate, a significant proportion of ladybugs must be male); a guinea pig is neither a pig nor from Guinea (it's a South American rodent); and a titmouse is neither mammal nor mammaried.

—RICHARD LEDERER, "English Is a Crazy Language"

Although the language and punctuation of this paragraph are playfully complex, the organization is simple: it is a series, or list, of brief examples in more or less random order.

In addition to using multiple examples to develop a paragraph, you can also focus on a single example, as in this paragraph from an essay on the limits of dictionary definitions:

Definitions are especially unhelpful to children. There's an oft-cited 1987 study in which fifth graders were given dictionary definitions and asked to write their own sentences using the words defined. The results were discouraging. One child, given the word *erode*, wrote, "Our family erodes a lot," because the definition given was "eat out, eat away."

—ERIN McKEAN, "Redefining Definition"

Here the writer states the point to be exemplified, identifies the source of the example she is going to use, comments on the significance of that source, and then gives the example: an exemplary use of example to develop a paragraph.

Classifying

With this method of development, you divide your subject into categories. In the following passage, a writer classifies the different kinds of English she uses:

Fortunately, for reasons I won't get into today, I later decided I should envision a reader for the stories I would write. And the reader I decided upon was my mother, because these were stories about mothers. So with this reader in mind—and in fact she did read my early drafts—I began to write stories using all the Englishes I grew up with: the English I spoke to my mother, which for lack of a better term might be described as "simple"; the English she used with me, which for lack of a better term might be described as "broken"; my translation of her Chinese, which could certainly be described as "watered down"; and what I imagined to be her translation of her Chinese if she could speak in perfect English, her internal language, and for that I sought to preserve the essence, but neither an English nor a Chinese structure. I wanted to capture what language ability tests can never reveal: her intent, her passion, her imagery, the rhythms of her speech and the nature of her thought.

Janet Wu tells another story about mothers and the limits of language on p. 206.

—AMY TAN, "Mother Tongue"

This is a complex paragraph, obviously; but the heart of it is the author's classification of her various "Englishes" into four specific types. The opening statements in the paragraph explain how this classification system came about, and the closing statement explains the purpose it serves.

Analyzing a Process

When you use PROCESS ANALYSIS (Chapter 8) to a develop a paragraph, you tell the reader how to do something—or how something works or is made—by breaking the process into steps. In the following paragraph, a young writer explains what she sees as the first steps in learning to be a writer:

To begin, don't write about yourself. I'm not saying you're uninteresting. I realize that your life has been so crazy no one could make this stuff up. But if you want to be a writer, start by writing about other people. Observe their faces, and the way they wave their hands around. Listen to the way they talk. Replay conversations in your mind—not just the words, but the silences as well. Imagine the lives of others. If you want to be a writer, you need to get over yourself. This is not just an artistic choice; it's a moral choice. A writer attempts to understand others from the inside.

—ALLEGRA GOODMAN, "So, You Want to Be a Writer? Here's How."

In a process analysis, the steps of the process are usually presented in the order in which they occur in time. Here the first step ("To begin") is something not to do: "don't write about yourself"; it is followed by five more steps in order: start, observe, listen, replay, imagine. At the end of the paragraph comes the end result of the process: (you will) "understand others from the inside."

Comparing

With a COMPARISON (Chapter 9) of two or more subjects, you point out their similarities and differences. In the following paragraph, a historian compares two Civil War generals, Ulysses S. Grant and Robert E. Lee:

So Grant and Lee were in complete contrast, representing two diametrically opposed elements in American life. Grant was the modern man emerging; beyond him, ready to come on the stage, was the great age of steel and machinery, of crowded cities and a restless burgeoning vitality. Lee might have ridden down from the old age of chivalry, lance in hand, silken banner fluttering over his head. Each man was the perfect champion of his cause, drawing both his strengths and his weaknesses from the people he led.

—BRUCE CATTON, "Grant and Lee"

Here the writer examines both of the subjects he is comparing in a single paragraph, moving systematically from the characteristics of one to those of the other.

Often, when comparing or contrasting two subjects, you will focus first on one of them, in one paragraph; and then on the other, in another paragraph, as in this comparison of two monkeys, Canto and Owen, who are being fed different diets in order to see which one will live the longer (if not happier) life:

Canto looks drawn, weary, ashen and miserable in his thinness, mouth slightly agape, features pinched, eyes blank, his expression screaming, "Please, no, not another plateful of seeds!"

Well-fed Owen, by contrast, is a happy camper with a wry smile, every inch the laid-back simian, plump, eyes twinkling, full mouth relaxed, skin glowing, exuding wisdom as if he's just read Kierkegaard and concluded that "Life must be lived forward, but can only be understood backward."

—ROGER COHEN, "The Meaning of Life"

The author of this comparison doesn't really believe that monkeys can read philosophy, but he fancifully assigns that power to the second monkey in order to sharpen the contrast between the two simians. Owen's wisdom is in opposition to Canto's despair ("not another plateful of seeds!"). So are the two monkeys' other traits, presented one by one in the same order from paragraph to paragraph.

For contrasting photos of Owen and Canto, see p. 407.

Defining

A DEFINITION (Chapter 10) explains what something is—or is not. Is a good waitress, or other skilled blue-collar worker, merely physically competent; or is she intellectually smart as well? According to the author of this paragraph from an essay on the "brilliance" of blue-collar workers, how we define intelligence depends on a number of factors:

I couldn't have put it in words when I was growing up, but what I observed in my mother's restaurant defined the world of adults, a place where competence was synonymous with physical work. I've since studied the working habits of blue-collar workers and have come to understand how much my mother's kind of work demands of both body and brain. A waitress acquires knowledge and intuition about the ways and the rhythms of the restaurant business. Waiting on seven to nine tables, each with two to six customers, Rosie devised memory strategies so that she could remember who ordered what.

And because she knew the average time it took to prepare different dishes, she could monitor an order that was taking too long at the service station.

—MIKE ROSE, "Blue-Collar Brilliance"

In this paragraph, the writer first presents an overly simplified definition of "competence" among "blue-collar workers" as the ability to do physical labor. He then redefines this key term to include a mental component ("knowledge and intuition"), concluding the paragraph by observing how his mother's work as a waitress demonstrates these defining traits.

A photo of Rosie is on p. 462.

Analyzing Causes and Effects

One of the most fundamental ways of developing a paragraph is to examine what caused your subject, or what effects it may have. In the following paragraph, from an essay about the power of words, the author speculates about the effects, among other subsequent events, of two public speeches—by Robert Kennedy on April 4, 1968, the night Martin Luther King Jr. was killed, and by King himself in Memphis the night before that:

After King's assassination, riots broke out in more than 100 U.S. cities—the worst destruction since the Civil War. But neither Memphis nor Indianapolis experienced that kind of damage. To this day, many believe that was due to the words spoken when so many were listening.

—TIM WENDEL, "King, Kennedy, and the Power of Words"

In a cause-and-effect analysis, the writer can proceed from cause to effect, or effect to cause. This brief but efficient paragraph does both, moving first from a known cause ("King's assassination") to a known effect ("destruction" in many U.S. cities), and then from a known effect (no destruction in two cities) to a possible cause ("words spoken when so many were listening").

INTRODUCTORY PARAGRAPHS

A well-constructed essay has a beginning, middle, and ending. Every paragraph plays an important role within this basic structure, but introductory paragraphs are particularly important because they represent your first chance to engage the reader.

In an introductory paragraph, you tell the reader what your essay is about—and otherwise seek to earn the reader's interest. The following famous introductory paragraph to an important document is as clear and stirring today as it was in 1776:

> When in the Course of human events, it becomes necessary for one people to dissolve the political bands which have connected them with another, and to assume among the powers of the earth, the separate and equal station to which the Laws of Nature and of Nature's God entitle them, a decent respect to the opinions of mankind requires that they should declare the causes which impel them to the separation.
>
> —THOMAS JEFFERSON, *The Declaration of Independence*

This paragraph tells the reader exactly what's coming in the text to follow: an inventory of the reasons for the Colonies' rebellion. It also seeks to justify the writer's cause and win the sympathy of the reader by invoking a higher authority: the "Laws" of God and nature trump those of Britain's King George III. Here are a few other ways to construct an introductory paragraph that may entice the reader to read on.

Tell a story that leads into what you have to say. This introductory paragraph, from a report about research on technology and literacy, begins with a story (actually two of them) about how today's students read and write:

> Two stories about young people, and especially college-age students, are circulating widely today. One script sees a generation of twitterers and texters, awash in self-indulgence and narcissistic twaddle, most of it riddled with errors. The other script doesn't diminish the effects of

technology, but it presents young people as running a rat race that is
fueled by the Internet and its toys, anxious kids who are inundated with
mountains of indigestible information yet obsessed with making the
grade, with success, with coming up with the "next big thing", but who
lack the writing and speaking skills they need to do so.
—ANDREA LUNSFORD, "Our Semi-literate Youth? Not So Fast"

The author of this paragraph considers both of the stories she is reporting
to be inaccurate; so after introducing them here, she goes on in the rest of
the essay to construct "alternative narratives" that are based upon her own
research.

Start with a quotation. In this example, the quotation is very short:

> Our leaders have asked for "shared sacrifice." But when they did
> the asking, they spared me. I checked with my mega-rich friends to
> learn what pain they were expecting. They, too, were left untouched.
> —WARREN BUFFETT, "Stop Coddling the Super-Rich"

The brief quotation in this paragraph is a reference to the following statement
on the deficit by President Barack Obama in an Internet address on July 16,
2011: "Simply put, it will take a balanced approach, shared sacrifice, and a will-
ingness to make unpopular choices on all our parts." Warren Buffett could have
quoted this entire statement in his introductory paragraph, of course, but Buffett's main rhetorical strategy here is to be direct and to the point.

Ask a question—or questions. This strategy should be used sparingly, but it
works especially well when you want to begin with a touch of humor—or otherwise suggest that you don't have all the answers. In this opening paragraph, a
food critic explores new territory:

> I've always wondered about dog food. Is a Gaines-burger really like a
> hamburger? Can you fry it? Does dog food "cheese" taste like real cheese"?

Does Gravy Train actually make gravy in the dog's bowl, or is that brown liquid just dissolved crumbs? And exactly what *are* by-products?

         —ANN HODGMAN, "No Wonder They Call Me a Bitch"

Sound appetizing? Even if your subject doesn't exactly appeal to everyone, a strong opening paragraph like this can leave readers eager for more—or at least willing to hear you out.

CONCLUDING PARAGRAPHS

The final paragraph of an essay should be just as satisfying as the opening paragraph. The conclusion of your essay is your last chance to drive home your point and to leave the reader with a sense of closure. Here are a few ways this is commonly done.

Restate your main point. Remind the reader what you've said, but don't just repeat your point. Add a little something new. In this closing paragraph from an essay about learning to be a detached scientific observer, a young researcher rehearses all the forms of restraint and professionalism she has practiced in the field—and then, for the first time, admits in the final clause that science has an emotional side, too:

Scientists are observers. We take notes, lots of notes. We look for patterns. We educate. We watch. We wait. And we weep.

         —JESSICA WALDEN, "Chasing Loons"

Show the broader significance of your subject. In an essay about why *The Oprah Winfrey Show* remains the most popular English-language program in Saudi Arabia, with reruns broadcast twice daily by satellite from Dubai, Jeff Jacoby comes to the following conclusion:

Is it any wonder that women trapped in a culture that treats them so wretchedly idolize someone like Oprah, who epitomizes so much that is absent from their lives? A nation that degrades its women degrades itself, and Oprah's message is an antidote to degradation.

Why do they love her? Because all the lies of the Wahhabists cannot stifle the truth she embodies: The blessings of liberty were made for women, too.

—JEFF JACOBY, "Watching Oprah from Behind the Veil"

Liberty for all, of course, is a much greater issue than why a particular television show is popular with a particular audience. By linking his limited topic to this broader one, the author greatly enlarges its significance.

End with a recommendation. This strategy is especially appropriate when you're winding up an argument. Before coming to the conclusion stated in the following paragraph, the author, a sportswriter, has made the claim that student athletes should be paid for their "work":

The republic will survive. Fans will still watch the NCAA tournament. Double-reverses will still be thrilling. Alabama will still hate Auburn. Everybody will still hate Duke. Let's do what's right and re-examine what we think is wrong.

—MICHAEL ROSENBERG, "Let Stars Get Paid"

Not only is he recommending pay for college athletes, the author of this paragraph asks the reader to rethink, and totally revise, the conventional wisdom that says paying them is morally wrong. (For an essay that comes to precisely the opposite conclusion, see p. 584.)

CHAPTER FOUR

DESCRIPTION

D ESCRIPTION* is the mode of writing that appeals most directly to the senses by showing us the physical characteristics of a subject—what it looks like, or how it sounds, smells, feels, or tastes. A good description *shows* us such characteristics; it doesn't just tell us about them. Description is especially useful for making an ABSTRACT or vague subject—such as freedom or truth or death—more CONCRETE or definite.

For example, if you were describing an old cemetery, you might say that it was a solemn and peaceful place. In order to show the reader what the cemetery actually looked or sounded like, however, you would need to focus on the physical aspects of the scene that evoked these more abstract qualities—the marble gravestones, the earth and trees, and perhaps the mourners at the site of a new grave.

Such concrete, physical details are the heart of any description. Those details can be presented either objectively or subjectively. Consider the following caption for a photograph from the website of Arlington National Cemetery:

> Six inches of snow blanket the rolling Virginia hillside as mourners gather at a fresh burial site in Arlington National Cemetery outside Washington, D.C. Rows of simple markers identify the more than 250,000 graves that make up the military portion of the cemetery. Visited annually by more than four million people, the cemetery conducts nearly 100 funerals each week.

*Words printed in SMALL CAPITALS are defined in the Glossary/Index.

In an OBJECTIVE description like this, the author stays out of the picture. The description shows what a detached observer would see and hear—snow, rolling hills, graves, and mourners—but it does not say what the observer thinks or feels *about* those things.

A SUBJECTIVE description, on the other hand, presents the author's thoughts and feelings along with the physical details of the scene or subject, as in this description by novelist John Updike of a cemetery in the town where he lived:

> The stones are marble, modernly glossy and simple, though I suppose that time will eventually reveal them as another fashion, dated and quaint. Now, the sod is still raw, the sutures of turf are unhealed, the earth still humped, the wreaths scarcely withered. . . . I remember my grandfather's funeral, the hurried cross of sand the minister drew on

the coffin lid, the whine of the lowering straps, the lengthening, cleanly cut sides of clay, the thought of air, the lack of air forever in the close dark space lined with pink satin. . . .

—JOHN UPDIKE, "Cemeteries"

This intimate description is far from detached. Not only does it give us a close-up view of the cemetery itself, it also reports the sensations that the newly dug graves evoke in the author's mind.

Whether the concrete details of a description are presented from a subjective or an objective POINT OF VIEW, every detail should contribute to some DOMINANT IMPRESSION that the writer wants the description to make upon the reader. The dominant impression we get from Updike's description, for example, is of the "foreverness" of the place. Consequently, every detail in Updike's description—from the enduring marble of the headstones to the dark, satin-lined interior of his grandfather's coffin—contributes to the sense of airless eternity that Updike recalls from his grandfather's funeral.

Brian Doyle's description of hummingbirds, p. 85, is both subjective and objective.

Updike's references to the "raw" sod and to unhealed "sutures" in the turf show how such figures of speech as METAPHOR, SIMILE, and PERSONIFICATION can be used to make a description more vivid and concrete. This is because we often describe something by telling what it is like. A thump in your closet at night sounds like an owl hitting a haystack. A crowd stirs like a jellyfish. The seams of turf on new graves are like the stitches closing a wound.

As Updike's description narrows in on his grandfather's grave, we get a feeling of suffocation that directly supports the main point that the author is making about the nature of death. Death, as Updike conceives it, is no abstraction; it is the slow extinction of personal life and breath.

Updike's painful reverie is suddenly interrupted by his young son, who is learning to ride a bicycle in the peaceful cemetery. As Updike tells the story of their joyful afternoon together, the gloom of the cemetery fades into the background—as descriptive writing often does. Description frequently plays a supporting role within other MODES OF WRITING; it may serve, for example, to set the scene for a NARRATIVE (as in Updike's essay) or it may provide the background for an ARGUMENT about the significance of a national cemetery.

Almost as important as the physical details in a description is the order in which those details are presented. Beginning with the glossy stones of the cemetery and the earth around them, Updike's description comes to focus on the interior of a particular grave. It moves from outside to inside and from the general to the specific. A good description can proceed from outside in, or inside out, top to bottom, front to back, or in any other direction—so long as it moves systematically in a way that is in keeping with the dominant impression it is supposed to give, and that supports the main point the description is intended to make.

The dominant impression of a description of farm machinery, p. 73, is fatigue and boredom.

In the following description of a boy's room, the writer is setting the stage for the larger narrative—in this case, a fairy tale:

> The room was so spare one could see everything at a glance: a closet door with a lock on it, a long table with five perfect constructions—three ships, two dragons—nothing else on the table but a neat stack of stainless-steel razor-blades. What defined all the rest, of course, was that immense desk and chair. They made it seem that the room itself was from a picture book, or better yet, a stage-set, for across one end hung a dark green curtain. Beyond that, presumably, the professor's son crouched, hiding. My gaze stopped and froze on an enormous bare foot that protruded, unbeknownst to its owner, no doubt, from behind the curtain. It was the largest human foot I'd ever seen or imagined. . . .
>
> —JOHN GARDNER, *Freddy's Book*

This description of the lair of a boy giant is pure fantasy, of course. What makes it appear so realistic is the systematic way in which Gardner presents the objects in the room. First we see the closet door, a feature we might find in any boy's bedroom. Next comes the lock. Even an ordinary boy might keep the contents of his closet under lock and key. The long table with the models and razor-blades is the first hint that something unusual may be at play. And when we see the oversized desk and chair, we truly begin to suspect that this is no ordinary room and no ordinary boy. But it is not until our gaze falls upon the enormous foot protruding from beneath the curtain that we know for sure we have entered the realm of make-believe.

Fanciful as the details of Gardner's description may be, his systematic method of presenting them is instructive for composing more down-to-earth descriptions. Also, by watching how Gardner presents the details of Freddy's room from a consistent VANTAGE POINT, we can see how he builds up to a dominant impression of awe and wonder.

A BRIEF GUIDE TO WRITING A DESCRIPTION

As you write a description, you need to identify who or what you're describing, say what your subject looks or feels like, and indicate the traits you plan to focus on. Cherokee Paul McDonald makes these basic moves of description in the beginning of his essay in this chapter:

> He was a lumpy little guy with baggy shorts, a faded T-shirt and heavy sweat socks falling down over old sneakers. . . . Covering his eyes and part of his face was a pair of those stupid-looking '50s-style wrap-around sunglasses.
>
> —CHEROKEE PAUL MCDONALD, "A View from the Bridge"

McDonald identifies what he's describing (a "little guy"); says what his subject looks like ("lumpy," "with baggy shorts, a faded T-shirt and heavy sweat socks"); and hints at characteristics (his "stupid-looking" sunglasses) that he might focus on. Here is one more example from this chapter:

> At the base of the tornado, dust and debris hovered, circling slowly, and I heard the sound of storm for the first time. It grew out of air, out of wind. It seemed as silent as noise can be, a faint howling that reached us over the rain, almost peaceful from a distance.
>
> —PAUL CRENSHAW, "Storm Country"

The following guidelines will help you to make these basic moves as you draft a description—and to come up with your subject, consider your purpose and audience, state your point, and create a dominant impression of your subject by organizing and presenting the details of your description effectively.

Coming Up with a Subject

A primary resource for finding a subject is your own experience. You will often want to describe something familiar from your past—the lake in which you learned to swim, the neighborhood where you grew up, a person from your hometown. Also consider more recent experiences or less familiar subjects that you might investigate further, such as crowd behavior at a hockey game, an unusual T-shirt, a popular bookstore. Whatever subject you choose, be sure that you will be able to describe it vividly for your readers by appealing to their senses.

For a taste of the unusual, Ann Hodgman describes pet food on p. 106.

Considering Your Purpose and Audience

Your PURPOSE in describing something—whether to view your subject objectively, express your feelings about it, convince the reader to visit it (or not), or simply to amuse your reader—will determine the details you include. Before you start composing, decide whether your purpose will be primarily objective (as in a lab report) or subjective (as in a personal essay about your grandmother's cooking). Although both approaches provide information, an OBJECTIVE description presents its subject impartially, whereas a SUBJECTIVE description conveys the writer's personal response to the subject.

Whatever your purpose, you need to take into account how much your AUDIENCE already knows (or does not know) about your subject. For example, if you want to describe to someone who has never been on your campus the mad rush that takes place when classes change, you're going to have to provide some background: the main quadrangle with its sun worshipers, the brick-and-stone classroom buildings on either side, the library looming at one end. On the other hand, if you were to describe this same locale to fellow students, you could skip the background description and go directly to the mob scene.

Generating Ideas: Asking What Something Looks, Sounds, Feels, Smells, and Tastes Like

Good descriptive writing is built on CONCRETE particulars rather than ABSTRACT qualities. So don't just write, "It was a dark and stormy night"; make your reader see, hear, and feel the wind and the rain, as Paul Crenshaw does in "Storm Country," pp. 79–83. To come up with specific details, observe your subject, ask questions, and take notes. Experience your subject as though you were a reporter on assignment or a traveler in a strange land.

One of your richest sources of ideas for a description—especially if you are describing something from the past—is memory. Ask friends or parents to help you remember details accurately and truthfully. Jog your own memory by asking, "What *did* the place (or object) look like exactly? What did it sound like? What did it smell or taste like?" Recovering the treasures of your memory is a little like fishing: think back to the spots you knew well; bait the hook by asking these key sensory questions; weigh and measure everything you pull up. Later on, you can throw back the ideas you can't use.

In "The Miss Dennis School of Writing," p. 96, Alice Steinbach draws upon her memories of a favorite teacher.

Templates for Describing

The following templates can help you to generate ideas for a description and then to start drafting. Don't take these as formulas where you just have to fill in the blanks. There are no easy formulas for good writing. But these templates can help you plot out some of the key moves of description and thus may serve as good starting points.

- ▶ The main physical characteristics of X are _____, _____, and _____.

- ▶ From the perspective of _____, however, X could be described as _____.

> ▶ In some ways, namely _____, X resembles _____; but in other ways, X is more like _____.
>
> ▶ X is not at all like _____ because _____.
>
> ▶ Mainly because of _____ and _____, X gives the impression of being _____.
>
> ▶ From this description of X, you can see that _____.

For more techniques to help you generate ideas and start writing a descriptive essay, see Chapter 2.

Stating Your Point

We usually describe something to someone for a reason. Why are you describing bloody footprints in the snow? You need to let the reader know, either formally or informally. One formal way is to include an explicit THESIS STATEMENT: "This description of Washington's ragged army at Yorktown shows that the American general faced many of the same challenges as Napoleon in the winter battle for Moscow, but Washington turned them to his advantage."

E. B. White makes his point about time and mortality with a single chilling phrase (p. 121, par. 13).

Or your reasons can be stated more informally. If you are writing a descriptive travel essay, for example, you might state your point as a personal observation: "Chicago is an architectural delight in any season, but I prefer to visit from April through October because of the city's brutal winters."

Creating a Dominant Impression

Some descriptions appeal to several senses: the sight of fireflies, the sound of crickets, the touch of a hand—all on a summer evening. Whether you appeal to a single sense or several, make sure they all contribute to the DOMINANT IMPRESSION you want your description to make upon the reader. For example, if you want an evening scene on the porch to convey an impression of danger, you probably won't include details about fireflies and crickets. Instead, you might call the reader's attention to dark clouds in the distance, the rising wind, crashing thunder, and the sound of footsteps drawing closer. In short, you will choose details that play an effective part in creating your dominant impression: a sense of danger and foreboding.

Even though you want to create a dominant impression, don't begin your description with a general statement of what that impression is supposed to be. Instead, start with descriptive details, and let your readers form the impression for themselves. Paul Crenshaw's description of tornadoes in "Storm Country," p. 79, conveys awe and wonder as well as danger. Remember that a good description doesn't tell readers what to think or feel; it *shows* them point by point. The dominant impression that John Gardner creates in his systematic description of Freddy's room, for instance, is a growing sense of awe and wonder. But he does so by taking us step by step into unfamiliar territory. If you were describing an actual room or other place—and you wanted to create a similar dominant impression in your reader's mind—you would likewise direct the reader's gaze to more familiar objects first (table, chairs, fireplace) and then to increasingly unfamiliar ones (a shotgun, polar bear skins on the floor, an elderly lady mending a reindeer harness).

Using Figurative Language

Figures of speech can help to make almost any description more vivid or colorful. The three figures of speech you are most likely to use in composing a description are similes, metaphors, and personification.

SIMILES tell the reader what something looks, sounds, or feels like, using *like* or *as*: "Suspicion climbed all over her face like a kitten, but not so playfully" (Raymond Chandler).

METAPHORS make implicit comparisons, without *like* or *as*: "All the world's a stage" (William Shakespeare). Like similes, metaphors have two parts: the subject of the description (*world*) and the thing (*stage*) to which that subject is being implicitly compared.

PERSONIFICATION assigns human qualities to inanimate objects, as in Sylvia Plath's poetic description of a mirror: "I have no preconceptions. / Whatever I see I swallow immediately."

Arranging the Details from a Consistent Vantage Point

The physical configuration of whatever you're describing will usually suggest a pattern of organization. Descriptions of places are often organized by direction—north to south, front to back, left to right, inside to outside, near to far, top to bottom. If you were describing a room, for example, you might use an outside-to-inside order, starting with the door or the door knob.

An object or person can also suggest an order of arrangement. If you were describing a large fish, for instance, you might let the anatomy of the fish guide your description, moving from its glistening scales to the mouth, eyes, belly, and tail. When constructing a description, you can go from whole to parts, or parts to whole; from most important to least important features (or vice versa); from largest to smallest, specific to general, or concrete to abstract—or vice versa.

Whatever organization you choose, be careful to maintain a consistent VANTAGE POINT. In other words, be sure to describe your subject from one position or perspective—across the room, from the bridge, face-to-face, under the bed, and so on. Do not include details that you are unable to see, hear, feel, smell, or taste from your particular vantage point. Before you fully reveal any objects or people that lie outside the reader's line of sight—such as a boy giant behind a curtain—you will need to cross the room and fling open the door or curtain that conceals them. If your vantage point (or that of your NARRATOR) changes while you are describing a subject, be sure to let your reader know that you have moved from one location to another, as in the following description of a robbery: "After I was pushed behind the counter of the Quik-Mart, I could no longer see the three men in ski masks, but I could hear them yelling at the owner to open up the register."

EDITING FOR COMMON ERRORS
IN DESCRIPTIVE WRITING

Like other kinds of writing, description uses distinctive patterns of language and punctuation—and thus invites typical kinds of errors. The following tips will help you to check for (and correct) these common errors in your own descriptive writing.

Check descriptive details to make sure they are concrete

> ▸ When I visited Great Pond, the lake in E. B. White's essay, it was so ~~amazing and incredible~~ clear and deep that floating on it in a boat seemed like floating on air.

Amazing and *incredible* are ABSTRACT terms; *clear* and *deep* describe the water in more CONCRETE terms.

> ▸ The Belgrade region is famous for its ~~charming views~~ panoramic views of fields, hills, and woodlands.

The revised sentence says more precisely what makes the views charming.

Check for filler words like *very, quite, really,* and *truly*

> ▸ The lake was ~~very much secluded~~ fifteen miles from the nearest village.

If you've used several adjectives together, be sure they are in the right order

Subjective adjectives (those that reflect the writer's own opinion) go before objective adjectives (those that are strictly factual): write "fabulous four-door Chevrolet" rather than "four-door fabulous Chevrolet." Beyond that, adjectives usually go in the following order: number, size, shape, age, color, nationality.

> ▸ The streets of Havana were lined with many ~~old, big~~ big, old American cars.

Check for common usage errors

UNIQUE, PERFECT

Don't use *more* or *most*, *less* or *least*, or *very* before words like *unique*, *equal*, *perfect*, or *infinite*. Either something is unique or it isn't.

▸ Their house at the lake was a ~~very~~ unique place.

AWESOME, COOL, INCREDIBLE

Not only are these modifiers too abstract, they're overused. You probably should delete them or replace them with fresher words no matter how grand the scene you're describing.

▸ The Ohio River is ~~an awesome river~~ approximately 981 miles long.

EVERYDAY DESCRIPTION
A Missing Cat

When you describe something, you tell what its main characteristics are. Spaz, the lost cat pictured on this poster, is a "mix," resembling a Russian blue, with a slit near the top of his left ear, a small patch of white on his chest, faint rings around his tail, and yellow-green eyes. If Spaz gets found and returned, it will be because his owner knows that a good description includes lots of specific details, down to his pet's ten-digit microchip number. Usually, when you describe something, you should give its important physical characteristics before getting into less tangible attributes.

GRACE WELTE

BRACKEN COUNTY, NORTHERN KENTUCKY

Grace Welte wrote "Bracken County, Northern Kentucky" for a first-year writing and rhetoric course at the University of Notre Dame. Her essay describes the tobacco fields on the farm where she grew up and the tedious work of setting each plant into holes made in the soil by constantly moving machinery—until the writer herself felt "like a machine."

When Welte first submitted her paper, she "expected to turn in the first draft, make some small revisions, and move on." Welte's teacher, John Dillon, had other ideas. Recognizing "the potential in my writing," says Welte, he guided her through multiple drafts—"like planting a seed and watching it germinate"—to the version reprinted here, a runner-up for the 2011 Norton Writer's Prize. The marginal annotations indicate some of Welte's main descriptive strategies.

Bracken County, Northern Kentucky

In the continuous cycle of tobacco farming, the month of   1
June means that it is time to set, or plant, the tobacco. My
mom, my brothers, and I climb out of the rusty old Chrysler
minivan, and we see my dad making his way down the dusty
road on one of the Ford tractors. The sun is just now above the
haze of morning, illuminating and warming the air around us.
It's going to be a hot one; I can tell by the way the humid air
feels—sticky and stifling—and by how seamless the sky
appears in the morning light. We can now see the chipped
blue-and-white paint of the dust-covered tractor as it
approaches the waterbeds, which hold trays of the valuable
tobacco plants. My dad already has everything hitched up,
loaded, and ready to go. He has tilled the acre of land to be
used for today's work. In the water tank on the front of the
tractor, the aqua blue fertilizer and beaded white pesticide
mingle to create manufactured blue water, ready to feed the
thirsty setter through tubes running underneath the tractor.
The red, grease-stained setter, with its sharpened plows and
rotating plant carousel, is well oiled. The original cherry red
sheen has dulled to crimson through years of use.

We know what to expect, so we don't waste time standing   2
around. The sooner we get started, the more we can do—
assuming that no machinery breaks down. We gather around
the rectangular water beds so that we can load the plants onto
the vertical tray mounts of the setter, four trays for each
person lucky enough to sit on one of the two seats of the setter.
This time the two lucky people are my third-oldest brother
and me. The black plastic-covered water beds contain the trays

> These DESCRIPTIVE details appeal primarily to the reader's senses of touch and sight

> Uses PERSONIFICATION to describe the plant setter

of plants that we need for the day. My brothers and I stand around the edge of the bed waiting to grab the trays, while my mom uses an old bowed PVC pipe to shove them across the scum-filled water. I pick up a single waterlogged tray at a time, carefully placing the short end on the lower mount of the setter while releasing the spring-loaded top mount on the upper half of the tray to secure it. My oldest brother, Simon, gets to drive the tractor, and the rest have the worst task of following the tractor and setter. The followers have to make sure that each plant is properly settled in the furrows made by the setter's plows. This job is tedious and tiring. It requires walking for hours on the uneven, loose soil. Each follower has to carry a bucket of plants to use as replacements for the scrawny ones that are carelessly planted, while constantly bending down to fix the never-ending mistakes left by the setter. The gummy residue that comes from the furry white tobacco stem covers the fingers and is quickly masked by a casing of mud after digging a new hole in the soil for the plant. The dirt and mud become like a glove on the hands.

My oldest brother lines the setter up with the edge of the field, making sure that not an inch of the ground goes to waste. Once the setter is lined up, we begin. The rotation of the carousel is in sync with the turning of the tractor wheels. We, in turn, are in sync with the carousel, our arms like wooden horses moving up and down from plant tray to carousel as if on an invisible pole—man and machine working in unison. Each mouth of the carousel reminds me of a giant popsicle tray, except these trays are made of thick metal, and the mouths are fused side by side and bent around a revolving

CONCRETE details in the rest of the paragraph flesh out this abstract description

This SIMILE shows what the dirt and mud felt like to the writer

3

metal rod protruding from the center. With each turn of the wheel, and each labored revolution of a gear, there is a hollow metal clink . . . clink . . . . clink, all in harmony with the wheel and married perfectly to the speed of the tractor. The fall of a small tobacco plant precedes each clink and never fails to do so, unless my brother or I fail to keep pace. We are good, though: seasoned by practice. As each grimy mouth-like hole comes around on the carousel to swallow a plant, we hasten to feed it. Only the healthiest plants must be selected. If the wrong plant is chosen, there is no chance of it surviving the heat of the afternoon. This exasperating routine repeats itself until the end of a row is reached, and then the plant trays and water tank are refilled. The cycle continues until the particular field is completed and there are elegant rows of tobacco plants in perfect order, winding along the furrows in the ground.

 By the time we finish the first field, it is noon. The sun is at its peak and the temperature is as well. It is the only time to escape the fiery sky and to take a twenty-minute lunch break. My mom is always the one to throw up her hands and signal that it's time to eat. Lunch itself is as predictable and bland as the work that we do in the fields every day. We take cover from the sun under the big maple tree next to the field, and I throw off my hat, plop down on the refreshing bed of grass, and grab a cold drink from the Kroger milk jug that holds our drinking water. As I lift the partially frozen jug to my mouth, I have to be careful so that the tobacco soil and mud surrounding the rim don't make their way into the water. My mom grabs our packed lunch out of the van and brings it over. I know exactly what will be in that brown, plastic Kroger bag:

These descriptive physical details are addressed to the reader's sense of hearing

Details up to this point are presented in the order of the planting PROCESS (Chapter 8)

4

A key point of Welte's description so far is to show how routine the work was bologna sandwiches, off-brand potato chips, apples—my dad's precursor to every meal—and either Big K pop or Citrus Drop. I am right, with one exception. My mom packed Little Debbie snack cakes this time; a rare and wonderful surprise for the day. I unwrap the paper towel covering my lunch and realize that among the warm, mayonnaise-slathered bologna and limp layer of lettuce, there is a fat slice of tomato. I can't understand why Mom insists on putting this slimy, tasteless vegetable on my food. When she turns her back, I quickly slide the tomato out and chuck it behind the tree.

The time spent setting tobacco always seems like forever. 5 Each plant that I plop into the carousel and each completed row in the field seem to get us no closer to finishing. After dropping a couple hundred plants into those rotating holes, things start to blur. I simply become a machine, programmed to repeat the same command. It is unbelievable to think that I have picked up one of those pale, fragile plants and continuously dropped it into a hole over a thousand times—a hundred thousand times.

To keep ourselves from dying of boredom, my brother and 6 I play word games or create raps that make us laugh like crazy. Sometimes I pick a famous country song like Jason Aldean's "Amarillo Sky," whose chorus goes, *"He just takes the tractor another round / And pulls the plow across the ground / And sends up another prayer,"* and my brother, with his burgundy Cynthiana Tobacco Warehouse hat lying backward on his thick head of ink-black hair, puts his twist on it and belts, *"And he takes the setter another round / And puts the plants into the ground / And sends up another prayer."* And instead

This detail breaks the routine

The writer's objective description is becoming more subjective

of, "*He says Lord I never complain / I never ask why / But please don't let my dream run dry / Underneath, underneath this Amarillo Sky,*" my brother sings, "*And then Grace complains / And she asks why / Do we have to set all night / Underneath, underneath this Shady Lane Sky?*"

They say creativity is born out of misery, but after long enough only irritation persists. Each timed click of the metal carousel. Each squeak produced by the plow disk below. Loneliness sets in, and I look to my brother to fill the silence in my head. I try to get his attention as he listens to his Sony cassette player, but he blows me off. Irritation persists. With irritation comes anger, and with anger comes action—pushes and shoves. I whine, "Jesse! Talk to me or something. I'm bored." He gives me a look as he raises his arm to lift one side of his headphones—"What?" "I'm bored. Let's play a game." Back down go his headphones to drown out my voice. "Jesse!" I cry as I lean over to give him a little punch on the arm. He just sits there plopping plants into the holes in front of him. "Jesse! . . . Jesse!"

Sometimes when it is all finished I stand at the edge where plowed dirt meets blue grass. Beyond this I see the cell-phone tower climbing its way to the sky till it comes to a blinking red speck. Telephone poles dot the hillside with arching wires in between them. In the distance I can hear the semis straying on the road, hitting the rumble strip of the AA. I see the expanse of earth before me as darkness stretches out towards the tree line. And before it has a chance to leave me, I seize the image of the winding rows of tobacco plants that reach as far as the eye can see. It is like an illustration on the pages of the

7   Develops the key point about the numbing effect of repetition and routine

8   Widens the descriptive range, but keeps same VANTAGE POINT

Reverts to the
familiar scene of
the fields and the
DOMINANT IMPRES-
SION of endless
routine

Burley Tobacco calendar hanging in my house, except the illustration doesn't show the pale green that I perceive or transmit the scent of the cultivated dirt in the air that I inhale with a sigh. No, it can never convey the experience that is so familiar to me—standing and gazing at the perfectly spaced plants whose shadows blend into one on the rolling hills around me, until my eyes can strain no further in the dim light, and all I am left with is the fertilized dirt, gritty between my teeth.

PAUL CRENSHAW

STORM COUNTRY

Paul Crenshaw grew up in Logan County, Arkansas, in the heart of "Tornado Alley," the region of spectacularly violent weather stretching from North Dakota to southern Texas and Louisiana that he describes in "Storm Country." Crenshaw's sense of geography—and of his entire childhood—was formed, he says, through late-night "radio reports of tornado warnings or sightings . . . in a storm cellar." A graduate of the MFA Writing Program at the University of North Carolina at Greensboro, Crenshaw teaches writing and literature at Elon University in North Carolina. His essays and stories have appeared in *Shenandoah, North American Review, Southern Humanities Review, Harper's Ferry Review,* and other publications. In the following two complete sections of "Storm Country" (*Southern Humanities Review,* 2004), Crenshaw describes a place and its people in rich physical and emotional detail—both as he observed them and as they linger "in my mind."

◇◇◇◇◇◇◇◇◇◇◇◇◇◇◇◇◇◇◇◇◇◇◇◇◇◇◇◇◇◇◇◇◇◇◇◇◇◇

M y grandfather could tell by the way leaves hung on the trees if it would   1
rain that day or not—an old-time meteorologist who watched the seasons and the sky simply because they were there.

"See there?" he said once. We were standing outside the cellar as the first storms began to fire up in the heat of late afternoon. Low green clouds hung silent in the distance, and I have since learned that when clouds turn green, one should take cover. A point hung from the cloud, a barb that looked ominous as the clouds passed on and we watched them go, and always after I have looked for low barbs hanging from dark green clouds, for silent formations that might spawn destruction. He knew, standing on the cellar stairs watching through the little window, when a tornado might drop from the clouds. He knew the feel of the air, the presence that announces a heavy storm.

Sometimes it will stop raining when the funnel falls. Sometimes the wind stops and the trees go still and the air settles on you as everything goes quiet. Then, faint at first as the storm gathers speed, you can hear the force as it spins itself into existence, touching earth, whirling out into the day or night. It sounds like rusted sirens, howling dogs, the call of a freight train on a long trip across the plains somewhere in the western night, pushing speed and sound before it, lonely and forlorn on its midnight ride.

A good description appeals to the physical senses; turn to p. 65 to learn how.

I've seen tornadoes drop from a clear blue sky. I've seen barns and houses and fields wiped out, cattle thrown for a distance to lie in the rain bawling with broken legs. Once I watched as a three- or four-hundred-pound cut of sheet metal floated across the highway, touched down once, then lifted off again, light as air. I've seen towns wrecked by tornadoes in November, houses swept away, all that was left of a church roof lying on the ground, unscathed but for a few shingles missing at one corner. One time I was almost struck by a bullet of hail the size of my fist. It crashed through the window and landed on our living-room floor. We all looked at it for a moment. My mother tried to protect the curtains as the rain came in, but my father herded us toward the cellar up the hill at my grandfather's house.

I know the sound of storms, the low growl of thunder that means storms in the distance, the loud quick clap that means storms overhead. I've blinked in the afterglow of forked lightning, watched flash lightning light the hills as night turns into day. I've seen the remains of exploded houses, nothing left of the house but kindling, from when the tornado drops and the air pressure changes and the air inside the house has to get out.

I've seen storms come with no warning, boiling up out of a western sky   6
rimmed with the red rays of the last sun, lightning flickering in the twilight,
the air gone heavy and still. I've seen them sweep through with hardly a ripple
but the wind in your hair, passing to other places and other times. I've huddled
in hallways and bathtubs and cellars listening to tornadoes pass overhead, and
when I see on television the remnants of a town destroyed by the force of storms,
I always offer, however briefly, a thanks that it was not my people, or my town.

The first tornado I can remember was when I was eight. The storm came   7
in the afternoon, as many storms do. It was early in March—a month that, as
the saying goes in Arkansas, enters like a lion, leaves like a lion. My father was
watching a basketball game on TV when the sound disappeared, followed by
the steady beep that means an announcement is coming. Thunderstorms are
moving through the area, the announcement ran at the bottom of the screen.
Tornadoes possible. Take shelter. When the announcement disappeared the
state of Arkansas appeared on the screen, the western counties lit like radiation.
My father went out to study the sky and came back in at a run.

"Let's go," he said.   8

The trees were dancing as we ran to the truck, leaves and small branches   9
swirling in the wind and falling all around. At the road up the hill to my grandfather's house a dust devil[1] danced before my father ran his truck through
it, dispersing the dust. A line of rain moved toward us through the fields. The
clouds in the distance were green.

By the time we reached the top of the hill the wind was rocking the truck   10
and the first drops of rain were hitting the hood, big and loud and hard. The
curtain of rain reached us, going from a few drops to a downpour in an instant.
The wind ripped the truck door from my father's hand. My grandfather ran out
from the cellar door, where he'd been watching for us, waiting. He took my
brother, my father took me. We couldn't see the cellar in the rain. Thunder
rumbled the hills, and lightning stabbed down, sharp and quick, splitting the
rain, everything quiet for an instant before the thunder struck.

1. A small, high-velocity swirl of wind made visible by the sand or dust that turns within it.

We splashed through the rain and into the cellar. I was wet, plastered to 11
my father's chest. My mother took us down the stairs. My father and grandfather stood, peering through the window at the rain. The day had gone
dark.

Downstairs, my grandmother was telling stories to my two younger cous- 12
ins, who were flinching in the sharp crashes of each thunder. The room smelled
of kerosene, of earth and wind and rain. My skin was wet, hair cold as my
mother wrapped me in a quilt. In the brief silences between thunderclaps,
we could hear the rain and my father and grandfather on the stairs. I peered
through the door and heard my father say, "There it is."

He turned and saw me standing at the bottom of the stairs and motioned 13
me up. The rain had slowed and was falling lightly now, the wind settled down
in the trees. I stood on the steps with my father as he pointed in the distance,
where a dark funnel coiled downward from the black clouds, like smoke, or
wind taking shape and color. At the base of the tornado dust and debris hovered, circling slowly, and I heard the sound of storm for the first time. It grew
out of air, out of wind. It seemed as silent as noise can be, a faint howling that
reached us over the rain, almost peaceful from a distance. But then it would
hit a line of trees, or a fence, shooting trees and fence posts and barbed wire
into the air. It crossed over a pond and water turned it almost white for an
instant. It hit an old barn like a fist, smashing boards and metal, slinging the
debris about.

We watched, not speaking, as the tornado moved over the empty fields in 14
the distance, leaving a swath of devastation in its wake. After a time it folded
itself back into the underbelly of the clouds, rising silently, dispersing like
smoke in the wind, the sound gone and the air still once again.

"It's over," my father said, but I could still see in my mind the black fun- 15
nel dropping from the clouds, twisting across the landscape, throwing trees and
dirt and anything in its path, tearing tracts of land as it went on its way. Before
me was the result, the path of the tornado, cut through the hills. And, for no
reason it seemed, it faded away, gone as surely as it had come.

We stood there for a long time after it was over, silent, watching the clouds 16
roll on through, speeding swiftly toward night. After a time—an hour or three
or four—the clouds peeled back, revealing bright stars flung across the sky.

My father, and my grandfather, had watched other tornadoes before, just   17
like that one, had seen them and knew what they could do. I had thought that
they were standing guard through the night, watching until it was safe for us to
come out, putting themselves between us and the danger that lurked outside.
But as we turned and went down the stairs together I realized they watched
from the window to see the terrible beauty of the storm rolling across the hills,
hail falling from the sky, streaks of lightning in the jagged edges of the storm,
the twisting funnel of clouds that held such power.

FOR DISCUSSION

1. Paul Crenshaw obviously knows a lot about the natural, physical conditions that
   generate storms, particularly tornadoes, in the midwestern and southern United
   States. How did he become such a skilled "meteorologist"(1)?
2. Why did Crenshaw and his family, generation after generation, need to acquire
   their expert knowledge of storms?
3. As a child, Crenshaw believed that his parents and grandparents were simply
   "standing guard" when they kept a close eye on a brewing storm (17). Later he
   discovered that they kept watch for another reason as well. What was it?
4. Crenshaw ascribes no significance, beyond the natural and human, to the phenomena he is describing. Should he have? Why or why not?

STRATEGIES AND STRUCTURES

1. Is Crenshaw's DESCRIPTION largely OBJECTIVE or SUBJECTIVE? Explain.
2. Crenshaw's description is composed mostly of sights and sounds. Point out
   passages that emphasize each of these physical senses. Why do you think he
   relies on these two senses in particular?
3. Point out passages in which Crenshaw captures his and his family's feelings and
   emotions during a storm. How does the scene in the storm cellar (11–16) contribute to the picture?
4. What DOMINANT IMPRESSION is Crenshaw's description likely to leave upon the
   reader: a sense of awe and wonder at the power of nature; of fear and trembling at

the helplessness of humans; of faith in the security of home and family; or some combination of these (or other) emotions? Explain why you think so.

5. Why, according to Crenshaw, do houses and other structures sometimes "explode" (5) in a tornado? Throughout his essay, how and how well does Crenshaw analyze the CAUSES and EFFECTS of the physical phenomena he is describing?

6. Crenshaw uses a FLASHBACK to recall the first time ("when I was eight") that he remembers actually witnessing a tornado (7). Where else in his essay does he use strategies of NARRATIVE like this?

WORDS AND FIGURES OF SPEECH

. . . .

1. Observers of oncoming tornadoes often describe them as sounding like a "freight train" (3). Does Crenshaw expand effectively on this common comparison? Or does he lapse into CLICHÉ? Explain.

2. Where else in his essay does Crenshaw use SIMILES to describe what he and his family see, hear, and feel? How, and how effectively, do these FIGURES OF SPEECH contribute to his description?

3. To what extent does Crenshaw's use of the term *meteorologist* (1) confirm what Richard Lederer says about English as a "crazy" language (pp. 216–19)?

4. "Sometimes," says Crenshaw, "it will stop raining when the funnel falls" (3). Why does he switch to the future tense here?

FOR WRITING

. . . .

1. In a paragraph or two, describe the first time you saw a storm, fire, waterfall, rainbow, or other impressive natural phenomenon. Be sure to describe your feelings and emotions as well as what you observed.

2. Write an essay describing how some specific knowledge or skill—for example, reading weather (or other) patterns in nature, fishing, cooking, playing a game or sport—was passed on to you by family members or friends. Set your description in a specific place, or places, and include specific moments in time.

BRIAN DOYLE

JOYAS VOLADORAS

Brian Doyle (b. 1956) is the editor of *Portland Magazine*, published by the University of Portland, Oregon. His collections of essays and stories—including *Spirited Men* (2004), *The Wet Engine* (2005), and *Grace Notes* (2011)—deal with topics ranging from marriage and homework to saints and miracles. Often described as a "spiritual" writer, Doyle grounds his revelations in a naturalist's minute observations of the physical world. In "Joyas Voladoras" (*American Scholar*, 2004), his eye is on the hummingbird, a native of the Americas that Doyle identifies by the descriptive name given to it by early European explorers.

<hr>

Consider the hummingbird for a long moment. A hummingbird's heart beats ten times a second. A hummingbird's heart is the size of a pencil eraser. A hummingbird's heart is a lot of the hummingbird. *Joyas Voladoras*, flying jewels, the first white explorers in the Americas called them, and the white men had never seen such creatures, for hummingbirds came into the world only in the Americas, nowhere else in the universe, more than three hundred species of them whirring and zooming and nectaring in hummer time zones nine times

1

removed from ours, their hearts hammering faster than we could clearly hear if we pressed our elephantine ears to their infinitesimal chests.

Each one visits a thousand flowers a day. They can dive at sixty miles an hour. They can fly backward. They can fly more than five hundred miles without pausing to rest. But when they rest they come close to death: on frigid nights, or when they are starving, they retreat into torpor, their metabolic rate slowing to a fifteenth of their normal sleep rate, their hearts sludging nearly to a halt, barely beating, and if they are not soon warmed, if they do not soon find that which is sweet, their hearts grow cold, and they cease to be. Consider for a moment those hummingbirds who did not open their eyes again today, this very day, in the Americas: bearded helmetcrests and booted racket-tails, violet-tailed sylphs and violet-capped woodnymphs, crimson topazes and purple-crowned fairies, red-tailed comets and amethyst woodstars, rainbow-bearded thornbills and glittering-bellied emeralds, velvet-purple coronets and golden-bellied star-frontlets, fiery-tailed awlbills and Andean hillstars, spatuletails and pufflegs,[1] each the most amazing thing you have never seen, each thunderous wild heart the size of an infant's fingernail, each mad heart silent, a brilliant music stilled. 2

Hummingbirds, like all flying birds but more so, have incredible enormous immense ferocious metabolisms. To drive those metabolisms they have racecar hearts that eat oxygen at an eye-popping rate. Their hearts are built of thinner, leaner fibers than ours; their arteries are stiffer and more taut. They have more mitochondria in their heart muscles—anything to gulp more oxygen. Their hearts are stripped to the skin for the war against gravity and inertia, the mad search for food, the insane idea of flight. The price of their ambition is a life closer to death; they suffer more heart attacks and aneurysms and ruptures than any other living creature. It's expensive to fly. You burn out. You fry the machine. You melt the engine. Every creature on earth has approximately two billion heartbeats to spend in a lifetime. You can spend them slowly, like a tortoise, and live to be two hundred years old, or you can spend them fast, like a hummingbird, and live to be two years old. 3

1. The names of some of the nearly 400 species of hummingbirds in the world.

A hummingbird feeds on a ginger flower.

The biggest heart in the world is inside the blue whale. It weighs more than seven tons. It's as big as a room. It *is* a room, with four chambers. A child could walk around it, head high, bending only to step through the valves. The valves are as big as the swinging doors in a saloon. This house of a heart drives a creature a hundred feet long. When this creature is born it is twenty feet long and weighs four tons. It is waaaaay bigger than your car. It drinks a hundred gallons of milk from its mama every day and gains two hundred pounds a day, and when it is seven or eight years old it endures an unimaginable puberty and then it essentially disappears from human ken, for next to nothing is known of the the mating habits, travel patterns, diet, social life, language, social structure, diseases, spirituality, wars, stories, despairs, and arts of the blue whale. There are perhaps ten thousand blue whales in the world, living in every ocean on earth, and of the largest animal who ever lived we know nearly nothing. But we know this: the animals with the largest hearts in the world generally travel in pairs, and their penetrating moaning cries, their piercing yearning tongue, can be heard underwater for miles and miles.

Mammals and birds have hearts with four chambers. Reptiles and turtles have hearts with three chambers. Fish have hearts with two chambers. Insects and mollusks have hearts with one chamber. Worms have hearts with one chamber, although they may have as many as eleven single-chambered hearts. Unicellular bacteria have no hearts at all; but even they have fluid eternally in motion, washing from one side of the cell to the other, swirling and whirling. No living being is without interior liquid motion. We all churn inside.

So much held in a heart in a lifetime. So much held in a heart in a day, an hour, a moment. We are utterly open with no one in the end—not mother and father, not wife or husband, not lover, not child, not friend. We open windows to each but we live alone in the house of the heart. Perhaps we must. Perhaps we could not bear to be so naked, for fear of a constantly harrowed heart. When young we think there will come one person who will savor and sustain us always; when we are older we know this is the dream of a child, that all hearts finally are bruised and scarred, scored and torn, repaired by time and will, patched by force of character, yet fragile and rickety forevermore, no matter how ferocious the defense and how many bricks you bring to the wall. You can brick up your heart as stout and tight and hard and cold and impregnable as you possibly can and down it comes in an instant, felled by a woman's second glance, a child's apple breath, the shatter of glass in the road, the words "I have something to tell you," a cat with a broken spine dragging itself into the forest to die, the brush of your mother's papery ancient hand in the thicket of your hair, the memory of your father's voice early in the morning echoing from the kitchen where he is making pancakes for his children.

Descriptive writing often uses figures of speech (p. 67) like this heart-as-house metaphor.

6

FOR DISCUSSION

. . . .

1. If hummingbirds are "like all flying birds," as Brian Doyle says, why does he single them out for special consideration (3)? What's so special about them?

2. According to Doyle, what price do hummingbirds pay for their ability to "eat oxygen at an eye-popping rate" (3)?

3. If every living creature has, as Doyle says, "two billion heartbeats to spend in a lifetime" (3), why is it that turtles, for example, live so much longer than birds?

STRATEGIES AND STRUCTURES

. . . .

1. "Consider the hummingbird for a long moment" (1). How and how well might such a statement serve to introduce a detailed DESCRIPTION of almost any subject?

2. What particular physical attribute of the hummingbird does Doyle select as most essential in describing the nature of the bird? Why this particular choice of detail?

3. What is the point of Doyle's description of the heart of the giant blue whale in paragraph 4?

4. In which paragraph of his essay does Doyle most clearly move from describing hummingbirds to describing numerous other animals and birds? How and how well does this paragraph serve as a TRANSITION between the two topics?

5. What is Doyle's point in comparing the hearts of hummingbirds with those of all other living creatures? Where does he state it most clearly and directly?

WORDS AND FIGURES OF SPEECH

1. "It's expensive to fly" (4). Anyone who has been on an airplane lately can appreciate this observation, but what, exactly, does Doyle mean by the phrase?

2. Doyle is a poet as well as a writer of prose. Point out places in his essay where Doyle seems to exercise his poet's license. How effectively does he blend such poetic language with the more prosaic kind? Explain.

3. In the beginning of his essay, Doyle describes the heart as an organ for pumping blood and circulating oxygen. How and why does the meaning of the word *heart*, as he uses it, change throughout the course of his description?

FOR WRITING

1. Write a paragraph or two describing a bird or other living creature in flight or some other characteristic act. Concentrate on the observable, physical aspects of your subject.

2. In a descriptive essay, bring together two or more different species of animals or plants (humans and dolphins, for example) and show what they have in common by focusing on one or two similar features (such as lungs and language).

CHEROKEE PAUL McDONALD

A VIEW FROM THE BRIDGE

Cherokee Paul McDonald (b. 1949) is a fiction writer and journalist. His most recent book, *Into the Green* (2001), recounts his months of combat as an Army lieutenant in Vietnam. One of the themes of the book, says McDonald, "is hate the war, but don't hate the soldier." After Vietnam, McDonald served for ten years on the police force of Fort Lauderdale, Florida, an experience that he draws upon in several crime novels and that he describes graphically in *Blue Truth* (1991). McDonald is also a fisherman and the father of three children, roles that come together in the following descriptive essay about a boy who helps the author see familiar objects in a new light. The essay was first published in 1990 in *Sunshine*, a Florida sporting magazine.

❖〰❖〰❖〰❖〰❖〰❖〰❖〰❖〰❖〰❖〰❖〰❖〰❖〰❖〰❖〰❖〰❖〰❖〰❖〰

I was coming up on the little bridge in the Rio Vista neighborhood of Fort Lauderdale, deepening my stride and my breathing to negotiate the slight incline without altering my pace. And then, as I neared the crest, I saw the kid.   1

He was a lumpy little guy with baggy shorts, a faded T-shirt, and heavy sweat socks falling down over old sneakers.   2

Partially covering his shaggy blond hair was one of those blue baseball caps with gold braid on the bill and a sailfish patch sewn onto the peak. Covering his eyes and part of his face was a pair of those stupid-looking '50s-style wrap-around sunglasses. [3]

He was fumbling with a beat-up rod and reel, and he had a little bait bucket by his feet. I puffed on by, glancing down into the empty bucket as I passed. [4]

"Hey, mister! Would you help me, please?" [5]

The shrill voice penetrated my jogger's concentration, and I was determined to ignore it. But for some reason, I stopped. [6]

With my hands on my hips and the sweat dripping from my nose I asked, "What do you want, kid?" [7]

"Would you please help me find my shrimp? It's my last one and I've been getting bites and I know I can catch a fish if I can just find that shrimp. He jumped outta my hand as I was getting him from the bucket." [8]

Exasperated, I walked slowly back to the kid, and pointed. [9]

"There's the damn shrimp by your left foot. You stopped me for *that?*" [10]

As I said it, the kid reached down and trapped the shrimp. [11]

"Thanks a lot, mister," he said. [12]

I watched as the kid dropped the baited hook down into the canal. Then I turned to start back down the bridge. [13]

That's when the kid let out a "Hey! Hey!" and the prettiest tarpon I'd ever seen came almost six feet out of the water, twisting and turning as he fell through the air. [14]

"I got one!" the kid yelled as the fish hit the water with a loud splash and took off down the canal. [15]

I watched the line being burned off the reel at an alarming rate. The kid's left hand held the crank while the extended fingers felt for the drag setting. [16]

"No, kid!" I shouted. "Leave the drag alone . . . just keep that damn rod tip up!" [17]

Then I glanced at the reel and saw there were just a few loops of line left on the spool. [18]

"Why don't you get yourself some decent equipment?" I said, but before 19
the kid could answer I saw the line go slack.

"Ohhh, I lost him," the kid said. I saw the flash of silver as the fish 20
turned.

"Crank, kid, crank! You didn't lose him. He's coming back toward you. 21
Bring in the slack!"

The kid cranked like mad, and a beautiful grin spread across his face. 22

"He's heading in for the pilings," I said. "Keep him out of those pilings!" 23

The kid played it perfectly. When the fish made its play for the pilings, 24
he kept just enough pressure on to force the fish out. When the water exploded
and the silver missile hurled into the air, the kid kept the rod tip up and the line
tight.

As the fish came to the surface and began a slow circle in the middle of the 25
canal, I said, "Whooee, is that a nice fish or what?"

The kid didn't say anything, so I said, "Okay, move to the edge of the 26
bridge and I'll climb down to the seawall and pull him out."

When I reached the seawall I pulled in the leader, leaving the fish lying on 27
its side in the water.

"How's that?" I said. 28

"Hey, mister, tell me what it looks like." 29

"Look down here and check him out," I said, "He's beautiful." 30

But then I looked up into those stupid-looking sunglasses and it hit me. 31
The kid was blind.

"Could you tell me what he looks like, mister?" he said again. 32

"Well, he's just under three, uh, he's about as long as one of your arms," 33
I said. "I'd guess he goes about 15, 20 pounds. He's mostly silver, but the silver
is somehow made up of *all* the colors, if you know what I mean." I stopped.
"Do you know what I mean by colors?"

The kid nodded. 34

"Okay. He has all these big scales, like armor all over his body. They're 35
silver too, and when he moves they sparkle. He has a strong body and a large
powerful tail. He has big round eyes, bigger than a quarter, and a lower jaw that
sticks out past the upper one and is very tough. His belly is almost white and his

back is a gunmetal gray. When he jumped he came out of the water about six feet, and his scales caught the sun and flashed it all over the place."

By now the fish had righted itself, and I could see the bright-red gills as the gill plates opened and closed. I explained this to the kid, and then said, more to myself, "He's a beauty." 36

"Can you get him off the hook?" the kid asked. "I don't want to kill him." 37

I watched as the tarpon began to slowly swim away, tired but still alive. 38

By the time I got back up to the top of the bridge the kid had his line secured and his bait bucket in one hand. 39

He grinned and said, "Just in time. My mom drops me off here, and she'll be back to pick me up any minute." 40

He used the back of one hand to wipe his nose. 41

"Thanks for helping me catch that tarpon," he said, "and for helping me to see it." 42

I looked at him, shook my head, and said, "No, my friend, thank you for letting *me* see that fish." 43

I took off, but before I got far the kid yelled again. 44

"Hey, mister!" 45

I stopped. 46

"Someday I'm gonna catch a sailfish and a blue marlin and a giant tuna and all those big sportfish!" 47

As I looked into those sunglasses I knew he probably would. I wished I could be there when it happened. 48

FOR DISCUSSION

. . . .

1. Which of the five senses does Cherokee Paul McDonald appeal to in his DESCRIPTION of the tarpon (35)? In this essay as a whole?

2. How much does the jogger seem to know about fish and fishing? About boys?

3. What is the attitude of the jogger toward the "kid" before he realizes the boy is blind (31)? As a reader, what is your attitude toward the jogger? Why?

4. How does the jogger feel about the kid when they part? How do you feel about the jogger? What, if anything, changes your view of him?

5. How does meticulously describing a small piece of the world help the grumpy jogger to see the world anew?

STRATEGIES AND STRUCTURES

1. McDonald serves as eyes for the boy (and us). Which physical details in his description of the scene at the bridge do you find to be visually most effective?

2. McDonald's description is part of a NARRATIVE. At first, the NARRATOR seems irritable and in a hurry. What makes him slow down? How does his behavior change? Why?

3. The narrator does not realize the boy is blind until paragraph 31, but we figure it out much sooner. What descriptive details lead us to realize that the boy is blind?

4. McDonald, of course, knew when he wrote this piece that the boy couldn't see. Why do you think he wrote from the POINT OF VIEW of the jogger, who doesn't know at first? How does he restrict the narrator's point of view in paragraph 6? Elsewhere in the essay?

5. How does the narrator's physical VANTAGE POINT change in paragraph 27? Why does this alter the way he sees the boy?

6. "No, my friend," says the jogger, "thank you for letting *me* see that fish" (43). So who is helping whom to see in this essay? How? Cite examples.

WORDS AND FIGURES OF SPEECH

1. METONYMY is a FIGURE OF SPEECH in which a word or object stands in for another associated with it. How might the blind boy's cap or sunglasses be seen as examples of metonymy?

2. Point out words and phrases in this essay—for example, "sparkle"—that refer to sights or acts of seeing (35).

3. What possible meanings are suggested by the word "view" in McDonald's title?

4. Besides its literal meaning, how else might we take the word "bridge" here? Who or what is being "bridged"?

FOR WRITING

. . . .

1. Suppose you had to describe a flower, bird, snake, butterfly, or other plant or animal to a blind person. In a paragraph, describe the object—its colors, smell, texture, movement, how the light strikes it—in sufficient physical detail so that the person could form an accurate mental picture of what you are describing.

2. Write an extended description of a scene in which you see a familiar object, person, or place in a new light because of someone else who brings a fresh viewpoint to the picture. For example, you might describe the scene at the dinner table when you bring home a new girlfriend or boyfriend. Or you might describe taking a tour of your campus, hometown, neighborhood, or workplace with a friend or relative who has never seen it before.

ALICE STEINBACH

THE MISS DENNIS SCHOOL
OF WRITING

Alice Steinbach (1933–2012) was a freelance writer whose essays and travel sketches often deal with what she called "lessons from a woman's life." As a reporter for the *Baltimore Sun*, where she won a Pulitzer Prize for feature writing in 1985, Steinbach wrote a column about her ninth-grade creative writing teacher. It became the title piece in a collection of personal essays, *The Miss Dennis School of Writing* (1996). Here the "lesson" is both a writing lesson and a life lesson. Miss Dennis taught that good descriptive writing (her specialty) makes the reader see what the writer sees. She also taught her students to find their unique personal voices. Steinbach's distinctive voice can be heard in her vivid descriptions of her former teacher. It is a perspective, she has said, that "tends to look at people with a child's eye."

"What kind of writing do you do?" asked the novelist sitting to my left at a writer's luncheon.   1

"I work for a newspaper in Baltimore," he was told.   2

"Oh, did you go to journalism school?"   3

"Well, yes." 4

"Columbia?" he asked, invoking the name of the most prestigious jour- 5
nalism school in the country.

"Actually, no," I heard myself telling him. "I'm one of the lucky ones. 6
I am a graduate of the Miss Dennis School of Writing."

Unimpressed, the novelist turned away. Clearly it was a credential that 7
did not measure up to his standards. But why should it? He was not one of the
lucky ones. He had never met Miss Dennis, my ninth-grade creative writing
teacher, or had the good fortune to be her student. Which meant he had never
experienced the sight of Miss Dennis chasing Dorothy Singer around the classroom, threatening her with a yardstick because Dorothy hadn't paid attention
and her writing showed it.

"You want to be a writer?" Miss Dennis would yell, out of breath from 8
all the running and yardstick-brandishing. "Then pay attention to what's going
on around you. Connect! You are not Switzerland—neutral, aloof, uninvolved.
Think Italy!"

Miss Dennis said things like this. If you had any sense, you wrote them 9
down.

"I can't teach you how to write, but I can tell you how to look at things, how 10
to pay attention," she would bark out at us, like a drill sergeant confronting a
group of undisciplined, wet-behind-the-ears[1] Marine recruits. To drive home her
point, she had us take turns writing a description of what we saw on
the way to school in the morning. Of course, you never knew which
morning would be your turn so—just to be on the safe side—you
got into the habit of looking things over carefully every morning and
making notes: "Saw a pot of red geraniums sitting in the sunlight on a white
stucco porch; an orange-striped cat curled like a comma beneath a black van; a
dark gray cloud scudding across a silver morning sky."

> Concrete details
> (p. 65) help to
> drive home the
> point of any
> description.

It's a lesson that I have returned to again and again throughout my writing 11
career. To this day, I think of Miss Dennis whenever I write a certain kind of

---

1. Young and inexperienced.

sentence. Or to be more precise, whenever I write a sentence that actually creates in words the picture I want readers to see.

Take, for instance, this sentence: Miss Dennis was a small, compact woman, about albatross height—or so it seemed to her students—with short, straight hair the color of apricots and huge eyeglasses that were always slipping down her nose. 12

Or this one: Miss Dennis always wore a variation of one outfit—a dark-colored, flared woolen skirt, a tailored white blouse and a cardigan sweater, usually black, thrown over her shoulders and held together by a little pearl chain. 13

Can you see her? I can. And the image of her makes me smile. Still. 14

But it was not Miss Dennis's appearance or her unusual teaching method—which had a lot in common with an out-of-control terrier—that made her so special. What set her apart was her deep commitment to liberating the individual writer in each student. 15

"What lies at the heart of good writing," she told us over and over again, "is the writer's ability to find his own unique voice. And then to use it to tell an interesting story." Somehow she made it clear that we were interesting people with interesting stories to tell. Most of us, of course, had never even known we had a story to tell, much less an interesting one. But soon the stories just started bubbling up from some inner wellspring. 16

Finding the material, however, was one thing; finding the individual voice was another. 17

Take me, for instance. I arrived in Miss Dennis's class trailing all sorts of literary baggage. My usual routine was to write like Colette on Monday, one of the Brontë sisters on Wednesday, and Mark Twain[2] on Friday. 18

Right away, Miss Dennis knocked me off my high horse. 19

2. Sidonie-Gabrielle Colette (1873–1954), French novelist known for her sophisticated depictions of female sexuality; Charlotte Brontë (1816–1855), Emily Brontë (1818–1848), and Anne Brontë (1820–1849), British writers of early Romantic novels; Mark Twain (1835–1910), American novelist and essayist known for his works of wit and satire.

"Why are you telling other people's stories?" she challenged me, peering   20
up into my face. (At fourteen I was already four inches taller than Miss Dennis.)
"You have your own stories to tell."

I was tremendously relieved to hear this and immediately proceeded to   21
write like my idol, E. B. White.[3] Miss Dennis, however, wasn't buying.

"How will you ever find out what you have to say if you keep trying to say   22
what other people have already said?" was the way she dispensed with my E. B.
White impersonation. By the third week of class, Miss Dennis knew my secret.
She knew I was afraid—afraid to pay attention to my own inner voice for fear
that when I finally heard it, it would have nothing to say.

What Miss Dennis told me—and I have carefully preserved these words   23
because they were then, and are now, so very important to me—was this: "Don't
be afraid to discover what you're saying in the act of saying it." Then, in her
inimitably breezy and endearing way, she added: "Trust me on this one."

From the beginning, she made it clear to us that it was not "right" or   24
"wrong" answers she was after. It was thinking.

"Don't be afraid to go out on a limb," she'd tell some poor kid struggling   25
to reason his way through an essay on friendship or courage. And eventually—
once we stopped being afraid that we'd be chopped off out there on that
limb—we needed no encouragement to say what we thought. In fact, after the
first month, I can't remember ever feeling afraid of failing in her class. Passing
or failing didn't seem to be the point of what she was teaching.

Miss Dennis spent as much time, maybe more, pointing out what was   26
right with your work as she did pointing out what was wrong. I can still hear her
critiquing my best friend's incredibly florid essay on nature. "You are a very
good observer of nature," she told the budding writer. "And if you just write
what you see without thinking so much about adjectives and comparisons, we
will see it through your attentive eyes."

3. American essayist and children's author (1899–1985), admired for his elegant style and
attention to detail.

By Thanksgiving vacation I think we were all a little infatuated with Miss   27
Dennis. And beyond that, infatuated with the way she made us feel about
ourselves—that we were interesting people worth listening to.

I, of course, fancied I had a special relationship with her. It was certainly   28
special to me. And, to tell the truth, I knew she felt the same way.

The first time we acknowledged this was one day after class when I   29
stayed behind to talk to her. I often did that and it seemed we talked about
everything—from the latest films to the last issue of the *New Yorker*. The one
thing we did not talk about was the sadness I felt about my father's death. He had
died a few years before and, although I did not know it then, I was still grieving
his absence. Without knowing the details, Miss Dennis somehow picked up on
my sadness. Maybe it was there in my writing. Looking back I see how that,
without my writing about it directly, my father's death hovered at the edges of all
my stories.

But on this particular day I found myself talking not about the movies or   30
about writing but instead pouring out my feelings about the loss of my father. I
shall never forget that late fall afternoon: the sound of the vanilla-colored blinds
flap, flap, flapping in the still classroom; sun falling in shafts through the windows, each ray illuminating tiny galaxies of chalk dust in the air; the smell of
wet blackboards; the teacher, small with apricot-colored hair, listening intently
to a young girl blurting out her grief. These memories are stored like vintage
photographs.

The words that passed between the young girl and the attentive teacher   31
are harder to recall. With this exception. "One day," Miss Dennis told me,
"you will write about this. Maybe not directly. But you will write about it. And
you will find that all this has made you a better writer and a stronger person."

After that day, it was as if Miss Dennis and I shared something. We never   32
talked again about my father but spent most of our time discussing our mutual
interests. We both loved poetry and discovered one afternoon that each of us
regarded Emily Dickinson with something approaching idolatry. Right then
and there, Miss Dennis gave me a crash course in why Emily Dickinson's
poems worked. I can still hear her talking about the "spare, slanted beauty" in
Dickinson's unique choice of words. She also told me about the rather cloistered

life led by this New England spinster, noting that nonetheless Emily Dickinson[4] knew the world as few others did. "She found her world within the word," is the way I remember Miss Dennis putting it. Of course, I could be making that part up.

That night, propped up in bed reading Emily Dickinson's poetry, I wondered if Miss Dennis, a spinster herself, identified in some way with the woman who wrote: 33

> Wild nights–Wild nights!
> Were I with thee
> Wild Nights should be
> Our luxury!

It seems strange, I know, but I never really knew anything about Miss Dennis' life outside of the classroom. Oh, once she confided in me that the initial "M" in her name stood for Mildred. And I was surprised when I passed by the teachers' lounge one day and saw her smoking a cigarette, one placed in a long, silver cigarette holder. It seemed an exceedingly sophisticated thing to do and it struck me then that she might be more worldly than I had previously thought. 34

But I didn't know how she spent her time or what she wanted from life or anything like that. And I never really wondered about it. Once I remember talking to some friends about her age. We guessed somewhere around fifty— which seemed really old to us. In reality, Miss Dennis was around forty. 35

It was Miss Dennis, by the way, who encouraged me to enter some writing contests. To my surprise, I took first place in a couple of them. Of course, taking first place is easy. What's hard is being rejected. But Miss Dennis helped me with that, too, citing all the examples of famous writers who'd been rejected time and time again. "Do you know what they told George Orwell[5] when they 36

4. American poet (1830–1886) who wrote almost 1,800 poems (and many letters). In later years, Dickinson seldom left her family home in Amherst, Massachusetts.

5. British novelist and essayist (1903–1950). Much of his major work, including the satiric novel *Animal Farm* (1945), reflects his opposition to repressive governments.

rejected *Animal Farm?"* she would ask me. Then without waiting for a reply, she'd answer her own question: "The publisher told him, 'It is impossible to sell animal stories in the U.S.A.'"

When I left her class at the end of the year, Miss Dennis gave me a pres-   37
ent: a book of poems by Emily Dickinson. I have it still. The spine is cracked and the front cover almost gone, but the inscription remains. On the inside fly-leaf, in her perfect Palmer Method handwriting,[6] she had written: "Say what you see. Yours in Emily Dickinson, Miss Dennis."

She had also placed little checks next to two or three poems. I took this to   38
mean she thought they contained a special message for me. One of those checked began this way:

> Hope is the thing with feathers
> That perches in the soul . . .

I can remember carefully copying out these lines onto a sheet of paper, one which I carried around in my handbag for almost a year. But time passed, the handbag fell apart and who knows what happened to the yellowing piece of paper with the words about hope.

The years went by. Other schools and other teachers came and went. But   39
one thing remained constant: My struggle to pay attention to my own inner life; to hear a voice that I would recognize finally as my own. Not only in my writing but in my life.

Only recently, I learned that Miss Dennis had died at the age of fifty.   40
When I heard this, it occurred to me that her life was close to being over when I met her. Neither of us knew this, of course. Or at least I didn't. But lately I've wondered if she knew something that day we talked about sadness and my father's death. "Write about it," she said. "It will help you."

And now, reading over these few observations, I think of Miss Dennis.   41
But not with sadness. Actually, thinking of Miss Dennis makes me smile. I

---

6. A form of standardized handwriting that became popular around 1900 but is rarely taught today.

think of her and see, with marked clarity, a small, compact woman with apricot-colored hair. She is with a young girl and she is saying something.

She is saying: "Pay attention."

42

FOR DISCUSSION

. . . .

1. When some teachers say, "Pay attention," they mean "Pay attention to what I am saying." According to her former pupil, Alice Steinbach, what did Miss Dennis mean when she told students to pay attention (8)?

2. It was neither Miss Dennis's appearance nor her teaching methods that made her so special as a teacher of writing, says Steinbach, but "her deep commitment to liberating the individual writer in each student" (15). How did Miss Dennis accomplish this feat in Steinbach's case?

3. Steinbach poses a direct question to the reader in paragraph 14: "Can you see her?" Well, can you? And if so, what exactly do you see—and hear? For example, what color was Miss Dennis's hair?

4. Steinbach thinks of her old teacher whenever she writes a sentence "that actually creates in words the picture I want readers to see" (11). This is precisely what good DESCRIPTIVE writing does, although it may appeal to other senses as well as sight. How did Miss Dennis teach this kind of writing?

5. Writing about old teachers who die can be an occasion for sentimentality or excessively emotional writing. Do you think Steinbach's tribute to her former teacher is overly emotional, or does she successfully avoid sentimentality? If she avoids it, in your opinion, explain how she does so. If not, explain why you think she doesn't. Find places in her essay that support your view.

STRATEGIES AND STRUCTURES

. . . .

1. Point out several descriptive passages in Steinbach's essay that follow her principle of creating in words what she wants the reader to see.

2. Why do you think Steinbach, looking back over her recollections of Miss Dennis, refers to them as "observations" (41)?

3. Description seldom stands alone. Often it shades into NARRATION, as here. Thus Miss Dennis, who greatly valued the writer's eye, urged the student, once she found her unique way of looking at the world, to use it "to tell an interesting story" (16). Besides Miss Dennis's, whose story is Steinbach telling? How interesting do you find *that* narrative?

4. What DOMINANT IMPRESSION of Miss Dennis do we get from Steinbach's description of her in paragraphs 12 through 14 and 41? Of Steinbach herself?

5. How informative do you find Steinbach's essay as a lesson on how to write, particularly on how to write good description? Where does Steinbach ANALYZE THE PROCESS?

WORDS AND FIGURES OF SPEECH

1. Which is more CONCRETE, to say that a woman has "hair the color of apricots" or to say that she is a redhead or blonde (12)? Which is more specific?

2. The orange-striped cat in young Steinbach's description of her walk to school is "curled like a comma" beneath a van (10). Such stated COMPARISONS, frequently using *like* or *as*, are called SIMILES. Implied comparisons, without like or as, are called METAPHORS. What metaphoric comparison does Steinbach make in the same description? What is she comparing to what?

3. Steinbach compares Miss Dennis to an "albatross" and "an out-of-control terrier" (12, 15). Besides describing Miss Dennis, what do these fanciful comparisons tell you about her former writing pupil?

4. Steinbach arrived in Miss Dennis's class "trailing all sorts of literary baggage" (18). To what is she comparing herself here?

5. How would you describe the words that Steinbach uses in paragraph 30 to describe the afternoon? Concrete or ABSTRACT? Specific or general?

FOR WRITING

1. On your next walk to or around school, pay close attention to your surroundings. Take notes, as young Steinbach does in paragraph 10. Describe what you see in a paragraph that "creates in words the picture" you want your reader to see (11).

Make it as free of literary or other baggage as you can, and try to select details that contribute to a single dominant impression.

2. Write a profile—a description of a person that not only tells but shows a piece of that person's life story—of one of your favorite (or most despised) teachers or coaches. Try to give your reader a clear sense of what that person looks like; of what he or she wears, says, and does; and of the dominant impression he or she makes on others. Be sure to show how you interact with that person and what he or she has (or has not) taught you.

ANN HODGMAN

NO WONDER THEY CALL
ME A BITCH

Ann Hodgman (b. 1956) is a freelance writer and former food critic for *Eating Well* magazine. Besides playing goalie on a women's hockey team, she is the author of more than forty children's books, several cookbooks, and two memoirs, *The House of a Million Pets* (2007) and *How to Die of Embarrassment Every Day* (2011). For reasons soon to be apparent, the following "tasteless" essay from 1990 did not appear in Hodgman's food column, "Sweet and Sour," but in the satiric magazine *Spy*, for which Hodgman was a contributing editor. A spoof on taste testing, it takes a blue ribbon for disgusting description that appeals to the grosser senses.

〉〈〉

I've always wondered about dog food. Is a Gaines-burger really like a hamburger? Can you fry it? Does dog food "cheese" taste like real cheese? Does Gravy Train actually make gravy in the dog's bowl, or is that brown liquid just dissolved crumbs? And exactly what *are* by-products?

    Having spent the better part of a week eating dog food, I'm sorry to say that I now know the answers to these questions. While my dachshund, Shortie, watched in agonies of yearning, I gagged my way through can after can of stinky, white-flecked mush and bag after bag of stinky, fat-drenched nuggets. And now I understand exactly why Shortie's breath is so bad.

Of course, Gaines-burgers are neither mush nor nuggets. They are, rather, a 3 miracle of beauty and packaging—or at least that's what I thought when I was little. I used to beg my mother to get them for our dogs, but she always said they were too expensive. When I finally bought a box of cheese-flavored Gaines-burgers—after twenty years of longing—I felt deliciously wicked.

"Dogs love real beef," the back of the box proclaimed proudly. "That's 4 why Gaines-burgers is the only beef burger for dogs with real beef and no meat by-products!" The copy was accurate: meat by-products did not appear in the list of ingredients. Poultry by-products did, though—right there next to preserved animal fat.

One Purina spokesman told me that poultry by-products consist of necks, 5 intestines, undeveloped eggs and other "carcass remnants," but not feathers, heads, or feet. When I told him I'd been eating dog food, he said, "Oh, you're kidding! Oh, *no!*" (I came to share his alarm when, weeks later, a second Purina spokesman said that Gaines-burgers *do* contain poultry heads and feet—but not undeveloped eggs.)

Up close my Gaines-burger didn't much resemble chopped beef. Rather, 6 it looked—and felt—like a single long, extruded piece of redness that had been chopped into segments and formed into a patty. You could make one at home if you had a Play-Doh Fun Factory.

I turned on the skillet. While I waited for it to heat up I pulled out a shred 7 of cheese-colored material and palpated it. Again, like Play-Doh, it was quite malleable. I made a little cheese bird out of it; then I counted to three and ate the bird.

There was a horrifying rush of cheddar taste, followed immediately by 8 the dull tang of soybean flour—the main ingredient in Gaines-burgers. Next I tried a piece of red extrusion. The main difference between the meat-flavored and cheese-flavored extrusions is one of texture. The "cheese" chews like fresh Play-Doh, whereas the "meat" chews like Play-Doh that's been sitting out on a rug for a couple of hours.

Frying only turned the Gaines-burger black. There was no melting, no siz- 9
zling, no warm meat smells. A cherished childhood illusion was gone. I flipped
the patty into the sink, where it immediately began leaking rivulets of red dye.

As alarming as the Gaines-burgers were, their soy meal began to seem 10
like an old friend when the time came to try some *canned* dog foods. I decided to
try the Cycle foods first. When I opened them, I thought about how rarely I use
can openers these days, and I was suddenly visited by a long-forgotten sensation
of can-opener distaste. *This* is the kind of unsavory place can openers spend
their time when you're not watching! Every time you open a can of, say, Italian
plum tomatoes, you infect them with invisible particles of by-product.

I had been expecting to see the usual homogeneous scrapple inside, but 11
each can of Cycle was packed with smooth, round, oily nuggets. As if someone
at Gaines had been tipped off that a human would be tasting the stuff, the four
Cycles really were different from one another. Cycle-1, for puppies, is wet and
soyish. Cycle-2, for adults, glistens nastily with fat, but it's passably edible—a
lot like some canned Swedish meatballs I once got in a care package at college.
Cycle-3, the "lite" one, for fatties, had no specific flavor; it just tasted like dog
food. But at least it didn't make me fat.

Cycle-4, for senior dogs, had the smallest nuggets. Maybe old dogs can't 12
open their mouths as wide. This kind was far sweeter than the other three
Cycles—almost like baked beans. It was also the only one to contain "dried beef
digest," a mysterious substance that the Purina spokesman defined as "enzymes"
and my dictionary defined as "the products of digestion."

Next on the menu was a can of Kal Kan Pedigree with Chunky Chicken. 13
Chunky *chicken?* There were chunks in the can, certainly—big, purplish-
brown chunks. I forked one chunk out (by now I was becoming more callous)
and found that while it had no discernible chicken flavor, it wasn't bad except
for its texture—like meat loaf with ground-up chicken bones.

In the world of canned dog food, a smooth consistency is a sign of low 14
quality—lots of cereal. A lumpy, frightening, bloody, stringy horror is a sign
of high quality—lots of meat. Nowhere in the world of wet dog foods was this
demonstrated better than in the fanciest I tried—Kal Kan's Pedigree Select
Dinners. These came not in a can but in a tiny foil packet with a picture of an

imperious Yorkie. When I pulled open the container, juice spurted all over my hand, and the first chunk I speared was trailing a long gray vein. I shrieked and went instead for a plain chunk, which I was able to swallow only after taking a break to read some suddenly fascinating office equipment catalogues. Once again, though, it tasted no more alarming than, say, canned hash.

Still, how pleasant it was to turn to *dry* dog food! Gravy Train was the first   15
I tried, and I'm happy to report that it really does make a "thick, rich, real beef gravy" when you mix it with water. Thick and rich, anyway. Except for a lingering rancid-fat flavor, the gravy wasn't beefy, but since it tasted primarily like tap water, it wasn't nauseating either.

My poor dachshund just gets plain old Purina Dog Chow, but Purina also   16
makes a dry food called Butcher's Blend that comes in Beef, Bacon & Chicken flavor. Here we see dog food's arcane semiotics at its best: a red triangle with a *T* stamped into it is supposed to suggest beef; a tan curl, chicken; and a brown *S*, a piece of bacon. Only dogs understand these messages. But Butcher's Blend does have an endearing slogan: "Great Meaty Tastes—without bothering the Butcher!" *You know, I wanted to buy some meat, but I just couldn't bring myself to bother the butcher . . .*

Purina O.N.E. ("Optimum Nutritional Effectiveness") is targeted at   17
people who are unlikely ever to worry about bothering a tradesperson. "We chose chicken as a primary ingredient in Purina O.N.E. for several reasonings," the long, long essay on the back of the bag announces. Chief among these reasonings, I'd guess, is the fact that chicken appeals to people who are—you know—*like us.* Although our dogs do nothing but spend eighteen-hour days alone in the apartment, we still want them to be *premium* dogs. We want them to cut down on red meat, too. We also want dog food that comes in a bag with an attractive design, a subtle typeface, and no kitschy pictures of slobbering golden retrievers.

Besides that, we want a list of the Nutritional Benefits of our dog food—   18
and we get it on O.N.E. One thing I especially like about this list is its constant references to a dog's "hair coat," as in "Beef tallow is good for the dog's skin and hair coat." (On the other hand, beef tallow merely provides palatability, while the dried beef digest in Cycle provides palatability *enhancement.*)

I hate to say it, but O.N.E. was pretty palatable. Maybe that's because it   19
has about 100 percent more fat than, say, Butcher's Blend. Or maybe I'd been
duped by the packaging; that's been known to happen before.

As with people food, dog snacks taste much better than dog meals.   20
They're better looking too. Take Milk-Bone Flavor Snacks. The loving-hands-
at-home prose describing each flavor is colorful; the writers practically choke on
their own exuberance. Of bacon they say, "It's so good, your dog will think it's
hot off the frying pan." Of liver: "The only taste your dog wants more than
liver—is even more liver!" Of poultry: "All those farm fresh flavors deliciously
mixed in one biscuit. Your dog will bark with delight!" And of vegetable: "Gar-
dens of taste! Specially blended to give your dog that vegetable flavor he wants—
but can rarely get!"

Well, I may be a sucker, but advertising this emphatic just doesn't con-   21
vince me. I lined up all seven flavors of Milk-Bone Flavor Snacks on the floor.
Unless my dog's palate is a lot more sensitive than mine—and considering that
she steals dirty diapers out of the trash and eats them, I'm loath to think it is—
she doesn't detect any more difference in the seven flavors than I did when I
tried them.

I much preferred Bonz, the hard-baked, bone-shaped snack stuffed with   22
simulated marrow. I liked the bone part, that is; it tasted almost exactly like the
cornmeal it was made of. The mock marrow inside was a bit more problematic:
in addition to looking like the sludge that collects in the treads of my running
shoes, it was bursting with tiny hairs.

I'm sure you have a few dog food questions of your own. To save us time,   23
I've answered them in advance.

Q. Are those little cans of Mighty Dog actually branded with the sizzling   24
word BEEF, *the way they show in the commercials?*

A. You should know by now that that kind of thing never happens.   25

Q. Does chicken-flavored dog food taste like chicken-flavored cat food?   26

A. To my surprise, chicken cat food was actually a little better—more   27
chickeny. It tasted like inferior canned pâté.

Q. Was there any dog food that you just couldn't bring yourself to try?   28

A. Alas, it was a can of Mighty Dog called Prime Entree with Bone   29
Marrow. The meat was dark, dark brown, and it was surrounded by gelatin that

was almost black. I knew I would die if I tasted it, so I put it outside for the raccoons.

FOR DISCUSSION

. . . .

1. Ann Hodgman's discourse on dog food may be a humorous, tongue-in-cheek play on conventional food reviews, but as DESCRIPTIVE writing do you agree that it is truly disgusting? Which do you find more effectively nauseating, her description of the tastes and textures of dry dog food or canned?

2. Most of Hodgman's "research" is done in her own laboratory kitchen. Where else does she go for information? Do you think her studies qualify her to speak expertly on the subject? How about vividly?

3. How do you suppose Hodgman knows what Play-Doh chews like after it's been "sitting out on a rug for a couple of hours"—that is, as opposed to fresh Play-Doh (8)?

4. What childhood fantasy does Hodgman fulfill by writing this essay? How does the reality COMPARE with the fantasy?

5. Do you find Hodgman's title in bad taste? Why or why not? How about her entire essay?

6. What question would you ask Hodgman about her research? For example, Q: *Why are you asking these unsavory questions?* A: Somebody has to honor those who do basic research in a new field.

STRATEGIES AND STRUCTURES

. . . .

1. "When I pulled open the container, juice spurted all over my hand, and the first chunk I speared was trailing a long gray vein" (14). Can you see, smell, and taste it? Cite other examples of Hodgman's descriptive skills and her direct appeal (if that's the right word) to the senses.

2. Notice the major shift that occurs when the description moves from canned dog food to dry. Where does the shift occur? Why does she find the change so "pleasant"? When does she shift again—to snacks?

3. Why do you suppose Hodgman never tells us why she is describing the ingredients, tastes, and textures of dog food with such scrupulous accuracy and OBJECTIVITY?

What is her PURPOSE in writing this piece, and how might her scrupulous objectivity be appropriate for that purpose?

4. Why do you think Hodgman shifts to a question-and-answer format at the end of her essay?

5. Hodgman is a professional food critic. What CONCRETE and specific words from her professional vocabulary does she use?

6. What is the DOMINANT IMPRESSION created by Hodgman's description of Bonz in paragraph 22?

7. Hodgman not only describes herself at work in her laboratory kitchen, she ANALYZES THE PROCESS of doing basic food research there. Besides tasting, what are some of the other steps in the process?

WORDS AND FIGURES OF SPEECH

. . . .

1. Hodgman refers to "some suddenly fascinating office equipment catalogues" that divert her from tasting Kal Kan's best (14). Is this IRONY?

2. How does your dictionary DEFINE "dried beef digest" (12)? Where else does Hodgman use the technical language of the industry she is SATIRIZING?

3. Hodgman says her Gaines-burger, when fried and flipped into the sink, "began leaking rivulets of red dye" (9). Is this scientific detachment or HYPERBOLE?

4. The opposite of intentional exaggeration is UNDERSTATEMENT. In Hodgman's analysis of the simulated marrow in Bonz, would "problematic" qualify as an example (22)?

5. Hodgman says Kal Kan Pedigree with Chunky Chicken tasted "like meat loaf with ground-up chicken bones" (13). Is this a SIMILE, or do you suppose the chicken could be literally chunky because of the bones?

FOR WRITING

. . . .

1. While Hodgman gags her way through sample after sample of premium dog food, her dachshund, Shortie, looks on "in agonies of yearning" (2). Describe the "data" in Hodgman's taste experiment from Shortie's POINT OF VIEW. How might Gaines-burgers and Kal Kan Pedigree with Chunky Chicken taste to

him? Is Hodgman right to say that Shortie cannot distinguish among the seven flavors of Milk-Bone Flavor Snacks? What would Shortie's palate tell us?

2. Conduct a program of research similar to Hodgman's but in the field of junk food. Write an unbiased description of your findings. Or, if you prefer, forget the taste tests, and follow Hodgman's lead in analyzing the claims of food advertisers. Choose a category of food products—gummy worms, breath mints, canned soup, frozen pizza, breakfast cereal, cookies—and study the packaging carefully. Write an essay in which you describe how the manufacturers of your samples typically describe their products.

E. B. WHITE

ONCE MORE TO THE LAKE

Elwyn Brooks White (1899–1985) was born in Mount Vernon, New York. After graduating from Cornell University in 1921, he worked as a journalist and advertising copywriter before joining the staff of the *New Yorker* in 1926. He also wrote a regular column for *Harper's*. White's numerous books include the children's classic *Charlotte's Web* (1952) and *The Elements of Style* (1959), a guide to writing that updates the work of his teacher William Strunk. "Once More to the Lake," which originally appeared in *Harper's*, was written in August 1941 on the eve of World War II. The lake described here is Great Pond, one of the Belgrade Lakes in south-central Maine. When White returns to the familiar scene, it seems unchanged—at first.

❖⟋❖⟍❖⟋❖⟍❖⟋❖⟍❖⟋❖⟍❖⟋❖⟍❖⟋❖⟍❖⟋❖⟍❖⟋❖⟍❖⟋❖⟍❖⟋❖⟍❖⟋❖

One summer, along about 1904, my father rented a camp on a lake in Maine and took us all there for the month of August. We all got ringworm from some kittens and had to rub Pond's Extract on our arms and legs night and morning, and my father rolled over in a canoe with all his clothes on; but outside of that the vacation was a success and from then on none of us ever thought there was any place in the world like that lake in Maine. We returned summer after summer—always on August 1 for one month. I have since become a salt-water man, but sometimes in summer there are days when the restlessness of the tides and the fearful cold of the sea water and the incessant wind that blows across the afternoon and into the evening make me wish for the placidity of a lake in the woods. A few weeks ago this feeling got so strong I bought myself a couple of bass hooks and a spinner and returned to the lake where we used to go, for a week's fishing and to revisit old haunts.

I took along my son, who had never had any fresh water up his nose and who had seen lily pads only from train windows. On the journey over to the lake I began to wonder what it would be like. I wondered how the time would have marred this unique, this holy spot—the coves and streams, the hills that the sun set behind, the camps and the paths behind the camps. I was sure that the tarred road would have found it out, and I wondered in what other ways it would be desolated. It is strange how much you can remember about places like that once you allow your mind to return into the grooves that lead back. You remember one thing, and that suddenly reminds you of another thing. I guess I remembered clearest of all the early mornings, when the lake was cool and motionless, remembered how the bedroom smelled of the lumber it was made of and of the wet woods whose scent entered through the screen. The partitions in the camp were thin and did not extend clear to the top of the rooms, and as I was always the first up I would dress softly so as not to wake the others, and sneak out into the sweet outdoors and start out in the canoe, keeping close along the shore in the long shadows of the pines. I remembered being very careful never to rub my paddle against the gunwale for fear of disturbing the stillness of the cathedral.

The lake had never been what you would call a wild lake. There were cottages sprinkled around the shores, and it was in farming country although the shores of the lake were quite heavily wooded. Some of the cottages were owned by nearby farmers, and you would live at the shore and eat your meals at the farmhouse. That's what our family did. But although it wasn't wild, it was a fairly large and undisturbed lake and there were places in it that, to a child at least, seemed infinitely remote and primeval.

I was right about the tar: it led to within half a mile of the shore. But when I got back there, with my boy, and we settled into a camp near a farmhouse and into the kind of summertime I had known, I could tell that it was going to be pretty much the same as it had been before—I knew it, lying in bed the first morning, smelling the bedroom and hearing the boy sneak quietly out and go off along the shore in a boat. I began to sustain the illusion that he was I, and therefore, by simple transposition, that I was my father. This sensation persisted, kept cropping up all the time we were there. It was not an entirely new feeling, but in this setting, it grew much stronger. I seemed to be living a dual existence. I would be in the middle of some simple act, I would be picking up a bait box or laying down a table fork, or I would be saying something, and suddenly it would be not I but my father who was saying the words or making the gesture. It gave me a creepy sensation.

We went fishing the first morning. I felt the same damp moss covering the worms in the bait can, and saw the dragonfly alight on the tip of my rod as it hovered a few inches from the surface of the water. It was the arrival of this fly that convinced me beyond any doubt that everything was as it always had been, that the years were a mirage and that there had been no years. The small waves were the same, chucking the rowboat under the chin as we fished at anchor, and the boat was the same boat, the same color green and the ribs broken in the same places, and under the floorboards the same freshwater leavings and débris—the dead helgramite, the wisps of moss, the rusty discarded fishhook, the dried blood from yesterday's catch. We stared silently at the tips of our rods, at the dragonflies that came and went. I lowered the tip of mine into the water, tentatively, pensively dislodging the fly, which darted two feet away, poised, darted two feet back, and came to rest again a little farther up the rod. There had been no years between the ducking of this dragonfly and the other one—the one that was part of memory. I looked at the boy, who was silently watching his fly, and it was my hands that held his rod, my eyes watching. I felt dizzy and didn't know which rod I was at the end of.

See p. 65 on how concrete physical details can bring abstract ideas down to earth.

We caught two bass, hauling them in briskly as though they were mackerel, pulling them over the side of the boat in a businesslike manner without any landing net, and stunning them with a blow on the back of the head. When we got back for a swim before lunch, the lake was exactly where we had left it, the same number of inches from the dock, and there was only the merest suggestion of a breeze. This seemed an utterly enchanted sea, this lake you could leave to its own devices for a few hours and come back to, and find that it had not stirred, this constant and trustworthy body of water. In the shallows, the dark, water-soaked sticks and twigs, smooth and old, were undulating in clusters on the bottom against the clean ribbed sand, and the track of the mussel was plain. A school of minnows swam by, each minnow with its small individual shadow, doubling the attendance, so clear and sharp in the sunlight. Some of the other campers were in swimming, along the shore, one of them with a cake of soap, and the water felt thin and clear and unsubstantial. Over the years there had been this person with the cake of soap, this cultist, and here he was. There had been no years.

Up to the farmhouse to dinner through the teeming, dusty field, the road under our sneakers was only a two-track road. The middle track was missing, the one with the marks of the hooves and the splotches of dried, flaky manure. There had always been three tracks to choose from in choosing which track to walk in; now the choice was narrowed down to two. For a moment I missed terribly the middle alternative. But the way led past the tennis court, and something about the way it lay there in the sun reassured me; the tape had loosened along the backline, the alleys were green with plantains and other weeds, and the net (installed in June and removed in September) sagged in the dry noon, and the whole place steamed with midday heat and hunger and emptiness. There was a choice of pie for dessert, and one was blueberry and one was apple, and the waitresses were the same country girls, there having been no passage of time, only the illusion of it as in a dropped curtain—the waitresses were still fifteen; their hair had been washed, that was the only difference—they had been to the movies and seen the pretty girls with the clean hair.

Summertime, oh, summertime, pattern of life indelible, the fade-proof lake, the woods unshatterable, the pasture with the sweetfern and the juniper forever and ever, summer without end; this was the background, and the life along the shore was the design, the cottages with their innocent and tranquil design, their tiny docks with the flagpole and the American flag floating against the white clouds in the blue sky, the little paths over the roots of the trees leading from camp to camp and the paths leading back to the outhouses and the can of lime for sprinkling, and at the souvenir counters at the store the miniature

Description

birch-bark canoes and the postcards that showed things looking a little better than they looked. This was the American family at play, escaping the city heat, wondering whether the newcomers in the camp at the head of the cove were "common" or "nice," wondering whether it was true that the people who drove up for Sunday dinner at the farmhouse were turned away because there wasn't enough chicken.

It seemed to me, as I kept remembering all this, that those times and those summers had been infinitely precious and worth saving. There had been jollity and peace and goodness. The arriving (at the beginning of August) had been so big a business in itself, at the railway station the farm wagon drawn up, the first smell of the pine-laden air, the first glimpse of the smiling farmer, and the great importance of the trunks and your father's enormous authority in such matters, and the feel of the wagon under you for the long ten-mile haul, and at the top of the last long hill catching the first view of the lake after eleven months of not seeing this cherished body of water. The shouts and cries of the other campers when they saw you, and the trunks to be unpacked, to give up their rich burden. (Arriving was less exciting nowadays, when you sneaked up in your car and parked it under a tree near the camp and took out the bags and in five minutes it was all over, no fuss, no loud wonderful fuss about trunks.) 9

See p. 66 on the importance of saying why you're describing "all this."

Peace and goodness and jollity. The only thing that was wrong now, really, was the sound of the place, an unfamiliar nervous sound of the outboard motors. This was the note that jarred, the one thing that would sometimes break the illusion and set the years moving. In those other summertimes all motors were inboard; and when they were at a little distance, the noise they made was a sedative, an ingredient of summer sleep. They were one-cylinder and two-cylinder engines, and some were make-and-break and some were jump-spark, but they all made a sleepy sound across the lake. The one-lungers throbbed and fluttered, and the twin-cylinder ones purred and purred, and that was a quiet sound, too. But now the campers all had outboards. In the daytime, in the hot mornings, these motors made a petulant, irritable sound; at night, in the still evening when the afterglow lit the water, they whined about one's ears like mosquitoes. My boy loved our rented outboard, and his great desire was to achieve 10 single-handed mastery over it, and authority, and he soon learned the trick of choking it a little (but not too much), and the adjustment of the needle valve. Watching him I would remember the things you could do with the old one-cylinder engine with the heavy flywheel, how you could have it eating out of your hand if you got really close to it spiritually. Motorboats in those days didn't have clutches, and you would make a landing by shutting off the motor at the proper time and coasting in with a dead rudder. But there was a way of reversing them, if you learned the trick, by cutting the switch and putting it on again exactly on the final dying revolution of the flywheel, so that it would kick back against compression and begin reversing. Approaching a dock in a strong following breeze, it was difficult to slow up sufficiently by the ordinary coasting method, and if a boy felt he had complete mastery over his motor, he was tempted to keep it running beyond its time and then reverse it a few feet from the dock. It took a cool nerve, because if you threw the switch a twentieth of a second too soon you would catch the flywheel when it still had speed enough to go up past center, and the boat would leap ahead, charging bull-fashion at the dock.

We had a good week at the camp. The bass were biting well and the sun shone endlessly, day after day. We would be tired at night and lie down in the accumulated heat of the little bedrooms after the long hot day and the breeze would stir almost imperceptibly outside and the smell of the swamp drift in through the rusty screens. Sleep would come easily and in the morning the red squirrel would be on the roof, tapping out his gay routine. I kept remembering everything, lying in bed in the mornings—the small steamboat that had a long rounded stern like the lip of a Ubangi, and how quietly she ran on the moonlight sails, when the older boys played their mandolins and the girls sang and we ate doughnuts dipped in sugar, and how sweet the music was on the water in the shining night, and what it had felt like to think about girls then. After breakfast, we would go up to the store and the things were in the same place—the minnows in a bottle, the plugs and spinners disarranged and pawed over by the youngsters from the boys' camp, the Fig Newtons and the Beeman's gum. Outside, the road was tarred and cars stood in front of the store. Inside, all was just as it had always been, except there was more

Coca-Cola and not so much Moxie[1] and root beer and birch beer and sarsa-
parilla. We would walk out with the bottle of pop apiece and sometimes the
pop would backfire up our noses and hurt. We explored the streams, quietly,
where the turtles slid off logs and dug their way into the soft bottom; and we
lay on the town wharf and fed worms to the tame bass. Everywhere we went
I had trouble making out which was I, the one walking at my side, the one
walking in my pants.

    One afternoon while we were there at that lake a thunderstorm came up. It 12
was like the revival of an old melodrama that I had seen long ago with childish
awe. The second-act climax of the drama of the electrical disturbance over a
lake in America has not changed in any important respect. This was the big
scene, still the big scene. The whole thing was so familiar, the first feeling of
oppression and heat and a general air around camp of not wanting to go very far
away. In midafternoon (it was all the same) a curious darkening of the sky, and a
lull in everything that had made life tick; and then the way the boats suddenly
swung the other way at their moorings with the coming of a breeze out of the
new quarter, and the premonitory rumble. Then the kettle drum, then the
snare, then the bass drum and cymbals, then crackling light against the dark,
and the gods grinning and licking their chops in the hills. Afterward the calm,
the rain steadily rustling in the calm lake, the return of light and hope and spir-
its, and the campers running out in joy and relief to go swimming in the rain,
their bright cries perpetuating the deathless joke about how they were getting
simply drenched, and the children screaming with delight at the new sensation
of bathing in the rain, and the joke about getting drenched linking the generations in a strong indestructible chain. And the comedian who waded in carrying an umbrella.

    When the others went swimming, my son said he was going in, too. He 13
pulled his dripping trunks from the line where they had hung all through the
shower and wrung them out. Languidly, and with no thought of going in, I
watched him, his hard little body, skinny and bare, saw him wince slightly as he

---

1. Brand name of an old-fashioned soft drink.

pulled up around his vitals the small, soggy, icy garment. As he buckled the swollen belt, suddenly my groin felt the chill of death.

FOR DISCUSSION

1. When and why did E. B. White return with his young son to the lake he himself had visited as a boy?
2. In paragraph 2, is White describing the lake as it was in the past, or as it is in the present time of his essay? How about in paragraphs 4–6? And in paragraph 11? Explain your answers.
3. In addition to the lake, White is also describing "the American family at play" (8). What qualities and attributes does he identify as particularly "American"?
4. Do American families still take summer vacations "at the lake"? How has the pattern of family play—on a lake or elsewhere—changed since White wrote his classic essay? How has it remained the same?

STRATEGIES AND STRUCTURES

1. In his description of the "primeval" lake, what qualities does White emphasize (3)? Point out particular details in his description that you find particularly effective. What is his main point in citing them?
2. Is White's description of the lake more OBJECTIVE or SUBJECTIVE? Or both at different times? Explain.
3. What DOMINANT IMPRESSION does White's description create in the reader? How?
4. When he returned to the lake with his young son, the two of them, says White, went fishing "the first morning" (5). Point out other direct references to time in White's essay. How does he use chronology and the passing of time to organize his entire description?
5. One way in which the lake of his childhood has definitely changed, says White, is in its sounds. What new sounds does he describe? How does he incorporate this change into his description of the lake as a timeless place?

6. How would White's essay be different without the last paragraph, in which he watches his young son get ready to go swimming?

WORDS AND FIGURES OF SPEECH

. . . .

1. What's the difference between an "illusion" and a "mirage" (5)? Which is White describing here at times? Explain.
2. When he describes the lake as not only "constant" but "trustworthy" (6), White has PERSONIFIED the natural scene. Where else does he use this figure of speech and why?
3. Why does White repeat the word *same* in paragraph 5?
4. As a boy on the lake, White did not want to disturb the "stillness of the cathedral" (2). What are the implications of this phrase? In what ways is White's son depicted as a chip off the old block?
5. How does White's reference to "a dropped curtain" (7) anticipate his description of the storm at the end of his essay?

FOR WRITING

. . . .

1. Think back to a memorable family vacation or other outing. What do you recall most clearly about it and why? Make a list of those details.
2. Recall a place that seemed "unique" and "holy" to you when you first visited it. Write an essay describing how it has changed since then and how it has remained the same. In choosing details to include, carefully consider what dominant impression you want to make.
3. Write an essay describing how a familiar sight, taste, or sound triggers your remembrance of things past. Be sure to show how what you find ties back in with the present.

CHAPTER FIVE

NARRATIVE

ᐯᐱᐯᐱᐯᐱᐯᐱᐯᐱᐯᐱᐯᐱᐯᐱᐯᐱᐯᐱᐯᐱᐯᐱᐯᐱᐯ

Narrative* writing tells a story; it reports "what happened." All of the essays in this chapter are narratives, telling about what happened to one New York writer on September 11, for example, and to one African American man when he refused to give up his seat on a bus in North Carolina in the 1940s. There is a big difference, however, between having something "happen" and writing about it, between an event and telling about an event.

In real life, events often occur randomly or chaotically. But in a narrative, they must be told or shown in some orderly sequence (the PLOT), by a particular person (the NARRATOR), from a particular perspective (the POINT OF VIEW), within a definite time and place (the SETTING). Let's look more closely at each of these elements.

Suppose we wanted to tell a story about a young woman sitting alone eating a snack. Our opening line might go something like this:

Little Miss Muffet sat on a tuffet, eating her curds and whey.

Here we have the bare bones of a narrative because we have someone (Miss Muffet) who is doing something (eating) at a particular time (the past) in a particular place (on a tuffet). The problem with our narrative is that it isn't very interesting. We have a character and a setting, but we don't really have a plot.

A good plot requires more than just sitting and eating. Plot can be achieved by introducing a conflict into the action, bringing the tension to a high

*Words printed in SMALL CAPITALS are defined in the Glossary/Index.

point (the CLIMAX), then releasing the tension—in other words, by giving the action of the story a beginning, middle, and end. In our story about Miss Muffet, we could achieve the necessary conflict by introducing an intruder:

> Along came a spider and sat down beside her . . .

You know what's coming next, but you can still feel the tension building up before we resolve the conflict and release the rising tension in the final line of our story:

> And frightened Miss Muffet away.

Well, that's better. We have a sequence of events now. Moreover, those events occur in our narrative in some sort of order—chronologically. But the events also have to be linked together in some meaningful way. In this case, the appearance of the intruder actually *causes* the departure of the heroine. There are many ways to connect the events in a narrative, but CAUSE AND EFFECT is one good approach (see Chapter 11).

Mary Mebane, p. 167, tells how segregation laws caused her to "live with terror."

We said earlier that a narrative must have a narrator. That narrator may be directly involved in the action of the narrative or may only report it. Do we have one here? Yes, we do; it is the narrator who refers to Miss Muffet as "her." But this narrator is never identified, and he or she plays no part in the action. Let's look at a narrator who does—Stephen King, in a passage from a narrative about an accident that almost killed him some years ago:

> Most of the sight lines along the mile-long stretch of Route 5 that I walk are good, but there is one place, a short steep hill, where a pedestrian heading north can see very little of what might be coming his way. I was three-quarters of the way up this hill when the van came over the crest. It wasn't on the road; it was on the shoulder. My shoulder. I had perhaps three-quarters of a second to register this.
>
> —STEPHEN KING, "On Impact"

Notice that the "I" in this piece is King himself, and he is very much involved in the action of the story he is telling. In fact, he is about to be hit by the van coming over the crest of the hill. That would introduce a conflict into his walk along Route 5, wouldn't it?

By narrating this story from a first-person point of view, King is putting himself in the center of the action. If he had said instead, "The van was closing in on him fast," we would have a third-person narrative, and the narrator would be reporting the action from the sidelines instead of bearing the brunt of it. What makes a chilling story here is that King is not only showing us what happened to him, he is showing us what he was thinking as he suddenly realized that the van was almost on top of him: "It wasn't on the road; it was on the shoulder. My shoulder." We look in as the narrator goes, in a few swift phrases, from startled disbelief to horrified certainty.

Another way in which King creates a compelling story is by using direct speech, or DIALOGUE. When King tells about his first day back at work, he lets his wife speak to us directly: "I can rig a table for you in the back hall, outside the pantry. There are plenty of outlets—you can have your Mac, the little printer, and a fan." Quoting direct speech like this helps readers to imagine the characters as real people.

But why does King end his narrative back at the writing desk? Because he knows that stories serve a larger PURPOSE than just telling what happened. The larger purpose of King's story is to make a point about writing and the writer's life. The van almost killed him, but writing, King demonstrates, helped him to recover and keeps him going.

Thomas Beller uses dialogue, p. 149, to introduce different people caught up in the events of 9/11.

Well-told stories are almost always told for some reason. The searing tale you heard earlier about Miss Muffet, for example, was told to make a point about narrative structure. A brief, illustrative story like this is called an ANECDOTE. All stories should have a point, but anecdotes in particular are used in all kinds of writing to give examples and to illustrate the greater subject at hand—writing, for instance.

When you use a story to make a point, don't forget to remind the reader exactly what that point is. When Annie Dillard recounts her adventures with spiders and moths in the essay from *Holy the Firm*, she explicitly tells us that she is making a point about the profession of writing and the dedication of the writer. That "one bald statement of motive," as Dillard says, "was unavoidable." Don't keep your reader in the dark. When your purpose is to explain something, don't get so wound up in the web of telling a good story that you forget to say what the moral is.

A BRIEF GUIDE TO WRITING A NARRATIVE

As you write a NARRATIVE, you need to say who or what the narrative is about, where it takes place, and what is happening. Mary Mebane makes these basic moves of narration in the following lines from her essay in this chapter:

> On this Saturday morning Esther and I set out for town for our music lesson. We were going on our weekly big adventure, all the way across town. . . . We walked the two miles from Wildwood to the bus line.
> —MARY MEBANE, "The Back of the Bus"

Mebane says *who* her story is about ("Esther and I"), *where* it takes place (on the bus line), and *what* is happening as the story opens (the two teenagers are heading for a "big adventure").

The following guidelines will help you to make these basic moves as you draft a narrative—and to come up with a subject for your story, consider your purpose and audience, state your point, and organize the specific details and events of your story into a compelling plot by using chronology, transitions, verb tenses, and dialogue.

Coming Up with a Subject

When you enjoy a well-told story, it is often because the author presents an everyday event in an interesting or even dramatic way. To come up with a subject for a story of your own, think of events, both big and small, that you have experienced. You might write a good story about a perfectly ordinary occurrence, such as buying a car, applying for a job, arguing with a friend—or even just doing your homework.

"No, no, no," the writer Frank McCourt, author of *Angela's Ashes*, used to say to his students when they complained that nothing had happened to them when they got home the night before. "What did you do when you walked in?" McCourt would ask. "You went through a door, didn't you? Did you have anything in your hands? A book bag? You didn't carry it with you all night, did you? Did you hang it on a hook? Did you throw it across the room and your mom yelled at you for it?" Even mundane details like these can provide the material for a good story if you use them to show what people said and did—and exactly where, why, and how they said and did it.

> Lynda Barry builds a narrative around the ordinary events of a school day (p. 177).

Considering Your Purpose and Audience

As you compose a narrative, think hard about the AUDIENCE you want to reach and the PURPOSE your narrative is intended to serve. Suppose you are emailing a friend about a visit to an electronics store in order to convince her to take advantage of the great deals you found there. You might tell your story this way: "When I walked into ComputerDaze, I couldn't believe my eyes. Printers everywhere! And the cheap prices! I went home with a printer under each arm." Or suppose you are writing a column in a computer magazine, and the purpose of your story is to show readers how to shop for a printer. You might write: "The first hurdle I encountered was the numbing variety of brands and models."

Whatever your purpose, think about how much your audience is likely to know about your subject so you can judge how much background information you need to give, what terms you need to DEFINE, and so on. If you are writing an ANECDOTE, make sure it is appropriate for your audience and illustrates your larger point.

Generating Ideas: Asking What Happened—and Who, Where, When, How, and Why

How do you come up with the raw materials for a narrative? To get started, ask yourself the questions that journalists typically ask when developing a story: who, what, where, when, how, and why? Your immediate answers will give you the beginnings of a narrative, but keep asking the questions over and over again. Try to recall lots of particular details, both visual and auditory. As the writer John Steinbeck once advised, "Try to remember [the situation] so clearly that you can see things: what colors and how warm or cold and how you got there . . . what people looked like, how they walked, what they wore, what they ate."

You will also want your readers to know *why* you're telling this particular story, so it's important to select details that support your point. For example, if you're trying to show why your sister is the funniest person in your family, your story might include specific, vivid details about the sound of her voice, her amusing facial expressions, and a practical joke she once pulled.

Templates for Narrating

The following templates can help you to generate ideas for a narrative and then to start drafting. Don't take these as formulas where you just have to fill in the blanks. There are no easy formulas for good writing. But these templates can help you plot out some of the key moves of narration and thus may serve as good starting points:

- ▸ This is a story about _____.
- ▸ My story takes place in _____ when _____.
- ▸ As the narrative opens, X is in the act of _____.
- ▸ What happened next was _____, followed by _____ and _____.

> ► At this point, _____ happened.

> ► The climax of these events was _____.

> ► When X understood what had happened, he/she said, "_____."

> ► The last thing that happened to X was _____.

> ► My point in telling this story is to show that _____.

For more techniques to help you generate ideas and start writing a narrative essay, see Chapter 2.

Stating Your Point

If you are writing a personal story about your sister, you might reveal your point implicitly through the details of the story. However, in much of the narrative writing you do as a student, you will want to state your point explicitly. If you are writing about information technology for a communications class, for example, you might include the story about going to an electronics store, and you would probably want to explain why in a THESIS STATEMENT like this: "Go into any computer store today, and you will discover that information technology is the main product of American business."

Developing a Plot Chronologically

As a general rule, arrange events in chronological order so your readers don't have to figure out what happened when. Chronology alone, however, is insufficient for organizing a good narrative. Events need to be related in such a way that one leads directly to, or causes, another. Taken together, the events should have a beginning, middle, and end. Then your narrative will form a complete action: a PLOT.

One of the best ways to plot a narrative is to set up a situation; introduce a conflict; build up the dramatic tension until it reaches a high point, or CLIMAX;

then release the tension and resolve the conflict. Even the little horror story about Miss Muffet is satisfying because it's tightly plotted with a keen sense of completion at the close.

Using Transitions and Verb Tenses

When you write a narrative, you will often incorporate direct references to time: *first, last, immediately, not long after, next, while, then, once upon a time.* References like these can be boring in a narrative if they become too predictable, as in *first, second, third.* But used judiciously, such TRAN-SITIONS provide smooth links from one event to another, as do other connecting words and phrases like *thus, therefore, consequently, what happened next, before I knew it,* and so on.

Barbara Kingsolver's narrative shifts from past to present when she writes, "And now look" (p. 146).

In addition to clear transitions, your verb tenses can help you to connect events in time. Remember that all actions that happen more or less at the same time in your narrative should be in the same tense: "I *was* three-quarters of the way up this hill when the van *came* over the crest. It *wasn't* on the road; it *was* on the shoulder." Don't shift tenses needlessly; but when you *do* need to indicate that one action happened before another, be sure to change tenses accordingly—and accurately. If you need to shift out of chronological order altogether—you might shift back in time in a FLASHBACK or shift forward in time in a FLASH-FORWARD—be sure to make the leap clear to your readers.

Maintaining a Consistent Point of View

As you construct a narrative, you need to maintain a logical and consistent POINT OF VIEW. In a narrative written in the first person ("I" or "we"), like Stephen King's, the NARRATOR can be both an observer of the scene ("Most of the sight lines along the mile-long stretch of Route 5 that I walk are good") *and* a participant in the action ("I had perhaps three-quarters of a second to register this"). In a narrative written in the third person ("he," "she," "it," or "they"), as is the case in most articles and history books, the narrator is often merely an observer, though sometimes an all-knowing one.

Whether you write in the first or third person, don't attribute perceptions to yourself or your narrator that are physically impossible. If you are narrating a story from the front seat of your car, don't pretend to see what is going on three blocks away. If you do claim to see (or know) more than you reasonably can from where you sit, your credibility with the reader will soon be strained.

On p. 136, Carrie Barker introduces two points of view by listening to "shoulder angels."

Adding Dialogue

You can introduce the points of view of other people into a story by using DIALOGUE. In a story about her childhood, for example, Annie Dillard lets her mother speak for herself: "Lie on your back," her mother tells young Dillard. "Look at the clouds and figure out what they look like."

As a first-person narrator, Dillard might have written, "My mother told me to look at the clouds and figure out what they look like." But these words would be a step removed from the person who said them and so would lack the immediacy of direct dialogue. If you let people in your narrative speak for themselves, your characters will come to life, and your whole narrative will have a greater dramatic impact.

EDITING FOR COMMON ERRORS IN NARRATIVE WRITING

Like other kinds of writing, narrative uses distinctive patterns of language and punctuation—and thus invites typical kinds of errors. The following tips will help you to check for (and correct) these errors in your narrative writing.

Check verb tenses to insure they accurately indicate when actions take place

Because narrative writing focuses on actions and events, it relies heavily on verbs. Don't get confused about when to use the simple past (She *arrived* at school), the present perfect (She *has arrived* at school), and the past perfect (She *had arrived* at school).

Use the simple past to indicate actions that were completed at a specified time in the past.

▶ He ~~has~~ completed the assignment this morning.

Use the present perfect to indicate actions begun and completed at some unspecified time in the past, or actions begun in the past and continuing into the present.

▶ The recession ~~comes~~ has come to an end.

▶ The recession ~~goes~~ has gone on for more than five years now.

Use the past perfect to indicate actions completed by a specific time in the past or before another past action occurred.

▶ The alligators arrived next, but by then the palm rats <u>had</u> moved out.

Check dialogue to be sure it's punctuated correctly

Narrative writing often includes the direct quotation of what people say. Punctuating dialogue can be challenging because you have to deal with the punctuation in the dialogue itself and also with any punctuation necessary to integrate the dialogue into the text.

Commas and periods always go inside the quotation marks.

▶ "Perspective is hard to define," my art history professor said.

▶ She noted that in Western painting "perspective means one thing."

Semicolons and colons always go outside the quotation marks.

▶ But in Asian painting, she said, "it means quite another"; then she went on to explain the differences.

▸ Asian painting presents the landscape "in layers": from the tops of mountains to the undersides of leaves in the same picture.

Question marks, exclamation points, and dashes go *inside* the quotation marks if they are part of the quoted text but *outside* if they are not part of the quoted text.

▸ The teacher asked, "Sam, how would you define perspective in art?"
▸ Did you say, "Divine perspective"?

EVERYDAY NARRATIVE
A Book Cover

MICHAEL LEWIS

Author of
THE BIG SHORT
★ ★ ★

Author of
THE BLIND SIDE
★ ★ ★

BOOMERANG

TRAVELS IN THE NEW THIRD WORLD

When you write a narrative, you tell what happened to somebody in a particular time and place. In the narrative illustrated on the cover of this book by best-selling author Michael Lewis, somebody has given George Washington a black eye. Lewis's title, *Boomerang*, implies that the wound is self-inflicted. Has George done something that's coming back to hit him in the face? Since the mug shot on this book cover is from a dollar bill, the offense must have been economic. A good narrative does more than simply tell what happened; it gives the story a plot with a beginning, middle, and end. In *Boomerang*, Lewis traces the rise and fall of the global economy before and after 2008. How will the story end? As indicated on this book cover, Lewis concludes that the boomerang effect of excessive borrowing and lending by the United States is harming the fragile economy and may leave the dollar with a semi-permanent black eye.

CARRIE BARKER

BUT TWO NEGATIVES EQUAL A POSITIVE

As a student at Kirkwood Community College, Carrie Barker wrote "But Two Negatives Equal a Positive" for a beginning composition course. Her narrative is about a life-altering decision, and it poses the difficult challenge of presenting a conflict that occurs largely in the narrator's thoughts. Barker's solution, which includes conjuring up a pair of "shoulder angels" who war for influence over the narrator's decision-making process, is indicated—along with some of the other narrative strategies she uses—in the marginal annotations that accompany her essay. "But Two Negatives Equal a Positive" won the W. W. Norton Writer's Prize in 2010.

But Two Negatives Equal a Positive

Oh my God. Oh my God. OH MY GOD! This cannot be 1
happening. Tears surged down my face, pelting my bare
thighs. Two different brands, two different stores, two
different bathrooms. Same results. *Are you frickin kidding
me?!* The second one only confirmed the first and the first only

First-person
POINT OF VIEW

confirmed what I'd recently begun to suspect.

How? I kept demanding. *How could this happen?* Okay, the 2
how wasn't the mystery. *This wasn't supposed to happen. Not
now.*

I must have sat there for a long time, numb. My head and 3
limbs felt far too heavy to get up, my brain incapable of
forming intelligent thought, eyes closed, head titled backward,

Descriptive details
help set opening
scene

positioned awkwardly against the tiled wall behind. At some
point, my eyes flickered open to the glare of a recessed flood
light directly above.

Was this the universe's idea of a sick joke? A test of some 4
kind?

I stared into the white hot light. Mesmerized by the orb, 5
I consented to it cauterizing the tears, scorching my corneas.

What words of wisdom might help here? I needed some- 6
thing. Anything. *When life hands you lemons, make lemon-
ade? What doesn't kill you will only make you stronger?*

"Shoulder angels"
indicate that the
main conflict of
Barker's PLOT is in
the narrator's mind

A shoulder angel whispered, "No one ever has to know." 7

"There *are* options," the other chimed in. 8

Activity a few feet away briefly interrupted the conversa- 9
tion only I could hear.

"But could she go through with it? Could she live with 10
herself afterward?" the first asked.

"Dunno. She never thought she'd be in this situation," the 11
second answered.

I closed my eyes and gently rubbed the black blobs out of 12
my vision. I dug the other contraption out from a small brown
sack at the bottom of my purse and discarded them both in
the receptacle mounted in the stall.

"A little different than the typical trash thrown in there," a 13
shoulder angel observed.

"It is ironic," the other agreed. 14

Go away, I told my shoulder angels. *I don't like you* 15
anymore.

I pulled myself together and made it to the sink. The 16
reflection in the mirror wasn't kind; twin mascara ruts flanked
each side of my face, eyelids swollen and naked, the whites
bloodshot and raw. The splash of cold water stung my pores.
Stalling, I wandered throughout the store and tried to come to
terms with this new reality. My loitering terminated in the
baby section.

> Narrator describes her own physical appearance in detail

How will Scott react? What will people think? What are we 17
going to do? I tried to put myself in his shoes. *We . . . will there*
continue to be a "we"? I just didn't know. . . .

> Introduces a second, external conflict into the plot

I slipped into the house and quickly scanned the rooms. 18
Scott was alone in the kitchen, cleaning out the refrigerator.
Damn, I had bad timing. I quietly crossed the room and
erected myself alongside the sweaty Tupperware and condi-
ment containers sitting on the counter.

> More descriptive details introduce a new character in a new SETTING

I crossed my arms and erupted, "You were right." 19

He backed out of the frig and shut the door, giving me his 20
full attention. "About what?" he asked.

Be strong; I told myself, *and do not cry.* 21

The instant our eyes met mine started to well up with 22
tears; I looked down and away, focusing on a few stray dust
bunnies gathering in the corner. I hesitated. Scott sighed
impatiently; he hated to be interrupted in the middle of
something. Briefly, my eyes met his arched brows then
darted back to the corner again. *For Christ's sake,* my brain
screamed, *he's your husband, not your father!* I took a deep
breath and purged, "You were right about me being pregnant." I stole another glance; his expression was impossible
to read. I took another breath and elaborated. "When you
suggested it earlier, I thought you'd lost your mind. But then
I got to thinking . . . the dates, not feeling well. I still
thought you were nuts, but I took a test. Two actually, and
they were both positive."

Just then, the patter of footsteps getting louder inter- 23
rupted my confession. "Mom, can I have some crackers?"

"Sure, buddy." I handed him the box, trying to buy us 24
more time alone. "Share with your brother and sister, okay?"

"Okay. Thanks, Mom!" and back to the living room he 25
went.

Scott's silence was unbearable. I forced myself to look 26
directly into his deep blue eyes.

"I haven't cheated on you," I offered. 27

"I wasn't thinking you did," he countered calmly. 28

"You weren't?" My brain couldn't comprehend. *How does* 29
a man with two surgically cut vas deferens not suspect his
knocked-up wife?

"You remember the numbers the doctor told us," he said. 30

Margin notes:

Internal DIALOGUE tells what narrator is thinking

Direct dialogue introduces additional points of view

"Yeah, I remember joking about our odds of having 31
another baby being greater than winning the lottery." *And
asking if I could do the honors,* I recalled. (After all, dads
were given the option of cutting the umbilical cord after a
baby was born; it seemed like a perfectly reasonable request
to me.)

"I can't believe I figured out you were pregnant before you 32
did," he said "What kind of woman are you?" He was teasing,
but I failed to see humor in the situation.

"The kind of woman who is done with that part of her 33
life," I belched, sounding defensive. "The kind that gave birth
to three babies in 33 months and likes eight hours of sleep a
night. The kind that is done changing diapers and washing
bottles and already got rid of every bit of baby stuff we ever
owned." I'm sure he was sorry he asked. "Why would being
pregnant even cross my mind?"

If he answered I didn't hear him. My brain was busy 34
cranking out reasons not to have this baby: *Because I was done
with that part of my life, because I finally owned clothes that
were stain-free, because I was a frazzled, overwhelmed mess
when the kids were babies. And because I was tired of feeling
like my sole purpose on this earth was to be someone's wife or
mother. What about me? When was it my turn?* I stopped,
realizing Scott was watching me shake my head back and
forth.

"Scott, I can't start over. I don't want to. They're all finally 35
in school." Guilt overwhelmed me. "And you know people are
going to assume I had an affair. Everyone knows you got a
vasectomy."

Dispells any remaining suspense about narrator's condition [margin note, ¶32]

Narrator begins to develop one side of the conflict [margin note, ¶34]

A potential external conflict in the plot is quickly resolved

"I don't give a shit what they think," he said. "Ultimately, 36
it's your decision and I'll support whatever you decide, but I
think we're in a better position now than when we had the first
three. Things are better now, right?"

It was true; we weren't exactly living the high life, but we 37
weren't nearly as broke as during those early years. And I
couldn't remember the last time we had an argument.

He continued, "I'd say I'm more mature now than at 25. 38
And more patient." I nodded. "Care, it's not like you're going
to have three babies again. Just one."

Also good points. Wait a minute—what the hell just hap- 39
pened? Since when is he the voice of reason? That's always been
my job!

"Come here," he said, gently pulling me into his protective 40
embrace.

Wow, I thought, dissolving into a blubbering train wreck, 41
I prepared for a whole slew of reactions, but that wasn't one of
them.

Narrator begins to explore the other side in her internal struggle

Exhausted and relieved, I agreed to let the idea of a fourth 42
child marinate a while.

I knew myself pretty well; I was capable of talking myself 43
into or out of just about anything. I had been known to
rationalize, justify, or just procrastinate until someone
decided for me. But I wasn't a fan of indecision either, and the
gravity of what Oprah called a "defining moment" weighed
heavily on my mind and gnawed at my brain stem. During
downtimes, my shoulder angels reappeared to duke it out; one
would throw out a legitimate objection and the other would
counter with an equally valid rebuttal.

In the shower: "She has no baby necessities; it would be   44
absurd to start from scratch."

"She learned the difference between a necessity and a   45
gadget the first time around."

"Has she looked at the prices of the stuff? This is going to   46
cost a bundle."

"It doesn't have to be brand new; there are always garage   47
sales and second-hand stores."

At a stoplight: "Another child is less than ideal in a   48
three-bedroom home; the boys are already sharing a room."

"Maybe it's a girl. Her daughter has always wanted a little   49
sister."

"Yeah, till she actually has one."   50

"People make do. Years ago, babies slept in dresser   51
drawers."

In line at the grocery store: "A new baby will totally mess   52
up the whole birth-order dynamic."

"It will. There will no longer be a middle child."   53

"The older kids may resent the baby."   54

"Maybe they'll be old enough to remember the experience   55
of having a new little brother or sister—being helpers,
teaching new things, reveling in all the firsts."

At night in bed: "She lives in a time where women can   56
choose. She doesn't have to blindly accept whatever card life
throws her."

"She considered all her options; she feels too often people   57
try to control every aspect of their lives. That's not life, that's
a spreadsheet. The bumps in the road are there to teach
things—about life, about adversity, about herself."

Extensive dialogue shows the intensity of narrator's internal debate

"But she said she doesn't want this." 58

"Well, it's not always about getting what you want. She 59
wants chocolate all the time. Wait, that's a bad example."

"But she said she was just starting to get her life back." 60

"It's true that the timing isn't convenient. But have you 61
noticed that things have a way of working out pretty terrific,
when given the chance?"

"Wait, does this mean she's having a baby?" 62

"She's decided; they're having a baby." 63

"I still can't go to sleep." 64

"Maybe it's because you consume too much caffeine." 65

"Maybe. Or maybe it's because I can't turn off my brain. 66
How is it that he can be lying next to her and snoring, sixty
seconds after his head hits the pillow? She's been lying here for
more than an hour."

"She's gonna have to get up to pee soon anyway, so she 67
may as well get used to it."

"Hey, what were all those girls' names we had picked out? 68
Do you remember?"

"Oh, the girl names were a piece of cake! We found lots of 69
names that we loved. It was the boys' names that were
tough . . . they had to sound masculine, but not too macho."

"Hmmm, I wonder where she put that name book." 70

Shut up! I scolded them. *I'm trying to fall asleep. Maybe* 71
I'll look for the book tomorrow.

Shoulder angels and narrator are all starting to agree as narrator resolves her inner debate in favor of having the baby

Playful TONE of ending contrasts sharply with anguish and doubt of opening paragraphs

BARBARA KINGSOLVER
IN CASE YOU EVER WANT
TO GO HOME AGAIN

Barbara Kingsolver (b. 1955) grew up in the small town of Carlisle in rural Kentucky, where she returns in "In Case You Ever Want to Go Home Again." Kingsolver attended DePauw University in Greencastle, Indiana, where she studied classical piano on a music scholarship until she switched to a major in biology. After graduate work in evolutionary biology and ecology at the University of Arizona, she became an essayist, novelist, and poet whose works include *The Poisonwood Bible* (1998); *Animal, Vegetable, Miracle* (2007); and *The Lacuna* (2009). In her first novel, *The Bean Trees* (1988), Kingsolver narrates the story of a young woman who leaves Kentucky for wider horizons in Arizona. The following narrative, a complete section from *High Tide in Tucson* (1995), tells how that novel and its young author were received by the townspeople of Carlisle when she returned home for a book signing.

◇◇◇◇◇◇◇◇◇◇◇◇◇◇◇◇◇◇◇◇◇◇◇◇◇◇◇◇◇◇◇◇◇◇◇◇◇

I n November 1988, bookstoreless though it was, my hometown hosted a big event. Paper banners announced it, and stores closed in honor of it. A crowd assembled in the town's largest public space—the railroad depot. The line went out the door and away down the tracks. At the front of the line they were plunking down $16.95 for signed copies of a certain book.

My family was there. The country's elected officials were there. My first-grade teacher. Miss Louella, was there, exclaiming to one and all: "I taught her to write!"   2

My old schoolmates were there. The handsome boys who'd spurned me at every homecoming dance were there.   3

It's relevant and slightly vengeful to confess here that I was not a hit in school, socially speaking. I was a bookworm who never quite fit her clothes. I managed to look fine in my school pictures, but as usual the truth lay elsewhere. In sixth grade I hit my present height of five feet almost nine, struck it like a gong, in fact, leaving behind self-confidence and any genuine need of a training bra. Elderly relatives used the term "fill out" when they spoke of me, as though they held out some hope I might eventually have some market value, like an underfed calf, if the hay crop was good. In my classroom I came to dread a game called Cooties, wherein one boy would brush against my shoulder and then chase the others around, threatening to pass on my apparently communicable lack of charisma. The other main victim of this game was a girl named Sandra, whose family subscribed to an unusual religion that mandated a Victorian dress code. In retrospect I can't say exactly what Sandra and I had in common that made us outcasts, except for extreme shyness, flat chests, and families who had their eyes on horizons pretty far beyond the hills of Nicholas County. Mine were not Latter-day Saints, but we read Thoreau[1] and Robert Burns[2] at home, and had lived for a while in Africa. My parents did not flinch from relocating us to a village beyond the reach of electricity, running water, or modern medicine (also, to my delight, conventional schooling) when they had a chance to do useful work there. They thought it was shameful to ignore a fellow human in need, or to waste money on trendy, frivolous things; they did not, on the other hand, think it was shameful to wear perfectly good hand-me-down dresses to school   4

---

1. Henry David Thoreau (1817–1862).
2. Scottish poet and lyricist (1759–1796).

in Nicholas Country. Ephemeral idols exalted by my peers, such as Batman, the Beatles, and the Hula Hoop, were not an issue at our house. And even if it took no more than a faint pulse to pass the fifth grade, my parents expected me to set my own academic goals, and then exceed them.

Possibly my parents were trying to make sure I didn't get pregnant in the eighth grade, as some of my classmates would shortly begin to do. If so, their efforts were a whale of a success. In my first three years of high school, the number of times I got asked out on a date was zero. This is not an approximate number. I'd caught up to other girls in social skills by that time, so I knew how to pretend I was dumber than I was, and make my own clothes. But these things helped only marginally. Popularity remained a frustrating mystery to me.

Nowadays, some of my city-bred friends muse about moving to a small town for the sake of their children. What's missing from their romantic picture of Grover's Corners[3] is the frightening impact of insulation upon a child who's not dead center in the mainstream. In a place such as my hometown, you file in and sit down to day one of kindergarten with the exact pool of boys who will be your potential dates for the prom. If you wet your pants a lot, your social life ten years later will be—as they say in government reports—impacted. I was sterling on bladder control, but somehow could never shake my sixth-grade stigma.

At age seventeen, I was free at last to hightail it for new social pastures, and you'd better believe I did. I attended summer classes at the University of Kentucky and landed a boyfriend before I knew what had hit me, or what on earth one did with the likes of such. When I went on to college in Indiana I was astonished to find a fresh set of peers who found me, by and large, likable and cootie-free.

I've never gotten over high school, to the extent that I'm still a little surprised that my friends want to hang out with me. But it made me what I am, for better and for worse. From living in a town that listened in on party lines, I learned both the price and value of community. And I gained things from my rocky school years: A fierce wish to look inside of people. An aptitude for

3. Fictional town in New Hampshire that is the setting for Thornton Wilder's *Our Town* (1938), a play about everyday life.

listening. The habit of my own company. The companionship of keeping a diary, in which I gossiped, fantasized, and invented myself. From the vantage point of invisibility I explored the psychology of the underdog, the one who can't be what others desire but who might still learn to chart her own hopes. Her story was my private treasure; when I wrote *The Bean Trees* I called her Lou Ann. I knew for sure that my classmates, all of them cool as Camaros[4] back then, would not relate to the dreadful insecurities of Lou Ann. But I liked her anyway.

And now, look. The boys who'd once fled howling from her cooties were 9 lined up for my autograph. Football captains, cheerleaders, homecoming queens were all there. The athlete who'd inspired in me a near-fatal crush for three years, during which time he never looked in the vicinity of my person, was there. The great wits who gave me the names Kingfish and Queen Sliver were there.

I took liberties with history. I wrote long, florid inscriptions referring to 10 our great friendship of days gone by. I wrote slowly. I made those guys wait in line *a long time.*

I can recall every sight, sound, minute of that day. Every open, generous 11 face. The way the afternoon light fell through the windows onto the shoes of the people in line. In my inventory of mental snapshots these images hold the place most people reserve for the wedding album. I don't know whether other people get to have Great Life Moments like this, but I was lucky enough to realize I was having mine, right while it happened. My identity was turning backward on its own axis. Never before or since have I felt all at the same time so cherished, so aware of old anguish, and so ready to let go of the past. My past had let go of *me,* so I could be something new: Poet Laureate and Queen for a Day in hometown Kentucky. The people who'd watched me grow up were proud of me, and exuberant over an event that put our little dot on the map, particularly since it wasn't an airline disaster or a child falling down a well. They didn't appear to mind that my novel discussed small-town life frankly, without gloss.

See p. 129 on building up to a high point in a narrative.

In fact, most people showed unsurpassed creativity in finding themselves, 12 literally, on the printed page. "That's my car isn't it?" they would ask. "My ser-

4. A high-powered Chevrolet sports car that debuted in 1967.

vice station!" Nobody presented himself as my Uncle Roscoe, but if he had, I happily would have claimed him.

FOR DISCUSSION

· ·

1. Among the "social skills" that she and the other girls acquired in high school, says Barbara Kingsolver, was learning "to pretend I was dumber than I was" (5). Is Kingsolver correct to describe such behavior as a valuable *skill*? Explain.

2. According to Kingsolver, idyllic conceptions of growing up in a small town ignore "the frightening impact of insulation upon a child who is not dead center in the mainstream" (6). What are the implications of this statement? Is it true? Why or why not?

3. Kingsolver says her NARRATIVE of a successful author returning to her hometown for a book signing is "slightly vengeful" (4). What's vengeful about it?

4. The title of Kingsolver's homecoming narrative echoes that of Thomas Wolfe's 1940 novel, *You Can't Go Home Again*, in which the hero writes a novel about his hometown and receives death threats because the townspeople find his narrative unflattering. How did Kingsolver, as she tells the story, avoid such a fate?

STRATEGIES AND STRUCTURES

· ·

1. Kingsolver says that the day of her homecoming is etched in her memory of "Great Life Moments" (11). As a NARRATOR, was Kingsolver wise to save this statement until near the end, or should she have started her narrative with it ("I'm going to tell about one of my Great Life Moments")? Explain.

2. The PLOT of Kingsolver's narrative has a definite beginning, middle, and end. What is the main, beginning action of the narrative (1–3)?

3. Which paragraphs constitute the middle section of Kingsolver's narrative? What happens there? Why does she spend most of her narrative on these events?

4. How and where does Kingsolver end her narrative? With what particular words does she signal a turn in her narrative from the middle action to the ending action?

5. Kingsolver says she has "never gotten over high school" (7). To what extent is her narrative also an analysis of CAUSE AND EFFECT? Explain.

WORDS AND FIGURES OF SPEECH

. . . .

1. As she was growing up, says Kingsolver, her adult height of "five feet almost nine" struck her "like a gong" (4). How, and how effectively, does this SIMILE capture the experience she is narrating?

2. What did Kingsolver's classmates have in mind when they used the term "cooties" (4)?

3. From whose POINT OF VIEW is Kingsolver speaking when she refers to "the vicinity of my person" (9)? Explain her use of such regal language.

4. In American speech, what are some of the implications of the phrase "You can't go home again"?

FOR WRITING

. . . .

1. In a paragraph or two, tell about a particular event—not necessarily a grand moment of triumph or despair, it can be an otherwise ordinary experience—that enabled you or someone else to come to terms (or not) with the past.

2. Using such a moment as your focal point, write a narrative that follows this pattern (or some variation): Open with the revealing event; go back to the past to explain how it came about; and end your narrative by returning to the event and expanding upon it, as Kingsolver does when she shows how the people of her hometown reacted to her book.

3. Write a narrative about the life lessons you learned from high school. Show in detail how particular events in your experience led to these specific effects.

THOMAS BELLER

THE ASHEN GUY: LOWER BROADWAY, SEPTEMBER 11, 2001

Thomas Beller (b. 1965) is the author of a collection of short stories, *Seduction Theory* (1995); a novel, *The Sleep-Over Artist* (2000); and the essay collections *How to Be a Man: Scenes from a Protracted Boyhood* (2005) and *Lost and Found: Stories from New York* (2009). He also runs mrbellersneighborhood.com, a website where New Yorkers can publish "true stories" of life in the big city. Following the events of September 11, 2001, Beller collected many of those personal narratives in a book, *Before & After: Stories from New York* (2002). "The Ashen Guy," written by Beller himself, is an "after" story; it takes place just after the first World Trade Center tower collapses but while the second one is still standing.

❖⌄◇⌄❖⌄◇⌄❖⌄◇⌄❖⌄◇⌄❖⌄◇⌄❖⌄◇⌄❖⌄◇⌄❖⌄◇⌄❖⌄◇⌄❖⌄◇⌄❖⌄◇⌄❖

At Broadway and Union Square a woman moved with the crowd talking on her cell phone. "It's a good thing," she began. I biked south. At Tenth Street the bells of Grace Church pealed ten times. Everyone was moving in the same direction, orderly, but with an element of panic and, beneath that, a nervous energy. Their clothes were crisp and unrumpled, their hair freshly combed. Below

Houston Street, a fleet of black shiny SUVs with sirens sped south, toward the smoky horizon somewhere south of Canal Street. A messenger biked beside me. I almost asked him if he was making a delivery.

At Thomas Street, about six blocks north of the World Trade Center, the nature of the crowd on the street changed. There was more urgency and less mirth. Cop cars parked at odd angles, their red sirens spinning. The policemen were waving their arms, shouting, and amidst the crowd was a guy who had been on the eighty-first floor of Two World Trade Center when the plane hit. It was just after 10 A.M. Two World Trade had just collapsed, and One World Trade stood smoldering behind him. 2

At first glance he looked like a snowman, except instead of snow he was covered in gray, asbestos-colored ash. He was moving along with the crowd, streaming north, up Broadway. His head and neck and shoulders and about halfway down his chest were covered in gray ash. You could make out a pair of bloodshot eyes, and he was running his hand over his head. A small plume of dust drifted off the top of his head as he walked, echoing the larger plume of smoke drifting off of One World Trade behind him. 3

"There were about 230 people on the eighty-first floor and I was one of the last ones out. We took the stairs. There was smoke, but it wasn't fire smoke, it was dry wall smoke and dust. The fire was above us." 4

He was shaking. His eyes were red from dust and maybe tears. He didn't seem like the sort of man who cried. He had fair skin and a sandy-colored crew cut. He was wearing chinos and Docksiders and his shirt was a checked button-down. 5

He was walking with the crowd, but his body language was a little different. Everyone, even those who weren't looking back, had about them a certain nervous desire to look behind them, to see, to communicate to their neighbor, but this guy had no interest in anything but in getting away from where he had just been. It radiated from every muscle in his body. To get away. 6

"I was almost out. I got down to the lobby, right near the Borders bookstore. And then there was this explosion. I don't know, I just got thrown to the ground and all this stuff fell on top of me." 7

By now he had dusted his head off and you could see his skin. It was pale   8
and ashen, one of his eyes was very red. At first I thought maybe it was the
dust and perhaps tears that had made his eyes bloodshot; looking closer I saw
that one eye was badly inflamed.

He was joined by another man, a blue oxford shirt with a tie, mid-forties,   9
lawyerly, who worked in the building across the street.

"I watched the whole thing. I saw the second plane hit, the See p. 131 on   10
explosion. No one told us to evacuate, and then the building just how to introduce people and
collapsed and I thought I better get out of here because my build- perspectives into a narrative.
ing could go too."

See p. 131 on how to introduce people and perspectives into a narrative.

On Franklin Street the police were screaming: "There's a package!   11
There's a package! Keep moving!"

They were herding everyone to the left, towards West Broadway. "People!   12
Trust me! Let's go! People let's go! There's an unidentified package across the
street!"

The view on West Broadway and Franklin was very good. One tower,   13
gray sky billowing, the sky darkening.

"Do you know which way the tower fell?" a woman asked. A tall man   14
stood behind her, scruffy beard and longish hair, his hand on her shoulder.

"It fell straight down!" someone said.   15

"Because we live one block away and . . . does anyone know which way   16
the building fell?"

The man behind her, her husband, I assumed, had this very sad look on his   17
face, as though he understood something she didn't. It was as if that consoling
hand on her shoulder was there to make sure she didn't try and make a run for it.

"I don't know what happened," said the ashen guy. "I just hit the ground,   18
don't know if something hit me or . . ."

"It was the force of the building collapsing," said the lawyer.   19

"I got up and just started walking," said the ashen guy.   20

There was a huge rumbling sound accompanied by the sound of people   21
shrieking. Everyone who wasn't already looking turned to see the remaining
building start to crumble in on itself, a huge ball of smoke rising out from beneath

it, a mushroom cloud in reverse. The whole street paused, froze, screamed, some people broke into tears, many people brought their hands up to their mouths, everyone was momentarily frozen, except for the ashen guy, who just kept walking.

FOR DISCUSSION

1. Who is telling this story? How does he identify himself in his NARRATIVE? How is he getting around?

2. Why does the NARRATOR single out the ashen guy from the rest of the crowd? Where was the ashen guy when the first plane hit? When did he get covered with ash?

3. The ashen guy is walking along with the crowd, "but his body language," says the narrator, "was a little different" from everyone else's (6). How and where does the narrator DESCRIBE the ashen guy's body? What does it "say"?

4. The identity of the ashen guy is never specified. Who might he be? What might he stand for?

5. The people in Thomas Beller's narrative walk as if they were in a dream. How appropriate do you find this dreamlike account of the events of September 11, 2001?

STRATEGIES AND STRUCTURES

1. This is a narrative about mass movement. In which direction is the narrator himself moving at first? When and where does he come closest to ground zero before moving back with the crowd? What role do the police play to move the narrative along?

2. When does the ashen guy first appear? How does the narrator create the impression in paragraph 8 that he is getting closer to this mysterious man who is the focal point of his narrative? In which paragraphs, before and after this close-up, does the narrator give a long perspective to the scene by looking back toward Ground Zero?

3. DIALOGUE is one of the most dramatic or playlike elements of narrative, introducing multiple POINTS OF VIEW, thus enabling the narrator to show us what other characters are thinking instead of just telling us about their thoughts. How many different speakers does Beller identify? What does each contribute to this narrative?

4. Dialogue also enables the narrator to convey new information to the reader. What crucial details does the ashen guy give us through what he says?

5. Why do you think Beller ends this tale of near mass hysteria with the fall of the second tower? What is the significance of his ending with the ashen guy "who just kept walking" (21)?

6. Beller's narrator seldom refers directly to himself. Why might Beller want his narrator to recede into the background? What's the focus of his story?

7. "At first glance he looked like a snowman, except instead of snow he was covered in gray, asbestos-colored ash" (3). Is this description or narration? Find some other passages in Beller's narrative where these two MODES OF WRITING shade into one another.

WORDS AND FIGURES OF SPEECH

. . . .

1. What are the implications of Beller's use of the word "ashen" in the story of a national nightmare?

2. Why do you suppose Beller calls the person at the center of his narrative a "guy," rather than a man or a gentleman or a citizen?

3. "A small plume of dust drifted off the top of his head as he walked, echoing the larger plume of smoke drifting off of One World Trade behind him" (3). What do you think of Beller's use of the word "echoing" in this sentence? What are the CONNOTATIONS of "plume"?

4. What are some other examples of Beller's figurative linking of "the ashen guy" with the tower? At the end of the narrative, the second World Trade Center tower falls. What happens to the ashen guy?

FOR WRITING

. . . .

1. In the days and months following the attacks on the World Trade Center, stories of survivors and eyewitnesses abounded. Of all the stories you heard, which one affected you most? In a brief narrative, tell what that survivor or witness did or saw on that fateful day.

2. People often recall their whereabouts at the time of significant events in a nation's history—such as where they were on September 11, 2001. Choose a significant event in recent history and write a narrative in which you recount where you were and tell what you and others did and felt. Try to remember the gist of what was said, and quote it directly as dialogue in your narrative.

HEIDI JULAVITS

TURNING JAPANESE

Heidi Julavits (b. 1968) is a novelist, freelance journalist, and founding editor of *The Believer*, a monthly magazine about books and culture. Her novels include *The Uses of Enchantment* (2006) and *The Vanishers* (2012). Julavits graduated from Dartmouth College in 1990, a time of global recession and imminent war in the Persian Gulf. With an unsure future and little in the way of marketable skills, Julavits decided to live in Japan and "reach a higher plane of existence while eating amazing food." First published in the *New York Times Magazine* in 2006, "Turning Japanese" tells the story of Julavits's "post-college limbo" and the understanding of Zen Buddhism she gained by eating a bean-cake dessert.

❖⌄❖⌄❖⌄❖⌄❖⌄❖⌄❖⌄❖⌄❖⌄❖⌄❖⌄❖⌄❖⌄❖⌄❖⌄❖⌄❖⌄❖⌄❖⌄❖

I graduated from college in 1990, an uncertain time indeed. Recession. Gulf War   1
imminent. In keeping with the shaky global mood, I haven't a clue what to do with my life. So I decide to move to Japan to teach the only thing I can confidently claim to know after four years of college: English. In America, I reason, the only thing more shameful than not knowing what you want is knowing, with absolute certainty, that stuffed animals turn you on. In Japan I'll be immersed in a

culture that nurtures uncertainty as a form of enlightenment.[1] I remind myself of the Zen-like quotation: "Emotional freedom comes with being aware of the certainty of uncertainty." I will go to Japan, I will be certainly uncertain and I will reach a higher plane of existence while eating amazing food.

I find a sublet in a functional-blah apartment building off Shijo Street in Kyoto, and two things happen: I remain unenlightened by my uncertainty, and I eat amazing food. A typical on-the-cheap lunch bowl, offered in local spots displaying dusty plastic food in the window, is katsu-don, a fried pork cutlet with scrambled eggs, served with rice and a sweet donburi sauce; or tekka-don, strips of raw tuna and pressed dried seaweed over rice. A Japanese family invites me to dinner each week for shabu shabu: a pot of water and enoki mushrooms, set on an electric tabletop coil, in which we poach very thin slices of beef or hacked-up Alaskan king crab; after the meat is finished, we dump our rice into the broth and slurp the resulting porridgy soup.

> In a narrative, "things happen," p. 123, whether they're extraordinary or just "blah."

As the months pass, I remain miserably uncertain about all things but one: I would kill for a trashy American sweet. I do not miss cheese or pasta or even my friends, but I do miss, with a maddening intensity, that blast of sugar that only a glazed cruller can provide. Plenty of Japanese bakeries offer deceptively Western-looking cakes and cookies, which reveal themselves to be gaggingly dry and possessing a slight aftertaste of fish, as if whatever fat the baker used came not from a cow or a pig but from a hake. I patronize a previously disdained restaurant called Spaghetti and Cake (Kyoto has a number of these "Western" establishments; another is Coffee and Golf) and am disappointed—huge shock. The best of the lousy bunch is ring cake, a rolled-up yellow sponge cut into slices. But one day while working as a movie extra in a period film (1850s Yokohama[2] being the period), I am forced to wear a bonnet and eat slice after slice of ring cake because the lead, a Japanese pop star, can't remember her three short lines. I come to hate ring cake. When another American tells me about a Western breakfast restaurant, I bike ten miles through a downpour and

1. From Zen Buddhism, an influential belief system in Japan, the idea that self-awareness of any sort is a fundamental goal.

2. Japanese town that developed as a major shipping port after the arrival of Westerners in the mid-nineteenth century.

order French toast as an excuse to deluge my plate with dyed-brown corn syrup, which I eat until I am headachingly ill.

I orchestrate my own intervention. I remind myself that everybody knows that ersatz American food, or ersatz any food, is a doomed proposition. You must play to a culture's strengths and not order a cataplana[3] of paella when in Green Bay, Wisconsin. Yet my first encounters with the native sweets are alienating. Gummy lime green bean blobs dusted in a flavorless white flour, for example, are not only not sweet, but they also do not appeal to any of my tongue's five regions and are all the more disappointing for appearing so pretty.

One dusky evening I am biking through Gion, Kyoto's geisha district,[4] examining the window displays with their meticulously wrapped I-don't-know-what. (Jewelry? Art supplies? Stew meat?) One helpfully exhibits what's concealed beneath the wrapping: a bloated Fig Newton look-alike bisected to reveal a dense and grainy maroon center. I buy what I learn, decades later, is called manju. The filling is a paste made from red azuki beans and sugar. I call it a bean cake. I bike to Gion every day and buy two.

And so it is that I come to grapple with that oldest of Zen mysteries: the bean-cake conundrum. Of course I've been paddling around this riddle for months, but it's not until I encounter the bean cake that it assumes its most potent form. While eating a bean cake, I reach a moment when I don't need, or want, another bite. I experience what I believe is contentment (rather than "no thought," think "no appetite"), and despite what my layman's notion of Zen Buddhist nongoal goals leads me to expect, it is no blissfest. My American relationship to sugar is always to want more of it; to encounter a sweet that doesn't court abuse in order to be enjoyed destabilizes my entire concept of craving-cruller-gluttony-happiness. I feel these moments of so-called contentment when I have no pointed desires—not a petit four to follow the chocolates to follow the tarte Tatin, not even a salt-funky cheese course as counterbalance—to be physically unbearable and thus, by quick extrapolation, existentially crippling. Does

4

5

6

3. Cooking dish used for preparing a Portuguese seafood specialty.

4. An area with many establishments featuring elaborately dressed women who are trained in traditional arts such as dance and music and who entertain male clientele.

this mean that contentment is anathema to my person? That contentment is a punishing mind-bender (to be content is to be less content than when you weren't content)? That this period of post-college limbo has been encapsulated, in all its dumb, stereotypical hand-wringing, by a bean cake?

Two months later I am spiritually annihilated by contentment. I haven't had a craving in months, and I'm so worried that I won't desire anything ever again that I forget to worry about my uncertain future. I pack my things, and within twenty-four hours I am on a dawn bus to Phuket, Thailand. Suddenly I am seized by a familiar sense of specific urgency, a hunger disconnected from appetite: I want tekka-don for breakfast. I am on a bus in the south of Thailand, and I want—no, must have—a bowl of Japanese rice and raw tuna. While I'm beside myself with relief, I'm simultaneously aware of the bear hug of my iffy future (no job, no place to live, running out of money) tightening around my chest again with an intensity I interpret as affection. My uncertain future missed me, too. I get off the bus at the beach and stare at the aptly blank horizon. I am broke and aimless, I am racked by doubt and worry, I crave a food that's three thousand miles away and I've never experienced such bliss in my life.

7

FOR DISCUSSION

. . . .

1. When Heidi Julavits graduated from college, all she could "confidently claim" was her knowledge of only one subject (1). Which one? Does her essay show that her confidence is justified?
2. Besides having a job there, why did Julavits go to Japan? Explain.
3. What did Julavits miss most about life back in America? How and how successfully did she attempt to make up for that loss?
4. How and when did Julavits realize that she had "turned Japanese"?
5. Why is Julavits so full of "bliss" at the end of her NARRATIVE (7)? Explain.

STRATEGIES AND STRUCTURES

. . . .

1. Almost all the events in Julavits's narrative pertain to food. How well do these adventures in eating support the Zen-like point that Julavits is making,

namely that "emotional freedom comes with being aware of the certainty of uncertainty" (1)?

2. Even though the events of Julavits's narrative took place in the past, many of her verbs are in the present tense. Point out several examples, and explain how and what they contribute to her narrative.

3. Should Julavits have said more about the other things (besides eating) that she did in Japan, such as her teaching or her work "as a movie extra" (3)? Why or why not?

4. In the last paragraph of her narrative, Julavits travels from Japan to Thailand, where she is suddenly "seized" by a hunger for "a bowl of Japanese rice and raw tuna" (7). How does this event serve as a CLIMAX to the main PLOT of Julavits's narrative? Explain.

5. How and how well does Julavits's narrative also serve as a DESCRIPTION of "post-college limbo" (6)?

WORDS AND FIGURES OF SPEECH

1. In Japan, Julavits knows that she will be "certainly uncertain" (1). Explain the implications of this OXYMORON for her narrative as a whole.

2. In Kyoto, Julavits finds an apartment in a "functional-blah" building (2). What does she mean by "functional-blah"? Point out other places in her narrative where she invents hyphenated words to convey concepts. How effective do you find this device? Explain.

3. Why would the Japanese name a restaurant "Spaghetti and Cake" or "Coffee and Golf" (3)? How apt do you find such names for supposedly "Western" establishments (3)?

4. At one point in her narrative, Julavits decides to "orchestrate my own intervention" (4). Why does she use such ABSTRACT language to say that she is trying the local desserts?

5. In Catholic and other Western theologies, "limbo" is a border state where some souls remain until they can enter heaven. How is Julavits DEFINING the term, and why does she use it here (6)?

6. A "conundrum" is a difficult and fascinating problem (6). How and why does eating bean cake pose such a problem for Julavits?

FOR WRITING

. . . .

1. Write a paragraph about the first time you tried a food from another country or culture. Explain what insights—if any—you gained about that culture through its food.

2. Write a narrative about a time when you became so wrapped up in the affairs and adventures of the moment that you forgot to worry about the uncertainties of the future.

YIYUN LI

ORANGE CRUSH

Yiyun Li (b. 1972) is a Chinese American writer who grew up in Beijing, China. In 1996, after attending Peking University, Li moved to the United States to study medicine at the University of Iowa, earning master's degrees in both immunology and the writing of creative nonfiction. Li's first collection of short stories, *A Thousand Years of Good Prayers* (2005), won numerous literary awards, and in 2009 she published her first novel, *The Vagrants* followed by *Gold Boy, Emerald Girl* in 2010. "Orange Crush" first appeared in the food and culture section of the *New York Times Magazine* in 2006. It tells the story of Li's encounter, as a teenager in China, with a new space-age drink from America—Tang.

◇◇◇◇◇◇◇◇◇◇◇◇◇◇◇◇◇◇◇◇◇◇◇◇◇◇◇◇◇◇◇◇◇◇◇◇◇◇

During the winter in Beijing, where I grew up, we always had orange and tangerine peels drying on our heater. Oranges were not cheap. My father, who believed that thrift was one of the best virtues, saved the dried peels in a jar; when we had a cough or cold, he would boil them until the water took on a bitter taste and a pale yellow cast, like the color of water drizzling out of a rusty faucet. It was the best cure for colds, he insisted.

1

I did not know then that I would do the same for my own children, prefer-   2
ring nature's provision over those orange- and pink- and purple-colored medi-
cines. I just felt ashamed, especially when he packed it in my lunch for the
annual field trip, where other children brought colorful flavored fruit drinks—
made with "chemicals," my father insisted.

The year I turned sixteen, a new product caught my eye. Fruit Treasure,   3
as Tang[1] was named for the Chinese market, instantly won everyone's heart.
Imagine real oranges condensed into a fine powder! Equally seductive was the
TV commercial, which gave us a glimpse of a life that most families, including
mine, could hardly afford. The kitchen was spacious and brightly lighted,
whereas ours was a small cube—but at least we had one; half the people we knew
cooked in the hallways of their apartment buildings, where every family's
dinner was on display and their financial states assessed by the number of
meals with meat they ate every week. The family on TV was beautiful, all three
of them with healthy complexions and toothy, carefree smiles (the young parents I saw on my bus ride to school were those who had to leave at six or even
earlier in the morning for the two-hour commute and who had to carry their
children, half-asleep and often screaming, with them because the only child
care they could afford was that provided by their employers).

The drink itself, steaming hot in an expensive-looking mug that was   4
held between the child's mittened hands, was a vivid orange. The mother
talked to the audience as if she were our best friend: "During the cold winter,
we need to pay more attention to the health of our family," she said. "That's
why I give my husband and my child hot Fruit Treasure for extra warmth and
vitamins." The drink's temperature was the only Chinese aspect of the commercial; iced drinks were considered unhealthful and believed to induce
stomach disease.

As if the images were not persuasive enough, near the end of the ad an   5
authoritative voice informed us that Tang was the only fruit drink used by
NASA for its astronauts—the exact information my father needed to prove his
theory that all orange-flavored drinks other than our orange peel water were
made of suspicious chemicals.

1. An orange-flavored powdered drink mix first marketed in the United States in 1959.

Until this point, all commercials were short and boring, with catchy phrases 6
like "Our Product Is Loved by People Around the World" flashing on screen.
The Tang ad was a revolution in itself: the lifestyle it represented—a more health-
ful and richer one, a Western luxury—was just starting to become legitimate in
China as it was beginning to embrace the West and its capitalism.

Even though Tang was the most expensive fruit drink available, its sales 7
soared. A simple bottle cost seventeen yuan, a month's worth of lunch money.
A boxed set of two became a status hostess gift. Even the sturdy glass containers that the powder came in were coveted. People used them as tea mugs, the
orange label still on, a sign that you could afford the modern American drink.
Even my mother had an empty Tang bottle with a snug orange nylon net over it,
a present from one of her fellow schoolteachers. She carried it from the office to
the classroom and back again as if our family had also consumed a full bottle.

The truth was, our family had never tasted Tang. Just think of how many 8
oranges we could buy with the money spent on a bottle, my father reasoned. His
resistance sent me into a long adolescent melancholy. I was ashamed by our lack
of style and our life, with its taste of orange peel water. I could not wait until I
grew up and could have my own Tang-filled life.

To add to my agony, our neighbor's son brought over his first girlfriend, 9
for whom he had just bought a bottle of Tang. He was five years older and a college sophomore; we had nothing in common and had not spoken more than ten
sentences. But this didn't stop me from having a painful crush on him. The
beautiful girlfriend opened the Tang in our flat and insisted that we all try it.
When it was my turn to scoop some into a glass of water, the fine orange powder
almost choked me to tears. It was the first time I had drunk Tang, and the taste
was not like real oranges but stronger, as if it were made of the essence of all the
oranges I had ever eaten. This would be the love I would seek, a boy unlike my
father, a boy who would not blink to buy a bottle of Tang for me. I looked at the
beautiful girlfriend and wished to replace her.

My agony and jealousy did not last long, however. Two
months later the beautiful girlfriend left the boy for an older and
richer man. Soon after, the boy's mother came to visit and was still
outraged about the Tang. "What a waste of money on someone
who didn't become his wife!" she said.

For tips on using chronological order and transitions like these in a narrative, see pp. 129–30. 10

"That's how it goes with young people," my mother said. "Once he has a   11
wife, he'll have a better brain and won't throw his money away."

"True. He's just like his father. When he courted me, he once invited me   12
to an expensive restaurant and ordered two fish for me. After we were married,
he wouldn't even allow two fish for the whole family for one meal!"

That was the end of my desire for a Tangy life. I realized that every dream   13
ended with this bland, ordinary existence, where a prince would one day become
a man who boiled orange peels for his family. I had not thought about the boy
much until I moved to America ten years later and discovered Tang in a grocery
store. It was just how I remembered it—fine powder in a sturdy bottle—but its
glamour had lost its gloss because, alas, it was neither expensive nor trendy. To
think that all the dreams of my youth were once contained in this commercial
drink! I picked up a bottle and then returned it to the shelf.

FOR DISCUSSION

. . . .

1. Yiyun Li was sixteen when she first heard about Tang, or "Fruit Treasure," as
   the American drink mix was marketed in her native China (3). How significant
   is the author's age to her story? Explain.
2. Why was Li's father against spending family money on the prestigious new drink?
   Was his position justified? Why or why not?
3. What happened to Li when she tasted Tang for the first time?
4. Why does Li change her mind about the importance of Tang in her life? What
   brings an end to her "agony and jealousy" (10)?
5. What life lesson does Li take from her early experience? How is her perspective
   on her experience influenced by her later life in America? Explain.

STRATEGIES AND STRUCTURES

. . . .

1. Why does Li begin her story with a DESCRIPTION of the orange and tangerine
   peels that her father saves to treat family coughs and colds—and of the water that

results when he boils them (1)? What role does this "orange peel water" play throughout her NARRATIVE?

2. What is the function of the TV commercial in Li's narrative (3–6)? Why does she describe it in such detail?

3. How does Li's crush on the neighbor's son contribute to the PLOT of her story?

4. Where and how effectively does Li use DIALOGUE? Explain.

5. In the last paragraph of her narrative, Li jumps ahead ten years in time. What is the PURPOSE of this FLASH-FORWARD? How does she anticipate this ending in the second paragraph of her story?

6. In her personal coming-of-age story, what point is Li making about the dreams of youth in general? How does she use CAUSE-AND-EFFECT analysis to help her make that point?

WORDS AND FIGURES OF SPEECH

1. Li gives her narrative the name of an American soft drink. Why? How does she connect this and the other "vivid orange" crush in her narrative to the "painful crush" she experienced as an adolescent (4, 9)?

2. How effective is Li's choice of a powdered American drink mix as a METAPHOR for the changes in her life and in the "lifestyle" of her native country (6)? Explain.

3. Explain the PUN in Li's reference to a "Tangy life" (13).

4. The Tang ad, says Li, was "a revolution" (6). What are the implications of this term, especially in a Communist culture such as China's?

5. What cultural differences do you find reflected in the different names for Tang in America and in China? Explain.

FOR WRITING

1. Have you or anyone you know ever purchased a product because you thought it would change your life? In a paragraph or two, tell about your encounter with this product and whether or not it met your expectations.

2. Write a narrative about an infatuation you've had with a particular person or lifestyle—or perhaps a person who represented a lifestyle. Tell what you did to act on your infatuation and how you got over it—or didn't.

3. Write a coming-of-age narrative about someone—such as a sibling, friend, or neighbor—whom you have seen change and grow over a period of time. Focus on specific actions and events that show your subject in the process of maturing.

MARY MEBANE

THE BACK OF THE BUS

Mary Mebane (1933–1992) was the daughter of a dirt farmer who sold junk to raise cash. She earned a Ph.D. from the University of North Carolina and became a professor of English at the University of Wisconsin-Milwaukee. In 1971 on the op-ed page of the *New York Times*, Mebane told the story of a bus ride from Durham, North Carolina, to Orangeburg, South Carolina, during the 1940s that "realized for me the enormousness of the change" since the Civil Rights Act of 1964. That bus ride was the germ of two autobiographical volumes, *Mary* (1981) and *Mary Wayfarer* (1983). The essay printed here is a complete chapter from the first book. It is a personal narrative of another, earlier bus ride that Mebane took when the segregation laws were still in place. Mebane said she wrote this piece because she "wanted to show what it was like to live under legal segregation *before* the Civil Rights Act of 1964."

᛫᛫᛫᛫᛫᛫᛫᛫᛫᛫᛫᛫᛫᛫᛫᛫᛫᛫᛫᛫᛫᛫᛫᛫᛫᛫᛫᛫᛫᛫

Historically, my lifetime is important because I was part of the last genera-tion born into a world of total legal segregation[1] in the Southern United

1. Government-endorsed policy that barred African Americans from white neighborhoods, schools, and other facilities, and required that African Americans sit in separate sections from whites in public spaces like buses and movie theaters.

States. When the Supreme Court outlawed segregation in the public schools in 1954, I was twenty-one. When Congress passed the Civil Rights Act of 1964, permitting blacks free access to public places, I was thirty-one. The world I was born into had been segregated for a long time—so long, in fact, that I never met anyone who had lived during the time when restrictive laws were not in existence, although some people spoke of parents and others who had lived during the "free" time. As far as anyone knew, the laws as they then existed would stand forever. They were meant to—and did—create a world that fixed black people at the bottom of society in all aspects of human life. It was a world without options.

Most Americans have never had to live with terror. I had had to live with it all my life—the psychological terror of segregation, in which there was a special set of laws governing your movements. You violated them at your peril, for you knew that if you broke one of them, knowingly or not, physical terror was just around the corner, in the form of policemen and jails, and in some cases and places white vigilante mobs formed for the exclusive purpose of keeping blacks in line.

It was Saturday morning, like any Saturday morning in dozens of Southern towns.

The town had a washed look. The street sweepers had been busy since six o'clock. Now, at eight, they were still slowly moving down the streets, white trucks with clouds of water coming from underneath the swelled tubular sides. Unwary motorists sometimes got a windowful of water as a truck passed by. As it moved on, it left in its wake a clear stream running in the gutters or splashed on the wheels of parked cars.

Homeowners, bent over industriously in the morning sun, were out pushing lawn mowers. The sun was bright, but it wasn't too hot. It was morning and it was May. Most of the mowers were glad that it was finally getting warm enough to go outside.

Traffic was brisk. Country people were coming into town early with their produce; clerks and service workers were getting to the job before the stores opened at ten o'clock. Though the big stores would not be open for another hour or so, the grocery stores, banks, open-air markets, dinettes, were already open and filling with staff and customers.

Everybody was moving toward the heart of Durham's downtown, which   7
waited to receive them rather complacently, little knowing that in a decade the
shopping centers far from the center of downtown Durham would create a
ghost town in the midst of the busiest blocks on Main Street.

Some moved by car, and some moved by bus. The more affluent used   8
cars, leaving the buses mainly to the poor, black and white, though there were
some businesspeople who avoided the trouble of trying to find a parking place
downtown by riding the bus.

I didn't mind taking the bus on Saturday. It wasn't so crowded. At night or   9
on Saturday or Sunday was the best time. If there were plenty of seats, the
blacks didn't have to worry about being asked to move so that a white person
could sit down. And the knot of hatred and fear didn't come into my stomach.

I knew the stop that was the safety point, both going and coming. Leaving   10
town, it was the Little Five Points, about five or six blocks north of the main
downtown section. That was the last stop at which four or five people might get
on. After the stop, the driver could sometimes pass two or three stops without
taking on or letting off a passenger. So the number of seats on the bus usually
remained constant on the trip from town to Braggtown. The nearer the bus got
to the end of the line, the more I relaxed. For if a white passenger got on near the
end of the line, often to catch the return trip back and avoid having to stand in the
sun at the bus stop until the bus turned around, he or she would usually stand
if there were not seats in the white section, and the driver would say nothing,
knowing that the end of the line was near and that the standee would get a seat
in a few minutes.

On the trip to town, the Mangum Street A&P[2] was the last point at which   11
the driver picked up more passengers than he let off. These people, though
they were just a few blocks from the downtown section, preferred to ride the
bus downtown. Those getting on at the A&P were usually on their way to work
at the Duke University Hospital—past the downtown section, through a residential neighborhood, and then past the university, before they got to Duke
Hospital.

2. Chain of supermarkets; originally called the Great Atlantic & Pacific Tea Company.

So whether the driver discharged more passengers than he took on near 12
the A&P on Mangum was of great importance. For if he took on more passengers than got off, it meant that some of the newcomers would have to stand. And if they were white, the driver was going to have to ask a black passenger to move so that a white passenger could sit down. Most of the drivers had a rule of thumb, though. By custom the seats behind the exit door had become "colored" seats, and no matter how many whites stood up, anyone sitting behind the exit door knew that he or she wouldn't have to move.

The disputed seat, though, was the one directly opposite the exit door. It 13
was "no-man's-land." White people sat there, and black people sat there. It all depended on whose section was fuller. If the back section was full, the next black passenger who got on sat in the no-man's-land seat; but if the white section filled up, a white person would take the seat. Another thing about the white people: they could sit anywhere they chose, even in the "colored" section. Only the black passengers had to obey segregation laws.

On this Saturday morning Esther[3] and I set out for town for our music les- 14
son. We were going on our weekly big adventure, all the way across town, through the white downtown, then across the railroad tracks, then through the "colored" downtown, a section of run-down dingy shops, through some fading high-class black neighborhoods, past North Carolina College, to Mrs. Shearin's house.

We walked the two miles from Wildwood to the bus line. Though it was a 15
warm day, in the early morning there was dew on the grass and the air still had the night's softness. So we walked along and talked and looked back constantly, hoping someone we knew would stop and pick us up.

I looked back furtively, for in one of the few instances that I remembered 16
my father criticizing me severely, it was for looking back. One day when I was walking from town he had passed in his old truck. I had been looking back and had seen him. "Don't look back," he had said. "People will think that you want them to pick you up." Though he said "people," I knew he meant men—not the men he knew, who lived in the black community, but the black men who were not part of the community, and all of the white men. To be picked up meant that

---

3. Mebane's sister.

something bad would happen to me. Still, two miles is a long walk and I occasionally joined Esther in looking back to see if anyone we knew was coming.

Esther and I got to the bus and sat on one of the long seats at the back that   17
faced each other. There were three such long seats—one on each side of the bus
and a third long seat at the very back that faced the front. I liked to sit on a long
seat facing the side because then I didn't have to look at the expressions on the
faces of the whites when they put their tokens in and looked at the blacks sitting
in the back of the bus. Often I studied my music, looking down and practicing
the fingering. I looked up at each stop to see who was getting on and to check
on the seating pattern. The seating pattern didn't really bother me that day
until the bus started to get unusually full for a Saturday morning. I wondered
what was happening, where all these people were coming from. They got on and
got on until the white section was almost full and the black section was full.

There was a black man in a blue windbreaker and a gray porkpie hat sit-   18
ting in no-man's-land, and my stomach tightened. I wondered what would happen. I had never been on a bus on which a black person was asked to give a seat
to a white person when there was no other seat empty. Usually, though, I had
seen a black person automatically get up and move to an empty seat farther
back. But this morning the only empty seat was beside a black person sitting in
no-man's-land.

The bus stopped at Little Five Points and one black got off. A young white   19
man was getting on. I tensed. What would happen now? Would the driver ask
the black man to get up and move to the empty seat farther back? The white
man had a businessman's air about him: suit, shirt, tie, polished brown shoes.
He saw the empty seat in the "colored" section and after just a little hesitation
went to it, put his briefcase down, and sat with his feet crossed. I relaxed a little
when the bus pulled off without the driver saying anything. Evidently he hadn't
seen what had happened, or since he was just a few stops from Main Street, he
figured the mass exodus there would solve all the problems. Still, I was afraid of
a scene.

The next stop was an open-air fruit stand just after Little Five Points, and   20
here another white man got on. Where would he sit? The only available seat was
beside the black man. Would he stand the few stops to Main Street or would the

driver make the black man move? The whole colored section tensed, but nobody said anything. I looked at Esther, who looked apprehensive. I looked at the other men and women, who studiously avoided my eyes and everybody else's as well, as they maintained a steady gaze at a far-distant land.

Just one woman caught my eye; I had noticed her before, and I had been ashamed of her. She was a stringy little black woman. She could have been forty; she could have been fifty. She looked as if she were a hard drinker. Flat black face with tight features. She was dressed with great insouciance in a tight boy's sweater with horizontal lines running across her flat chest. It pulled down over a nondescript skirt. Laced-up shoes, socks, and a head rag completed her outfit. She looked tense.

The white man who had just gotten on the bus walked to the seat in no-man's-land and stood there. He wouldn't sit down, just stood there. Two adult males, living in the most highly industrialized, most technologically advanced nation in the world, a nation that had devastated two other industrial giants in World War II[4] and had flirted with taking on China in Korea. Both these men, either of whom could have fought for the United States in Germany or Korea, faced each other in mutual rage and hostility. The white one wanted to sit down, but he was going to exert his authority and force the black one to get up first. I watched the driver in the rearview mirror. He was about the same age as the antagonists. The driver wasn't looking for trouble, either.

"Say there, buddy, how about moving back," the driver said, meanwhile driving his bus just as fast as he could. The whole bus froze—whites at the front, blacks at the rear. They didn't want to believe what was happening was really happening.

The seated black man said nothing. The standing white man said nothing.

"Say, buddy, did you hear me? What about moving on back." The driver was scared to death. I could tell that.

21

22

23

24

25

4. The United States and its allies defeated "industrial giants" Germany and Japan, as well as Italy, in World War II (1939–45).

"These is the niggers' seats!" the little lady in the strange outfit started 26
screaming. I jumped. I had to shift my attention from the driver to the frieze of
the black man seated and white man standing to the articulate little woman who
had joined in the fray.

"The government gave us these seats! These is the niggers' seats." I was 27
startled at her statement and her tone. "The president said that these are the
niggers' seats!" I expected her to start fighting at any moment.

Evidently the bus driver did, too, because he was driving faster and faster. 28
I believe that he forgot he was driving a bus and wanted desperately to pull to
the side of the street and get out and run.

"I'm going to take you down to the station, buddy," the driver said. 29

The white man with the briefcase and the polished brown shoes who had 30
taken a seat in the "colored" section looked as though he might die of embarrassment at any moment.

As scared and upset as I was, I didn't miss a thing. 31

By that time we had come to the stop before Main Street, and the black 32
passenger rose to get off.

"You're not getting off, buddy. I'm going to take you downtown." The 33
driver kept driving as he talked and seemed to be trying to get downtown as fast
as he could.

"These are the niggers' seats! The government plainly said these are the 34
niggers' seats!" screamed the little woman in rage.

I was embarrassed at the use of the word "nigger" but I was proud of the 35
lady. I was also proud of the man who wouldn't get up.

The bus driver was afraid, trying to hold on to his job but plainly not will- 36
ing to get into a row with the blacks.

The bus seemed to be going a hundred miles an hour and everybody was 37
anxious to get off, though only the lady and the driver were saying anything.

The black man stood at the exit door; the driver drove right past the A&P 38
stop. I was terrified. I was sure that the bus was going to the police station to put
the black man in jail. The little woman had her hands on her hips and she never
stopped yelling. The bus driver kept driving as fast as he could.

Then, somewhere in the back of his mind, he decided to forget the whole thing. The next stop was Main Street, and when he got there, in what seemed to be a flash of lightning, he flung both doors open wide. He and his black antagonist looked at each other in the rearview mirror; in a second the windbreaker and porkpie hat were gone. The little woman was standing, preaching to the whole bus about the government's gift of these seats to the blacks; the man with the brown shoes practically fell out of the door in his hurry; and Esther and I followed the hurrying footsteps.

We walked about three doors down the block, then caught a bus to the black neighborhood. Here we sat on one of the two long seats facing each other, directly behind the driver. It was the custom. Since this bus had a route from a black neighborhood to the downtown section and back, passing through no white residential areas, blacks could sit where they chose. One minute we had been on a bus in which violence was threatened over a seat near the exit door; the next minute we were sitting in the very front behind the driver.

The people who devised this system thought that it was going to last forever.

39

40

41

FOR DISCUSSION

1. Why does the bus driver threaten to drive to the police station? What was his official duty under segregation?
2. Why does the businessman with the briefcase and brown shoes take the separate seat in the back of the bus instead of the place on the bench across from the exit? Was he upholding or violating segregation customs by doing so?
3. What is the main confrontation of the NARRATIVE? What emotion(s) does it arouse in young Mary Mebane and her sister as witnesses?
4. Who are the "people" to whom Mebane refers in paragraph 41?
5. Why does Mebane claim a national significance for the events of her private life as narrated here? Is her CLAIM justified? How does this claim relate to her PURPOSE for writing?

STRATEGIES AND STRUCTURES

. . . .

1. In which paragraph does Mebane begin telling the story of the bus ride? Why do you think she starts with the routine of the street sweepers and the homeowners doing yard work?

2. List several passages in Mebane's text that seem to be told from young Mary's POINT OF VIEW. Then list others that are told from the point of view of the adult author looking back at an event in her youth. Besides time, what is the main difference in their perspectives?

3. Why does Mebane refer to the black passenger who confronts the bus driver as "the windbreaker and porkpie hat" (39)? Whose point of view is she capturing? Is she showing or telling here—and what difference does it make in her essay?

4. How does Mebane use the increasing speed of the bus to show rather than tell about the precariousness of the segregation system?

5. Mebane interrupts her narrative of the events of that Saturday morning in paragraphs 10 through 13. What is she explaining to her AUDIENCE, and why is it necessary that she do so? Where else does she interrupt her narrative with EXPOSITION?

WORDS AND FIGURES OF SPEECH

. . . .

1. Why does Mebane refer to the seat across from the exit as a "no-man's land" (13)? What does this term mean?

2. Mebane COMPARES the seated black man and the standing white man to a "frieze," a decorative horizontal band, often molded or carved, along the upper part of a wall (26). Why is the METAPHOR appropriate here?

3. Look up "insouciance" in your dictionary (21). Does the use of this word prepare you for the rebellious behavior of the "stringy" little woman (21)? How?

4. What are the two possible meanings of "scene" (19)? How might Mebane's personal narrative be said to illustrate both kinds?

5. Which of the many meanings of "articulate" in your dictionary best fits the woman who screams back at the bus driver (26)?

FOR WRITING

1. In a brief ANECDOTE, recount a ride you have taken on a bus, train, plane, roller coaster, boat, or other vehicle. Focus on the vehicle itself and the people who were on it with you.

2. Write a personal narrative about an experience you had with racial tension in a public place. Be sure to describe the physical place and tell what you saw and heard and did there.

LYNDA BARRY

THE SANCTUARY OF SCHOOL

Lynda Barry (b. 1956) is a cartoonist, novelist, and teacher of writing. She was born in Wisconsin but spent most of her adolescence in Seattle, where she supported herself at age 16 as a janitor. As a student at Evergreen State College in Olympia, Washington, Barry began drawing *Ernie Pook's Comeek*, the comic strip for which she is perhaps best known. Her first novel, *Cruddy* (2000), was about a teenager and her troubled family life "in the cruddiest part of town." Barry tells how she first discovered the therapeutic value of art—and of good teachers—in "The Sanctuary of School," which first appeared in the education section of the *New York Times* in January 1992. This narrative about her early school days also carries a pointed message for those who would cut costs in the public school system by eliminating art from the curriculum.

❧◇◇◇◇◇◇◇◇◇◇◇◇◇◇◇◇◇◇◇◇◇◇◇◇◇◇◇◇◇◇◇◇◇◇❧

I WAS SEVEN YEARS OLD the first time I snuck out of the house in the dark. It   1
was winter and my parents had been fighting all night. They were short on money and long on relatives who kept "temporarily" moving into our house because they had nowhere else to go.

My brother and I were used to giving up our bedroom. We slept on the 2
couch, something we actually liked because it put us that much closer to the light
of our lives, our television.

At night when everyone was asleep, we lay on our pillows watching it with the 3
sound off. We watched Steve Allen's[1] mouth moving. We watched Johnny Car-
son's[2] mouth moving. We watched movies filled with gangsters shooting machine
guns into packed rooms, dying soldiers hurling a last grenade, and beautiful
women crying at windows. Then the sign-off finally came and we tried to sleep.

The morning I snuck out, I woke up filled with a panic about needing to 4
get to school. The sun wasn't quite up yet but my anxiety was so fierce that I just
got dressed, walked quietly across the kitchen and let myself out the back door.

It was quiet outside. Stars were still out. Nothing moved and no one was 5
in the street. It was as if someone had turned the sound off on the world.

I walked the alley, breaking thin ice over the puddles with my shoes. I 6
didn't know why I was walking to school in the dark. I didn't think about it. All
I knew was a feeling of panic, like the panic that strikes kids when they realize
they are lost.

That feeling eased the moment I turned the corner and saw the dark out- 7
line of my school at the top of the hill. My school was made up of about 15 nondescript portable classrooms set down on a fenced concrete lot in a rundown
Seattle neighborhood, but it had the most beautiful view of the Cascade Mountains. You could see them from anywhere on the playfield and you could see
them from the windows of my classroom—Room 2.

I walked over to the monkey bars and hooked my arms around the cold 8
metal. I stood for a long time just looking across Rainier Valley. The sky was
beginning to whiten and I could hear a few birds.

In a perfect world my absence at home would not have gone unnoticed. I would 9
have had two parents in a panic to locate me, instead of two parents in a panic to

1. American actor and musician (1921–2000) best known for his work on late night television.
2. American comedian and television personality (1924–2005) who hosted *The Tonight Show*
for thirty years.

locate an answer to the hard question of survival during a deep financial and emotional crisis.

But in an overcrowded and unhappy home, it's incredibly easy for any 10 child to slip away. The high levels of frustration, depression, and anger in my house made my brother and me invisible. We were children with the sound turned off. And for us, as for the steadily increasing number of neglected children in this country, the only place where we could count on being noticed was at school.

"Hey there, young lady. Did you forget to go home last night?" It was Mr. 11 Gunderson, our janitor, whom we all loved. He was nice and he was funny and he was old with white hair, thick glasses and an unbelievable number of keys. I could hear them jingling as he walked across the playfield. I felt incredibly happy to see him.

He let me push his wheeled garbage can between the different portables as 12 he unlocked each room. He let me turn on the lights and raise the window shades and I saw my school slowly come to life. I saw Mrs. Holman, our school secretary, walk into the office without her orange lipstick on yet. She waved.

I saw the fifth-grade teacher, Mr. Cunningham, walking under the breeze- 13 way eating a hard roll. He waved.

And I saw my teacher, Mrs. Claire LeSane, walking toward us in a red 14 coat and calling my name in a very happy and surprised way, and suddenly my throat got tight and my eyes stung and I ran toward her crying. It was something that surprised us both.

It's only thinking about it now, 28 years later, that I realize I was crying 15 from relief. I was with my teacher, and in a while I was going to sit at my desk, with my crayons and pencils and books and classmates all around me, and for the next six hours I was going to enjoy a thoroughly secure, warm and stable world. It was a world I absolutely relied on. Without it, I don't know where I would have gone that morning.

Mrs. LeSane asked me what was wrong and when I said "Nothing," she 16 seemingly left it at that. But she asked me if I would carry her purse for her, an honor above all honors, and she asked if I wanted to come into Room 2 early and paint.

She believed in the natural healing power of painting and drawing for troubled   17
children. In the back of her room there was always a drawing table and an easel
with plenty of supplies, and sometimes during the day she would come up to
you for what seemed like no good reason and quietly ask if you wanted to go
to the back table and "make some pictures for Mrs. LeSane." We all had a chance
at it—to sit apart from the class for a while to paint, draw and silently work out
impossible problems on 11 × 17 sheets of newsprint.

Drawing came to mean everything to me. At the back table in Room 2, I   18
learned to build myself a life preserver that I could carry into my home.

We all know that a good education system saves lives, but the people of   19
this country are still told that cutting the budget for public schools
is necessary, that poor salaries for teachers are all we can manage
and that art, music and all creative activities must be the first to go
when times are lean.

When you tell a story, it should have a point (p. 66).

Before- and after-school programs are cut and we are told that public schools are   20
not made for baby-sitting children. If parents are neglectful temporarily or permanently, for whatever reason, it's certainly sad, but their unlucky children must
fend for themselves. Or slip through the cracks. Or wander in a dark night alone.

We are told in a thousand ways that not only are public schools not impor-   21
tant, but that the children who attend them, the children who need them most,
are not important either. We leave them to learn from the blind eye of a television, or to the mercy of "a thousand points of light"[3] that can be as far away as
stars.

I was lucky. I had Mrs. LeSane. I had Mr. Gunderson. I had an abun-   22
dance of art supplies. And I had a particular brand of neglect in my home that
allowed me to slip away and get to them. But what about the rest of the kids who
weren't as lucky? What happened to them?

By the time the bell rang that morning I had finished my drawing and   23
Mrs. LeSane pinned it up on the special bulletin board she reserved for drawings from the back table. It was the same picture I always drew—a sun in the
corner of a blue sky over a nice house with flowers all around it.

Mrs. LeSane asked us to please stand, face the flag, place our right hands   24
over our hearts and say the Pledge of Allegiance. Children across the country
do it faithfully. I wonder now when the country will face its children and say a
pledge right back.

---

3. In his inaugural address on January 20, 1989, President George H. W. Bush used this
phrase to refer to "all the community organizations that are spread like stars throughout the
Nation, doing good."

FOR DISCUSSION

1. As a seven-year-old leaving home in the dark in a fit of panic and anxiety, why did young Barry instinctively head for her school?

2. Why does Barry say, "We were children with the sound turned off" (10)? Who fails to hear them?

3. Barry always drew the same picture when she sat at the art table in the back of Mrs. LeSane's classroom. What's the significance of that picture? Explain.

4. Why does Barry refer to the Pledge of Allegiance in the last paragraph of her essay?

STRATEGIES AND STRUCTURES

1. Why does Barry begin her NARRATIVE with an account of watching television with her sister? Where else does she refer to watching TV? Why?

2. Most of Barry's narrative takes place at her school, which she pictures in some detail. Which of these physical details do you find most revealing, and how do they help to present the place as a sanctuary"?

3. Point out several places in her narrative where Barry characterizes Mrs. LeSane, Mr. Gunderson, and others through their gestures and bits of DIALOGUE. What do these small acts and brief words reveal about the people Barry is portraying?

4. What does young Barry's sense of panic and anxiety contribute to the PLOT of her narrative?

5. Where and how does Barry's narrative morph into an ARGUMENT about public schools in America? What's the point of that argument, and where does she state it most directly?

WORDS AND FIGURES OF SPEECH

1. Is Barry speaking literally or metaphorically (or both) when she refers to children who "wander in a dark night alone" (20)? How and how well does she pave the way for this statement at the end of her narrative?

2. What does Barry mean when she says that the "points of light" in a child's life can be "as far away as stars" (21)? How and where does the word *light* take on different implications during the course of her narrative?

3. Barry characterizes her old school as a *sanctuary* instead of, for example, a *haven* or *safehouse*. Why do you think she chooses this term? Is it apt? Why or why not?

4. Why does Barry refer to the "blind eye" of television (21)?

FOR WRITING

. . . .

1. In a few paragraphs, tell about a time when you found school to be a sanctuary, or the opposite. Be sure to DESCRIBE the physical place and what people said and did there.

2. Write a narrative essay in which you use your experience at school to make a point about the importance of some aspect of the school curriculum that you fear may be changed or lost. If possible, expand your argument to include schools in general, not just your own.

CHAPTER SIX

EXAMPLE

⟡⟡⟡⟡⟡⟡⟡⟡⟡⟡⟡⟡⟡⟡⟡⟡⟡⟡⟡⟡⟡⟡⟡⟡⟡⟡

I T'S difficult to write about any subject, however familiar, without giving EXAMPLES.* Take hiccups, for example. The most prolonged case of hiccups in a human being is that of an Iowa man who hiccupped from 1922 to 1990. We know this is a true case because it is documented in the *Guinness World Records*, which is a compendium of examples, however unique. That is, a typical entry consists of a category (largest pizza, oldest cat, longest bout of hiccups) and a person or thing that fits that category.

This is what examples are and do: they're individuals (a man from Iowa who hiccupped for 68 years) taken out of a larger category or group (serious cases of hiccupping) to represent the whole group. Nobody knows for sure what causes hiccups—eating too fast is only one possibility—but why we use examples in writing is pretty clear.

To represent the idea of "family," David Sedaris (p. 227) uses the example of singing "Kookaburra" with his sister.

For most of us, it is easier to digest a piece of pie than the whole pie at once. The same goes for examples. Good examples are *representative:* they exhibit all of the main, important characteristics of the group they exemplify. That is, they give the flavor of the whole subject in a single bite. This makes it easier for the reader to grasp (if not swallow) what we have to say—assuming, of course, that our examples are interesting and compelling. Or at least vivid.

Good examples vivify—or give life to—a subject by making general statements ("cats can live a long time") more specific ("the oldest cat on record is Creme Puff of Austin, Texas, who lived to be 38 years old"). They also help to

*Words printed in SMALL CAPITALS are defined in the Glossary/Index.

make ABSTRACT concepts more CONCRETE. In the following humorous passage, Dave Barry is explaining the abstract concept of "neat stuff":

> By "neat," I mean "mechanical and unnecessarily complex." I'll give you an example. Right now I'm typing these words on an *extremely* powerful computer. It's the latest in a line of maybe ten computers I've owned, each one more powerful than the last. My computer is chock full of RAM and ROM and bytes and megahertzes and various other items that enable a computer to kick data-processing butt. It is probably capable of supervising the entire U.S. air-defense apparatus while simultaneously processing the tax return of every resident of Ohio. I use it mainly to write a newspaper column.
>
> —DAVE BARRY, "Guys vs. Men"

Abstractions are concepts, such as "neat stuff," that are more or less detached from our five senses. Concrete examples, such as Barry's computer, help to make them more immediately perceptible, especially to our eyes and ears.

As the *Guinness World Records* demonstrates, concrete examples can be interesting in their own right. In most kinds of writing, however, we do not use examples for their own sake but to make a point. Barry's point here is that "guys like neat stuff" and that this characteristic distinguishes them from "men," who are generally "way too serious" to care about mere stuff, however neat. Elsewhere in "Guys vs. Men," Barry uses a similar concrete example to distinguish guys from women: "Guys do not have a basic need to rearrange furniture. Whereas a woman who could cheerfully use the same computer for fifty-three years will rearrange her furniture on almost a weekly basis, sometimes in the dead of night."

Whether or not you agree with Barry's conclusions about masculinity and other issues of gender, his examples make an entertaining, if not absolutely decisive, argument. How many examples are sufficient to prove your point?

As with other kinds of evidence, that will depend on the complexity of your subject, the nature of your audience, and your purpose in writing. Are you merely seeking to convince readers that guys like "mechanical and unnecessarily complex" devices? Or are you saying that guys are behaviorally different from women in fundamental ways? (For this, even Barry feels the need to qualify:

"I realize that I'm making gender-based generalizations here, but my feeling is that if God did not want us to make gender-based generalizations, She would not have given us genders.")

Sometimes a single example can suffice—and even provide a focal point for an essay or an entire book—if it is truly representative and sufficiently appealing to your audience. Take the example of J. P. Morgan's nose, for instance. In her introduction to *Morgan, American Financier* (1999), the prize-winning biographer Jean Strouse discusses the difficulties she faced in writing a life of the banker who almost single-handedly ran the American economy a hundred years ago. In addition to the sheer bulk of biographical material, there were also countless stories and legends that had grown up around Morgan.

Strouse did not solve the problem of organizing all this material by focusing on Morgan's unusual nose; but she did effectively use the nose example to introduce the legendary nature of her subject to her readers:

> Even Morgan's personal appearance gave rise to legend. He had a skin disease called rhinophyma that in his fifties turned his nose into a hideous purple bulb. One day the wife of his partner Dwight Morrow reportedly invited him to tea. She wanted her daughter Anne to meet the great man, and for weeks coached the girl about what would happen. Anne would come into the room and say good afternoon; she would not stare at Mr. Morgan's nose, she would not say anything about his nose, and she would leave.

The appointed day came, as Strouse tells the story, and the Morrows' young daughter, Anne, played her part flawlessly. Mrs. Morrow herself, however, had more difficulty:

> Mrs. Morrow and Mr. Morgan sat on a sofa by the tea tray. Anne came in, said hello, did not look at Morgan's nose, did not say anything about his nose, and left the room. Sighing in relief, Mrs. Morrow asked, "Mr. Morgan, do you take one lump or two in your nose?"

The usefulness of this story as an example of how examples can help to organize and focus our writing is only enhanced by the fact that it never happened.

When she grew up, Anne Morrow went on to become the writer Anne Morrow Lindbergh, wife of aviator Charles Lindbergh, who made the first solo transatlantic flight. "This ridiculous story has not a grain of truth in it," Mrs. Lindbergh told Morgan's biographer many years later; but "it is so funny I am sure it will continue."

Brief NARRATIVES, or ANECDOTES, such as the story of Mrs. Morrow and J. P. Morgan's nose, often make good organizing examples because they link generalities or abstractions—gender differences, principles of biography—to specific people and concrete events. By citing just this one story among the many inspired by Morgan's appearance and personality, Strouse accomplishes several things with one stroke: she paints a clear picture of how his contemporaries regarded the man whose life story she is introducing; she shows how difficult it was to see her controversial subject through the legends that enshrouded him; and she finds a focal point for organizing the introduction to her entire book. Evidently, Strouse has a good nose for examples.

A BRIEF GUIDE TO WRITING
AN ESSAY BASED ON EXAMPLES

As you write an essay based on examples, you need to identify your subject, say what its main characteristics are, and give specific instances that exhibit those characteristics. The editors of the *Onion* make these basic moves of exemplification in the following tongue-in-cheek passage from an essay in this chapter:

> In total, 347 individual acts of sin were committed at the bake sale, with nearly every attendee committing at least one of the seven deadly sins as outlined by Gregory the Great in the Fifth Century.
> —THE ONION, *All Seven Deadly Sins Committed at Church Bake Sale*

The editors of the *Onion* identify their subject ("the seven deadly sins"), define it or state its main characteristics ("as outlined by Gregory the Great"), and give specific instances that exhibit these characteristics ("347 individual acts of sin").

The following guidelines will help you to make these basic moves as you draft an exemplification essay. They will also help you to ensure that your examples fit your purpose and audience, are sufficient to make your point, are truly representative of your subject, and are effectively organized with appropriate transitions.

Coming Up with a Subject

To come up with a subject for your essay, take any subject you're interested in—the presidency of Abraham Lincoln, for example—and consider whether it can be narrowed down to focus on a specific aspect of the subject (such as Lincoln's humor in office) for which you can find a reasonable number of examples. Then choose examples that show the characteristics of that narrower topic. In this case, a good example of the presidential humor might be the time a well-dressed lady visited the White House and inadvertently sat on Lincoln's hat. "Madame," the president is supposed to have responded, "I could have told you it wouldn't fit."

The author of "My Technologically Challenged Life," p. 194, had all the examples she needed at home and work. If you have personal knowledge of your topic, you may already have a store of exemplary facts or stories about it. Or you may need to do some research. As you look for examples, choose ones that truly represent the qualities and characteristics you're trying to illustrate—and that are most likely to appeal to your AUDIENCE.

Considering Your Purpose and Audience

Before you begin writing, think about your PURPOSE. Is it to entertain? inform? persuade? For instance, the purpose of "All Seven Deadly Sins Committed at Church Bake Sale" on page 200 is to entertain, so the writer offers humorous examples of incidents at the bake sale. But if you were writing about the bake sale in order to persuade others to participate next time, you might offer examples of the money earned at various booths, how much fun participants had, and the good causes the money will be used for. In every case, your purpose determines the kinds of examples you use.

Before you select examples, you need to take into account how much your AUDIENCE already knows about your topic and how sympathetic they are likely to be to your position. If you are writing to demonstrate that the health of Americans has declined over the past decade, and your audience consists of doctors and nutritionists, a few key examples would probably suffice. For a general audience, however, such as your classmates, you would need to give more background information and cite more (and more basic) examples. And if your readers are unlikely to view your topic as you do, you will have to work even harder to come up with convincing examples.

Generating Ideas: Finding Good Examples

Try to find examples that display as many of the typical characteristics of your topic as possible. Suppose you were writing an essay on the seven deadly sins, and you decided to focus on gluttony. One characteristic of gluttony is overeating, so you might look for examples of people who overeat. Great athletes eat large quantities of food; however, we don't consider them gluttons because they're fit and energetic. In this case, you would need to consider other characteristics of gluttony: obesity and lethargy. Perhaps Jabba the Hutt, the obese alien of *Star Wars* fame, would make a good example of gluttony because he not only overeats but also is fat and lazy.

Templates for Exemplifying

The following templates can help you to generate ideas for an exemplification essay and then to start drafting. Don't take these as formulas where you just have to fill in the blanks. There are no easy formulas for good writing. But these templates can help you plot out some of the key moves of exemplification and thus may serve as good starting points.

> ▸ About X, it can generally be said that _____; a good example would be _____.
>
> ▸ The main characteristics of X are _____ and _____, as exemplified by _____, _____, and _____.

> ▶ For the best example(s) of X, we can turn to _____.
>
> ▶ Additional examples of X include _____, _____, and _____.
>
> ▶ From these examples of X, we can conclude that _____.

For more techniques to help you generate ideas and start writing with examples, see Chapter 2.

Stating Your Point

In an exemplification essay, you usually state your point directly in a THESIS STATEMENT in your introduction. For example:

> College teams depend more on excellent teamwork than on star athletes for success.
>
> In general, the health of most Americans has declined in the last ten years.
>
> Mitt Romney's 2012 campaign for the U.S. presidency made a number of tactical errors.

Each of these thesis statements calls for specific examples to support it. How many examples do you need—and what kinds?

Using Sufficient Examples

As you select examples to support a thesis, you can use either multiple brief examples or one or two extended examples. The approach you take will depend, in part, on the kind of generalization you're making. Multiple examples work well when you are dealing with different aspects of a large topic (the Romney presidential campaign strategy) or with trends involving large numbers of people (Americans' declining health, college athletes). Extended examples work better when you are writing about a particular case, such as a single scene in a novel.

For an essay made up almost entirely of examples, see p. 216.

Keep in mind that sufficiency isn't strictly a matter of numbers. Often a few good examples will suffice, which is what sufficiency implies: enough to do the job, and no more. In other words, whether or not your examples are sufficient to support your thesis is not determined by the number of examples but by how persuasive those examples seem to your readers. Choose examples that you think they will find vivid and convincing.

Using Representative Examples

Be sure that your examples fairly and accurately support the point you're making. In an essay on how college athletic teams depend on teamwork, for instance, you would want to choose examples from several teams and sports. Similarly, if you are trying to convince readers that a candidate made many tactical errors in a political campaign, you would need to show a number of errors from different points in the campaign. And if you're exemplifying an ABSTRACT concept, such as gluttony, be sure to choose CONCRETE examples that possess all of its distinguishing characteristics.

Another way to make sure that your examples are representative is to steer clear of highly unusual examples. In an essay about the benefits of swimming every day, for instance, Michael Phelps might not be the best example since he is not a typical swimmer. Better to cite several swimmers who can demonstrate a variety of benefits.

Organizing Examples and Using Transitions

Once you have stated your thesis and chosen your examples, you need to put them in some kind of order. You might present them in order of increasing importance or interest, perhaps saving the best for last. Or if you have a large number of examples, you might organize them into categories. Or you might arrange them chronologically, if you are citing errors made during a campaign, for example.

Regardless of the organization you choose, you need to relate your examples to each other and to the point you're making by using clear TRANSITIONS and other connecting words and phrases. You can always use the phrases *for example* and *for instance*. But consider using other transitions as well, such as *more specifically, exactly, precisely, thus, namely, indeed, that is, in other words, in fact, in particular:* "Obesity, in fact, has caused a dramatic increase in the incidence of diabetes." Or try using a RHETORICAL QUESTION, which you then answer with an example: "So what factor has contributed the most to the declining health of Americans?"

EDITING FOR COMMON ERRORS IN EXEMPLIFICATION

Exemplification invites certain typical errors, especially with lists or series of examples. The following tips will help you to check and correct your writing for these common problems.

When you list a series of examples, make sure they are parallel in structure

> ► Animals avoid predators in many ways. They travel in groups, move fast, blend~~ing~~ in with their surroundings, and look~~ing~~ threatening.

Edit out *etc., and so forth,* or *and so on* when they don't add materially to your sentence

> ► Animals typically avoid predators by traveling in groups, moving fast, <u>and</u> blending in with their surroundings~~, etc~~.

Check your use of *i.e.* and *e.g.*

These abbreviations of Latin phrases are often used interchangeably to introduce examples, but they do not mean the same thing: *i.e.* means "that is" and *e.g.* means "for example." Since most of your readers do not likely speak Latin, it is a good idea to use the English equivalents.

> ► The tree sloth is an animal that uses protective coloring to hide—~~i.e.~~ <u>that is</u>, it lets green algae grow on its fur in order to blend in with the tree leaves.

> ► Some animals use protective coloring to hide—~~e.g.~~ <u>for example</u>, the tree sloth.

EVERYDAY EXAMPLE
A Lighted Billboard

Use
Electricity
Wisely

Eskom

By illuminating only one of the spotlights on this billboard, a utility company sets a good example for consumers—and gives a "for instance" of the general point it is making here. You can use examples to shed light on almost any subject by making abstract concepts (energy conservation) more concrete (turning off extra lights) and by focusing the reader's attention on a particular illuminating instance or illustration of your subject.

MONICA WUNDERLICH

MY TECHNOLOGICALLY CHALLENGED LIFE

Monica Wunderlich's "My Technologically Challenged Life" appeared in 2004 in *Delta Winds*, an anthology of student writing published each year by the English department of San Joaquin Delta College in Stockton, California. Wunderlich first wrote the essay as an assignment for an English course. It gives many humorous examples of the difficulties she has encountered with ordinary technology (or the lack of it) in her everyday life. At the nursing facility where the author worked while attending college, however, the lack of up-to-date equipment was no laughing matter—as Wunderlich's more disturbing examples make clear.

My Technologically Challenged Life

It probably seems easy for someone to use a computer to solve a task or call a friend on a cellular phone for the solution. I, however, do not have access to such luxuries. My home, workplace, and automobile are almost barren of anything electronic. It's not as if I don't want technology in my life, but I feel as if technology has taken on the role of a rabbit, and I am the fox with three legs that just can't seem to get it. And after many useless attempts at trying to figure it out, I have almost given up.

1

> Three-category organization promises multiple examples and suggests the order in which they'll appear

In my house, technology does not exist, at least not for my parents. In fact it was 1995 when my father finally had to part with his beloved rotary phone,[1] not because it was worn out, but because it would not work with the new automated menus that companies were using. Reaching an actual person was difficult the old way because of the physical impossibility of being able to *push* 1, 2, or 3 when a phone possesses no buttons. It was quite embarrassing, especially since I was fifteen and all of my friends had "normal" phones. My dad's biggest argument was that "It's a privacy issue. No one can tap into our phone calls and listen to our conversations." Well, the last time I had checked, none of us were trafficking dope.

2

> Example: rotary phone

I also had the privilege of not using a computer. It was hard going through high school without one, for I had many teachers who demanded many essays from me. Yet I had no way to type them. My sister was in the same boat, so we tried

3

> Example: no computer

---

1. *Rotary phone*: A dial-faced style of telephone in widespread use throughout much of the twentieth century.

tag-teaming[2] my parents into getting us a computer. But to no avail. We kept getting things like "They're too expensive," or "We have no room for one," or "We'll get one later." Later! My parents should have just said NEVER! So my sister and I resorted to spending hours at our friends' houses, because their parents were nice to them and bought computers. The only problem was that our friends had lives and weren't always around at our disposal. So Plan B for essay completion was using a cheesy electronic word processor that my dad had borrowed from my *grandparents* to supposedly "help us out." This beast of a machine wasn't much help, though, because it was a pain in the neck to use. It had a teeny tiny little screen that wouldn't show the entire typed line, so by the time the line was printed, I'd find about ten uncorrected mistakes, and I'd have to start over. However, nothing is permanent and walls do come down, and so be it—the Wunderlichs buy their first computer! Two years after I graduate high school. As of yet, we still do not have the Internet.

My job is another place where technology is lacking. I   4
work in a home for the elderly, and I take care of about eight to ten patients a night. I have to take some of these patients' vital signs, and I speak on behalf of anyone who has ever worked in the medical profession when I say that the most efficient way to take vital signs is electronically. However, my employers do not grant us the equipment for electronic vitals.

Example: glass thermometers ·······• We are still using glass thermometers, which are not only a waste of time (3 seconds vs. 3 minutes for an oral temp), but

2. *Tag-teaming*: A wrestling term referring to two people working as a team in alternate turns.

they are extremely dangerous. Residents are known to bite down on the thermometers, exposing themselves to harmful mercury. I can't even begin to count how many thermometers I have dropped and broken since I've worked there. One time I dropped a thermometer and didn't realize I had broken it. So I picked it up to shake it down, but instead I flung mercury everywhere. An electronic thermometer just makes more sense when trying to make the residents' environment as safe as possible.

We also have to use manual blood pressure cuffs. They're just the normal cuffs that are wrapped around the arm, pumped up, and read using the bouncing needle. The problem is that none of our blood pressure cuffs are calibrated correctly, and the needles are way out of kilter. This makes it impossible to get an accurate reading. An ingenious solution would be digital cuffs, but that is highly unlikely. Actually, the home did try to supply some digital cuffs, but they were stolen. One man's sticky fingers equals inconvenience for the rest of us, and the home no longer supplied us with such time-saving technology. Using manual equipment is hard not only for us but also for the nurses. The care home does not allow feeding machines in the facility, yet people who need to be fed by a stomach tube are still admitted. This means that the nurses have to allot a special time from their med pass to hook up a syringe to the patient's stomach tube and pour their "steak dinner in a can" down the tube little by little. This tedious process takes about twenty minutes, and nurses don't really have twenty minutes to throw around, so it really crowds their schedules. If we had feeding machines, the

5 ····· Example: manual blood pressure cuffs

•····· Example: no feeding machines

nurses would only have to change a bag when a machine beeps. Problem solved if things went my way.

Another part of my life that is technologically crippled is my car. As much as I like my car, I still think it could use a few more bells and whistles. I drive a 2002 Volkswagen Jetta, which would probably make the reader think, "Oh, a new car. There must be plenty of technology in that new car?" My answer to that is "No, there isn't." The only technology is the 5 billion standard airbags for when I do something really stupid. Other than that I have to shift it manually. If I want to roll down my window, I have to turn a crank. My car did not come with a CD player, so I shelled out $500 for one. I've had this stereo since last May, and I still can't figure out how to set the clock or preset stations. Volkswagen technology could not stop my car from exercising its "check engine light" once every three weeks. Even though the design techs included a cute warning light, my blood still boiled every time the light would come on proudly, and I made yet another pilgrimage to the dealership . . . on my day off. It would be nice if my car came equipped with one of those Global Positioning System things as well. I am really good at getting lost, and if I had one of these systems a year ago, I would not have found myself driving over both the Bay Bridge and the Golden Gate Bridge when I was supposed to be on the Richmond Bridge. (Ironically enough, I did this during the weekend that terrorists were supposed to be blowing up the Bay and Golden Gate Bridges.) And if I had had any passengers while tempting fate that day, I could have kept them distracted from the fact that we were lost (and possibly going to die) by letting them watch

6

RHETORICAL QUESTION indicates more examples to come

Examples presented in cluster: manual transmission and windows, after-market stereo, faulty engine light, no GPS

a movie on one of those in-car DVD players. But of course I don't have an in-car DVD player, so my hypothetical passengers would probably have been frantic.

No matter how much technology is out there, I seem to be getting through the day without most of it. It would seem hard to imagine someone else living without such modern conveniences, and, yes, at times I feel very primitive. However, I am slowly catching on to what's new out there even though incorporating every modern convenience into my day is out of the question. I am learning even though it is at a snail's pace. Hopefully I'll have it all figured out by the time cars fly, or else I will be walking.

7 •······ Final example: flying cars

THE ONION

ALL SEVEN DEADLY SINS COMMITTED AT CHURCH BAKE SALE

The *Onion* is a SATIRICAL newspaper that originated in Madison, home of the University of Wisconsin. In a typical issue, the paper pokes fun at everything from politics ("Obama Practices Looking-Off-Into-Future Pose") and American lifestyles ("TV Helps Build Valuable Looking Skills") to medicine ("Colonoscopy Offers Non-Fantastic Voyage through Human Body") and religion (which is what this selection is about—sort of). According to the Catholic Church, there are basically two types of sins: "venial" ones that are easily forgiven and "deadly" ones that, well, are not. In the fifth century, Pope Gregory the Great identified what he, and the Church ever since, took to be the seven worst of the worst: pride, envy, wrath, sloth, avarice (or greed), gluttony, and lust. As originally conceived, the seven deadlies are highly abstract concepts. In this tongue-in-cheek news release from a church bake sale in Gadsden, Alabama, the roving *Onion* reporter, who knows sin when he sees it, finds concrete, specific examples of each of them.

G ADSDEN, AL—The seven deadly sins—avarice, sloth, envy, lust, gluttony, pride, and wrath—were all committed Sunday during the twice-annual bake sale at St. Mary's of the Immaculate Conception Church.

Page 189 explains how to state the point of your example.

In total, 347 individual acts of sin were committed at the bake sale, with nearly every attendee committing at least one of the seven deadly sins as outlined by Gregory the Great in the Fifth Century.

"My cookies, cakes, and brownies are always the highlight of our church bake sales, and everyone says so," said parishioner Connie Barrett, 49, openly committing the sin of pride. "Sometimes, even I'm amazed by how well my goodies turn out."

Fellow parishioner Betty Wicks agreed.

"Every time I go past Connie's table, I just have to buy something," said the 245-pound Wicks, who commits the sin of gluttony at every St. Mary's bake sale, as well as most Friday nights at Old Country Buffet. "I simply can't help myself—it's all so delicious."

The popularity of Barrett's mouth-watering wares elicited the sin of envy in many of her fellow vendors.

"Connie has this fantastic book of recipes her grandmother gave her, and she won't share them with anyone," church organist Georgia Brandt said. "This year, I made white-chocolate blondies and thought they'd be a big hit. But most people just went straight to Connie's table, got what they wanted, and left. All the while, Connie just stood there with this look of smug satisfaction on her face. It took every ounce of strength in my body to keep from going over there and really telling her off."

While the sins of wrath and avarice were each committed dozens of times at the event, Barrett and longtime bake-sale rival Penny Cox brought them together in full force.

"Penny said she wanted to make a bet over whose table would make the most money," said Barrett, exhibiting avarice. "Whoever lost would have to sit in the dunk tank at the St. Mary's Summer Fun Festival. I figured it's for such a good cause, a little wager couldn't hurt. Besides, I always bring the church more money anyway, so I couldn't possibly lose."

Patti George (far right) commits the sin of envy as she eyes fellow parishioner Mary Hoelchst's suprior strawbery rhubarb pie.

Moments after agreeing to the wager, Cox became wrathful when Barrett,   10
the bake sale's co-chair, grabbed the best table location under the pretense of having to keep the coffee machine full. Cox attempted to exact revenge by reporting an alleged Barrett misdeed to the church's priest.

"I mentioned to Father Mark [O'Connor] that I've seen candles at Connie's   11
house that I wouldn't be surprised one bit if she stole from the church's storage closet," said Cox, who also committed the sin of sloth by forcing her daughter to set up and man her booth while she gossiped with friends. "Perhaps if he investigates this, by this time next year, Connie won't be co-chair of the bake sale and in her place we'll have someone who's willing to rotate the choice table spots."

The sin of lust also reared its ugly head at the bake sale, largely due to the   12
presence of Melissa Wyckoff, a shapely 20-year-old redhead whose family recently joined the church. While male attendees ogled Wyckoff, the primary object of lust for females was the personable, boyish Father Mark.

Though attendees' feelings of lust for Wyckoff and O'Connor were never 13
acted on, they did not go unnoticed.

"There's something not right about that Melissa Wyckoff," said envious 14
and wrathful bake-sale participant Jilly Brandon, after her husband Craig
offered Wyckoff one of her Rice Krispie treats to "welcome [her] to the parish."
"She might have just moved here from California, but that red dress of hers
should get her kicked out of the church."

According to St. Mary's treasurer Beth Ellen Coyle, informal church- 15
sponsored events are a notorious breeding ground for the seven deadly sins.

"Bake sales, haunted houses, pancake breakfasts . . . such church events 16
are rife with potential for sin," Coyle said. "This year, we had to eliminate the
'Guess Your Weight' booth from the annual church carnival because the envy
and pride had gotten so out of hand. Church events are about glorifying God,
not violating His word. If you want to do that, you're no better than that cheap
strumpet Melissa Wyckoff."

FOR DISCUSSION

. . . .

1. The *Onion* reporter gives bake-sale-specific EXAMPLES for each of the Deadly
   Sins. How well do you think these examples represent the sins they're meant to
   illustrate?

2. Statistics is the science of analyzing numerical examples. In all, says *Onion*
   reporter, parishioners at the St. Mary's bake sale committed "347 individual acts
   of sin" (2). Anything suspicious about these stats? How do you suppose they
   were determined?

3. All of the seven deadly sins are identified in the first paragraph of the *Onion's*
   spoof. In what order are they explained after that? Which one does the watchful
   reporter come back to at the end?

4. Which specific deadly sin is the only one unacted upon at the bake sale? Who
   inspired it?

STRATEGIES AND STRUCTURES

. . . .

1. Pope Gregory might object that the *Onion*'s examples are a bit trivial. But how CONCRETE and specific are they?

2. SATIRE is writing that makes fun of vice or folly for the PURPOSE of exposing and correcting it. To the extent that the *Onion* is satirizing the behavior of people at "church-sponsored events," what less-than-truly-deadly "sins" is the paper actually making fun of (15)?

3. A *spoof* is a gentle parody or mildly satirical imitation. What kind of writing or reporting is the *Onion* spoofing here? Who is the AUDIENCE for this spoof?

4. As a Catholic priest, "boyish Father Mark" would probably say that all the other deadly sins are examples of pride (12). How might pride be thought of as the overarchingly general "deadly sin"?

5. As a "news" story, this one has elements of NARRATIVE. What are some of them, specifically?

WORDS AND FIGURES OF SPEECH

. . . .

1. What, exactly, is a "strumpet" (16)?

2. *Deadly* (or *mortal*) sins are to be distinguished from *venial* sins. According to your dictionary, what kind of sins would be venial sins? Give several examples.

3. Give a SYNONYM for each of the following words: "avarice," "sloth," "gluttony," and "wrath" (1).

4. Another word for *pride* is *hubris*. What language does it derive from? What's the distinction between the two?

5. *Hypocrisy* is not one of the seven deadly sins, but how would you DEFINE it? Which of the St. Mary's parishioners might be said to commit *this* sin?

FOR WRITING

. . . .

1. Imagine a strip mall called the Seven Deadly Sins Shopping Center, where each item on Pope Gregory's list is represented by a store selling ordinary products

and services. Draw up a list of store names that would exemplify each of the seven deadlies—for example, Big Joe's Eats. You might also compose some signs or other advertising to place in the windows of each shop.

2. Using examples, write an essay entitled "All Seven Deadly Sins Committed at _____." Fill in the blank with any venue you choose—"School Cafeteria," for example, or "College Library." Give at least one example for each offense.

3. According to somebody's critical theory, the characters on Gilligan's Island each represent one of the seven deadly sins. If you've seen enough reruns of the show to have an opinion, write an essay either questioning or supporting this reading.

JANET WU

HOMEWARD BOUND

Janet Wu, a reporter for Boston television, was twelve years old when she first met her Chinese grandmother. Wu's father had escaped China during the communist revolution at the end of World War II, and for the next twenty-five years, because of strained relations between China and the United States, Chinese Americans were not allowed to return to their homeland. "Homeward Bound," first published in the *New York Times Magazine* in 1999, is about Wu's visits with a relative she did not know she had. In this essay, Wu looks at the vast differences between two cultures through a single, extended example—the ancient practice, now outlawed, of breaking and binding the feet of upper-class Chinese girls. These "lotus feet" were a symbol of status and beauty.

◇◈◇◈◇◈◇◈◇◈◇◈◇◈◇◈◇◈◇◈◇◈◇◈◇◈◇◈◇◈◇◈◇◈◇

M y grandmother has bound feet. Cruelly tethered since her birth, they   1
are like bonsai trees, miniature versions of what should have been. She is a relic even in China, where foot binding was first banned more than 80 years ago when the country could no longer afford a population that had to be carried. Her slow, delicate hobble betrays her age and the status she held and lost.

My own size 5 feet are huge in comparison. The marks and callouses they bear come from running and jumping, neither of which my grandmother has ever done. The difference between our feet reminds me of the incredible history we hold between us like living bookends. We stand like sentries on either side of a vast gulf.

For most of my childhood, I didn't even know she existed. My father was a young man when he left his family's village in northern China, disappearing into the chaos of the Japanese invasion and the Communist revolution[1] that followed. He fled to Taiwan and eventually made his way to America, alone. To me, his second child, it seemed he had no family or history other than his American-born wife and four children. I didn't know that he had been writing years of unanswered letters to China.

I was still a young girl when he finally got a response, and with it the news that his father and six of his seven siblings had died in those years of war and revolution. But the letter also contained an unexpected blessing: somehow his mother had survived. So 30 years after he left home, and in the wake of President Nixon's visit,[2] my father gathered us up and we rushed to China to find her.

I saw my grandmother for the very first time when I was 12. She was almost 80, surprisingly alien and shockingly small. I searched her wrinkled face for something familiar, some physical proof that we belonged to each other. She stared at me the same way. Did she feel cheated, I wondered, by the distance, by the time we had not spent together? I did. With too many lost years to reclaim, we had everything and nothing to say. She politely listened as I struggled with scraps of formal Chinese and smiled as I fell back on "Wo bu dong" ("I don't understand you"). And yet we communicated something strange and beautiful. I found it easy to love this person I had barely met.

---

1. The Japanese invasion of China began in the late 1930s and lasted until Japan surrendered to the Allied forces at the close of World War II. In the years following this surrender, the Chinese Nationalist and Communist parties battled for control, with the communists seizing power in 1949.

2. In 1972, Richard Nixon became the first U.S. president to meet with Communist leaders on Chinese soil, opening relations between countries that had been enemies since the revolution.

The second time I saw her I was 23, arriving in China on an indulgent post-graduate-school adventure, with a Caucasian boyfriend in tow. My grandmother sat on my hotel bed, shrunken and wise, looking as if she belonged in a museum case. She stroked my asymmetrically cropped hair. I touched her feet, and her face contorted with the memory of her childhood pain. "You are lucky," she said. We both understood that she was thinking of far more than the bindings that long ago made her cry. I wanted to share even the smallest part of her life's journey, but I could not conceive of surviving a dynasty and a revolution, just as she could not imagine my life in a country she had never seen. In our mutual isolation of language and experience, we could only gaze in wonder, mystified that we had come to be sitting together.

I last saw her almost five years ago. At 95, she was even smaller, and her frailty frightened me. I was painfully aware that I probably would never see her again, that I would soon lose this person I never really had. So I mentally logged every second we spent together and jockeyed with my siblings for the chance to hold her hand or touch her shoulder. Our departure date loomed like some kind of sentence. And when it came, she broke down, her face bowed into her gnarled hands. I went home, and with resignation awaited the inevitable news that she was gone.

But two months after that trip, it was my father who died. For me, his loss was doubly cruel: his death deprived me of both my foundation and the bridge to my faraway grandmother. For her, it was the second time she had lost him. For the 30 years they were separated, she had feared her son was dead. This time, there was no ambiguity, no hope. When she heard the news, my uncle later wrote us, she wept quietly.

When I hear friends complain about having to visit their nearby relatives, I think of how far away my grandmother is and how untouched our relationship remains by the modern age. My brief handwritten notes are agonizingly slow to reach her. When they do arrive, she cannot read them. I cannot call her. I cannot see, hear or touch her.

But last month my mother called to tell me to brush up on my Chinese. Refusing to let go of our tenuous connection to my father's family, she has decided to take us all back to China in October for my grandmother's 100th birthday. And so every night, I sit at my desk and study, thinking of her tiny doll-like feet, of the miles and differences that separate us, of the moments we'll share when we meet one last time. And I beg her to hold on until I get there.

FOR DISCUSSION

1. Janet Wu's feet are calloused from exercise. What does this difference between her feet and her grandmother's show about the differences in their lives?

2. Why does Wu touch her grandmother's feet in paragraph 6? What is her grandmother's response? What happens to the "vast gulf" between them (2)?

3. What is the CONCRETE EXAMPLE Wu's essay is organized around? How does this example illustrate the differences between her and her grandmother, and their connection as family? Refer to particular passages.

STRATEGIES AND STRUCTURES

1. Where does Wu mention her grandmother's feet for the last time in her essay? How does this mention serve as an example of bridging two disparate thoughts?

2. Wu is separated from her grandmother by culture, physical distance, and *time*. Point out several of the many references to time and the passage of time in her essay. How do these references help Wu to organize her essay?

3. Wu's NARRATIVE takes an unexpected turn in paragraph 8. What is it? How does the physical frailty of her grandmother contribute to the IRONY of this turn of events?

4. A big part of the cultural difference that separates Wu and her grandmother is *language*. List some of the examples Wu gives of this separation. Why do you think Wu says, in the last paragraph of her essay, that "every night, I sit at my desk and study" (10)?

5. Wu uses the example of her grandmother's bound feet as the basis of an extended COMPARISON AND CONTRAST. Besides feet, what is she comparing to what? What specific similarities and differences does she touch on? What other examples does she use?

WORDS AND FIGURES OF SPEECH

1. Explain the PUN(s), or play(s) on words, in Wu's title.

2. Wu compares her grandmother's feet to "bonsai trees" (1). What is a bonsai, and what do the grandmother's feet have in common with one?

3. Wu says her wrinkled, shrunken grandmother looks like she belongs in "a museum case" (6). Why? To what is she comparing her grandmother?

4. If Wu and her grandmother are "living bookends," what do they hold between them (2)? What connection(s) between books and "history" does Wu's use of this METAPHOR imply (2)?

5. When is Wu using her grandmother's bound feet as a metaphor, and when are the feet simply serving her as a literal example? Cite specific passages.

FOR WRITING

1. In a paragraph or two, give several examples of distinctive traits, gestures, or physical features shared by members of your family.

2. Write a personal narrative about a meeting between you and a relative or family friend that exemplifies both the differences separating you and the ties binding you together. Use lots of examples to illustrate those similarities and differences.

ALEX HORTON

METAL MEMORIALS

Alex Horton (b. 1985) is a native Texan and a U.S. Army veteran of the war in Iraq. In 2006, Horton started a blog, *Army of Dude*, as a way of keeping in touch with his family and telling them about Army life. Horton disliked writing in high school, but in the military, he says, "writing became my only creative out-let, a way to relay thoughts and experiences that I would never dare speak out loud. . . . This blog was a closely guarded secret." "Metal Memorials" is Hor-ton's Memorial Day post for May 31, 2010, written after he was back in school under the GI Bill. This tribute to a fallen comrade, Brian ("Chevy") Chevalier, also exemplifies one soldier's mixed feelings about memorials, whether marked by a public holiday, inscribed on a bracelet, or "emblazoned in the memories of those who called them brothers" (4).

❖⌄◇⌄❖⌄◇⌄❖⌄◇⌄❖⌄◇⌄❖⌄◇⌄❖⌄◇⌄❖⌄◇⌄❖⌄◇⌄❖⌄◇⌄❖⌄◇⌄❖⌄◇⌄❖⌄◇⌄❖

"Hey man, just so you know, I'm going to set this thing off."   1

    I don't have a metal plate in my head or shrapnel in my legs, but   2
I carry with me something that might as well be lodged deep under my skin.
After Vietnam, soldiers and civilians alike would wear bracelets etched with the
names of prisoners of war so their memory would live on even if they never

came home. Veterans of the wars in Iraq and Afghanistan continued the practice, but with a twist. The same bracelets are adorned with the names of friends killed in action. The date and the place are also included as a testament to where they took their last steps. One of the first things my platoon did after coming home was order memorial bracelets from the few websites that specialize in military memorabilia. You don't even have to type in the name or the date; their system uses the DOD[1] casualty list. All you have to do is filter by name and a software-aided laser will burn the selection onto an aluminum or steel bracelet. What emerges out of this casual and disinterested practice is jewelry teeming with the amount of love and commitment found in ten wedding rings.

Every trip to the airport has the same outcome: additional security checks   3
and a pat-down from a TSA agent. I tell them it's the bracelet that the metal detector shrieks at. "Can you take it off?" is always the question. "I don't want to take it off" is always the answer. To some screeners my answer is a poke in the eye of their authority, a wrench in the system of their daily routine. Others recognize the bracelet and give me a gentle nod and a quick pat-down. I suspect they have encountered other veterans like me and realize the futility of asking to have it removed. In a glass booth at the security gate is where I most often get the question, "Who's on the bracelet?" Those who realize the significance of it usually want to know the name. I stare down and rub my fingers over the lettering. "Brian Chevalier, but we called him Chevy."

At times the memorial bracelets seem almost redundant. The names of   4
the fallen are written on steel and skin, but are they not also carved into the hearts of men? Are the faces of the valiant not emblazoned in the memories of those who called them brothers? No amount of ink or steel can be used to represent what those days signify. My bracelet says "14 March 2007," but it does not describe the blazing heat that day, or the smell of open sewers trampled underfoot, or the sight of a Stryker,[2] overturned and smoke-filled as the school adjacent exploded under tremendous fire. It was as if God chose to end

1. Department of Defense.
2. Eight-wheeled armored vehicle used by the U.S. Army.

the world within one city block. When Chevy was lovingly placed into a body bag under exploding RPGs[3] and machine gun tracers, worlds ended. Others began.

The concept of Memorial Day nearly approaches superfluous ritual to some veterans. It's absurd to ask a combat veteran to take out a single day to remember those who fell in battle, as if the other 364 days were not marked by their memories in one way or another. I try to look at pictures of my friends, both alive and dead, at least once a day to remember their smiles or the way they wore their kits. I talk to them online and send emails and texts and, on rare occasions, visit them in person. We drink and laugh and recall the old days and tell the same war stories everyone has heard a thousand times but still manage to produce streams of furious laughter. I get the same feeling with them; Memorial Day does not begin or end on a single day. It ebbs and flows in torrents of memory, sometimes to a crippling degree. Most of us have become talented at hiding our service and we safeguard the moments when we become awash in memories like March 14. The bracelet is the only physical reminder of the tide we find ourselves in.

See p. 191 for tips on using concrete examples to explain abstract concepts like memorial and memorialize.

Perhaps it's best to let civilians hold onto Memorial Day and hope they use the time to reflect wisely. A time to remember old friends or distant relatives whom they did not necessarily serve with, but still honor their sacrifice. Not just soldiers are touched by war. Chevy was a father and a son, and his loss not only rippled through the platoon and company but a small town in Georgia. The day serves as a reminder that there are men and women who have only come back as memories. Maybe the reflection on those who did not return is a key to helping civilians bridge the gap with veterans. Occasionally my bracelet spurs conversations with friends and co-workers who did not know I was in the army or deployed to Iraq. I still don't feel completely comfortable answering their questions but I'm always happy to talk about the name on my wrist. His name was Brian Chevalier, but we called him Chevy.

---

3. Rocket-propelled grenades.

FOR DISCUSSION

. . . .

1. According to Alex Horton, why does Memorial Day seem "absurd" to some military veterans (5)? What does Horton himself think about the value and purpose of the day?

2. In addition to wearing "metal memorials," how else do Horton and his fellow veterans remember and celebrate their comrades?

3. Why and under what circumstances might Horton and other veterans sometimes strive to "become talented at hiding" their service and memories (5)? Is this caution justified? Why or why not?

STRATEGIES AND STRUCTURES

. . . .

1. Horton begins his post with a bit of DIALOGUE, presumably spoken by his friend just before he was killed. What do these words exemplify about the speaker? Is this a fitting way to introduce what follows? Explain.

2. Like his bracelet, Horton's post is a tribute to the memory of Brian Chevalier. What point about memorials in general is he also making by citing the EXAMPLE of his lost friend? Explain.

3. Where and how does Horton discuss the limitations of even the most lovingly crafted memorials? What are some of them?

4. An example is an individual chosen to represent a whole group. How and how well has Horton chosen his main example? Is this single example sufficient to make his point? Explain.

WORDS AND FIGURES OF SPEECH

. . . .

1. A "testament" is something that serves as tangible proof (2). Why might Horton have choosen this word to DESCRIBE the inscription on his bracelet?

2. "Emblazoned" refers, literally, to heraldic figures inscribed or painted on a shield, banner, or other surface (4). Is Horton speaking METAPHORICALLY here? Explain.

3. Why do you think Horton ends his post by repeating a name and phrase he has used many times before? Is this an effective ending? Why or why not?

FOR WRITING

· ·

1. Write the text you would inscribe on a bracelet or other memorial to someone you wish to remember.

2. Using specific examples of your own, write an essay illustrating the true meaning, as you see it, of Memorial Day, Thanksgiving, New Year's Day, or some other holiday or public "ritual" (5). If you feel that even your best examples do not fully represent your subject, be sure to explain how and why they fall short.

RICHARD LEDERER

ENGLISH IS A CRAZY LANGUAGE

Richard Lederer (b. 1938) taught for many years at St. Paul's, a boarding school in New Hampshire. He retired in 1989 to carry on his "mission as a user-friendly English teacher" by writing and speaking extensively and humorously about the peculiarities of the English language. He coined the term *verbivore* to describe those who, like himself, "devour words." Lederer is the author of *Anguished English* (1994) and *Get Thee to a Punnery* (2006), among many other books. This essay, made up of one rapid-fire example after another, is the opening chapter of his best-selling *Crazy English* (1989).

English is the most widely spoken language in the history of our planet, used in some way by at least one out of every seven human beings around the globe. Half of the world's books are written in English, and the majority of international telephone calls are made in English. English is the language of over 60 percent of the world's radio programs, many of them beamed, ironically, by the Russians, who know that to win friends and influence nations, they're best off using English. More than 70 percent of international mail is written and addressed in English, and 80 percent of all computer text is stored in English.

English has acquired the largest vocabulary of all the world's languages, perhaps as many as two million words, and has generated one of the noblest bodies of literature in the annals of the human race.

Nonetheless, it is now time to face the fact that English is a crazy language.   2

In the crazy English language, the blackbird hen is brown, blackboards can be blue or green, and blackberries are green and then red before they are ripe. Even if blackberries were really black and blueberries really blue, what are strawberries, cranberries, elderberries, huckleberries, raspberries, boysenberries, mulberries, and gooseberries supposed to look like?   3

For tips on when and how to use multiple examples like these, see p. 190.

To add to the insanity, there is no butter in buttermilk, no egg in eggplant, no grape in grapefruit, neither worms nor wood in wormwood, neither pine nor apple in pineapple, neither peas nor nuts in peanuts, and no ham in a hamburger. (In fact, if somebody invented a sandwich consisting of a ham patty in a bun, we would have a hard time finding a name for it.) To make matters worse, English muffins weren't invented in England, french fries in France, or danish pastries in Denmark. And we discover even more culinary madness in the revelations that sweetmeat is candy, while sweetbread, which isn't sweet, is made from meat.   4

In this unreliable English tongue, greyhounds aren't always grey (or gray); panda bears and koala bears aren't bears (they're marsupials); a woodchuck is a groundhog, which is not a hog; a horned toad is a lizard; glowworms are fireflies, but fireflies are not flies (they're beetles); ladybugs and lightning bugs are also beetles (and to propagate, a significant proportion of ladybugs must be male); a guinea pig is neither a pig nor from Guinea (it's a South American rodent); and a titmouse is neither mammal nor mammaried.   5

Language is like the air we breathe. It's invisible, inescapable, indispensable, and we take it for granted. But when we take the time, step back, and listen to the sounds that escape from the holes in people's faces and explore the paradoxes and vagaries of English, we find that hot dogs can be cold, darkrooms can be lit, homework can be done in school, nightmares can take place in broad daylight, while morning sickness and daydreaming can take place at night, tomboys are girls, midwives can be men, hours—especially happy hours and rush hours—can last longer than sixty minutes, quicksand works *very* slowly, boxing   6 rings are square, silverware can be made of plastic and tablecloths of paper, most telephones are dialed by being punched (or pushed?), and most bathrooms don't have any baths in them. In fact, a dog can go to the bathroom under a tree—no bath, no room; it's still going to the bathroom. And doesn't it seem at least a little bizarre that we go to the bathroom in order to go to the bathroom?

Why is it that a woman can man a station but a man can't woman one, that a man can father a movement but a woman can't mother one, and that a king rules a kingdom but a queen doesn't rule a queendom? How did all those Renaissance men reproduce when there don't seem to have been any Renaissance women?

A writer is someone who writes, and a stinger is something that stings. But fingers don't fing, grocers don't groce, hammers don't ham, and humdingers don't humding. If the plural of *tooth* is *teeth*, shouldn't the plural of *booth* be *beeth*? One goose, two geese—so one moose, two meese? One index, two indices—one Kleenex, two Kleenices? If people ring a bell today and rang a bell yesterday, why don't we say that they flang a ball? If they wrote a letter, perhaps they also bote their tongue. If the teacher taught, why isn't it also true that the preacher praught? Why is it that the sun shone yesterday while I shined my shoes, that I treaded water and then trod on soil, and that I flew out to see a World Series game in which my favorite player flied out?

If we conceive a conception and receive at a reception, why don't we grieve a greption and believe a beleption? If a horsehair mat is made from the hair of horses and a camel's hair brush from the hair of camels, from what is a mohair coat made? If a vegetarian eats vegetables, what does a humanitarian eat? If a firefighter fights fire, what does a freedom fighter fight? If a weightlifter lifts weights, what does a shoplifter lift? If *pro* and *con* are opposites, is congress the opposite of progress?

Sometimes you have to believe that all English speakers should be committed to an asylum for the verbally insane. In what other language do people drive in a parkway and park in a driveway? In what other language do people recite at a play and play at a recital? In what other language do privates eat in the general mess and generals eat in the private mess? In what other language do men get hernias and women get hysterectomies? In what other language do people ship by truck and send cargo by ship? In what other language can your nose run and your feet smell?

How can a slim chance and a fat chance be the same, "what's going on?" 11
and "what's coming off?" be the same, and a bad licking and a good licking be
the same, while a wise man and a wise guy are opposites? How can sharp speech
and blunt speech be the same and *quite a lot* and *quite a few* the same, while
overlook and *oversee* are opposites? How can the weather be hot as hell one day
and cold as hell the next?

If *button* and *unbutton* and *tie* and *untie* are opposites, why are *loosen* and 12
unloosen and *ravel* and *unravel* the same? If *bad* is the opposite of *good*, *hard* the
opposite of *soft*, and *up* the opposite of *down*, why are *badly* and *goodly*, *hardly* and
softly, and *upright* and *downright* not opposing pairs? If harmless actions are the
opposite of harmful actions, why are shameless and shameful behavior the same
and pricey objects less expensive than priceless ones? If appropriate and inappropriate remarks and passable and impassable mountain trails are opposites, why
are flammable and inflammable materials, heritable and inheritable property,
and passive and impassive people the same and valuable objects less treasured
than invaluable ones? If *uplift* is the same as *lift up*, why are *upset* and *set up*
opposite in meaning? Why are *pertinent* and *impertinent*, *canny* and *uncanny*,
and *famous* and *infamous* neither opposites nor the same? How can *raise* and
raze and *reckless* and *wreckless* be opposites when each pair contains the same
sound?

Why is it that when the sun or the moon or the stars are out, they are vis- 13
ible, but when the lights are out, they are invisible, and that when I wind up my
watch, I start it, but when I wind up this essay, I shall end it?

English is a crazy language. 14

FOR DISCUSSION

· ·

1. Most of the time, Richard Lederer is illustrating his main point that "English is
   a crazy language" (2). But what does he say about its widespread influence?
   What EXAMPLES does he give?

2. Do you think English is as crazy as Lederer says it is? Why or why not? Give
   several examples to support your opinion.

3. How seriously do you think Lederer actually intends for us to take the general proposition of his essay? Why do you think he gives so many crazy examples?

4. Linguists hold that the meanings of words are arbitrary, determined by convention rather than by any innate qualities. Do you think the examples in Lederer's essay represent this principle? Refer to specific passages in his essay that support your position.

5. List several examples of your own of the craziness of the English language.

STRATEGIES AND STRUCTURES

1. What is the PURPOSE of the opening paragraph of Lederer's essay? How does the opening paragraph color the rest of what he says about the craziness of the English language?

2. Lederer's essay is made up almost entirely of clusters of examples. What do the examples in paragraph 3 have in common? Are the examples in paragraph 4 more like those in paragraph 3 or paragraph 5? Explain.

3. In paragraph 8, Lederer pretends to be upset with irregular verbs and irregular plurals of nouns. Which are examples of which? Make a list of his examples for both categories.

4. Which examples have to do primarily with gender? What connects all the examples in paragraph 12?

5. In paragraph 6, Lederer refers to two related aspects of the English language that all of his examples might be said to illustrate. What are these aspects? Where else in his essay does Lederer actually name the aspects of English he is exemplifying?

6. Lederer gives his essay the form of a logical ARGUMENT. The proposition he intends to prove is stated in paragraph 2. Where does he state it again as a conclusion? Is the argument in between primarily INDUCTIVE (reasoning from specific examples to a general conclusion) or DEDUCTIVE (reasoning from general principles to a more specific conclusion)? Explain.

WORDS AND FIGURES OF SPEECH

1. In American English (speaking of contradictions), a *rant* is a form of vehement speech; in British English (speaking of redundancies), a *rant* can also mean an outburst of wild merriment. Which meaning or meanings apply to Lederer's essay?

2. A *misnomer* is a term that implies a meaning or interpretation that is actually untrue or inaccurate—"koala bear," for example. Choose one of the following misnomers that Lederer mentions and explain why you think the object it refers to has this inaccurate name—and why the name persists: "eggplant," "peanut," "french fries," "horned toad," "firefly," "guinea pig" (4, 5).

3. How does your dictionary DEFINE the word "vagaries" (6)? How is it related to the word "vagabonds"?

4. Lederer "winds up" his essay in paragraph 13. Could he be said, just as accurately, to "wind it down"?

FOR WRITING

1. Write an essay illustrating the craziness of some language other than English—one you speak and/or have studied. For example, one way to say you're welcome in French is "Je vous en prie," which means, literally, "I beg of you."

2. For all its "craziness," Lederer asserts that "English is the most widely spoken language in the history of our planet" (1). Write an essay that supports or contests this proposition. Be sure to include sufficient examples of who uses the language, where, and for what purposes.

JOANNA WEISS

HAPPY MEALS AND OLD SPICE GUY

Joanna Weiss (b. 1972) is a reporter and columnist for the *Boston Globe* who writes mostly about gender and pop culture. A 1994 graduate of Harvard, she recently published a satiric novel, *Milkshake* (2011), about "breastfeeding, politics, and female competition." In this *Globe* column from 2010, Weiss focuses on two examples—McDonald's Happy Meals and Proctor and Gamble's "Old Spice Guy"—of the advertising and marketing strategies of large corporations as they learn to deal with social media such as *YouTube* and *Twitter*. Are the new techniques working with consumers? "It's too early to know," says Weiss, "if we're buying or not."

〰〰〰〰〰〰〰〰〰〰〰〰〰〰〰〰〰〰〰〰〰〰〰〰〰〰〰〰〰〰

In the laudable quest to fight childhood obesity, it's hard to get kids to exercise, control their portions, and hold the salt. It's easy to blame the Happy Meal toy. This spring, officials in Santa Clara, California, banned toy giveaways with kids' fast-food meals. Last month, the Center for Science in the Public Interest threatened to sue McDonald's, saying the toys are a deceptive marketing practice.

Of course, there has been backlash, and not just from kids who fear they might miss out on "Last Airbender" figurines. A group of competing Save-The-Happy-Meal-Toys *Facebook* pages has sprung up, each with a fan base of nostalgic hipsters. The Happy Meal, it turns out, isn't just a bundle of adorably packaged calories. It's a bundle of adorably packaged calories that represents childhood.

There's something to be said for the power of marketing, the ways it can influence us even when we think we're too smart and too cool. Notre Dame University marketing professor Carol Phillips says that when her students brag that they aren't susceptible to advertising, she points to their shoes, their hats, and their computers.

And she tells them that marketing isn't limited to ads; it's packaging, store placement, associations. And entertainment, too, as in last weekend's brilliant Old Spice social media campaign, in which the suave and shirtless "Old Spice

The manly man on a white horse in this ad from Procter & Gamble's 2010 Old Spice campaign is a good example of advertising informed by marketing research, which shows that men's body wash is usually purchased by wives and girlfriends.

Guy" posted *YouTube* responses to questions asked through *Twitter*. He offered image advice to President Obama. He helped a guy propose to his girlfriend. He might be the most beloved man in America, even though we know he's trying to sell us body wash.

It's too early to know if we're buying or not, though some old-school marketing gurus have noted that sales of Old Spice are down. For all of its power, advertising has its limits—and ads are a reflection of the marketplace as much as they're an influence. Ad agencies do assiduous research into what people already want; "Old Spice Guy" came about because Procter & Gamble understood that women buy most of their husbands' body wash, and presumably want it to smell manly.

For advice on when and how to use extended examples, see p. 190.

McDonald's is buffeted by market forces, too, which is why the fast-food giant has taken some baby steps into the wholesome-food game. One way the chain turned sluggish sales around in the early 2000s, Phillips notes, is by putting a few salads on the menu.

Campaigns against obesity have affected the Happy Meal, too: In 2006, the *Los Angeles Times* reported that Disney executives were balking over Happy Meal tie-ins, in part because they feared an association with fatty food. Today, the main Happy Meals web page mentions fries and soft drinks, but only shows pictures of lowfat milk and apples.

Is it bait-and-switch advertising? Sure. And McDonald's could be far more aggressive in pushing apples over fries in actual stores. But at this point, are parents really unaware that French fries aren't a health food?

The anti-Happy Meal types prefer to paint parents as wimps, powerless against a corporate marketing campaign. One anti-Ronald McDonald polemic, issued by a group called Corporate Accountability International, says McDonald's "undermines parental values" and creates "a fundamental restructuring of the family dynamic." The evidence: "Every time a parent has to say no to a child, it's another let down, another way that a parent has to feel bad about not making that child happy."

Well, my kids don't like it when I tell them they can't play with knives, but I don't let it get to me. I also understand that the secret to survival in an ad-heavy world isn't avoiding marketing, but understanding it. Kids can be taught that what's on an ad isn't necessarily what they need. And the power of ads can be harnessed for good. If a *YouTube* video can make us talk about Old Spice, the right viral campaign could boost the market power of the nectarine.

A healthy lifestyle, after all, has clear appeal, which a clever marketer   11
could surely harness. Today, kids are lured by the Happy Meal in all of its weight-adding splendor. But after a few years, isn't it likely they'll want to look like Old Spice Guy, instead?

FOR DISCUSSION

1. Joanna Weiss focuses on two main EXAMPLES—McDonald's Happy Meals and Procter & Gamble's bare-chested Old Spice Guy. What do they exemplify about the buying habits of modern consumers?

2. The marketing of fast food, body wash, and other consumer products, says Weiss, is not limited to advertising. What else does she think it entails, according to the marketing experts she cites?

3. Retail giants like Procter & Gamble are always looking for new ways to sell their products. What are some of them, as exemplified by the Old Spice marketing campaign?

4. What does Weiss mean when she says that "the secret to survival in an ad-heavy world isn't avoiding marketing, but understanding it" (10). Do you agree? Why or why not?

STRATEGIES AND STRUCTURES

1. Procter & Gamble uses the Old Spice Guy to suggest who might need their body wash. Weiss uses him as an example of "a healthy lifestyle" (11). For what AUDI-ENCES and PURPOSES, respectively?

2. What point is Weiss making with her don't-play-with-knives example (10)? With the example of the "nectarine" (10)?

3. Weiss says it's "too early" to tell what EFFECT the Procter & Gamble campaign will have on the sale of Old Spice products (5). Where and how does she explain what CAUSED the company to launch this particular campaign?

4. According to Weiss, the Old Spice campaign exemplifies the "limits" of advertising (5). How and how well does she use this example to make her point?

5. Weiss uses a number of specific examples to show "the power of marketing," including its power to deceive (3). How and where does she also construct an ARGUMENT about harnessing that power to do "good" (10)?

WORDS AND FIGURES OF SPEECH

. . . .

1. Why does Weiss ask if parents are "really unaware that French fries aren't a health food" (8)? Where else does she use RHETORICAL QUESTIONS in her essay? For what purpose?

2. What is "bait-and-switch advertising" (8)? Why is it called that?

3. Why does Weiss use terms like "wimps" and "ad-heavy" when referring to attitudes toward consumer products (9, 10)?

FOR WRITING

. . . .

1. Choose an advertisement for a product aimed at children and write a paragraph or two explaining how you would use that ad as an example to show young consumers that "what's on an ad isn't necessarily what they need" (10).

2. Write an exemplification essay showing typical marketing strategies and techniques that companies use to successfully (or unsuccessfully) sell their products. Choose your examples from ad campaigns that you find especially effective (or misdirected).

DAVID SEDARIS

LAUGH, KOOKABURRA

David Sedaris (b. 1956) grew up in the suburbs of Raleigh, North Carolina, the second of six siblings, including the actress Amy Sedaris, with whom he illicitly sang the Kookaburra song at age eleven and for which he was duly punished by his father, Lou. In 1992, Sedaris made a name for himself with the *SantaLand Diaries*, a hilarious account of his adventures as a Christmas elf at Macy's that he read on National Public Radio. Sedaris's collections of essays—from *Barrel Fever* (1994) to *Me Talk Pretty One Day* (2000) and *When You Are Engulfed in Flames* (2008)—have all been bestsellers. His most recent collection is *Squirrel-Seeks Chipmunk* (2010). In "Laugh, Kookaburra" (from the *New Yorker* magazine, 2009), Sedaris writes about a trip to Australia with his partner, Hugh Hamrick. How to feed raw duck meat to an Australian kingfisher, or kookaburra, is just one example of what he learned about a faraway place. Many of his examples, however, hit closer to home.

I've been to Australia twice so far, but according to my father I've never actu-   1
ally seen it. He made this observation at the home of my cousin Joan, whom
he and I visited just before Christmas last year, and it came on the heels of an

equally aggressive comment. "Well," he said, "David's a better *reader* than he is a writer." This from someone who hasn't opened a book since *Dave Stockton's Putt to Win* in 1996. He's never been to Australia, either. Never even come close.

"No matter," he told me. "In order to see the country, you have to see the countryside, and you've only been to Sydney." 2

"And Melbourne. And Brisbane," I said. "And I have too gone into the country." 3

"Like hell you have." 4

"All right," I said. "Let's get Hugh on the phone. He'll tell you. He'll even send you pictures." 5

Joan and her family live in Binghamton, New York. They don't see my father and me that often, so it was pretty lousy to sit at their table, he and I bickering like an old married couple. Ashamed by the bad impression we were making, I dropped the countryside business, and as my dad moved on to other people's shortcomings I thought back to the previous summer, and my twenty-three-hour flight from London to Sydney. I was in Australia on business, and because someone else was paying for the ticket, and it would be possible to stop in Japan on the way home, Hugh joined me. This is not to put Australia down, but he'd already gone once before. Then, too, spend that much time on a plane and you're entitled to a whole new world when you step off at the other end—the planet Mercury, say, or, at the very least, Mexico City. For an American, though, Australia seems pretty familiar: same wide streets, same office towers. It's Canada in a thong, or that's the initial impression. 6

I hate to admit it, but my dad was right about the countryside. Hugh and I didn't see much of it, but we wouldn't have seen anything were it not for a woman named Pat, who was born in Melbourne and has lived there for most of her life. We'd met her a few years earlier, in Paris, where she'd come to spend a mid-July vacation. Over drinks in our living room, her face dewed with sweat, she taught us the term "shout," as in "I'm shouting lunch." This means that you're treating, and that you don't want any lip about it. "You can also say, 'It's my shout,' or, 'I'll shout the next round,'" she told us. 7

We kept in touch after her visit, and when my work was done, and I was given a day and a half to spend as I liked, Pat offered herself as a guide. On that 8 first afternoon, she showed us around Melbourne, and shouted coffee. The following morning, she picked us up at our hotel, and drove us into what she called "the bush." I expected a wasteland of dust and human bones, but it was nothing like that. When Australians say "the bush," they mean the woods. The forest.

First, though, we had to get out of Melbourne, and drive beyond the seemingly endless suburbs. It was August, the dead of winter, and so we had the windows rolled up. The homes we passed were made of wood, many with high fences around the back yards. They didn't look exactly like American houses, but I couldn't quite identify the difference. Was it the roofs? I wondered. The siding? Pat was driving, and as we passed the turnoff for a shopping center she invited us to picture a four-burner stove. 9

"Gas or electric?" Hugh asked, and she said that it didn't matter. 10

This was not a real stove but a symbolic one, used to prove a point at a management seminar she'd once attended. "One burner represents your family, one is your friends, the third is your health, and the fourth is your work." The gist, she said, was that in order to be successful you have to cut off one of your burners. And in order to be *really* successful you have to cut off two. 11

Pat has her own business, a good one that's allowing her to retire at fifty-five. She owns three houses, and two cars, but, even without the stuff, she seems like a genuinely happy person. And that alone constitutes success. 12

I asked which two burners she had cut off, and she said that the first to go had been family. After that, she switched off her health. "How about you?" 13

I thought for a moment, and said that I'd cut off my friends. "It's nothing to be proud of, but after meeting Hugh I quit making an effort." 14

"And what else?" she asked. 15

"Health, I guess." 16

Hugh's answer was work. 17

"And?" 18

"Just work," he said. 19

I asked Pat why she'd cut off her family, and with no trace of bitterness she talked about her parents, both severe alcoholics. They drank away their jobs and credit, and because they were broke they moved a lot, most often in the 20 middle of the night. This made it hard to have a pet, though for a short time Pat and her sister managed to own a sheep. It was an old, beat-up ram they named Mr. Preston. "He was lovely and good-natured, until my father sent him off to be shorn," Pat said. "When he returned, there were bald patches and horrible deep cuts, like stab wounds, in his skin. Then we moved to an apartment, and had to get rid of him." She looked at her hands on the steering wheel. "Poor old Mr. Preston. I hadn't thought about him in years."

It was around this time that we finally entered the bush. Hugh pointed out the window, at a lump of dirty fur lying beside a fallen tree, and Pat carolled, "Roadkill!" Then she pulled over, so we could take a closer look. Since leaving Melbourne, we'd been climbing higher into the foothills. The temperature had dropped, and there were graying patches of snow on the ground. I had on a sweater and a jacket, but they weren't quite enough, and I shivered as we walked toward the body, and saw that it was a . . . what, exactly? "A teen-age kangaroo?"

"A wallaby," Pat corrected me.

The thing had been struck but not run over. It hadn't decomposed, or been disfigured, and I was surprised by the shoddiness of its coat. It was as if you'd bred a rabbit with a mule. Then there was the tail, which reminded me of a lance.

"Hugh," I called. "Come here and look at the wallaby."

It's his belief that in marveling at a dead animal on the roadside you may as well have killed it yourself—not accidentally but on purpose, cackling, most likely, as you ran it down. Therefore, he stayed in the car.

"It's your loss," I called, and a great cloud of steam issued from my mouth.

Our destination that afternoon was a place called Daylesford, which looked, when we arrived, more like a movie set than like an actual working town. The buildings on the main street were two stories tall, and made of wood, like buildings in the Old West, but brightly painted. Here was the shop selling handmade soaps shaped like petit fours. Here was the fudgery, the jammery, your source for moisturizer. If Dodge City had been founded and maintained by homosexuals, this is what it might have looked like. "The spas are fantastic," Pat said, and she parked the car in front of a puppet shop. From there we walked down a slight hill, passing a flock of sulfur-crested cockatoos, just milling about, pulling worms from the front lawn of a bed-and-breakfast. This was the moment when familiarity slipped away, and Australia seemed not just distant but impossibly foreign. "Will you look at that," I said.

It was Pat who had made the lunch reservation. The restaurant was   28
attached to a hotel, and on arriving we were seated beside a picture window. The view was of a wooden deck and, immediately beyond it, a small lake. On a sunny day, it was probably blinding, but the winter sky was like brushed aluminum. The water beneath it had the same dull sheen, and its surface reflected nothing.

Even before the menus were handed out, you could see what sort of a place   29
this was. Order the pork and it might resemble a rough-hewn raft, stranded by tides on a narrow beach of polenta. Fish might come with shredded turnips or a pabulum of coddled fruit. The younger an ingredient, the more highly it was valued, thus the baby chicken, the baby spinach, the newborn asparagus, each pale stalk as slender as a fang.

As always in a fancy restaurant, I asked Hugh to order for me. "Whatever   30
you think," I told him. "Just so long as there's no chocolate in it."

He and Pat weighed our options, and I watched the hostess seat a party of   31
eight. Bringing up the rear was a woman in her mid-thirties, pretty, and with a baby on her shoulder. Its back was covered with a shawl, but to judge from the size it looked extremely young—a month old, tops.

Keep it away from the chef, I thought.   32

A short while later, I noticed that the child hadn't shifted position. Its   33
mother was running her hand over its back, almost as if she were feeling for a switch, and when the top of the shawl fell away I saw that this was not a baby but a baby doll.

"*Psssst,*" I whispered, and when Pat raised her eyes I directed them to the   34
other side of the room.

"Is that normal in Australia?" I asked.   35

"Maybe it's a grieving thing," she offered. "Maybe she lost a baby in   36
childbirth and this is helping her to work through it."

There's a definite line between looking and staring, and after I was caught crossing it I turned toward the window. On the highest rail of the deck was a wooden platform, and standing upon it, looking directly into my eyes, was what I knew to be a kookaburra. This thing was as big as a seagull, but squatter, squarer, and all done up in earth tones, the complete spectrum from beige to dark walnut. When seen full on, the feathers atop his head looked like brush-cut hair, and that gave him a brutish, almost conservative look. If owls were the professors of the avian kingdom, then kookaburras, I thought, might well be the gym teachers.

A Laughing Kookaburra

When the waitress arrived, I pointed out the window and asked her a half-dozen questions, all of them fear-based. "Oh," she said, "that bird's not going to hurt anybody." She took our orders and then she must have spoken to one of the waiters. He was a tall fellow, college age, and he approached our table with a covered bowl in his hands. I assumed that it was an appetizer, but it seemed instead that it was for the kookaburra. "Would you like to step outside and feed him?" he asked.

I wanted to say that between the wallaby and the baby doll I was already overstimulated, but how often in life do you get such an offer? That's how I found myself on the deck, holding a bowl of raw duck meat cut into slender strips. At the sight of it, the bird stood up and flew onto my arm, which buckled slightly beneath the weight.

"Don't be afraid," the waiter said, and he talked to the kookaburra in a soothing, respectful voice, the way you might to a child with a switchblade in his hand. For that's what this thing's beak was—a serious weapon. I held a strip of raw duck, and after yanking it from my fingers the bird flew back to the railing. Then he took the meat and began slamming it against his wooden platform. *Whap, whap, whap.* Over and over, as if he were tenderizing it.

"This is what he'd do in the wild with snakes and lizards and such," the 41
waiter said. "He thinks it's still alive, see. He thinks he's killing it."

The kookaburra must have slammed the meat against the wooden plat- 42
form a good ten times. Only then did he swallow it, and look up, expectantly,
for more.

I took another strip from the bowl, and the action repeated itself. *Whap,* 43
whap, whap. On or about his third helping, I got used to the feel of a bird on my
arm, and started thinking about other things, starting with the word "kookaburra." I first heard it in the fifth grade, when our music teacher went on an
Australian kick. She taught us to sing "Waltzing Matilda," "Tie Me Kangaroo
Down, Sport," and what we called, simply, "Kookaburra." I'd never heard such
craziness in my life. The first song, for instance, included the words "jum-
buck," "billabong," "swagman," and "tucker bag," none of which were ever
explained. The more nonsensical the lyric, the harder it was to remember, and
that, most likely, is why I retained the song about the kookaburra—it was less
abstract than the others.

I recall that after school that day I taught it to my sister Amy, who must 44
have been in the first grade at the time. We sang it in the car, we sang it at the
table, and then, one night, we sang it in her bed, the two of us lying side by side
and rocking back and forth. "Kookaburra sits in the old gum tree . . ."

We'd been at it for half an hour, when the door flung open. "What the hell is 45
going on?" It was our father, one hand resting, teapot style, on his hip, and the
other—what would be the spout—formed into a fist. He was dressed in his
standard around-the-house outfit, which is to say, his underpants. No matter
the season, he wore them without a shirt or socks, the way a toddler might pad
about in a diaper. For as long as any of us could remember, this was the way it
went: he returned home from work and stepped out of his slacks, sighing with
relief, as if they were oppressive, like high heels. All said, my father looked good
in his underpants, better than the guys in the Penney's catalogue, who were, in
my opinion, consistently weak in the leg department. Silhouetted in the doorway,

he resembled a wrestler. Maybe not one in tip-top condition, but he was closer than any of the other dads on our street. "It's one o'clock in the morning, for God's sake. David, get to your room."

Lou Sedaris claiming it was 1 A.M. meant that it was, at best, ten-thirty. Still, though, there was no point in arguing. Down in the basement, I went to my room and he resumed his position in front of the TV. Within a few minutes he was snoring, and I crept back upstairs to join Amy for another twenty rounds. "Kookaburra sits in the old gum tree, merry merry king of the bush is he—"

It didn't take long for our father to rally. "Did I not tell you to go to your room?"

What would strike me afterward was the innocence of it. If I had children and they stayed up late, singing a song about a bird, I believe I would find it charming. "I knew I had those two for a reason," I think I'd say to myself. I might go so far as to secretly record them, and submit the tape in a My Kids Are Cuter Than Yours competition. My dad, by contrast, clearly didn't see it that way, which was strange to me. It's not like we were ruining his TV reception. He couldn't even hear us from that distance, so what did he have to complain about? "All right, sonny, I'm giving you ten seconds. One. Two . . ."

I guess what he resented was being dismissed. Had our mother told us to shut up, we'd probably have done it. He, on the other hand, sitting around in his underpants—it just didn't seem that important.

At the count of six, I pushed back the covers. "I'm going," I spat, and once again I followed my father downstairs.

Ten minutes later, I was back. Amy cleared a space for me, and we picked up where we had left off. "Laugh, Kookaburra! Laugh, Kookaburra! Gay your life must be."

Actually, maybe it was that last bit that bothered him. An eleven-year-old boy in bed with his sister, not just singing about a bird but doing it as best he could, rocking back and forth and imagining himself onstage, possibly wearing a cape, and performing before a multitude.

The third time he came into the room, our father was a wild man. Even worse, he was wielding a prop, the dreaded fraternity paddle. It looked like

46

47

48

49

50

51

52

53

a beaver's tail made out of wood. In my memory, there were Greek letters burned into one side, and crowded around them were the signatures of other Beta Epsilons, men we'd never met, with old-fashioned nicknames like Lefty and Slivers—names, to me, as synonymous with misfortune as Smith and Wesson. Our father didn't bring out the paddle very often, but when he did he always used it.

54

"All right, you, let's get this over with." Amy knew that she had nothing to worry about. He was after me, the instigator, and so she propped herself against the pillows, drawing up her legs as I scooted to the other side of the bed, then stood there, dancing from foot to foot. It was the worst possible strategy, as evasion only made him angrier. Still, who in his right mind would surrender to such a punishment?

He got me eventually, the first blows landing just beneath my kneecaps. 55 Then down I went, and he moved in on my upper thigh. *Whap, whap, whap.* And while it certainly hurt, I have to say that he didn't go overboard. He never did. I asked him about it once, when I was around fourteen, and he chalked it up to a combination of common sense and remarkable self-control. "I know that if I don't stop myself early I'll kill you," he said.

As always after a paddling, I returned to my room vowing never to talk to 56 my father again. To hell with him, to hell with my mother, who'd done nothing to stop him, to hell with Amy for not taking a few licks herself, and to hell with the others, who were, by now, certainly whispering about it.

I didn't have the analogy of the stovetop back then, but what I'd done was 57 turn off the burner marked "family." Then I'd locked my door and sat there simmering, knowing even then that without them I was nothing. Not a son or a brother but just a boy—and how could that ever be enough? As a full-grown man, it seems no different. Cut off your family, and how would you know who you are? Cut them off in order to gain success, and how could that success be measured? What would it possibly mean?

I thought of this as the kookaburra, finally full, swallowed his last strip of 58 duck meat, and took off over the lake. Inside the restaurant, our first courses had arrived, and I watched through the window as Hugh and Pat considered their plates. I should have gone inside right then, but I needed another minute to take it all in, and acknowledge, if only to myself, that I really did have it made. A storybook town on the far side of the world, enough in my pocket to shout a fancy lunch, and the sound of that bird in the distant trees, laughing. Laughing.

FOR DISCUSSION

. . . .

1. David Sedaris recognizes a kookaburra when he sees one for the first time (37). How and when did he first learn about this exotic (to a North American) creature?
2. When they see the woman in the restaurant with the doll, Sedaris's friend Pat says, "Maybe it's a grieving thing" (36). Is this a satisfactory explanation of the woman's behavior? Why or why not?
3. Which burner on Pat's "symbolic" stove would you turn off first (11)? Why?
4. Sedaris's partner Hugh says he would cut off the "work" burner (17). What view of success does he EXEMPLIFY?
5. Sedaris's essay is about travel in a strange land. What else, closer to home, is it also about? Explain.

STRATEGIES AND STRUCTURES

. . . .

1. The kookaburra is one example of the "impossibly foreign" quality of Australia as Sedaris sees it (27). Point out other examples in his NARRATIVE that you find particularly revealing.
2. What is Sedaris exemplifying about himself and his family when he recalls the night his father paddled him?
3. By CONTRAST with the four-burner stove, what does the example of "poor old Mr. Preston" tell the reader about Sedaris's friend Pat (20)?

4. How and how well does Sedaris use the kookaburra song and his experience at the restaurant as examples showing that "I really did have it made" (58)?

5. What main point about the nature of success and happiness is Sedaris making by citing all these examples? Explain.

WORDS AND FIGURES OF SPEECH

1. At first, Australia seems somewhat familiar to Sedaris: "It's Canada in a thong" (6). What are some of the implications of this METAPHOR? Explain.

2. Why is Sedaris so interested in words like "shout" and "bush" (7, 8)? What do they say to him about the place he's visiting? Point out other examples of his use of words as guides to culture.

3. Why does Sedaris say that kookaburras are the "gym teachers" of "the avian kingdom" (37)?

4. When he was a boy at home, says Sedaris, his father padded about in his underwear like a toddler "in a diaper" (45). Where else does Sedaris use humorous images like this to describe his family's quirks? Point out several examples and explain how they support his point about family and "who you are" (57).

5. Sedaris ends his essay with a single word, "Laughing" (58). Is this an appropriate conclusion? Why or why not?

FOR WRITING

1. Think of a person or place that seemed particularly strange or foreign when you first met him or her or went there. Make a list of specific examples showing what gave you this impression.

2. Write an essay about living or working with family or friends that makes the point that happiness alone constitutes (or does not constitute) success. Be sure to include copious examples.

CHAPTER SEVEN
CLASSIFICATION

◇◇◇◇◇◇◇◇◇◇◇◇◇◇◇◇◇◇◇◇◇◇◇◇◇◇◇◇◇◇◇◇◇◇◇◇

WHEN WE CLASSIFY* things, we say what categories they belong to. Dogs, for instance, can be classified as Great Danes, Labrador retrievers, Chihuahuas, and so on. A category is a group with similar characteristics. Thus, to be classified as a Labrador, a dog must be sturdily built, have soft jaws for carrying game, and have a yellow, black, or chocolate coat because these are the characteristics, among others, that distinguish its group—or breed.

Dogs, like anything else, can be classified in more than one way. We can also classify dogs as working dogs, show dogs, and mutts that make good family pets. Or simply as small, medium, and large dogs—or as males and females. The categories into which we divide any subject will depend upon the basis on which we classify it. In the case of dogs, our principle of classification is often by breed, but it can also be by role, size, sex, or some other principle.

No matter your subject or your principle of classification, the categories in your system must be inclusive and not overlap. You wouldn't classify dogs as hunting dogs, show dogs, or retrievers, because some dogs, such as most family pets, would be left out—while others, such as Irish setters, would belong to more than one category, since setters are both hunting dogs and retrievers.

Humans, too, can be classified as David Brooks notes on p. 279.

The categories in any classification system will vary with who is doing the classifying and for what PURPOSE. A teacher divides a group of thirty students according to grades: A, B, C, D, and F. A basketball coach might divide the

*Words printed in SMALL CAPITALS are defined in the Glossary/Index.

same group of students into forwards, guards, and centers. The director of a student drama group would have another set of criteria. Yet all three systems are valid for the purposes they are intended to serve. And classification must serve some larger purpose, or it becomes an empty game.

Systems of classification can help us organize our thoughts about the world around us. They can also help us organize our thoughts in writing, whether in a single paragraph or a whole essay. For example, you might organize a paragraph by introducing your subject, dividing it into types, and then giving the distinguishing features of each type. Here is a paragraph that follows such a pattern. The subject is lightning:

> There are several types of lightning named according to where the discharge takes place. Among them are intracloud lightning, by far the most common type, in which the flash occurs within the thundercloud; air-discharge lightning, in which the flash occurs between the cloud and the surrounding air; and cloud-to-ground lightning, in which the discharge takes place between the cloud and the ground.
> —RICHARD ORVILLE, "Bolts from the Blue"

This short paragraph could be the opening of an essay that goes on to discuss each of the three types of lightning in order, devoting a paragraph or more to each type. If the author's purpose were simply to help us understand the different types, he would probably spend more time on the first kind of lightning— perhaps coming back to it in detail later in his essay—because "intracloud lightning" is the most common variety.

In this case, however, Richard Orville, a meteorologist at Texas A&M University, chose to develop his essay by writing several additional paragraphs on the third type of lightning, "in which the discharge takes place between the cloud and the ground." Why emphasize this category?

Meteorologists classify storms—especially hurricanes, tornadoes, and thunderstorms—not only to understand them but also to predict where they are most likely to occur. As Orville says, his main point in classifying lightning is to "tell what parts on the ground will be most threatened by the lightning activity." Based on this information, the meteorologist can then warn people to take shelter. He can also alert the power companies, so they can deploy power crews more effectively, or reroute electricity away from a power plant even before it is hit.

Given this purpose—to predict weather activity so he can issue accurate warnings and advisories—Orville first classifies his subject into types based on the location of the electrical discharge, or "flash." He then devotes most of his essay to the third type of lightning (cloud-to-ground) because it is the most dangerous kind—to property, to natural resources such as forests, and to people.

Meteorologists divide the subject of lightning into groups or kinds—intracloud, air-discharge, cloud-to-ground. This is the equivalent of classifying dogs by dividing them into distinct breeds. Meteorologists also sort individual bolts of lightning according to the group or kind they belong to: "The bolt of lightning that just destroyed the oak tree in your yard was the cloud-to-ground kind." This is the equivalent of saying that a particular dog is a Lab or a husky or a Portuguese water dog. In this chapter, we will use the term *classification* whether we are dividing a subject into groups or sorting individuals according to the group they belong to—because in either case we are organizing a subject into categories.

A BRIEF GUIDE TO WRITING
A CLASSIFICATION ESSAY

As you write a classification essay, you need to identify your subject and explain the basis on which you're classifying it. David Brooks makes these basic moves of classification in the first paragraph of his essay in this chapter:

> The world can be divided in many ways—rich and poor, democratic and authoritarian—but one of the most striking is the divide between the societies with an individualist mentality and the ones with a collectivist mentality.
>
> —DAVID BROOKS, "Harmony and the Dream"

Brooks identifies his subject (societies of the world) and explains the basis on which he is classifying it (their basic philosophies, or "mentalities").

The following guidelines will help you to make these basic moves as you draft a classification essay. They'll also help you to come up with your subject and to select categories that fit your purpose and audience, are effectively organized, support your main point, and are sufficiently inclusive yet don't overlap.

Coming Up with a Subject

Almost any subject—lightning, convertibles, TV dramas—can be classified in some way. As you consider subjects to classify, think about what you might learn from doing so—your PURPOSE for classifying. For example, you might want to classify something in order to evaluate it (Which dog breeds are appropriate for families with young children?); to determine causes (Was the crash due to mechanical failure, weather, or pilot error?); or to make sense of events (What kinds of economic recessions has the United States historically experienced?). Choose a subject that interests you, but also ask yourself, "Why is this subject worth classifying?"

Considering Your Purpose and Audience

The specific traits you focus on and the categories you divide your subject into will be determined largely by your purpose and audience. Suppose the roof of your town's city hall blows off in a hurricane, and your PURPOSE is to determine—and write an article for your neighborhood newsletter explaining—what kind of roof will stay on best in the next hurricane. In this case, you'd look closely at such traits as weight and wind resistance and pay less attention to such traits as color or energy efficiency.

Once you've determined the kind of roof that has the highest wind rating, you probably will not have a hard time convincing your AUDIENCE (some of whom also lost their roofs) that this is the kind to buy. However, since your audience of homeowners may not be experts in roofing materials, you'll want to DEFINE any technical terms and use language they're familiar with. Keep in mind that readers will not always agree with the way you classify a subject. So you may need to explain why they should accept the criteria you've used.

Generating Ideas:
Considering What Categories There Are

Once you have a subject in mind and a reason for classifying it, consider what categories there are and choose the ones that best suit your purpose and audience. For example, if your purpose is to evaluate different kinds of movies for a film course, you might classify them by genre—drama, comedy, romance, horror, thriller, musical. But if you are reviewing movies for the campus newspaper, you would probably base your classification on quality, perhaps dividing them into these five categories: "must see," "excellent," "good," "mediocre," and "to be avoided at all costs."

When you devise categories for a classification essay, make sure they adhere to a consistent principle (or basis) of classification. For example, if the basis of your movie classification is "movies appropriate for young children," you might use categories such as "good for all ages," "pre-school," "six and up," and "not suitable for children." But you should avoid mixing such categories with those based on genre or quality. In other words, you wouldn't use "drama," "excellent," and "not suitable for children" as the categories.

Templates for Classifying

The following templates can help you to generate ideas for a classification essay and then to start drafting. Don't take these as formulas where you just have to fill in the blanks. There are no easy formulas for good writing. But these templates can help you plot out some of the key moves of classification and thus may serve as good starting points.

- ► X can be classified on the basis of _____.

- ► Classified on the basis of _____, some of the most common types of X are _____, _____, and _____.

- ► X can be divided into two basic types, _____ and _____.

- ► Experts in the field typically divide X into _____, _____, and _____.

- ► This particular X clearly belongs in the _____ category, since it is _____, _____, and _____.

- ► _____ and _____ are examples of this type of X.

- ► By classifying X in this way, we can see that _____.

For more techniques to help you generate ideas and start writing a classification essay, see Chapter 2.

Organizing a Classification Essay

In the opening paragraphs of your essay, tell the reader what you're classifying and why, and explain your classification system. If you were writing an essay classifying types of environmentally friendly cars, for example, you might use an introduction like this:

> If you are considering buying an environmentally friendly car, you need to know which types of fueling are available in order to find a car that meets your goals for a green lifestyle. Green cars can best be divided into the following categories: petrol cars, diesel cars, electric cars, hybrid cars, and biofuel cars. If you understand these five basic types and the differences among them, you can make an informed decision for the good of both the environment and your wallet.

Typically, the body of a classification essay is devoted to a point-by-point discussion of each of the categories that make up your classification system. Thus if you are classifying green cars, you would spend a paragraph, or at least several sentences, explaining the most important characteristics of each type.

Once you've laid out the categories in some detail, remind the reader of the point you are making. The point of classifying cars by fuel type, for example, is to help readers choose the green car that best meets their goals for an environmentally friendly lifestyle.

Stating Your Point

When you compose a classification essay, you should have in mind what you learned about your subject by classifying it in a particular way. Tell the reader in a THESIS STATEMENT what your main point is and why you're dividing up your subject as you do. Usually, you'll want to state your main point in the introduction as you explain your classification system. In the opening paragraph of the essay on green cars, for instance, the main point is stated in the last sentence: "If you can understand these five basic types . . . you can make an informed decision."

Choosing Significant Characteristics

Whatever classification system you use, base your categories on the most significant characteristics of your subject—ones that explain something important about it. For example, you probably would not discuss color when classifying environmentally friendly cars because this attribute does not tell the reader anything about a car's impact on the environment. After all, every kind of car comes in more or less the same colors. Instead, you would probably use such attributes as fuel type, miles-per-gallon, and types of emissions—traits that differentiate, say, a hybrid car from other kinds of green cars.

Choosing Categories That Are Inclusive and Don't Overlap

When you divide your subject into categories, those categories must be inclusive enough to cover most cases, and they must not overlap. For example, classifying ice cream into chocolate and vanilla alone isn't very useful because this system leaves out many other important kinds, such as strawberry, pistachio, and rum raisin. The categories in a good classification system include all kinds: for instance, no-fat, low-fat, and full-fat ice cream. And they should not overlap. Thus, chocolate, vanilla, homemade, and Ben and Jerry's do not make a good classification system because the same scoop of ice cream could fit into more than one category.

EDITING FOR COMMON ERRORS IN A CLASSIFICATION ESSAY

Classification invites problems with listing groups or traits. Here are some common errors to check for and correct when you write a classification essay.

When you list categories or traits in a classification system, make sure they are parallel in form

- ▸ How much income tax you pay each year depends largely on whether your income is taxed as wages or ~~you have a lot of~~ capital gains.
- ▸ Capital gains are classified according to whether the earnings are long-term (more than a year) or ~~are produced over the~~ short-term (a year or less).

Check that traits used to describe or define categories are in the following order: size, age, color, region

- ▸ His preferred type of headgear was ~~Panama, old, big, white~~ <u>big, old, white Panama</u> hats.

EVERYDAY CLASSIFICATION
Drunk or Buzzed?

Drunk Driving

Buzzed Driving

Buzzed driving is drunk driving.

Driving home a point with classification. When we classify things, we divide them into categories based on their distinguishing characteristics. Those with different traits go into different categories: "Officer, I'm not drunk, just buzzed." When two things are essentially alike, however, we put them in the *same* category, as on this poster from a U.S. Department of Transportation campaign against impaired driving: "Buzzed driving *is* drunk driving."

ERIC A. WATTS

THE COLOR OF SUCCESS

A native of Springfield, Massachusetts, Eric A. Watts wrote the following essay about racial stereotyping when he was a sophomore at Brown University. In it, Watts argues that African Americans who criticize each other for "acting white" and who say that success based on academic achievement is "not black" are misclassifying themselves as "victims." After tracing the historical roots of this "outdated" system, Watts assesses its damaging effects and examines more recent ways of classifying (and achieving) success that are based more on economics than race. "The Color of Success" originally appeared in the Brown *Alumni Monthly*.

The Color of Success

When I was a black student at a primarily white high
school, I occasionally confronted the stereotypes and prejudice that some whites aimed at those of my race. These
incidents came as no particular surprise—after all, prejudice,
though less prevalent than in the past, is ages old.

What did surprise me during those years was the
profound disapproval that some of my black peers expressed
toward my studious behavior. "Hitting the books," expressing oneself articulately, and, at times, displaying more than a
modest amount of intelligence—these traits were derided as
"acting white."

Once, while I was traveling with other black students, a
young woman asked me what I thought of one of our teachers.
My answer, phrased in what one might call "standard"
English, caused considerable discomfort among my audience.
Finally, the young woman exploded: "Eric," she said, "stop
talking like a white boy! You're with us now!"

Another time, again in a group of black students, a friend
asked how I intended to spend the weekend. When I answered
that I would study, my friend's reaction was swift: "Eric, you
need to stop all this studying; you need to stop acting so
white." The others laughed in agreement.

Signithea Fordham's 1986 ethnographic study of a mostly
black high school in Washington, D.C., *Black Students'
School Success,* concluded that many behaviors associated
with high achievement—speaking standard English, studying
long hours, striving to get good grades—were regarded as
"acting white." Fordham further concluded that "many black

Sidebar annotations:

- Inroduces the general topic of Watts's essay: false categories
- Identifies the particular false category that the writer will emphasize
- Gives the first in a series of traits that define "acting white"

students limit their academic success so their peers won't think they are 'acting white.' "

Frankly, I never took the "acting white" accusation seriously. It seemed to me that certain things I valued—hard work, initiative, articulateness, education—were not solely white people's prerogative.

6

Rejects "acting-white" as a valid category

Trouble begins, however, when students lower their standards in response to peer pressure. Such a retreat from achievement has potentially horrendous effects on the black community.

7

The writer's purpose in examining a false classification system is to examine its harmful effects

Even more disturbing is the rationale behind the "acting white" accusation. It seems that, on a subconscious level, some black students wonder whether success—in particular, academic success—is a purely white domain.

8

In his essay "On Being Black and Middle Class," in *The Content of Our Character* (1990), Shelby Steele, a black scholar at San Jose State University, argues that certain "middle-class" values—the work ethic, education, initiative—by encouraging "individualism," encourage identification with American society, rather than with race. The ultimate result is integration.

9

But, Steele argues, the racial identification that emerged during the 1960s, and that still persists, urges middle-class blacks to view themselves as an embattled minority: to take an adversarial stance toward the mainstream. It emphasizes ethnic consciousness over individualism.

10

Analyzes CAUSES that led to self-stereotyping

Steele says that this form of black identification emerged in the civil rights effort to obtain full racial equality, an effort that demanded that blacks present themselves (by and large)

11

as a racial monolith: a single mass with the common experience of oppression. So blackness became virtually synonymous with victimization and the characteristics associated with it: lack of education and poverty.

I agree with Steele that a monolithic form of racial   12
identification persists. The ideas of the black as a victim and the black as inferior have been too much entrenched in cultural imagery and too much enforced by custom and law not to have damaged the collective black psyche.

This damage is so severe that some black adolescents still   13
believe that success is a white prerogative—the white "turf." These young people view the turf as inaccessible, both because (among other reasons) they doubt their own abilities and because they generally envision whites as, if not outspoken racists, people who are mildly interested in "keeping blacks down."

States the main damaging effect of believing in the stereotypes ······•

The result of identifying oneself as a victim can be, "Why   14
even try? It's a white man's world."

Several years ago I was talking to an old friend, a   15
black male. He justified dropping out of school and failing to look for a job on the basis of one factor: the cold, heartless, white power structure. When I suggested that such a power structure might indeed exist, but that opportunity for blacks was at an unprecedented level, he laughed. Doomed, he felt, to a life of defeat, my friend soon eased his melancholy with crack.

Gives an example from personal experience ······•

The most frustrating aspect of the "acting white" accusa-   16
tion is that its main premise—that academic and subsequent

success are "white"—is demonstrably false. And so is the broader premise: that blacks are the victims of whites.

That academic success is "not black" is easily seen as false if one takes a brisk walk through the Brown University campus and looks at the faces one passes. Indeed, the most comprehensive text concerning blacks in decades, *A Common Destiny* (1989), states, "Despite large gaps . . . whether the baseline is the 1940s, 1950s, or 1960s, the achievement outcomes . . . of black schooling have greatly improved." That subsequent success in the world belongs to blacks as well as whites is exemplified today by such blacks as Jesse Jackson, Douglas Wilder, Norman Rice, Anne Wortham, Sara Lawrence Lightfoot, David Dinkins, August Wilson, Andrew Young . . .

17 · · · · · · Attacks the premises of the "victims" argument

The idea of a victimized black race is slowly becoming outdated. Today's black adolescents were born after the *Brown v. Board of Education* decision of 1954; after the passage of the Civil Rights Act; after the Economic Opportunity Act of 1964. With these rulings and laws, whites' attitudes toward blacks have also greatly improved. Although I cannot say that my life has been free of racism on the part of whites, good racial relations in my experience have far outweighed the bad. I refuse to apologize for or retreat from this truth.

18

The result of changes in policies and attitudes has been to provide more opportunities for black Americans than at any other point in their history. As early as 1978, William Julius Wilson, in *The Declining Significance of Race,* concluded that "the recent mobility patterns of blacks lend strong support to

19 · · · · · · Argues that racial conditions in America have changed

the view that economic class is clearly more important than race in predetermining . . . occupational mobility."

There are, of course, many factors, often socioeconomic, that still impede the progress of blacks. High schools in black neighborhoods receive less local, state, and federal support than those in white areas; there is evidence that the high school diplomas of blacks are little valued by employers.

We should rally against all such remaining racism, confronting particularly the economic obstacles to black success. But we must also realize that racism is not nearly as profound as it once was, and that opportunities for blacks (where opportunity equals jobs and acceptance for the educated and qualified) have increased. Furthermore, we should know that even a lack of resources is no excuse for passivity.

As the syndicated columnist William Raspberry (who is black) says, it is time for certain black adolescents to "shift their focus": to move from an identity rooted in victimization to an identity rooted in individualism and hard work.

Simply put, the black community must eradicate the "you're-acting white" syndrome. Until it does, black Americans will never realize their potential.

Marginal notes:

Anticipates objections to his position

The writer concludes by saying what should be done

Paragraph numbers: 20, 21, 22, 23

AMY TAN

MOTHER TONGUE

Amy Tan (b. 1952) is a native of California. In her best-selling first novel, *The Joy Luck Club* (1989), Tan used all of the different forms of the English language she had spoken since childhood with her mother, whose native language was Chinese. In "Mother Tongue," which first appeared in the *Threepenny Review* (1990), Tan not only *uses* her family's different "Englishes," she classifies them into their various kinds and explains how each type lends itself to a different form of communication. Tan's other novels include *Saving Fish from Drowning* (2006) and *The Valley of Amazement* (2012).

◇◇◇◇◇◇◇◇◇◇◇◇◇◇◇◇◇◇◇◇◇◇◇◇◇◇◇◇◇◇◇

I am not a scholar of English or literature. I cannot give you much more than   1
personal opinions on the English language and its variations in this country
or others.

I am a writer. And by that definition, I am someone who has always loved   2
language. I am fascinated by language in daily life. I spend a great deal of my
time thinking about the power of language—the way it can evoke an emotion, a
visual image, a complex idea, or a simple truth. Language is the tool of my trade.
And I use them all—all the Englishes I grew up with.

Recently, I was made keenly aware of the different Englishes I do use. I   3
was giving a talk to a large group of people, the same talk I had already given to
half a dozen other groups. The nature of the talk was about my writing, my life,
and my book, *The Joy Luck Club*. The talk was going along well enough, until I
remembered one major difference that made the whole talk sound wrong. My
mother was in the room. And it was perhaps the first time she had heard me
give a lengthy speech, using the kind of English I have never used with her. I
was saying things like, "The intersection of memory upon imagination" and
"There is an aspect of my fiction that relates to thus-and-thus"—a speech filled
with carefully wrought grammatical phrases, burdened, it suddenly seemed to
me, with nominalized forms, past perfect tenses, conditional phrases, all the
forms of standard English that I had learned in school and through books,
the forms of English I did not use at home with my mother.

Just last week, I was walking down the street with my mother, and I again   4
found myself conscious of the English I was using, the English I do use with
her. We were talking about the price of new and used furniture and I heard
myself saying this: "Not waste money that way." My husband was with us as
well, and he didn't notice any switch in my English. And then I realized why.
It's because over the twenty years we've been together I've often used the same
kind of English with him, and sometimes he even uses it with me. It has become
our language of intimacy, a different sort of English that relates to family talk,
the language I grew up with.

So you'll have some idea of what this family talk I heard sounds like, I'll   5
quote what my mother said during a recent conversation which I videotaped
and then transcribed. During this conversation, my mother was talking about a
political gangster in Shanghai who had the same last name as her family's, Du,
and how the gangster in his early years wanted to be adopted by her family,
which was rich by comparison. Later, the gangster became more powerful, far
richer than my mother's family, and one day showed up at my mother's wedding
to pay his respects. Here's what she said in part:

"Du Yusong having business like fruit stand. Like off the street kind. He   6
is Du like Du Zong—but not Tsung-ming Island people. The local people call
putong, the river east side, he belong to that side local people. That man want to

ask Du Zong father take him in like become own family. Du Zong father wasn't look down on him, but didn't take seriously, until that man big like become a mafia. Now important person, very hard to inviting him. Chinese way, came only to show respect, don't stay for dinner. Respect for making big celebration, he shows up. Mean gives lots of respect. Chinese custom. Chinese social life that way. If too important won't have to stay too long. He come to my wedding. I didn't see, I heard it. I gone to boy's side, they have YMCA dinner. Chinese age I was nineteen."

You should know that my mother's expressive command of English belies how much she actually understands. She reads the *Forbes*[1] report, listens to *Wall Street Week*, converses daily with her stockbroker, reads all of Shirley MacLaine's[2] books with ease—all kinds of things I can't begin to understand. Yet some of my friends tell me they understand 50 percent of what my mother says. Some say they understand 80 to 90 percent. Some say they understand none of it, as if she were speaking pure Chinese. But to me, my mother's English is perfectly clear, perfectly natural. It's my mother tongue. Her language, as I hear it, is vivid, direct, full of observation and imagery. That was the language that helped shape the way I saw things, expressed things, made sense of the world.

Lately, I've been giving more thought to the kind of English my mother speaks. Like others, I have described it to people as "broken" or "fractured" English. But I wince when I say that. It has always bothered me that I can think of no way to describe it other than "broken," as if it were damaged and needed to be fixed, as if it lacked a certain wholeness and soundness. I've heard other terms used, "limited English," for example. But they seem just as bad, as if everything is limited, including people's perceptions of the limited English speaker.

I know this for a fact, because when I was growing up, my mother's "limited" English limited *my* perception of her. I was ashamed of her English. I believed that her English reflected the quality of what she had to say. That is, because she expressed them imperfectly her thoughts were imperfect. And I

1. Business magazine popular with corporate executives and investors.
2. American film actress (b. 1934) who has written a number of memoirs.

had plenty of empirical evidence to support me: the fact that people in department stores, at banks, and at restaurants did not take her seriously, did not give her good service, pretended not to understand her, or even acted as if they did not hear her.

My mother has long realized the limitations of her English as well. When I was fifteen, she used to have me call people on the phone to pretend I was she. In this guise, I was forced to ask for information or even to complain and yell at people who had been rude to her. One time it was a call to her stockbroker in New York. She had cashed out her small portfolio and it just so happened we were going to go to New York the next week, our very first trip outside California. I had to get on the phone and say in an adolescent voice that was not very convincing, "This is Mrs. Tan."

And my mother was standing in the back whispering loudly, "Why he don't send me check, already two weeks late. So mad he lie to me, losing me money."

And then I said in perfect English, "Yes, I'm getting rather concerned. You had agreed to send the check two weeks ago, but it hasn't arrived."

Then she began to talk more loudly. "What he want, I come to New York tell him front of his boss, you cheating me?" And I was trying to calm her down, make her be quiet, while telling the stockbroker, "I can't tolerate any more excuses. If I don't receive the check immediately, I am going to have to speak to your manager when I'm in New York next week." And sure enough, the following week there we were in front of this astonished stockbroker, and I was sitting there red-faced and quiet, and my mother, the real Mrs. Tan, was shouting at his boss in her impeccable broken English.

We used a similar routine just five days ago, for a situation that was far less humorous. My mother had gone to the hospital for an appointment, to find out about a benign brain tumor a CAT scan had revealed a month ago. She said she had spoken very good English, her best English, no mistakes. Still, she said, the hospital did not apologize when they said they had lost the CAT scan and she had come for nothing. She said they did not seem to have any sympathy when she told them she was anxious to know the exact diagnosis, since her husband and son had both died of brain tumors. She said they would not give her any more information until the next time and she would have to make another appointment for that. So she said she would not leave until the doctor called her daughter. She wouldn't budge. And when the doctor finally called her daughter, me, who spoke in perfect English—lo and behold—we had assurances the CAT scan would be found, promises that a conference call on Monday would be held, and apologies for any suffering my mother had gone through for a most regrettable mistake.

I think my mother's English almost had an effect on limiting my possibilities in life as well. Sociologists and linguists probably will tell you that a person's developing language skills are more influenced by peers. But I do think that the language spoken in the family, especially in immigrant families which are more insular, plays a large role in shaping the language of the child. And I believe that it affected my results on achievement tests, IQ tests, and the SAT. While my English skills were never judged as poor, compared to math, English could not be considered my strong suit. In grade school I did moderately well, getting perhaps B's, sometimes B-pluses, in English and scoring perhaps in the sixtieth or seventieth percentile on achievement tests. But those scores were not good enough to override the opinion that my true abilities lay in math and science, because in those areas I achieved A's and scored in the ninetieth percentile or higher.

This was understandable. Math is precise; there is only one correct answer. Whereas, for me at least, the answers on English tests were always a judgment call, a matter of opinion and personal experience. Those tests were constructed around items like fill-in-the-blank sentence completion, such as, "Even though Tom was _____, Mary thought he was _____." And the correct answer always seemed to be the most bland combinations of thoughts, for example, "Even though Tom was shy, Mary thought he was charming," with the grammatical structure "even though" limiting the correct answer to some sort of semantic opposites, so you wouldn't get answers like, "Even though Tom was foolish, Mary thought he was ridiculous." Well, according to my mother, there were very few limitations as to what Tom could have been and what Mary might have thought of him. So I never did well on tests like that.

The same was true with word analogies, pairs of words in which you were supposed to find some sort of logical, semantic relationship—for example, "*Sunset* is to *nightfall* as _____ is to _____." And here you would be presented

See p. 245 on choosing categories that don't overlap.

15

16

17

with a list of four possible pairs, one of which showed the same kind of relationship: *red* is to *stoplight*, *bus* is to *arrival*, *chills* is to *fever*, *yawn* is to *boring*. Well, I could never think that way. I knew what the tests were asking, but I could not block out of my mind the images already created by the first pair, *"sunset* is to *nightfall"*—and I would see a burst of colors against a darkening sky, the moon rising, the lowering of a curtain of stars. And all the other pairs of words—red, bus, stoplight, boring—just threw up a mass of confusing images, making it impossible for me to sort out something as logical as saying: "A sunset precedes nightfall" is the same as "a chill precedes a fever." The only way I would have gotten that answer right would have been to imagine an associative situation, for example, my being disobedient and staying out past sunset, catching a chill at night, which turns into feverish pneumonia as punishment, which indeed did happen to me.

I have been thinking about all this lately, about my mother's English, about achievement tests. Because lately I've been asked, as a writer, why there are not more Asian Americans represented in American literature. Why are there few Asian Americans enrolled in creative writing programs? Why do so many Chinese students go into engineering? Well, these are broad sociological questions I can't begin to answer. But I have noticed in surveys—in fact, just last week—that Asian students, as a whole, always do significantly better on math achievement tests than in English. And this makes me think that there are other Asian-American students whose English spoken in the home might also be described as "broken" or "limited." And perhaps they also have teachers who are steering them away from writing and into math and science, which is what happened to me.

Fortunately, I happen to be rebellious in nature and enjoy the challenge of disproving assumptions made about me. I became an English major my first year in college, after being enrolled as pre-med. I started writing nonfiction as a freelancer the week after I was told by my former boss that writing was my worst skill and I should hone my talents toward account management.

But it wasn't until 1985 that I finally began to write fiction. And at first I wrote using what I thought to be wittily crafted sentences, sentences that would finally prove I had mastery over the English language. Here's an example from the first draft of a story that later made its way into *The Joy Luck Club*, but without this line: "That was my mental quandary in its nascent state." A terrible line, which I can barely pronounce.

Fortunately, for reasons I won't get into today, I later decided I should envision a reader for the stories I would write. And the reader I decided upon was my mother, because these were stories about mothers. So with this reader in mind—and in fact she did read my early drafts—I began to write stories using all the Englishes I grew up with: the English I spoke to my mother, which for lack of a better term might be described as "simple"; the English she used with me, which for lack of a better term might be described as "broken"; my translation of her Chinese, which could certainly be described as "watered down"; and what I imagined to be her translation of her Chinese if she could speak in perfect English, her internal language, and for that I sought to preserve the essence, but neither an English nor a Chinese structure. I wanted to capture what language ability tests can never reveal: her intent, her passion, her imagery, the rhythms of her speech and the nature of her thoughts. 21

Apart from what any critic had to say about my writing, I knew I had succeeded where it counted when my mother finished reading my book and gave me her verdict: "So easy to read." 22

FOR DISCUSSION

1. Into what two basic categories does Amy Tan CLASSIFY all the Englishes that she uses in writing and speaking?

2. How many Englishes did Tan learn at home from conversing with her mother, a native speaker of Chinese? How does she distinguish among them?

3. According to Tan, what are the significant characteristics of "standard" English (3)? How and where did she learn standard English?

4. Tan tells us that she envisions her mother as the AUDIENCE for her stories, using "all the Englishes I grew up with" in writing them (21). For what audience did Tan write this essay? How would you classify the English she uses in it?

STRATEGIES AND STRUCTURES

. . . .

1. Why do you think Tan begins her essay with the disclaimer that she is "not a scholar" of the English language (1)? How does she otherwise establish her authority on the subject? How well does she do it?
2. Tan first gives EXAMPLES of "family talk" and only later classifies them (4, 21). Why do you think she follows this order? Why not give the categories first, then the specific examples?
3. What specific kind of English, by Tan's classification, is represented by paragraph 6 of her essay?
4. Besides classifying Englishes, Tan also includes NARRATIVES about using them. What do the narratives contribute to her essay? How would the essay be different without the stories?
5. In which paragraphs is Tan advancing an ARGUMENT about achievement tests? What is her point here, and how does she use her different Englishes to support that point?

WORDS AND FIGURES OF SPEECH

. . . .

1. Explain the PUN in Tan's title. What does it tell us about the essay?
2. By what standards, according to Tan, is "standard" English to be established and measured (3)?
3. What are some of the implications of using such terms as "broken" or "fractured" to refer to nonstandard forms of speech or writing (8)?
4. Do you find "simple" to be better or worse than "broken"? How about "watered down" (21)? Explain.
5. Tan does not give a term for the kind of English she uses to represent her mother's "internal language" (21). What name would you give it? Why?

FOR WRITING

. . . .

1. Many families have private jokes, code words, gestures, even family whistles. In a paragraph or two, give examples of your family's private speech or language. How does each function within the family? In relation to the family and the outside world?

2. How many different Englishes (and other languages) do you use at home, at school, among friends, and elsewhere? Write an essay classifying them, giving the characteristics of each, and explaining how and when each is used.

THE DOLLAR-STORE ECONOMY

Jack Hitt (b. 1957) grew up in Charleston, South Carolina, and graduated from the University of the South in Sewanee, Tennessee, in 1979. His articles and essays appear frequently in such magazines as *Rolling Stone, Wired,* and *Outside.* As a contributing editor to the *New York Times, Harper's,* and *This American Life,* Hitt has covered everything from undergraduate drinking and presidential politics to Internet spam and featherless chickens. He is the author, most recently, of *Bunch of Amateurs: A Search for the American Character* (2012). In "The Dollar-Store Economy" (*New York Times,* 2011), Hitt classifies retail outlets in "the basement of American capitalism." Like an archeologist digging through "the detritus of a hyperproductive global manufacturing system," he divides this "stratum" into various levels—and uncovers a new breed of shopper inspired by the recession.

Heather Mann writes a blog called Dollar Store Crafts, which evolved from her occasional trips to the extreme-discount dollar stores near her home in Salem, Oregon. Her readers admire her gift for buying really cheap stuff   1

and then making cool and beautiful things from the pile. Her knockoff "alien abduction lamp" is jury-rigged from a small light fixture, two plastic bowls (flying saucer), a clear acrylic tumbler (tractor beam) and a small plastic toy cow (abductee)—all purchased for about five bucks.

As we entered her favorite store, a Dollar Tree in Salem, Mann warned me that I'd have to hustle to keep up with her. "Look at these," she said. "Cute." Before I could even examine her find—a rack of smushy yellow chickens on sticks (plastic toy? garden ornament? edible peeps?)—she had ricocheted down another aisle, where I found her studying a prominent display garishly pushing a superabsorbent shammy. Mann noted that this was not the famously kitschy ShamWow! but a very cheap imitation called, merely, Wow. The display boasted, "As Seen on TV."

"As in, you've seen the *real* ad on TV," she said.

All around, the stacks of products and aisles of merchandise screamed a technicolor siren song. I found four AA batteries for my tape recorder for a dollar ($5.49 when I spotted them the next day at RadioShack), and dish towels that might have sold for $5 elsewhere were just a buck. Mann now brandished something called a "wineglass holder" the way Jacques Cousteau might have held up a starfish. It was a small aluminum device meant to clip onto your plastic picnic plate "for hands-free dining and socializing." At a price of four for a dollar, it's a good deal if your world is overrun with miserly wine connoisseurs.

When I looked up, Mann was already around the corner, having fun with a bottle of discount detergent boasting a "bingo bango mango" scent. Just up the way was a bin of brown bags marked either "A Surprise for a Boy" or "A Surprise for a Girl." Mann's five-year-old niece accompanied us on our tour and was crazed with excitement over these, and the truth is, we were all in the same exact mood. All around

See p. 241 on how your purpose affects your classification.

us, strange things hung here and there, urging us on an unending treasure hunt. Perhaps, like me, you have driven by and occasionally stopped in a dollar store and assumed that there were two kinds of customers, those there for the kitschy pleasure of it all—the Heather Manns of the world—and those for whom the dollar store affords a low-rent version of the American Consumer Experience, a

2

3

4

5

A young woman scans an aisle in a Dollar Tree store.

place where the poor can splurge. That's true. But current developments in this, the low end of retail, suggest that a larger shift in the American consumer market is under way.

We are awakening to a dollar-store economy. For years the dollar store has not only made a market out of the detritus of a hyperproductive global manufacturing system, but it has also made it appealing—by making it amazingly cheap. Before the market meltdown of 2008 and the stagnant, jobless recovery that followed, the conventional wisdom about dollar stores—whether one of the three big corporate chains (Dollar General, Family Dollar and Dollar Tree) or any of the smaller chains (like "99 Cents Only Stores") or the world of independents—was that they appeal to only poor people. And while it's true that low-wage earners still make up the core of dollar-store customers (42 percent earn $30,000 or less), what has turned this sector into a nearly recession-proof corner of the economy is a new customer base. "What's driving the growth," says James Russo, a vice president with the Nielsen Company, a consumer survey firm, "is affluent households."

The affluent are not just quirky D.I.Y.[1] types. These new customers are people who, though they have money, feel as if they don't, or soon won't. This anxiety—sure to be restoked by the recent stock-market gyrations and generally abysmal predictions for the economy—creates a kind of fear-induced pleasure in selective bargain-hunting. Rick Dreiling, the chief executive of Dollar General, the largest chain, with more than 9,500 stores, calls this idea the New Consumerism. "Savings is fashionable again," Dreiling told me. "A gallon of Clorox bleach, say, is $1.44 at a drugstore or $1.24 at a grocery store, and you pay a buck for it at the Dollar General. When the neighbors come over, they can't tell where you bought it, and you save anywhere from 20 to 40 cents, right?"

Financial anxiety—or the New Consumerism, if you like—has been a boon to dollar stores. Same-store sales, a key measure of a retailer's health, spiked at the three large, publicly traded chains in this year's first quarter—all were up by at least 5 percent—while Walmart had its eighth straight quarterly decline. Dreiling says that much of Dollar General's growth is generated by what he calls "fill-in trips"—increasingly made by wealthier people. Why linger in the canyons of Wal-Mart or Target when you can pop into a dollar store? Dreiling says that 22 percent of his customers make more than $70,000 a year and added, "That 22 percent is our fastest-growing segment."

This growth has led to a building campaign. At a time when few businesses seem to be investing in new equipment or ventures or jobs, Dreiling's company announced a few months ago that it would be creating 6,000 new jobs by building 625 new stores this year. Kiley Rawlins, vice president for investor relations at Family Dollar, said her company would add 300 new stores this year, giving it more than 7,000 in 44 states.

And yet, how do dollar stores expand and make impressive returns, all the while dealing in an inventory that still largely retails for a few dollars? How does a store sell four AA batteries for $1? In part this market takes advantage of the economy degrading all around it. When I asked Dreiling about the difference

1. Abbreviation for "do it yourself," rather than hire a specialist.

in the cost of RadioShack batteries, he said that "RadioShack is probably in a better spot in the same shopping center," while Dollar General might be in a "C+, B site." RadioShack pays the high rent, while the dollar stores inhabit a "no-frills box."

The dollar-store combination has more to it than low store rents and really cheap products. The labor force needed to run a dollar store is a tiny, low-wage staff. Do the math of Dreiling's announcement: 6,000 jobs divided by 625 stores equals about 10 jobs per store. 11

Perhaps this is all merely our grandparents' Woolworth's[2] five-and-dime updated by inflation to a dollar and adapted, like any good weed, to distressed areas of the landscape. But a new and eroding reality in American life underwrites this growing market. Yet even deep discounters have limits. In early June, Dollar General predicted that its sales growth would slow slightly for the rest of the year. Dreiling told analysts in a conference call that his company would be very careful about raising prices, even though its costs for fuel and such were rising. "This sounds almost silly," he said, "but a $1 item going to $1.15 in our channel is a major change for our customer." Such delicate price sensitivity suggests what is changing. Howard Levine, the chief executive of Family Dollar, said to me, although "not necessarily a good thing for our country, more and more people are living paycheck to paycheck." 12

Profit margins have always been thin in the dollar stores. But now that they are competing for the shrinking disposable income of the middle class, there is a new kind of consultant out there—the dollar-store fixer. Bob Hamilton advises the troubled independent-dollar-store manager on the tactics needed to survive and thrive in the dollar-store economy. One afternoon he drove me to Beaverton, Oregon, to give me a tour of a Dollar Tree store whose layout and strategy he thinks is exemplary in its competitive cunning. 13

In Hamilton's view, the secret of a good dollar store is an obsessive manager who can monitor 8,000 to 10,000 items, constantly varying product display 14

---

2. The original five-and-dime discount chain that sold general merchandise in stores across the United States for most of the twentieth century.

tactics, and sense the changing interests of a local customer base. This frenzied drama requires a sharp eye for tiny details. "The market is moving all the time," Hamilton said as we entered the store. Right away, he threw up his arms, thrilled. This was just before Easter, and he pointed out the big holiday display practically in the doorway, an in-our-face explosion of color and delight that herded us away from the exit. "The natural inclination is to move to the right," Hamilton said, nodding at the cash registers on the left. The hunt was on.

Hamilton pointed out that the aisles are about two inches wider than two shopping carts, which themselves are comically tiny, giving the buyer a sense that even a small pile of goods is lavish. Despite the dollar store's reputation for shoddy products, the *mise-en-scène* nevertheless suggests a kind of luxury, if only of quantity. "The first thing you feel is this thing is packed with merchandise," Hamilton said, pointing out the high shelves along the walls. Helium

15

An aisle in a Dollar Store in North Arlington, New Jersey

balloons strained upward, everywhere. Any empty wall space was filled with paper signage proclaiming savings or "$1" and framing the store's goods.

But wait! There, in the middle of the aisle, was a tower of candy boxes, razored open and overflowing with cheap sweets. "They do this a lot with facial tissue or back-to-school items," Hamilton said. But it was blocking the aisle—a deadly error in his view. Worse are the managers who deliberately create cul-de-sacs by closing off the back of an aisle with goods. "You have to turn around and come back!" Hamilton said, shaking his head in disbelief. "You just watch the customers, and they will skip the aisle, every one of them." 16

The idea, Hamilton explained, is to create a kind of primal experience and a certain meditative flow. "My theory was to get them in a pattern, and they will just go up and down and go, 'Oh, I forgot I need that,' and pick it up." 17

At one point in the tour, Hamilton spotted patches of bare shelf space and was practically ashamed. His model store was committing egregious mistakes. "This is probably the worst aisle we've been down," he whispered. He dashed to a single barren metal hook and pointed in horror. "They have an empty peg! People are thinking, I'm getting the last one!" The stuffed bins, the boxes on wood pallets sitting on the floor, the merchandise piled to the ceiling—all this breeds an excited sense that everything just got here and you're getting to it first. 18

"You always keep things full," he said. And always keep the higher part of the shelves engorged with product. "People buy at eye level," he added. Hamilton advised that products should be hung in vertical strips so that in a walk up the aisle, the eye can distinguish one item from the next. We arrived to a back wall covered entirely in plastic, pillar after pillar of household cleaning supplies, a kaleidoscopic blaze of primary colors. Bob Hamilton was one happy man. 19

"Shopping is our hunting and gathering," says Sharon Zukin, a professor of sociology at Brooklyn College who specializes in consumer culture and suggests that the dollar-store experience is a mere updating of our evolutionary instincts. "This bare-bones aesthetic puts across the idea that there is nothing between you the consumer and the goods that you desire. You are a bargain hunter, and it's not like a bazaar or open-market situation in other regions of the world. It doesn't require personal haggling between the shopkeeper and the 20 shoppers. Right? The price is set, and it's there for the taking. In many cases the cartons there have not been unpacked! You are getting the product direct from the anonymous large-scale producer. You have bagged the deer: you have your carton of 36 rolls of toilet paper."

As strange as sociological metaphors sound in this context, this is very close to how the corporate chain executives describe the next stage of dollar-store evolution, as they try to please their new, more affluent customer. Both Dollar General and Family Dollar are moving toward uniformity in their design and layout, throwing off the serendipity that came of buying random lots and salvage goods and was so admired by, say, crafts bloggers. The new design has opened up the front of the stores "for those whose trip is all about, 'I'm getting what I need and getting out,'" said Rawlins of Family Dollar. As a result, the design of the store is no longer catch-as-catch-can but built around groupings of products that all make sense for the mission-oriented hunter. Store designers call these groupings "adjacencies" and draw them up in fine detail in an architectural schematic called a planogram. Toys, wrapping paper and gift cards, for instance, are laid out in a logical sequence that has been revealed by elaborate customer research and designed with precision.

"A hundred percent of our stores are planogrammed," Dreiling of Dollar General says. "We used to have what was called 'flex space,' and 25 percent of the store was where the store manager could put in whatever they wanted." No more. "Everything is planogrammed now." '

"Today we have very little in terms of closeouts," said Family Dollar's Rawlins. "Forty-five percent of our merchandise are national brands that we carry every day." Even though the goods are still deeply discounted, the stores will begin to have a similar look and layout—like the higher-end stores already do. Same inventory, same layout, same experience—from coast to coast.

As all these stores expand into really cheap food, they are creating their own store brands. Just as A&P long ago, or Target more recently, pronounced its market significance by creating store brands like Ann Page or Archer Farms foods, Family Dollar now sells Family Gourmet packaged meals, and Dollar General promotes its line of discounted packaged foods with the bucolic handle Clover Valley.

What does all this mean for the independent dollar stores? Is there a place for them in the evolving dollar-store economy? There is, but only if they are willing to hustle for pennies. 25

I called JC Sales, one of the big warehouse suppliers of independent dollar stores located south of Los Angeles, and talked to Wally Lee, director of marketing and technology. He agreed there was little room for error now. If I wanted to open a dollar store, I asked him, where would he suggest I locate it? "Right next to a Wal-Mart or a Target," he said. And how large should my new store be? "If you want to be profitable, start with an 8,000-square-foot store," he said. "That is the most optimally profitable among all our customers." Stores can be as small as 1,000 square feet and go up to 20,000, but Lee implied that there is practically an algorithm of size, labor and expenses—8,000 to 10,000 square feet is profitability's sweet spot. But it's not all science, Lee said. The very absence of a planogram is the other advantage independents can have. 26

"You need to have a good store manager who loves to talk to people," Lee said. "If it is a Spanish market, then it has to be a Spanish manager to speak to them to see what their needs are. If you don't do that, you'll never beat anybody else." 27

In other words, even as the corporate chains standardize their inventory and planogram their stores down to the last Wow shammy, the independents flourish by retaining a Bob Hamilton-like sensibility—the sense that the market is in motion—with managers buzzing about the store, constantly tweaking the inventory, moving stuff around, ordering things that people request, changing the lineup again, trying out a different placement, listening, yakking, and hand-trucking more product onto the floor. 28

In the basement of American capitalism, you can see the invisible hand at work, except it's not invisible. It's actually your hand. 29

The streamlining of the big dollar stores opens up, for other outlets, their original source of cheap merchandise: distressed goods, closeouts, overstock, salvage merchandize, department-store returns, liquidated goods, discontinued lines, clearance items, ex-catalog stock, freight-damaged goods, irregulars, salvage cosmetics, test-market items and bankruptcy inventories. 30

This secondary market supplies another stratum of retail chains below the 31
dollar-store channel, one of the best known being Big Lots. Hamilton explained
that if these guys don't sell the merchandise, it bumps on down the line to another
level known as liquidators.

Hamilton drove me out to Steve's Liquidators outside Portland, Oregon. It 32
was marked by only a sign on the road. The store itself was an unadorned massive warehouse, with not even a sign over the door, a Euclidean concrete cube
painted a bright lime green with lemon yellow trim.

As we entered, a scruffy man exited, pushing a busted cart—each palsied 33
wheel pulling in a different direction—into a busy parking lot brimming with
older-model automobiles. Inside, the store could not have been more spare, a
decrepit imitation of a standard suburban grocery store. Exposed warehouse
ceilings above, and below, an unfinished shop floor occupied by metal industrial
shelving with aisles wide and deep enough to forklift in the goods. Here is where
food products minutes away from expiration hover, on the cusp of becoming
compost.

A pallet of giant restaurant-grade cans formed a giant ingot of eggplant in 34
tomato sauce. Hamilton examined the cans, each dented and dinged, labels
torn—all still sitting on a wooden pallet, partly in its shrink-wrap. "Must have
fallen off a truck," he mused. There were sparse fruits and vegetables and rows
of salvaged canned goods. Scattered throughout and along the sides were whatever else had been left behind at the dollar stores and then the closeout stores
and maybe even the thrift shops—dozens of princess night lights, a single mattress leaning against a wall, a pallet of car oil, an array of carpets, a thousand
boxes of the same generic cornflakes, a leaf blower. Back in the car, I asked Hamilton where the merchandise would go if it didn't sell here.

"The Dumpster," he said. 35

FOR DISCUSSION

. . . .

1. Why, according to Jack Hitt, are Americans, even affluent ones, shopping more and more frequently in dollar stores? Is his assessment accurate? Explain.

2. Do you agree that "shopping is our hunting and gathering" (20)? Why or why not?

3. Hitt says that the economy represented by dollar stores, particularly the larger chains, is "evolving" (25). In what ways? For what PURPOSE do species usually evolve?

4. Dollar stores have low profit margins, so how do the successful ones make money (13)? What are some of the earmarks of a successful dollar store, according to Hitt?

STRATEGIES AND STRUCTURES

. . . .

1. What is Hitt's main purpose in exploring the lower ranks of retail outlets in America? Where does he first state the general point he is making by CLASSIFYING different types of discount stores?

2. Hitt divides dollar stores into two basic categories. What are they, and what are some of the main traits that distinguish the two types?

3. If independent dollar stores constitute "the basement of American capitalism," what is the sub-sub-sub-basement (29)? Where does a chain like Big Lots fit in this secondary classification system? How about Steve's Liquidators outside Portland, Oregon (32)? Explain.

4. By what specific traits does Hitt distinguish among various types in the "stratum of retail chains below the dollar-store channel" (31)? Point out several EXAMPLES, including ones that occupy an entire paragraph.

5. As Hitt delves into the nether regions of the dollar-store economy, he talks about encounters with various guides, such as the crafts blogger Heather Mann (1–5). How and how well do these ANECDOTES help the reader sort out and understand the different categories Hitt is identifying?

WORDS AND FIGURES OF SPEECH

. . . .

1. Comment on the irony of Hitt's reference to a Dollar Tree store that is "exemplary in its competitive cunning" (13).

2. The French term *mise-en-scène* (literally "put in the scene"), refers to the staging of a play (15). Why does Hitt appropriate this term from the theater to DESCRIBE a dollar store in Beaverton, Oregon?

3. "You have bagged the deer," says the sociology professor whom Hitt cites as an expert on consumer culture (20). What deer? Explain her METAPHOR.

4. Google "invisible hand" and Adam Smith, the Scottish philosopher who coined it (29). What did Smith mean by the term, and how has it come to be used by modern economists?

5. At the bottom of the dollar-store food chain, Hitt finds dated goods "on the cusp of becoming compost" (33). In what sense is he using the word "cusp" in an essay about trends in retailing?

FOR WRITING

. . . .

1. Visit a Sears, Walmart, or other department store and make a list of the main categories of goods and services it provides as suggested by the store's signage, including "planograms."

2. Choose a "stratum" (high-end, low-end, middle, other) of retail outlets, including car dealerships, and write an essay classifying the different kinds of businesses you find in that stratum. Mention particular people you encounter, and try to relate your classification to the economy in general.

WARREN BUFFETT

STOP CODDLING THE SUPER-RICH

Warren Buffett (b. 1930) is the CEO of Berkshire Hathaway, a holding company headquartered in Omaha, Nebraska, with total assets of over $300 billion. One of the richest men in the world and widely regarded as the most successful investor of his generation, the "Sage of Omaha" has pledged to donate approximately 99 percent of his wealth to charitable causes. He once said, "I want to give my kids just enough so that they would feel that they could do anything, but not so much that they would feel like doing nothing." Except for a private jet named *The Indefensible*, Buffett lives modestly in a house he purchased in 1957 for $31,500. In "Stop Coddling the Super-Rich" (*New York Times*, 2011), Buffett uses a classification system based on income (and equity) to argue for an increase in taxes for the wealthiest Americans, classifying them in general as "those making more than $1 million." A version of this "Buffett rule" was considered by the U.S. Senate as part of the Paying a Fair Share Act of 2012, but it did not receive enough votes to move forward. The bill would have raised approximately $46.7 billion in tax revenue over the next 10 years, according to an estimate by the bipartisan Joint Committee on Taxation in March 2012.

Our leaders have asked for "shared sacrifice." But when they did the asking, they spared me. I checked with my mega-rich friends to learn what pain they were expecting. They, too, were left untouched.

While the poor and middle class fight for us in Afghanistan, and while most Americans struggle to make ends meet, we mega-rich continue to get our extraordinary tax breaks. Some of us are investment managers who earn billions from our daily labors but are allowed to classify our income as "carried interest," thereby getting a bargain 15 percent tax rate. Others own stock index futures for 10 minutes and have 60 percent of their gain taxed at 15 percent, as if they'd been long-term investors.

These and other blessings are showered upon us by legislators in Washington who feel compelled to protect us, much as if we were spotted owls or some other endangered species. It's nice to have friends in high places.

To belong to a particular species, one must exhibit *all* its significant traits, p. 244. Billionaires are rare but not endangered.

Last year my federal tax bill—the income tax I paid, as well as payroll taxes paid by me and on my behalf—was $6,938,744. That sounds like a lot of money. But what I paid was only 17.4 percent of my taxable income—and that's actually a lower percentage than was paid by any of the other 20 people in our office. Their tax burdens ranged from 33 percent to 41 percent and averaged 36 percent.

If you make money with money, as some of my super-rich friends do, your percentage may be a bit lower than mine. But if you earn money from a job, your percentage will surely exceed mine—most likely by a lot.

To understand why, you need to examine the sources of government revenue. Last year about 80 percent of these revenues came from personal income taxes and payroll taxes. The mega-rich pay income taxes at a rate of 15 percent on most of their earnings but pay practically nothing in payroll taxes. It's a different story for the middle class: typically, they fall into the 15 percent and 25 percent income-tax brackets, and then are hit with heavy payroll taxes to boot.

Back in the 1980s and 1990s, tax rates for the rich were far higher, and my percentage rate was in the middle of the pack. According to a theory I sometimes hear, I should have thrown a fit and refused to invest because of the elevated tax rates on capital gains and dividends.

I didn't refuse, nor did others. I have worked with investors for 60 years 8 and I have yet to see anyone—not even when capital gains rates were 39.9 percent in 1976–77—shy away from a sensible investment because of the tax rate on the potential gain. People invest to make money, and potential taxes have never scared them off. And to those who argue that higher rates hurt job creation, I would note that a net of nearly 40 million jobs were added between 1980 and 2000. You know what's happened since then: lower tax rates and far lower job creation.

Since 1992, the I.R.S. has compiled data from the returns of the 400 Ameri- 9 cans reporting the largest income. In 1992, the top 400 had aggregate taxable income of $16.9 billion and paid federal taxes of 29.2 percent on that sum. In 2008, the aggregate income of the highest 400 had soared to $90.9 billion—a staggering $227.4 million on average—but the rate paid had fallen to 21.5 percent.

The taxes I refer to here include only federal income tax, but you can be 10 sure that any payroll tax for the 400 was inconsequential compared to income. In fact, 88 of the 400 in 2008 reported no wages at all, though every one of them reported capital gains. Some of my brethren may shun work but they all like to invest. (I can relate to that.)

I know well many of the mega-rich and, by and large, they are very decent 11 people. They love America and appreciate the opportunity this country has given them. Many have joined the Giving Pledge, promising to give most of their wealth to philanthropy. Most wouldn't mind being told to pay more in taxes as well, particularly when so many of their fellow citizens are truly suffering.

Twelve members of Congress will soon take on the crucial job of 12 rearranging our country's finances.[1] They've been instructed to devise a plan that reduces the 10-year deficit by at least $1.5 trillion. It's vital, however, that they achieve far more than that. Americans are rapidly losing faith in the ability of Congress to deal with our country's fiscal problems. Only action that is imme- diate, real, and very substantial will prevent that doubt from morphing into hopelessness. That feeling can create its own reality.

Job one for the 12 is to pare down some future promises that even a rich 13 America can't fulfill. Big money must be saved here. The 12 should then turn to

1. Reference to the Congress's Joint Select Committee on Deficit Reduction (popularly known as the "Supercommittee"), which was unable to come to an agreement on how best to handle the U.S. budget deficit and disbanded in November 2011.

the issue of revenues. I would leave rates for 99.7 percent of taxpayers unchanged and continue the current 2-percentage-point reduction in the employee contribution to the payroll tax. This cut helps the poor and the middle class, who need every break they can get.

But for those making more than $1 million—there were 236,883 such households in 2009—I would raise rates immediately on taxable income in excess of $1 million, including, of course, dividends and capital gains. And for those who make $10 million or more—there were 8,274 in 2009—I would suggest an additional increase in rate.

My friends and I have been coddled long enough by a billionaire-friendly Congress. It's time for our government to get serious about shared sacrifice.

FOR DISCUSSION

1. Why does Warren Buffett think legislators in Washington should stop "coddling" the country's richest taxpayers? Do you agree? Why or why not?
2. According to Buffett, how has the federal tax system changed since the 1980s? Should he have said more about the causes of those changes, or is he wise to leave them largely unspecified? Explain.
3. What economic "theory" is Buffett referring to in paragraph 7? Why does he think this view of investment is incorrect? What evidence does he give?
4. According to Buffett, what specific actions should Congress take in order to do "the crucial job of rearranging our country's finances" (12)? Why does Buffett think these steps are especially needed now?

STRATEGIES AND STRUCTURES

1. An income tax system is, by definition, a CLASSIFICATION system. As laid out by Buffett, what are some of the principle categories of the present system of classifying taxpayers and their incomes in the United States?
2. How and how well does Buffett use these various categories to support his ARGUMENT that the system needs to be changed? Point out specific examples in the text that you find particularly effective.

3. When and where does Buffett use mainly anecdotal evidence to make his case? When does he turn to statistics? Should he have included more (or fewer) numbers? Explain.

4. Many wealthy people, says Buffett, "classify our income as 'carried interest'" (2). How and how well does this example support Buffett's claim that such a classification system is faulty?

5. "I know well many of the 'mega-rich' and, by and large, they are very decent people" (11). How and how well does Buffett establish his credibility as someone qualified to speak authoritatively about each of these categories? Explain.

WORDS AND FIGURES OF SPEECH

1. If the "mega-rich," according to Buffett's classification system, are "those who make $10 million or more" (14), how does the system define the merely "super-rich"?

2. *Coddled* is a word usually reserved for children. What does it mean, and why does Buffett use the term to refer to a particular economic class (or classes)?

3. In Buffett's accounting of the traits and conditions that define the super-rich, what are the implications of the word "blessings" (3)? Of "showered" (3)?

4. Why does Buffett put "shared sacrifice" in quotation marks at the beginning of his essay but not at the end (1, 15)?

FOR WRITING

1. Check out the Internal Revenue Service's website at www.irs.gov. Make a list of the main categories of information and services on the site.

2. Many banks and lending institutions in the United States identify a category of customers whom they call the "mass affluent." Write a classification essay about this socio-economic group that explains its common traits and divides this general category into subgroups. Be sure to explain why bankers and stockbrokers might be particularly interested in this segment of the American population.

DAVID BROOKS

HARMONY AND THE DREAM

David Brooks (b. 1961) is a political columnist for the *New York Times* and a regular commentator on National Public Radio. He is the author of several books, including *Bobos in Paradise* (2000), a book of cultural commentary about wealth in the United States, and most recently *The Social Animal* (2011). In "Harmony and the Dream," an op-ed column published in the *Times* in 2008, Brooks takes a more global view, classifying the societies of the world, particularly China and the United States, as either "collectivist" or "individualistic." Brooks wrote this essay in Chengdu, China, while on assignment at the 2008 Olympic Games.

T he world can be divided in many ways—rich and poor, democratic and authoritarian—but one of the most striking is the divide between the societies with an individualist mentality and the ones with a collectivist mentality.

    This is a divide that goes deeper than economics into the way people perceive the world. If you show an American an image of a fish tank, the American will usually describe the biggest fish in the tank and what it is doing. If you ask a Chinese person to describe a fish tank, the Chinese will usually describe the context in which the fish swim.

These sorts of experiments have been done over and over again, and the results reveal the same underlying pattern. Americans usually see individuals; Chinese and other Asians see contexts.

3

When the psychologist Richard Nisbett[1] showed Americans individual pictures of a chicken, a cow, and hay and asked the subjects to pick out the two that go together, the Americans would usually pick out the chicken and the cow. They're both animals. Most Asian people, on the other hand, would pick out the cow and the hay, since cows depend on hay. Americans are more likely to see categories. Asians are more likely to see relationships.

4

You can create a global continuum with the most individualistic societies— like the United States or Britain—on one end, and the most collectivist societies— like China or Japan—on the other.

5

The individualistic countries tend to put rights and privacy first. People in these societies tend to overvalue their own skills and overestimate their own importance to any group effort. People in collective societies tend to value harmony and duty. They tend to underestimate their own skills and are more self-effacing when describing their contributions to group efforts.

6

Researchers argue about why certain cultures have become more individualistic than others. Some say that Western cultures draw their values from ancient Greece, with its emphasis on individual heroism, while other cultures draw more on tribal philosophies. Recently, some scientists have theorized that it all goes back to microbes. Collectivist societies tend to pop up in parts of the world, especially around the equator, with plenty of disease-causing microbes. In such an environment, you'd want to shun outsiders, who might bring strange diseases, and enforce a certain conformity over eating rituals and social behavior.

7

Either way, individualistic societies have tended to do better economically. We in the West have a narrative that involves the development of individual reason and conscience during the Renaissance and the Enlightenment,[2]

8

1. Professor of social psychology (b. 1940) and co-director of the Culture and Cognition program at the University of Michigan.

2. During the Enlightenment, which began in the late 1600s, European philosophers questioned conventional ways of thinking about morality, social systems, religion, and individual freedom. The Renaissance refers to a rebirth in learning and the arts in the fifteenth century.

and then the subsequent flourishing of capitalism. According to this narrative, societies get more individualistic as they develop.

But what happens if collectivist societies snap out of their economic stagnation? What happens if collectivist societies, especially those in Asia, rise economically and come to rival the West? A new sort of global conversation develops. 9

The opening ceremony in Beijing was a statement in that conversation. It was part of China's assertion that development doesn't come only through Western, liberal means, but also through Eastern and collective ones. 10

The ceremony drew from China's long history, but surely the most striking features were the images of thousands of Chinese moving as one—drumming as one, dancing as one, sprinting on precise formations without ever stumbling or colliding. We've seen displays of mass conformity before, but this was collectivism of the present—a high-tech vision of the harmonious society performed in the context of China's miraculous growth. 11

If Asia's success reopens the debate between individualism and collectivism (which seemed closed after the cold war[3]), then it's unlikely that the forces of individualism will sweep the field or even gain an edge. 12

For one thing, there are relatively few individualistic societies on earth. For another, the essence of a lot of the latest scientific research is that the Western idea of individual choice is an illusion and the Chinese are right to put first emphasis on social contexts. 13

Scientists have delighted to show that so-called rational choice is shaped by a whole range of subconscious influences, like emotional contagions[4] and priming effects[5] (people who think of a professor before taking a test do better than people who think of a criminal). Meanwhile, human brains turn out to be extremely permeable (they naturally mimic the neural firings of people around them). Relationships are the key to happiness. People who live in the densest social networks tend to flourish, while people who live with few social bonds are much more prone to depression and suicide. 14

3. A period of intense hostility between the United States and the communist-led Soviet Union that lasted from the mid-1940s until the fall of the Soviet Union in 1991.

4. Concept that people subconsciously mimic the emotions of others they interact with.

5. Concept that a previous stimulus can prompt the human brain to perform in certain ways.

The rise of China isn't only an economic event. It's a cultural one. The 15
ideal of a harmonious collective may turn out to be as attractive as the ideal of
the American Dream.[6]

It's certainly a useful ideology for aspiring autocrats. 16

FOR DISCUSSION

. . . .

1. Why, according to David Brooks, does the "divide" between China and the
   United States go "deeper than economics" (2)?
2. What does Brooks mean when he says that "the debate between individualism and
   collectivism . . . seemed closed after the cold war" (12)? In his view, what would
   reopen the "global conversation" (9) between the two types of societies? Explain.
3. In what ways does recent scientific research suggest that "the Chinese are right to
   put first emphasis on social contexts" (13)?
4. How does this same research suggest that "the American Dream" might be an
   "illusion" (15, 13)? Explain.

STRATEGIES AND STRUCTURES

. . . .

1. What is Brooks's main point in dividing the world into "collectivist societies"
   and "individualistic societies" (5)? Where does he state it most directly?
2. On what basis is Brooks classifying the societies of the world into these two categories? What's his main principle of CLASSIFICATION here?
3. According to Brooks, what are some of the main characteristics of collectivist
   societies? Of individualistic societies?
4. How effective is Brooks's EXAMPLE of the fish tank (2) for explaining the differences between the two categories that he examines? Point to other similar examples throughout his essay. How and how well do they help explain the characteristics that distinguish each of the groups he discusses?
5. Brooks's classification system is made up of two basic categories, which he places at
   opposite ends of a "global continuum" (5). Is this an effective strategy for enlarging

6. American ideal that through hard work, persistence, and good moral character, anyone
can succeed, even from humble beginnings.

the scope of his classification system? What problems might arise from this strategy, and what are the benefits of it?

6. Who does Brooks assume is his main AUDIENCE? What cultural background does this audience share? Point to specific passages that support your answer.

7. What possible CAUSES does Brooks give for the development of collectivist societies? How about individualistic societies? What do his explanations contribute to his essay?

WORDS AND FIGURES OF SPEECH

1. What does Brooks mean by "mentality" (1)? How does his use of this term fit with his later references to psychology and the human brain?

2. Brooks chooses the word "harmony" to describe the ideology of collectivism (6). What alternate terms might he have chosen? Why do you think he chose this one?

3. What are the implications of describing the "economic stagnation" of collectivist societies as a condition they can "snap out" of (9)?

4. Why do you think Brooks refers to a new global "conversation" rather than a new global *standoff, conflict,* or *confrontation* (9)?

5. Explain the different CONNOTATIONS of the following words: "idea," "ideal," and "ideology" (13, 15, 16).

6. What is an "autocrat," and why might he or she find the ideology of a collective society to be "useful" (16)?

FOR WRITING

1. Have you ever been in a situation where a group of people exhibited signs of "mass conformity" (11)? Describe that situation or event in a paragraph or two. Be sure to say what was "collectivist" about it.

2. Using Brooks's categories of individualistic and collectivist groups, write an essay classifying the clubs and other student organizations in your school. Be sure to account for groups that share characteristics of both categories, and consider adding additional categories to your system, if necessary.

ROBERT LUSTIG, LAURA SCHMIDT,
AND CLAIRE BRINDIS

THE TOXIC TRUTH ABOUT SUGAR

Robert Lustig is a professor of clinical pediatrics at the University of California, San Francisco, and his specialty is childhood obesity. Laura Schmidt and Claire Brindis also teach at UCSF in the Philip R. Lee Institute for Health Policy, which Brindis directs. In this article, first published in *Nature* in 2012, these three health experts put sugar in the same category as alcohol and tobacco. Classified this way, they argue, sugar likewise "warrants some form of societal intervention" and should be regulated like the other two substances.

◇◇◇◇◇◇◇◇◇◇◇◇◇◇◇◇◇◇◇◇◇◇◇◇◇◇

L ast September, the United Nations declared that, for the first time in human history, chronic noncommunicable diseases such as heart disease, cancer, and diabetes pose a greater health burden worldwide than do infectious diseases, contributing to 35 million deaths annually.

This is not just a problem of the developed world. Every country that has adopted the Western diet—one dominated by low-cost, highly processed food— has witnessed rising rates of obesity and related diseases. There are now 30 percent more people who are obese than who are undernourished. Economic development means that the populations of low- and middle-income countries are living longer, and therefore are more susceptible to noncommunicable diseases; 80 percent of deaths attributable to them occur in these countries. Many people think that obesity is the root cause of these diseases. But 20 percent of obese people have normal metabolism and will have a normal lifespan. Conversely, up to 40 percent of normal-weight people develop the diseases that constitute the metabolic syndrome: diabetes, hypertension, lipid problems, cardiovascular disease and nonalcoholic fatty liver disease. Obesity is not the cause; rather, it is a marker for metabolic dysfunction, which is even more prevalent.

The UN announcement targets tobacco, alcohol, and diet as the central risk factors in noncommunicable disease. Two of these three—tobacco and alcohol—are regulated by governments to protect public health, leaving one of the primary culprits behind this worldwide health crisis unchecked. Of course, regulating food is more complicated—food is required, whereas tobacco and alcohol are nonessential consumables. The key question is: what aspects of the Western diet should be the focus of intervention?

In October 2011, Denmark chose to tax foods high in saturated fat, despite the fact that most medical professionals no longer believe that fat is the primary culprit. But now the country is considering taxing sugar as well—a more plausible and defensible step. Indeed, rather than focusing on fat and salt—the current dietary "bogeymen" of the US Department of Agriculture (USDA) and the European Food Safety Authority—we believe that attention should be turned to "added sugar," defined as any sweetener containing the molecule fructose that is added to food in processing.

Over the past 50 years consumption of sugar has tripled worldwide. In the United States, there is fierce controversy over the pervasive use of one particular added sugar—high-fructose corn syrup (HFCS). It is manufactured from corn syrup (glucose), processed to yield a roughly equal mixture of glucose and fructose. Most other developed countries eschew HFCS, relying on naturally occurring sucrose as an added sugar, which also consists of equal parts glucose and fructose.

Authorities consider sugar as "empty calories"—but there is nothing empty about these calories. A growing body of scientific evidence is showing that fructose can trigger processes that lead to liver toxicity and a host of other chronic diseases.[1] A little is not a problem, but a lot kills—slowly. If international bodies are truly concerned about public health, they must consider limiting fructose—and its main delivery vehicles, the added sugars HFCS and sucrose—which pose dangers to individuals and to society as a whole.

No Ordinary Commodity

In 2003, social psychologist Thomas Babor and his colleagues published a landmark book called *Alcohol: No Ordinary Commodity*, in which they established four criteria, now largely accepted by the public-health community, that justify the regulation of alcohol—unavoidability (or pervasiveness throughout society), toxicity, potential for abuse, and negative impact on society.[2] Sugar meets the same criteria, and we believe that it similarly warrants some form of societal intervention.

See p. 243 on organizing a classification essay by distinguishing features.

7

First, consider unavoidability. Evolutionarily, sugar was available to our ancestors as fruit for only a few months a year (at harvest time), or as honey, which was guarded by bees. But in recent years, sugar has been added to nearly all processed foods, limiting consumer choice.[3] Nature made sugar hard to get; man made it easy. In many parts of the world, people are consuming an average of more than 500 calories per day from added sugar alone.

8

Now, let's consider toxicity. A growing body of evidence argues that excessive sugar consumption affects human health beyond simply adding calories.[4] Importantly, sugar induces all of the diseases associated with metabolic syndrome.[5] This includes: hypertension (fructose increases uric acid, which raises blood pressure); high triglycerides and insulin resistance through synthesis of fat in the liver; diabetes from increased liver glucose production combined with insulin resistance; and the aging process, caused by damage to lipids, proteins, and DNA through non-enzymatic binding of fructose to these molecules. It can also be argued that fructose exerts toxic effects on the liver that are similar to those of alcohol.[6] This is no surprise, because alcohol is derived from the fermentation of sugar. Some early studies have also linked sugar consumption to human cancer and cognitive decline.

9

Sugar also has clear potential for abuse. Like tobacco and alcohol, it acts on the brain to encourage subsequent intake. There are now numerous stud-

10

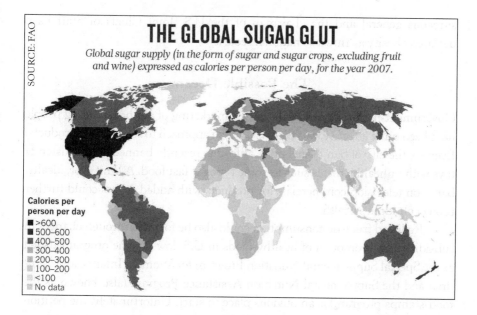

THE GLOBAL SUGAR GLUT

Global sugar supply (in the form of sugar and sugar crops, excluding fruit and wine) expressed as calories per person per day, for the year 2007.

SOURCE: FAO

Calories per
person per day
■ >600
■ 500–600
■ 400–500
■ 300–400
■ 200–300
■ 100–200
■ <100
■ No data

ies examining the dependence-producing properties of sugar in humans.[7] Specifically, sugar dampens the suppression of the hormone ghrelin, which signals hunger to the brain. It also interferes with the normal transport and signaling of the hormone leptin, which helps to produce the feeling of satiety. And it reduces dopamine signaling in the brain's reward centre, thereby decreasing the pleasure derived from food and compelling the individual to consume more.[8]

Finally, consider the negative effects of sugar on society. Passive smoking and drunk-driving fatalities provided strong arguments for tobacco and alcohol control, respectively. The long-term economic, health-care, and human costs of metabolic syndrome place sugar overconsumption in the same category.[9] The United States spends $65 billion in lost productivity and $150 billion on health-care resources annually for morbidities associated with metabolic syndrome. Seventy-five percent of all U.S. health-care dollars are now spent on treating these diseases and their resultant disabilities. Because about 25 percent of military applicants are now rejected for obesity-related reasons, the past three U.S.

11

surgeons general and the chairman of the U.S. Joint Chiefs of Staff have declared obesity a "threat to national security."

The Possible Dream

Government-imposed regulations on the marketing of alcohol to young people have been quite effective, but there is no such approach to sugar-laden products. Even so, the city of San Francisco, California, recently banned the inclusion of toys with unhealthy meals such as some types of fast food. A limit—or, ideally, ban—on television commercials for products with added sugars could further protect children's health.

    Reduced fructose consumption could also be fostered through changes in subsidization. Promotion of healthy foods in U.S. low-income programs, such as the Special Supplemental Nutrition Program for Women, Infants, and Children and the Supplemental Nutrition Assistance Program (also known as the food-stamps program) is an obvious place to start. Unfortunately, the petition by New York City to remove soft drinks from the food-stamp program was denied by the USDA.

    Ultimately, food producers and distributors must reduce the amount of sugar added to foods. But sugar is cheap, sugar tastes good and sugar sells, so companies have little incentive to change. Although one institution alone can't turn this juggernaut around, the US Food and Drug Administration could "set the table" for change.[10] To start, it should consider removing fructose from the Generally Regarded as Safe (GRAS) list, which allows food manufacturers to add unlimited amounts to any food. Opponents will argue that other nutrients on the GRAS list, such as iron and vitamins A and D, can also be toxic when overconsumed. However, unlike sugar, these substances have no abuse potential. Removal from the GRAS list would send a powerful signal to the European Food Safety Authority and the rest of the world.

    Regulating sugar will not be easy—particularly in the "emerging markets" of developing countries where soft drinks are often cheaper than potable water or milk. We recognize that societal intervention to reduce the supply and demand for sugar faces an uphill political battle against a powerful sugar lobby, and will

12

13

14

1

require active engagement from all stakeholders. Still, the food industry knows that it has a problem—even vigorous lobbying by fast-food companies couldn't defeat the toy ban in San Francisco. With enough clamor for change, tectonic shifts in policy become possible. Take, for instance, bans on smoking in public places and the use of designated drivers, not to mention airbags in cars and condom dispensers in public bathrooms. These simple measures—which have all been on the battleground of American politics—are now taken for granted as essential tools for our public health and well-being. It's time to turn our attention to sugar.

Notes

1. R. H. Lustig, "Fructose: Metabolic, Hedonic, and Societal Parallels with Ethanol," *Journal of the American Dietary Association* 110 (2010): 1307–21.

2. T. Babor et al., *Alcohol: No Ordinary Commodity: Research and Public Policy* (New York: Oxford University Press, 2003).

3. F. Vio and R. Uauy, "The Sugar Controversy," in *Food Policy for Developing Countries: Case Studies*, eds. P. Pinstrup-Andersen and F. Cheng, no. 9-5 (Ithaca, NY: Cornell University, 2007).

4. Joint WHO/FAO Expert Consultation, *Diet, Nutrition, and the Prevention of Chronic Diseases*, WHO Technical Report Series 916 (Geneva: WHO, 2003).

5. Lustig, "Fructose"; see also: L. Tappy, K. A. Lê, C. Tran, and N. Paquot, "Fructose and Metabolic Diseases: New Findings, New Questions," *Nutrition* 26 (2010): 1044–49.

6. Lustig, "Fructose."

7. A. K. Garber and R. H. Lustig, "Is Fast Food Addictive?" *Current Drug Abuse Reviews* 4 (2011): 146–62.

8. Lustig, "Fructose"; Garber and Lustig, "Is Fast Food Addictive?"

9. E. A. Finkelstein, I. C. Fiebelkorn, and G. Wang, "National Medical Spending Attributable to Overweight and Obesity: How Much, and Who's Paying?" *Health Affairs* W3 (suppl., 2003): 219–26.

10. C. L. Engelhard, A. Garson Jr., and S. Dorn, *Reducing Obesity: Policy Strategies from the Tobacco Wars* (Urban Institute, 2009); see go.nature.com/w4o5uk.

FOR DISCUSSION

. . . .

1. Why are Robert Lustig, Laura Schmidt, and Claire Brindis so concerned about the added sugar or other sweeteners in commercially available food and drinks (7–11)? Are their fears justified? Explain.

2. What solutions do they propose? Are these measures likely to work? Explain.

3. How do health experts define "added sugar" (5)? How does high-fructose corn syrup (HFCS) fit into this category?

4. According to Lustig, Schmidt, and Brindis, why is it more difficult to regulate food than alcohol and tobacco? Do you agree that added sugars should be regulated? Why or why not?

STRATEGIES AND STRUCTURES

. . . .

1. Lustig and his colleagues argue that sugar should be classified like alcohol and tobacco. Why? On what basis would they put sugar in the same general category as these other two commodities? Explain.

2. In a binary CLASSIFICATION system, a subject like "commodities" is divided into two basic categories. One of the basic categories here is "no ordinary commodity"; what is the other one (7)? According to Lustig and his colleagues, what is the fundamental difference between these two categories?

3. Lustig and his colleagues list four "criteria" for belonging to the special group they're concerned about (7–11). What are those criteria? Why do these researchers think sugar belongs in this special group?

4. In the second section of their essay, the authors devote an entire paragraph to each of the four traits that, in their view, characterize commodities that should be regulated. Is this a good strategy, or should they have simply listed the traits and moved on? Explain.

5. The authors of "The Toxic Truth about Sugar" use classification to make an ARGUMENT for regulating the production and consumption of sugar. How and how well is this claim supported by the classification system they propose?

6. If Lustig and his colleagues have already made their point about the need to regulate sugar, what is their purpose—and how well do they achieve it—in the final section of their essay? Explain.

WORDS AND FIGURES OF SPEECH

. . . .

1. "The Toxic Truth about Sugar" is an essay about food and diet. Why do the authors use the term *toxic* instead of *unhealthy* or *non-nutritious?* Why do they pair this harsh term with *truth?*

2. Lustig and his colleagues say that alcohol, tobacco, and sugar are "central risk factors in noncommunicable diseases" (3). What kind of language is this? How would you classify it, and where else do they use it? Point out several specific examples.

3. How would you classify terms like *culprit, empty,* and *cheaper* (4, 6, 15)? Explain why such terms might belong in a different category (or categories) from ones like *central risk factors* (3).

4. Why is the phrase "set the table" in quotation marks (14)?

FOR WRITING

. . . .

1. Make a list of the criteria you would use to classify "ordinary commodities" that do not need to be controlled or regulated.

2. You are the CEO of a large food or sugar company (Conglomerated Foods, Total Sugar). Using a classification system of your own—or modifying theirs—write a rebuttal to the argument of Lustig, Schmidt, and Brindis. Be sure to cite your sources as they do.

CHAPTER EIGHT

PROCESS ANALYSIS

◊∧◊∨◊∧◊∨◊∧◊∨◊∧◊∨◊∧◊∨◊∧◊∨◊∧◊∨◊∧◊∨◊∧◊∨◊∧◊∨◊∧◊∨◊

T HE essays in this chapter are examples of PROCESS ANALYSIS* or "how to" writing. Basically, there are two kinds of process analysis: *directive* and *explanatory*. A directive process analysis explains how to make or do something—for instance, how to throw a boomerang. ("Bring the boomerang back behind you and snap it forward as if you were throwing a baseball."— howstuffworks.com) An explanatory process analysis explains how something works; it tells you what makes the boomerang come back.

Both kinds of analysis break a process into the sequence of actions that lead to its end result. In her sassy memoir *Bossypants*, for example, the comedian Tina Fey explains how to do improvisational comedy by breaking the process into four basic rules. "The first rule of improvisation," Fey writes, "is AGREE. Always agree and SAY YES." Then "add something of your own" (rule 2), continue to make positive statements (rule 3), and treat all "mistakes" as "opportunities" (rule 4).

The end result of improvisational comedy, of course, is the audience's laughter. Here's an example of how Fey follows her own "rules" to achieve this end:

> If I start a scene as what I think is very clearly a cop riding a bicycle, but you think I am a hamster in a hamster wheel, guess what? Now I'm a hamster in a hamster wheel. I'm not going to stop everything to explain

*Words printed in SMALL CAPITALS are defined in the Glossary/Index.

that it was really supposed to be a bike. Who knows? Maybe I'll end up being a police hamster who's been put on "hamster wheel" duty because I'm "too much of a loose cannon" in the field. In improv there are no mistakes, only beautiful happy accidents. And many of the world's greatest discoveries have been by accident. I mean, look at the Reese's Peanut Butter Cup, or Botox.

— TINA FEY, *Bossypants*

In a directive process analysis, you typically use the second-person pronoun (*you*) because you're giving instructions directly to the reader. Sometimes the *you* is understood, as in a recipe: *[you] combine the milk with the eggs, then add a pinch of salt and the juice of one lemon.* In an explanatory process analysis, you typically use the third-person pronoun (*he, she, it*) because you're giving information *about* something to the reader:

Allegra Goodman, p. 322, uses the second-person to tell you how to be a good writer.

The uneven force caused by the difference in speed between the two wings applies a constant force at the top of the spinning boomerang. . . . Like a leaning bicycle wheel, the boomerang is constantly turning to the left or right, so that it travels in a circle and comes back to its starting point.

—howstuffworks.com

Bring behind head, then snap forward

Sometimes a process is best explained by *showing* how it works, so you may want to add diagrams or drawings to the written text. An analysis of how to throw a boomerang, for example, might benefit from a clearly labeled diagram.

Most processes that you analyze will be linear rather than cyclical. Even if the process is repeatable, your analysis will proceed chronologically step by step, stage by stage to an end result that is different from the starting point. Consider this explanatory analysis of how fresh oranges are turned into orange juice concentrate:

> As the fruit starts to move along a concentrate plant's assembly line, it is first culled. . . . Moving up a conveyer belt, oranges are scrubbed with detergent before they roll on into juicing machines. There are several kinds of juicing machines, and they are something to see. One is called the Brown Seven Hundred. Seven hundred oranges a minute go into it and are split and reamed on the same kind of rosettes that are in the centers of ordinary kitchen reamers. The rinds that come pelting out the bottom are integral halves, just like the rinds of oranges squeezed in a kitchen. Another machine is the Food Machinery Corporation's FMC In-line Extractor. It has a shining row of aluminum teeth. When an orange tumbles in, the upper jaw comes crunching down on it while at the same time the orange is penetrated from below by a perforated steel tube. As the jaws crush the outside, the juice goes through the perforations in the tube and down into the plumbing of the concentrate plant. All in a second, the juice has been removed and the rind has been crushed and shredded beyond recognition.
>
> From either machine, the juice flows on into a thing called the finisher, where seeds, rag, and pulp are removed. The finisher has a big stainless-steel screw that steadily drives the juice through a fine-mesh screen. From the finisher, it flows on into holding tanks.
>
> —JOHN McPHEE, *Oranges*

John McPhee divides the process of making orange juice concentrate from fresh fruit into five stages: (1) culling, (2) scrubbing, (3) extracting, (4) straining,

(5) storing. When you plan an essay that analyzes a process, make a list of all the stages or phases in the process you are analyzing. Make sure that they are separate and distinct and that you haven't left any out. When you are satisfied that your list is complete, you are ready to decide upon the order in which you will present the steps.

The usual order of process analysis is chronological, beginning with the earliest stage of the process (the culling of the split and rotten oranges from the rest) and ending with the last, or with the finished product (concentrated orange juice in holding tanks). Notice that after they leave the conveyer belt, McPhee's oranges come to a fork in the road. They can go in different directions, depending upon what kind of juicing machine is being used. McPhee briefly follows the oranges into one kind of juicer and then comes back to the other. He has stopped time and forward motion for a moment. Now he picks them up again and proceeds down the line: "from either machine, the juice flows on into a thing called the finisher" where it is strained. From the straining stage, the orange concentrate goes into the fifth (and final) holding stage, where it is stored in large tanks.

An early stage in becoming a man, says Jon Katz, p. 316, is learning to show no fear.

Another lesson to take away here: if the order of the process you are analyzing is controlled by a piece of machinery or other mechanism, let it work for you. McPhee, in fact, lets several machines—conveyor belt, extractor, and finisher—help him organize his analysis.

Some stages in a process analysis may be more complicated than others. Suppose you are explaining to someone how to replace a light switch. You might break the process down into six stages: (1) select and purchase the new switch; (2) turn off the power at the breaker box; (3) remove the switch plate; (4) disconnect the old switch and install the new one; (5) replace the switch plate; (6) turn the power back on. Obviously, one of these stages—"disconnect the old switch and install the new one"—is more complicated than the others. When this happens, you can break down the more complicated stage into its constituent steps, as McPhee does with his analysis of the production of orange juice concentrate.

The most complicated stage in McPhee's process analysis is the third one, extracting. He breaks it into the following steps: (1) an orange enters the extractor; (2) it is crushed by the extractor's steel jaws; (3) at the same time, the orange is "penetrated from below by a perforated steel tube"; (4) the extracted juice flows on to the next stage of the process. All of this happens "in a second," says McPhee; but for purposes of analysis and explanation, the steps must be presented in sequence, using such TRANSITIONS as "when," "while at the same time," "all in a second," "from . . . to," "next," and "then."

McPhee's process analysis is explanatory; it tells how orange juice concentrate is made. When you are telling someone how to do something (a directive process analysis), the method of breaking the process into steps and stages is the same. Here's how our analysis of how to change a light switch might break down the most complicated step in the process, the one where the old switch is removed and replaced. The transitions and other words that signal the order and timing of the steps *within* this stage are printed in italics:

Jeffrey Skinner uses this kind of process analysis to explain how to write poetry, p. 327.

> To remove the old switch, *first* unscrew the two terminal screws on the sides. *If* the wires are attached to the back of the switch, *instead* clip off the old wires as close to the switch as possible. As necessary, strip the insulation from the ends of the wires *until* approximately half an inch is exposed. *Next,* unscrew the green grounding screw, *and* disconnect the bare wire attached to it. You are *now* ready to remove the old switch and replace it with the new one. *Either* insert the ends of the insulated wires into the holes on the back of the new switch, *or* bend the ends of the wires around the terminal screws *and* tighten the screws. *Reattach* the bare wire to the green terminal. *Finally,* secure the new switch by tightening the two long screws at top and bottom into the ears on the old switch box.

Explaining this stage in our analysis is further complicated because we have to stop the flow of information (with "if . . . instead"; "either . . . or . . . and") to go down a fork in the road—the wires can be attached either to the screws on the sides of the switch or to holes in the rear—before getting back on track. And we now have to signal a move on to the next stage: "Once the new switch is installed, replacing the switch plate is a snap."

Actually, this simple next-to-last stage (before turning the power back on) requires a *twist* of the little screw in the center of the switch plate, which can serve to remind us that the forward movement of a process analysis, step

by step, from beginning to end, is much like the twisting and turning of the
PLOT in a NARRATIVE. Like plot in narrative, a process is a sequence of events
or actions. You are the NARRATOR, and you are telling the exciting story of
how something is made or done or how it works. Also as with a narrative, you
will want your process analysis to make a point so the reader
knows why you're analyzing the process and what to expect.
When Tina Fey analyzes how to do improv, for example, she is
also careful to explain that "the rules of improvisation appealed
to me not only as a way of creating comedy, but as a worldview."

"The Pizza Plot,"
p. 342, combines
narrative and
process analysis—
but not to tell how
to make pizza.

You may simply conclude your story with the product or end result of the
process you've been analyzing. But you may want to round out your account by
summarizing the stages you have just gone through or by encouraging the reader
to follow your directions—"Changing a light switch yourself is easy, and it can
save money"—or by explaining why the process is important. The production
of orange juice concentrate, for example, transformed Florida's citrus industry.
In what is called "the old fresh-fruit days," 40 percent of the oranges grown in
Florida were left to rot in the fields because they couldn't travel well. "Now," as
McPhee notes, "with the exception of split and rotten fruit, all of Florida's orange
crop is used." This is not exactly the end product of the process McPhee is analyzing, but it is an important consequence and one that makes technical advances
in the citrus industry seem more worth reading about.

One other detail, though a minor one, in McPhee's analysis that you may
find interesting: when all that fresh fruit was left to rot on the ground because it
couldn't be shipped and local people couldn't use it all, the cows stepped in to
help. Thus McPhee notes that in the days before orange juice concentrate,
"Florida milk tasted like orangeade." Details like this may not make the process
you are analyzing clearer or more accurate, but they may well make the reader
more interested in the process itself.

A BRIEF GUIDE TO WRITING
A PROCESS ANALYSIS

As you write a PROCESS ANALYSIS, you need to say what process you're analyzing
and to identify some of its most important steps. These moves are fundamental

to any process analysis. Allegra Goodman makes these basic moves of process analysis in her essay in this chapter:

> Forthwith, some advice for those of you who have always wanted to write. . . . To begin, don't write about yourself. . . . [I]f you want to be a writer, start by writing about other people. . . . Find a peaceful place to work. . . . Read widely. . . . value your own time.
> — ALLEGRA GOODMAN, "So, You Want to be a Writer? Here's How."

Goodman identifies the process she's analyzing (how "to be a writer") and indicates the most important steps that make up the process (write "about other people," "find a peaceful place to work," "read widely," "value your own time").

The following guidelines will help you to make these basic moves as you draft a process analysis. They will also help you to choose a process to analyze, divide it into steps, and put those steps in order, using appropriate transitions and pronouns.

Coming Up with a Subject

Your first challenge is to find a process worth analyzing. You might start by considering processes you are already familiar with, such as running a marathon, training a puppy, or playing a video game. Or you might think about processes you are interested in and want to learn more about. Do you wonder how bees make honey, how to tune a guitar, how to change the oil in a car engine, or how the oil and gas in your car are produced and refined? Whatever process you choose, you will need to understand it fully yourself before you can explain it clearly to your readers.

Considering Your Purpose and Audience

When your PURPOSE is to tell readers how to do something, a basic set of instructions will usually do the job, as when you give someone the recipe for your Aunt Mary's famous pound cake. When, however, you want your AUDIENCE to understand, not duplicate, a complicated process—such as the chemistry that makes a cake rise—your analysis should be explanatory. So instead of giving instructions ("add the sugar to the butter"), you would go over the inner workings of the process in some detail, telling readers, for example, what happens when they add baking powder to the cake mixture.

The nature of your audience will also influence the information you include. How much do your intended readers already know about the process? Why might they want to know more, or less? If you are giving a set of instructions, will they require any special tools or equipment? What problems are they likely to encounter? Will they need to know where to find more information on your topic? Asking questions like these will help you select the appropriate steps and details.

Generating Ideas: Asking How Something Works

When you analyze a process, the essential question to ask yourself is *how*. How does a cake rise? How do I back out of the garage?

Or catch a loon (p. 306)? Or conduct industrial espionage (p. 342)?

To get started, ask yourself a "how" question about your subject, research the answer (if necessary), and write down all the steps involved. For instance, "How do I back out of the garage?" might result in a list like this: put the car in reverse, step on the gas, turn the key in the ignition, look in the rearview mirror. Although this list includes all the essential steps for backing a car out of a garage, you wouldn't want your reader to follow them in this order. Once you have a complete list of steps, think about the best order in which to present them to your reader. Usually it will be chronological: turn the key in the ignition, put the car in reverse, look in the rearview mirror, step lightly on the gas pedal.

Also think about whether you should demonstrate the process—or a complex part of it—visually. If you decide to include one or more diagrams or drawings, make sure there are words to accompany each visual. Either DESCRIBE what the visual shows, or label the parts of a diagram (the parts of an engine, for instance).

Templates for Analyzing a Process

The following templates can help you to generate ideas for an essay that analyzes a process and then to start drafting. Don't take these as formulas where you just have to fill in the blanks. There are no easy formulas for good writing. But these templates can help you plot out some of the key moves of process analysis and thus may serve as good starting points.

> ► In order to understand how process X works, we can divide it into the following steps: _____, _____, and _____.
>
> ► The various steps that make up X can be grouped into the following stages: _____, _____, and _____.
>
> ► The end result of X is _____.
>
> ► In order to repeat X, you must first _____; then _____ and _____; and finally _____.
>
> ► The tools and materials you will need to replicate X include _____, _____, and _____.
>
> ► The most important reasons for understanding/repeating X are _____, _____, and _____.

For more techniques to help you generate ideas and start writing a process analysis, see Chapter 2.

Putting the Steps in Order

When you write about a process, you must present its main steps in order. If the process is a linear one, such as backing out of a garage or driving to a particular address in Dallas, you simply start at the earliest point in time and move forward chronologically, step by step, to the end result. If the process is cyclical, such as what's happening in your car engine as you drive, you will have to pick a logical point in the process and then proceed through the rest of the cycle. If, however, the process you are analyzing does not naturally follow chronology, try arranging the steps from most important to least important, or the other way around.

Stating Your Point

A good process analysis should have a point to make, and that point should be clearly expressed in a THESIS STATEMENT. Make sure your thesis statement identifies the process, indicates its end result, and tells the reader why you're analyzing it. For example:

In "How to Get Out of a Locked Trunk," p. 333, the writer is probing his fear of tight situations—such as marriage.

> You cannot understand how the Florida citrus industry works without understanding how fresh orange juice gets processed into "concentrate."
> — JOHN MCPHEE, *Oranges*

McPhee's thesis statement clearly tells the reader what process he's analyzing (making "concentrate" from fresh oranges), its end result (orange juice concentrate), and why he is analyzing it (to understand the Florida citrus industry).

Using Appropriate Transitions

As you move from one step to another, include clear TRANSITIONS, such as *next, from there, after five minutes, then*. Because the actions and events that make up a process are repeatable, you will frequently use such expressions as *usually, normally, in most cases, whenever*. Also, use transitions like *sometimes, rarely*, and *in one instance* to note any deviations from the normal order.

Using Appropriate Pronouns

In addition to appropriate transition words, be careful to use pronouns that fit the kind of analysis you are writing. In an explanatory process analysis, you will focus on the things (oranges) and activities (culling and scrubbing) that make up the process. Thus, you will usually write about the process in the third person (*he, she, it*, and *they*), as John McPhee does: "Moving up a conveyor belt, oranges are scrubbed with detergent before *they* roll on into the juicing machines." In a directive process analysis, by contrast, you are telling the reader directly how to do something as when Tina Fey tells readers how to do improv comedy. So you should typically use the second person (*you*): "When you're improvising . . . *you* are required to agree with whatever your partner has created."

Concluding a Process Analysis

A process analysis is not complete until it explains how the process ends—and the significance of that result. For example, in concluding a process analysis about training a puppy, you might say not only what the result will be but why it is important or desirable: "A well-trained dog will behave when guests visit, won't destroy your carpeting and furniture, and will make less work for you in the long run." In the case of processing oranges into concentrate, John McPhee concludes his essay by telling readers not only that the process yielded a new, concentrated form of orange juice, but that it totally changed the Florida citrus industry and saved much of the crop from going to waste—or winding up as orange-flavored milk.

EDITING FOR COMMON ERRORS IN A PROCESS ANALYSIS

Like other kinds of writing, process analysis uses distinctive patterns of language and punctuation—and thus invites typical kinds of errors. The following tips will help you to check for (and correct) these common errors when you analyze a process in your own writing.

Check to insure you've used the right pronouns

When you're explaining how something works or is done, make sure you use mostly third-person pronouns (*he, she, it, they*). When you're explaining how to do something, make sure you emphasize the second-person pronoun (*you*).

Here, readers are being told how oranges are processed by others.

▶ When fresh oranges are turned into concentrate, ~~you first scrub them~~ they are first scrubbed with detergent.

Here, readers are being told how to make orange concentrate for themselves.

▶ To turn fresh oranges into concentrate, ~~they are first scrubbed~~ <u>you must first scrub them</u> with detergent.

Check your verbs to make sure you haven't shifted needlessly between the indicative and the imperative moods

▶ According to my mother's recipe, ~~add~~ the nuts <u>are added</u>, and then the cinnamon is sprinkled on top.

▶ According to my mother's recipe, add the nuts, and then <u>sprinkle</u> the cinnamon ~~is sprinkled~~ on top.

EVERYDAY PROCESS ANALYSIS
How to Draw Cartoons

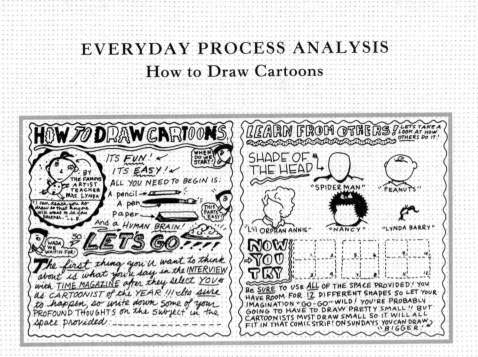

Process analysis is "how to" writing. In these tongue-in-cheek panels from a Lynda Barry cartoon, the process being analyzed is . . . how to draw cartoons. (Barry tells the more serious story of how she herself learned to draw in "The Sanctuary of School," p. 177.) When you write a process analysis that gives directions like this, you should inform readers, usually at the beginning, what ingredients or equipment they'll need to do the job. For drawing cartoons, according to Barry, these are simply "a pencil, pen, paper, and a human brain." (This last is useful with any sort of writing or illustration, not just process analysis.) You then break the process you're analyzing into steps, as Barry does. Because Barry is giving instructions directly to the reader, she uses the second-person *you*. If she were writing an explanatory process analysis instead of a directive one, she would focus on the third-person (*he, she, it*). For fun, Barry puts the last step of the process first—the one even beyond the end result of drawing a particular cartoon, where the reader, now a famous writer-cartoonist, thinks up what she wants to say to the media. So let's go—"Wada we waitin' for!"

JESSICA WALDEN

CHASING LOONS

After her sophomore year at Cornell University, Jessica Walden took an unusual summer job doing field work with a team of researchers studying the common loon on the lakes of northern Wisconsin. ("Some girls waited tables and came home with tips; I waded through bogs and came home with ticks.") Written for an advanced writing class, "Chasing Loons" is Walden's detailed analysis of the process she and her fellow researchers went through when looking for—and occasionally finding—an elusive quarry in the wild.

Chasing Loons

I drove into Rhinelander, Wisconsin, at seven in the 1
evening on May 21. My sophomore year of college behind me,
I headed out to the Midwest for a summer of field work, living
in a house with two other undergraduates and three primary
investigators from three different American universities. My
directions took me on the main highway through town, so that
I was greeted by a huge sign: "Welcome to Rhinelander, WI,
Home of the Hodag!" I'd been warned about the Hodag, a
legendary lizard-like beast covered with black hair with two
huge fangs, large horns, green eyes, and spikes running down
its spine. It is the local scapegoat for anything and everything
that goes wrong.

Rhinelander is in Oneida County, the heart of the 2
Wisconsin Northwoods, which means that it is quiet and
sparsely populated. Half the roads are unpaved, with names
like Sheep Ranch Road and South Lost Lake Lane. Apparently there are 1,129 lakes in Oneida County; I can personally
vouch for a tenth of them. The dry, matter-of-fact Northwoods sense of humor is evident in the lakes' names: Clear
Lake, Mud Lake, Lost Lake, Long Lake, another Long Lake
(even longer than the first), Madeline and Carrol Lakes, Lake
Seventeen (apparently they ran out of names), North Two and
South Two Lakes, and my personal favorite, Wind Pudding
Lake. Life in the Northwoods is centered on the water. Some
residents were born in the houses on the lakes that their
grandchildren now visit; many people greet the morning by
fishing, rowing, or slipping into the water for an early swim.

The writer identi-
fies the general
process (summer
field work) that
she is analyzing

Our team of biologists, too, was drawn to the lakes. We came for the loons.

Up before dawn every day, keys in the ignition by four-thirty, paddle in the water by five. Binoculars, clipboard, data sheets, pencils, map, GPS, compass, PB&J, directions to lakes, field notebook—my daily accessories for an average day's work. Some girls waited tables and came home with tips; I waded through bogs and came home with ticks.

Professional Loon Chaser. That is a distinction that most college juniors cannot add to their resumes. Yet, from May 21, 2007, through August 2, 2007, my personal and professional lives revolved around birds, one particular species of bird, the common loon. Taxonomically speaking, loons are in an order (Gaviiformes), family (Gaviidae), and genus (*Gavia*) of their own. Loons come in five varieties: arctic, pacific, yellow-billed, red-throated, and common. The most numerous of the five may be *Gavia immer*, or the common loon, but it is everything but usual. The word "common" suggests an ordinary thief, unrefined and unwelcome. That is assuredly not the case.

At first glance, when you cast your eyes over a calm lake glittering, like shattered glass on a bright predawn morning, you don't see the loons at all. Each of the small lakes in the study area harbored only one pair of loons, as they are territorial birds with no tolerance for nosy neighbors dropping by for a look around. It is almost dawn and the loons are out there, somewhere, but what are you looking for? You are hoping to catch a glimpse of a bird whose black head and neck, silhouetted against the glow that precedes sunrise, have

3

Identifies the specific objective of the field work

Explains the equipment she and her team will use in the field

4

Uses CLASSIFICATION to help identify the specific kind of loon the team is seeking

5

The process begins

the elegant arch of the f-holes in a Stradivari violin. A loon's head and neck are an ancient black, pure and regal, shimmering in sapphire and amethyst tones to offset faultless rubies set in as eyes. Through these crimson lenses, the loons see well enough to dive for over two minutes at a time to fish for yellow perch 200 feet down. Under a loon's slender, pointed bill, the curve sloping down to its plush, cream-colored chest resembles half a heart, so that when the pair members pass each other face to face, for just an instant the two halves make a whole heart.

Each loon, male or female, has at the base of its neck a   6
pearl choker necklace composed of white feathers strung in short vertical stripes. A checkerboard cape of onyx and opal drapes over a loon's broad back; since the weight of the loon's solid bones pulls its body down, it settles low in the water so that its milky white chest is unexposed. Hidden underwater are the loon's leathery black legs and flipper feet. Natural selection has endowed the loon with legs that have been flattened to slice through the water. The webbing folds up tight as the bird pulls its foot forward, fanning out with each stroke to the size of a grown man's outstretched hand. A loon participating in our study often wears on its legs a unique combination of brightly colored plastic identification bands that look like jewelry, as well as a silvery aluminum Fish and Wildlife Service band with an identification number.

Uses DESCRIPTION to identify the quarry in detail

Loons have forgone life on land. A loon cannot walk.   7
Those paddle-like limbs are fixed to the rear-most point of the loon's body: the position is optimal for darting after crayfish but it is dreadfully awkward for scurrying about on shore.

Three feet long from bill to toe, ten pounds of feathers, muscle, and bone, a loon on land can do nothing but scoot along the ground on its chest. Fortunately, its only residual land-bound habit is nesting, so you may find a loon settled atop two mottled eggs on a mound of grass and mud no more than a yard from the water's edge. With one strong push from its powerful legs, the loon regains its preferred environment. A loon can fly well enough to escape the bitter winter chill and settle in the Gulf of Mexico until the ice melts off the lakes up north. Ducks can leap out of the water and take off flying, but a loon is not a duck: a loon turns to face the wind and sprints across the lake until it gains enough momentum to go aloft.

Explains the only place to look for loons on land

Take off is a noisy process, and on a calm day there are very few loons in the skies.

If for some reason you cannot see your loon, you may catch 8 its long mournful wail, or its cackling tremolo, or—if it is a male—its maniacal yodeling to scare off unwelcome visitors. The sound echoes from shore to shore and surrounds you in your canoe. The loon is there, somewhere. You can hear it.

> The first step in chasing loons is to listen for them

On June 10, 2007, my first stop was Madeline and Carrol 9 Lakes. By the time I shoved off it was 5:15 a.m. The sun had already peeked above the pines. The water was so smooth that the opposite shore of the lake a mile away seemed only a paddle's length beyond my bow. I remember the pair of juvenile bald eagles chasing each other through the white pine branches. Juveniles are the same size as their piebald parents, but their feathers are the color of pine bark. If their white-and-black-feathered parents always look as if they were dressed for a white-tie affair, the immature eagles seem dressed in their play clothes and covered in mud. Our national bird cackles like a squeaky spinning wheel in need of some WD-40. I paddled out to the trio of islands 100 meters from shore, where the loons had nested just the week before. It should have been a quick paddle out to the nest. My directions to it were: NE shore of NE of 3 islands off of boat landing, under bush. No loons. Two eggs the size of a man's fist, the color of chocolate milk speckled with cocoa powder, sat alone in a bowl scooped out by the loons on the muddy shore. The eggs were cold to the touch from being left unattended on the cloudless night. Such abandonment is not unusual in loons, as they are known to leave a nest if there are too many eagles or humans nearby.

> With this specific example, Walden echoes Thoreau's famous loon chase on Walden Pond

In this case, the nest was directly under a white pine that served as a hangout for the delinquent eagles living on Carrol Lake. Eagle droppings spackled the eggs, so I knew that the loons had been gone for more than a few hours.

On a day like that my job was pleasant. It was a perfect   10
Sunday morning because there was no wind, an ideal day for canoeing. Carrol Lake and Madeline Lake compose a broad territory. Combined, the two lakes are over 500 acres of open water, water that has been stocked with walleye, large-mouthed bass, and muskellunge for the enjoyment of local anglers and weekenders from Milwaukee and Chicago. A male loon who chooses to settle there has to defend water the size of nearly 400 football fields.

Paddling on Carrol Lake was serene and loonless. Then a   11
sharp wail struck my ears from the direction of Madeline
Lake. I paddled through the connecting channel and found my birds 40 feet off shore in a sheltered little bay full of cattails and lily pads. The scene would have been beautiful if not for the RV park 50 meters up shore. At slips littered with tackle and fading life vests, summer residents docked their boats: pontoon party boats, jet boats with huge engines for waterskiing, mid-life-crisis yachts with every GPS/radar/sonar gadget in the catalog, and simple aluminum-hull fishing boats complete with one seat, a tackle box, and a cooler. It was still only 7:45 a.m. on a Sunday, so the few empty slips were explained by the diehard anglers out on the water. The only activity on shore was provided by children exploring the crevices of old oak trees and their parents savoring mugs of coffee and murmuring about the weather.

> Listening to the cry of the loons leads to the first sighting

Still, there she was, with him, diving short and shallow 12
and never straying further than a few meters from her
beloved. The wail I'd heard from Carrol Lake must have been
hers, tinny and frantic. Because she was diving, she gave me a
few good looks at her legs. The high mid-summer sun, the
cloudless sky, and the calm water made for perfect conditions
to spot jewel-colored ankle bands. This particular female had
none. Though we did not know her history, she was important
to the study because she had paired up with a male on a study
lake. What a good mate she was. She was in an absolute tizzy
and became ever more fretful as I floated towards the two of
them. Her mate, a big strong buck of a loon with a broad
back and a proud chest, looked like a sidelined football
player, and she was his tireless cheerleader. She dived around
him encouragingly.

Listlessly, he paddled with his left leg only and his right 13
leg tucked up under his wing. Trailing him with my binoculars, I could identify the bright red-striped and blue-striped
bands on his left leg, which was paddling like the pendulum of
an old grandfather clock that someone forgot to wind. The
swinging limb barely had enough momentum to make it to
the next stroke. When he was almost within arms' reach, he
turned and extended his right leg. When he waggled his foot,
I could see why he had been cradling it. A six-inch, jointed,
shiny, apple-green muskie lure was embedded in the webbing
of his right foot just below his green and silver bands. Each
end of the lure sprouted three pronged hooks like miniature
chandeliers with barbs instead of candles. That lure was
meant to latch onto the gills of a thirty-pound carnivorous

Walden finds a
particular pair of
birds—and an
unexpected
problem

fish. Heavy-test line twined around his ankle, tightening the lure's grip. Dejected and resigned to his condition, he drifted with his head resting on his back between his wings and his eyes half-lidded. Each time he waved his foot the lure flopped like a banner of callous ignorance and waste.

How do you catch a loon and not tell anyone? How do you pull a threatened bird out of the water, cut the line—a line the bird could not have broken on its own—and walk away? Someone peered over the edge of his boat into the roiling water and saw white and black wings thrashing and heard the loon's frantic wails. And then he severed the line. He did not call the police or the Department of Natural Resources. No one knew. 14

You catch a loon by sneaking up behind it in a small boat and scooping it up in a thirty-inch wide fishing net. Loons dive, so you can catch one only if it is staying with a chick or too ill to sneak under water. I tried to catch the male on Madeline Lake, but he was able to dive when he felt threatened. He was too strong to capture, but the lure would stop him from diving deep enough to eat well. It would stop him from defending his territory, and it would stop him from flying. 15

Explains how to actually catch a loon and why Walden can't attempt it here

So I left him. 16

Some two weeks later I returned to Carrol and Madeline Lakes to check on my birds. At the state campground boat landing, I met a bored teenaged boy fishing off the dock. I mentioned the injured loon, and he told me that he and his family had taken a loon with a lure in its foot to the Northwoods Wildlife Clinic the day before. The bird had been 17 starving with its head resting on its shoulder when they found it beached by their campsite.

I was relieved. I expressed my gratitude to the family and 18 hopped into my canoe to identify a loon I saw wailing and diving out by the nesting islands on Carrol Lake. I had guessed that the distraught loon would be my injured male's caring mate. Diving frantically and shallow, the lone loon keened pitifully. I set down my paddle and lifted my binoculars. Red- and blue-striped bands on the left leg, a green and a silver band on the right—and a glittering green and silver lure dragging from one foot.

The family had rescued the unbanded female. 19

Two loons. Two lures. One territory. One month. 20

I visited her at the wildlife clinic. She was their most 21 expensive patient, eating over a hundred dollars' worth of minnows a day. She gained a kilo over the weekend she spent in the clinic. We put pretty periwinkle and yellow bands on her, so that her ankles looked like a patch of irises in the spring. We released her back onto her lake, but none of us saw her for the rest of the summer.

Her mate was not so lucky. On July 22 he was still just 22 barely alive. His feathers were water-logged and his crimson red eyes were dull: too weak to preen and too exhausted to eat. He looked like a bird from the pages of *National Geographic* after the Exxon Valdez oil spill in Alaska. The shiny black cap of feathers on his head was rumpled and greasy as if someone had dragged a comb through it. We went out as a team to

---

Marginal notes:

Sums up the results of Walden's field work so far

Gives the researchers' final contact with the female loon

rescue him on the evening of July 27. It was too late. We found his body floating by the shore among beef jerky wrappers and Mountain Dew cans.

Gives the end result of catching a loon on a fishing line

The lure was gone. Maybe someone salvaged it after he died. Maybe someone tried to help him out. Who knows? Infection had spread and his whole leg was septic. His joints were inflamed and rock hard. The fishing line had cut deep gashes in the thick leathery flaps of skin on his legs. The hooks had ripped gaping holes in the webbing of both feet.

23

It is illegal to handle a loon, even a dead loon, without special permits. I could not legally take him to a taxidermist and have him stuffed in a lifelike pose, even though he would be a welcome addition to any natural history museum collection or any living room in the Northwoods. I picked him up by the ankles and tossed him into the boat. He is now in the freezer at the Department of Natural Resources office in Rhinelander, along with more dead loons and other threatened species collected over the past two decades.

24

Gives the researchers' final contact with the male loon

Two loons snagged on two lakes in one territory in one breeding season. They had had a nest on a very successful site. They probably would have had chicks. They probably had at least ten years left to breed.

25

Scientists are observers. We take notes, lots of notes. We look for patterns. We educate. We watch. We wait. And we weep.

26

Explains the result of the process

JON KATZ

HOW BOYS BECOME MEN

Jon Katz (b. 1947) is a mystery writer and media critic. A former executive producer for *CBS Morning News,* he has also written a number of books about dogs, including *Izzy and Lenore* (2008), as well as columns for *Rolling Stone, HotWired,* and slashdot.org, a website dedicated to "News for Nerds." For Katz, the Internet is different from other, more traditional media, such as books and newspapers, because it is interactive. Interactivity, however, is not a trait that most men come by naturally in their personal lives, says Katz. Why? Because "sensitivity" has been beaten out of them as boys. Katz analyzes this male maturation process in "How Boys Become Men," first published in 1993 in *Glamour,* a magazine for young women.

◇◇◇◇◇◇◇◇◇◇◇◇◇◇◇◇◇◇◇◇◇◇◇◇◇◇◇◇

1   Two nine-year-old boys, neighbors and friends, were walking home from school. The one in the bright blue windbreaker was laughing and swinging a heavy-looking book bag toward the head of his friend, who kept ducking and stepping back. "What's the matter?" asked the kid with the bag, whooshing it over his head. "You chicken?"

2   His friend stopped, stood still and braced himself. The bag slammed into the side of his face, the thump audible all the way across the street where I stood

watching. The impact knocked him to the ground, where he lay mildly stunned for a second. Then he struggled up, rubbing the side of his head. "See?" he said proudly. "I'm no chicken."

No. A chicken would probably have had the sense to get out of the way. This boy was already well on the road to becoming a *man*, having learned one of the central ethics of his gender: Experience pain rather than show fear. 3

Women tend to see men as a giant problem in need of solution. They tell us that we're remote and uncommunicative, that we need to demonstrate less machismo and more commitment, more humanity. But if you don't understand something about boys, you can't understand why men are the way we are, why we find it so difficult to make friends or to acknowledge our fears and problems. 4

Boys live in a world with its own Code of Conduct, a set of ruthless, unspoken, and unyielding rules: 5

Don't be a goody-goody.

Never rat. If your parents ask about bruises, shrug.

Never admit fear. Ride the roller coaster, join the fistfight, do what you have to do. Asking for help is for sissies.

Empathy is for nerds. You can help your best buddy, under certain circumstances. Everyone else is on his own.

Never discuss anything of substance with anybody. Grunt, shrug, dump on teachers, laugh at wimps, talk about comic books. Anything else is risky.

See p. 300 for tips on putting the steps of a process in order.

Boys are rewarded for throwing hard. Most other activities—reading, befriending girls, or just thinking—are considered weird. And if there's one thing boys don't want to be, it's weird.

More than anything else, boys are supposed to learn how to handle themselves. I remember the bitter fifth-grade conflict I touched off by elbowing aside a bigger boy named Barry and seizing the cafeteria's last carton of chocolate milk. Teased for getting aced out by a wimp, he had to reclaim his place in the pack. Our fistfight, at recess, ended with my knees buckling and 6 my lip bleeding while my friends, sympathetic but out of range, watched resignedly.

When I got home, my mother took one look at my swollen face and screamed. 7 I wouldn't tell her anything, but when my father got home I cracked and confessed, pleading with them to do nothing. Instead, they called Barry's parents, who restricted his television for a week.

The following morning, Barry and six of his pals stepped out from behind 8 a stand of trees. "It's the rat," said Barry.

I bled a little more. *Rat* was scrawled in crayon across my desk. 9

They were waiting for me after school for a number of afternoons to follow. 10 I tried varying my routes and avoiding bushes and hedges. It usually didn't work.

I was as ashamed for telling as I was frightened. "You did ask for it," said 11 my best friend. Frontier Justice has nothing on Boy Justice.

In panic, I appealed to a cousin who was several years older. He followed 12 me home from school, and when Barry's gang surrounded me, he came barreling toward us. "Stay away from my cousin," he shouted, "or I'll kill you."

After they were gone, however, my cousin could barely stop laughing. 13 "You were afraid of *them?*" he howled. "They barely came up to my waist."

Men remember receiving little mercy as boys; maybe that's why it's some- 14 times difficult for them to show any.

"I know lots of men who had happy childhoods, but none who have happy 15 memories of the way other boys treated them," says a friend. "It's a macho marathon from third grade up, when you start butting each other in the stomach."

"The thing is," adds another friend, "you learn early on to hide what you 16 feel. It's never safe to say, 'I'm scared.' My girlfriend asks me why I don't talk more about what I'm feeling. I've gotten better at it, but it will *never* come naturally."

You don't need to be a shrink to see how the lessons boys learn affect their 17 behavior as men. Men are being asked, more and more, to show sensitivity, but they dread the very word. They struggle to build their increasingly uncertain work lives but will deny they're in trouble. They want love, affection, and support but don't know how to ask for them. They hide their weaknesses and fears from all, even those they care for. They've learned to be wary of intervening when they see others in trouble. They often still balk at being stigmatized as weird.

Some men get shocked into sensitivity—when they lose their jobs, their wives, or their lovers. Others learn it through a strong marriage, or through their own children.

It may be a long while, however, before male culture evolves to the point that boys can learn more from one another than how to hit curve balls. Last month, walking my dog past the playground near my house, I saw three boys encircling a fourth, laughing and pushing him. He was skinny and rumpled, and he looked frightened. One boy knelt behind him while another pushed him from the front, a trick familiar to any former boy. He fell backward.

When the others ran off, he brushed the dirt off his elbows and walked toward the swings. His eyes were moist and he was struggling for control.

"Hi," I said through the chain-link fence. "How ya doing?"

"Fine," he said quickly, kicking his legs out and beginning his swing.

18

19

20

21

22

FOR DISCUSSION

1. In order to explain how boys become men, Jon Katz must first explain how boys become boys. By what specific "rules" does this process occur, according to him (5)?

2. Is Katz right, do you think, in his PROCESS ANALYSIS of how boys are brought up? Why or why not?

3. The end result of how they learn to behave as boys, says Katz, is that men find it difficult "to make friends or to acknowledge our fears and problems" (4). They lack "sensitivity" (18). Do you agree? In your experience, is Katz's analysis accurate or inaccurate? Explain.

4. According to Katz, women are puzzled by "male culture" (19). How, in his view, do women regard men? Do you agree or disagree with this analysis? Why?

5. What evidence, if any, can you find in Katz's essay to indicate that the author has learned as an adult male to behave in ways he was not taught as a boy? By what processes, according to Katz, do men sometimes learn such new kinds of behavior?

STRATEGIES AND STRUCTURE

. . . .

1. Katz tells the story in paragraphs 1 and 2 of a boy who prefers to get knocked down rather than be called a "chicken." Why do you think he begins with this incident? What stage or aspect of the boy-training process is he illustrating?

2. The longest of the ANECDOTES that Katz tells to show how boys learn to behave is the one about himself. Where does it begin and end? By what process or processes is he being taught here?

3. What is the role of the older cousin in the NARRATIVE Katz tells about himself as a boy? How does the cousin's response in paragraph 13 illustrate the process Katz is analyzing?

4. Where else in his essay does Katz tell a brief story to illustrate what he is saying about how boys are trained? How do these stories support his main point? What would the essay be like without any of the stories?

5. "If you don't understand something about boys, you can't understand why men are the way we are . . ." (4). To whom is Katz speaking here? What PURPOSES might he have for explaining the male maturation process to this particular AUDIENCE?

6. Besides analyzing the processes by which boys learn to behave according to a rigid "Code of Conduct," Katz's essay also analyzes the lasting effects caused by this early training (5). What are some of these effects?

WORDS AND FIGURES OF SPEECH

. . . .

1. How does your dictionary define "machismo" (4)? What language(s) does it derive from?

2. To feel *sympathy* for someone means to have feelings and emotions similar to theirs. What does "empathy" mean (5)?

3. How does Katz's use of the various meanings of the words "chicken" and "rat" help him to make his point about how boys become men (1–3, 5, 8–9)?

4. Verbal IRONY is the use of one word or phrase to imply another with a quite different meaning. What's ironic about the boy's reply to Katz's question in paragraph 22?

FOR WRITING

1. Write a brief Code of Conduct like the one in paragraph 5 that lays out the unspoken rules of the "culture," male or female, in which you grew up.

2. Write an essay that analyzes the process of how boys become men, as *you* see it. Or, alternatively, write an analysis of the process(es) by which *girls* are typically socialized to become women in America or somewhere else. Draw on your own personal experience, or what you know from others, or both. Feel free to use ANECDOTES and other elements of narrative as appropriate to illustrate your analysis.

ALLEGRA GOODMAN

SO, YOU WANT TO BE A WRITER?
HERE'S HOW.

Allegra Goodman (b. 1967) is a novelist, short-story writer, and mother of four. After growing up in Honolulu, she studied at Harvard, then earned a Ph.D. in English from Stanford University. Her most recent novels include *The Other Side of the Island* (2008) and *The Cookbook Collector* (2010). "If there's one thing I've learned over the years," says Goodman, who is fascinated by the writing process, "it's the value of revision. I write draft after draft, rereading, rethinking, rephrasing every step of the way." In the following essay, published in the *Boston Globe* in 2008, Goodman gives advice on the process of becoming a writer.

When people hear that I'm a novelist, I get one comment more than any other. "I'm a physician (or a third-grade teacher, or a venture capitalist) but what I really want to do is write." A mother of three muses: "I've always loved writing since I was a little girl." A physicist declares, "I've got a great idea for a mystery-thriller-philosophical-love story—if I only had the time." I nod, resisting the temptation to reply: "And I have a great idea for a unified field theory—if I just had a moment to work it out on paper."

Book sales are down, but creative writing enrollments are booming. The longing to write knows no bounds. A lactation consultant[1] told me, "I have a story inside of me. I mean, I know everybody has a story, but I really have a story."

Forthwith, some advice for those of you who have always wanted to write, those with best-selling ideas, and those who really have a story.

To begin, don't write about yourself. I'm not saying you're uninteresting. I realize that your life has been so crazy no one could make this stuff up. But if you want to be a writer, start by writing about other people. Observe their faces, and the way they wave their hands around. Listen to the way they talk. Replay conversations in your mind—not just the words, but the silences as well. Imagine the lives of others. If you want to be a writer, you need to get over yourself. This is not just an artistic choice; it's a moral choice. A writer attempts to understand others from the inside.

Find a peaceful place to work. Peace does not necessarily entail an artists' colony or an island off the coast of Maine. You might find peace in your basement, or at a cafe in Davis Square,[2] or amid old ladies rustling magazines at the public library. Peace is not the same as quiet. Peace means you avoid checking your e-mail every ten seconds. Peace means you are willing to work offline, screen calls, and forget your to-do list for an hour. If this is difficult, turn off your Web browser, or try writing without a computer altogether. Treat yourself to pen and paper and make a mess, crossing out sentences, crumpling pages, inserting paragraphs in margins. Remember spiral-bound notebooks, and thank-you notes with stamps? Handwriting is arcane in all the best ways. Writing in ink doesn't feel like work; it feels like secret diaries and treasure maps and art.

> Always tell readers when they will need special equipment, p. 300.

Read widely, and dissect books in your mind. What, exactly, makes David Sedaris[3] funny? How does George Orwell[4] fill us with dread? If you want to be a novelist, read novels new and old, satirical, experimental, Victorian, American.

---

1. Someone who advises mothers about nursing their infants.

2. Central intersection in Somerville, Massachusetts, a city north of Boston.

3. Best-selling American author (b. 1956), known for his witty autobiographical writing.

4. British novelist and essayist (1903–1950), whose dystopian novel *1984* is a foreboding story of a repressive totalitarian government.

Read nonfiction as well. Consider how biographers select details to illuminate a life in time. If you want to write nonfiction, study histories and essays, but also read novels and think about narrative, and the novelist's artful release of information. Don't forget poetry. Why? Because it's good to go where words are worshipped, and essential to remember that you are not a poet. Lyric poets linger on a mood or fragmentary phrase; prose writers must move along to tell their story, and catch their train.

And this is true for everyone, but especially for women: If you don't value your own time, other people won't either. Trust me, you can't write a novel in stolen minutes outside your daughter's tap class. Virginia Woolf[5] declared that a woman needs a room of her own. Well, the room won't help, if you don't shut the door. Post a note. "Book in progress, please do not disturb unless you're bleeding." Or these lines from Samuel Taylor Coleridge,[6] which I have adapted for writing mothers: ". . . Beware! Beware! / Her flashing eyes, her floating hair! / Weave a circle round her thrice, / And close your eyes with holy dread, / For she on honey-dew hath fed, / and drunk the milk of Paradise."

7

FOR DISCUSSION

1. Why, according to Allegra Goodman, should aspiring writers write about other people instead of themselves? Do you think this is sensible advice? Why or why not?

2. What PROCESS is Goodman ANALYZING exactly—how to write or how to become a writer? Is her analysis explanatory or directive? Explain.

3. Why does Goodman recommend writing by hand in ink?

4. Why does Goodman think all writers should study poetry? Is she right? Why or why not?

5. British novelist and essayist (1882–1941). In her book *A Room of One's Own* (1929), Woolf noted that "a woman must have money and a room of her own if she is to write fiction."

6. British Romantic poet and critic (1772–1834). Goodman adapts lines from his poem "Kubla Khan" (1816), which Coleridge claimed he was unable to complete after being interrupted by a knock at the door during its composition.

5. What special advice does Goodman have for women writers? Why, in her view, do they need such advice even more than men do?

STRATEGIES AND STRUCTURES

. . . .

1. What is the end result of the process that Goodman is analyzing? Where and how does she first introduce it?

2. In the beginning of her essay, Goodman tells about all the people she has met who want to be writers. Is this an effective way to begin? Why or why not?

3. Goodman tells us early on who she has in mind as her main AUDIENCE for the advice she gives. Who is it? In what ways is her essay directed toward this audience? Explain.

4. Goodman divides the process that she is analyzing into four basic stages. What are they? Does she use chronology to organize them? If not, how are they organized?

5. Into what steps is the reading stage of the process further broken down? What about the other stages? Why does Goodman break them down in this way?

6. Why does Goodman end her analysis with the words of another writer? Is this an effective strategy? Why or why not?

7. In paragraph 6, Goodman COMPARES the writer of prose to the writer of poetry. Which kind of writer—or aspiring writer—is her advice aimed at? How does she DEFINE the kind of writer she has in mind?

WORDS AND FIGURES OF SPEECH

. . . .

1. Why is writing about other people rather than oneself a "moral" choice, according to Goodman (4)? What's moral about it?

2. The writer, says Goodman, needs "a peaceful place to work" (5). How does she define "peaceful"?

3. Why does Goodman use the word "arcane" instead of *old-fashioned* or *outmoded* to DESCRIBE handwriting (5)?

4. What does Goodman mean by "artful" when she uses it to describe how the novelist releases information in a NARRATIVE (6)?

5. Explain the ALLUSION to Virginia Woolf in the last paragraph of Goodman's essay. What PURPOSE does it serve in her analysis?

FOR WRITING

. . . .

1. In a paragraph or two, analyze the process you follow for managing your time when you write.

2. Write an essay analyzing the process you have gone through so far in learning how to be a writer. Be sure to say how much further you have to go in order to reach your goal and what advice you have for other writers.

JEFFREY SKINNER

SOME STEPPING-STONES TO WRITING A POEM

Jeffrey Skinner is a poet, playwright, and teacher of writing at the University of Louisville. Skinner grew up in Levittown, New York, which he describes as "a working-class bastion with young dads and moms just starting out, the dads back from the war, able to buy their Levitt house because of Levitt's genius and the G.I. bill." A graduate of Rollins College in Winter Park, Florida, Skinner worked as a private detective in his father's security firm while earning an MFA in poetry writing at Columbia University. His sixth collection of poems, *Glaciology*, is scheduled for publication in 2013. "Some Stepping-Stones to Writing a Poem" (editor's title) is a complete section from Skinner's hilarious but also erudite (and modest) "self-help memoir," *The 6.5 Practices of Moderately Successful Poets* (2012). In this selection, Skinner analyzes the process that his friend and fellow poet Kiki Petrosino (b. 1979), who also teaches creative writing at Louisville, went through to produce a single poetic line. The process, says Skinner, is typical of how most poets write, including himself.

I asked my friend, colleague, and fellow poet Kiki Petrosino for her thoughts   1
on "research" in poetry. Here is how she replied:

> *My research is pretty unscientific. Right now I'm in the office, working*
> *on a new poem. So far, I've looked up information on skeletonization, the*
> *ancient demon Astaroth, carnivorous beetles, sunfish, the mallow plant,*
> *and the Lesser Key of Solomon. Much of this has been through Google,*
> *because I only want to know a little bit about each thing right now . . . just*
> *enough to complete an image and move on to the next line. I look something*
> *up, think about it for a few minutes, turn it over a few times in my imagi-*
> *nation, and then test out a phrase. Undoubtedly, what I come up with has*
> *very little to do with facts and much more to do with making noise! I count*
> *Susan Howe as one of the major poets in my constellation, but I rarely*
> *devote myself to the painstaking research on single topics that she is so*
> *adept at. My method is to do a lot of jumping around (literally—moving*
> *from my desk to the computer, to the dictionary, etc.).*

Kiki's informal method is, I think, the method of *most* poets, a matter of what
we might call "research by association."

Poems can begin in a variety of ways: with a line, an image, a rhythm, a   2
piece of speech, an obsessive dream, or worry. Poems can even begin with an
idea, though this may be the rarest of incitements. But in most cases the actual
work of the poem doesn't *really* begin until some words appear on a page. In this
instance Kiki had obviously started, had already written down a few words that
interested her. She looked these words up. She mulled over her findings. She
delighted in parts of it, and allowed those parts to suggest further words, rhythms,
lines, or targets of research.

And so she went, moving blissfully on a kind of poetry scavenger hunt,   3
where the prize at the end is the larger mystery of the newborn poem itself. On
the way, one clue leads by association to the next, and the explorer keeps moving, even though the "correct" number of clues is unknown, it's up to the poet
to decide even what a *clue* is, and even some of those unearthed treasures that
seemed most promising will be discarded in the final work.

Crossing a stream, rock by rock, throwing down each new stepping-stone   4
as you go . . . which brings us to the second part of Kiki's answer, and an even
better simile:

> One line leads to another (at least, on good days), like a rope of scarves
> through a magician's hands. Some piece of language will come up—for
> example, the word "swamp," which I love. And then I think to myself, what
> grows in the swamp? And I remember a Workshop friend of mine, Nellie.
> She has this recipe for "real" marshmallows that uses the mallow plant as
> an ingredient. Nellie hunts the mallow in the marshes near her childhood
> home in the countryside. So then I look up the word "mallow" to see what
> comes up, not because I'm going to talk about Nellie—or marshmallows—in
> my poem, but because I like the sound of the word "mallow" and think it
> might be spooky enough to work well in this line I'm trying to write about

the swamp. The word "mallow" leads me to the word "stem," and suddenly I'm thinking, "what else has stems?" And that thought eventually leads me to this line: "I hear your old jaws snag on the stem of a grin." Did I mention this is a completely arbitrary & weird process?? Research is not the map (there is no map), but it might function as a kind of compass through the field of language. A terrifically broken compass, of course.

"I hear your old jaws snag on the stem of a grin"—an interesting line, and what a journey Kiki took to arrive at it. I really don't know of a better, more specific description of the odd and intuitive way poems may be made. In one compressed paragraph (well, now two) we see clearly how the associative process moves in many directions at once in the poet's brain—the sound of one word leads to contemplation of its literal meaning, then to all that the signified "thing itself" (*swamp*) contains. This leads to a memory of a friend whose interesting habit Kiki associates with *swamp*. Then the why of the association brings up a specific, lovely word—*mallow*—which the poet "likes the sound of." The poet then looks this word up. The results of this bit of "research" lead the poet to consider one part or implication of that word, again shifting from desirable sound to a more literal, material denotation. Finally, Kiki asks herself to think of other contexts or categories in which this last clue in the trail might appear. When she finds the right one, the line comes to her, presto—as if by magic.

5

A process can move "in many directions" in the brain; on paper it must be presented in a particular order, p. 300.

FOR DISCUSSION

. . . .

1. Jeffrey Skinner says that the way Kiki Petrosino writes is "the method of *most* poets" (1). Is he right? How and how adequately does Skinner take into account the element of "poetic inspiration"? Explain.

2. What does Petrosino mean when she says that "right now" her research "has very little to do with facts and much more to do with making noise" (1)? Why might a poet be particularly interested in sound?

3. Under what circumstances might Petrosino do more, and more systematic, research—like the "historical" poet Susan Howe, whose work she admires?

4. Like most poets, says Skinner, his friend writes "by association" (1). Where and how does this process take place; and what, according to Skinner (and Petrosino), does the poet associate with what? Explain.

STRATEGIES AND STRUCTURES

1. To illustrate how poets write poetry, Skinner cites a single detailed EXAMPLE, including the specific words that prompted a fellow poet to come up with a particular poetic line. Is this a good strategy, given the brevity of his analysis; or should Skinner have cited more, shorter examples about the practices of several different poets? Explain.

2. Skinner says that Petrosino had "obviously started" writing her poem before she described the process to him (2). What had she already done?

3. According to Skinner, what are some of the various ways that poets typically begin to write poems? In his view, when does "the actual work of the poem" begin (2)?

3. Once the poet has some words down on paper, what does he or she do next? Where and how does Skinner identify these steps in the writing process?

4. Skinner compares writing a poem to a "journey" (5). On what basis? How valid is the COMPARISON, and how does he develop it?

WORDS AND FIGURES OF SPEECH

1. How does the word *mallow* lead the poet to the word *stem* (4)? Explain the associative process that is operating here.

2. After she has the word *stem* in mind, the poet finds herself wondering "what else has stems?" (4). How does she get from there to "the stem of a grin"—and to "*snag*" (4)?

3. Explain Skinner's use of the "stepping-stone" METAPHOR (4). Why does he say that each new stone has to be thrown down "as you go" (4)?

FOR WRITING

1. Choose one of the following words, and make a list of the other words that come to mind when you "think about it for a few minutes": *swamp, spooky, marshmallow, stream, map, broken compass* (1). Look up the words on your list, and make notes of any new meanings or associations you discover.

2. Write a process analysis explaining how you typically write. Choose a particular piece of writing you've done, or are working on—it doesn't have to be a poem but certainly can be—and use it as an example of the process. Be sure to include specific words and phrases from your text.

PHILIP WEISS

HOW TO GET OUT OF
A LOCKED TRUNK

Philip Weiss is an investigative journalist and former columnist for the *New York Observer*. He has also been a contributor to the *Jewish World Review*, *Esquire*, and *Harper's*, in which "How to Get Out of a Locked Trunk" was first published (1992). Weiss is the author of the political novel *Cock-A-Doodle-Doo* (1995) and the investigative work *American Taboo: A Murder in the Peace Corps* (2004). About to be married when he wrote this essay, Weiss obsessively analyzes his way out of the trunks of locked cars, a strange fixation that suggests his bachelor self may be carrying some extra baggage. The essay also analyzes how Weiss got out of his condition.

O n a hot Sunday last summer my friend Tony and I drove my rental car, a '91 Buick, from St. Paul to the small town of Waconia, Minnesota, forty miles southwest. We each had a project. Waconia is Tony's boyhood home, and his sister had recently given him a panoramic postcard of Lake Waconia as seen from a high point in the town early in the century. He wanted to duplicate the

1

photograph's vantage point, then hang the two pictures together in his house in Frogtown. I was hoping to see Tony's father, Emmett, a retired mechanic, in order to settle a question that had been nagging me: Is it possible to get out of a locked car trunk?

We tried to call ahead to Emmett twice, but he wasn't home. Tony thought he was probably golfing but that there was a good chance he'd be back by the time we got there. So we set out.

I parked the Buick, which was a silver sedan with a red interior, by the graveyard near where Tony thought the picture had been taken. He took his picture and I wandered among the headstones, reading the epitaphs. One of them was chillingly anti-individualist. It said, "Not to do my will, but thine."

Trunk lockings had been on my mind for a few weeks. It seemed to me that the fear of being locked in a car trunk had a particular hold on the American imagination. Trunk lockings occur in many movies and books—from *Goodfellas* to *Thelma and Louise* to *Humboldt's Gift*.[1] And while the highbrow national newspapers generally shy away from trunk lockings, the attention they receive in local papers suggests a widespread anxiety surrounding the subject. In an afternoon at the New York Public Library I found numerous stories about trunk lockings. A Los Angeles man is discovered, bloodshot, banging the trunk of his white Eldorado following a night and a day trapped inside; he says his captors went on joyrides and picked up women. A forty-eight-year-old Houston doctor is forced into her trunk at a bank ATM and then the car is abandoned, parked near the Astrodome.[2] A New Orleans woman tells police she gave birth in a trunk while being abducted to Texas. Tests undermine her story, the police drop the investigation. But so what if it's a fantasy? That only shows the idea's hold on us.

Every culture comes up with tests of a person's ability to get out of a sticky situation. The English plant mazes. Tropical resorts market those straw finger-grabbers that tighten their grip the harder you pull on them, and Viennese

1. *Humboldt's Gift* (1975), a novel by Saul Bellow about a spiritually empty writer whose life is reawakened by a mob member; *Goodfellas* (1990), a gangster movie; *Thelma and Louise* (1991), a road movie about two women trying to escape oppressive marriages.

2. A large sports arena in Houston, Texas.

intellectuals gave us the concept of childhood sexuality—figure it out, or remain neurotic for life.

At least you could puzzle your way out of those predicaments. When they slam the trunk, though, you're helpless unless someone finds you. You would think that such a common worry should have a ready fix, and that the secret of getting out of a locked trunk is something we should all know about. 6

I phoned experts but they were very discouraging. 7

"You cannot get out. If you got a pair of pliers and bat's eyes, yes. But you have to have a lot of knowledge of the lock," said James Foote at Automotive Locksmiths in New York City. 8

Jim Frens, whom I reached at the technical section of *Car and Driver*[3] in Detroit, told me the magazine had not dealt with this question. But he echoed the opinion of experts elsewhere when he said that the best hope for escape would be to try and kick out the panel between the trunk and the backseat. That angle didn't seem worth pursuing. What if your enemies were in the car, crumpling beer cans and laughing at your fate? It didn't make sense to join them. 9

The people who deal with rules on auto design were uncomfortable with my scenarios. Debra Barclay of the Center for Auto Safety, an organization founded by Ralph Nader,[4] had certainly heard of cases, but she was not aware of any regulations on the matter. "Now, if there was a defect involved—" she said, her voice trailing off, implying that trunk locking was all phobia. This must be one of the few issues on which she and the auto industry agree. Ann Carlson of the Motor Vehicle Manufacturers Association became alarmed at the thought that I was going to play up a non-problem: "In reality this very rarely happens. As you say, in the movies it's a wonderful plot device," she said. "But in reality apparently this is not that frequent an occurrence. So they have not designed that feature into vehicles in a specific way." 10

When we got to Emmett's one-story house it was full of people. Tony's sister, Carol, was on the floor with her two small children. Her husband, Charlie, had 11

---

3. A monthly magazine for car enthusiasts.

4. American attorney and political activist (b. 1934) who was an early advocate of automobile safety.

one eye on the golf tournament on TV, and Emmett was at the kitchen counter, trimming fat from meat for lunch. I have known Emmett for fifteen years. He looked better than ever. In his retirement he had sharply changed his diet and lost a lot of weight. He had on shorts. His legs were tanned and muscular. As always, his manner was humorous, if opaque.

Tony told his family my news: I was getting married in three weeks. 12
Charlie wanted to know where my fiancée was. Back East, getting everything ready. A big-time hatter was fitting her for a new hat.

Emmett sat on the couch, watching me. "Do you want my advice?" 13

"Sure." 14

He just grinned. A gold tooth glinted. Carol and Charlie pressed him to 15
yield his wisdom.

Finally he said, "Once you get to be thirty, you make your own mistakes." 16

He got out several cans of beer, and then I brought up what was on my 17
mind.

Emmett nodded and took off his glasses, then cleaned them and put them 18
back on.

We went out to his car, a Mercury Grand Marquis, and Emmett opened 19
the trunk. His golf clubs were sitting on top of the spare tire in a green golf bag. Next to them was a toolbox and what he called his "burglar tools," a set of elbowed rods with red plastic handles he used to open door locks when people locked their keys inside.

Tony and Charlie stood watching. Charlie is a banker in Minneapolis. He 20
enjoys gizmos and is extremely practical. I would describe him as unflappable. That's a word I always wanted to apply to myself, but my fiancée had recently informed me that I am high-strung. Though that surprised me, I didn't quarrel with her.

For a while we studied the latch assembly. The lock closed in much the 21
same way that a lobster might clamp on to a pencil. The claw portion, the jaws of the lock, was mounted inside the trunk lid. When you shut the lid, the jaws locked on to the bend of a U-shaped piece of metal mounted on the body of the car. Emmett said my best bet would be to unscrew the bolts. That way the U-shaped piece would come loose and the lock's jaws would swing up with it still in their grasp.

"But you'd need a wrench," he said. 22

It was already getting too technical. Emmett had an air of endless patience, 23
but I felt defeated. I could only imagine bloodied fingers, cracked teeth. I had
hoped for a simple trick.

Charlie stepped forward. He reached out and squeezed the lock's jaws. 24
They clicked shut in the air, bound together by heavy springs. Charlie now
prodded the upper part of the left-hand jaw, the thicker part. With a rough flick
of his thumb, he was able to force the jaws to snap open. Great.

Unfortunately, the jaws were mounted behind a steel plate the size of 25
your palm in such a way that while they were accessible to us, standing outside
the car, had we been inside the trunk the plate would be in our way, blocking
the jaws.

This time Emmett saw the way out. He fingered a hole in the plate. It was 26
no bigger than the tip of your little finger. But the hole was close enough to the
latch itself that it might be possible to angle something through the hole from
inside the trunk and nudge the jaws apart. We tried with one of my keys. The
lock jumped open.

It was time for a full-dress test. Emmett swung the clubs out of the trunk, 27
and I set my can of Schmidt's on the rear bumper and climbed in. Everyone
gathered around, and Emmett lowered the trunk on me, then pressed it shut
with his meaty hands. Total darkness. I couldn't hear the people outside. I thought
I was going to panic. But the big trunk felt comfortable. I was pressed against a
sort of black carpet that softened the angles against my back.

I could almost stretch out in the trunk, and it seemed to me I could make 28
them sweat if I took my time. Even Emmett, that sphinx, would give way to
curiosity. Once I was out he'd ask how it had been and I'd just grin. There were
some things you could only learn by doing.

It took a while to find the hole. I slipped the key in and angled it to one 29
side. The trunk gasped open.

Emmett motioned the others away, then levered me out with his big right 30
forearm. Though I'd only been inside for a minute, I was disoriented—as much
as anything because someone had moved my beer while I was gone, setting it
down on the cement floor of the garage. It was just a little thing, but I could not
be entirely sure I had gotten my own beer back.

Charlie was now raring to try other cars. We examined the latch on his   31
Toyota, which was entirely shielded to the trunk occupant (i.e., no hole in the
plate), and on the neighbor's Honda (ditto). But a 1991 Dodge Dynasty was
doable. The trunk was tight, but its lock had a feature one of the mechanics I'd
phoned described as a "tailpiece": a finger-like extension of the lock mechanism
itself that stuck out a half inch into the trunk cavity; simply by twisting the
tailpiece I could free the lock. I was even faster on a 1984 Subaru that had a little
lever device on the latch.

We went out to my rental on Oak Street. The Skylark was in direct sun and   32
the trunk was hot to the touch, but when we got it open we could see that its latch
plate had a perfect hole, a square in which the edge of the lock's jaw appeared like
a face in a window.

The trunk was shallow and hot. Emmett had to push my knees down   33
before he could close the lid. This one was a little suffocating. I imagined being
trapped for hours, and even before he had got it closed I regretted the decision
with a slightly nauseous feeling. I thought of Edgar Allan Poe's live burials,[5]
and then about something my fiancée had said more than a year and a half before.
I had been on her case to get married. She was divorced, and at every opportunity
I would reissue my proposal—even during a commercial. She'd interrupted one
of these chirps to tell me, in a cold, throaty voice, that she had no intention of
ever going through another divorce: "This time, it's death out." I'd carried those
words around like a lump of wet clay.

As it happened, the Skylark trunk was the easiest of all. The hole was right   34
where it was supposed to be. The trunk popped open, and I felt great satisfaction that we'd been able to figure out a rule that seemed to apply about 60 percent of the time. If we publicized our success, it might get the attention it
deserved. All trunks would be fitted with such a hole. Kids would learn about
it in school. The grip of the fear would relax. Before long a successful trunk-
locking scene would date a movie like a fedora[6] dates one today.

---

5. American author (1809–1849) known for his eerie short stories and poems; his story "The
Premature Burial" recounts the terror of a man buried alive.
6. Brimmed men's hat popular from the 1920s through the 1950s, often worn by gangsters
and detectives in movies from that era.

When I got back East I was caught up in wedding preparations. I live in New   35
York, and the wedding was to take place in Philadelphia. We set up camp there
with five days to go. A friend had lent my fiancée her BMW, and we drove it
south with all our things. I unloaded the car in my parents' driveway. The last
thing I pulled out of the trunk was my fiancée's hat in its heavy cardboard shipping box. She'd warned me I was not allowed to look. The lid was free but I
didn't open it. I was willing to be surprised.

When the trunk was empty it occurred to me I might hop in and give it a   36
try. First I looked over the mechanism. The jaws of the BMW's lock were
shielded, but there seemed to be some kind of cable coming off it that you might
be able to manipulate so as to cause the lock to open. The same cable that
allowed the driver to open the trunk remotely . . .

I fingered it for a moment or two but decided I didn't need to test out the   37
theory.

FOR DISCUSSION

. . . .

1. So, according to Philip Weiss, how *do* you get out of a locked trunk? How,
   according to his fiancée, do you get out of a marriage? What is the implication of
   Weiss's addressing these two problems in the same essay?
2. Of the cars he tests, which one alarms Weiss most yet turns out to be the easiest
   to get out of? Why is he so alarmed, do you think? Why is he so anxious to find
   a "simple trick" that will fit all instances (23)?
3. Why does Weiss say, "There were some things you could only learn by doing"
   (28)? What might some of them be?
4. Why do you think Weiss refrains from taking a peek at his fiancée's new hat, since
   the lid is "free" and the box would be so easy to open (35)? Incidentally, how does
   Weiss know that the lid is free?

STRATEGIES AND STRUCTURES

. . . .

1. What is Weiss's PURPOSE in ANALYZING THE PROCESS of getting out of a locked
   trunk? What AUDIENCE does Weiss think will be interested in his analysis? Why?

2. Weiss's essay is divided into three parts—paragraphs 1 through 10, 11 through 34, and 35 through 37. In which section does Weiss most fully analyze the process of getting out of a locked car trunk? Is his analysis explanatory or directive? Explain.

3. Why do you think the last section of Weiss's essay is the shortest? How—and how effectively—does it bring the essay to a satisfying conclusion?

4. What is Weiss's purpose in citing several "experts" in paragraphs 7 through 10? What is Emmett's role in the big experiment?

5. "It's a wonderful plot device," Weiss quotes one expert as saying about being locked in a car trunk (10). Is she right? Where in his essay is Weiss telling a story, and where is he analyzing a process? Give specific EXAMPLES from the text.

6. Like NARRATIVES, which often report events chronologically, process analyses are often organized in the chronological order of the steps or stages of the process that is being analyzed. Where does Weiss use chronology either to tell a story or to analyze a process? Give specific examples from the text.

WORDS AND FIGURES OF SPEECH

1. The lock on the trunk of Emmett's Mercury Grand Marquis, says Weiss, "closed in much the same way that a lobster might clamp on to a pencil" (21). How effective do you find this SIMILE for explaining how this particular trunk locks? Where else does Weiss use FIGURES OF SPEECH as a tool of process analysis?

2. A phobia is an irrational fear (10). Point out specific EXAMPLES in his essay where Weiss (or his persona) might be said to exhibit phobic behavior. What's he afraid of?

3. To whom is Weiss referring when he mentions "Viennese intellectuals" (5)? Why is he ALLUDING to them? Why does he allude to Poe in paragraph 33?

4. "Not to do my will, but thine" (3). What are the implications of this inscription, which Weiss reads on a tombstone at the beginning of his essay?

5. "Case," "reissue," "chirp," and "death out" (33): why does Weiss use these words in the ANECDOTE about his proposals? What about "willing" (35)?

FOR WRITING

. . . .

1. Has anyone you know ever exhibited phobic behavior? Explain how the phobia manifested itself and what specific steps the victim took to deal with it.

2. "Every culture," writes Weiss, "comes up with tests of a person's ability to get out of a sticky situation" (5). Have you ever been in such a situation? How did you get out of it? Write an essay analyzing the process.

ADAM PENENBERG AND MARC BARRY

THE PIZZA PLOT

Adam Penenberg (b. 1962) is an investigative journalist and professor of journalism at New York University. Marc Barry is a spy, or rather a "competitive intelligence professional," who specializes in corporate espionage. (Not surprisingly, we've been unable to find much information about him, nevermind a photo.) Penenberg, the principal author of this selection, has written articles and essays for, among others, *Forbes*, the *New York Times*, *Slate*, and *Wired*. His latest book, about how smart businesses "grow themselves," is *Viral Loop: From Facebook to Twitter* (2009). "The Pizza Plot" is from *Spooked: Espionage in Corporate America* (2000), a book written by Penenberg with Barry as a constant consultant. In "The Pizza Plot," Penenberg and Barry explain, in step-by-step detail, the surreptitious process by which Barry quickly obtained vital corporate secrets from one of the largest food corporations in America.

◇◇◇◇◇◇◇◇◇◇◇◇◇◇◇◇◇◇◇◇◇◇◇◇◇

A lmost every Fortune 500[1] company these days has a "competitive intelli- 1
gence" (or C.I.) unit or farms out its spy activities. Coca-Cola, 3M, Dow Chemical, General Electric, and Intel all maintain a staff dedicated to uncovering

1. The 500 largest U.S. corporations (in terms of gross revenue), as listed by *Fortune* magazine.

what business rivals are up to. Motorola hired away a star from the Central Intelligence Agency to create its corporate intelligence division. Ernst & Young, the accounting firm, boasts a 25-member competitive intelligence arm.

Although the word "espionage" conjures images of shady characters in overcoats who are hired to steal nuclear secrets, today's corporate spies are decidedly less glamorous. For one, they are hired to find out prosaic things like a company's marketing plan, the state of its R and D[2] or a factory's production capacity. (Valuable, yes, but not sexy.) And instead of fancy gizmos like exploding pens and secret decoder rings, often all they need to get the job done is a telephone.

When companies don't have in-house C.I. units, they often turn to independent consultants, most of whom received their training from the Department of Defense, the C.I.A. or the F.B.I. Three years ago, Schwan's Sales Enterprises, a food company based in Marshall, Minnesota, hired a consultant who runs his own firm. Schwan's wanted to find out about a new product that promised to revolutionize frozen pizza. The target was Kraft, the largest packaged-food company in the country. It already sold pizza under the brands Tombstone and Jack's and had perfected a new type of "rising crust" pizza it had been test-marketing under the name DiGiorno. It was the winter of 1997, and up to then it was often hard to taste the difference between a frozen pizza and the cardboard box it came in.

Schwan's, which marketed store-bought pizza under the brand name Tony's, already knew the secret behind DiGiorno: pumping yeast into the raw crust, which Schwan's was also working on with its rising-crust pizza offering, Freschetta. If Schwan's was to have any chance against its hulking rival, however, it would have to know how fast Kraft planned to roll out DiGiorno nationwide, so that it could create a counterstrategy. To do this, the company had to learn the production capacity of a plant it knew Kraft had constructed somewhere in Sussex, Wisconsin. Specifically, Schwan's needed to know the type of equipment the plant housed, the number of production lines, what types and sizes of pizzas were being produced there, and, most important, how many pies were coming off the assembly line each day.

2. Research and Development.

Schwan's needed the information fast, but the consultant knew it would   5
be nearly impossible for him to get it without resorting to subterfuge. As a
member of the Society of Competitive Intelligence Professionals, or SCIP, the
C.I. industry's governing body, the consultant knew he was supposed to abide
by rules that prohibit misrepresentation or deception when interviewing a target on behalf of a client. SCIP stresses the "ethical" acquisition of information
"from publicly available" or "open-source" materials like published documents,
public filings, patents, and annual reports. The purpose of SCIP's spin control
is to make industrial spying more palatable to P.R.-conscious[3] corporations. It
also makes spying more difficult.

This doesn't mean that breaking SCIP rules is against the law. The Eco-   6
nomic Espionage Act of 1996 was passed to deal with foreign agents stealing trade
secrets from American companies. But "to prove trade secrecy theft, you first
have to prove there is a trade secret," says Mark Halligan, a Chicago lawyer and
author of *Trade Secrets Case Digest*. The formula for Coca-Cola and the source
code for Microsoft Windows are trade secrets. Factory production, the information Schwan's wanted, isn't, and this loophole allowed the consultant, and the
7,000 other members of SCIP, to earn a living.

The consultant decided to subcontract the work to a "kite" or "go-to guy,"   7
who, in addition to being able to get the information the job required, would
provide the consultant with plausible deniability. The consultant could fly the
kite out there and let him do whatever needed doing to get the information, but
if he got caught, the consultant could claim he had no idea what his subcontractor was up to. With Schwan's eagerly awaiting the information, the consultant
hired one of us, Marc Barry, founder of the corporate intelligence firm C3I
Analytics of New York, who had gotten the job done for the consultant half a
dozen times in the past.

Barry, a streetwise Irish redhead in his early 30s, had made a name for   8
himself as an expert "humint" (human intelligence) man. Working undercover
for years at a time, he had infiltrated Asian organized crime networks that controlled the distribution of counterfeit goods in the United States, as well as tracked

---

3. That is, conscious of public relations.

phony pharmaceuticals and airplane parts. To Barry, collecting intelligence on companies was a snap compared with gathering information on violent gangs.

After doing some initial Internet research, Barry bought a $10 prepaid phone card from a nearby grocery so his calls couldn't be traced. He set up bogus voice-mail and fax-forwarding lines with a company called Ameri- can Voice Mail. Both accounts were created under the 414 area code, which covered Sussex, Wisconsin. This way, Barry could collect his messages and faxes from his office in New York, yet his targets would be under the impression he was local.

For tips on combining process analysis and narrative, see p. 297.

9

Barry figured someone in the Sussex town government would know details about the plant. "Politicians are easily manipulated because they are usually eager to take credit for things," Barry says. He phoned the Sussex Chamber of Commerce and posed as a reporter from the *Wall Street Journal*. It took him one minute to get the address of the Tombstone pizza plant, located on Sussex Road. Then he dialed the Sussex town assessor's office, where he learned from an employee that Kraft was being assessed taxes for a new 143,914-foot plant.

10

Barry knew that, America being America, Kraft wouldn't be able to begin construction of its plant without permits, so he created a persona, an environ- mentalist he called Curtis Walton. He wrote it down because often at the end of a phone conversation a person will ask, "What was your name again?" and he didn't want to forget. (It had happened before.) Barry dialed the fire department and town building inspectors, since both usually have blueprints for local man- ufacturing plants. He claimed he was calling on behalf of an environmental advocacy nonprofit organization called EcoNet and was researching an article about excessive fluorohydrocarbons being emitted from the Sussex plant for the *EcoNews*. The fire department didn't bite, and the building inspectors weren't in. After several calls, Barry managed to get a secretary at the building inspec- tor's office on the line, who told him there was nothing she could do until her boss returned.

11

"But I'm on deadline," Barry cum[4] Walton said. "Isn't there anything you can do?"

12

4. *With, as* (Latin).

"My boss is so much better at reading these plans than I am," she said. 13
"I'm afraid I'd miss something."

"Any help you could give would be greatly appreciated." 14

"I really should wait for my boss." 15

"But it will be too late by then," Barry said, letting a tinge of desperation 16
color his voice. "And I just don't have the time to drive out to you and pull the
plans myself. You know how deadlines are." Eventually Barry wore her down.
As she read off the contents of the plans, even though he was recording the conversation, Barry scrawled notes just in case there was a glitch with the tape
recorder. "This was not a new plant, but rather additions are being added onto
an existing plant," the secretary informed him. This made sense. To keep transportation costs down, Kraft would want to keep its pizza production in a central-
ized location, and close to key ingredients. "The 143,914-square-foot addition
was designed by Stahlman Engineering of New London, New Hampshire—"

"Stallman? How do you spell that?" Barry asked. 17

"S-t-a-h-l-m-a-n." 18

She recited the details the expansion permit covered: additional ware- 19
housing, more bakery space, a new recycling building. When she got into the
nitty-gritty of what equipment was going to be housed in the new facility, Barry
peppered her with questions and began to draw a map.

"Three compressor rooms," she said, "a 10-below-zero freezer and high- 20
rise freezers—"

"How many?" 21

"Two. A label paste room, meat cooler and cheese coolers, a chemical stor- 22
age room, something called a vestibule conveyor belt system, bakery waterfall
oiler, several sauce and topping lines—"

"How many sauce and topping lines?" 23

"It doesn't say." 24

"O.K., go on." 25

"A Grotter PepperMatic, four spiral freezers—" 26

"How far from the conveyor belt are the freezers?" 27

"Around the corner, about eight feet away, a wheat dock, a loading dock—" 28

"How big is the loading dock?" 29

"Um, 1,906 square feet." 30

"Where is it?" 31

"It's been relocated between the bakery and the recycling room." 32

Delighted by his score, Barry thanked the secretary and hung up. Four 33
spiral and two high-rise freezers? A 2,000-square-foot loading dock? A bakery
waterfall oiler? Although Barry didn't know anything about pizza production,
Schwan's certainly did and would be able to make good use of this information.

But Barry wasn't done. Now came the tricky part: how would he be able to 34
measure how many pizzas the plant was producing daily? He mulled over a strategy. What, he wondered, do all frozen pizzas require? Labels. How would he track
labels though? Besides, there were at least three different styles of pizza. Cheese?
No way. Too complicated. Kraft used tons of it, and didn't it manufacture a four-
cheese pie? Besides, cheese could be stored for a while, so it wouldn't be much use
in trying to figure out how many pizzas came off those conveyor belts. Wheat?
Yeast? Oil? Nah, those wouldn't do it. The cardboard boxes? Maybe, except that
Tombstone pizzas were packaged in shrink-wrapped plastic, not in a box. Then it
came to him: diskettes. Every pizza, whether it came in a box or in shrink-
wrapped plastic, sat on a round, cardboard diskette. This was the one constant.

Barry picked up the receiver and dialed the Sussex plant. He asked for 35
"accounts payable" and got a voice-mail line. Immediately he punched zero, and
when an operator picked up he requested "accounts receivable." After another
voice mail he ordered the operator to hook him up with the "purchasing department," where an older woman picked up. "Hi, this is Bobby Royce," Barry said,
looking at the name he had just scrawled in his notebook, alongside a fictitious
company. "I'm president of Presidential Corrugated Box."

"What can I do for you, Mr. Royce?" the woman asked cheerfully. 36

Good, Barry thought. "Well, you see, I own a cardboard manufacturing 37
plant, nothing too big, mind you. A local family business. And I figured since I
was a local business and you're a local business, well, maybe we could do business together."

"I dunno, sir," she said. "We use an awful lot of cardboard." 38

"Hmm, I see. What do you think you'd need? Ten, 20 thousand units a 39
month?"

"Oh, no, we'd need more than that." 40

"How much more?" 41

"A lot more. We go through hundreds of thousands of units a day. We use Weyerhaeuser. They're the largest." 42

Barry tried to sound disappointed. "Weyerhaeuser, huh? That's way too much output for our plant. But in case you get any spillover and need more, I'll send over some literature." 43

He got off the phone and logged on to the Internet, where he plugged Weyerhaeuser into Yahoo's search engine to locate its corporate Web site. One call to Weyerhaeuser's corporate headquarters and he was given the number of the White Bear Lake facility near Minneapolis, the plant that serviced Wisconsin. He posed as an employee of the purchasing department of Kraft's Tombstone pizza plant who had just taken over the account and claimed there was a discrepancy on some paperwork. He asked how many boxes and disks Weyerhaeuser had shipped to the plant in the last month. But the number the accounts payable department gave him—the equivalent of a few hundred thousand a day—was too low when compared with what the woman from the purchasing department had told him. It didn't make sense. Barry dialed the Kraft Tombstone loading dock. 44

After a few rings, someone picked up, and Barry could hear heavy machinery grinding in the background. Reprising his role as Bobby Royce, Barry and the Tombstone worker fell into small talk. Barry figured the guy must be a Green Bay Packers fan, so he pretended the Minnesota Vikings, whom the Packers were scheduled to play that week, were his favorite team. The conversation shifted from the Packer legend Vince Lombardi to the right kind of thermos for Wisconsin winters to who manufactures the best work boot. Barry, who had worked as an undercover agent on dozens of loading docks for cargo theft investigations, said he liked Timberlands, but his new friend wore Wolverines. 45

Finally, Barry started asking questions about cardboard, specifically how much of it was handled by the loading dock. But the dock worker gave him a number even lower than the one Weyerhaeuser had supplied. Now Barry was really confused. 46

"They come in only once or twice a week," the guy said, trying to be helpful. 47

"What do you mean?" Barry asked. 48

"We recycle the boxes." 49

"I don't get it. You sell your pizzas in the box, right?"   50

"These are different boxes. These ones get used four times each. We use   51
them to ship the crusts up from Little Chute."

"What the hell is Little Chute?"   52

"Our crust-manufacturing plant. But we're not going to be using card-   53
board for much longer. We've started moving to plastic for interplant shipping,
which doesn't have to be recycled." He told Barry the Little Chute factory made
most of the crusts, although some came from the Sussex plant, which is where
Kraft manufactured the pizzas.

"So," Barry asked gently, but taking a more direct approach, "how many   54
pizzas are we talking about here?"

"Since September, about 300,000 pizzas per day at the Sussex plant," the   55
man said, blithely unaware of the value of the information he was giving up.
"That includes the 12-inch Jack's Pizza, as well as 8- and 12-inch DiGiorno."

This was the number Barry had been looking for. Without letting on to   56
his target that he'd been taken, Barry calmly continued with small talk, thanked
his new friend and got off the phone. Then he lit up a macanudo[5] and fired up
his espresso maker, pondering what this information meant, and what his next
step would be.

He realized that knowing the number of pizzas the Sussex plant was pro-   57
ducing right now—its operating capacity—wasn't enough. He needed to find
out its full production capacity. This would tell his client how many rising-
crust pizzas Kraft could potentially make at any given time.

Barry donned his next phone disguise—that of a graduate student work-   58
ing on a research paper on food production—and dialed the Sussex plant's production lines manager. After making his pitch for academic assistance, Barry
said: "I know you are cranking out 300,000 pizzas a day. How many production
lines is that?"

The answer was five, but only three ran at any one time. Barry did some   59
quick number-crunching in his head and calculated that Kraft's Sussex plant
was operating at 60 percent of capacity, and that Kraft could increase pizza pro-

---

5. Type of premium cigar produced in the Dominican Republic.

duction to 500,000 pizzas a day. The manager also told Barry that DiGiorno wasn't the only rising-crust pizza Kraft planned to market. It had subcontracted the manufacture of rising crusts to Nation Pizza in Chicago for Tombstone, another hot-selling line.

Now this was big, Barry realized. The potential production numbers, coupled with its plan to market rising-crust pizzas under two brands, indicated that Kraft hoped to flood the market and establish itself as the primo player in rising-crust frozen pizza. If the information that Barry sucked up showed that Kraft was taking its time in bringing rising-crust pizzas to market, Schwan's could afford to move slowly. But since Kraft was diving headlong into the rising-crust market, Schwan's had no choice but to be aggressive.

Though Schwan's entry, Freschetta, was a new brand, the company decided to take a chance and plow resources into production and marketing. The information that Barry provided turned out to be key to Freschetta's ultimate success. Although DiGiorno was the first of the rising-crust pizzas, Freschetta became an immediate contender, spurred on by an intensive media campaign. Rising-crust pizzas became the fastest-growing food category and now account for more than 30 percent of frozen-pizza sales in the United States—about $2.3 billion. DiGiorno quickly became the No. 1 selling pizza in the nation, but the covert information helped Freschetta rise from No. 6 to No. 2 by the end of 1999. And all it took was a day and a half worth of phone work by Marc Barry.

FOR DISCUSSION

1. According to Adam Penenberg and Marc Barry, why do major U.S. companies often hire spies, or rather, "competitive intelligence" agents (1)?

2. The agency that hired Barry as a corporate spy belonged to the Society of Competitive Intelligence Professionals (SCIP), a trade organization that prohibits its members from obtaining information by "misrepresentation or deception" (5). By what "loophole" in the law did Barry and his employer get around this rule?

3. We are told that the spying Barry did for his client was not illegal. Was it ethical? Why or why not?

4. In the rising-crust pizza sweepstakes, a $2.3 billion dollar industry, according to Barry, his client's entry rose from sixth place to become the number-two seller. "And all it took was a day and a half worth of phone work by Marc Barry" (61). How accurate is this claim? Explain.

STRATEGIES AND STRUCTURES

1. Barry was not looking for Kraft's secret recipe for rising-crust pizza. What information *was* he seeking? Before the hunt even begins, where do he and Penenberg specify the end result Barry hoped to achieve in the spying process?

2. After Barry learns how many pizzas are produced every day at Kraft's Sussex plant, he ponders "his next step" (56). Starting with "doing some initial Internet research," list the main steps of the process Barry goes through to achieve his goal (9).

3. Of the various steps in the process that Penenberg and Barry are analyzing, which one is the most "tricky" (34)? How and when does Barry find a solution to this part of the problem?

4. "Wheat? Yeast? Oil? Nah, those wouldn't do it" (34). Point out other places like this in their essay where Penenberg and Barry show not only the various actions that went into spying for Schwan's but the thought processes behind those actions as well. What does this depiction contribute to their analysis?

5. In an explanatory process analysis, the writer typically uses the third-person (*he, she, it*). How might "The Pizza Plot" be said to illustrate this principle in the extreme? Explain.

6. Comment on Penenberg and Barry's use of NARRATIVE strategies, particularly dialogue, in their analysis of the process by which Barry obtained sensitive information about Kraft foods.

WORDS AND FIGURES OF SPEECH

1. How and how well does calling the Kraft foods conglomerate a "hulking rival" help Penenberg and Barry to justify using dirty tricks to gain information about the company (4)?

2. Why did Schwan's chose the name *Freschetta* for its new, rising-crust frozen pizza (4)? What is the name supposed to connote?

3. Why do intelligence firms call the subcontractor that actually does the dirty work a "kite" (7)? Is the term appropriate?

4. According to *Cigar Choice* magazine, a *macanudo* (56) is a cigar "known for its mild flavor and body as well as its unparalleled consistency." What does this and other personal details about Barry—such as his choice of an accompanying espresso rather than, say, a scotch or vodka—tell the reader about the *persona* he is projecting through the essay (11)? Explain by pointing to particular words and phrases in the text.

5. What are the implications of the word *plot* in Penenberg and Barry's account of Barry's forays into corporate spying? What does the term connote in addition to "espionage" (2)? How appropriate is it for describing their piece?

FOR WRITING

. . . .

1. You are an employee at Corrugated Cardboard, and a caller asks how many boxes you sell per day on average. You suspect corporate espionage. Hoping to catch the suspect in the act, you prolong the conversation and record it. Write a transcript of what was said between you and the caller.

2. Write a process analysis explaining how you (or someone else) obtained sensitive, secret information in a particular case, whether in business, love, war, or some other enterprise. Be sure to say exactly what was learned and how that information was ultimately used.

CHAPTER NINE

COMPARISON AND CONTRAST

⋎⋏⋎⋏⋎⋏⋎⋏⋎⋏⋎⋏⋎⋏⋎⋏⋎⋏⋎⋏⋎⋏⋎⋏⋎⋏⋎⋏⋎⋏⋎⋏

I F you are thinking of buying a new car, you will probably want to do some COMPARISON* shopping. You might compare the Mazda Miata to the Mitsubishi Eclipse, for example: both are sporty convertibles with similar features in about the same price range. If you're in the market for a convertible, you would be wasting your time getting a quote on a van or pickup. That would be comparing apples to oranges, and true comparisons can be made only among like kinds. Your final decision, however, will be based more on differences (in acceleration, fuel economy, trunk space) than on the similarities. Your comparison, that is, will also entail CONTRAST. (Strictly speaking, a *comparison* looks at both the similarities and the differences between two subjects, whereas a *contrast* looks mainly at the differences.)

Drawing comparisons in writing is a lot like comparison shopping. It points out similarities in different subjects and differences in similar ones. Consider the following comparison between two items we might normally think of as identical:

> The common yo-yo is crudely made, with a thick shank between two widely spaced wooden disks. The string is knotted or stapled to the shank. With such an instrument nothing can be done except the simple up-down movement. My yo-yo, on the other hand, was a perfectly

*Words printed in SMALL CAPITALS are defined in the Glossary/Index.

balanced construction of hard wood, slightly weighted, flat, with only a sixteenth of an inch between the halves. The string was not attached to the shank, but looped over it in such a way as to allow the wooden part to spin freely on its own axis. The gyroscopic effect thus created kept the yo-yo stable in all attitudes.

— FRANK CONROY, *Stop-Time*

Why is Frank Conroy comparing yo-yos here? He is not going to buy one, nor is he telling the reader what kind to buy. Conroy is a man with a message: all yo-yos are not created equal. They may look alike and they may all go up and down on a string, but he points out meaningful (if you are interested in yo-yos) differences between them. There are good yo-yos, Conroy is saying, and bad yo-yos.

Once Conroy has brought together like kinds (apples to apples, yo-yos to yo-yos) and established in his own mind a basis for comparing them (the "common" kind versus "my" kind), he can proceed in one of two ways. He can dispense his information in "chunks" or in "slices" (as when selling bologna). These basic methods of organizing a comparison or contrast are sometimes called the subject-by-subject and the point-by-point methods. The subject-by-subject method treats several aspects of one subject, then discusses the same aspects of the other. So the author provides chunks of information all about one subject before moving on to the other subject. Point-by-point organization shifts back and forth between each subject, treating each point of similarity and difference before going on to the next one.

Dan Treadway uses this method in "Football vs. Asian Studies," p. 364.

In his comparison, Conroy uses the subject-by-subject method. He first gives several traits of the inferior, "common" yo-yo ("crudely made," string fixed to the shank, only goes up and down); then he gives contrasting traits of his superior yo-yo ("perfectly balanced," string loops over the shank, "spins freely on its own axis"). Now let's look at an example of a comparison that uses the point-by-point method to compare two great basketball players, Wilt ("the Stilt") Chamberlain and Bill Russell:

Russell has been above all a team player—a man of discipline, self-denial and killer instinct; in short, a *winner*, in the best American Calvinist tradition. Whereas Russell has been able somehow to squeeze out his last ounce of ability, Chamberlain's performances have been marked by a seeming nonchalance—as if, recognizing his Gigantic fate, he were more concerned with personal style than with winning. "I never want to set records. The only thing I strive for is perfection," Chamberlain has said.

— JAMEY LARNER, "David vs. Goliath"

Paragraph by paragraph, Jamey Larner goes on like this, alternating "slices" of information about each player: Chamberlain's free throws were always uncertain; Russell's were always accurate in the clutch. Chamberlain was efficient; Russell was more so. Chamberlain was fast; Russell was faster. Chamberlain was Goliath at 7-feet-3-inches tall; Russell was David at 6-feet-9. The fans expected Chamberlain to lose; they expected Russell to win.

Point by point, Larner goes back and forth between his two subjects, making one meaningful (to basketball fans) distinction after another. But why, finally, is he bringing these two players together? What's his reason for comparing them at all? Larner has a point to make, just as Conroy does when he compares two yo-yos and just as you should when you draw comparisons in your writing. The author compares these two in order to ARGUE that although the giant Chamberlain was "typecast" by the fans to lose to Russell the giant-killer, it was Wilt "the Stilt," defying all expectations, who (arguably) became the greatest basketball player ever. (This decision was made without consulting Michael Jordan or LeBron James.)

Whether you use chunks or slices, you can take a number of other hints from Conroy and Larner. First, choose subjects that belong to the same general class or category: two toys, two athletes, two religions, two mammals. You might point out many differences between a mattress and motorcycle, but any distinctions you make between them are not likely to be meaningful because there is little logical basis for comparing them.

Even more important, you need to have a good reason for bringing your subjects together in the first place—and a main point to make about them. Then, whether you proceed subject by subject or point by point, stick to two and only two subjects at a time.

Gary Soto compared ethnic groups, p. 390, because he wanted to get married.

And, finally, don't feel that you must always give equal weight to similarities and differences. You might want to pay more attention to the similarities if you wish to convince your parents that a two-seater convertible actually has a lot in common with the big, safe SUV they want you to consider—they both have wheels, brakes, and an engine, for example. But you might want to emphasize the differences between your two subjects if the similarities are readily apparent, as between two yo-yos and two basketball stars.

A BRIEF GUIDE TO WRITING A COMPARISON-AND-CONTRAST ESSAY

As you begin to write a comparison, you need to identify your subjects, state the basis on which you're comparing them, and indicate whether you plan to emphasize their similarities or their differences. Roger Cohen makes these basic moves of comparison in the second paragraph of his essay in this chapter:

> The monkeys are part of a protracted experiment in aging being con-
> ducted by a University of Wisconsin team. Canto gets a restricted diet
> with 30 percent fewer calories than usual while Owen gets to eat what-
> ever the heck he pleases.
> — ROGER COHEN, "The Meaning of Life"

Cohen identifies his subjects (two monkeys), states the basis on which he is comparing them (as part of a study on aging), and indicates that he is planning to emphasize their differences (Cato's diet is restricted; Owen eats whatever he likes). Here is one more example from this chapter:

> They were two strong men, these oddly different generals, and they
> represented the strengths of two conflicting currents that, through them,
> had come into final collision.
> — BRUCE CATTON, "Grant and Lee: A Study in Contrasts"

The following guidelines will help you to make these basic moves as you draft a comparison. They will also help you to come up with two subjects to compare, present their similarities and differences in an organized way, and state your point in comparing them.

Coming Up with Your Subjects

The first thing you need to do when composing a comparison essay is to choose two subjects that are different in significant ways but that also have enough in common to provide a solid basis of comparison. A cruise ship and a jet, for instance, are very different machines; but both are modes of transportation, and that shared characteristic can become the basis for comparing them.

When you look for two subjects that have shared characteristics, don't stretch your comparison too far. The Duchess in Lewis Carroll's *Alice in Wonderland* compares mustard to flamingos because they "both bite." In the real world, however, there's no point in bringing two subjects together when the differences between them are far more significant than the similarities. Better to compare mustard and ketchup or flamingos and roseate spoonbills.

Considering Your Purpose and Audience

Suppose that you are comparing smartphones because the screen cracked on your old one and you need to replace it. In this case, your PURPOSE is to evaluate them and decide which smartphone fits your needs best. However, if you were writing the comparison for *Consumer Reports*, you would be comparing and contrasting smartphones in order to inform readers about their various functions and capabilities.

With comparisons, one size does not fit all. Whether you're writing a comparison to inform, to evaluate, or for some other purpose, always keep the specific needs of your AUDIENCE in mind. How much do your readers already know about your topic? Why should they want or need to know more? What distinctions can you make that they haven't already thought of?

Deborah Tannen talks to teachers, p. 397, so they'll teach differently.

Generating Ideas: Asking How Two Things Are Alike or Different

Once you have a clear basis for comparing two subjects—flamingos and roseate spoonbills are both large pink birds; mustard and ketchup are both condiments; cruise ships and jets are both modes of transportation—look for specific points of comparison between them. Ask yourself: How, specifically, are my two subjects alike? How do they differ?

As you answer these questions, make a point-by-point list of the similarities and differences between your subjects. When you draw up your list, make sure you look at the same elements in both subjects. For example, if you are comparing two smartphone models, you might list such elements as the price, size, and accessories available for each one. Preparing such a list will help you to determine whether your two subjects are actually worth comparing—and will also help you to get the similarities and differences straight in your own mind before attempting to explain them to your audience.

Templates for Comparing

The following templates can help you to generate ideas for a comparison and then to start drafting. Don't take these as formulas where you just have to fill in the blanks. There are no easy formulas for good writing. But these templates can help you plot out some of the key moves of comparison and contrast and thus may serve as good starting points.

- ► X and Y can be compared on the grounds that both are _____.

- ► Like X, Y is also _____, _____, and _____.

- ► Although X and Y are both _____, the differences between them far outweigh the similarities. For example, X is _____, _____, and _____, while Y is _____, _____, and _____.

> ▸ Unlike X, Y is _____.

> ▸ Despite their obvious differences, X and Y are basically alike in that _____.

> ▸ At first glance, X and Y seem _____; however, a closer look reveals _____.

> ▸ In comparing X and Y, we can clearly see that _____.

For more techniques to help you generate ideas and start writing a comparison essay, see Chapter 2.

Organizing a Comparison

As we discussed earlier, there are fundamentally two ways to organize a comparison: point by point or subject by subject. With a point-by-point organization (like Larner's comparison of Wilt Chamberlain and Bill Russell), you discuss each point of comparison (or contrast) between your two subjects before going on to the next point. With the subject-by-subject method, you discuss each subject individually, making a number of points about one subject and then covering more or less the same points about the other subject. This is the organization Conroy follows in his comparison of yo-yos.

Which method of organization should you use? You will probably find that the point-by-point method works best for beginning and ending an essay, while the subject-by-subject method serves you well for longer stretches in the main body.

One reason for using the subject-by-subject method to organize most of your essay is that the point-by-point method, when relentlessly applied, can make the reader a little seasick as you jump back and forth from your first subject to your second. With the subject-by-subject method, you do not have to give equal weight to both subjects. The subject-by-subject method is, thus, indispensable for treating a subject in depth, whereas the point-by-point

Jeff Jacoby begins
with this method
on p. 368.
method is an efficient way to establish a basis of comparison at the beginning, to remind readers along the way why two subjects are being compared, and to sum up your essay at the end.

Stating Your Point

Your main point in drawing a comparison will determine whether you emphasize similarities or differences. For instance, if your thesis is that there are certain fundamental qualities that all successful coaches share—and you're comparing the best coaches from your own high school days to make this point—you will focus on the similarities among them. However, if you're comparing blind dates to make the point that it's difficult to be prepared for a blind date because no two are alike, you would focus on the differences among the blind dates you've had.

Whatever the main point of your comparison might be, state it clearly right away in an explicit THESIS STATEMENT: "Blind dates are inherently unpredictable; since no two are alike, the best way to go into one is with no expectations at all." Be sure to indicate to readers which you are going to emphasize—the similarities or differences between your subjects. Then, in the body of your essay, use specific points of comparison to show those similarities or differences and to prove your main point.

Providing Sufficient Points of Comparison

No matter how you organize a comparison essay, you will have to provide a sufficient number of points of comparison between your subjects to demonstrate that they are truly comparable and to justify your reasons for comparing them. How many points of comparison are enough to do the job?

Sufficiency isn't strictly a matter of numbers. It depends, in part, on just how inclined your audience is to accept (or reject) the main point your comparison is intended to make. If you are comparing subjects that your readers are not familiar with, you may have to give more examples of similarities or differences than you would if your readers already knew a lot about your subjects. For instance, if you're comparing the racing styles of cyclists Bradley Wiggins and Mark Cavendish, readers who think the Tour de France is a vacation package are going to require more (and more basic) points of comparison than avid cycling fans will.

To determine how many points of comparison you need to make, consider your intended readers, and choose the points of comparison you think they will find most useful, interesting, or otherwise convincing. Then give a sufficient number to get your larger point across, but not so many that you run the comparison into the ground.

EDITING FOR COMMON ERRORS IN COMPARISONS

Like other kinds of writing, comparison uses distinctive patterns of language and punctuation—and thus invites typical kinds of errors. The following tips will help you to check for (and correct) these common errors when you draw comparisons in your own writing.

Make sure all comparisons are complete

Comparisons examine at least two things at once. Check to make sure you've identified both of them; otherwise, readers may not fully understand what is being compared.

- ► When you enter a chapel, expect more solitude and silence <u>than in the world outside</u>.
- ► Most public chapels are not as quiet <u>as those attached to monasteries</u>.

Check that all comparisons are grammatically consistent

When you compare items, they should be grammatically parallel—that is, similar in grammatical form. The original version of this sentence unintentionally compares churches to a country.

- ► In Italy the churches seemed even older than <u>those in</u> France.

Check for common errors in usage

GOOD, WELL, BETTER

Good is an adjective; *well* is the adverb form. *Better* can be either an adjective or an adverb.

▸ Celeste plays the clarinet ~~good~~ *well*, but Angela plays even *better*.

BETWEEN, AMONG

Use *between* when you're comparing two items; use *among* when you're comparing three or more.

▸ *Between* France and Germany, Germany has the larger economy.
▸ *Among* all the countries in the euro zone, Germany has the largest economy.

EVERYDAY COMPARISON
A Coffee Mug

This coffee mug, purchased in the campus bookstore of Kenyon College in Gambier, Ohio, quotes the novelist E. L. Doctorow, who graduated from—Kenyon. When you draw a comparison like Doctorow's, you need to choose two subjects (Kenyon and Ohio State) that are in the same general category (schools in Ohio) but that are different enough in their particular details (poetry, football) to make the comparison interesting. Which details you choose to emphasize, however, will depend on your purpose in drawing the comparison. The purpose of the Kenyon coffee mug is to promote the liberal arts: "We grapple with metaphors," as one Kenyon administrator put it; "they clench in the mud." Down the road at Ohio State, however, a competing coffee mug might emphasize the range of academic programs offered by a large state university: "The way they do poetry at Kenyon, we do football at Ohio State—and medieval literature, metallurgy, aviation, law, business, and medicine."

DAN TREADWAY

FOOTBALL VS. ASIAN STUDIES

Dan Treadway wrote "Football vs. Asian Studies" as a senior majoring in communication studies at the University of Texas, Austin. Far from comparing apples to oranges, his essay uses strategies of comparison to uncover unexpected similarities between sports and academics at a large state university. "Sadly," argues Treadway, an associate editor of the *Daily Texan*, those similarities are generally ignored. "Football vs. Asian Studies" was a finalist in a student writing contest sponsored in 2010 by the *Nation* magazine.

Football vs. Asian Studies

The University of Texas football team is among the best in the nation. It has been a beloved part of the university since 1894, and has grown each year since its inception. The program is seemingly larger than life, making more money last year than any other athletic program in history. Its place at this university is defined and unquestioned. If one attends the University of Texas, it's impossible to not know about the importance of the football team.

The University of Texas Asian Studies program is one of the best in the nation. It's been a part of the university since 1994, and is already among the most distinguished academic departments of its kind. Its place at this university is defined to those who know about the major, but it's quite possible to study on campus for four years and never become aware of the fact that the Asian Studies program even exists.

Italics indicate change from subject A (football) to subject B (Asian Studies)

The football team is comprised of eighty-five student-athletes who receive full scholarships to attend the university.

While there is limited funding for those who study abroad, the Department of Asian Studies does not have the funds to offer scholarships specifically aimed at students within the major to help them pay for classes at UT.

Covers the same points in the same order, here and throughout, for each subject

To bolster the team's defense, the University recently recruited Will Muschamp, the former defensive coordinator at Auburn University, to stabilize the shaky unit. Muschamp was offered a salary of $425,000 annually to bring his unique services to the program. Entering only his third year at the University, Muschamp has already become a team favorite among players and fans alike.

To bolster an incomplete Asian Studies program, students 6
along with faculty lobbied tirelessly for the university to adopt a
class that would teach the Vietnamese language. After two
years of diligent campaigning, the university decided to add the
language to the curriculum in the Department of Asian Studies
in 2006. Dr. Hoang Ngo was selected to teach both the regular
and advanced Vietnamese courses at the University. He was
offered a salary of a little more than $45,000 for his unique
services. Ngo quickly became a favorite among his students for
his knowledge and patience.

Football is the most popular spectator sport in the state of 7
Texas without rival. The sport's importance to our heritage is
well known and documented.

Vietnamese is the third-most-spoken language in the state of 8
Texas behind English and Spanish. This is a fact that is not
well-known or documented.

Under head coach Mack Brown, the Longhorns football 9
program has soared to new heights. In the past decade, the
Longhorns have won more games than in any other ten-year
stretch in the program's history. Brown's smart coaching and
savvy recruiting have built a seemingly unstoppable athletic
machine in the city of Austin. His success has distinguished
this era of Texas football as the golden age, unmatched by
teams from past generations.

Under Dr. Hoang Ngo, the Vietnamese language course 10
had grown quite popular in a short period of time. According to
Nickie Tran, a former student in Ngo's class, "[Teaching the
Vietnamese language] is important because if you talk to a lot
of second-generation Asian-Americans, you hear it's hard for
them to retain their native language." Teaching Vietnamese at
the University of Texas has enabled this generation of

Frequent repetition of phrases establishes a firm basis of comparison

Vietnamese-Americans to develop a special connection to generations past.

Mack Brown recently received a $2.1 million pay raise on 11 his $3 million base salary to reward all of his success. The University of Texas's football program is thriving—last year it generated $120 million in revenue.

Dr. Ngo has now moved back to Vietnam to seek new 12 *employment. The Vietnamese language program at UT has been discontinued. A casualty of budget cuts, the administration felt that the program was expendable because of its small size—its absence will save the university approximately $50,000 a year.*

> Frames Asian Studies as a bargain by comparison

A 2009 study revealed that less than 50 percent of football 13 players at the University of Texas ultimately graduated and received a degree.

With the elimination of the Vietnamese language program, 14 *dozens of students will be forced to take courses in a different foreign language so that they may fulfill their academic requirement and graduate with a degree.*

Come September, when students come back to campus, 15 the most popular sport in Texas will be put on display before an ecstatic crowd of more than 100,000 screaming people in Darrell K. Royal-Texas Memorial Stadium, which recently received $179 million in renovations.

Come September, when students come back to campus, the 16 *third most spoken language in Texas will no longer be taught due to budgetary constraints and sadly, hardly anybody will ask questions or even notice.*

> Conclusion emphasizes points of contrast between the two subjects

JEFF JACOBY

WATCHING OPRAH FROM BEHIND THE VEIL

Jeff Jacoby (b. 1959) is a columnist for the *Boston Globe*. Before turning to journalism, Jacoby practiced law, worked on a political campaign, assisted the president of Boston University, and hosted a television show, *Talk of New England*. In 2004 he received the Thomas Paine Award, presented to journalists dedicated "to the preservation and championing of individual liberty." First published in the *Globe* in 2008, "Watching Oprah from Behind the Veil" compares the life and circumstances of an American icon with those of the Arab women who have made her show the most popular English-language program in Saudi Arabia.

$\diamond\!\wedge\!\diamond\!\wedge\!\diamond\!\wedge\!\diamond\!\wedge\!\diamond\!\wedge\!\diamond\!\wedge\!\diamond\!\wedge\!\diamond\!\wedge\!\diamond\!\wedge\!\diamond\!\wedge\!\diamond\!\wedge\!\diamond\!\wedge\!\diamond\!\wedge\!\diamond\!\wedge\!\diamond$

S he has been called the most influential woman of our time. They are among   1
the most disempowered women on earth.

    She is a self-made billionaire, with worldwide interests that range from   2
television to publishing to education. They are forbidden to get a job without
the permission of a male "guardian," and the overwhelming majority of them
are unemployed.

She has a face that is recognized the world over. They cannot leave home 3
without covering their face and obscuring their figure in a cloak.

She is famous for her message of confidence, self-improvement, and spiri- 4
tual uplift. They are denied the right to make the simplest decisions, treated
by law like children who cannot be trusted with authority over their own
well-being.

She, of course, is Oprah Winfrey. They are the multitude of Saudi Ara- 5
bian women whose devotion to her has made *The Oprah Winfrey Show*—
broadcast twice daily on a Dubai-based satellite channel—the highest-rated
English-language program in the kingdom.

A recent *New York Times* story—"Veiled Saudi Women Are Discover- 6
ing an Unlikely Role Model in Oprah Winfrey"—explored the appeal of
America's iconic talk-show host for the marginalized women of the Arabian
peninsula.

"In a country where the sexes are rigorously separated, where topics like 7
sex and race are rarely discussed openly, and where a strict code of public
morality is enforced by religious police," the *Times* noted, "Ms. Winfrey provides many young Saudi women with new ways of thinking about the way local
taboos affect their lives. . . . Some women here say Ms. Winfrey's assurances to
her viewers—that no matter how restricted or even abusive their circumstances
may be, they can take control in small ways and create lives of value—help
them find meaning in their cramped, veiled existence."

And so they avidly analyze Oprah's clothes and hairstyles, 8
and circulate "dog-eared copies" of her magazine, *O*, and write let- | Jacoby is now using the subject-by-subject method, p. 354.
ters telling her of their dreams and disappointments. Many
undoubtedly dream of doing what she did—freeing themselves
from the shackling circumstances into which they were born and rising as high
as their talents can take them.

But the television star never faced the obstacles that confront her Saudi 9
fans.

That is not to minimize the daunting odds Oprah overcame. She was 10
born to an unwed teenage housemaid in pre-civil rights Mississippi, and spent
her first years in such poverty that at times she wore dresses made from potato
sacks. She was sexually molested as a child, and ran away from home as a young

teen. It was a squalid beginning, one that would have defeated many people not blessed with Oprah's intelligence and drive and native gifts.

But whatever else may be said of Oprah's life, it was never crippled by 11 Wahhabism, the fundamentalist strain of Islam that dominates Saudi Arabia and immiserates Saudi women in ruthless gender apartheid. Strict sex segregation is the law of the land. Women are forbidden to drive, to vote, to freely marry or divorce, to appear in public without a husband or other male guardian, or to attend university without their father's permission. They can be jailed—or worse—for riding in a car with a man to whom they are unrelated. Their testimony in court carries less weight than a man's. They cannot even file a criminal complaint without a male guardian's permission—not even in cases of domestic abuse, when it is their "guardian" who has attacked them.

Could Oprah herself have surmounted such pervasive repression? 12

Some Saudi women manage to find jobs, but Wahhabist opposition is 13 fierce. In 2006, Youssef Ibrahim reported in the *New York Sun* on Nabil Ramadan, the owner of a fast-food restaurant in Ranoosh who hired two women to take telephone orders. Within twenty-four hours, the religious police had him arrested and shut down the restaurant for "promoting lewdness." Ramadan was sentenced by a religious court to ninety lashes on his back and buttocks.

Is it any wonder that women trapped in a culture that treats them so 14 wretchedly idolize someone like Oprah, who epitomizes so much that is absent from their lives? A nation that degrades its women degrades itself, and Oprah's message is an antidote to degradation. Why do they love her? Because all the lies of the Wahhabists cannot stifle the truth she embodies: The blessings of liberty were made for women, too.

FOR DISCUSSION

. . . .

1. According to Jeff Jacoby, why do Oprah Winfrey and her show appeal to so many women in Saudi Arabia?
2. What particular lesson about living in "restricted or even abusive" circumstances does Oprah have to teach these women (7)?

3. What obstacles do Saudi women face that Oprah did not, even though she grew up poor in "pre-civil rights Mississippi" (10)?

4. What is the root cause, according to Jacoby, of the "ruthless gender apartheid" that many Saudi women must contend with (11)?

STRATEGIES AND STRUCTURES

1. Do you think Jacoby's intended AUDIENCE for this COMPARISON essay is mostly female, mostly male, or both? Why do you think so?

2. On what basis is Jacoby comparing some of "the most disempowered women on earth" to the "influential" Oprah Winfrey (1)? What common ground do they share?

3. Why does Jacoby wait until the fifth paragraph to name his subjects? What is the effect of referring to them at first as "she" and "they"? What does this contribute to his comparison?

4. Does Jacoby rely more on the point-by-point or subject-by-subject method for organizing his comparison? Is this method of organization effective for this essay? Explain.

5. What is the main point of Jacoby's comparison? Where does he state it most directly?

6. What are some of Jacoby's most effective points of comparison? Does he give a sufficient number of them to support his point? Explain.

7. Jacoby includes a brief NARRATIVE about Oprah's life in paragraph 10. What purpose does this story serve in his comparison? Where else does Jacoby incorporate narrative in his essay?

WORDS AND FIGURES OF SPEECH

1. Though many Arab women wear veils, Jacoby is not simply referring to their attire in his title. Explain the METAPHORIC implications of the phrase "from behind the veil."

2. Why does Jacoby put the word *guardian* in quotation marks (2)?

3. "Immiserates," meaning makes miserable, probably does not appear in your dictionary (11). Why not? Should Jacoby have used a more common word? Explain.

4. "Apartheid" is a South African term that refers to a systematic policy of discrimination based on race (11). How valid do you find Jacoby's use of this term in the context of gender? Explain.

FOR WRITING

. . . .

1. Compile a list of the points of comparison you would make if you were comparing Oprah Winfrey to those who watched her show and read her magazine in the United States.

2. Write an essay comparing the characteristics and values of an influential (or notorious) public figure with those of a particular group of his or her most avid admirers (or detractors).

BRUCE CATTON

GRANT AND LEE: A STUDY IN CONTRASTS

Bruce Catton (1899–1979) was a distinguished historian of the Civil War, winner of both the Pulitzer Prize and the National Book Award for *A Stillness at Appomattox* (1953). Among Catton's many other Civil War books are *This Hallowed Ground* (1956), *The Army of the Potomac* (1962), *Terrible Swift Sword* (1963), and *Grant Takes Command* (1969). It was not, said Catton, "the strategy or political meanings" of the Civil War that most fascinated him, but the "almost incomprehensible emotional experience which this war brought to our country." First published in the essay collection *The American Story* (1955), "Grant and Lee: A Study in Contrasts" looks at two great Americans—one "the modern man emerging," the other from "the age of chivalry."

When Ulysses S. Grant and Robert E. Lee met in the parlor of a modest house at Appomattox Court House, Virginia, on April 9, 1865, to work out the terms for the surrender of Lee's Army of Northern Virginia, a great chapter in American life came to a close, and a great new chapter began.

These men were bringing the Civil War[1] to its virtual finish. To be sure, 2
other armies had yet to surrender, and for a few days the fugitive Confederate
government would struggle desperately and vainly, trying to find some way to
go on living now that its chief support was gone. But in effect it was all over
when Grant and Lee signed the papers. And the little room where they wrote
out the terms was the scene of one of the poignant, dramatic contrasts in American history.

They were two strong men, these oddly different generals, and they rep- 3
resented the strengths of two conflicting currents that, through them, had come
into final collision.

Back of Robert E. Lee was the notion that the old aristocratic concept 4
might somehow survive and be dominant in American life.

Lee was tidewater Virginia,[2] and in his background were family, culture, 5
and tradition . . . the age of chivalry transplanted to a New World which was
making its own legends and its own myths. He embodied a way of life that had
come down through the age of knighthood and the English country squire.
America was a land that was beginning all over again, dedicated to nothing
much more complicated than the rather hazy belief that all men had equal
rights and should have an equal chance in the world. In such a land Lee stood
for the feeling that it was somehow of advantage to human society to have a
pronounced inequality in the social structure. There should be a leisure class,
backed by ownership of land; in turn, society itself should be keyed to the land
as the chief source of wealth and influence. It would bring forth (according to
this ideal) a class of men with a strong sense of obligation to the community;
men who lived not to gain advantage for themselves, but to meet the solemn
obligations which had been laid on them by the very fact that they were privi-
leged. From them the country would get its leadership; to them it could look for

1. Fought between "the Union" (Northern states that stayed loyal to the federal government
under President Abraham Lincoln) and "the Confederacy" (eleven slave-holding Southern
states and their sympathizers that formed a separate government under Jefferson Davis)
(1861–1865).

2. Coastal region of eastern Virginia. Jamestown, the first British colony in North America,
was settled in this region in 1607.

the higher values—of thought, of conduct, of personal deportment—to give it strength and virtue.

Lee embodied the noblest elements of this aristocratic ideal. Through him, the landed nobility justified itself. For four years, the Southern states had fought a desperate war to uphold the ideals for which Lee stood. In the end, it almost seemed as if the Confederacy fought for Lee; as if he himself was the Confederacy . . . the best thing that the way of life for which the Confederacy stood could ever have to offer. He had passed into legend before Appomattox. Thousands of tired, underfed, poorly clothed Confederate soldiers, long since past the simple enthusiasm of the early days of the struggle, somehow considered Lee the symbol of everything for which they had been willing to die. But they could not quite put this feeling into words. If the Lost Cause, sanctified by so much heroism and so many deaths, had a living justification, its justification was General Lee.

Grant, the son of a tanner on the Western frontier, was everything Lee was not. He had come up the hard way and embodied nothing in particular except the eternal toughness and sinewy fiber of the men who grew up beyond the mountains. He was one of a body of men who owed reverence and obeisance to no one, who were self-reliant to a fault, who cared hardly anything for the past but who had a sharp eye for the future.

These frontier men were the precise opposites of the tidewater aristocrats. Back of them, in the great surge that had taken people over the Alleghenies[3] and into the opening Western country, there was a deep, implicit dissatisfaction with a past that had settled into grooves. They stood for democracy, not from any reasoned conclusion about the proper ordering of human society, but simply because they had grown up in the middle of democracy and knew how it worked. Their society might have privileges, but they would be privileges each man had won for himself. Forms and patterns meant nothing. No man was born to anything, except perhaps to a chance to show how far he could rise. Life was competition.

Yet along with this feeling had come a deep sense of belonging to a national community. The Westerner who developed a farm, opened a shop, or

---

3. Mountain range that runs from north-central Pennsylvania to southwestern Virginia.

set up in business as a trader, could hope to prosper only as his own community prospered—and his community ran from the Atlantic to the Pacific and from Canada down to Mexico. If the land was settled, with towns and highways and accessible markets, he could better himself. He saw his fate in terms of the nation's own destiny. As its horizons expanded, so did his. He had, in other words, an acute dollars-and-cents stake in the continued growth and development of his country.

And that, perhaps, is where the contrast between Grant and Lee becomes most striking. The Virginia aristocrat, inevitably, saw himself in relation to his own region. He lived in a static society which could endure almost anything except change. Instinctively, his first loyalty would go to the locality in which that society existed. He would fight to the limit of endurance to defend it, because in defending it he was defending everything that gave his own life its deepest meaning. **10**

The Westerner, on the other hand, would fight with an equal tenacity for the broader concept of society. He fought so because everything he lived by was tied to growth, expansion, and a constantly widening horizon. What he lived by would survive or fall with the nation itself. He could not possibly stand by unmoved in the face of an attempt to destroy the Union. He would combat it with everything he had, because he could only see it as an effort to cut the ground out from under his feet. **11**

So Grant and Lee were in complete contrast, representing two diametrically opposed elements in American life. Grant was the modern man emerging; beyond him, ready to come on the stage, was the great age of steel and machinery, of crowded cities and a restless burgeoning vitality. Lee might have ridden down from the old age of chivalry, lance in hand, silken banner fluttering over his head. Each man was the perfect champion of his cause, drawing both his strengths and his weaknesses from the people he led. **12**

Yet it was not all contrast, after all. Different as they were—in background, in personality, in underlying aspiration—these two great soldiers had much in common. Under everything else, they were marvelous fighters. Furthermore, their fighting qualities were really very much alike. **13**

A balanced comparison includes both similarities and differences.

Each man had, to begin with, the great virtue of utter tenacity and fidelity. Grant fought his way down the Mississippi Valley in spite of acute personal **14**

Union general Ulysses S. Grant, 1864. Photograph by Mathew Brady.

Confederate general Robert E. Lee, 1860.

discouragement and profound military handicaps. Lee hung on in the trenches at Petersburg after hope itself had died. In each man there was an indomitable quality . . . the born fighter's refusal to give up as long as he can still remain on his feet and lift his two fists.

Daring and resourcefulness they had, too; the ability to think faster and move faster than the enemy. These were the qualities which gave Lee the dazzling campaigns of Second Manassas and Chancellorsville and won Vicksburg for Grant. 15

Lastly, and perhaps greatest of all, there was the ability, at the end, to turn quickly from war to peace once the fighting was over. Out of the way these two men behaved at Appomattox came the possibility of a peace of reconciliation. It was a possibility not wholly realized, in the years to come, but which did, in the end, help the two sections to become one nation again . . . after a war whose bitterness might have seemed to make such a reunion wholly impossible. No part of either man's life became him more than the part he played in this brief meeting in the McLean house at Appomattox. Their behavior there put all succeeding generations of Americans in their debt. Two great Americans, Grant and Lee—very different, yet under everything very much alike. Their encounter at Appomattox was one of the great moments of American history. 16

FOR DISCUSSION

1. Bruce Catton writes that Generals Lee and Grant represented two conflicting currents of American culture. What were these currents? What CONTRASTING qualities and ideals does Catton associate with each man?

2. What qualities, according to Catton, did Grant and Lee have in common? What did these shared qualities enable each man to accomplish?

3. With Lee's surrender, says Catton, "a great new chapter" of American history began (1). What characteristics of the new era does Catton anticipate in his DESCRIPTION of Grant?

4. Catton does not describe, in any detail, how Grant and Lee behaved as they worked out the terms of peace at Appomattox. What does he imply about the conduct of the two men in general?

STRATEGIES AND STRUCTURES

. . . .

1. Beginning with paragraph 3, Catton gets down to the particulars of his contrast between the two generals. How does Catton organize his contrast—point by point or subject by subject? In what paragraphs does he turn to the similarities between the two men and how are they organized?

2. Which sentence in the final paragraph brings together both the differences and the similarities outlined in the preceding paragraphs? How does this paragraph recall the opening paragraphs of the essay? Why might Catton end with an echo of his beginning?

3. Catton does not really give specific reasons for the Confederacy's defeat. What general explanation does he hint at, however, when he associates Lee with a "static society" and Grant with a society of "restless burgeoning vitality" (10, 12)? What is Catton's purpose in drawing this extensive comparison?

4. In comparing and contrasting the two generals in this essay, Catton also describes two regional types. What are some of the specific personal characteristics Catton ascribes to Grant and Lee that, at the same time, make them representative figures?

WORDS AND FIGURES OF SPEECH

. . . .

1. Catton describes the parlor where Grant and Lee met as the "scene" of a "dramatic" contrast, and he says that a new era was ready to come on stage (2). What view of history is suggested by these METAPHORS?

2. What does Catton mean by "the Lost Cause" in paragraph 6?

3. What is the precise meaning of "obeisance" (7)? Why might Catton choose this term instead of the more common *obedience* when describing General Grant?

4. Look up any of the following words with which you are not on easy terms: "fugitive" (2), "poignant" (2), "chivalry" (5), "sinewy" (7), "implicit" (8), "tenacity" (11), "diametrically" (12), "acute" (14), "profound" (14), "indomitable" (14). What words would you substitute to help make the TONE of the essay less formal?

FOR WRITING

1. Photographs of Grant and Lee are included with this essay. Consider what each photograph contributes to your understanding of the men and their roles in history. Write several paragraphs comparing and contrasting the two photographs and what they reveal about each man.

2. Write an essay comparing and contrasting a pair of important historical or public figures with whom you are familiar—Thomas Jefferson and Alexander Hamilton or Hillary Clinton and Michelle Obama, for example.

PICO IYER

CHAPELS: ON THE REWARDS
OF BEING QUIET

Pico Iyer (b. 1957) is a novelist and travel writer known for his spirituality. Iyer's travels began at an early age when his family moved to California from Oxford, England. As a seven-year-old, Iyer remained in school in Britain but flew back and forth to his new home on holidays. A graduate of Harvard, Iyer taught writing there before joining *Time* magazine in 1982. Though he now mainly resides in Japan, Iyer still writes for *Time*, as well as numerous other periodicals in the United States and elsewhere. On the road, Iyer makes his home in various temples and monasteries from California to Tibet. His most recent books include *The Open Road* (2008), a meditation on the spiritual journey of his family friend the Dalai Lama, and *The Man Within My Head* (2012). In the following two complete sections from "Chapels" (*Portland Magazine*, Winter 2010), Iyer compares the two different worlds he encounters wherever he travels. One is noisy, chaotic, and always changing; the other is silent, orderly, and changeless.

Giant figures are talking and strutting and singing on enormous screens above me, and someone is chattering away on the miniscreen in the cab from which I just stepped. Nine people at this street corner are shouting into thin air, wearing wires around their chins and jabbing at screens in their hands. One teenager in Sacramento, I read recently, sent 300,000 text messages in a month—or ten a minute for every minute of her waking day, assuming she was awake sixteen hours a day. There are more cell phones than people on the planet now, almost (ten mobiles for every one at the beginning of the century). Even by the end of the last century, the average human being in a country such as ours saw as many images in a day as a Victorian inhaled in a lifetime.

Sometimes a comparison requires special information.

1

And then I walk off crowded Fifth Avenue and into the capacious silence of St. Patrick's. Candles are flickering here and there, intensifying my sense of all I cannot see. Figures are on their knees, heads bowed, drawing my attention to what cannot be said. Light is flooding through the great blue windows, and I

2

Saint Patrick's Cathedral in New York City

have entered a realm where no I or realm exists. I notice everything around me: the worn stones, the little crosses, the hymnbooks, the upturned faces; then I sit down, close my eyes—and step out of time, into everything that stretches beyond it.

* * *

Many years ago, when I was too young to know better, I worked in a twenty-fifth-floor office four blocks from Times Square, in New York City. Teletypes juddered the news furiously into our midst every second—this was the World Affairs department of *Time* magazine—and messengers breathlessly brought the latest reports from our correspondents to our offices. Editors barked, early computers sputtered, televisions in our senior editors' offices gave us the news as it was breaking. We spoke and conferred and checked facts and wrote, often, twenty or twenty-five pages in an evening.

I left all that for a monastery on the back streets of Kyoto. I wanted to learn about silence. I wanted to learn about who I was when I wasn't thinking about it. The Japanese are masters of not saying anything, both because their attention is always on listening, on saying little, even on speaking generically, and because when they do talk, they are very eager to say nothing offensive, outrageous, or confrontational. They're like talk-show hosts in a nation where self-display is almost forbidden. You learn more by listening than talking, they know; you create a wider circle not by thinking about yourself, but about the people around you, and how you can find common ground with them. The Japanese idea of a dream date—I've been with my Japanese sweetheart for twenty-three years and I've learned the hard way—is to go to a movie and come out saying nothing.

Perhaps I wouldn't need this kind of training in paying attention and keeping quiet were it not for the fact that I used to love babbling, and my colleges and friends in England and the U.S. trained and encouraged me to talk, to thrust myself forward, to assert my little self in all its puny glory. Perhaps we wouldn't need chapels if our lives were already clear and calm (a saint or a Jesus may never need to go into a church; he's always carrying one inside himself). Chapels are emergency rooms for the soul. They are the one place we can reliably go to find who we are and what we should be doing with our lives—usually by finding all we aren't, and what is much greater than us, to which we can only give ourselves up.

Times Square

"I like the silent church," Emerson[1] wrote "before the service begins." 6

* * *

We've always needed chapels, however confused or contradictory we may be in 7
the way we define our religious affiliations; we've always had to have quietness
and stillness to undertake our journeys into battle, or just the tumult of the
world. How can we act in the world, if we haven't had the time and chance to
find out who we are and what the world and action might be?

But now Times Square is with us everywhere. The whole world is clamor- 8
ing at our door even on a mountaintop (my monastery has wireless Internet, its
workers downloaded so much of the world recently that the system crashed, and
the monastery has a digital address, www.contemplation.com). Even in my cell

---

1. Ralph Waldo Emerson (1803–1882), American essayist and poet.

in Japan, I can feel more than 6 billion voices, plus the Library of Alexandria,[2] CNN, MSNBC, everything, in that inoffensive little white box with the apple on it. Take a bite, and you fall into the realm of Knowledge, and Ignorance, and Division.

The high-tech firm Intel experimented for seven months with enforcing "Quiet Time" for all of its workers for at least four consecutive hours a week (no e-mails were allowed, no phone calls accepted). It tried banning all e-mail checks on Fridays and assuring its workers that they had twenty-four hours, not twenty-four minutes, in which to respond to any internal e-mail. If people are always running to catch up, they will never have the time and space to create a world worth catching up with. Some colleges have now instituted a vespers hour, though often without a church; even in the most secular framework, what people require is the quietness to sink beneath the rush of the brain. Journalist friends of mine switch off their modems from Friday evening to Monday morning, every week, and I bow before them silently; I know that when I hop around the Web, watch *YouTube* videos, surf the TV set, I turn away and feel agitated. I go for a walk, enjoy a real conversation with a friend, turn off the lights and listen to Bach or Leonard Cohen, and I feel palpably richer, deeper, fuller, happier.

Happiness is absorption, being entirely yourself and entirely in one place. That is the chapel that we crave.

Long after my home had burned down, and I had begun going four times a year to my monastery up the coast, long after I'd constructed a more or less unplugged life in Japan—figuring that a journalist could write about the news best by not following its every convulsion, and writing from the chapel and not the madness of Times Square—I found a Christian retreat house in my own hometown. Sometimes, when I had an hour free in the day, or was running from errand to errand, I drove up into the silent hills and parked there, and just sat for a few minutes in its garden. Encircled by flowers. In a slice of light next to a statue of the Virgin.

2. The largest and most significant library of the ancient world, located in Egypt.

Instantly, everything was okay. I had more reassurance than I would ever   12
need. I was thinking of something more than an "I" I could never entirely
respect.

Later, I opened the heavy doors and walked into the chapel, again when   13
no one was there. It sat next to a sunlit courtyard overlooking the dry hills and
far-off blue ocean of what could have been a space in Andalusia. A heavy bell
spoke of the church's private sense of time. A row of blond-wood chairs was
gathered in a circle. I knelt and closed my eyes and thought of the candle flickering in one corner of the chapel I loved in the monastery up the coast.

When I had to go to Sri Lanka, in the midst of its civil war, I went to the   14
chapel to be still; to gather my resources and protection, as it were. I went there
when I was forcibly evacuated from the house that my family had rebuilt after
our earlier structure had burned down, and our new home was surrounded by
wild flames driven by seventy-mile-per-hour winds. In the very same week, my
monastery in Big Sur was also encircled by fire.

I went there even when I was halfway across the world, because I had   15
reconstituted the chapel in my head, my heart; it was where I went to be held by
something profound. Then another wildfire struck up, and a newspaper editor
called me in Japan: the retreat house near my home was gone.

Where does one go when one's chapel is reduced to ash? Perhaps it is the   16
first and main question before us all. There are still chapels everywhere. And I
go to them. But like the best of teachers or friends, they always have the gift of
making themselves immaterial, invisible—even, perhaps, immortal. I sit in
Nara, the capital of Japan thirteen centuries ago, and I see a candle flickering. I
feel the light descending from a skylight in the rotunda roof. I hear a fountain in
the courtyard. I close my eyes and sit very still, by the side of my bed, and sense
the chapel take shape around me.

If your silence is deep enough, bells toll all the way through it.   17

FOR DISCUSSION

1. As a young journalist, why did Pico Iyer leave a bustling news room at *Time* magazine in New York City and go to stay in a monastery (3–4)? Was this a wise decision? Explain.

2. Why did Iyer choose a monastery in Japan instead of simply retreating to St. Patrick's Cathedral or some other local sanctuary? What does Iyer's example of going to a movie with his "Japanese sweetheart" show about the character, as he sees it, of the Japanese people (4)?

3. According to Iyer, how does normal social behavior in Japan differ from the way young people are "trained" to behave in England and the United States (5)?

4. What does Iyer mean when he says, "But now Times Square is with us everywhere" (8)? In his view, what are some of the CAUSES of this state of affairs?

5. What is Iyer's answer to the final question he raises about what to do "when one's chapel is reduced to ash" (16)?

STRATEGIES AND STRUCTURES

1. Iyer begins his essay by comparing the sensations that bombard today's "average human being" with those experienced by "a Victorian" (1). Is this an effective introduction? Why or why not?

2. What is the point of Iyer's extended comparison between chapels and the outside world? Where does he state that point most clearly?

3. Iyer's essay focuses on vastly different types of places. On what basis is he comparing them—as, for example, when he says, "I have entered a realm where no I or realm exists" (2)?

4. If chapels are realms of silence and timelessness, what are the typical attributes, according to Iyer, of other, more worldly places such as Times Square or his old newsroom at *Time* magazine? Point to specific examples, and explain how they help him to sharpen the contrast.

5. Iyer ends each section of his essay with a brief summary statement. How and how well does this strategy fit in with his general message about "paying attention and keeping quiet" (5)?

6. Iyer defines happiness as "being entirely yourself and entirely in one place" (10). Where else in his essay does Iyer use DEFINITIONS like this to help make comparisons? Explain by pointing to specific examples in the text.

WORDS AND FIGURES OF SPEECH

1. Why does Iyer find it IRONIC that the name of a monastery's website is www.contemplation.com (8)?
2. Iyer says of the apple logo on his computer, "Take a bite, and you fall into the realm of Knowledge, and Ignorance, and Division" (8). Explain the ALLUSION. How appropriate is it?
3. Iyer describes his life in Japan as *"unplugged"* (11). How and how well does this term fit what he says about chapels as sanctuaries?
4. "If your silence is deep enough, bells toll all the way through it" (17). How does Iyer resolve the apparent contradiction of this OXYMORON?

FOR WRITING

1. Visit a chapel or other place of sanctuary. Take notes on what you see, hear, and feel there. When you come out, review your notes and make a list of the most important attributes of the scene.
2. Write an essay comparing a particular place as you first experienced it with the same place as you came to know it more completely over time. Be sure to explain how you learned to see the place in a different light.

GARY SOTO

LIKE MEXICANS

Gary Soto (b. 1952), who grew up in Fresno, California, taught creative writing
at the University of California at Riverside. He is the author of eleven books of
poetry, numerous stories for children and young adults, and several novels,
including *Nickel and Dime* (2000), *Poetry Lover* (2001), and *Amnesia in a Republican Country* (2003). Soto's memoir, *Living up the Street* (1985), won an American
Book Award. In "Like Mexicans," from *Small Faces* (1986), another collection of
reminiscences about growing up in the barrio, Soto compares his future wife's
Japanese American family with his own Mexican American one.

◇◇◇◇◇◇◇◇◇◇◇◇◇◇◇◇◇◇◇◇◇◇◇◇◇◇◇◇◇

My grandmother gave me bad advice and good advice when I was in my   1
early teens. For the bad advice, she said that I should become a barber
because they made good money and listened to the radio all day. "Honey, they
don't work como burros," she would say every time I visited her. She made the
sound of donkeys braying. "Like that, honey!" For the good advice, she said
that I should marry a Mexican girl. "No Okies, hijo"—she would say—"Look,
my son. He marry one and they fight every day about I don't know what and I
don't know what." For her, everyone who wasn't Mexican, black, or Asian were

Okies. The French were Okies, the Italians in suits were Okies. When I asked about Jews, whom I had read about, she asked for a picture. I rode home on my bicycle and returned with a calendar depicting the important races of the world. "Pues si, son Okies tambien!"[1] she said, nodding her head. She waved the calendar away and we went to the living room where she lectured me on the virtues of the Mexican girl: first, she could cook and, second, she acted like a woman, not a man, in her husband's home. She said she would tell me about a third when I got a little older.

I asked my mother about it—becoming a barber and marrying Mexican. 2
She was in the kitchen. Steam curled from a pot of boiling beans, the radio was on, looking as squat as a loaf of bread. "Well, if you want to be a barber—they say they make good money." She slapped a round steak with a knife, her glasses slipping down with each strike. She stopped and looked up. "If you find a good Mexican girl, marry her of course." She returned to slapping the meat and I went to the backyard where my brother and David King were sitting on the lawn feeling the inside of their cheeks.

"This is what girls feel like," my brother said, rubbing the inside of his 3
cheek. David put three fingers inside his mouth and scratched. I ignored them and climbed the back fence to see my best friend, Scott, a second-generation Okie. I called him and his mother pointed to the side of the house where his bedroom was, a small aluminum trailer, the kind you gawk at when they're flipped over on the freeway, wheels spinning in the air. I went around to find Scott pitching horseshoes.

I picked up a set of rusty ones and joined him. While we played, we talked 4
about school and friends and record albums. The horseshoes scuffed up dirt, sometimes ringing the iron that threw out a meager shadow like a sundial. After three argued-over games, we pulled two oranges apiece from his tree and started down the alley still talking school and friends and record albums. We pulled more oranges from the alley and talked about who we would marry. "No offense, Scott," I said with an orange slice in my mouth, "but I would never marry an Okie." We walked in step, almost touching, with a sled of shadows

1. Well yes, they're Okies, too.

dragging behind us. "No offense, Gary," Scott said, "but I would *never* marry a Mexican." I looked at him: a fang of orange slice showed from his munching mouth. I didn't think anything of it. He had his girl and I had mine. But our seventh-grade vision was the same: to marry, get jobs, buy cars and maybe a house if we had money left over.

We talked about our future lives until, to our surprise, we were on the downtown mall, two miles from home. We bought a bag of popcorn at Penney's and sat on a bench near the fountain watching Mexican and Okie girls pass. "That one's mine," I pointed with my chin when a girl with eyebrows arched into black rainbows ambled by. "She's cute," Scott said about a girl with yellow hair and a mouthful of gum. We dreamed aloud, our chins busy pointing out girls. We agreed that we couldn't wait to become men and lift them onto our laps.

But the woman I married was not Mexican but Japanese. It was a surprise to me. For years, I went about wide-eyed in my search for the brown girl in a white dress at a dance. I searched the playground at the baseball diamond. When the girls raced for grounders, their hair bounced like something that couldn't be caught. When they sat together in the lunchroom, heads pressed together, I knew they were talking about us Mexican guys. I saw them and dreamed them. I threw my face into my pillow, making up sentences that were good as in the movies.

But when I was twenty, I fell in love with this other girl who worried my mother, who had my grandmother asking once again to see the calendar of the Important Races of the World. I told her I had thrown it away years before. I took a much-glanced-at snapshot from my wallet. We looked at it together, in silence. Then Grandma reclined in her chair, lit a cigarette, and said, "Es pretty." She blew and asked with all her worry pushed up to her forehead: "Chinese?"

I was in love and there was no looking back. She was the one. I told my mother who was slapping hamburger into patties. "Well, sure if you want to marry her," she said. But the more I talked, the more concerned she became. Later I began to worry. Was it all a mistake? "Marry a Mexican girl," I heard my mother say in my mind. I heard it at breakfast. I heard it over math problems, between Western Civilization and cultural geography. But then one afternoon while I was hitchhiking home from school, it struck me like a base-ball in the back: my mother wanted me to marry someone of my own social class—a poor girl. I considered my fiancée, Carolyn, and she didn't look poor, though I knew she came from a family of farm workers and pull-yourself-up-by-your-bootstraps ranchers. I asked my brother, who was marrying Mexican poor that fall, if I should marry a poor girl. He screamed "Yeah" above his ter-rible guitar playing in his bedroom. I considered my sister who had married Mexican. Cousins were dating Mexican. Uncles were remarrying poor women. I asked Scott, who was still my best friend, and he said, "She's too good for you, so you better not."

I worried about it until Carolyn took me home to meet her parents. We 9 drove in her Plymouth until the houses gave way to farms and ranches and finally her house fifty feet from the highway. When we pulled into the drive, I panicked and begged Carolyn to make a U-turn and go back so we could talk about it over a soda. She pinched my cheek, calling me a "silly boy." I felt better, though, when I got out of the car and saw the house: the chipped paint, a cracked window, boards for a walk to the back door. There were rusting cars near the barn. A tractor with a net of spiderwebs under a mulberry. A field. A bale of barbed wire like children's scribbling leaning against an empty chicken coop. Carolyn took my hand and pulled me to my future mother-in-law who was coming out to greet us.

We had lunch: sandwiches, potato chips, and iced tea. Carolyn and her 10 mother talked mostly about neighbors and the congregation at the Japanese Methodist Church in West Fresno. Her father, who was in khaki work clothes, excused himself with a wave that was almost a salute and went outside. I heard a truck start, a dog bark, and then the truck rattle away.

Carolyn's mother offered another sandwich, but I declined with a shake of 11 my head and a smile. I looked around when I could, when I was not saying over and over that I was a college student, hinting that I could take care of her daughter. I shifted my chair. I saw newspapers piled in corners,

Soto is clearly stating his basis of comparison, p. 357.

dusty cereal boxes and vinegar bottles in corners. The wallpaper was bubbled from rain that had come in from a bad roof. Dust. Dust lay on lamp shades and window sills. These people are just like Mexicans, I thought. Poor people.

Carolyn's mother asked me through Carolyn if I would like a *sushi*. A   12
plate of black and white things were held in front of me. I took one, wide-eyed,
and turned it over like a foreign coin. I was biting into one when I saw a kitten
crawl up the window screen over the sink. I chewed and the kitten opened its
mouth of terror as she crawled higher, wanting in to paw the leftovers from our
plates. I looked at Carolyn who said that the cat was just showing off. I looked
up in time to see it fall. It crawled up, then fell again.

We talked for an hour and had apple pie and coffee, slowly. Finally, we got   13
up with Carolyn taking my hand. Slightly embarrassed, I tried to pull away but
her grip held me. I let her have her way as she led me down the hallway with her
mother right behind me. When I opened the door, I was startled by a kitten clinging to the screen door, its mouth screaming "cat food, dog biscuits, *sushi*. . . ." I
opened the door and the kitten, still holding on, whined in the language of
hungry animals. When I got into Carolyn's car, I looked back: the cat was still
clinging. I asked Carolyn if it were possibly hungry, but she said the cat was
being silly. She started the car, waved to her mother, and bounced us over the
rain-pocked drive, patting my thigh for being her lover baby. Carolyn waved
again. I looked back, waving, then gawking at a window screen where there
were now three kittens clawing and screaming to get in. Like Mexicans, I
thought. I remembered the Molinas and how the cats clung to their screens—
cats they shot down with squirt guns. On the highway, I felt happy, pleased by
it all. I patted Carolyn's thigh. Her people were like Mexicans, only different.

FOR DISCUSSION

. . . .

1. After COMPARING his future wife's family to his own, Gary Soto concludes that
   they are much alike, "only different" (13). How and how well does this conclusion summarize the main point of Soto's comparison? Explain.

2. How does Soto's grandmother DEFINE an "Okie" (1)? Why doesn't she want him
   to marry one?

3. Why does Soto say that his grandmother gave him bad and good advice (1)?
   Which is which, and why?

4. "It was a surprise to me," says Soto about marrying a girl of Japanese descent (6). Why didn't he marry a Mexican girl, as his grandmother advised?

5. What does Soto imply about ethnic and racial stereotypes when he refers to the calendar showing the "Important Races of the World" (1, 7)? Why does his grandmother ask for the calendar again?

STRATEGIES AND STRUCTURES

1. Before comparing them with Japanese Americans, Soto explains what Mexican Americans are "like." What are some of the specifics by which he characterizes himself and his family? What is his PURPOSE for citing these particular traits?

2. We meet Carolyn's family in paragraph 10. How has Soto already prepared us to expect more similarities than differences between the two families? Cite details by which Soto explains what Carolyn's people are "like."

3. Why does Soto refer so often to the kittens of Carolyn's family's house? What role do they play in his comparison?

4. Besides giving advice, Soto's grandmother, like all the other adult women in "Like Mexicans," is engaged in what activity? Why do you think Soto focuses on this?

5. Soto's comparison of two American families has many elements of NARRATIVE. Who is the NARRATOR: a young man growing up in a Mexican American neighborhood, an older man looking back at him, or both? Explain.

WORDS AND FIGURES OF SPEECH

1. What is the effect of Soto's DESCRIPTION of the orange slice in Scott's mouth as a "fang" (4)? Why do you think he says, "I didn't think anything of it" (4)?

2. What does Soto mean by the term "social class" in paragraph 8?

3. Why do you think Soto compares *sushi* to a foreign coin (12)? Give examples of other SIMILES like this one in his essay.

4. What is the derivation of Soto's grandmother's favorite ethnic slur, "Okies"?

5. When Soto mentions Jews to his grandmother, she calls for the calendar of the races. Is "Jews" a racial or an ethnic category? What's the difference? How about "Hispanic" or "Japanese American"?

FOR WRITING

1. Write a paragraph comparing and contrasting your family with that of a close friend, spouse, or partner. Choose one specific point of comparison—how or what they eat, how they interact within their family, how they celebrate special occasions, and so forth.

2. Whether or not you grew up in a racially or ethnically diverse neighborhood, you may recall friends and acquaintances who differed from each other in social, economic, physical, religious, or other ways. Write an essay comparing and contrasting several of these friends.

DEBORAH TANNEN

GENDER IN THE CLASSROOM

Deborah Tannen (b. 1945) is a linguist at Georgetown University. She specializes, as she says, in "the language of everyday conversation." "Gender in the Classroom," which originally appeared in the *Chronicle of Higher Education*, grew out of her research for *You Just Don't Understand* (1990), a book about the various conversational styles of men and women. In the United States, says Tannen, the sexes bond differently. Women do it by talking with each other about their troubles; men do it by exchanging "playful insults." In this essay, Tannen compares and contrasts the various behaviors that result from gender-related styles of talking and then explains how she changes her teaching methods to accommodate these behaviors.

W̲hen I researched and wrote my latest book, *You Just Don't Understand: Women and Men in Conversation*, the furthest thing from my mind was reevaluating my teaching strategies. But that has been one of the direct benefits of having written the book.

The primary focus of my linguistic research always has been the language of everyday conversation. One facet of this is conversational style: how different regional, ethnic, and class backgrounds, as well as age and gender, result in different ways of using language to communicate. *You Just Don't Understand* is about the conversational styles of women and men. As I gained more insight into typically male and female ways of using language, I began to suspect some of the causes of the troubling facts that women who go to single-sex schools do better in later life, and that when young women sit next to young men in classrooms, the males talk more. This is not to say that all men talk in class, nor that no women do. It is simply that a greater percentage of discussion time is taken by men's voices.

The research of sociologists and anthropologists such as Janet Lever, Marjorie Harness Goodwin, and Donna Eder has shown that girls and boys learn to use language differently in their sex-separate peer groups. Typically, a girl has a best friend with whom she sits and talks, frequently telling secrets. It's the telling of secrets, the fact and the way that they talk to each other, that makes them best friends. For boys, activities are central: Their best friends are the ones they do things with. Boys also tend to play in larger groups that are hierarchical. High-status boys give orders and push low-status boys around. So boys are expected to use language to seize center stage: by exhibiting their skill, displaying their knowledge, and challenging and resisting challenges.

These patterns have stunning implications for classroom interaction. Most faculty members assume that participating in class discussion is a necessary part of successful performance. Yet speaking in a classroom is more congenial to boys' language experience than to girls', since it entails putting oneself forward in front of a large group of people, many of whom are strangers and at least one of whom is sure to judge speakers' knowledge and intelligence by their verbal display.

Another aspect of many classrooms that makes them more hospitable to most men than to most women is the use of debate-like formats as a learning tool. Our educational system, as Walter Ong[1] argues persuasively in his book *Fighting for Life* (Cornell University Press, 1981), is fundamentally male in that

---

1. Cultural historian, philosopher, and Jesuit priest (1912–2003); a long-time faculty member at St. Louis University.

the pursuit of knowledge is believed to be achieved by ritual opposition: public display followed by argument and challenge. Father Ong demonstrates that ritual opposition—what he calls "adversativeness" or "agonism"—is fundamental to the way most males approach almost any activity. (Consider, for example, the little boy who shows he likes a little girl by pulling her braids and shoving her.) But ritual opposition is antithetical to the way most females learn and like to interact. It is not that females don't fight, but that they don't fight for fun. They don't *ritualize* opposition.

Anthropologists working in widely disparate parts of the world have found contrasting verbal rituals for women and men. Women in completely unrelated cultures (for example, Greece and Bali) engage in ritual laments: spontaneously produced rhyming couplets that express their pain, for example, over the loss of loved ones. Men do not take part in laments. They have their own, very different verbal ritual: a contest, a war of words in which they vie with each other to devise clever insults.   6

When discussing these phenomena with a colleague, I commented that I see these two styles in American conversation: Many women bond by talking about troubles, and many men bond by exchanging playful insults and put-downs, and other sorts of verbal sparring. He exclaimed: "I never thought of this, but that's the way I teach: I have students read an article, and then I invite them to tear it apart. After we've torn it to shreds, we talk about how to build a better model."   7

This contrasts sharply with the way I teach: I open the discussion of readings by asking, "What did you find useful in this? What can we use in our own theory building and our own methods?" I note what I see as weaknesses in the author's approach, but I also point out that the writer's discipline and purposes might be different from ours. Finally, I offer personal anecdotes illustrating the phenomena under discussion and praise students' anecdotes as well as their critical acumen.   8

These different teaching styles must make our classrooms wildly different places and hospitable to different students. Male students are more likely to be comfortable attacking the readings and might find the inclusion of personal anecdotes irrelevant and "soft." Women are more likely to resist discussion they   9 perceive as hostile, and, indeed, it is women in my classes who are most likely to offer personal anecdotes.

A colleague who read my book commented that he had always taken for granted that the best way to deal with students' comments is to challenge them: this, he felt, was self-evident, sharpens their minds and helps them develop debating skills. But he had noticed that women were relatively silent in his classes, so he decided to try beginning discussion with relatively open-ended questions and letting comments go unchallenged. He found, to his amazement and satisfaction, that more women began to speak up.

Though some of the women in his class clearly liked this better, perhaps some of the men liked it less. One young man in my class wrote in a questionnaire about a history professor who gave students questions to think about and called on people to answer them: "He would then play devil's advocate . . . i.e., he debated us. . . . That class *really* sharpened me intellectually. . . . We as students do need to know how to defend ourselves." This young man valued the experience of being attacked and challenged publicly. Many, if not most, women would shrink from such a "challenge," experiencing it as a public humiliation.

A professor at Hamilton College told me of a young man who was upset because he felt his class presentation had been a failure. The professor was puzzled because he had observed that class members had listened attentively and agreed with the student's observations. It turned out that it was this very agreement that the student interpreted as failure: Since no one had engaged his ideas by arguing with him, he felt they had found them unworthy of attention.

So one reason men speak in class more than women is that many of them find the "public" classroom setting more conducive to speaking, whereas most women are more comfortable speaking in private to a small group of people they know well. A second reason is that men are more likely to be comfortable with the debate-like form that discussion may take. Yet another reason is the different attitudes toward speaking in class that typify women and men.

Students who speak frequently in class, many of whom are men, assume that it is their job to think of contributions and try to get the floor to express them. But many women monitor their participation not only to get the floor but to avoid getting it. Women students in my class tell me that if they have spoken up once or twice, they hold back for the rest of the class because they don't want to dominate. If they have spoken a lot one week, they will remain silent the next. These different ethics of participation are, of course, unstated, so those who speak freely assume that those who remain silent have nothing to say, and those who are reining themselves in assume that the big talkers are selfish and hoggish.

When I looked around my classes, I could see these differing ethics and habits at work. For example, my graduate class in analyzing conversation had twenty students, eleven women and nine men. Of the men, four were foreign students: two Japanese, one Chinese, and one Syrian. With the exception of the three Asian men, all the men spoke in class at least occasionally. The biggest talker in the class was a woman, but there were also five women who never spoke at all, only one of whom was Japanese. I decided to try something different.

I broke the class into small groups to discuss the issues raised in the readings and to analyze their own conversational transcripts. I devised three ways of dividing the students into groups: one by the degree program they were in, one by gender, and one by conversational style, as closely as I could guess it. This meant that when the class was grouped according to conversational style, I put Asian students together, fast talkers together, and quiet students together. The class split into groups six times during the semester, so they met in each grouping twice. I told students to regard the groups as examples of interactional data and to note the different ways in which they participated in the different groups. Toward the end of the term, I gave them a questionnaire asking about their class and group participation.

I could see plainly from my observation of the groups at work that women who never opened their mouths in class were talking away in the small groups. In fact, the Japanese woman commented that she found it particularly hard to contribute to the all-woman group she was in because "I was overwhelmed by how talkative the female students were in the female-only group." This is particularly revealing because it highlights that the same person who can be "oppressed" into silence in one context can become the talkative "oppressor" in another. No one's conversational style is absolute; everyone's style changes in response to the context and others' styles.

15

16

17

Some of the students (seven) said they preferred the same-gender groups; others preferred the same-style groups. In answer to the question "Would you have liked to speak in class more than you did?" six of the seven who said yes were women; the one man was Japanese. Most startlingly, this response did not come only from quiet women; it came from women who had indicated they had spoken in class never, rarely, sometimes, and often. Of the eleven students who said the amount they had spoken was fine, seven were men. Of the four women who checked "fine," two added qualifications indicating it wasn't completely fine: One wrote in "maybe more," and one wrote, "I have an urge to participate often but feel I should have something more interesting/relevant/wonderful/intelligent to say!"

18

I counted my experiment a success. Everyone in the class found the small groups interesting, and no one indicated he or she would have preferred that the class not break into groups. Perhaps most instructive, however, was the fact that the experience of breaking into groups, and of talking about participation in class, raised everyone's awareness about classroom participation. After we had talked about it, some of the quietest women in the class made a few voluntary contributions, though sometimes I had to insure their participation by interrupting the students who were exuberantly speaking out.

19

Americans are often proud that they discount the significance of cultural differences: "We're all individuals," many people boast. Ignoring such issues as gender and ethnicity becomes a source of pride: "I treat everyone the same." But treating people the same is not equal treatment if they are not the same.

20

The classroom is a different environment for those who feel comfortable putting themselves forward in a group than it is for those who find the prospect of doing so chastening, or even terrifying. When a professor asks, "Are there any questions?," students who can formulate statements the fastest have the greatest opportunity to respond. Those who need significant time to do so have not really been given a chance at all, since by the time they are ready to speak, someone else has taken the floor.

21

In a class where some students speak out without raising hands, those who feel they must raise their hands and wait to be recognized do not have equal opportunity to speak. Telling them to feel free to jump in will not make them

22

feel free; one's sense of timing, of one's rights and obligations in a classroom, are automatic, learned over years of interaction. They may be changed over time, with motivation and effort, but they cannot be changed on the spot. And everyone assumes his or her own way is best. When I asked my students how the class could be changed to make it easier for them to speak more, the most talkative woman said she would prefer it if no one had to raise hands, and a foreign student said he wished people would raise their hands and wait to be recognized.

My experience in this class has convinced me that small-group interaction should be part of any class that is not a small seminar. I also am convinced that having the students become observers of their own interaction is a crucial part of their education. Talking about ways of talking in class makes students aware that their ways of talking affect other students, that the motivations they impute to others may not truly reflect others' motives, and that the behaviors they assume to be self-evidently right are not universal norms.

The goal of complete equal opportunity in class may not be attainable, but realizing that one monolithic classroom-participation structure is not equal opportunity is itself a powerful motivation to find more diverse methods to serve diverse students—and every classroom is diverse.

23

24

A comparison should have a goal even if it's not entirely attainable.

FOR DISCUSSION

. . . .

1. According to Deborah Tannen, speaking up in class is typically more "congenial" to whom, women or men (4)? What accounts for this difference, according to her COMPARISON of "the language experience" (4)?

2. Men, says Tannen, "ritualize opposition"; women don't (5). Why not? What is the difference, according to the authorities she cites, between how men fight and how women fight? Do you agree?

3. One of Tannen's colleagues teaches by asking students to read an article and then "tear it apart" (7). How does Tannen say this compares with the way she teaches?

4. Tannen CONTRASTS the "ethics of [class] participation" by men with those of women (14). What differences does she find? What are the consequences of their being "unstated" (14)?

5. Tannen, in paragraph 18, presents the results of her questionnaire about class and group participation. What are some of those results? What do you think of her findings?

6. Tannen says that her research in the conversation of men and women caused her to change her classroom teaching strategies. What are some of the changes she made? How compelling do you find her reasons for making them?

STRATEGIES AND STRUCTURES

1. Tannen's title announces that she is comparing men and women on the basis of their classroom behavior. Where does she first indicate what particular aspects of this behavior she will focus on? What are some of them?

2. This essay was originally published in the *Chronicle of Higher Education*, a periodical read by teachers and other educators. In what ways does Tannen tailor her essay to suit this AUDIENCE? How might this essay be different if she had written it for an audience of first-year college students?

3. In paragraph 13, Tannen sums up two of the points of comparison that she has previously made. What are they, and why do you think she summarizes them here? What new point of comparison does she then introduce, and how does she develop it in the next paragraph(s)?

4. "No one's conversational style is absolute," says Tannen; "everyone's style changes in response to the context and others' styles" (17). How does the EXAMPLE of the Japanese woman in her class illustrate the principle that people have different styles of conversation in different situations?

5. Besides comparing and contrasting the behavior of men and women, Tannen is advancing an ARGUMENT about equal opportunity in the classroom (24). What is the main point of her argument? How and how well does she support her main point?

6. "I broke the class into small groups," says Tannen in paragraph 16. Where else in her essay do you find Tannen telling a brief, illustrative story or ANECDOTE about what she did or said? How do the NARRATIVE elements in her essay support the comparison she is making in it?

WORDS AND FIGURES OF SPEECH

1. Roughly speaking, one's "sex" is biological while one's "gender" is not, or not entirely. Why do you think Tannen uses the second term in her essay rather than the first one?

2. "Behavior" usually functions a collective noun, as in the sentence "Their behavior last night was atrocious." Why do you suppose social scientists like Tannen often use the plural form, "behaviors," in their writing (23)? What is the significance of this difference in terminology?

3. Like that of other social scientists, Tannen's writing style is peppered with compound nouns and nouns used as adjectives—for example, "single-sex schools" and "sex-separate peer groups" (2, 3). Point out other expressions like these throughout her essay.

4. What is the meaning of the word "hierarchical" (3), and why does Tannen use it to refer to boys?

5. What is the difference between "ritual opposition" as Tannen uses the term and just plain opposition (5)? What other behaviors does Tannen cite that might be considered rituals?

FOR WRITING

1. How do Tannen's observations on gender in the classroom compare with your own? Write a paragraph comparing and contrasting some aspect of the classroom behaviors of the two genders.

2. Commenting on the differences in the ways girls and boys use language to make friends, Tannen writes: "Typically, a girl has a best friend with whom she sits and talks, frequently telling secrets" (3). Talking together makes them best friends. Boys, she says, make friends through "activities" (3). Consequently, they "use language to seize center stage," to take control (3). How do Tannen's observations square with your experience of making friends while growing up? Write an essay in which you compare and contrast how you made same-sex friends with the way, as you recall, the "opposite" gender did so. Give specific examples and include anecdotes when possible.

ROGER COHEN

THE MEANING OF LIFE

Roger Cohen (b. 1955) is a regular columnist for the *New York Times* and the *International Herald Tribune*. A native of Britain, he studied history and French at Oxford, receiving a master's degree in 1977. After working for the *Wall Street Journal* in Italy and Beirut, Cohen joined the staff of the *Times* in 1980. He is the coauthor of *In the Eye of the Storm* (1991), a biography of General Norman Schwarzkopf, and the author of two other books on war and warfare: *Hearts Grown Brutal* (1998), about the conflict in the former Yugoslavia, and *Soldiers and Slaves* (2005), an account of American POWs in World War II. In "The Meaning of Life," a 2009 op-ed column from the *Times*, Cohen compares Canto and Owen, two rhesus monkeys involved in a study of aging at the University of Wisconsin.

⟡◇⟡

What's life for? That question stirred as I contemplated two rhesus monkeys, Canto, aged 27, and Owen, aged 29, whose photographs appeared last week in the *New York Times*.   1

    The monkeys are part of a protracted experiment in aging being conducted   2
by a University of Wisconsin team. Canto gets a restricted diet with 30 percent
fewer calories than usual while Owen gets to eat whatever the heck he pleases.

Preliminary conclusions, published in *Science* two decades after the 3
experiment began, "demonstrate that caloric restriction slows aging in a pri-
mate species," the scientists leading the experiment wrote. While just 13 percent of the dieting group has died in ways judged due to old age, 37 percent of
the feasting monkeys are already dead.

These conclusions have been contested by other scientists for various rea- 4
sons I won't bore you with—boredom definitely shortens life spans.

Meanwhile, before everyone holds the French fries, the issue arises of how 5
these primates—whose average life span in the wild is 27 (with a maximum of
40)—are feeling and whether these feelings impact their desire to live.

Monkeys' emotions were part of my childhood. My father, a 6
doctor, worked with them all his life. His thesis at the University of
Witwatersrand in Johannesburg, South Africa, was on the men-
strual cycle of baboons. When he settled in Britain in the 1950s, he

With some
subjects, you
look for small
differences
among the
similarities.

*Canto and Owen, two rhesus monkeys who are the subjects of experiments in aging
at the University of Wisconsin.*

had some of his baboons (average life span 30) shipped over, ultimately donating a couple to the London Zoo.

Upon visiting the zoo much later, he got a full-throated greeting from the baboons, who rushed to the front of their cage to tell him they'd missed him. Moral of story: Don't underestimate monkeys' feelings. 7

Which brings me to low-cal Canto and high-cal Owen: Canto looks drawn, weary, ashen, and miserable in his thinness, mouth slightly agape, features pinched, eyes blank, his expression screaming, "Please, no, not another plateful of seeds!" 8

Well-fed Owen, by contrast, is a happy camper with a wry smile, every inch the laid-back simian, plump, eyes twinkling, full mouth relaxed, skin glowing, exuding wisdom as if he's just read Kierkegaard[1] and concluded that "Life must be lived forward, but can only be understood backward." 9

It's the difference between the guy who got the marbleized rib-eye and the guy who got the oh-so-lean filet. Or between the guy who got a Château Grand Pontet St. Emilion with his brie and the guy who got water. As Edgar notes in *King Lear*, "Ripeness is all."[2] You don't get to ripeness by eating apple peel for breakfast. 10

Speaking of St. Emilion, scientists, aware that most human beings don't have the discipline to slash their calorie intake by almost a third, have been looking for substances that might mimic the effects of caloric restriction. They have found one candidate, resveratrol, in red wine. 11

The thing is there's not enough resveratrol in wine to do the trick, so scientists are trying to concentrate it, or produce a chemical like it in order to offer people the gain (in life expectancy) without the pain (of dieting). 12

I don't buy this gain-without-pain notion. Duality resides, indissoluble, at life's core—Faust's two souls within his breast, Anna Karenina's[3] shifting 13

---

1. Søren Kierkegaard (1813–1855), Danish philosopher and theologian.

2. Shakespeare's *King Lear* (c. 1608), 5.2.11.

3. Title character in 1878 novel by Russian writer Leo Tolstoy. *Faust*: A figure in German legend who serves as the basis for many literary works; an ambitious scholar, Faust gives his soul to the devil in exchange for unlimited knowledge and magical powers.

essence. Life without death would be miserable. Its beauty is bound to its fragility. Dawn is unimaginable without the dusk.

When life extension supplants life quality as a goal, you get the desolation of Canto the monkey. Living to 120 holds zero appeal for me. Canto looks like he's itching to be put out of his misery. 14

There's an alternative to resveratrol. Something is secreted in the lovesick that causes rapid loss of appetite—caloric restriction—yet scientists have been unable to reproduce this miracle substance, for if they did they would be decoding love. Because love is too close to the divine, life's essence, it seems to defy such breakdown. 15

My mother died of cancer at 69. Her father lived to 98, her mother to 104. I said my mother died of cancer. But that's not true. She was bipolar and depression devastated her. What took her life was misery. 16

We don't understand what the mind secretes. The process of aging remains full of enigma. But I'd bet on jovial Owen outliving wretched Canto. I suspect those dissenting scientists I didn't bore you with are right. 17

My 98-year-old grandfather had a party trick, making crisscross incisions into a watermelon, before allowing it to fall open in a giant red blossom. It was as beautiful as a lily opening—and, still vivid, close to what life is for. 18

When my father went to pick up his baboons at Heathrow airport, he stopped at a grocery store to buy them a treat. "Two pounds of bananas, please," he said. But there were none. "O.K.," he said, "Then I'll take two pounds of carrots." The shop-keeper gave him a very strange look before hurriedly handing over the carrots. 19

I can hear my 88-year-old father's laughter as he tells this story. Laughter extends life. There's little of it in the low-cal world and little doubt pudgy Owen will have the last laugh. 20

FOR DISCUSSION

· ·

1. Although he admits that Canto may live longer, Cohen says that, of the two monkeys under study, he would prefer to be Owen. Why? Is he right or wrong?

2. What is Cohen's answer to the profound question raised at the beginning of his essay (1)? How adequate is it?

3. "Life must be lived forward, but can only be understood backward" (9). Why (and how appropriately) does Cohen quote this statement by the Danish philosopher Soren Kierkegaard?

4. "Duality resides," says Cohen, "at life's core" (13). How does Cohen DEFINE that duality—and why?

STRATEGIES AND STRUCTURES

. . . .

1. Point out specific details in Cohen's COMPARISON of Canto and Owen that highlight their differences especially well. Why do you find them so effective?

2. Does Cohen give sufficient evidence for the claims, based a comparison of two rhesus monkeys, that he is making about the meaning of life? Why or why not?

3. Visual elements in an essay should be more than mere decoration. How about the photo of Canto and Owen? How and how well does it support Cohen's comparison?

4. What is the "moral" of the story that Cohen tells about his father at the London Zoo (6–7)? How and how well does it apply to the rest of his essay?

5. Point out other ANECDOTES in Cohen's essay, such as that of his grandfather and the watermelon (18). What, if anything, do they add to the comparison?

WORDS AND FIGURES OF SPEECH

. . . .

1. The statement "Ripeness is all," from Shakespeare's *King Lear*, has been variously interpreted (10). What does Cohen take it to mean? Is this interpretation justified?

2. What is the purpose of Cohen's ALLUSIONS to Faust and Anna Karenina in his musings on the "duality" of life (13)?

3. Look up the word *enigma* in your dictionary (17). How does it differ in meaning from the related *conundrum*? Has Cohen chosen the right word here? Why or why not?

FOR WRITING

. . . .

1. Examine the photo of Canto and Owen on p. 407. Write one paragraph each on the physical characteristics of the two monkeys.

2. Using their physical characteristics as a basis, write a comparison of Canto and Owen that speculates about other aspects of their (and the human) condition. Be sure to refer to the scientists' claim that "caloric restriction slows aging" (3).

CHAPTER TEN

DEFINITION

◇◇◇◇◇◇◇◇◇◇◇◇◇◇◇◇◇◇◇◇◇◇◇◇◇◇◇◇◇◇◇◇◇◇◇◇◇◇

W HEN you DEFINE* something, you tell what it is—and what it is not—as in the following famous definitions:

Happiness is a warm puppy.
—CHARLES M. SCHULZ

Man is a biped without feathers.
—PLATO

Hope is the thing with feathers.
—EMILY DICKINSON

Golf is a good walk spoiled.
—MARK TWAIN

All of these model definitions, you'll notice, work in the same way. They place the thing to be defined (happiness, man, hope, golf) into a general class (puppy, biped, thing, walk) and then add characteristics (warm, without feathers, with feathers, spoiled) that distinguish it from others in the same class.

This is the kind of defining—by general class and characteristics—that dictionaries do. *The American Heritage Dictionary*, for example, defines the word *scepter* as "a staff held by a sovereign . . . as an emblem of authority." Here the general class is "staff," and the characteristics that differentiate it from other

*Words printed in SMALL CAPITALS are defined in the Glossary/Index.

staffs—such as those carried by shepherds—are "held by a sovereign" and "as an emblem of authority."

The problem with a basic dictionary definition like this is that it often doesn't tell us everything we need to know. You might begin an essay with one, but you are not going to get very far with a topic unless you *extend* your definition. One way to give an extended definition is to name other similar items in the same category as the item you are defining.

Take the term *folklore*, for example. A standard definition of *folklore* is "the study of traditional materials." This basic definition is not likely to enlighten anyone who is not already familiar with what those "materials" are, however. So one folklorist defines his field by listing a host of similar items that all belong to it:

> Folklore includes myths, legends, folktales, jokes, proverbs, riddles, chants, charms, blessings, curses, oaths, insults, retorts, taunts, teases, toasts, tongue-twisters, and greeting and leave-taking formulas (e.g., See you later, alligator). It also includes folk costumes, folk dance, folk drama (and mime), folk art, folk belief (or superstition), folk medicine, folk instrumental music (e.g., fiddle tunes), folksongs (e.g., lullabies, ballads), folk speech (e.g., to paint the town red), and names (e.g., nicknames and place names).
>
> —ALAN DUNDES, *The Study of Folklore*

Dundes's extended definition does not stop here; it goes on to include "latrinalia (writings on the walls of public bathrooms)," "envelope sealers (e.g., SWAK—Sealed With A Kiss)," "comments made after body emissions (e.g., after burps or sneezes)," and many others items that populate the field he is defining.

Another way to extend a basic definition is to specify additional characteristics of the item or idea you are defining. *Hydroponic tomatoes*, for example, are tomatoes grown mostly in water. Food expert Raymond Sokolov further defines this kind of tomato as one that is "mass-produced, artificially ripened, mechanically picked, and long-hauled." "It has no taste," he says, "and it won't go splat" (all additional

Dave Barry does this with the term *guys* in "Guys vs. Men," p. 427.

negative characteristics). *Organic tomatoes*, by contrast, says Sokolov, are to be defined as tomatoes that are "squishable, blotchy, tart, and sometimes green-dappled."

To extend your definition further, you might give SYNONYMS for the word or concept you're defining, or trace its ETYMOLOGY, or word history. *Tomatoes*, for example, are commonly defined as "vegetables," but an extended definition might point out that they are actually synonymous with "berries" or "fleshy fruits" and that they derive their name from the Nahuatl word *tomatl*. How do we know this last obscure fact? Because most standard dictionaries include etymologies along with basic definitions. Etymologies trace the origins of a word and sometimes can help organize an entire essay.

For example, here is the beginning of an essay by biologist Stephen Jay Gould on the concept of evolution:

> The exegesis [interpretation] of evolution as a concept has occupied the lifetimes of a thousand scientists. In this essay, I present something almost laughably narrow in comparison—an exegesis of the word itself. I shall trace how organic change came to be called *evolution*. The tale is complex and fascinating as a pure antiquarian exercise in etymological detection. But more is at stake, for a past usage of this word has contributed to the most common, current misunderstanding among laymen of what scientists mean by evolution.
>
> —STEPHEN JAY GOULD, *Ever Since Darwin*

The misunderstanding to which this paragraph refers is the idea that *evolution* means "progress." Among scientists, the term signifies simply "organic change," adaptation—without any implication of improvement.

Gould could make this point by tracing the history of evolution "as a concept"; but that might take another scientific lifetime, and he is only writing an essay. So he chooses the much narrower topic of tracing the origins of "the word itself." Following the etymology of a key term like this is an efficient way to reach a larger conclusion—in this case, the modern scientific understanding of evolution. And it can provide a road map for organizing the rest of an essay as a tale of "detection" that uncovers and explains how various related terms have been used in the past.

There is no set formula for writing good definitions, but there are some questions to keep in mind when you are working on one: What is the essential nature or main use of the thing you are defining? What are its distinguishing characteristics? How is it different from other things like it? And, perhaps most important, why do your readers need to know about it, and what point do you want to make?

A BRIEF GUIDE TO WRITING
A DEFINITION ESSAY

As you write a definition, you need to identify your subject, assign it to a general class, and specify particular characteristics that distinguish it from others in that same class. Erin McKean makes these fundamental moves in her essay in this chapter.

> But the traditional dictionary definition, although it bears all the trappings of authority, is in fact a highly stylized, overly compressed, and often tentative stab at capturing the consensus on what a particular word "means."
>
> —ERIN McKEAN, "Redefining Definition"

McKean identifies the term she is defining ("the traditional dictionary definition"), assigns it to a particular class ("stab" at the accepted meaning), and specifies particular characteristics ("highly stylized, overly compressed, and often tentative") that distinguish it from others in that class.

Basic definitions like this can be useful in almost any kind of essay. To define a concept in depth, however, you will need to explain why you're defining it—McKean's purpose in "Redefining Definition" is to advocate the use of online dictionaries—and to extend your definition by adding other distinguishing characteristics, by giving synonyms, and by tracing the etymology of key terms. The following guidelines will help you to make these and other key moves of definition as you draft an essay.

Mike Rose's purpose in "Blue-Collar Brilliance," p. 459, is to question traditional definitions of intelligence.

Coming Up with a Subject

When you compose a definition essay, a good strategy is to look for a concept or term that you think has been defined incorrectly or inadequately—as Gould and McKean do with *evolution* and *dictionary definition*—or that is complex enough in meaning to leave room for discussion and debate. For example: What constitutes *racism* or *sexual harassment*? What characterizes *friendship*? What is *intelligent design*? Whatever term you choose, you will need to discover its essential characteristics (such as the trust and loyalty involved in friendship) and make a specific point about it.

Considering Your Purpose and Audience

When you define something, you may be conveying useful information, demonstrating that you understand the term's meaning, arguing for a particular definition, or just entertaining the reader. Keep your PURPOSE in mind as you construct your definition, and adapt the TONE of your essay accordingly—objective when you want to inform, persuasive when you are arguing, humorous when you want the reader to smile.

Also consider why your AUDIENCE might want (or be reluctant) to know more about your term and what it means. How might the reader already define the term? What information can you supply to make it easier for the reader to understand your definition, or be more receptive to it? For example, a definition of *acid* in a lab manual for chemistry students would be considerably different from a definition of *acid* for a general audience. Whatever term you are defining, be sure to focus on those aspects of it that your audience is most likely to find interesting and useful.

Generating Ideas: Asking What Something Is—and Is Not

In order to define a term or concept, you need to know what its distinguishing characteristics are—what makes it different from other things in the same general class. For instance, suppose you wanted to define what a bodybuilder is. It might occur to you to say that bodybuilders are athletes who need to keep their body fat under control and to build up muscle strength. But these characteristics also apply to runners and swimmers. Among these three types of athletes, however, only bodybuilders train primarily for muscle definition and bulk. In other words, training for muscle definition and bulk is a characteristic that distinguishes bodybuilders from other athletes. Runners and swimmers need strong muscles, too, but what distinguishes them is their speed on the track or in the pool, characteristics that do *not* apply to bodybuilders. As you list the essential characteristics for your term, remember that definitions set up boundaries. They say, in effect: "This is the territory occupied by my concept, and everything outside these boundaries is something else."

What distinguishes "dyslexics," says Jack Horner, p. 454, is their other "extraordinary" abilities.

Once you have identified the distinguishing characteristics for your term or concept, you can construct a basic definition of it—and then extend it from there. So a good basic definition of a bodybuilder might be "an athlete who trains primarily for muscle definition and bulk."

Templates for Defining

The following templates can help you to generate ideas for a definition and then to start drafting. Don't take these as formulas where you just have to fill in the blanks. There are no easy formulas for good writing. But these templates can help you plot out some of the key moves of definition and thus may serve as good starting points.

> ▶ In general, X can be defined as a kind of _____.
>
> ▶ What specifically distinguishes X from others in this category is _____.
>
> ▶ Other important distinguishing characteristics of X are _____, _____, and _____.

- ▶ X is often used to mean _____, but a better synonym would be _____ or _____.
- ▶ One way to define X is as the opposite of _____, the distinguishing characteristics of which are _____, _____, and _____.
- ▶ If we define X as _____, we can then define Y as _____.
- ▶ By defining X in this way, we can see that _____.

For more techniques to help you generate ideas and start writing effective definitions, see Chapter 2.

Stating Your Point

In any definition essay, you need to explain the point your definition is intended to make. A THESIS STATEMENT—usually in the introduction of your essay and perhaps reiterated with variations at the end—is a good way to do this. The following example is from an essay defining a farmer, written by Craig Schafer, an Ohio State student who grew up on a farm in the Midwest: "By definition, a farmer is someone who tills the soil for a living, but I define a true farmer according to his or her attitudes toward the land." This is a good thesis statement because it defines the subject in an interesting way that may draw the reader in to the rest of the essay.

Adding Other Distinguishing Characteristics

Of all the ways you can extend a basic definition, perhaps the most effective is simply to specify additional characteristics that set your subject apart. To support his definition of a farmer as a person with certain attitudes toward the land, Schafer goes on to specify what those attitudes are, devoting a paragraph to each: A farmer is a born optimist, planting his crops "with no assurances that nature will cooperate." A farmer is devoted to the soil, sifting it through his fingers and "sniffing the fresh clean aroma of a newly plowed field." A farmer is self-denying, with a barn that is often "more modern than his house." And so on. As you compose a definition essay, make sure you provide enough characteristics to identify your subject thoroughly and completely.

Using Synonyms and Etymologies

Another way to extend a definition is by offering SYNONYMS. For example, if you were defining *zine* for readers who are unfamiliar with the term, you might say that it is short for *magazine*. You could then explain which characteristics of magazines apply to zines and which ones don't. Both zines and magazines, you might point out, include printed articles and artwork; but zines, unlike magazines, are typically self-published, are photocopied and bound by hand, have very small circulations and are rarely sold at newsstands, and include both original work and work appropriated from other sources.

Often you can extend the definition of a term by tracing its history, or ETYMOLOGY. This is what one engineer did when he asked: "Who are we who have been calling ourselves engineers since the early nineteenth century?" Here's part of his answer:

> The word *engineering* probably derives from the Latin word *ingeniatorum*. In 1325 a contriver of siege towers was called by the Norman word *engynours*. By 1420 the English were calling a trickster a *yngynore*. By 1592 we find the word *enginer* being given to a designer of phrases—a wordsmith.
>
> —JOHN H. LIENHARD, "The Polytechnic Legacy"

Knowing the history of a word and its earlier variations can often help you with a current definition. You can find the etymology of a word in most dictionaries.

CORRECTING COMMON ERRORS IN DEFINITIONS

Like other kinds of writing, definitions use distinctive patterns of language and punctuation—and thus invite typical kinds of errors. The following tips will help you to check for (and correct) these common errors in your own definitions.

Make sure that words referred to as words are in italics

▸ An expert in evolution, Gould defines the term *evolution* by explaining how it has been misused.

▸ Often used as a synonym for *progress*, says Gould, *evolution* simply means change.

Be sure each basic definition includes the general class to which the term belongs

▸ Engineering <u>is a professional field that</u> applies science for practical purposes.

▸ A thoroughbred is<u> a breed of horse</u> capable of racing at high speeds for long distances.

Without *professional field* and *breed of horse*, the preceding sentences are statements about their subjects rather than definitions of them.

Check for common usage errors

IS WHERE, IS WHEN

Where and *when* should not be used to introduce definitions.

▸ Engineering is ~~where you put~~ <u>the practice of putting</u> science to use.

▸ A recession is ~~when~~ <u>the economic condition in which</u> both prices and sales go down.

COMPRISE, COMPOSE

Comprise means "to consist of." *Compose* means "to make up." The whole *comprises* the parts; the parts *compose* the whole.

▸ The federal government ~~composes~~ <u>comprises</u> three branches.

▸ Three branches ~~comprise~~ <u>compose</u> the federal government.

EVERYDAY DEFINITION
Social Media Explained with Donuts

SOCIAL MEDIA EXPLAINED

TWITTER   I'M EATING A #DONUT

FACEBOOK   I LIKE DONUTS

FOURSQURE   THIS IS WHERE
            I EAT DONUTS

INSTAGRAM   HERE'S A VINTAGE
            PHOTO OF MY PONUT

YOUTUBE   HERE I AM EATING A DONUT

LINKED N   MY SKILLS INCLUDE DONUT EATING

PINTEREST   HERE'S A PONUT RECIPE

LAST FM   NOW LISTENING TO "DONUTS"

G+   I'M A GOOGLE EMPLOYEE
            WHO EATS DONUTS.

When you define something, you explain what general category it belongs to; then you give specific characteristics (and examples) of your subject that distinguish it from others in that same category. *Twitter* and *YouTube*, for example—like the other technologies defined by donuts here—both belong to the general category *social media*. As with selecting a donut, however, it is the differences that really define them. With *Twitter*, of course, you're limited to 140-character messages. With *YouTube*, you can post actual videos of yourself engaged in some activity. ("Here I am eating a donut.") Videos on *YouTube*, however, are always posted after the fact. If you want to tell people what's happening in real time, *Twitter*, though plainer, may be the better selection. ("I'm eating a #donut.") Ultimately, the best medium to choose is the one that best suits the purpose or need your message is intended to serve. Ditto for definitions—and for donuts.

LAWRENCE COLLERD

CITY OF BIG SHOULDERS

Lawrence Collerd grew up in the outskirts of Chicago, the city he defines in the following essay as having "big shoulders," among other distinguishing characteristics drawn from Carl Sandburg's famous poem. Collerd expands and updates Sandburg's definition of Chicago as the "Hog Butcher for the World," however, by adding defining features of his own, including Wrigley Field, Michael Jordan, and the high-rise office buildings along the river. "City of Big Shoulders," which Collerd wrote in 2008 as a junior at Ithaca College in New York, won a prize in an annual competition sponsored by the school's Department of Writing.

City of Big Shoulders

Title names the
characteristic that
most clearly
defines the city for
Collerd

I miss stoops. My family moved to the near-west suburbs of
Chicago when I was in kindergarten, in a modest split-level just
beyond the city limits. Before we retreated to the boring, safe
streets of River Forest, we lived in Wrigleyville, the section of
Chicago that surrounds the Home of the Cubs. Sitting on the
stoop with my family during the summer, hands slowly
congealing to Popsicle sticks or chocolate bars, we could gauge
homeruns by the roar of the crowd a few blocks away. During
the seventh inning stretch, Harry Caray's voice caromed over
the houses and apartment buildings to tell us how many strikes
it took in the old ball game.

Mark Grace played first base lankily back then, proving
to me that my build had a chance in the major leagues. Sammy
Sosa hadn't turned to syringes yet, Ryne Sandburg was still
flipping double-plays, and Shawon Dunston wore prescription
glasses with hinged shades, flicking them down casually before
chasing a fly ball. I've never worn glasses, but that didn't stop
me from imitating that flick every time the tennis ball popped
off my neighbor's waffle bat in our front yard.

Wrigleyville is a funny place. It's only a couple miles north
of the Loop, the heart of Chicago, and at that time it was just
becoming quaint—families proliferated among picturesque
flats, raising kids as though it were a suburb. We had back-
yards with swing sets and basketball hoops in the alley behind.
I could stick out my tongue during the day, trying to make that
Michael Jordan fade-away jumper even though the ball was
bigger than my torso, but I had to come in at dusk. Once the
sun set, there could be a different kind of jumper in the alley;

Tells what kind of
place the author
lived in within the
larger city

one who had fists and maybe a knife, and had been said to jump kids just for their red-and-white Jordans. Occasionally a car got stolen, but more often only its radio. Some carried a transistor in the car, leaving the tape deck empty.

Those first five years of life were my introduction to Chicago, the place I consider home, the city where I want to raise my kids, the town I feel inseparable from. When a friend from Colorado was looking for an apartment on the north side, I sent her one of my favorite poems, an urban battle cry by Carl Sandburg, telling her that she couldn't live here unless she'd read it. Describing an early twentieth-century Chicago, he wrote,

4

> Sandburg's poem is a series of brief definitions

> *Hog Butcher for the World,*
> *Tool Maker, Stacker of Wheat,*
> *Player with Railroads and the Nation's Freight Handler;*
> *Stormy, husky, brawling,*
> *City of the Big Shoulders . . .*

> Builds on "big shoulders" definition by giving additional characteristics of the city

The city doesn't reek anymore from the slaughterhouses and stockyards of the south side, but Sandburg's description still rings true. I have much of this poem memorized, mostly because the percussive words pound like black boots on pavement if you say them right. They go particularly well with the dotted eighth-note rhythm of the el—the elevated public train system that connects most neighborhoods to the loop. It's a dying system, delays racking up under the stress of decades and growing populations, but normally I don't mind the pauses, the waits for signal clearance. They force you to take in the reality of the west side—if you're headed east on the green line—a no man's land of the struggling. Gangs run this section, operating drug dens in abandoned apartment buildings that make McDonalds look slow. I watch fifteen-year-old Men trudge the alleys, looking for trouble whether they want it or not, stormy, husky, brawling, heads high, chests out, trying to make their shoulders big enough for the history they've got to carry.

Farther east, I can see the United Center where Michael Jordan used to wield a basketball like a trumpet, a scalpel, a paintbrush. There was only One Basketball Team in the Midwest back then, named for the animal that made the city stink, but it brought revenues that blossomed skyscrapers. If you don't believe Michael Jordan was a magician on the basketball court, consider it a little more thoroughly. He made every crew-cut suburban white kid dream of being bald and black.

5 · · · · · Distinguishing features are organized mainly by geography

When the train pushes closer to the river, poverty goes underground and the highrises begin. These are the buildings with Big Shoulders, reflecting communally like senators basking in each other's power. These are the buildings in which Things Happen.

6

Below on the avenues, a certain metallic cacophony rises, all shapes and forms of People Moving: going, coming, running, dawdling, laughing, sobbing, looking stern, hailing a taxi, asking for change, catching another's eye for a second and then disappearing. At this point I get off the train to transfer to another line; this is the hub, the Loop, the center. There's not much to say about it, because you only understand when you've

7

· · · · · Conclusion characterizes the core of the city

been Here, when you've descended the el stairs to street level, the bottom of an urban canyon, and closed your eyes for a second, felt the Wind pull you towards the river like a magnet, ruffling your hair, making your eyes water, stealing part of your identity and giving it to The City.

DAVE BARRY

GUYS VS. MEN

Dave Barry (b. 1947) is a widely published humorist and former columnist for the *Miami Herald*, where he won a Pulitzer Prize for commentary in 1988. He is the author of many humor books, including *Dave Barry's Complete Guide to Guys* (1995), the introduction of which is included here. Despite its title, "Guys vs. Men" is not a comparative study of these two basic types of males. Men and manhood have been written about far too much already, says Barry. But guys and guyhood are neglected topics, and even though he "can't define exactly what it means to be a guy," Barry's essay lays out "certain guy characteristics" that distinguish his quarry from other warm-blooded animals in the field.

⋎⬦⋀⋎⬦⋀⋎⬦⋀⋎⬦⋀⋎⬦⋀⋎⬦⋀⋎⬦⋀⋎⬦⋀⋎⬦⋀⋎⬦⋀⋎⬦⋀⋎⬦⋀⋎

T his is a book about guys. It's *not* a book about men. There are already way   1
too many books about men, and most of them are *way* too serious.

Men itself is a serious word, not to mention *manhood* and *manly*. Such   2
words make being male sound like a very important activity, as opposed to what it primarily consists of, namely, possessing a set of minor and frequently unreliable organs.

But men tend to attach great significance to Manhood. This results in cer-   3
tain characteristically masculine, by which I mean stupid, behavioral patterns

that can produce unfortunate results such as violent crime, war, spitting, and ice hockey. These things have given males a bad name.[1] And the "Men's Movement," which is supposed to bring out the more positive aspects of Manliness, seems to be densely populated with loons and goobers.

So I'm saying that there's another way to look at males: not as aggressive macho dominators; not as sensitive, liberated, hugging drummers; but as *guys.*

And what, exactly, do I mean by "guys"? I don't know. I haven't thought that much about it. One of the major characteristics of guyhood is that we guys don't spend a lot of time pondering our deep innermost feelings. There is a serious question in my mind about whether guys actually *have* deep innermost feelings, unless you count, for example, loyalty to the Detroit Tigers,[2] or fear of bridal showers.

Giving synonyms is always a good way to define a key term, p. 419.

But although I can't define exactly what it means to be a guy, I can describe certain guy characteristics, such as:

Guys Like Neat Stuff

By "neat," I mean "mechanical and unnecessarily complex." I'll give you an example. Right now I'm typing these words on an *extremely* powerful computer. It's the latest in a line of maybe ten computers I've owned, each one more powerful than the last. My computer is chock full of RAM and ROM and bytes and megahertzes and various other items that enable a computer to kick data-processing butt. It is probably capable of supervising the entire U.S. air-defense apparatus while simultaneously processing the tax return of every resident of Ohio. I use it mainly to write a newspaper column. This is an activity wherein I sit and stare at the screen for maybe ten minutes, then, using only my forefingers, slowly type something like:

Henry Kissinger[3] *looks like a big wart.*

1. Specifically, "asshole" [Barry's note].
2. Major league baseball team that last won the World Series in 1984.
3. Henry Kissinger (b. 1923), U.S. Secretary of State 1973–1977.

I stare at this for another ten minutes, have an inspiration, then amplify the original thought as follows:

Henry Kissinger looks like a big fat wart.

Then I stare at that for another ten minutes pondering whether I should try to work in the concept of "hairy."

This is absurdly simple work for my computer. It sits there, humming ⁸ impatiently, bored to death, passing the time between keystrokes via brain-teaser activities such as developing a Unified Field Theory of the universe and translating the complete works of Shakespeare into rap.[4]

In other words, this computer is absurdly overqualified to work for me, ⁹ and yet soon, I guarantee, I will buy an *even more powerful* one. I won't be able to stop myself, I'm a guy.

Probably the ultimate example of the fundamental guy drive to have neat ¹⁰ stuff is the Space Shuttle. Granted, the guys in charge of this program *claim* it has a Higher Scientific Purpose, namely to see how humans function in space. But of course we have known for years how humans function in space: They float around and say things like: "Looks real good, Houston!"

No, the real reason for the existence of the Space Shuttle is that it is one ¹¹ humongous and spectacularly gizmo-intensive item of hardware. Guys can tinker with it practically forever, and occasionally even get it to work, and use it to place *other* complex mechanical items into orbit, where they almost immediately break, which provides a great excuse to send the Space Shuttle up *again*. It's Guy Heaven.

Other results of the guy need to have stuff are Star Wars,[5] the recreational ¹² boating industry, monorails, nuclear weapons, and wristwatches that indicate the phase of the moon. I am not saying that women haven't been involved in the development or use of this stuff. I'm saying that, without guys, this stuff probably

---

4. To be or not? I got to *know*. Might kill myself by the end of the *show* [Barry's note].

5. Popular term for the Strategic Defense Initiative, a 1980s-era program to develop a space-based, antimissile system for the United States.

would not exist; just as, without women, virtually every piece of furniture in the world would still be in its original position. Guys do not have a basic need to rearrange furniture. Whereas a woman who could cheerfully use the same computer for fifty-three years will rearrange her furniture on almost a weekly basis, sometimes in the dead of night. She'll be sound asleep in bed, and suddenly, at 2 a.m., she'll be awakened by the urgent thought: *The blue-green sofa needs to go perpendicular to the wall instead of parallel, and it needs to go there* RIGHT NOW. So she'll get up and move it, which of course necessitates moving other furniture, and soon she has rearranged her entire living room, shifting great big heavy pieces that ordinarily would require several burly men to lift, because there are few forces in Nature more powerful than a woman who needs to rearrange furniture. Every so often a guy will wake up to discover that, because of his wife's overnight efforts, he now lives in an entirely different house.

(I realize that I'm making gender-based generalizations here, but my feeling is that if God did not want us to make gender-based generalizations, She would not have given us genders.)

13

Guys Like a Really Pointless Challenge

Not long ago I was sitting in my office at the *Miami Herald*'s Sunday magazine, *Tropic*, reading my fan mail[6] when I heard several of my guy coworkers in the hallway talking about how fast they could run the forty-yard dash. These are guys in their thirties and forties who work in journalism, where the most demanding physical requirement is the ability to digest vending-machine food. In other words, these guys have absolutely no need to run the forty-yard dash.

14

But one of them, Mike Wilson, was writing a story about a star high-school football player who could run it in 4.38 seconds. Now if Mike had written a story about, say, a star high-school poet, none of my guy coworkers would have suddenly decided to find out how well they could write sonnets. But when Mike turned in his story, they became *deeply* concerned about how fast they could run the forty-yard dash. They were so concerned that the magazine editor, Tom Shroder, decided that they should get a stopwatch and go out to a nearby park

15

6. Typical fan letter: "Who cuts your hair? Beavers?" [Barry's note].

and find out. Which they did, a bunch of guys taking off their shoes and running around barefoot in a public park on company time.

This is what I heard them talking about, out in the hall. I heard Tom, who was thirty-eight years old, saying that his time in the forty had been 5.75 seconds. And I thought to myself: This is ridiculous. These are middle-aged guys, supposedly adults, and they're out there *bragging* about their performance in this stupid juvenile footrace. Finally I couldn't stand it anymore.

"Hey!" I shouted. "*I* could beat 5.75 seconds."

So we went out to the park and measured off forty yards, and the guys told me that I had three chances to make my best time. On the first try my time was 5.78 seconds, just three-hundredths of a second slower than Tom's, even though, at forty-five, I was seven years older than he. So I just *knew* I'd beat him on the second attempt if I ran really, really hard, which I did for a solid ten yards, at which point my left hamstring muscle, which had not yet shifted into Spring Mode from Mail-Reading Mode, went, and I quote, "pop."

I had to be helped off the field. I was in considerable pain, and I was obviously not going to be able to walk right for weeks. The other guys were very sympathetic, especially Tom, who took the time to call me at home, where I was sitting with an ice pack on my leg and twenty-three Advil in my bloodstream, so he could express his concern.

"Just remember," he said, "*you didn't beat my time.*"

There are countless other examples of guys rising to meet pointless challenges. Virtually all sports fall into this category, as well as a large part of U.S. foreign policy ("I'll bet you can't capture Manuel Noriega!"[7] "Oh YEAH??")

Guys Do Not Have a Rigid and Well-Defined Moral Code

This is not the same as saying that guys are bad. Guys *are* capable of doing bad things, but this generally happens when they try to be Men and start becoming manly and aggressive and stupid. When they're being just plain guys, they aren't so much actively *evil* as they are *lost*. Because guys have never really grasped the

---

7. Manuel Noriega (b. 1934), Panamanian dictator removed from power by armed U.S. intervention in 1989.

Basic Human Moral Code, which I believe was invented by women millions of years ago when all the guys were out engaging in some other activity, such as seeing who could burp the loudest. When they came back, there were certain rules that they were expected to follow unless they wanted to get into Big Trouble, and they have been trying to follow these rules ever since, with extremely irregular results. Because guys have never *internalized* these rules. Guys are similar to my small auxiliary backup dog, Zippy, a guy dog[8] who has been told numerous times that he is *not* supposed to (1) get into the kitchen garbage or (2) poop on the floor. He knows that these are the rules, but he has never really understood *why*, and sometimes he gets to thinking: Sure, I am *ordinarily* not supposed to get into the garbage, but obviously this rule is not meant to apply when there are certain extenuating[9] circumstances, such as (1) somebody just threw away some perfectly good seven-week-old Kung Pao Chicken, and (2) I am home alone.

And so when the humans come home, the kitchen floor has been trans- 23
formed into Garbage-Fest USA, and Zippy, who usually comes rushing up, is off in a corner disguised in a wig and sunglasses, hoping to get into the Federal Bad Dog Relocation Program before the humans discover the scene of the crime.

When I yell at him, he frequently becomes so upset that he poops on the 24
floor.

Morally, most guys are just like Zippy, only taller and usually less hairy. 25
Guys are *aware* of the rules of moral behavior, but they have trouble keeping these rules in the forefronts of their minds at certain times, especially the present. This is especially true in the area of faithfulness to one's mate. I realize, of course, that there are countless examples of guys being faithful to their mates until they die, usually as a result of being eaten by their mates immediately following copulation. Guys outside of the spider community, however, do not have a terrific record of faithfulness.

I'm not saying guys are scum. I'm saying that many guys who consider 26
themselves to be committed to their marriages will stray if they are confronted with overwhelming temptation, defined as "virtually any temptation."

8. I also have a female dog, Earnest, who *never* breaks the rules [Barry's note].

9. I am taking some liberties here with Zippy's vocabulary. More likely, in his mind, he uses the term *mitigating* [Barry's note].

Okay, so maybe I *am* saying guys are scum. But they're not *mean-spirited*   27
scum. And few of them—even when they are out of town on business trips, far
from their wives, and have a clear-cut opportunity—will poop on the floor.

FOR DISCUSSION

1. Dave Barry starts to DEFINE what he means by "guys" and then says, "I don't
   know. I haven't thought that much about it" (5). He's being funny, right? Does
   his extended definition of *guys* lead you to believe that he has thought intelli-
   gently about what guys are? How so?
2. Males, says Barry, can be divided into two basic classes. What are the distinguishing characteristics of each?
3. To write his humor column, Barry doesn't ever need to buy a new, more powerful computer. But he says in paragraph 13 that he will do it anyway. What
   principle of guy behavior is he illustrating here?
4. In paragraph 16, Barry develops his definition of guys as neat-stuff-buying
   animals by CONTRASTING them with women. How does he define women in
   this paragraph? Do you think his definition is accurate? If not, how would you
   revise what he says?
5. Do you agree or disagree with Barry that "virtually all" sports fall into the
   "pointless challenge" category (25)? What about U.S. foreign policy?
6. Guys, says Barry, "are similar" to his dog Zippy (26). This is a definition by
   ANALOGY. What specific characteristics, according to Barry, do guys and Zippy
   have in common? Do you think the COMPARISON is just? In what one way does
   even Barry admit that unleashed guys are generally superior to dogs?

STRATEGIES AND STRUCTURES

1. Beginning in paragraph 6, Barry defines guys by citing three of their distinguishing "guy characteristics." What are they? How does Barry use these characteristics to organize his entire essay?
2. The basic logic behind defining something is to put it into a set of ever-narrower
   categories or classes. In Barry's definition, guys belong to the class of males
   who like challenges. But this is still a very broad class, so Barry narrows it

down further by adding the qualifier "pointless." Following this logic, why can't the high-school poet in paragraph 19 be defined as a guy? Point out other examples of this logic of elimination in Barry's essay, such as his definition of guys as "scum" in paragraph 31.

3. Why do you think Barry is so careful to specify the gender of God in paragraph 17? What AUDIENCE does he have in mind here?

4. From reading Barry's title, you might expect "Guys vs. Men" to be primarily a comparison and contrast essay. Where and *why* does Barry switch from drawing a comparison between the two kinds of males to defining one kind to the exclusion of the other?

5. Barry's humor often comes from his use of specific examples, as in "violent crime, war, spitting, and ice hockey" (3). Point out where his scrupulous examples help define specific terms. What would this essay be like *without* all the examples? What is Barry's PURPOSE in being (or pretending to be) so rigorous?

WORDS AND FIGURES OF SPEECH

1. How does Barry define "male" (2)? How about "manly" (2)? So, according to Barry's definitions, is "manly male" an OXYMORON? (Barry would probably make a joke here, one that would not be complimentary either to males or to oxen.)

2. How would you define "loons" (3)? How do they differ from "goobers" (3)?

3. Why does Barry capitalize "Big Trouble" in paragraph 26?

4. Translate the following Barry phrase into standard English: "one humongous and spectacularly gizmo-intensive item of hardware" (15).

FOR WRITING

1. Rightly or wrongly, Barry has been called a humorist. How would you define one? Make a list of the distinguishing characteristics that make a good humorist in your view, and give examples of humorists who you think represent these characteristics (you might want to use Barry as an example, or not).

2. How would you define "guys"? What characteristics does Barry leave out? Can a female be a "guy" (as in "When we go shopping, my grandmother is just one of the guys")? Write an essay setting forth your definition of "guys." Or choose another gender term (such as *men, women, girls,* or *girlfriends*), and write an essay that gives "another way to look" at gender through your definition of this term.

SE HABLA ESPAÑOL

Tanya Maria Barrientos (b. 1960) is a novelist, a columnist for the *Philadelphia Inquirer*, and a writing teacher at Arcadia University. She is the author of *Frontera Street* (2002) and *Family Resemblance* (2003). "Se Habla Español" is from a 2004 issue of the bilingual magazine *Latina*. The title refers to the sign, often seen in store windows, announcing that "Spanish is spoken" here. In this essay, Barrientos raises a basic question of self-definition and ethnic identity: Can a woman born in Guatemala who grew up in the United States speaking English instead of Spanish be legitimately considered a *Latina*?

The man on the other end of the phone line is telling me the classes I've 1
called about are first-rate: native speakers in charge, no more than six students per group. I tell him that will be fine and yes, I've studied a bit of Spanish in the past. He asks for my name and I supply it, rolling the double "r" in "Barrientos" like a pro. That's when I hear the silent snag, the momentary hesitation I've come to expect at this part of the exchange. Should I go into it again? Should I explain, the way I have to half a dozen others, that I am Guatemalan by birth but *pura gringa*[1] by circumstance?

1. *Pura* is Spanish for "pure"; *gringa*, the feminine form of *gringo*, is used to refer to someone of non-Latino background.

This will be the sixth time I've signed up to learn the language my parents 2
speak to each other. It will be the sixth time I've bought workbooks and notebooks and textbooks listing 501 conjugated verbs in alphabetical order, in
hopes that the subjunctive tense will finally take root in my mind. In class
I will sit across a table from the "native speaker," who will wonder what to
make of me. "Look," I'll want to say (but never do). "Forget the dark skin.
Ignore the obsidian eyes. Pretend I'm a pink-cheeked, blue-eyed blonde whose
name tag says 'Shannon.'" Because that is what a person who doesn't innately
know the difference between *corre, corra,* and *corri*[2] is supposed to look like,
isn't it?

I came to the United States in 1963 at age three with my family and imme- 3
diately stopped speaking Spanish. College-educated and seamlessly bilingual
when they settled in west Texas, my parents (a psychology professor and an artist)
wholeheartedly embraced the notion of the American melting pot. They declared
that their two children would speak nothing but *inglés.* They'd read in English,
write in English, and fit into Angelo society beautifully.

It sounds politically incorrect now. But America was not a hyphenated 4
nation back them. People who called themselves Mexican Americans or Afro
Americans were considered dangerous radicals, while law-abiding citizens were
expected to drop their cultural baggage at the border and erase any lingering
ethnic traits.

To be honest, for most of my childhood I liked being the brown girl who 5
defied expectations. When I was seven, my mother returned my older brother
and me to elementary school one week after the school year had already begun.
We'd been on vacation in Washington, D.C., visiting the Smithsonian, the
Capitol, and the home of Edgar Allan Poe. In the Volkswagen on the way home,
I'd memorized "The Raven," and I would recite it with melodramatic flair to
any poor soul duped into sitting through my performance. At the school's
office, the registrar frowned when we arrived.

"You people. Your children are always behind, and you have the nerve to 6
bring them in late?"

2. Verb forms of "run."

"My children," my mother answered in a clear, curt tone, "will be at the 7
top of their classes in two weeks." 8

The registrar filed our cards, shaking her head.

I did not live in a neighborhood with other Latinos, and the public school 9
I attended attracted very few. I saw the world through the clear, cruel vision of a
child. To me, speaking Spanish translated into being poor. It meant waiting
tables and cleaning hotel rooms. It meant being left off the cheerleading squad
and receiving a condescending smile from the guidance counselor when you
said you planned on becoming a lawyer or a doctor. My best friends' names
were Heidi and Leslie and Kim. They told me I didn't seem "Mexican" to them,
and I took it a as compliment. I enjoyed looking into the faces of Latino store
clerks and waitresses and, yes, even our maid and saying *"Yo no hablo español."*[3] It
made me feel superior. It made me feel American. It made me feel white. I
thought if I stayed away from Spanish, stereotypes would stay away from me.

Then came the backlash. During the two decades when I'd worked hard 10
to isolate myself from the stereotype I'd constructed in my own head, society

Stereotypes cite defining traits (p. 354) that are false or over-simplified. shifted. The nation changed its views on ethnic identity. College professors started teaching history through African American and Native American eyes. Children were told to forget about the melting pot and picture America as a multicolored quilt instead. Hyphens

suddenly had muscle, and I was left wondering where I fit in.

The Spanish language was supposedly the glue that held the new Latino 11
community together. But in my case it was what kept me apart. I felt awkward
among groups whose conversations flowed in and out of Spanish. I'd be asked a
question in Spanish and I'd have to answer in English, knowing this raised a
mountain of questions. I wanted to call myself Latina, to finally take pride, but it
felt like a lie. So I set out to learn the language that people assumed I already knew.

After my first set of lessons, I could function in the present tense. *"Hola,* 12
Paco. ¿Qué tal? ¿Qué color es tu cuaderno? El mío es azul."[4] My vocabulary built
quickly, but when I spoke, my tongue felt thick inside my mouth—and if I

---

3. I don't speak Spanish.

4. Hello, Paco. How are you? What color is your notebook? Mine is blue.

needed to deal with anything in the future or the past, I was sunk. I enrolled in a three-month submersion program in Mexico and emerged able to speak like a sixth-grader with a solid C average. I could read Gabriel García Márquez[5] with a Spanish-English dictionary at my elbow, and I could follow 90 percent of the melodrama on any given telenovela.[6] But true speakers discover my limitations the moment I stumble over a difficult construction, and that is when I get the look. The one that raises the wall between us. The one that makes me think I'll never really belong. Spanish has become a litmus test showing how far from your roots you've strayed.

My bilingual friends say I make too much of it. They tell me that my Guatemalan heritage and unmistakable Mayan features are enough to legitimize my membership in the Latin American club. After all, not all Poles speak Polish. Not all Italians speak Italian. And as this nation grows more and more Hispanic, not all Latinos will share one language. But I don't believe them.   13

There must be other Latinas like me. But I haven't met any. Or, I should say, I haven't met any who have fessed up. Maybe they are secretly struggling to fit in, the same way I am. Maybe they are hiring tutors and listening to tapes behind locked doors, just like me. I wish we all had the courage to come out of our hiding places and claim our rightful spot in the broad Latino spectrum. Without being called hopeless gringas. Without having to offer apologies or show remorse.   14

If it will help, I will go first.   15

Aquí estoy.[7] Spanish-challenged and *pura* Latina.   16

---

5. Columbian novelist and short-story writer (b. 1928).

6. Spanish-language TV soap opera.

7. Here I am.

FOR DISCUSSION

. . . .

1. Tanya Maria Barrientos is not a native speaker of Spanish, though both of her parents were. Why didn't they encourage her to learn the language as a child? Should they have? Why or why not?

2. According to Barrientos, how were "hyphenated" Americans DEFINED when she and her family first came to the United States from Guatemala in 1963 (4)? How did young Barrientos herself define Latinos who spoke Spanish?

3. In the decades following her arrival in the United States, says Barrientos, societal views toward ethnic identity "shifted" (10). What are some of the more significant aspects of that shift, according to Barrientos?

4. In your opinion, is Barrientos a legitimate member of "the Latin American club" (13)? That is, can she and others with similar backgrounds rightfully define themselves as Latinas or Latinos? Why or why not?

STRATEGIES AND STRUCTURES

. . . .

1. What is Barrientos's PURPOSE in "Se Habla Español": to explain why she does not speak Spanish with the fluency of a native speaker? to persuade readers that she is a true Latina? to define the ambiguous condition of being both "Spanish-challenged and *pura* Latina" (16)? Explain.

2. Is Barrientos's essay aimed mainly at a multilingual AUDIENCE or a largely English-speaking one? Why do you say so?

3. Throughout her essay, how does Barrientos use the Spanish language itself to help define who and what she is? Give several examples that you find particularly effective.

4. Where and how does Barrientos construct a stereotypical definition of "Latin American?" Where and how does she reveal the shortcomings of this definition?

5. Barrientos's essay includes many NARRATIVE elements. What are some of them, and how do they help her to define herself and her condition?

WORDS AND FIGURES OF SPEECH

1. Once defined as a "melting-pot," the United States, says Barrientos, is now a "multicolored quilt" (10). What are some of the implications of this shift in METAPHORS for national diversity?

2. When Barrientos refers to the Spanish language as "glue," is she avoiding CLICHÉS or getting stuck in one (11)? Explain.

3. In printing, a *stereotype* was a cast metal plate used to reproduce blocks of type or crude images. How does this early meaning of the term carry over into the modern definition as Barrientos uses it (10)?

4. Barrientos sometimes groups herself with other "Latinos," sometimes with other "Latinas" (9, 14). Why the difference?

FOR WRITING

1. Write a paragraph or two about an incident in which someone defined you on the basis of your choice of words, your accent, or some other aspect of your speech or appearance.

2. Write an essay about your experience learning, or attempting to learn, a language other than your native tongue—and how that experience affected your own self-definition or cultural identity.

GEETA KOTHARI

IF YOU ARE WHAT YOU EAT,
THEN WHAT AM I?

Geeta Kothari teaches writing at the University of Pittsburgh. She is the editor
of *Did My Mama Like to Dance? and Other Stories about Mothers and Daughters*
(1994). Her stories and essays have appeared in various newspapers and journals,
including the *Toronto South Asian Review* and the *Kenyon Review*, from which
these complete sections of a longer article are taken. Kothari's essay (1999) presents a problem in personal definition. The Indian food she eats, says Kothari, is
not really Indian like her mother's; nor is the American food she eats really
American like her husband's. So, Kothari wonders, if we are defined by what we
eat—and the culture it represents—how are she and her culture to be defined?

❖ᐱᐯᐱᐯ❖ᐯᐱᐯ❖ᐯᐱᐯ❖ᐯᐱᐯ❖ᐯᐱᐯ❖ᐯᐱᐯ❖ᐯᐱᐯ❖ᐯᐱᐯ❖ᐯᐱᐯ❖

> To belong is to understand the tacit codes of the people you live with.
> —MICHAEL IGNATIEFF, *Blood and Belonging*

The first time my mother and I open a can of tuna, I am nine years old. We   1
stand in the doorway of the kitchen, in semidarkness, the can tilted toward
daylight. I want to eat what the kids at school eat: bologna, hot dogs, salami—

foods my parents find repugnant because they contain pork and meat byproducts, crushed bone and hair glued together by chemicals and fat. Although she has never been able to tolerate the smell of fish, my mother buys the tuna, hoping to satisfy my longing for American food.

Indians, of course, do not eat such things. 2

The tuna smells fishy, which surprises me because I can't remember anyone's tuna sandwich actually smelling like fish. And the tuna in those sandwiches doesn't look like this, pink and shiny, like an internal organ. In fact, this looks similar to the bad foods my mother doesn't want me to eat. She is silent, holding her face away from the can while peering into it like a half-blind bird. 3

For tips on writing pithy definitions like this, see p. 416.

"What's wrong with it?" I ask. 4

She has no idea. My mother does not know that the tuna everyone else's mothers made for them was tuna *salad*. 5

"Do you think it's botulism?" 6

I have never seen botulism, but I have read about it, just as I have read about but never eaten steak and kidney pie. 7

There is so much my parents don't know. They are not like other parents, and they disappoint me and my sister. They are supposed to help us negotiate the world outside, teach us the signs, the clues to proper behavior: what to eat and how to eat it. 8

We have expectations, and my parents fail to meet them, especially my mother, who works full-time. I don't understand what it means, to have a mother who works outside and inside the home; I notice only the ways in which she disappoints me. She doesn't show up for school plays. She doesn't make chocolate-frosted cupcakes for my class. At night, if I want her attention, I have to sit in the kitchen and talk to her while she cooks the evening meal, attentive to every third or fourth word I say. 9

We throw the tuna away. This time my mother is disappointed. I go to school with tuna eaters. I see their sandwiches, yet cannot explain the discrepancy between them and the stinking, oily fish in my mother's hand. We do not understand so many things, my mother and I. 10

When we visit our relatives in India, food prepared outside the house is carefully monitored. In the hot, sticky monsoon months in New Delhi and Bombay, we 11 cannot eat ice cream, salad, cold food, or any fruit that can't be peeled. Definitely no meat. People die from amoebic dysentery, unexplained fevers, strange boils on their bodies. We drink boiled water only, no ice. No sweets except for jalebi, thin fried twists of dough in dripping hot sugar syrup. If we're caught outside with nothing to drink, Fanta, Limca, Thums Up (after Coca-Cola is thrown out by Mrs. Gandhi[1]) will do. Hot tea sweetened with sugar, served with thick creamy buffalo milk, is preferable. It should be boiled, to kill the germs on the cup.

My mother talks about "back home" as a safe place, a silk cocoon frozen in time where we are sheltered by family and friends. Back home, my sister and I do not argue about food with my parents. Home is where they know all the rules. We trust them to guide us safely through the maze of city streets for which they have no map, and we trust them to feed and take care of us, the way parents should.   12

Finally, though, one of us will get sick, hungry for the food we see our cousins and friends eating, too thirsty to ask for a straw, too polite to insist on properly boiled water.   13

At my uncle's diner in New Delhi, someone hands me a plate of aloo tikki, fried potato patties filled with mashed channa dal and served with a sweet and a sour chutney. The channa, mixed with hot chilies and spices, burns my tongue and throat. I reach for my Fanta, discard the paper straw, and gulp the sweet orange soda down, huge drafts that sting rather than soothe.   14

When I throw up later that day (or is it the next morning, when a stomachache wakes me from deep sleep?), I cry over the frustration of being singled out, not from the pain my mother assumes I'm feeling as she holds my hair back from my face. The taste of orange lingers in my mouth, and I remember my lips touching the cold glass of the Fanta bottle.   15

At that moment, more than anything, I want to be like my cousins.   16

In New York, at the first Indian restaurant in our neighborhood, my father orders with confidence, and my sister and I play with the silverware until the steaming plates of lamb biryani arrive.   17

What is Indian food? my friends ask, their noses crinkling up.   18

1. Coca-Cola was banned in India for twenty years beginning in the mid-1970s, when Indira Gandhi was prime minister, because the company would not reveal its formula to the government. Fanta, Limca, and Thums Up are other soft drinks popular in India.

Later, this restaurant is run out of business by the new Indo-Pak-Bangladeshi   19
combinations up and down the street, which serve similar food. They use plastic cutlery and Styrofoam cups. They do not distinguish between North and South
Indian cooking, or between Indian, Pakistani, and Bangladeshi cooking, and
their customers do not care. The food is fast, cheap, and tasty. Dosa, a rice flour
crepe stuffed with masala potato, appears on the same trays as chicken makhani.

Now my friends want to know, Do you eat curry at home?   20

One time my mother makes lamb vindaloo for guests. Like dosa, this is a   21
South Indian dish, one that my Punjabi[2] mother has to learn from a cookbook.
For us, she cooks everyday food—yellow dal, rice, chapati, bhaji. Lentils, rice,
bread, and vegetables. She has never referred to anything on our table as "curry"
or "curried," but I know she has made chicken curry for guests. Vindaloo, she
explains, is a curry too. I understand then that curry is a dish created for guests,
outsiders, a food for people who eat in restaurants.

I look around my boyfriend's freezer one day and find meat: pork chops, ground   22
beef, chicken pieces, Italian sausage. Ham in the refrigerator, next to the homemade bolognese sauce. Tupperware filled with chili made from ground beef and
pork.

He smells different from me. Foreign. Strange.   23

I marry him anyway.   24

He has inherited blue eyes that turn gray in bad weather, light brown hair,   25
a sharp pointy nose, and excellent teeth. He learns to make chili with ground
turkey and tofu, tomato sauce with red wine and portobello mushrooms, roast
chicken with rosemary and slivers of garlic under the skin.

He eats steak when we are in separate cities, roast beef at his mother's   26
house, hamburgers at work. Sometimes I smell them on his skin. I hope he
doesn't notice me turning my face, a cheek instead of my lips, my nose wrinkled
at the unfamiliar, musky smell.

I have inherited brown eyes, black hair, a long nose with a crooked bridge, and   27
soft teeth with thin enamel. I am in my twenties, moving to a city far from my

2. Native of the state of Punjab, in northern India.

parents, before it occurs to me that jeera, the spice my sister avoids, must have an English name. I have to learn that haldi = turmeric, methi = fenugreek. What to make with fenugreek, I do not know. My grandmother used to make methi roti for our breakfast, cornbread with fresh fenugreek leaves served with a lump of homemade butter. No one makes it now that she's gone, though once in a while my mother will get a craving for it and produce a facsimile ("The cornmeal here is wrong") that only highlights what she's really missing: the smells and tastes of her mother's house.

I will never make my grandmother's methi roti or even my mother's   28
unsatisfactory imitation of it. I attempt chapati; it takes six hours, three phone calls home, and leaves me with an aching back. I have to write translations down: jeera = cumin. My memory is unreliable. But I have always known garam = hot.

If I really want to make myself sick, I worry that my husband will one day leave   29
me for a meat-eater, for someone familiar who doesn't sniff him suspiciously for signs of alimentary infidelity.

Indians eat lentils. I understand this as absolute, a decree from an unidentifi-   30
able authority that watches and judges me.

So what does it mean that I cannot replicate my mother's dal? She and my   31
father show me repeatedly, in their kitchen, in my kitchen. They coach me over the phone, buy me the best cookbooks, and finally write down their secrets. Things I'm supposed to know but don't. Recipes that should be, by now, engraved on my heart.

Living far from the comfort of people who require no explanation for   32
what I do and who I am, I crave the foods we have shared. My mother convinces me that moong is the easiest dal to prepare, and yet it fails me every time: bland, watery, a sickly greenish yellow mush. These imperfect imitations remind me only of what I'm missing.

But I have never been fond of moong dal. At my mother's table it is the last   33
thing I reach for. Now I worry that this antipathy toward dal signals something deeper, that somehow I am not my parents' daughter, not Indian, and because

I cannot bear the touch and smell of raw meat, though I can eat it cooked (charred, dry, and overdone), I am not American either.

I worry about a lifetime purgatory in Indian restaurants where I will complain that all the food looks and tastes the same because they've used the same masala. 34

FOR DISCUSSION

. . . .

1. How does Geeta Kothari DEFINE "meat byproducts" (1)? Why is she so concerned with different kinds of food? Who or what is she trying to define?

2. How do Kothari and her mother define "back home" in paragraph 12?

3. Why is Kothari angry with herself in paragraphs 15 and 16? What "rule" has she momentarily forgotten?

4. Kothari's friends ask for a definition of Indian food in paragraph 18. How does she answer them (and us)?

5. What's wrong, from Kothari's POINT OF VIEW, with the "Indo-Pak-Bangladeshi" restaurants that spring up in her neighborhood (19)?

6. Marriage is an important event in anyone's biography, but why is it especially central in Kothari's case?

STRATEGIES AND STRUCTURES

. . . .

1. How does Kothari go about answering the definition question that she raises in her title? Give specific examples of her strategy. What point is she making in answering this question?

2. Why does Kothari recall the tuna incident in paragraphs 1 through 10? What does this ANECDOTE illustrate about her relationship with her mother? About her "Americanness"?

3. Why does Kothari introduce the matter of heredity in paragraphs 25 and 27? How do these paragraphs anticipate the reference to "something deeper" in paragraph 33?

4. According to Kothari, is culture something we inherit or something we learn? How do paragraphs 31 and 32 contribute to her definition of culture?

5. Kothari's essay is largely made up of specific EXAMPLES, particularly culinary ones. How do they relate to the matters of personal and cultural identity she is defining? Should she have made these connections more explicit? Why?

WORDS AND FIGURES OF SPEECH

1. What is usually meant by the saying "You are what you eat"? How is Kothari interpreting this adage?

2. What does Kothari mean by "alimentary infidelity" (29)? What ANALOGY is she drawing here?

3. What is "purgatory" (34)? Why does Kothari end her essay with a reference to it?

4. *Synecdoche* is the FIGURE OF SPEECH that substitutes a part for the whole. What part does Kothari substitute for what whole when she uses the phrase "meat-eater" (29)? Can we say her entire essay works by means of synecdoche? Why or why not?

5. Kothari provides both the Indian word and its English equivalent for several terms in her essay—"garam" for "hot" in paragraph 28, for example. Why? What do these translations contribute to her definition of cultural identity? Point out several other examples in the text.

FOR WRITING

1. Write an extended definition of your favorite type of food. Be sure to relate how your food and food customs help to define who you are.

2. Food and food customs are often regional, as Kothari points out. Write an essay in which you define one of the following: New England, Southern, or Midwestern cooking; California cuisine; Tex-Mex, French, or Chinese food; fast food; or some other distinctive cuisine.

3. Write an essay about food and eating in your neighborhood. Use the food customs of specific individuals and groups to help define them—personally, ethnically, socially, or in some other way.

ERIN McKEAN

REDEFINING DEFINITION

Erin McKean (b. 1971), formerly editor-in-chief for American dictionaries at Oxford University Press, is a founder of the online dictionary *Wordnik* and editor of the language quarterly *Verbatim*. McKean studied linguistics at the University of Chicago, graduating in 1993. Her books include *Totally Weird and Wonderful Words* (2006) and *The Secret Lives of Dresses* (2011). A self-anointed "language evangelist," McKean is a modern equivalent of Noah Webster, the nineteenth-century American dictionary maker whose name is invoked (too often in McKean's view) in the phrase "according to Webster." As a lexicographer, McKean is an authority on dictionary definitions, which she thinks should be redefined in such a way as to make them more accurate and flexible. "Redefining Definition" first appeared in the On Language section of the *New York Times* in December 2009.

⋄∿

If anything is guaranteed to annoy a lexicographer, it is the journalistic habit of starting a story with a dictionary definition. "According to Webster's" begins a piece, blithely, and the lexicographer shudders, because she knows that a dictionary is about to be invoked as an incontrovertible authority. Although we may profess to believe, as the linguist Dwight Bolinger once put it, that dictionaries "do not exist to define but to help people grasp meanings," we don't often act on that belief. Typically we treat a definition as the final arbiter of meaning, a scientific pronouncement of a word's essence.

But the traditional dictionary definition, although it bears all the trappings of authority, is in fact a highly stylized, overly compressed, and often tentative stab at capturing the consensus on what a particular word "means." A good dictionary derives its reputation from careful analysis of examples of words in use, in the form of sentences, also called *citations*. The lexicographer looks at as many citations for each word as she can find (or, more likely, can review in the time allotted) and then creates what is, in effect, a dense abstract, collapsing into a few general statements all the ways in which the word behaves. A definition is as convention-bound as a sonnet and usually more compact. Writing one is considered, at least by anyone who has ever tried it, something of an art.

Despite all the thought and hard work that go into them, definitions, surprisingly, turn out to be ill suited for many of the tasks they have been set to— including their ostensible purpose of telling you the meaning of a word. Overly abstract definitions are often helpful only if you come to them already primed by context. It's difficult to read a definition like "(esp. of a change or distinction) so delicate or precise as to be difficult to analyze or describe," and have *subtle* immediately spring to mind; or to come across "reduce the force, effect or value of" and think of *attenuate*.

Definitions are especially unhelpful to children. There's an oft-cited 1987 study in which fifth graders were given dictionary definitions and asked to write their own sentences using the words defined. The results were discouraging. One child, given the word *erode*, wrote, "Our family erodes a lot," because the definition given was "eat out, eat away."

Neither are definitions complete pictures of all the possible meanings of a word. One study found that in a set of arbitrarily chosen passages from modern fiction, an average of 13 percent of the nouns, verbs, and adjectives were used in senses not found in a large desk dictionary. And of course there are some words that simply elude definition, a problem even Samuel Johnson[1] faced. In the pref-

1. English writer and lexicographer (1709–1784).

ace to his groundbreaking *Dictionary of the English Language*, he wrote, "Ideas of the same race, though not exactly alike, are sometimes so little different that no words can express the dissimilitude, though the mind easily perceives it when they are exhibited together." We all have had Johnson's experience of "easily perceiving" differences between words that we cannot as easily describe—quick: what's the difference between *louche* and *raffish*? Most people, when asked what a word means, resort to using it in a sentence, because that's the way we learn words best: by encountering them in their natural context.

Given these shortcomings of definitions, and the advantages of examples, why do we still cling to definitions? The short answer, for hundreds of years, has been a practical one: space—specifically the lack thereof. Print dictionaries have never had sufficient page-room to show enough real, live, useful examples to create an optimal and natural word-learning experience. Even the expert lexicographers at the *Oxford English Dictionary*, which famously includes "illustrative quotations" alongside its definitions, still put the definition and its needs first, making new words wait their turn to make it through the definition bottleneck. 6

The near-infinite space of the web gives us a chance to change all this. Imagine if lexicographers were to create online resources that give, in addition to definitions, many living examples of word use, drawn not just from literature and newspapers but from real-time sources of language like Web sites, blogs, and social networks. We could build For other useful ways of extending definitions, see p. 413. people's confidence in their ability to understand and use words naturally, from the variety of contexts in which words occur. Indeed, this is what my colleagues and I are trying to accomplish at the online dictionary *Wordnik.com*: we're using text-mining techniques and the unlimited space of the Internet to show as many real examples of word use as we can, as fast as we can. 7

This approach is especially useful for grasping new words and uses: if you look up *tweet* on a site like mine, for example, you understand that the word is used to refer to messages sent via *Twitter*; there's no waiting for an editor to write you a definition; plus there are examples of tweets right on the page. Online, you can also look up just the form of a word you're interested in—say, *sniped* instead of *snipe*—and find precise examples. A word is so much more 8 than its meaning: it's also who uses it, when it was used, what words appear alongside it, and what kinds of texts it appears in.

Without privileging definitions, dictionary-making would involve more curation and less abridgment, less false precision, and more organic understanding. If we stop pretending definitions are science, we can enjoy them as a kind of literature—think of them as extremely nerdy poems—without burdening them with tasks for which they are unsuited.

9

FOR DISCUSSION

. . . .

1. A long-standing debate among lexicographers is whether dictionaries should be *prescriptive* (tell readers how they ought to use words) or *descriptive* (tell readers how words are actually used). Where does Erin McKean come down in this debate? Explain.

2. According to McKean, changes in technology have changed how dictionaries can (and should) DEFINE words. What are some of these technological changes, and how, according to McKean, can they help to make dictionaries better definers?

3. In her career, McKean has gone from editing print dictionaries at Oxford University Press to founding and editing an online dictionary called *Wordnik*. Is this career move an ARGUMENT for or against her authority as a critic of print dictionaries? Explain.

STRATEGIES AND STRUCTURES

. . . .

1. McKean defines "the traditional dictionary definition" of a word as "often" a "tentative stab" at explaining the meaning of the word (2). How does McKean define the kind of online definition she is advocating? Point to specific characteristics and attributes in her definition.

2. Words are best defined, says McKean, by EXAMPLE. Among the numerous examples she cites to make this point, which ones do you find particularly effective? Why?

3. If McKean is writing a new job description for dictionary makers, why does she cite the "groundbreaking" work of the eighteenth-century essayist and lexicographer Samuel Johnson, who defined a lexicographer as "a harmless drudge" (5)?

4. What is McKean's point in COMPARING traditional dictionary definitions to "extremely nerdy poems" (9)? How and how well does she support the claim that dictionary definitions constitute a "kind of literature" (9)?

WORDS AND FIGURES OF SPEECH

1. What are the connotations of *stab* in McKean's definition of traditional dictionary definitions (2)? Why does she use the term here?

2. Why do you think McKean used the example of *sniped* and *snipe* instead of, for example, *snip* and *snipped* to make her point about the virtues of looking up words online (8)?

3. Look up *curation* in your dictionary (9). In which sense is McKean using the term? Why?

4. McKean says old-fashioned dictionary definitions are like "nerdy poems" (9). Why *nerdy*? Explain.

FOR WRITING

1. In a paragraph or two, cite several of your own examples of dictionary definitions that don't help much in defining a word unless you already know what the word means, and explain why.

2. Write a definition essay arguing that dictionary definitions should (or should not) be "the final arbiter" in defining a word (1). Be sure to define what you mean by *dictionary* and by *definition*.

THE EXTRAORDINARY
CHARACTERISTICS OF DYSLEXIA

Jack Horner (b. 1946) is a native of Shelby, Montana. He studied geology and zoology at the University of Montana and is now a professor at the Montana State University and curator of the Museum of the Rockies, which has the largest dinosaur collection in the United States. A technical advisor for the *Jurassic Park* movies, Horner and his research partner were the first to discover dinosaur eggs in the Western Hemisphere. Horner's research specialty is dinosaur growth, and he is currently working with a team of geneticists to "nudge" the DNA of a chicken into a dinosaur-like creature that he calls a "chickenosaurus." Despite his academic credentials, Horner did not actually complete his bachelor's degree due to a common learning disorder often called *dyslexia*. Caused by differences in the way the brain processes symbolic information, dyslexia does not indicate a lack of intelligence. In fact, says Horner in "The Extraordinary Characteristics of Dyslexia" (published in 2008 by the International Dyslexia Association in *Perspectives on Language and Literacy*), dyslexia may even be defined as a way of understanding the world that is, in some respects, superior to the norm.

E ach of us can narrate an early experience of failure in schools. Because of it, most of us have known some form of peer persecution. But what most non-dyslexics don't know about us, besides the fact that we simply process information differently, is that our early failures often give us an important edge as we grow older. It is not uncommon that we "dyslexics" go on to succeed at the highest of levels.

I don't care much for the word *dyslexia*. I generally think of "us" as spatial thinkers and non-dyslexics as linear thinkers, or people who could be most often described as being *dys-spatios*. For spatial thinkers, reading is clearly necessary but overrated. Most of us would rather write about our own adventures than read about someone else's. Most spatial thinkers are extremely visual, highly imaginative, and work in three dimensions, none of which has anything to do with time. Linear thinkers (*dys-spatics*) generally operate in a two-dimensional world where time is of the utmost importance. We spatial thinkers fail tests given by linear thinkers because we don't think in terms of time or in terms of written text. Instead, our perception is multidimensional, and we do best when we can touch, observe, and analyze. If we were to give spatial tests to linear thinkers, they would have just as much trouble with our tests as we do with theirs. It is unfortunate that we are the minority and have to deal with the linear-thinkers' exams in order to enter the marketplace to find jobs. Even though we often fail or do miserably on these linear-thinker tests, we often end up in life achieving exceptional accomplishments. From the perspective of the linear thinkers, we spatial thinkers seem to "think outside the box," and this accounts for our accomplishments. However, we think outside the box precisely because we have never been in one. Our minds are not clogged up by preconceived ideas acquired through excessive reading. We are, therefore, free to have original thoughts enhanced by personal observations.

> How to use root meanings in a definition is discussed on p. 419.

In 1993, I was inducted into the American Academy of Achievement, an organization started in 1964, that annually brings together the highest achievers in America with the brightest American high-school students. The achievers included United States presidents, Nobel Laureates, movie stars, sports figures, and other famous people. The high school students were winners of the best scholarships like the Rhodes, the Westinghouse, the Truman, and so on. In other words, it was supposed to be a meeting of the best of the best according to the linear thinkers who "judge" such things. The idea was that the achievers would somehow, over the course of a three-day meeting, influence the students, and push them on to extraordinary achievement. Interestingly, however, most of us "achievers" admitted that we would never have qualified to be in such a student group. The largest percentage of the achievers were actually people who had difficulties in school and didn't get scholarships, or awards, or other accolades. Most of the achievers were spatial thinkers, while most of the students were linear thinkers. From 1964 until 2000, fewer than half a dozen students broke the barrier to be inducted at the American Academy of Achievement's annual get-together. How could it be that so many promising students, judged by the linear thinkers themselves, failed to reach the highest levels of achievement?

I think the answer is simple. Linear thinkers are burdened by high expectations from everyone, including themselves. They go out and get good jobs, but they seldom follow their dreams because dream-following is risk-taking, and risk-taking carries the possible burden of failure. 4

We spatial thinkers have known failure our entire lives and have grown up without expectations, not from our teachers, often not from our parents, and, sometimes, not even from ourselves. We don't meet the expectations of linear thinkers and are free to take risks. We are the people who most often follow our dreams, who think differently, spatially, inquisitively. 5

Personally, I think dyslexia and the consequences of dyslexia—learning to deal with failure—explains my own success. From my failures, I've learned where I need help, such as reading and math. But I've also learned from my accomplishments what I'm better at than the linear thinkers. When I'm teaching linear thinkers here at Montana State University, I know to be patient, as they have just as hard a time with spatial problems as I have with linear ones. We both have learning talents and learning challenges, but I would never think of trading my spatial way of thinking for their linear way of thinking. I think dyslexia is an extraordinary characteristic, and it is certainly not something that needs to be fixed, or cured, or suppressed! Maybe it's time for a revolution! 6

Take us out of classes for special ed, and put us in classes for spatial ed, taught of course, by spatial thinkers!

FOR DISCUSSION

1. Whereas "non-dyslexics" are "linear thinkers," people with dyslexia, says Jack Horner, are "spatial thinkers" (2). What does he mean by this distinction?
2. Why does Horner think his spatial perspective has helped him to succeed in his life and career? Is he right? Why or why not?
3. According to Horner, why do some linear thinkers, including "many promising students," fail "to reach the highest levels of achievement" in their fields (3)?

STRATEGIES AND STRUCTURES

1. Horner does not cite a standard textbook DEFINITION of *dyslexia*. In addition to its "extraordinary characteristics," should he have given the ordinary characteristics of dyslexia in his definition as well? Why or why not?
2. What is Horner's (and the International Dyslexia Association's) purpose in defining dyslexia in positive terms? Explain.
3. People with dyslexia, according to Horner, have other distinguishing characteristics besides "spatial" thinking. What are some of them, and which ones seem particularly effective for extending Horner's basic definition?
4. Horner uses his own life and career as an EXAMPLE of his positive definition of dyslexia. How and how effectively does he do so?
5. What EVIDENCE does Horner offer to support his CLAIM that having (or not having) dyslexia actually causes one to succeed (or fail) to reach "the highest levels of achievement" (3)? How sufficient and PERSUASIVE is that evidence? Explain.

WORDS AND FIGURES OF SPEECH

. . . .

1. Horner derives the word "dys-spatics" by analogy—with what (2)?
2. Thinking "outside the box" could be considered a CLICHÉ (2). Should Horner have avoided the phrase? Why or why not?
3. What are the implications of *burdened* (4)? How IRONIC is Horner being here?
4. Explain the PUN in "spatial ed" (6).

FOR WRITING

. . . .

1. Write a paragraph or two explaining how you have been given "an important edge" now by an "early experience of failure" in school or by "peer persecution"— or both (1).
2. Write a definition essay explaining the nature of dyslexia, what its causes are thought to be, and how it is usually treated. Cite your sources carefully and, where appropriate, an interesting case or two—whether "extraordinary" or typical.

MIKE ROSE

BLUE-COLLAR BRILLIANCE

Mike Rose (b. 1944) is a professor of education at the UCLA Graduate School of Education and Information Studies. When he was seven, Rose moved with his parents from Altoona, Pennsylvania, to Los Angeles, where his mother worked as a waitress, and he "watched the cooks and waitresses and listened to what they said." After graduating from Loyola University, Rose earned advanced degrees from the University of Southern California and UCLA. His books on language, literacy, and cognition include *The Mind at Work: Valuing the Intelligence of the American Worker* (2004) and the forthcoming *Back to School: Second Chances at Higher Ed*. Based on years of teaching and close observations of the workplace, Rose is convinced that people can be smart in many different ways. In "Blue-Collar Brilliance," from the *American Scholar* (2009), he offers a definition of intelligence that does not separate the mind from the body, a shortcoming, in his view, of more conventional definitions.

᳗᳙᳗᳙᳗᳙᳗᳙᳗᳙᳗᳙᳗᳙᳗᳙᳗᳙᳗᳙᳗᳙᳗᳙᳗᳙᳗᳙᳗᳙᳗᳙᳗᳙᳗᳙᳗᳙

M y mother, Rose Meraglio Rose (Rosie), shaped her adult identity as a waitress in coffee shops and family restaurants. When I was growing up in Los Angeles during the 1950s, my father and I would occasionally hang out at the restaurant until her shift ended, and then we'd ride the bus home with her. Sometimes she worked the register and the counter, and we sat there; when she waited booths and tables, we found a booth in the back where the waitresses took their breaks.

There wasn't much for a child to do at the restaurants, and so as the hours stretched out, I watched the cooks and waitresses and listened to what they said. At mealtimes, the pace of the kitchen staff and the din from customers picked up. Weaving in and out around the room, waitresses warned *behind you* in impassive but urgent voices. Standing at the service window facing the kitchen, they called out abbreviated orders. *Fry four on two,* my mother would say as she clipped a check onto the metal wheel. Her tables were *deuces, four-tops,* or *six-tops* according to their size; seating areas also were nicknamed. The *racetrack,* for instance, was the fast-turnover front section. Lingo conferred authority and signaled know-how.

Rosie took customers' orders, pencil poised over pad, while fielding questions about the food. She walked full tilt through the room with plates stretching up her left arm and two cups of coffee somehow cradled in her right hand. She stood at a table or booth and removed a plate for this person, another for that person, then another, remembering who had the hamburger, who had the fried shrimp, almost always getting it right. She would haggle with the cook about a returned order and rush by us, saying, *He gave me lip, but I got him.* She'd take a minute to flop down in the booth next to my father. *I'm all in,* she'd say, and whisper something about a customer. Gripping the outer edge of the table with one hand, she'd watch the room and note, in the flow of our conversation, who needed a refill, whose order was taking longer to prepare than it should, who was finishing up.

I couldn't have put it in words when I was growing up, but what I observed in my mother's restaurant defined the world of adults, a place where competence was synonymous with physical work. I've since studied the working habits of blue-collar workers and have come to understand how much my mother's kind of work demands of both body and brain. A waitress acquires knowledge and intuition about the ways and the rhythms of the restaurant business. Waiting on seven to nine tables, each with two to six customers, Rosie devised memory strategies so that she could remember who ordered what. And because she knew the average time it took to prepare different dishes, she could monitor an order that was taking too long at the service station.

Page 419 offers advice on using synonyms to start a definition.

2

3

4

Like anyone who is effective at physical work, my mother learned *to work*   5
smart, as she put it, *to make every move count*. She'd sequence and group tasks:
What could she do first, then second, then third as she circled through her station? What tasks could be clustered? She did everything on the fly, and when
problems arose—technical or human—she solved them within the flow of
work, while taking into account the emotional state of her co-workers. Was the
manager in a good mood? Did the cook wake up on the wrong side of the bed? If
so, how could she make an extra request or effectively return an order?

And then, of course, there were the customers who entered the restaurant   6
with all sorts of needs, from physiological ones, including the emotions that
accompany hunger, to a sometimes complicated desire for human contact. Her
tip depended on how well she responded to these needs, and so she became
adept at reading social cues and managing feelings, both the customers' and her
own. No wonder, then, that Rosie was intrigued by psychology. The restaurant
became the place where she studied human behavior, puzzling over the problems of her regular customers and refining her ability to deal with people in a
difficult world. She took pride in *being among the public*, she'd say. *There isn't a
day that goes by in the restaurant that you don't learn something.*

My mother quit school in the seventh grade to help raise her brothers and sis-   7
ters. Some of those siblings made it through high school, and some dropped out
to find work in railroad yards, factories, or restaurants. My father finished a grade
or two in primary school in Italy and never darkened the schoolhouse door
again. I didn't do well in school, either. By high school I had accumulated a
spotty academic record and many hours of hazy disaffection. I spent a few years
on the vocational track, but in my senior year I was inspired by my English
teacher and managed to squeak into a small college on probation.

My freshman year was academically bumpy, but gradually I began to see   8
formal education as a means of fulfillment and as a road toward making a living. I
studied the humanities and later the social and psychological sciences and taught
for ten years in a range of situations—elementary school, adult education courses,
tutoring centers, a program for Vietnam veterans who wanted to go to college.
Those students had socioeconomic and educational backgrounds similar to mine.

Rosie solved technical and human problems on the fly.

Then I went back to graduate school to study education and cognitive psychology and eventually became a faculty member in a school of education.

Intelligence is closely associated with formal education—the type of schooling a person has, how much and how long—and most people seem to move comfortably from that notion to a belief that work requiring less schooling requires less intelligence. These assumptions run through our cultural history, from the post–Revolutionary War period, when mechanics were characterized by political rivals as illiterate and therefore incapable of participating in government, until today. More than once I've heard a manager label his workers as "a bunch of dummies." Generalizations about intelligence, work, and social class deeply affect our assumptions about ourselves and each other, guiding the ways we use our minds to learn, build knowledge, solve problems, and make our way through the world.

Although writers and scholars have often looked at the working class, they have generally focused on the values such workers exhibit rather than on the thought their work requires—a subtle but pervasive omission. Our cultural iconography promotes the muscled arm, sleeve rolled tight against biceps, but no brightness behind the eye, no image that links hand and brain.

One of my mother's brothers, Joe Meraglio, left school in the ninth grade to work for the Pennsylvania Railroad. From there he joined the Navy, returned to the railroad, which was already in decline, and eventually joined his older brother at General Motors where, over a 33-year career, he moved from working on the assembly line to supervising the paint-and-body department. When I was a young man, Joe took me on a tour of the factory. The floor was loud—in some places deafening—and when I turned a corner or opened a door, the smell of chemicals knocked my head back. The work was repetitive and taxing, and the pace was inhumane. 11

This famous poster by J. Howard Miller, later called "Rosie the Riveter," was created to boost morale among factory workers during World War II. "Our cultural iconography," writes Mike Rose, "promotes the muscled arm, sleeve rolled tight against biceps, but no brightness behind the eye, no image that links hand and brain." With the feminist movement of the 1960s and later, however, "Rosie" came to represent what Rose himself calls "blue-collar brilliance"—a blending of muscle and intelligence.

Still, for Joe the shop floor provided what school did not; it was *like school-* 12
ing, he said, a place where *you're constantly learning.* Joe learned the most efficient
way to use his body by acquiring a set of routines that were quick and preserved
energy. Otherwise he would never have survived on the line.

As a foreman, Joe constantly faced new problems and became a consum- 13
mate multi-tasker, evaluating a flurry of demands quickly, parceling out physical and mental resources, keeping a number of ongoing events in his mind,
returning to whatever task had been interrupted, and maintaining a cool head
under the pressure of grueling production schedules. In the midst of all this, Joe
learned more and more about the auto industry, the technological and social
dynamics of the shop floor, the machinery and production processes, and the
basics of paint chemistry and of plating and baking. With further promotions,
he not only solved problems but also began to find problems to solve: Joe initi-
ated the redesign of the nozzle on a paint sprayer, thereby eliminating costly
and unhealthy overspray. And he found a way to reduce energy costs on the
baking ovens without affecting the quality of the paint. He lacked formal
knowledge of how the machines under his supervision worked, but he had direct
experience with them, hands-on knowledge, and was savvy about their quirks
and operational capabilities. He could experiment with them.

In addition, Joe learned about budgets and management. Coming off the 14
line as he did, he had a perspective of workers' needs and management's demands,
and this led him to think of ways to improve efficiency on the line while relieving
some of the stress on the assemblers. He had each worker in a unit learn his or
her co-workers' jobs so they could rotate across stations to relieve some of the
monotony. He believed that rotation would allow assemblers to get longer and
more frequent breaks. It was an easy sell to the people on the line. The union,
however, had to approve any modification in job duties, and the managers were
wary of the change. Joe had to argue his case on a number of fronts, providing
him a kind of rhetorical education.

Eight years ago I began a study of the thought processes involved in work 15
like that of my mother and uncle. I catalogued the cognitive demands of a range
of blue-collar and service jobs, from waitressing and hair styling to plumbing
and welding. To gain a sense of how knowledge and skill develop, I observed
experts as well as novices. From the details of this close examination, I tried to

fashion what I called "cognitive biographies" of blue-collar workers. Biographical accounts of the lives of scientists, lawyers, entrepreneurs, and other professionals are rich with detail about the intellectual dimension of their work. But the life stories of working-class people are few and are typically accounts of hardship and courage or the achievements wrought by hard work.

Our culture—in Cartesian fashion[1]—separates the body from the mind, so that, for example, we assume that the use of a tool does not involve abstraction. We reinforce this notion by defining intelligence solely on grades in school and numbers on IQ tests. And we employ social biases pertaining to a person's place on the occupational ladder. The distinctions among blue, pink, and white collars carry with them attributions of character, motivation, and intelligence. Although we rightly acknowledge and amply compensate the play of mind in white-collar and professional work, we diminish or erase it in considerations about other endeavors—physical and service work particularly. We also often ignore the experience of everyday work in administrative deliberations and policymaking.

16

But here's what we find when we get in close. The plumber seeking leverage in order to work in tight quarters and the hair stylist adroitly handling scissors and comb manage their bodies strategically. Though work-related actions become routine with experience, they were learned at some point through observation, trial and error, and, often, physical or verbal assistance from a co-worker or trainer. I've frequently observed novices talking to themselves as they take on a task, or shaking their head or hand as if to erase an attempt before trying again. In fact, our traditional notions of routine performance could keep us from appreciating the many instances within routine where quick decisions and adjustments are made. I'm struck by the thinking-in-motion that some work requires, by all the mental activity that can be involved in simply getting from one place to another: the waitress rushing back through her station to the kitchen or the foreman walking the line.

17

The use of tools requires the studied refinement of stance, grip, balance, and fine-motor skills. But manipulating tools is intimately tied to knowledge of what a particular instrument can do in a particular situation and do better than

18

1. After French philosopher René Descartes (1596–1650), who proposed the dualism of mind and body.

With an eighth-grade education. Joe (hands together) advanced to supervisor of a G.M. paint-and-body department.

other similar tools. A worker must also know the characteristics of the material one is engaging—how it reacts to various cutting or compressing devices, to degrees of heat, or to lines of force. Some of these things demand judgment, the weighing of options, the consideration of multiple variables, and, occasionally, the creative use of a tool in an unexpected way.

In manipulating material, the worker becomes attuned to aspects of the environment, a training or disciplining of perception that both enhances knowledge and informs perception. Carpenters have an eye for length, line, and angle; mechanics troubleshoot by listening; hair stylists are attuned to shape, texture, and motion. Sensory data merge with concept, as when an auto mechanic relies on sound, vibration, and even smell to understand what cannot be observed.   19

Planning and problem solving have been studied since the earliest days of modern cognitive psychology and are considered core elements in Western definitions of intelligence. To work is to solve problems. The big difference between the psychologist's laboratory and the workplace is that in the former the problems   20 are isolated and in the latter they are embedded in the real-time flow of work with all its messiness and social complexity.

Much of physical work is social and interactive. Movers determining how 21 to get an electric range down a flight of stairs require coordination, negotiation, planning, and the establishing of incremental goals. Words, gestures, and sometimes a quick pencil sketch are involved, if only to get the rhythm right. How important it is, then, to consider the social and communicative dimension of physical work, for it provides the medium for so much of work's intelligence.

Given the ridicule heaped on blue-collar speech, it might seem odd to value 22 its cognitive content. Yet, the flow of talk at work provides the channel for organizing and distributing tasks, for troubleshooting and problem solving, for learning new information and revising old. A significant amount of teaching, often informal and indirect, takes place at work. Joe Meraglio saw that much of his job as a supervisor involved instruction. In some service occupations, language and communication are central: observing and interpreting behavior and expression, inferring mood and motive, taking on the perspective of others, responding appropriately to social cues, and knowing when you're understood. A good hair stylist, for instance, has the ability to convert vague requests (*I want something light and summery*) into an appropriate cut through questions, pictures, and hand gestures.

Verbal and mathematical skills drive measures of intelligence in the Western Hemisphere, and many of the kinds of work I studied are thought to require relatively little proficiency in either. Compared to certain kinds of white-collar occupations, that's true. But written symbols flow through physical work.

Numbers are rife in most workplaces: on tools and gauges, as measurements, as indicators of pressure or concentration or temperature, as guides to sequence, on ingredient labels, on lists and spreadsheets, as markers of quantity and price. Certain jobs require workers to make, check, and verify calculations, and to collect and interpret data. Basic math can be involved, and some workers develop a good sense of numbers and patterns. Consider, as well, what might be called material mathematics: mathematical functions embodied in materials and actions, as when a carpenter builds a cabinet or a flight of stairs. A simple mathematical act can extend quickly beyond itself. Measuring, for example, can involve more than recording the dimensions of an object. As I watched a cabinetmaker measure a long strip of wood, he read a number off the tape out loud, looked back over his shoulder to the kitchen wall, turned back to his task, took another measurement, and paused for a moment in thought. He was solving a problem involving the molding, and the measurement was important to his deliberation about structure and appearance.

In the blue-collar workplace, directions, plans, and reference books rely on illustrations, some representational and others, like blueprints, that require training to interpret. Esoteric symbols—visual jargon—depict switches and receptacles, pipe fittings, or types of welds. Workers themselves often make sketches on the job. I frequently observed them grab a pencil to sketch something on a scrap of paper or on a piece of the material they were installing.

Though many kinds of physical work don't require a high literacy level, more reading occurs in the blue-collar workplace than is generally thought, from manuals and catalogues to work orders and invoices, to lists, labels, and forms. With routine tasks, for example, reading is integral to understanding production quotas, learning how to use an instrument, or applying a product. Written notes can initiate action, as in restaurant orders or reports of machine malfunction, or they can serve as memory aids.

True, many uses of writing are abbreviated, routine, and repetitive, and they infrequently require interpretation or analysis. But analytic moments can be part of routine activities, and seemingly basic reading and writing can be cognitively rich. Because workplace language is used in the flow of other activities, we can overlook the remarkable coordination of words, numbers, and drawings required to initiate and direct action.

If we believe everyday work to be mindless, then that will affect the work we create in the future. When we devalue the full range of everyday cognition, we offer limited educational opportunities and fail to make fresh and meaningful instructional connections among disparate kinds of skill and knowledge. If we think that whole categories of people—identified by class or occupation— are not that bright, then we reinforce social separations and cripple our ability to talk across cultural divides.

Affirmation of diverse intelligence is not a retreat to a softhearted definition of the mind. To acknowledge a broader range of intellectual capacity is to take seriously the concept of cognitive variability, to appreciate in all the Rosies and Joes the thought that drives their accomplishments and defines who they are. This is a model of the mind that is worthy of a democratic society.

FOR DISCUSSION

1. Is Mike Rose correct when he says that DEFINITIONS of human intelligence should not be based solely "on grades in school and numbers on IQ tests" (16)? Why or why not?

2. According to Rose, how *should* intelligence be defined, especially among workers whose tasks are not "closely associated with formal education" (9)? What would he add to more traditional definitions?

3. Why is Rose concerned with definitions of intelligence that consider "everyday work to be mindless" (28)? What EFFECTS are such misguided (in his view) conceptions likely to have on society "in the future" (28)?

4. What does Rose mean by the "concept of cognitive variability" (29), and where— aside from watching his mother wait tables in a restaurant—did he likely learn about it?

STRATEGIES AND STRUCTURES

1. Why does Rose begin his essay with an account of his mother's experience as a waitress (1–6)? Where else does he use elements of NARRATIVE to support his definition of intelligence? How effective are they? Explain.

2. What are some of the main traits of "blue-collar brilliance" as Rose defines it? Point to specific passages in the text where he identifies those traits.

3. "There wasn't much for a child to do at the restaurants," says Rose, "and so as the hours stretched out, I watched the cooks and waitresses and listened to what they said" (2). How does his childhood role as an observer at his mother's restaurant anticipate the adult role that Rose adopts as a scholar who tells "the life stories of working-class people" (15)?

4. "I couldn't have put it into words," Rose says of this early experience of the workplace (4). How *did* he learn to put his observations into words, and what kind of language does he typically use to do it? Point to specific examples in the text.

5. Rose's definition of blue-collar intelligence is based on "a model of the mind" that, he claims at the end of his essay, is "worthy of a democratic society" (29). How and how well does Rose anticipate this ARGUMENT? Should he have stated this major point more directly earlier? Why or why not?

6. Rose's essay first appeared in the *American Scholar*, a journal aimed at readers who are interested in intellectual subjects beyond their narrow fields of expertise. How appropriate are the language and writing style of his essay to this intended AUDIENCE? Explain.

WORDS AND FIGURES OF SPEECH

. . . .

1. How and how well does Rose capture the "lingo" of the workplace (2)? Point to specific words and phrases in the text that do (or don't do) the job particularly well.

2. SYNONYMS are different words that have essentially the same meaning. What is Rose defining when he refers to "a place where competence was synonymous with physical work" (4)?

3. Look up the word *iconography* in your dictionary (10). Who or what did it pertain to before the rock stars and television celebrities of today?

4. Rose says that he has long observed blue-collar workers for the purpose of writing their "cognitive biographies" (15). Judging from the context in which he uses it, what does Rose mean by this term? Which parts of his essay (if any) would you point to as examples of this type of writing? Why?

FOR WRITING

. . . .

1. Spend an hour or so watching and listening to the workers in a diner, factory, store, hair salon, or other everyday workplace. Take notes on what they say and do, and write a paragraph or two capturing the scene as Rose does in the opening paragraphs of his essay.

2. Write an essay explaining how a group of workers you have observed, blue-collar or otherwise, defines some important aspect of their work. For example, you might explain how they define competency in their field—or failure, loyalty, or some other broad concept. Cite particular cases and conversations in some detail.

CHAPTER ELEVEN
CAUSE AND EFFECT

◈▽◈◈◈▽◈◈◈▽◈◈◈▽◈◈◈▽◈◈◈▽◈◈◈▽◈◈◈▽◈◈◈▽◈◈◈▽◈◈◈▽◈◈

I F you were at home on vacation and read in the morning paper that the phys-ics building at your school had burned, your first questions would probably be about the *effects* of the fire: "How much damage was done? Was anyone hurt?" Once you knew what the effects were—the building burned to the ground, but the blaze broke out in the middle of the night when nobody was in it—your next questions would likely be about the *causes*: "What caused the fire? Lightning? A short circuit in the electrical system? An arsonist's match?"

If the newspaper went on to say that the fire was set by your old room-mate, Larry, you would probably have some more questions, such as "Why did Larry do it? What will happen to Larry as a result of his action?" When you write a CAUSE-AND-EFFECT* essay, you answer fundamental questions like these about the *what* and *why* of an event or phenomenon. The questions may be simple, but answering them fully and adequately may require you to consider a variety of possible causes and effects—and to distinguish one type of cause from another.

In our example, Larry struck a match, which caused the building to catch fire. That effect in turn caused another effect—the building burned down. Larry's striking the match is the *immediate* cause of the fire—the one closest to the event in time. A *remote* cause, on the other hand, might be Larry's failure on a physics test two weeks earlier. But which cause is the *main* cause, the most important one, and which causes are less important—merely *contributing*? Was Larry depressed and angry before he took the physics test? What were his

*Words printed in SMALL CAPITALS are defined in the Glossary/Index.

◀ 471 ▶

feelings toward his father, the physics professor? Often you will need to run through a whole chain of related causes and effects like these before deciding to emphasize one or two.

How do you make sure that the causes you choose to emphasize actually account for the particular event or phenomenon you're analyzing? Two basic conditions have to be met to prove causation. A main cause has to be both *necessary* and *sufficient* to produce the effect in question. That is, it must be shown that (1) the alleged cause *always* accompanies the effect, and (2) that the alleged cause (and only the alleged cause) has the power to produce the effect. Let's look at these conditions in the following passage from a 2009 article on statistics in the *New York Times*. The author is recalling a time before the Salk vaccine defeated polio:

> For example, in the late 1940s, before there was a polio vaccine, public health experts in America noted that polio cases increased in step with the consumption of ice cream and soft drinks. . . . Eliminating such treats was even recommended as part of an anti-polio diet. It turned out that polio outbreaks were most common in the hot months of summer, when people naturally ate more ice cream. . . .
>
> —STEVE LOHR, "For Today's Graduates, Just One Word: Statistics"

The health experts who thought that ice cream and soft drinks *caused* polio failed to distinguish between causation and mere correlation. Although outbreaks of polio always seemed to be accompanied by an increase in the consumption of cool summer treats, ice cream and soft drinks did not actually have the power to cause the disease. And though the *heat* was the clear cause of the increased consumption of ice cream and soft drinks, Jonas Salk and his colleagues suspected that normal summer weather was not sufficiently harmful to induce paralysis. Eventually they isolated the *main* cause—the poliomyelitis virus. This tiny killer met both tests for true causality: it appeared in every case, and it was the only factor capable of producing the dire effect ascribed to it. It was both necessary and sufficient.

As Dr. Salk knew from the beginning, mere sequences in time—cases of polio increase as, or immediately after, the consumption of ice cream

Tim Wendel makes this distinction in "King, Kennedy, and the Power of Words," p. 487.

and soft drinks increases—is not sufficient to prove causation. This mistake in causal analysis is commonly referred to as the *post hoc, ergo propter hoc* FALLACY, Latin for "after this, therefore because of this." Salk understood the two conditions that must be met before causation may be accurately inferred.

These two conditions can be expressed as a simple formula:

B cannot have happened without A;
Whenever A happens, B must happen.

When we are dealing with psychological and social rather than purely physical factors, the main cause may defy simple analysis. Or it may turn out that there are a number of causes working together. Suppose we looked for an answer to the following question: Why does Maria smoke? This looks like a simple question, but it is a difficult one to answer because there are so many complicated reasons why a young woman like Maria might smoke. The best way for a writer to approach this kind of causal analysis might be to list as many of the contributing causes as he or she can turn up:

MARIA: I smoke because I need to do something with my hands.

MARIA'S BOYFRIEND: Maria smokes because she thinks it looks sophisticated.

MEDICAL DOCTOR: Because Maria has developed a physical addiction to tobacco.

PSYCHOLOGIST: Because of peer pressure.

SOCIOLOGIST: Because Maria is Hispanic; in recent years tobacco companies have spent billions in advertising to attract more Hispanic smokers.

When you list particular causes like this, be as specific as you can. When you list effects, be even more specific. Instead of saying "Smoking is bad for your health," be particular. In an essay on the evils of tobacco, for example, Erik

Eckholm provides a grim effect. "The most potentially tragic victims," he writes, "are the infants of mothers who smoke. They are more likely than the babies of nonsmoking mothers to be born underweight and thus to encounter death or disease at birth or during the initial months of life."

In singling out the effects of smoking upon unwitting infants, Eckholm uses an EXAMPLE that might be just powerful enough to convince some smokers to quit. Though your examples may not be as dramatic as Eckholm's, they must be specific to be powerful. And they must be selected with your AUDIENCE in mind. In the previous example, Eckholm addresses young women who smoke. If he were writing for a middle-aged audience, however, he might point out that the incidence of cancer and heart disease is 70 percent higher among one-pack-a-day men and women than among nonsmokers.

Your audience needs to be taken into account when you analyze causes and effects because, among other reasons, you are usually making an ARGU-MENT about the causes or effects of a phenomenon or event. Thus, you must carry the reader step by step through some kind of proof. Your explanation may be instructive, amusing, or startling; but if your analysis is to make the point you want it to make, it must also be persuasive.

A BRIEF GUIDE TO WRITING A CAUSE-AND-EFFECT ESSAY

When you analyze causes or effects, you explain why something happened or what its results are. So as you write a cause-and-effect essay, you need to iden-tify your subject and indicate which you plan to emphasize—causes or effects. Myriam Marquez makes these basic moves in the opening paragraphs of her essay in this chapter:

> When I'm shopping with my mother or standing in line with my step-dad to order fast food or anywhere else we might be together, we're going to speak Spanish. . . . Let me explain why we haven't adopted English as our official family language.
> —MYRIAM MARQUEZ, "Why and When We Speak Spanish in Public"

Marquez identifies the subject of her analysis (speaking Spanish in public) and indicates that she plans to emphasize the causes of this phenomenon ("why").

Whether you emphasize causes or effects, remember that the effect of one event may become the cause of a subsequent event, forming a CAUSAL CHAIN that you will need to follow link by link in order to fully analyze why something happened. For example: Two cars collide, killing the driver of the second car. The first driver's excessive speed is the cause; the death of the second driver is the effect. That effect, in turn, causes another dire effect—the children of the second driver grow up without that parent.

> Elisa Gonzales traces a chain of causes and effects in "Family History," p. 482.

The following guidelines will help you make the basic moves of cause and effect as you draft an essay. They will also help you come up with your subject, explain why you're analyzing causes and effects, distinguish between different kinds of causes, and present your analysis in an organized way.

Coming Up with a Subject

To find a subject for an essay that analyzes cause and effect, start with your own curiosity—about the physical world or about history, sociology, or any other field that interests you. Look for specific phenomena or events—climate change, President Truman's decision to drop the atomic bomb on Japan in 1945, growing obesity among young children in the United States—that you find intriguing. In order to narrow your subject down into a topic that is specific enough to investigate within the time allotted by your instructor, begin by asking yourself what its main causes (or effects) are likely to be. You may need to do some research on your subject; you'll find guidelines for doing research in the Appendix of this book.

Considering Your Purpose and Audience

As you examine particular causes and effects, think about why you're analyzing them. Is your PURPOSE to inform your readers? Amuse them? ARGUE that one set of causes (or effects) is more likely than another? One writer, for example, may try to persuade readers that autism is caused by inherent biological factors, while another writer might argue for environmental causes.

You'll also need to consider the AUDIENCE you want to reach. Are your readers already familiar with the topic, or will you need to provide background information and DEFINE unfamiliar terms? Are they likely to be receptive to the point you're making, or opposed to it? An article on the causes of autism may have a very different slant depending on whether the intended readers are parents of autistic children, medical doctors, psychologists, or the general public.

Myriam Marquez, p. 506, assumes a reader who knows little about her subject.

Generating Ideas: Asking Why, What, and What If

When you want to figure out what caused something, the essential question to ask is *why*. Why does a curveball drop as it crosses home plate? Why was Napoleon defeated in his invasion of Russia in 1812? If, on the other hand, you want to figure out what the effects of something are, or will be, then the basic question to ask is *what*, or *what if*. What will happen if the curveball fails to drop? What effect did the weather have on Napoleon's campaign?

As you ask *why* or *what* about your subject, keep in mind that a single effect may have multiple causes, or vice versa. Be sure to write down as many causes or effects as you can think of. If you were to ask why the U.S. financial system almost collapsed in the fall of 2008, for example, you would need to consider a number of possible causes, including greed on Wall Street, vastly inflated real estate values, subprime mortgages offered to unqualified borrowers, and a widespread credit crunch. Similarly, if you were analyzing the effects of the financial crisis, you would need to consider several of them, such as widespread unemployment, falling stock prices, and the loss of consumer confidence.

Templates for Analyzing Causes and Effects

The following templates can help you to generate ideas for a cause-and-effect essay and then to start drafting. Don't take these as formulas where you just have to fill in the blanks. There are no easy formulas for good writing. But these templates can help you plot out some of the key moves of cause and effect and thus may serve as good starting points.

- ► The main cause/effect of X is _____.
- ► X would also seem to have a number of contributing causes, including _____, _____, and _____.
- ► One effect of X is _____, which in turn causes _____.
- ► Some additional effects of X are _____, _____, and _____.
- ► Although the causes of X are not known, we can speculate that a key factor is _____.
- ► X cannot be attributed to mere chance or coincidence because _____.
- ► Once we know what causes X, we are in a position to say that _____.

For more techniques to help you generate ideas and start writing a cause-and-effect analysis, see Chapter 2.

Stating Your Point

As you draft an essay that analyzes cause and effect, tell readers at the outset whether you are going to focus on causes or effects—or both. Also make clear what your main point, or THESIS, is. For example, if you are analyzing the causes of the financial meltdown in the United States in 2008, you might signal your main point in a THESIS STATEMENT like this one:

> The main cause of the financial meltdown in the United States in 2008 was the freezing of credit, which made it impossible for anyone to borrow money.

Once you have stated your thesis, you are ready to present the analysis that supports it.

Distinguishing One Type of Cause from Another

To help your reader understand how a number of causes work together to produce a particular effect, you can distinguish among causes based on their relative importance in producing the effect and on their occurrence in time.

MAIN AND CONTRIBUTING CAUSES. The *main cause* is the one that has the greatest power to produce the effect. It must be both necessary to cause the effect and sufficient to do so. On August 1, 2007, a bridge collapsed on Interstate 35W in Minneapolis, Minnesota. Most investigators now agree that the main cause of the collapse was a flaw in the bridge's design. A *contributing cause* is a secondary cause—it helps to produce the effect but is not sufficient to do it alone. In the Minnesota bridge collapse, a contributing cause was the weight of construction supplies and equipment on the bridge at the time. Although it would have been wise to locate at least some of the construction equipment off the bridge, the added weight alone did not cause the collapse. As one investigator pointed out, "If the bridge had not been improperly designed, everybody says it would have held up that weight easily."

IMMEDIATE AND REMOTE CAUSES. The *immediate cause* is the one closest in time and most directly responsible for producing the effect, whereas *remote causes* are less apparent and more removed in time. The immediate cause of the financial meltdown of 2008 was the drying up of credit, but several remote causes were in play as well, such as subprime lending, the burst in the housing bubble, and recklessness on Wall Street.

Keep in mind, however, that these two ways of distinguishing causes aren't mutually exclusive. For example, the weight of the construction equipment on the bridge was both a contributing cause and an immediate one—though not the main cause, it immediately triggered the collapse of the bridge.

As you link together causes and effects, be careful not to confuse causation with coincidence. Just because one event (increased sales of soft drinks) comes before another (higher incidence of polio) does not mean the first event actually caused the second.

Organizing a Cause-and-Effect Essay

One way to present the effects of a given cause is by arranging them in chronological order. If you were tracing the effects of the credit crisis of 2008, for example, you would start with the crisis itself (the freezing of credit) and then proceed chronologically, detailing its effects in the order in which they occurred: first several investment banks collapsed, then the stock market plummeted, then the federal government stepped in with a massive bailout, and so on.

Reverse chronological order, in which you begin with a known effect and work backward through the possible causes, can also be effective. In the case of the 2007 Minnesota bridge collapse, you would start with the collapse itself (the known effect) and work backward in time through all of the possible causes: heavy construction equipment overloaded the bridge; the bridge structure was already weakened by corrosion; corrosion had not been discovered because of lack of inspections and maintenance; the capacity of the bridge was reduced at the outset by an error in design.

> Henry Louis Gates Jr. traces causes back in time in "A Giant Step," p. 499.

Often you will want to organize your analysis around various types of causes or effects. You might, for instance, explore the immediate cause before moving on to the remote causes, or vice versa. Or you might explore the contributing causes before the main cause, or vice versa. Whatever method you choose, be sure to organize your analysis in a way that makes the relationship between causes and effects as clear to your reader as possible.

EDITING FOR COMMON ERRORS IN A CAUSE-AND-EFFECT ANALYSIS

Like other kinds of writing, a cause-and-effect analysis uses distinctive patterns of language and punctuation—and thus invites typical kinds of errors. The following tips will help you to check for (and correct) these common errors when you analyze causes and effects in your own writing.

Check your verbs to make sure they clearly express causation

Some verbs express causation clearly and directly, whereas other verbs merely imply that one thing causes another.

VERBS THAT EXPRESS CAUSATION	VERBS THAT IMPLY CAUSATION
account for	follow
bring about	happen
cause	imply
effect	involve
make	implicate
result	influence

Using verbs that clearly express causation makes your analysis more precise.

▸ The collapse of the bridge on Interstate 35 W ~~involved~~ <u>was caused by</u> faulty design.

Check for common usage errors

AFFECT, EFFECT

In cause-and-effect analysis, *affect* is a verb meaning "influence." *Effect* is usually a noun meaning "result," but it can also be a verb meaning "bring about."

▸ Failing the course did not *affect* his graduation.

▸ Failing the course did not have the *effect* he feared most.

▸ Failing the course, however, did *effect* a change in his class standing.

REASON IS BECAUSE, REASON WHY

Both of these expressions are redundant. In the first case, use *that* instead of *because*. In the second, use *reason* alone.

▸ The reason the bridge collapsed was ~~because~~ <u>that</u> it was poorly designed.

▸ Faulty design is the reason ~~why~~ the bridge collapsed.

EVERYDAY CAUSE AND EFFECT
A Poster

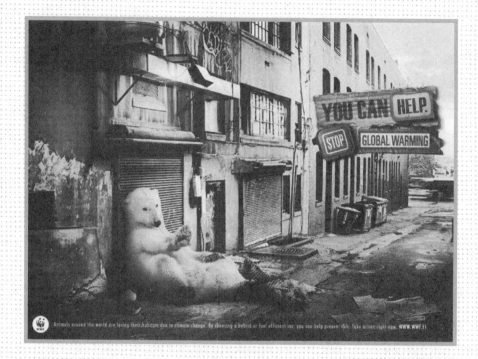

In this poster, sponsored by WWF, a world wildlife foundation, a polar bear sleeps on a seedy backstreet. The sign in the background suggests that one cause of his predicament is global warming. How has global warming left the bear on the skids? The fine print at the bottom of the poster explains: "Animals around the world are losing their habitats due to climate change. By choosing a hybrid or fuel-efficient car, you can help prevent this. Take action right now." When you analyze causes and effects, follow the lead of the WWF: identify the particular effect you plan to look into (homeless polar bear) and the causes of this effect (loss of habitat due to climate change). You may also want to explain how readers can prevent undesirable causes and their effects "right now"—so that polar bears and other animals can get back to their own neighborhoods.

ELISA GONZALES

FAMILY HISTORY

In "Family History," which she wrote for an undergraduate writing class at Yale University, Elisa Gonzales explores the causes and effects of bipolar disorder in two members of the same family. Gonzales does not try to determine if such psychological conditions are inherited, but she does find sufficient evidence in her family's history to suggest that the effects of one person's disorder may become causes of the same disorder in another family member. "Family History," along with other work by Gonzales, won the 2011 Norman Mailer College Writing prize, sponsored jointly by the National Council of Teachers of English and the Mailer Center.

Family History

1 By the time I am diagnosed with bipolar disorder type II, I have known Dr. Bradley for years. I know that he is divorced with two children, that he dated a beautiful Russian nurse who quit last year under obscure circumstances, that he colors his hair to stop the gray from infringing on his catalogue-model looks. He delivered my littlest sister, now seven, and he cried when my youngest brother died after several days in an incubator, his lungs hesitantly fluttering like moth wings before they finally deflated. Dr. Bradley has spent years counseling my mother after suicide attempts. In many ways, he knows us better than my closest friends who, blithe and unsuspecting, have always accepted my selective disclosures about my family. So when he pauses, clears his throat, and asks if I have a family history of bipolar disorder, I stare at him without speaking. It seems impossible that he doesn't know about my father.

First line introduces a serious effect of yet unknown cause(s)

Probes for possible causes of the disorder

2 For several minutes, I have trouble comprehending what he's saying, though he's kind and clear. Based on what I've told him—that I've had to leave parties because the urge to scream was so uncontrollable I felt I might disintegrate, that I've stayed up for days without speaking or going to class, that I've frightened my boyfriend with my bursts of rage—bipolar disorder seems probable. It often manifests in people around my age, especially in creative high-achieving people. There is no blood test; he will give me medication, a combination of new antipsychotic drugs and traditional lithium pills, and see if I improve. Confirming my family history is the last piece of the diagnosis. Heredity strikes most people as soon as they look in the mirror, in how much the jawline protrudes or how adamantly

Gives specific effects that might confirm the diagnosis

the earlobes crease, so I should not be so surprised at being confronted with my own history. Studying a chart of the cardiovascular system, I briefly wonder if I have always known that I carried with me more than my father's curly hair and dry sense of humor. But this is impossible, and far too mystical for the sterility of the exam table. It is true, though, that I have always feared my father, not just the physical reality of him—those thick hands that have left bruises around my throat and shoved my mother's teeth through her cheeks—but the lingering effects of his presence.

Introduces a significant probable cause of the disorder

When I was six, I went to the kitchen expecting breakfast and found my father frying Sesame Street videotapes in the cast-iron skillet. The charred plastic littered the kitchen for days and smoke stained the walls for the whole summer, until my father was released from his month-long stay in the hospital and repainted the entire house as penance. He also mended the holes he'd made in the walls and bought a new couch to replace the one he'd gutted with a butcher knife one night while we were sleeping. To celebrate, we ate store-bought pecan pie in a kitchen that smelled of fresh white paint. He talked about repairing the furnace and my sister showed him the stuffed dog named Rosie she'd gotten for her birthday. Although this cycle—destruction, then rehabilitation—has happened many times, I have always recalled the precision of his hands as he stood so calmly by the stove stirring twisted plastic with a metal spatula.

Implies that immediate effects of one disorder may be remote causes of the other

A month before my diagnosis, my sister and I fought about who would use the car, a typical sibling fight, except in its escalation. I started screaming and threw a book at her

3

4

head, threatening to call the police on her and report the car stolen if she took it. When she moved toward the door, I got a knife from the kitchen and told her I would slash the tires before I would let her leave. She stopped arguing with me to say, disbelievingly, "You're just like Daddy." I wanted to tell her that I couldn't be like him because he is crazy and I am not. Instead, I began to weep soundlessly, collapsing to the ground, my mouth gaping and silent. Now, in the exam room, I feel that type of ache again, beyond expression because no noise can cure it. It is here that I realize my entire life has converged in a dark pattern newly revealed.

> Suggests a cause-and-effect relationship between the two disorders

When my father was nineteen—the same age I am now—he cut up houseplants in precise segments and neatly ate a plateful with a fork before his brother found him and rushed him to the hospital. Later that month, after the doctors bandied around the word "schizophrenia" for a while, he received his own proper diagnosis. In 1979, lithium pharmacology had been approved for the treatment of manic depression, as bipolar disorder was called then, so his illness was manageable if he took his pills. But he never liked lithium, or the other medications his doctors prescribed. I wonder if I too will feel blunted and blurred without other forces sharpening themselves on my mind. Dr. Bradley asks if I have any questions before he writes me a prescription, and I say no. I am familiar with the required monthly checkups and learned the difference between the words "manic" and "maniac" when I was seven. Years before I grew up a little and participated in the national spelling bee, I was awed by the crucial distinction created through the addition of an *A*.

5

> Gives early symptoms of the father's disorder

> Anticipates possible future effects upon the daughter

> Suggests that the old name for the disorder confused cause and effect

The strangest part of hearing the diagnosis is that I   6
suddenly want something I haven't wanted in years: to talk to
my father. I know that he ran away after the doctors told him
the news and his brothers found him four days later on a
beach in California, but I know nothing else. I would like to
call my father and say, "I know I've always hated you, but as it
turns out, I'm just like you." Perhaps he would tell me how he
felt when he found out, if he slept on the beach and wandered
through a shabby town looking for the anonymity that would
let him lose his label, or if he blurted his diagnosis to people to
try it out. Mostly, I would like to know if he would have come
back, had they not found him, or if instead he would have
woken up and walked into the ocean one day, the only person
to separate the sky from all that water. The lure of water in the
lungs, of the non-breathing world, is one that I too will face in
the months after the diagnosis.

But my father and I haven't exchanged more than a few   7
words since I was fourteen, when he tried to strangle me,
saying that he had brought me into this world and he could
take me out of it. After that, he left us, hauled out by police
officers and kept away by court orders; I no longer know his
number. I will not call him, nor mention when I see him for a
few minutes at Christmas that I am also bipolar. Yet months
after, when I am assigned *Paradise Lost* for a class, I will start
to cry upon reading a piece of the poet's invocation:

> *though fallen on evil days,*
> *on evil days though fallen, and evil tongues;*
> *in darkness, and with dangers compass'd round,*
> *and solitude; yet not alone.*

Confronts one of the worst remote effects the daughter may face ·······•

Ends with a positive effect of the daughter's discovery that her condition is shared ·······•

TIM WENDEL

KING, KENNEDY, AND
THE POWER OF WORDS

Tim Wendel is a novelist, sportswriter, and teacher of writing. He was born in Philadelphia and grew up in Lockport, New York. After graduating from Syracuse University as a journalism major, Wendel earned an MFA from Johns Hopkins University, where he now teaches writing. His articles and essays have appeared in *Esquire, Go, Gargoyle*, the *New York Times*, the *Washington Post*, and *USA Today*. Author of *Summer of '68: The Season That Changed Baseball, and America, Forever* (2012), among other books, Wendel believes that American discourse, especially political discourse, has changed significantly in the decades since the assassinations of John F. Kennedy, Martin Luther King Jr., and Robert F. Kennedy. In "King, Kennedy, and the Power of Words" (from the website of the *American Scholar*, April 2012), Wendel analyzes some of the specific causes and effects of those changes, particularly what he sees as the tendency of politicians today to slip into "passive-voice mode."

The night of April 4, 1968, presidential candidate Robert Kennedy received the news that Martin Luther King Jr. had been assassinated. Kennedy was about to speak in Indianapolis and some in his campaign wondered if they should go ahead with the rally.

Moments before Kennedy climbed onto a flatbed truck to address the crowd, which had gathered in a light rain, press secretary Frank Mankiewicz gave the candidate a sheet of paper with ideas of what he might say. Kennedy slid it into his pocket without looking at it. Another aide approached with more notes and the candidate waved him away.

"Do they know about Martin Luther King?" Kennedy asked those gathered on the platform. No, came the reply.

After asking the crowd to lower its campaign signs, Kennedy told his audience that King had been shot and killed earlier in Memphis. Gasps went up from the crowd and for a moment everything seemed ready to come apart. Indianapolis might have joined other cities across America that burned on that awful night.

But then Kennedy, beginning in a trembling, halting voice, slowly brought the people back around and somehow held them together. Listening to the speech decades later is to be reminded of the real power of words. How they can heal, how they can still bring us together, but only if they are spoken with conviction and from the heart.

Compare what we often hear from politicians today to what Kennedy said on that tragic night in Indianapolis. He told the crowd how he "had a member of my family killed"—a reference to his brother John, who had been assassinated less than five years before.

Later on, Kennedy recited a poem by Aeschylus, which he had memorized long before that trying night in Indianapolis:

> Even in our sleep, pain which cannot forget
> Falls drop by drop upon the heart,
> Until, in our own despair, against our will,
> Comes wisdom through the awful grace of God.

Martin Luther King Jr.

Kennedy's heartfelt speech came only hours after King's last address. The night before, the civil rights leader had reluctantly taken to the dais at the Mason Temple in Memphis. The weather that evening had been miserable—thunderstorms and tornado warnings. As a result, King arrived late and was just going to say a few words and then tell everyone to please go home.   8

Visibly tired and with no notes in hand, King stumbled at first. The shutters hitting against the temple walls sounded like gun shots to him. So much so that King's friend, the Reverend Billy Kyles, found a custodian to stop the noise. Only then, at the crowd's urging, did the words begin to come together for King.   9

"We've got some difficult days ahead," he said that night. "But it really doesn't matter with me now. Because I've been to the mountaintop."   10

King closed by telling the crowd," We as a people will get to the Promised Land. So I'm happy tonight. I'm not worried about anything. I'm not fearing any man. . . ."   11

Novelist Charles Baxter contends that the greatest influence on American 12
writing and discourse in recent memory can be traced back to the phrase "Mistakes were made." Of course, that's from Watergate and the shadowy

Remote causes
are discussed
on p. 478.

intrigue inside the Nixon White House.[1] In his essay "Burning Down
the House," Baxter compares that "quasi-confessional passive-voice-
mode sentence" to what Robert E. Lee said after the battle of Gettysburg and
the disastrous decision of Pickett's Charge.[2]

"All of this has been my fault," the Confederate general said. "I asked 13
more of the men than should have been asked of them."

In Lee's words, and those of King and Kennedy, we hear a refreshing can- 14
dor and directness that we miss today. In 1968, people responded to what King
and Kennedy told them. During that tumultuous 24-hour period in 1968, people cried aloud and chanted in Memphis. Words struck a chord in Indianapolis, too, and decades later former mayor (and now U.S. Senator) Richard Lugar
told writer Thurston Clarke that Kennedy's speech was "a turning point" for
his city.

After King's assassination, riots broke out in more than 100 U.S. cities— 15
the worst destruction since the Civil War. But neither Memphis nor Indianapolis experienced that kind of damage. To this day, many believe that was due to
the words spoken when so many were listening.

1. Shortly after President Richard Nixon (1913–1994), a Republican, began his second term
in office, it was discovered that operatives of his campaign had broken into offices of the
Democratic Party in the Watergate office complex in June 1972. The resulting scandal,
popularly known as Watergate, prompted Nixon to resign from office in 1974, the only U.S.
president ever to do so.

2. On July 3, 1863, Confederate commander Robert E. Lee ordered General George Pickett
to lead an infantry assault against Union positions at Gettysburg, Pennsylvania. The attack
failed and the battle of Gettysburg was lost. Many historians consider this to be the turning
point of the Civil War.

FOR DISCUSSION

1. Beginning with the title of his essay, Tim Wendel CLAIMS that words have "power." To do what, according to his analysis?

2. When and how, in Wendel's view, can words have the EFFECT he ascribes to them? Under what circumstances, and spoken by whom? Explain.

3. Why, according to Wendel, did the cities of Memphis and Indianapolis escape destruction, by and large, during the riots that followed the assassination of Martin Luther King Jr. in April 1968? Is his analysis of CAUSE AND EFFECT correct? Why or why not?

4. Wendel's essay is ultimately about RHETORIC, which can be defined as the use of words to move an audience to action or belief. According to Wendel, "American writing and discourse" have changed since April 1968 (12). How does he explain the causes of this effect?

STRATEGIES AND STRUCTURES

1. Wendel's essay was written for Martin Luther King Day 2012. How and how well do his words speak to that occasion? Explain.

2. Wendel criticizes the rhetoric of "politicians today"; but aside from alluding to "the Nixon White House," he does not name names (6, 12). Should he have? Why or why not?

3. "To this day, many believe that was due to the words spoken when so many were listening" (15). As proof of this conclusion about cause and effect, Wendel cites three main EXAMPLES of speech and speeches by King, Kennedy, and Robert E. Lee. Is this evidence sufficient to make his point? Why or why not?

4. Wendel does not mention that on June 5, 1968, just two months after the death of Martin Luther King Jr., the other man who had spoken so eloquently that night—Robert Kennedy—was himself shot while campaigning for the presidency, and he died the next day. Is this a glaring omission, or does it contribute in some way to the rhetorical effect of Wendel's essay? Explain.

WORDS AND FIGURES OF SPEECH

. . . .

1. The word *awful* comes up twice in Wendel's essay (4, 7). In what different senses does he use it?

2. Martin Luther King Jr. said he had been to the "mountaintop" (10). What mountaintop was he referring to? Explain the ALLUSION.

3. Look up *discourse* in your dictionary (12). In what sense is Wendel using the term here?

4. Why does Wendel refer to the phrase "mistakes were made" as a "quasi-confessional passive-voice-mode sentence" (12)? What is passive about this verbal phrase, and how does this grammatical construction fit in with Wendel's overall argument about the use of words by public figures?

FOR WRITING

. . . .

1. Martin Luther King Jr.'s famous "I Have a Dream" speech is reprinted in Chapter 13. Comb through King's speech and make a list of the words and phrases that confirm (or call into question) the power of words when "spoken with conviction and from the heart" (5).

2. Choose one (or more) of the classic speeches or essays in Chapter 13, and write an analysis of how the author achieves (or fails to achieve) the effect his or her words are apparently intended to produce upon the audience. For example, the writer might seek to establish his or her credibility by convincing readers that they are listening to a person of good moral character—or of great feeling or intellect. Cite specific passages from the text to support your analysis.

MARISSA NUÑEZ

CLIMBING THE GOLDEN ARCHES

Marissa Nuñez (b. 1974) was nineteen when she wrote this essay about working for McDonald's. Nuñez started at the bottom (the "fried products" station) and worked her way up to management training. "Climbing the Golden Arches" not only tells the story of this ascent, it also analyzes the effects, personal and professional, of learning to do a job, dealing with the public, and being part of a team. An essay about making choices and becoming oneself, "Climbing the Golden Arches" originally appeared in 1997 in *New Youth Connections*, a magazine that publishes work by student authors.

Two years ago, while my cousin Susie and I were doing our Christmas shopping on Fourteenth Street, we decided to have lunch at McDonald's. 1

"Yo, check it out," Susie said. "They're hiring. Let's give it a try." I looked at her and said, "Are you serious?" She gave me this look that made it clear that she was. 2

After we ate our food, I went over to the counter and asked the manager for two applications. I took them back to our table and we filled them out. When we finished, we handed them in to the manager and he told us he'd be calling. 3

When Susie and I got home from school one day about a month later, my mother told us that McDonald's had called. They wanted to interview us both. We walked straight over there. They asked us why we wanted to work at McDonald's and how we felt about specific tasks, like cleaning the bathrooms. Then they told us to wait for a while. Finally the manager came out and said we had the job.

When we got outside, I looked over at Susie and laughed because I hadn't thought it would work. But I was happy to have a job. I would be able to buy my own stuff and I wouldn't have to ask my mother for money anymore.

A week and a half later we went to pick up our uniforms (a blue and white striped shirt with blue pants or a blue skirt) and to find out what days we'd be working. We were also told the rules and regulations of the work place. "No stealing" was at the top of the list. A couple of the others were: "Leave all your problems at home" and "Respect everyone you work with."

Before you can officially start working, you have to get trained on every station. I started on "fried products," which are the chicken nuggets, chicken sandwiches, and Filet-o-Fish. Then I learned to work the grill, which is where we cook the burgers. Next was the assembly table where we put all the condiments (pickles, onions, lettuce, etc.) on the sandwiches. After all that, you have to learn the french fry station. Then finally you can learn to work the register. It was a month before I could be left alone at any station.

The most difficult thing was learning how to work the grill area. We use a grill called a clamshell, which has a cover. It cooks the whole burger in forty-four seconds without having to flip it over. At first I didn't like doing this. Either I wouldn't lay the meat down right on the grill and it wouldn't cook all the way through or I would get burned. It took a few weeks of practicing before I got the hang of it. Now, after a lot more practice, I can do it with no problem.

My first real day at work was a lot of fun. The store had been closed for remodeling and it was the grand opening. A lot of people were outside waiting for the store to open. I walked around just to get the feel of things before we let the customers come in. I was working a register all by myself. My cousin was at the station next to me and we raced to see who could get the most customers and who could fill the orders in fifty-nine seconds. I really enjoyed myself.

Susie worked for only three months after our grand opening, but I stayed   10
on. I liked having a job because I was learning how to be a responsible person. I
was meeting all kinds of people and learning a lot about them. I
started making friends with my co-workers and getting to know
many of the customers on a first-name basis. And I was in charge
of my own money for the first time. I didn't have to go asking Mom
for money when I wanted something anymore. I could just go and buy it.

Page 472 analyzes
how and *why* one
event causes or
results from
another.

Working at McDonald's does have its down side. The worst thing about   11
the job is that the customers can be real jerks sometimes. They just don't seem to
understand the pressure we're under. At times they will try to jerk you or make you
look stupid. Or they will blame you for a mistake they made. If you don't watch
and listen carefully, some of them will try to short-change you for some money.

The most obnoxious customer I ever had came in one day when it was really   12
busy. She started saying that one of my co-workers had overcharged her. I knew
that wasn't the case, so I asked her what the problem was. She told me to mind my
own business, so I told her that she was my business. She started calling me
a "Spanish b-tch" and kept on calling me names until I walked away to get the
manager. If I had said anything back to her, I would have gotten in trouble.

Another time, a woman wanted to pay for a $2.99 Value Meal with a $100   13
bill. No problem, we changed it. She walked away from the counter with her
food and then came back a few minutes later saying we had given her a counterfeit $20 bill in her change. We knew it was a lie. She wouldn't back down and
even started yelling at the manager. He decided that we should call the cops and
get them to settle it. That got her so mad that she threw her tray over the counter at us. Then she left. Of course, not all our customers are like this. Some are
very nice and even take the time to tell the manager good things about me.

Sometimes we make up special events to make the job more fun for every-   14
one. For example, we'll have what we call a "battle of the sexes." On those days,
the women will work the grill area and the french fry station and all the other
kitchen jobs and the men will work the registers. For some reason, the guys usually like to hide in the grill area. The only time they'll come up front and pretend they are working there is to see some female customer they are interested
in. Still, they always act like working the grill is so much harder than working

the register. I say the grill is no problem compared to working face-to-face with customers all day. After a battle of the sexes, the guys start to give the girls more respect because they see how much pressure we're under.

Every six months, our job performance is reviewed. If you get a good review, you get a raise and sometimes a promotion. After my first six months on the job I got a raise and was made a crew trainer. I became the one who would show new employees how to work the register, fry station, and, yes, even the grill area. 15

When I made a year and a half, I was asked if I would like to become a manager-trainee. To move to that level, your performance has to be one hundred percent on all stations of the store. That means doing every job by the book with no shortcuts. The managers have to trust you, and you have to set a good example for your co-workers. I was so happy. Of course I said yes. 16

Now that I've been there two years, the managers trust me to run a shift by myself. I am working to get certified as a manager myself. To do that I have to attend a class and take an exam, and my manager and supervisor have to observe the way I work with everyone else and grade my performance. I have been in the program for nine months now and expect to get certified this month. I'm thinking about staying on full-time after I graduate from high school. 17

Working at McDonald's has taught me a lot. The most important thing I've learned is that you have to start at the bottom and work your way up. I've learned to take this seriously—if you're going to run a business, you need to know how to do all the other jobs. I also have more patience than ever and have learned how to control my emotions. I've learned to get along with all different kinds of people. I'd like to have my own business someday, and working at McDonald's is what showed me I could do that. 18

FOR DISCUSSION

. . . .

1. Marissa Nuñez had been working for McDonald's for two years when she wrote this essay. What EFFECTS did the experience have on her? What were some of the main CAUSES of those effects?

2. What particular work experiences did Nuñez find most instructive? How did they help bring about the personal changes she mentions?

3. What does Nuñez hope to become by working at McDonald's? How does she expect to accomplish that goal?

4. What do you think of Nuñez's response to the customer who calls her a name?

5. This essay was originally published in a magazine for teenagers. How does it appeal to the attitudes and values of that AUDIENCE?

STRATEGIES AND STRUCTURES

. . . .

1. In paragraph 10, Nuñez sums up what she is learning in her new job. Where does she sum up what she *has* learned? If Nuñez had left out these two paragraphs, how would the focus and direction of her essay be changed?

2. How does the following sentence, which comes approximately halfway through her essay, help Nuñez to present different aspects of her work experience: "Working at McDonald's does have its down side" (11)? What sort of causes is she analyzing now? What effect do they have on her?

3. In addition to analyzing causes and effects, "Climbing the Golden Arches" tells a story. What is the role of the "most obnoxious customer" and of the woman who throws her tray (12, 13)? What roles do these people play in her analysis of causes and effects?

4. Nuñez's essay covers a two-year work period that might be broken down into application, apprenticeship, "officially working," management training, future plans. Where does each stage begin and end? How effective do you find this strategy for organizing this analysis?

5. The phases of Nuñez's NARRATIVE resemble the steps or stages of much PROCESS ANALYSIS, or how-to writing (Chapter 8). Why is this? Besides examining the effects on her life of working at McDonald's, what process or processes does she analyze by telling her story?

WORDS AND FIGURES OF SPEECH

. . . .

1. Why does Nuñez put "battle of the sexes" in quotation marks (14)?

2. What does the word "station" mean in connection with restaurant work (7)?

3. Explain the METAPHOR in Nuñez's title. What figurative meaning does the word "arches" take on in an account of someone's career goals? How about "golden" arches?

4. How does Nuñez DEFINE the word *fun* in this essay (9, 14)? What specific EXAMPLES does she give? What does her distinctive use of the word indicate about her attitude toward work?

FOR WRITING

. . . .

1. Write a letter of application for your ideal job. Explain your qualifications, your career goals, and how you expect to achieve them.

2. Write a personal narrative of your work experience or some other experience that taught you a lot. Break it into phases, if appropriate, and explain how specific aspects and events of the experience caused you to become who you are. In other words, tell what happened to you, but also analyze the specific EFFECTS the experience had on you and your life.

HENRY LOUIS GATES JR.

A GIANT STEP

Henry Louis Gates Jr. (b. 1950) is the director of the W. E. B. Du Bois Institute for African and African American Research at Harvard. He is the author or editor of many works on black literature and history and of literary criticism, including *The Signifying Monkey: A Theory of Afro-American Literary Criticism* (1988) and *The Norton Anthology of African American Literature* (2nd ed., 2004). Gates grew up in Piedmont, West Virginia, the small town depicted in this personal narrative from the *New York Times Magazine*. He later incorporated this essay into *Colored People: A Memoir* (1994), a book that tells of events and people in the author's past from the standpoint of the present. But "A Giant Step" is also an essay in cause and effect, playfully examining the social attitudes that caused young Gates to be misdiagnosed as an "overachiever" and showing how he sidestepped the potentially crippling effects of both physical disability and racial prejudice on his way to becoming a distinguished scholar.

"What's this?" the hospital janitor said to me as he stumbled over my right shoe. 1

"My shoes," I said. 2

"That's not a shoe, brother," he replied, holding it to the light. "That's a brick." 3

It *did* look like a brick, sort of. 4

"Well, we can throw these in the trash now," he said. 5

"I guess so." 6

We had been together since 1975, those shoes and I. They were orthopedic shoes built around molds of my feet, and they had a 2¼-inch lift. I had mixed feelings about them. On the one hand, they had given me a more or less even gait for the first time in 10 years. On the other hand, they had marked me as a "handicapped person," complete with cane and special license plates. I went through a pair a year, but it was always the same shoe, black, wide, weighing about four pounds. 7

Tracing a casual chain of events back in time is discussed on p. 479.

It all started 26 years ago in Piedmont, West Virginia, a backwoods town of 2,000 people. While playing a game of touch football at a Methodist summer camp, I incurred a hairline fracture. Thing is, I didn't know it yet. I was 14 and had finally lost the chubbiness of my youth. I was just learning tennis and beginning to date, and who knew where that might lead? 8

Not too far. A few weeks later, I was returning to school from lunch when, out of the blue, the ball-and-socket joint of my hip sheared apart. It was instant agony, and from that time on nothing in my life would be quite the same. 9

I propped myself against the brick wall of the schoolhouse, where the school delinquent found me. He was black as slate, twice my size, mean as the day was long and beat up kids just because he could. But the look on my face told him something was seriously wrong, and—bless him—he stayed by my side for the two hours it took to get me into a taxi. 10

"It's a torn ligament in your knee," the surgeon said. (One of the signs of what I had—a "slipped epithysis"—is intense knee pain, I later learned.) So he scheduled me for a walking cast. 11

I was wheeled into surgery and placed on the operating table. As the doctor wrapped my leg with wet plaster strips, he asked about my schoolwork. 12

"Boy," he said, "I understand you want to be a doctor." 13

I said, "Yessir." Where I came from, you always said "sir" to white people, 14
unless you were trying to make a statement.

Had I taken a lot of science courses? 15

"Yessir. I enjoy science." 16

"Are you good at it?" 17

"Yessir, I believe so." 18

"Tell me, who was the father of sterilization?" 19

"Oh, that's easy, Joseph Lister." 20

Then he asked who discovered penicillin. 21

Alexander Fleming. 22

And what about DNA? 23

Watson and Crick. 24

The interview went on like this, and I thought my answers might get me 25
a pat on the head. Actually, they just confirmed the diagnosis he'd come to.

He stood me on my feet and insisted that I walked. When I tried, the joint 26
ripped apart and I fell on the floor. It hurt like nothing I'd ever known.

The doctor shook his head. "Pauline," he said to my mother, his voice 27
kindly but amused, "there's not a thing wrong with that child. The problem's
psychosomatic. Your son's an overachiever."

Back then, the term didn't mean what it usually means today. In Appa- 28
lachia,[1] in 1964, "overachiever" designated a sort of pathology: the overstraining
of your natural capacity. A colored kid who thought he could be a doctor—just
for instance—was headed for a breakdown.

What made the pain abate was my mother's reaction. I'd never, ever heard 29
her talk back to a white person before. And doctors, well, their words were
scripture.

Not this time. Pauline Gates stared at him for a moment. "Get his clothes, 30
pack his bags—we're going to the University Medical Center," which was 60
miles away.

---

1. Rural area of the eastern United States that stretches from New England to northern
Alabama, Mississippi, and Georgia; named for the mountain range that passes through it.

Not great news: the one thing I knew was that they only moved you to the University Medical Center when you were going to die. I had three operations that year. I gave my tennis racket to the delinquent, which he probably used to club little kids with. So I wasn't going to make it to Wimbledon.[2] But at least I wasn't going to die, though sometimes I wanted to. Following the last operation, which fitted me for a metal ball, I was confined to bed, flat on my back, immobilized by a complex system of weights and pulleys. It was six weeks of bondage—and bedpans. I spent my time reading James Baldwin,[3] learning to play chess and quarreling daily with my mother, who had rented a small room—which we could ill afford—in a motel just down the hill from the hospital.

I think we both came to realize that our quarreling was a sort of ritual. We'd argue about everything—what time of day it was—but the arguments kept me from thinking about that traction system.

I limped through the next decade—through Yale and Cambridge . . . as far away from Piedmont as I could get. But I couldn't escape the pain, which increased as the joint calcified and began to fuse over the next 15 years. My leg grew shorter, as the muscles atrophied and the ball of the ball-and-socket joint migrated into my pelvis. Aspirin, then Motrin, heating pads and massages, became my traveling companions.

Most frustrating was passing store windows full of fine shoes. I used to dream about walking into one of those stores and buying a pair of shoes. "Give me two pairs, one black, one cordovan," I'd say. "Wrap 'em up." No six-week wait as with the orthotics in which I was confined. These would be real shoes. Not bricks.

In the meantime, hip-joint technology progressed dramatically. But no surgeon wanted to operate on me until I was significantly older, or until the pain was so great that surgery was unavoidable. After all, a new hip would last only for 15 years, and I'd already lost too much bone. It wasn't a procedure they were sure they'd be able to repeat.

This year, my 40th, the doctors decided the time had come.

I increased my life insurance and made the plunge.

31

32

33

34

35

36

37

2. The world's oldest tennis tournament, named for the London suburb in which it is held.

3. African American novelist and essayist (1924–1987).

The nights before my operations are the longest nights of my life—but never long enough. Jerking awake, grabbing for my watch, I experience a delicious sense of relief as I discover that only a minute or two have passed. You never want 6 a.m. to come. 38

And then the door swings open. "Good morning, Mr. Gates," the nurse says. "It's time." 39

The last thing I remember, just vaguely, was wondering where amnesiac minutes go in one's consciousness, wondering if I experienced the pain and sounds, then forgot them, or if these were somehow blocked out, dividing the self on the operating table from the conscious self in the recovery room. I didn't like that idea very much. I was about to protest when I blinked. 40

"It's over, Mr. Gates," says a voice. But how could it be over? I had merely *blinked.* "You talked to us several times," the surgeon had told me, and that was the scariest part of all. 41

Twenty-four hours later, they get me out of bed and help me into a "walker." As they stand me on my feet, my wife bursts into tears. "Your foot is touching the ground!" I am afraid to look, but it is true: the surgeon has lengthened my leg with that gleaming titanium and chrome-cobalt alloy ball-and-socket-joint. 42

"You'll need new shoes," the surgeon says. "Get a pair of Dock-Sides; they have a secure grip. You'll need a ¾-inch lift in the heel, which can be as discreet as you want." 43

I can't help thinking about those window displays of shoes, those elegant shoes that, suddenly, I will be able to wear. Dock-Sides and sneakers, boots and loafers, sandals and brogues. I feel, at last, a furtive sympathy for Imelda Marcos,[4] the queen of soles. 44

The next day, I walk over to the trash can, and take a long look at the brick. I don't want to seem ungracious or unappreciative. We have walked long miles together. I feel disloyal, as if I am abandoning an old friend. I take a second look. 45

Maybe I'll have them bronzed. 46

---

4. Wife and government ambassador (b. 1929) of Philippine dictator Ferdinand Marcos. When his regime fell in 1986, evidence of the extravagance of Imelda Marcos's lifestyle included some 5,500 pairs of shoes.

FOR DISCUSSION

. . . .

1. The doctor misdiagnoses Henry Louis Gates's injury in paragraph 11. What does he misdiagnose in paragraph 27? What CAUSES the doctor to make the first mistake? The second?

2. What EFFECTS did each misdiagnosis have on Gates? On his mother, Pauline?

3. "Where I came from," says Gates, "you always said 'sir' to white people, unless you were trying to make a statement" (14). What "statement," or point, is Gates making about race and "natural capacity" in this essay (28)?

4. Why does Gates think of having his old shoes "bronzed" (46)?

STRATEGIES AND STRUCTURES

. . . .

1. What is the PURPOSE of Gates's essay? To inform? Persuade? Amuse? Something else? How do you know?

2. Gates takes a giant step when he gets a new hip. Up until then, however, his life story has been shaped around an earlier turning point. What is it? How do the two "steps" differ? What effect does each have on his life?

3. Besides the effects of physical pain, young Gates also had to deal with the effects of racism. How does the incident involving his mother and the doctor who "interviews" him show both what he is up against and what strengths he has that will enable him to succeed (13–30)?

4. Gates begins his essay by relating the moment he threw away his orthopedic shoes—the end of the chain of events that begins with the incident he relates in paragraph 8. Is this an effective strategy for beginning this essay? Why or why not?

5. How much time elapses between when the "bricks" first go in the trash can and when Gates thinks of having them bronzed (5, 46)? How many distinct time periods does Gates identify? What do these elements of NARRATIVE contribute to Gates's essay?

WORDS AND FIGURES OF SPEECH

1. How, according to Gates, has the meaning of "overachiever" changed since 1964 (28)?

2. A "slipped epithysis" is a medical pathology (11). What kind of pathology is Gates referring to in paragraph 28?

3. What are the multiple meanings of each of the following words as Gates uses them here: "breakdown," "bondage," "limped" (28, 31, 33)?

4. Why does Gates profess to feel "disloyal" in paragraph 45? What does it mean to say to someone, "You've been a brick"?

FOR WRITING

1. Write a paragraph about an object you might like to have bronzed. Be sure to analyze the effects it has had on your life.

2. Write an essay that examines the effects of dealing with some kind of adversity. Those effects might be physical, psychological, or both. Give specific EXAMPLES, as Gates does when he tells about his mixed feelings toward his old shoes.

MYRIAM MARQUEZ

WHY AND WHEN WE SPEAK
SPANISH IN PUBLIC

Myriam Marquez is in charge of the editorial pages of the *Miami Herald*. Born
in Cuba, Marquez fled to the United States with her parents in 1959. After
graduating from the University of Maryland, where she studied journalism and
political science, Marquez worked for eighteen years at the *Orlando Sentinel*,
joining the staff of the *Herald* in 2005. In "Why and When We Speak Spanish
in Public" (*Orlando Sentinel*, June 28, 1999), Marquez examines the causes
and effects of her family's decision not to adopt English as "our official family
language."

W hen I'm shopping with my mother or standing in line with my stepdad   1
to order fast food or anywhere else we might be together, we're going to
speak to one another in Spanish.

That may appear rude to those who don't understand Spanish and over-   2
hear us in public places.

Those around us may get the impression that we're talking about them. 3
They may wonder why we would insist on speaking in a foreign tongue, especially
if they knew that my family has lived in the United States for forty years and
that my parents do understand English and speak it, albeit with
difficulty and a heavy accent.

> A true cause must
> be sufficient *and*
> necessary (p. 472)
> to produce an
> alleged effect.

Let me explain why we haven't adopted English as our offi- 4
cial family language. For me and most of the bilingual people I
know, it's a matter of respect for our parents and comfort in our cultural roots.

It's not meant to be rude to others. It's not meant to alienate anyone or to 5
Balkanize America.

It's certainly not meant to be un-American—what constitutes an "Ameri- 6
can" being defined by English speakers from North America.

Being an American has very little to do with what language we use during 7
our free time in a free country. From its inception, this country was careful not
to promote a government-mandated official language.

We understand that English is the common language of this country and 8
the one most often heard in international-business circles from Peru to Norway.
We know that, to get ahead here, one must learn English.

But that ought not mean that somehow we must stop speaking in our 9
native tongue whenever we're in a public area, as if we were ashamed of who we
are, where we're from. As if talking in Spanish—or any other language, for
that matter—is some sort of litmus test used to gauge American patriotism.

Throughout this nation's history, most immigrants—whether from Poland 10
or Finland or Italy or wherever else—kept their language through the first generation and, often, the second. I suspect that they spoke among themselves in
their native tongue—in public. Pennsylvania even provided voting ballots written in German during much of the 1800s for those who weren't fluent in English.

In this century, Latin American immigrants and others have fought for 11
this country in U.S.-led wars. They have participated fully in this nation's democracy by voting, holding political office, and paying taxes. And they have watched
their children and grandchildren become so "American" that they resist speaking in Spanish.

You know what's rude? 12

When there are two or more people who are bilingual and another person 13
who speaks only English and the bilingual folks all of a sudden start speaking
Spanish, which effectively leaves out the English-only speaker. I don't tolerate
that.

One thing's for sure. If I'm ever in a public place with my mom or dad and 14
bump into an acquaintance who doesn't speak Spanish, I will switch to English
and introduce that person to my parents. They will respond in English and do
so with respect.

FOR DISCUSSION

. . . .

1. Even though they have lived in the United States for many years, Myriam Marquez and her parents have not adopted English as their "official family language" (4). Should they have? Why or why not?

2. Marquez defends her family's right to speak Spanish among themselves, but she
   nevertheless insists that "one must learn English" (8). Why? What are the consequences of doing so—or of not doing so—in her view?

3. "I don't tolerate that," Marquez says of people who continue to speak Spanish in
   the presence of others who speak only English (13). Why does she think this is
   "rude" (12)? Do you agree? Why or why not?

STRATEGIES AND STRUCTURES

. . . .

1. Marquez gives specific EFFECTS ("we're going to speak to one another in Spanish")
   before she gives particular CAUSES ("respect for our parents and comfort in our
   cultural roots") (1, 4). Is this a logical order of presentation? Why or why not?

2. Why does Marquez cite immigrants from Poland, Finland, Italy, and "wherever
   else" (10)? Is this additional evidence sufficient to justify her CLAIM that it's okay
   for her family to speak their native language in public? Why or why not?

3. Marquez makes a point of saying that immigrants from Latin America have
   "fought for this country" and "participated fully in this nation's democracy by
   voting, holding political office, and paying taxes" (11). What potential objection
   to her claim is she anticipating here? How effective is this strategy?

4. How and how effectively does Marquez use elements of NARRATIVE to develop her analysis of causes and effects? Point to specific passages in the text that support your answer.

WORDS AND FIGURES OF SPEECH

1. To "Balkanize" means to divide a region into small, less powerful states (5). Where does the meaning of this word come from, and how appropriate is Marquez's use of the term here? Explain.
2. A "litmus test" is a test in which the outcome is based on only one factor (9). Why might Marquez be reluctant to apply such an either/or test to a person's "patriotism" (6)?
3. Why does Marquez make a point of describing certain behavior as "rude" (2, 12)? How does her choice of this word affect her credibility as someone who can judge when social behavior is proper or not?

FOR WRITING

1. In a paragraph or two, explain why it would (or would not) be rude to continue speaking rapidly in English (or some other language) in the presence of others who have difficulty understanding the language being spoken.
2. Write an essay analyzing how and why you and your family (or friends) might speak or behave in a fashion that could seem exclusive to others but that is not intended to be disrespectful. Give specific circumstances under which you think such conduct would (and would not) be appropriate.

ANN HOOD

LONG BEAUTIFUL HAIR

Ann Hood (b. 1956) is a novelist, essayist, and teacher of writing at the New School in New York City and at New York University. A native of Warwick, Rhode Island, Hood graduated from the University of Rhode Island with a major in English and went on to study American literature in graduate school at NYU. On April 18, 2002, Hood's five-year-old daughter Grace contracted a virulent form of strep and died suddenly. Among other works, *The Knitting Circle* (2007), *Comfort: A Journey Through Grief* (2008), and *The Red Thread* (2010) are Hood's attempts, in both fiction and nonfiction, to work through her loss. At first glance, "Long Beautiful Hair" appears to trace the causes and effects of mundane events familiar to anyone who has had a bad hair day. The depth and direction of Hood's analysis changes, however, when she recalls a hair pact with her daughter. "Long Beautiful Hair" first appeared in the Spring 2010 issue of *Amoskeag*, the literary journal of Southern New Hampshire University.

✧◇✧◇✧◇✧◇✧◇✧◇✧◇✧◇✧◇✧◇✧◇✧◇✧◇✧◇✧◇✧◇✧◇

I blame Kathy Connor for over 30 years of hair disasters. When I met her, back in 1975, I was a hair virgin. I had very long, dirty blond locks that had   1 remained exactly that long for my entire 19 years. Kathy took one look, lifted a hank of hair in her hands, and examined it. "Your hair," she said, "is a mess. Dry. Damaged. Split." Kathy was one of those people who seem infinitely wiser and older than everyone else. She did not wear jeans or Izod shirts. She liked Frank Sinatra music. She knew how to prepare flank steak and cherries jubilee. So when she delivered my hair diagnosis, I listened.

"You need to cut it," she said. I began to sweat. My hair, thick and high-lighted with gold streaks that I carefully painted on every six weeks, was my best feature.

"Like a trim?" I managed to ask. Once a year, I went to the hair salon at the Jordan Marsh department store and let a hairdresser cut an inch or two. This, I believed, kept my tresses looking good. Apparently, I was wrong.

Kathy leaned in for a closer examination. Her face filled with disgust. "At least six inches," she announced.

If only I had been the kind of 19-year-old who did not listen to someone simply because she knew the words to "My Kind of Town,"[1] this story would have ended right there in the living room of the Alpha Xi Delta sorority. Instead, I followed Kathy to the telephone and let her make an appointment for me with a man named Tony at a salon in nearby Providence. A week later, I walked onto South Main Street a different person. My long, beautiful hair had been cut into a Dorothy Hamill wedge.[2] Even worse, as the blond locks fell to the floor, I was left with what lay beneath them: mousy brown roots.

"You look so much better," Kathy said, swinging her own still-long hair. She had gotten a one-inch trim. I had been scalped.

"Uh-huh," I said, peering at my reflection in various store windows as we walked by them. I was skinny back then, and with my hair so short and wearing my standard uniform of khaki pants and a polo shirt, I no longer looked like a pretty girl. To be honest, I didn't look much like a girl at all.

---

1. A song about the city of Chicago made popular by Frank Sinatra.
2. Dorothy Hamill is a U. S. figure skater who won a gold medal in the 1976 Olympics. Her short, wedge-like hairstyle became popular in the 1970s.

That haircut stayed with me throughout college. Whenever I tried to grow it out, I got weird wings on the sides of my face that made me look like the Flying Nun. I tried to adapt to the change: I replaced my Long & Silky shampoo with Short & Sassy. I painted on highlights more frequently, trying to make the best of a bad situation. I pretended I was glad that I attracted attention because of my wit and smarts, rather than a gorgeous head of hair. Truth be told, I missed the weight of all that hair on my shoulders. I missed the way boys grabbed onto it when we kissed. I even missed my split ends, which I held up in the sunlight on lazy afternoons, a book open on my lap, and pulled apart.

Putting unruled events in chronological order, p. 479, can help to straighten out their causes.

After college, when I interviewed with airlines for a job as a flight attendant, the woman at United told me the highlights had to go. "Too brassy," she said, with the same tone of distaste as Kathy Connor.

To remedy my so-called brassy hair, Tony (don't ask me why I went back to him) stripped it completely and recolored it a dishwater-dull ash blond. It was my first real chemical process. And it was just the beginning. War had been declared; my hair was now the enemy.

Shortly after visiting Tony, I decided to grow it long again, thereby kicking off a protracted, torturous growing-out process. Over the next few years, I tried bangs, braids, and bobs. (Why? Because one hairdresser said I had to "go short to go long.") I had perms, highlights, lowlights, root color, and foils. Once I even got the top spiked, which left me with a mullet that could be fixed only by chopping my hair short again. All this was in an effort to have my hair resemble what it had looked like before I met Kathy Connor. But no matter what I did, my 19-year-old self's hair remained elusive.

Or it did until one day when, at the age of 30, I wandered into a fancy New York City salon, saw a beautiful, long-haired stylist named Joy, and told her: "I want your hair." Joy did not believe that you had to go short in order to go long. She worked her magic, and within a few months I had long, gentle layers of blond hair—exactly the way I had wanted it.

I had missed this Me in my decade of short and medium-length hair. Call me shallow and narcissistic, but I liked the way men admired it. I liked walking down a city street in my jeans, cowboy boots, and black leather jacket. And, yes, abundant blond hair.

That should have been the end of my hair saga. Goal achieved; move on to   14
the next thing. But life is not so simple. And so, at age 35, I found myself once
again sitting in a hair salon, wearing a kimono and a towel pinned around my
shoulders. I was pregnant, and suddenly my hair was dull and uncooperative
again. The products that once gave it volume made it so full that I looked like a
country-western singer. And my doctor said no hair color until the baby was
born.

"To the collarbone," I told the stylist. She lifted her scissors and cut.   15

By the time I had my second baby, a few years later, my hair was as short   16
as a British schoolboy's. And, surprisingly, I was OK with that. It was much
easier to care for and kind of sexy, I decided. Plus, it was blonder than ever
before.

That second baby was a girl, whom my husband and I named Grace. And   17
she was blessed with the real thing: pale blond hair that never betrays you by
turning brown. To keep her tangles under control, we cut her hair chin-length
in a chic cut that had longer points in front.

When Grace turned five, she announced that she wanted long hair. It   18
would be beautiful, I thought. Fine and golden. "You grow yours, too," Grace
said. "We'll be even more the same." Grace looked exactly like me. "Deal," I
told her. She didn't have to know how I kept my own hair blond. We sealed our
plan with a sticky kiss.

Grace and I did not get very far in our journey. Before her hair reached her   19
shoulders, she got a virulent form of strep and died within 36 hours. The day of
her funeral, my hairdresser, Jenny, came to our house to fix my hair.

"Cut it," I told her.   20

"Really?" Jenny asked. Her eyes were red and puffy from crying.   21

I couldn't bear to tell her the deal Grace and I had made. I couldn't bear to   22
keep my end of it, alone now. "Really," I said.

Jenny cut it, and for the next two years, as grief kept me in its terrible   23
grasp, I kept it short and dark, as if even my hair had to wear my sorrow.

Time passed. Somehow, it does that. And one spring day in 2007, five years after   24
Grace's death, I walked into a new salon and told the owner, Kim, that I wanted
to grow out my hair. And I wanted it to be blond. Although that might sound as

if I had not traveled very far at all, in fact, that day turned out to be one of the first tentative steps I took back into the world.

Patiently, over the next year, Kim trimmed and shaped so that the 25 growing-out process did not make me look too bad. "You'll be able to wear a ponytail this summer," she said. She was right. That summer I walked along the ocean with my wet hair pulled back. By winter it fell below my collarbone. And now it hangs gently down my back.

Thirty-one years ago, I was a 19-year-old without the self-confidence to 26 ignore bad advice. The fact that, at 50, I have the same hair that I so foolishly relinquished decades earlier does not mean that I am holding on to my youth or am unable to grow older gracefully. No. It means that I am a woman who has teased and sprayed and snipped her way through the decades, to finally land at the place where she feels most herself: as an unapologetic, long-haired blond; as a mother who lost her daughter, slowly, slowly reclaiming the torn pieces of herself.

FOR DISCUSSION

1. When she was nineteen, says Ann Hood, a "friend" instructed her to cut off her long hair (1–4). Hood did as she was told. Why? What should she have done?

2. Hood spent the next decade fretting over the loss of her hair—and trying fruitlessly to get it back. "Call me shallow and narcissistic," she writes (13). Is this a fair assessment? Why or why not?

3. As her "hair saga" unfolds, Hood tells about several occasions when she had her hair shorn or otherwise altered (11, 14–16). In each case, what was the immediate cause of her hair trauma? What were some of the remote causes?

4. That she still wants, more than thirty years later, to have "the same hair" she had at nineteen, says Hood, "does not mean that I am holding on to my youth or am unable to grow older gracefully" (26). What *does* it mean? Explain.

STRATEGIES AND STRUCTURES

. . . .

1. Hood gives no hint at the beginning of her essay that she will be writing, in part, about her reaction to her daughter's death. Should she have? Why or why not?

2. Hood presents major hair events of her life in chronological order. Within each episode, however, she generally gives effects ("I found myself once again sitting in a hair salon") before she gives causes ("I was pregnant") (14). How, and how effectively, does this strategy help to draw the reader into her analysis?

3. In addition to presenting effects before causes in time, Hood presents them in greater detail. Should she have given equal play to causes? Explain.

4. Point out specific passages in her essay where Hood *does* explain (or at least suggest) what caused her to react as she did. Which passages do you find particularly revealing? Why?

5. Hood's hair troubles can be seen as side effects of the events she chronicles. What point is she making by dwelling on these rather than the main effects or their causes?

6. In the last paragraph of her essay, Hood allows her hair to grow back. What are the causes of this final effect? How and how well does it help her to tie up the loose ends, so to speak?

WORDS AND FIGURES OF SPEECH

. . . .

1. Hood's hair references can be seen as instances of METONOMY: her hair is to be associated with, or "stands in for," something of which it is a part. What might that might be? Explain.

2. A *saga* is an epic tale, usually about the adventures of Vikings or other Norsemen (14). Is it inappropriate for Hood to use this term for a mere hair story? Why or why not?

3. What are the implications, in context, of each of the following terms: *virgin* (1), *betrays* (17), *journey* (19)?

4. The "torn pieces" in the last sentence of Hood's essay refer explicitly to her grief over the loss of her daughter. What else might they recall? Explain.

FOR WRITING

. . . .

1. In a paragraph or two, write about an occasion when you allowed someone to convince you to do something that went against your better judgment. Be sure to explain what caused you to give in despite your misgivings.

2. Write a CAUSE-AND-EFFECT analysis of the difficulties (or triumphs) you have experienced as the result of trying to maintain a particular image of yourself—or perception of someone else. Focus on physical causes and consequences, if you like, but try to touch on mental and emotional ones as well.

CHAPTER TWELVE

ARGUMENT

ARGUMENT* is the strategic use of language to convince an AUDIENCE to agree with you on an issue or to act in a way that you think is right—or at least to hear you out, even if they disagree with you. You can convince people in three ways: (1) by appealing to their sense of reason, (2) by appealing to their emotions, and (3) by appealing to their sense of ethics (their standards of what constitutes proper behavior). The essays in this chapter illustrate all three appeals.

When you appeal to a reader's sense of reason, you don't simply declare, "Be reasonable; agree with what I say." You must supply solid EVIDENCE for your claim in the form of facts, examples, statistics, expert testimony, and personal experience. And you must use logical reasoning in presenting that evidence. There are basically two kinds of logical reasoning: INDUCTION and DEDUC-TION. When we use induction, we reason from particulars to generalities: "You have a gun in your house; this whole neighborhood must be vio-lent." When we deduce something, we reason from general premises to particular conclusions: "All guns are dangerous; your family is in danger because you have one in your house."

Nicholas Carr reasons inductively when he examines how he uses the Internet, p. 563.

Of course, a proposition can be logically valid without neces-sarily being true. If "all guns are dangerous," then logically a particular gun must be dangerous as well. Given this general premise (or assumption) about guns, the conclusion about any particular gun's being dangerous is a valid conclusion. The same is true of the following argument: "*No* guns are dangerous; this par-

*Words printed in SMALL CAPITALS are defined in the Glossary/Index.

ticular gun is *not* dangerous." This is a valid argument, too; but here, again, not everyone will accept the first (or major) premise about guns in general. Most real-life debates, in fact, take place because rational people disagree about the truth of one or more of the premises on which their conclusions are based.

Whether an argument uses induction or deduction, it must make an arguable statement or CLAIM. Take, for example, the idea that the world's leaders "should start an international campaign to promote imports from sweatshops." Nicholas D. Kristof argued in favor of this controversial proposition in an article published in the *New York Times* in 2002 entitled "Let Them Sweat." Kristof's essay is an instructive example of how all the techniques of argumentation can work together.

Kristof knows that arguing in favor of sweatshops is likely to be an uphill battle. Like any writer with a point to make, especially a controversial one, he needs to win the reader's trust. One way to do this is to anticipate objections that the reader might raise. So before anyone can accuse him of being totally out of his head for promoting sweatshops, Kristof writes: "The Gentle Reader will think I've been smoking Pakistani opium. But sweatshops are the only hope of kids like Ahmed Zia, 14, here in Attock, a gritty center for carpet weaving."

Right away, Kristof is hoping to convince his audience that they are hearing the words of an ethical person who deserves to be heeded. Next, he tugs at the readers' heartstrings:

> Ahmed earns $2 a day hunched over the loom, laboring over a rug that will adorn some American's living room. It is a pittance, but the American campaign against sweatshops could make his life much more wretched by inadvertently encouraging mechanization that could cost him his job.
>
> "Carpet-making is much better than farm work," Ahmed said. "This makes much more money and is more comfortable."

Underlying Kristof's emotional appeal in citing Ahmed's case is the logical claim that Ahmed's plight is representative of that of most factory workers in poor countries. "Indeed," writes Kristof, "talk to Third World factory workers and the whole idea of 'sweatshops' seems a misnomer. It is farmers and brick-makers who really sweat under the broiling sun, while sweatshop workers merely glow."

The same claim—that other cases are like this one—also lies behind Kristof's second example: "But before you spurn a shirt made by someone like Kamis Saboor, 8, an Afghan refugee whose father is dead and who is the sole breadwinner in the family, answer this question: How does shunning sweatshop products help Kamis? All the alternatives for him are worse." Kristof is appealing to the reader's emotions and sense of ethics, and he is using logical reasoning. If we grant Kristof's premise that in really poor countries "all the alternatives" to sweatshop labor are worse, we must logically concede his main point that, for these workers, "a sweatshop job is the first step on life's escalator" and, therefore, that sweatshops are to be supported.

Kristof has not finished marshaling his reasons and evidence yet. To strengthen his argument, he introduces another, broader example, one that Americans are more likely to be familiar with:

Nike has 35 contract factories in Taiwan, 49 in South Korea, only three in Pakistan, and none at all in Afghanistan—if it did, critics would immediately fulminate about low wages, glue vapors, the mistreatment of women.

But the losers are the Afghans, and especially Afghan women. The country is full of starving widows who can find no jobs. If Nike hired them at 10 cents an hour to fill all-female sweatshops, they and their country would be hugely better off.

Nike used to have two contract factories in impoverished Cambodia, among the neediest countries in the world. Then there was an outcry after BBC reported that three girls in one factory were under 15 years old. So Nike fled controversy by ceasing production in Cambodia.

The result was that some of the 2,000 Cambodians (90 percent of them young women) who worked in three factories faced layoffs. Some who lost their jobs probably were ensnared in Cambodia's huge sex slave industry—which leaves many girls dead of AIDS by the end of their teenage years.

We can object to Kristof's premises. Can the widows of Afghanistan find no decent jobs whatsoever? Will they actually starve if they don't? Will some of the young women of Cambodia die of AIDS because Nike has pulled out of their impoverished country? (Notice that Kristof qualifies this assertion with "probably.") We can even dispute Kristof's reasoning based on statistics. In statistics, when it is not possible to poll every individual in the set being analyzed, sound practice requires at least a representative sampling. Has Kristof given us a truly representative sampling of *all* the workers in Third World sweatshops?

We can pick away at Kristof's logic—as have many of his critics since this article was first published. But with the exception of a court of law, a good argument does not have to prove its point beyond a shadow of a doubt. It only has to convince the reader. Whether or not you're convinced by Kristof's argument, you can learn from the tactics he uses to support his position.

A BRIEF GUIDE TO WRITING AN ARGUMENT

When you construct an ARGUMENT, you take a position on an issue and then support that position, as Nicholas D. Kristof does in his argument in favor of sweatshops. So the first moves you need to make as you write an argument are to identify the subject or issue you are addressing and to state the claim you are making about it. Here's how Mark D. White and Robert Arp make these fundamental moves near the beginning of their argument in this chapter:

> Pop culture, such as the Batman comics and movies, provides an opportunity to think philosophically about issues and topics that parallel the real world. For instance, thinking about why Batman has never killed the Joker may help us reflect on the nation's issues with terror and torture, specifically their ethics.
> —MARK D. WHITE AND ROBERT ARP, "Should Batman Kill the Joker?"

White and Arp identify the subject of their argument (pop culture) and state their claim about it ("provides an opportunity to think philosophically about issues and topics"). Next they narrow the broad field of pop culture to a specific topic ("why Batman has never killed the Joker") and a more limited claim ("may help us reflect on the nation's issues with terror and torture").

The following guidelines will help you make these basic moves as you draft an argument. They will also help you support your claim with reasoning and evidence, avoid logical fallacies, appeal to your readers' emotions and sense of ethics, and anticipate other arguments.

Coming Up with a Claim

Unlike a statement of fact (broccoli is a vegetable) or personal taste (I hate broccoli), a CLAIM is a statement that is debatable, that rational people can disagree with. We can all agree, for example, that pop culture has something to teach us. We might reasonably disagree, however, on what those lessons are. To come up with a claim, think of issues that are debatable: Batman is (is not) a sterling model of ethical behavior. Broccoli provides (does not provide) more health benefits than any other vegetable. Genetic factors are (are not) the main determiners of personality. The risks of climate change have (have not) been exaggerated by the scientific community. Before you decide on a particular claim, make sure it is one you actually care about enough to argue it persuasively. If you don't care much about your topic, your readers probably won't either.

For more debatable claims, see the debate clusters on pp. 558 and 577.

Considering Your Purpose and Audience

The PURPOSE of an argument is to convince other people to listen thoughtfully to what you have to say—even if they don't completely accept your views. Whatever your claim, your argument is more likely to appeal to your audience if it is tailored to their particular needs and interests. Suppose, for example, that you have a friend who habitually sends text messages while driving even though she knows it's dangerous. You think your friend should put down her phone while driving—or pull over when she needs to text. Your friend might be more likely to agree with you if, in addition to citing statistics on increased traffic deaths due to driving while texting, you also pointed out that she was setting a bad example for her younger sister.

So think about what your audience's views on the particular issue are likely to be. Of all the evidence you might present in support of your case, what kind would your intended readers most likely find reasonable and, thus, convincing?

Generating Ideas: Finding Effective Evidence

Suppose you want to argue that the SAT is unfair because it is biased in favor of the wealthy. To support a claim like this effectively, you can use *facts, statistics, examples, expert testimony,* and *personal experience.*

FACTS. To argue that the SAT favors the wealthy, you might cite facts about the cost of tutors for the test: "In New York City, a company called Advantage charges $500 for 50 minutes of coaching with their most experienced tutors."

STATISTICS. You could cite statistics about income and text scores: "On the 2008 SAT, students with family incomes of more than $200,000 had an average math score of 570, while those with family incomes up to $20,000 had an average score of 456."

EXAMPLES. You could discuss a question from an actual SAT exam that might show SAT bias. The following question asks the test taker to select a pair of words whose relationship matches the relationship expressed by RUNNER : MARA-THON. The choices are (A) envoy : embassy; (B) martyr : massacre; (C) oars-man : regatta; (D) referee : tournament; (E) horse : stable. The correct answer is C: an oarsman competes in a regatta, an organized boat race, in much the same way as a runner competes in a marathon. But because regattas are largely a pursuit of the wealthy, you could argue that the question favors the wealthy test taker.

EXPERT TESTIMONY. You might quote a statement like this one by Richard Atkinson, former president of the University of California: "Anyone involved in education should be concerned about how overemphasis on the SAT is distorting educational priorities and practices [and] how the test is perceived by many as unfair. . . ."

A works-cited list like the one on p. 574 can help to identify your sources.

PERSONAL EXPERIENCE. The following anecdote reveals, in a personal way, how the SAT favors certain socioeconomic groups: "No one in my family ever participated in a regatta—as a high school student, I didn't even know the meaning of the word. So when I took the SAT and encountered analogy questions that referred to regattas and other unfamiliar things, I barely broke 600 on the verbal aptitude section."

No matter what type of evidence you present, it must be pertinent to your argument and sufficient to convince your audience that your claim is worth taking seriously. It should also be presented to the reader in a well-organized fashion that makes sense logically.

Templates for Arguing

The following templates can help you to generate ideas for an argument and then to start drafting. Don't take these as formulas where you just have to fill in the blanks. There are no easy formulas for good writing, though these templates can help you plot out some of the key moves of argumentation and thus may serve as good starting points.

> ▶ In this argument about X, the main point I want to make is _____.
>
> ▶ Others may say _____, but I would argue that _____.
>
> ▶ My contention about X is supported by the fact that _____.
>
> ▶ Additional facts that support this view of X are _____, _____, and _____.
>
> ▶ My own experience with X shows that _____ because _____.
>
> ▶ My view of X is supported by _____, who says that X is _____.
>
> ▶ What you should do about X is _____.

For more techniques to help you generate ideas and start writing an argument, see Chapter 2.

Organizing an Argument

Any well-constructed argument is organized around a claim and support for that claim. Here is a straightforward plan that can be effective for most argument essays. You may, of course, need to supplement or modify this plan to fit a particular topic.

1. In your *introduction*, identify your topic and state your claim clearly. Indicate why you're making this claim and why the reader should be interested in it. Make sure your topic is narrow enough to be covered in the time and space allotted.

2. In the main *body* of your argument, introduce an important example, or a solid piece of evidence, that is likely to catch your reader's attention; then use a clear, logical organization to present the rest of your support. For example, move from your weakest point to your strongest. Or vice versa.

3. Deal with *counterarguments* at appropriate points throughout your essay.

4. In the *conclusion*, restate your claim—and why you're making it—and sum up how the evidence supports that claim.

Narrowing and Stating Your Claim

State your claim clearly at the beginning of your argument—and take care not to claim more than you can possibly prove in one essay. "Sweatshops are acceptable," for example, is too broad to work as an arguable claim. Acceptable for whom, we might ask? Under what circumstances?

To narrow this claim, we could restate it as follows: "In very poor countries, sweatshops are acceptable." This claim could be still more restricted, however: "In very poor countries, sweatshops are acceptable *when the alternatives are even worse.*" Because it is narrower, this is a more supportable claim than the one we started with.

Using Logical Reasoning: Induction and Deduction

In many writing situations, logical reasoning is indispensable for persuading others that your ideas and opinions are valid. As we noted in the introduction, there are two main kinds of logical reasoning, induction and deduction. Induction is reasoning from particular evidence to a general conclusion. It is based on probability and draws a conclusion from a limited number of specific cases. You reason inductively when you observe the cost of a gallon of gas at half a dozen service stations and conclude that the price of gas is uniformly high. In contrast to induction, deduction moves from general principles to a particular conclusion. You reason deductively when your car stops running and—knowing that cars need fuel, that you started with half a tank and have been driving all day—you conclude that you are out of gas.

Deductive arguments can be stated as SYLLOGISMS, which have a major premise, a minor premise, and a conclusion. For example:

> **Major premise:** All scientific theories should be taught in science classes.
> **Minor premise:** Intelligent design is a scientific theory.
> **Conclusion:** Intelligent design should be taught in science classes.

According to Steven Pinker, p. 559, the major premise of most media critics is "You are what you eat."

This is a valid syllogism, meaning that the conclusion follows logically from the premises. (Remember however, that *validity* in a deductive argument is not the same as *truth.*)

The great advantage of deduction over induction is that it deals with logical certainty rather than mere probability. As long as a deductive argument is properly constructed, the conclusion must be valid. The conclusion can still be untrue, however, if one or more of the premises is false. The following syllogism, for example, is properly constructed (the conclusion follows logically from the premises), but not everyone would agree that the major premise is true:

Major premise: Only people who have tattoos are cool.
Minor premise: Robin got a tattoo on her shoulder last weekend.
Conclusion: Robin is cool.

Advertisers use this kind of faulty reasoning all the time to try to convince you that you must buy their products if you want to be a cool person. Many people, however, would consider the major premise false; there are lots of cool people who don't have tattoos at all, so the reasoning is faulty.

You can also run into trouble when you know that some of your readers may disagree with your premises but you still want to convince them to accept (or at least think seriously about) your conclusion. For example, if you are arguing that a particular firearm is not dangerous because "no guns are dangerous," many readers are likely to take exception with your reasoning. What to do?

One tactic would be to tone down your major premise. Your ultimate purpose in constructing any argument, after all, is to convince readers to accept your *conclusion.* So instead of the (obviously loaded) premise that "no guns are dangerous," you might instead restate your premise as follows: "Not all guns are dangerous." That a particular gun is safe does not necessarily follow from this premise, but more readers may be inclined to accept it—and thus more likely to take your conclusion seriously—especially if the rest of your evidence is strong, and you avoid obvious blunders in logic.

Avoiding Logical Fallacies

LOGICAL FALLACIES are errors in logical reasoning. Here are some of the most common logical fallacies to watch out for:

POST HOC, ERGO PROPTER HOC.　Assuming that just because one event (such as rain) comes after another event (a rain dance), it therefore occurs *because* of the first event: "From 1995 to 2005, as the Internet grew, the number of new babies named Jennifer grew by 30 percent." The increase in "Jennifers" may have followed the spread of the Internet, but the greater Internet use didn't necessarily *cause* the increase.

NON SEQUITUR.   A statement that has no logical connection to the preceding statement: "The early Egyptians were masters of architecture. Thus they created a vast network of trade throughout the ancient world." Since mastering architecture has little to do with expanding trade, this second statement is a *non sequitur.*

BEGGING THE QUESTION.   Taking for granted what is supposed to be proved: "Americans should be required to carry ID cards because Americans need to be prepared to prove their identity." Instead of addressing the claim that Americans should be required to prove their identity by having an ID card that verifies it, the "because" statement takes that claim for granted.

APPEAL TO DOUBTFUL AUTHORITY.   Citing as expert testimony the opinions of people who are not experts on the issue: "According to David Letterman, the candidate who takes Ohio will win the election." Letterman isn't an expert on politics.

AD HOMINEM.   Attacking the person making an argument instead of addressing the actual issue: "She's too young to be head of the teachers' union, so why listen to her views on wages?" Saying she's too young focuses on her as a person rather than on her views on the issue.

To avoid this fallacy, Joe Posnanski refers to a fellow sportswriter as "my great good friend," p. 584.

EITHER/OR REASONING.   Treating a complicated issue as if it had only two sides: "Either you believe that God created the universe, or you believe that the universe evolved randomly." This statement doesn't allow for beliefs outside of these two options.

HASTY GENERALIZATION.   Drawing a conclusion based on far too little evidence: "In the four stories by Edgar Allan Poe that we read, the narrator is mentally ill. Poe himself must have been insane." There is not nearly enough evidence here to determine Poe's mental health.

FALSE ANALOGY.   Making a faulty comparison: "Children are like dogs. A happy dog is a disciplined dog, and a happy child is one who knows the rules and is taught to obey them." Dogs and children aren't alike enough to assume that what is good for one is necessarily good for the other.

RED HERRING.   Leading the reader off on a false scent, away from the main argument: "Sure, my paper is full of spelling errors. But English is not a very phonetic language. Now if we were writing in Spanish . . ."

OVERSIMPLIFICATION.   Assigning insufficient causes to explain an effect or justify a conclusion: "In a school budget crunch, art and music classes should be eliminated first because these subjects are not very practical." This argument is oversimplified because it doesn't admit that there are other reasons, besides practicality, for keeping a subject in the school curriculum.

Appealing to Your Readers' Emotions

Sound logical reasoning is hard to refute, but appealing to your readers' emotions can also be an effective way to convince them to accept—or at least listen to—your argument. In a January 2009 follow-up to his 2002 argument in favor of sweatshops, Nicholas D. Kristof writes:

> The miasma of toxic stink leaves you gasping, breezes batter you with filth, and even the rats look forlorn. Then the smoke parts and you come across a child ambling barefoot, searching for old plastic cups that recyclers will buy for five cents a pound.
> —NICHOLAS D. KRISTOF, "Where Sweatshops Are a Dream"

Kristof is describing a gigantic garbage dump in Phnom Penh, Cambodia, where whole families try to eke out a living under inhumane conditions. Compared to this "Dante-like vision of hell," Kristof argues, "sweltering at a sewing machine" seems like an unattainable dream. By making us feel the desperation of the people he describes, Kristof is clearly tugging at the readers' heartstrings—before going on to supply more facts and examples to support his claim.

Establishing Your Own Credibility

When you construct an argument, you can demonstrate with irrefutable logic that what you have to say is valid and true. And you can appeal to your readers' emotions with genuine fervor. Your words may still fall on deaf ears, however, if your readers don't fully trust you. Here are a few tips to help you establish trust:

- *Present issues objectively.* Acknowledge opposing points of view, and treat them fairly and accurately. If you have experience or expertise in your subject, let your readers know. For example, Kristof tells his readers, "My views on sweatshops are shaped by years living in East Asia, watching as living standards soared—including those in my wife's ancestral village in southern China—because of sweatshop jobs."

- *Pay close attention to the* TONE *of your argument.* Whether you come across as calm and reasonable or full of righteous anger, your tone will say much about your own values and motives for writing—and about you as a person.

- *Convince your readers* that they are listening to the words of a moral and ethical person who shares their values and understands their concerns.

Anticipating Other Arguments

As you construct an argument, it's important to consider viewpoints other than your own, including objections that others might raise. Anticipating other arguments, in fact, is yet another way to establish your credibility. Readers are more likely to see you as trustworthy if, instead of ignoring an opposing argument, you state it fairly and accurately and then refute it. Kristof knows that many readers will disagree with his position on sweatshops, so he acknowledges the opposition up front before going on to give his evidence for his position:

Johnson C. Montgomery admits, p. 542, that opponents may find his position "inhumane."

> When I defend sweatshops, people always ask me: But would you want to work in a sweatshop? No, of course not. But I would want even less to pull a rickshaw. . . . I often hear the argument: Labor standards can

improve wages and working conditions, without greatly affecting the eventual retail cost of goods. That's true. But . . .

—NICHOLAS D. KRISTOF, "Where Sweatshops Are a Dream"

You still may not agree with Kristof's position that sweatshops are a good idea. But you're more likely to listen to what he, or any other writer, has to say if you think that person has thought carefully about all aspects of the issue, including points of view opposed to his or her own.

EDITING FOR COMMON ERRORS IN ARGUMENTS

As with other modes of writing, certain errors in punctuation and usage are common in arguments. The following guidelines will help you spot such problems and edit them appropriately.

Check to see that you've correctly punctuated the following connecting words: *if, therefore, thus, consequently, however, nevertheless*, and *because*

When the connecting word comes at the beginning of a sentence and links the statement you're making to earlier statements, it should be followed by a comma:

- ▶ Therefore, stronger immigration laws will not be necessary.
- ▶ Consequently, the minimum drinking age should be lowered to age 18.

When the connecting word comes at the beginning of a sentence and is part of an introductory clause—a group of words that includes a subject and a verb—the entire clause should be followed by a comma:

- ▶ Because guest workers will be legally registered, stronger immigration laws will be unnecessary.
- ▶ If people are old enough to vote and go to war, they're old enough to drink responsibly.

▶ If recent statistics from the Department of Transportation are accurate, far fewer people die when the legal drinking age is 21 instead of 18.

When the connecting word indicates a relationship—such as cause and effect, logical sequence, or comparison—between two independent clauses, it is usually preceded by a semicolon and followed by a comma:

▶ Many of the best surgeons have the highest rates of malpractice; thus, the three-strikes-and-you're-out rule for taking away a doctor's license may do more harm than good.

When the connecting word comes in the middle of an independent clause, it should usually be set off by commas:

▶ A surgeon who removes the wrong leg, however, deserves a somewhat harsher penalty than one who forgets to remove a sponge.

Check for common errors in usage

HOWEVER, NEVERTHELESS

Use *however* when you acknowledge a different argument but want to minimize its consequence:

▶ The surgeon may have been negligent; ~~nevertheless,~~ <u>however,</u> he should not lose his license because the patient lied about the dosage he was taking.

Use *nevertheless* when you acknowledge a different argument but wish to argue for a harsher consequence anyway:

▶ The surgeon may not have been negligent; ~~however,~~ <u>nevertheless,</u> he should lose his license because the patient died.

IMPLY, INFER

Use *imply* when you mean "to state indirectly":

- The coach's speech ~~inferred~~ implied that he expected the team to lose the game.

Use *infer* when you mean "to draw a conclusion":

- From the coach's speech, I ~~implied~~ inferred that the team would lose the game.

EVERYDAY ARGUMENT
T-shirt on a Stick

When you construct an argument, you make a claim and support it with evidence. Your purpose is to convince readers to accept your claim and perhaps even to act on it. The main purpose of the folks who run the shop in Des Moines, Iowa, where this T-shirt was purchased is, of course, to sell T-shirts. Iowa, however, is home to one of the grandest state fairs in the country. This T-shirt, featuring . . . a T-shirt on a stick, is also intended, in a tongue-in-check way, to promote the fair. Yessiree, Bob. Been there, done that—and got the T-shirt? What about a hot dog (or pretzel or fried ice cream) on a stick? Makes it mighty handy to walk around and see all the booths—or the butter cow, tractor pull, llama judging, giant tomatoes, and chain-saw art.

LIZ ADDISON

TWO YEARS ARE BETTER THAN FOUR

In "Two Years Are Better Than Four," Liz Addison argues that community colleges are "one of America's great institutions." A graduate of Southern Maine Community College, Addison submitted her essay to a national college writing contest sponsored by the *New York Times* magazine. The topic: to respond to "What's the Matter with College," an opinion piece by the historian Rick Perlstein, published online by the *Times* in July 2007. A graduate of an elite four-year university, Perlstein argued that colleges "seem to have lost their centrality" in American culture. Approximately 600 students from institutions across the country took up the challenge, and Addison's rebuttal was chosen as one of four runners-up.

Two Years Are Better Than Four

Oh, the hand wringing. "College as America used to understand it is coming to an end," bemoans Rick Perlstein and his beatnik friend of fallen face. Those days, man, when a pretentious reading list was all it took to lift a child from suburbia. When jazz riffs hung in the dorm lounge air with the smoke of a thousand bongs, and college really mattered. Really mattered?

Rick Perlstein thinks so. It mattered so much to him that he never got over his four years at the University of Privilege. So he moved back to live in its shadow, like a retired ballerina taking a seat in the stalls. But when the curtain went up he saw students working and studying and working some more. Adults before their time. Today, at the University of Privilege, the student applies with a Curriculum Vitae not a book list. Shudder.

Thus, Mr. Perlstein concludes, the college experience—a rite of passage as it was meant it to be—must have come to an end. But he is wrong. For Mr. Perlstein, so rooted in his own nostalgia, is looking for himself—and he would never think to look for himself in the one place left where the college experience of self-discovery does still matter to those who get there. My guess, reading between the lines, is that Mr. Perlstein has never set foot in an American community college.

The philosophy of the community college, and I have been to two of them, is one that unconditionally allows its students to begin. Just begin. Implicit in this belief is the understanding that anything and everything is possible. Just follow any one of the 1,655 road signs, and pop your head inside—yes, they let anyone in—and there you will find discoveries of a first independent film, a first independent thought, a first independent study. This college experience remains as it should. This college brochure is not marketing for the parents—because the parents, nor grandparents, probably never went to college themselves.

Upon entry to my first community college I had but one   5
O'level to my name. These now disbanded qualifications once marked the transition from lower to upper high school in the Great British education system. It was customary for the average student to proceed forward with a clutch of O'levels, say eight or nine. On a score of one, I left school hurriedly at sixteen. Thomas Jefferson once wrote, "Everybody should have an education proportional to their life." In my case, my life became proportional to my education. But, in doing so, it had the good fortune to land me in an American community college and now, from that priceless springboard, I too seek admission to the University of Privilege. Enter on empty and leave with a head full of dreams? How can Mr. Perlstein say college does not matter anymore?

Writer's claim is based on an ideal of "public service"

The community college system is America's hidden public   6
service gem. If I were a candidate for office I would campaign from every campus. Not to score political points, but simply to make sure that anyone who is looking to go to college in this country knows where to find one. Just recently, I read an article in the *New York Times* describing a "college application essay" workshop for low-income students. I was strangely disturbed that those interviewed made no mention of community college. Mr. Perlstein might have been equally disturbed,

for the thrust of the workshop was no different to that of an essay coach to the affluent. "Make Life Stories Shine," beams the headline. Or, in other words, prove yourself worldly, insightful, cultured, mature, before you get to college.

Yet, down at X.Y.C.C. it is still possible to enter the college experience as a rookie. That is the understanding— that you will grow up a little bit with your first English class, a bit more with your first psychology class, a whole lot more with your first biology, physics, chemistry. That you may shoot through the roof with calculus, philosophy, or genetics. "College is the key," a young African American student writes for the umpteenth torturous revision of his college essay, "as well as hope." Oh, I wanted desperately to say, please tell him about community college. Please tell him that hope can begin with just one placement test.

7

When Mr. Perlstein and friends say college no longer holds importance, they mourn for both the individual and society. Yet, arguably, the community college experience is more critical to the nation than that of former beatnik types who, lest we forget, did not change the world. The community colleges of America cover this country college by college and community by community. They offer a network of affordable future, of accessible hope, and an option to dream. In the cold light of day, is it perhaps not more important to foster students with dreams rather than a building take-over?

8

I believe so. I believe the community college system to be one of America's uniquely great institutions. I believe it should be celebrated as such. "For those who find it necessary

9

Conclusion restates the writer's claim as a matter of "belief" to go to a two-year college," begins one University of Privilege admissions paragraph. None too subtle in its implication, but very true. For some students, from many backgrounds, would never breathe the college experience if it were not for the community college. Yes, it is here that Mr. Perlstein will find his college years of self-discovery, and it is here he will find that college does still matter.

JOHNSON C. MONTGOMERY

THE ISLAND OF PLENTY

Johnson C. Montgomery (1934–1974) was a California attorney and an early member of the organization Zero Population Growth. Montgomery's "The Island of Plenty," which first appeared as a "My Turn" column in *Newsweek* in 1974, is an argument in favor of American social isolationism. Until we have enough food to feed all Americans plentifully, Montgomery reasons, Americans should not share their material resources with other countries of the world.

◈◇◈◇◈◇◈◇◈◇◈◇◈◇◈◇◈◇◈◇◈◇◈◇◈◇◈◇◈◇◈◇◈◇◈◇◈

T he United States should remain an island of plenty in a sea of hunger. The   1
future of mankind is at stake. We are not responsible for the   A good argument
rest of humanity. We should not accept responsibility for all human-   makes a claim that
ity. We owe more to the hundreds of billions of *Homo futurans* than   rational people can
disagree with.
we do to the hungry millions—soon to be billions—of our own generations.

Ample food and resources exist to nourish man and all other creatures   2
indefinitely into the future. This planet is indeed an Eden—to date our only
Eden. Admittedly our Eden is plagued by pollution. Some of us have polluted
the planet by reproducing too many of us. Too many people have made excessive demands on the long-range carrying capacity of our garden; and during the

last 200 years there has been dramatic, ever-increasing destruction of the web of life on earth. If we try to save the starving millions today, we will simply destroy what's left of Eden.

The problem is not that there is too little food. The problem is there are too many people—many too many. It is not that the children should never have been born. It is simply that we have mindlessly tried to cram too many of us into too short a time span. Four billion humans are fine—but they should have been spread over several hundred years.[1]

But the billions are already here. What should we do about them? Should we send food, knowing that each child saved in Southeast Asia, India or Africa will probably live to reproduce and thereby bring more people into the world to live even more miserably? Should we eat the last tuna fish, the last ear of corn, and utterly destroy the garden? That is what we have been doing for a long time and all the misguided efforts have merely increased the number who go to bed hungry each night. There have never been more miserable, deprived people in the world than there are right now.

It was obvious even in the late 1950s that the famine the world now faces was coming unless people immediately began exercising responsibility for reducing population levels. It was also obvious that too many people contributed to the risk of nuclear war, global pestilence, illiteracy, and even to many problems that are usually classified as purely economic. For example, unemployment is having too many people for the available jobs. Inflation is in part the result of too much demand from too many people. But in the 1950s, population control was taboo and those who warned of impending disasters received a cool reception.

By the time Zero Population Growth, Inc.,[2] was formed, those of us who wanted to do something useful decided to concentrate our initial efforts on our own families and friends and then on the white American middle and upper classes. Our belief was that by setting an example, we could later insist that others pay attention to our proposals.

---

1. World population is estimated to have surpassed seven billion in 2012.

2. International movement founded in 1968; its original goal was to limit the birth rate in the United States and other developed countries.

I think I was the first in the original ZPG group to have had a vasectomy. 7
Nancy and I had two children—each doing superbly well and each getting all
the advantages of the best nutrition, education, attention, love, and other resources
available. I think Paul Ehrlich[3] (one child) was the next. Now don't ask me to
cut my children back to the same number of calories that children from large
families eat. In fact, don't ask me to cut my children back on anything. I won't
do it without a fight; and in today's world, power is in knowledge, not numbers.
Nancy and I made a conscious decision to limit the number of our children so
each child could have a larger share of whatever we could make available. We
intend to keep the best for them.

The future of mankind is indeed with the children. But it is with the 8
nourished, educated, and loved children. It is not with the starving, uneducated,
and ignored. This is of course a highly elitist point of view. But that doesn't make
the view incorrect. As a matter of fact, the lowest reproductive rate in the nation
is that of one of the most elite groups in the world—black, female Ph.D.'s. They
had to be smart and effective to make it. Having made it, they are smart enough
not to wreck it with too many kids.

We in the United States have made great progress in lowering our birth 9
rates. But now, because we have been responsible, it seems to some that we
have a great surplus. There is, indeed, waste that should be eliminated, but
there is not as much fat in our system as most people think. Yet we are being
asked to share our resources with the hungry peoples of the world. But why
should we share? The nations having the greatest needs are those that have
been the least responsible in cutting down on births. Famine is one of nature's
ways of telling profligate peoples that they have been irresponsible in their
breeding habits.

Naturally, we would like to help; and if we could, perhaps we should. But 10
we can't be of any use in the long run—particularly if we weaken ourselves.

Until we have at least a couple of years' supply of food and other resources 11
on hand to take care of our own people and until those asking for handouts are
doing at least as well as we are at reducing existing excessive population-

3. Biology professor at Stanford, founder and past president of Zero Population Growth.

growth rates, we should not give away our resources—not so much as one bushel of wheat. Certainly we should not participate in any programs that will increase the burden that mankind is already placing on the earth. We should not deplete our own soils to save those who will only die equally miserably a decade or so down the line—and in many cases only after reproducing more children who are inevitably doomed to live and die in misery.

We know the world is finite. There is only so much pie. We may be able to expand the pie, but at any point in time, the pie is finite. How big a piece each person gets depends in part on how many people there are. At least for the foreseeable future, the fewer of us there are, the more there will be for each. That is true on a family, community, state, national, and global basis.

At the moment, the future of mankind seems to depend on our maintaining the island of plenty in a sea of deprivation. If everyone shared equally, we would all be suffering from protein-deficiency brain damage—and that would probably be true even if we ate every last animal on earth.

As compassionate human beings, we grieve for the condition of mankind. But our grief must not interfere with our perception of reality and our planning for a better future for those who will come after us. Someone must protect the material and intellectual seed grain for the future. It seems to me that that someone is the U.S. We owe it to our children—and to their children's children's children's children.

These conclusions will be attacked, as they have been within Zero Population Growth, as simplistic and inhumane. But truth is often very simple and reality often inhumane.

FOR DISCUSSION

. . . .

1. What is Johnson C. Montgomery's main CLAIM?

2. Which of Montgomery's reasons for his position do you find most PERSUASIVE? Why? What counterarguments would you make?

3. In paragraph 4, what is the last sentence intended to prove? Why do you think Montgomery includes it?

4. Montgomery warns us not to ask him "to cut my children back on anything" (7). How is this position consistent with what he says about there not being enough food to go around?

STRATEGIES AND STRUCTURES

1. The logic of Montgomery's ARGUMENT can be represented by a SYLLOGISM:

> **Major premise:** To provide undamaged human stock for the future, some people must remain healthy.
>
> **Minor premise:** All will suffer if all share equally in the world's limited bounty.
>
> **Conclusion:** Therefore, some must not share what they have.

How sound is this logic? Do you think Montgomery's premises, particularly the second one, are true? Why or why not?

2. The purpose of Montgomery's essay is not only to present his version of "reality," but also to convince us to act (15). What would Montgomery have us do?

3. Logic is only part of Montgomery's persuasive arsenal. Where does he appeal more to emotion and ethics than to logic? Give examples from the text.

4. Montgomery seems to be speaking from a position of authority. Where does he get his authority, and how much weight does it carry, in your opinion?

5. Montgomery admits that his position is elitist (8). How does he anticipate the objection that it is racist?

6. Montgomery's argument is based on a COMPARISON. What is he comparing to what? Which points of his comparison do you find most convincing? Least convincing? Why?

WORDS AND FIGURES OF SPEECH

1. How does the METAPHOR of the island contribute to the author's argument?

2. For the sake of the future, he says we must save "material and intellectual seed grain" (14). Explain this metaphor. What does he compare to what?

3. Montgomery's coinage *Homo futurans*, meaning "man of the future," is modeled after such scientific terms as *Homo erectus* ("upright man") and *Homo sapiens* ("thinking man"). Why do you think Montgomery uses the language of science at the beginning of his argument?

4. How does Montgomery's use of the word "mindlessly" epitomize his entire argument (3)?

5. What is the meaning of "profligate" (9)? Why does Montgomery use this term?

FOR WRITING

1. Write an essay agreeing or disagreeing with Montgomery's position, particularly his assumption that "the future of mankind seems to depend on our maintaining the island of plenty in a sea of deprivation" (13).

2. Read Jonathan Swift's "A Modest Proposal" in the next chapter, and write a "modest proposal" of your own in which you argue for a way to solve one of the world's great problems—such as feeding the masses, sharing the world's wealth, regulating human breeding habits, reversing climate change, or eliminating terrorism.

MARK D. WHITE AND ROBERT ARP

SHOULD BATMAN KILL
THE JOKER?

Mark D. White is a professor of political science, economics, and philosophy at the College of Staten Island of the City University of New York. He is the co-editor with Irene van Staveren of *Ethics and Economics* (2009). Robert Arp is a specialist in biomedical ethics and the philosophy of biology and an associate of the Analysis Group of Falls Church, Virginia, a company that provides technical and operational support for national security clients. He is the author of *Scenario Visualization: An Evolutionary Account of Creative Problem Solving* (2008). Together, White and Arp have edited a collection of essays, *Batman and Philosophy: The Dark Knight of the Soul* (2008). In "Should Batman Kill the Joker?" first published in the *Boston Globe* in 2008, they argue for the value of pop culture in helping us explore ethical approaches to real-world issues.

❖∿∧∿∧∿❖∿∧∿∧∿❖∿∧∿∧∿❖∿∧∿∧∿❖∿∧∿∧∿❖∿∧∿∧∿❖∿∧∿∧∿❖∿∧∿❖∿∧∿❖

Batman should kill the Joker. How many of us would agree with that? Quite a few, we'd wager. Even Heath Ledger's Joker in *The Dark Knight* marvels at Batman's refusal to kill him. After all, the Joker is a murderous psychopath,   1 and Batman could save countless innocent lives by ending his miserable existence once and for all.

Of course, there are plenty of masked loonies ready to take the Joker's place, but none of them has ever shown the same twisted devotion to chaos and tragedy as the Clown Prince of Crime.

But if we say that Batman should kill the Joker, doesn't that imply that we should torture terror suspects if there's a chance of getting information that could save innocent lives? Of course, terror is all too present in the real world, and Batman only exists in the comics and movies. So maybe we're just too detached from the Dark Knight and the problems of Gotham City, so we can say "go ahead, kill him." But, if anything, that detachment implies that there's more at stake in the real world—so why aren't we tougher on actual terrorists than we are on the make-believe Joker?

Pop culture, such as the Batman comics and movies, provides an opportunity to think philosophically about issues and topics that parallel the real world. For instance, thinking about why Batman has never killed the Joker may help us reflect on the nation's issues with terror and torture, specifically their ethics.

Three major schools of ethics provide some perspective on Batman's quandary.

Utilitarianism, based on the work of Jeremy Bentham and John Stuart Mill,[1] would probably endorse killing the Joker, based on comparing the many lives saved against the one life lost.

Deontology, stemming largely from the writings of Immanuel Kant,[2] would focus on the act of murder itself, rather than the consequences. Kant's position would be more ambiguous than the utilitarian's: While it may be preferable for the Joker to be dead, it may not be morally right for any person (such as Batman) to kill him. If the Joker is to be punished, it should be through official procedures, not vigilante justice. More generally, while the Joker is evil, he is still a human being, and is thus deserving of at least a minimal level of respect and humanity.

For advice on appealing to the reader's sense of ethics, see p. 517.

---

1. Mill (1806–1873) and Bentham (1748–1832) were British philosophers and social reformers.

2. German philosopher (1724–1804) whose works include treatises on reason and ethics.

Finally, virtue ethics, dating back to the ancient Greeks (such as Aristotle[3]), would highlight the character of the person who kills the Joker. Does Batman want to be the kind of person that takes his enemies' lives? If he killed the Joker, would he be able to stop there, or would every two-bit thug get the same treatment? 8

Taking these three ethical perspectives together, we see that while there are good reasons to kill the Joker, in terms of innocent lives saved, there are also good reasons not to kill him, based on what killing him would mean about Batman and his motives, mission, and character. 9

The same arguments apply to the debate over torture: While there are good reasons to do it, based on the positive consequences that may come from it, there are also good reasons not to, especially those based on our national character. Many Americans who oppose torture explain their position by saying, "It's not who we are" or "We don't want to turn into them." Batman often says the same thing when asked why he hasn't killed the Joker: "I don't want to become that which I hate." 10

Applying philosophy to Batman, *South Park*, or other pop culture phenomena may seem silly or frivolous, but philosophers have used fanciful examples and thought experiments for centuries. The point is making philosophy accessible, and helping us think through difficult topics by casting them in a different light. 11

Regardless of your position, torture is an uncomfortable and emotional topic. If translating the core issue to another venue, such as Batman and the Joker, helps us focus on the key aspects of the problem, that can only help refine our thinking. And Batman would definitely approve of that. 12

---

3. Classical Greek philosopher (384–322 B.C.E.) whose work was foundational for Western philosophy and culture.

FOR DISCUSSION

. . . .

1. Mark D. White and Robert Arp do not give a final answer to the question posed in their title. Should they have? Why or why not?

2. Of the three schools of philosophy cited by White and Arp, which one(s) best support Batman's CLAIM that if he kills the Joker he will become "that which I hate" (10)? Explain your answer.

3. Are White and Arp being "silly or frivolous" when they take Batman's adventures as a serious guide to moral and ethical behavior (11)? Why or why not?

4. So *is* Batman morally and ethically right to let the Joker live? Or should he kill the Joker at the first opportunity? Why do you think so?

STRATEGIES AND STRUCTURES

. . . .

1. What AUDIENCE in particular do White and Arp have in mind when they use pop culture to examine complex ethical and philosophical questions?

2. What is White and Arp's main CLAIM in comparing the actions and decisions of a comic book character to those that real-life leaders must make in government and society? Where in the text is that claim directly stated?

3. Throughout their ARGUMENT, White and Arp rely heavily on logical reasoning, both INDUCTIVE and DEDUCTIVE. Where in their argument do they reason inductively? Where is their reasoning more deductive? Point to specific instances of each type of reasoning.

4. "Should Batman Kill the Joker?" is primarily a moral and ethical argument. How and how well do White and Arp present themselves as knowledgeable and ethical people who deserve to be heard? Point to specific passages in the text where they establish (or fail to establish) their credibility.

5. Is it logical to say that a person who condones torture is in danger of becoming that which he or she hates? Or does such reasoning introduce a red herring, or some other LOGICAL FALLACY? Explain.

6. Arguments by ANALOGY draw comparisons, as White and Arp do in comparing Batman's dilemma to the debate over torture and terrorism. The PURPOSE of such arguments, as they say, is to help us "think through difficult topics by

casting them in a different light" (11). How effective is this strategy in helping White and Arp to clarify the difficult issue of torture?

7. In general, arguments by analogy are only as strong as the analogy, or likeness between the terms being compared, is close. How close is the analogy—and, thus, how strong is the argument—in "Should Batman Kill the Joker?" Explain.

8. How do the DEFINITIONS that White and Arp provide in paragraphs 6–8 support their argument about the value of pop culture for understanding ethical and philosophical issues?

WORDS AND FIGURES OF SPEECH

1. A "psychopath" is someone who is antisocial and self-centered to the point of having no regard for the rules of society or the needs of other people (1). In what ways does the Joker, as White and Arp DESCRIBE him, exhibit the behavior of a psychopath?

2. "Utilitarianism" stresses the welfare of the majority over the special interests of the few (6). How and how well does White and Arp's summary of this philosophy fit this definition?

3. "Deontology" takes its name from the Greek word for *obligation* or *duty* (7). How does this root meaning apply to the school of ethics by that name as White and Arp define it?

4. Look up the root meanings of *ethics* and *ethnic* in your dictionary. What do the two terms have in common? What does their ETYMOLOGY tell you about the nature of *ethical* arguments, as opposed to *emotional* arguments and arguments that appeal to the reader's sense of logic?

FOR WRITING

1. Choose a pop culture icon whose adventures you find particularly enlightening. Write an argument for why that figure's deeds and moral standards (or lack thereof) can teach us moral, ethical, or practical lessons.

2. Write an argument condemning (or justifying) the use of torture when dealing with terrorists. Consider applying one or more of the schools of philosophy outlined by White and Arp—or any other that you choose—to make your argument.

ARIANNA HUFFINGTON

EMPATHY: WHAT WE NEED NOW

Arianna Huffington (b. 1950) is the founder and chief executive of the *Huffing-ton Post*, a news and commentary website. Huffington was born in Athens, Greece, and studied economics as an undergraduate at Cambridge University in England before moving to the United States in 1980. In the recall election of 2003, Huffington ran unsuccessfully for governor of California against Arnold Schwarzenegger, a race she described, in reference to their personal vehicles, as "the hybrid versus the Hummer." Among her other regular media appearances, Huffington is cohost of the weekly public radio program *Both Sides Now*. In the following selection from her book *Third World America* (2010), Huffington calls for a return, "in this time of economic hardship, political instability, and rapid technological change," to a form of social activism that is based, in her view, on a mixture of capitalism and caring.

◊◊◊◊◊◊◊◊◊◊◊◊◊◊◊◊◊◊◊◊◊◊◊◊◊◊◊◊◊

I n *The Empathic Civilization*, Jeremy Rifkin[1] describes empathy as "the will-ingness of an observer to become part of another's experience, to share the feeling of that experience."

1. Jeremy Rifkin (b. 1945): American economist and political activist; author, among other books, of *The Empathetic Civilization: The Race to Global Consciousness in a World in Crisis* (2010).

Unlike sympathy, which is passive, empathy is active, engaged, and dynamic. New scientific data tells us that empathy is not a quaint behavior trotted out during intermittent visits to a food bank or during a heart-tugging telethon. Instead, it lies at the very core of human existence.

2

Since the economic crisis, the role empathy plays in our lives has only grown more important. In fact, in this time of economic hardship, political instability, and rapid technological change, empathy is the one quality we most need if we're going to flourish in the twenty-first century. "An individual," said Martin Luther King, "has not started living until he can rise above the narrow confines of his own individualistic concerns to the broader concerns of all humanity."

3

Arguments that appeal to feeling and emotions are discussed on p. 519.

* * *

"We are on the cusp of an epic shift," writes Jeremy Rifkin. "The Age of Reason is being eclipsed by the Age of Empathy." He makes the case that as technology is increasingly connecting us to one another, we need to understand what the goal of all this connectivity is. "Seven billion individual connections," he says, "absent any overall unifying purpose, seem a colossal waste of human energy."

4

That sense of purpose, which must include expanding the narrow confines of our own concerns, can have powerful social implications. Dr. King showed that for a social movement to become broad-based enough to produce real change, it must be fueled by empathy.

5

In his 1963 work "Letter from a Birmingham Jail," King lamented the failure of "the white moderate" to "understand that the present tension in the South is a necessary phase of the transition from an obnoxious negative peace, in which the Negro passively accepted his unjust plight, to a substantive and positive peace, in which all men will respect the dignity and worth of human personality."

6

King understood that he needed to tap into the empathy of whole constituencies that would not themselves be the direct beneficiaries of the civil rights movement. He set about making a compelling moral case by forcing many in white America to see for the first time that millions of their fellow citizens were effectively living in a different world—a different America—than they were. He created pathways for empathy and then used them to create a better country for everybody.

7

Conservative commentator Tony Blankley once remarked—only half-seriously—that "evolution, cruel as it is, determined that empathy is not a survival trait." If you've been paying attention to the actions of many of our CEOs—from those running big banks to those running Massey Energy and BP[2]—you would be inclined to agree. But if we are to continue as a thriving democratic society, we will need all the empathy we can get. Without it, we'll never be able to create the kind of national consensus required to tackle the enormous problems that face us, rescue the middle class, and stop our descent into Third World America.

As America's Misery Index[3] soars, so must our Empathy Index.

"We have to lean on one another and look out for one another and love one another and pray for one another," Barack Obama said when he delivered the eulogy for the fallen West Virginia miners in April 2010. This is a call that transcends left and right political divisions.

David Brooks has written about the need to replace our "atomized, segmented society" with a society "oriented around relationships and associations"—an approach advocated by conservative British writer Phillip Blond in his book *Red Tory.* "Volunteering, especially among professional classes and the young," Blond wrote, "has doubled in recent months"—proof, he suggests, that "the wish to make a difference is a common and rising aspiration."

Those who are working to address the devastation in their own communities are willing to experiment, try many things, fail, and try again, the way you do when you really care. And there is extraordinary creativity in local philanthropy.

In 2002 in San Francisco's Mission district, author Dave Eggers and teacher Nínive Calegari opened 826 Valencia, a writing lab that provides free tutoring to local kids and has attracted hundreds of skilled volunteer instructors. Offering drop-in, one-on-one instruction with a focus on the creative and

2. The Massey Energy Company owned and operated the Upper Big Branch Mine in West Virginia where, in April 2010, 29 coal miners were killed in an explosion; BP (British Petroleum) was responsible for the largest marine oil spill in history that, also in April 2012, killed 11 workers and released nearly 5 million barrels of oil into the Gulf of Mexico.

3. An economic indicator calculated by adding the unemployment rate to the inflation rate.

fun aspects of writing, as well as other learning programs including field trips and in-class learning, 826 Valencia has since fanned out across the country, opening chapters—and enlisting volunteer tutors—in Los Angeles, New York City, Ann Arbor, Seattle, Chicago, and Boston.

In Brooklyn, New York, FEAST (Funding Emerging Art with Sustainable Tactics) hosts volunteer-prepared dinner parties in a church basement, where locals are invited to pitch ideas for community art and improvement projects. The 250+ dinner-goers pay ten to twenty dollars to attend the fetes, where they feast on local food, listen to live music, socialize, and vote on their favorite proposals. At the end of the dinner, FEAST organizers present the winner with the prize money, raised from that night's admission proceeds, for the implementation of the project. 14

Matthew Bishop, U.S. business editor for the *Economist*, in his book *Philanthrocapitalism*, explored how this moment of crisis for capitalism and philanthropy could be used to transform both—how capitalism could be imbued with a social mission, and philanthropy could be reinvigorated with the best practices of capitalism. And in seeking to blend the efficiency of enterprise with the benefits of philanthropy, the burgeoning social entrepreneurship movement does precisely that. Social entrepreneurs pinpoint social problems and, rather than waiting for government action, apply market principles to solve them in original ways. Supported by investment funds from organizations such as Echoing Green, Ashoka, and Investors' Circle, trailblazing social ventures are reenvisioning the way social change happens, not only abroad, but here at home, too. 15

Providing microcredit to small businesses is an innovation for which Muhammad Yunus won the Nobel Peace Prize in 2006. In 2008, Yunus's Grameen Bank opened a branch in New York. In 2010 it opened a branch in Omaha, Nebraska. The Grameen Bank's slogan: "Banking for the unbanked." Hoping to serve one million American entrepreneurs, Grameen America plans to expand into more than fifty cities across the country, including Washington, D.C., and San Francisco. A practice most closely associated with helping struggling Third World countries has now arrived in America. By February 2010, the New York branch had extended loans to 2,500 clients, mostly women. The average loan 16 amount is $1,500 (no collateral necessary) and more than 99 percent of the recipients make their payments on time.

Grameen Bank is not the only organization committed to providing micro- credit to small businesses here at home. Since 1991, ACCION USA has lent over $119 million, in the form of more than 19,500 small-business loans, to low- and moderate-income entrepreneurs. Luis Zapeda Alvarez, for example, who was once homeless and out of work, now runs his own business delivering baked goods to New York City restaurants and delis—in large part due to the assis- tance he received. After banks refused to lend him start-up capital, Alvarez approached ACCION and borrowed enough money to buy the delivery truck he needed to get his business off the ground. When his truck needed new insu- lation, ACCION USA helped him secure a $5,600 loan to make the improve- ments. Alvarez's business has expanded to three daily delivery routes—he's now so busy that he had to hire a part-time employee—and his success as an entrepreneur has helped cement his relationship with his children.

Another New Yorker, Lyn Genet Recitas, opened Neighborhood Holis- tic, a yoga studio and spa, in Harlem with the help of a microloan from ACCION USA. Within a year, the studio was profitable, and Recitas expanded her ven- ture, bringing on twelve part-time employees and providing yoga scholarships for low-income community members.

Some of the most exciting social advocacy and "citizen philanthropy" is happening on the Web. DonorsChoose.org, for example, invites public school teachers from around the country to post funding proposals for classroom needs. Users browse the listings—for things such as notebooks and pencils, LCD projectors for math instruction, or mirrors so that art students can prac- tice drawing self-portraits—and donate however much they'd like to their cho- sen projects. By May 2010, just a decade after the site was started by Bronx high school social studies teacher Charles Best, DonorsChoose.org had raised over $52 million across more than 130,000 different proposals.

* * *

Taken together, these efforts, and thousands of others like them, are helping turn the country around. And it would be great if more of America's super affluent—the wealthiest 1 percent, who hold 35 percent of the nation's wealth—

also tapped into their reserves of empathy and acted on Andrew Carnegie's assertion that "he who dies rich dies disgraced."

That's a sentiment that Bill Gates and Warren Buffett[3] clearly share. The pair has launched The Giving Pledge, a campaign to convince the world's billionaires to give at least 50 percent of their money away. Buffett has promised to give 99 percent of his roughly $46 billion to charity; Gates has made a similar pledge. And others are starting to join in, including Michael Bloomberg,[4] who, echoing Carnegie, says: "I am a big believer in giving it all away and have always said that the best financial planning ends with bouncing the check to the undertaker." If The Giving Pledge catches on, Gates and Buffett believe they can generate $600 billion for philanthropic causes.

At the tail end of the last Gilded Age, the opulently rich—men like Andrew Carnegie, Cornelius Vanderbilt, John D. Rockefeller and Andrew W. Mellon[5]—led a nationwide wave of philanthropy. If Buffett and Gates are successful, as our own Gilded Age nears its end, a second great wave of giving is coming. And it couldn't be more timely.

21

22

3. Gates (b. 1955), cofounder of Microsoft, and Buffet (b. 1930), CEO of Berkshire Hathaway, are among the world's wealthiest individuals; they have teamed up on a number of philanthropic projects.

4. Billionaire businessman (b. 1942); mayor of New York City since 2002.

5. American industrial magnates of the late nineteenth and early twentieth centuries.

FOR DISCUSSION

. . . .

1. According to Arianna Huffington, what is *empathy*? How does it differ from the related idea of *sympathy*?

2. Why does Huffington think empathy as a social ideal is particularly important today? Do you agree? Why or why not?

3. Many of the people whom Huffington cites as EXAMPLES of empathy in action are what she calls "social entrepreneurs" (15). What does Huffington mean by this term? In particular, what do "social entrepreneurs" borrow from capitalism? What, in Huffington's view, should capitalism borrow from them?

STRATEGIES AND STRUCTURES

. . . .

1. Before Huffington argues that empathy is "more important" than ever before, she DEFINES what she means by this key term (1–3). Is this a good strategy? Why or why not?

2. What is Huffington's main PURPOSE in promoting social empathy? What does she claim it can accomplish? Where does she state this claim most clearly and directly?

3. Huffington quotes the work of economist Jeremy Rifkin to help define her subject. What is her RHETORICAL PURPOSE in citing the work of Martin Luther King Jr. (3, 5–7)? How and how well does the King citation serve that purpose?

4. Why does Huffington admit that she is "inclined to agree" with Tony Blankley's ARGUMENT that "empathy is not a survival trait"—and then proceed to make her own case (8)? How does this admission affect her credibility? Explain.

5. The bulk of Huffington's argument is devoted to particular examples of people and organizations that practice social empathy. Which ones do you find particularly effective (or ineffective)? Why?

6. Huffington waits until the end of her essay to bring out her big guns, such as Gates and Buffet (20–22). Is this a wise strategy? Why or why not?

WORDS AND FIGURES OF SPEECH

1. Some arguments arise because of differences of opinion about the meaning of a key term or concept, such as *evolution* or *survival of the fittest*—or *empathy*. Is Huffington's essay such an argument of definition, or is she mainly using the term *empathy* to argue another claim? Explain.

2. Michael Bloomberg, mayor of New York City, is a billionaire. What is the tone and likely purpose of his remark about "bouncing the check to the undertaker" (21)?

3. The "gilded age" of industrial capitalism in America—the term was coined by Mark Twain and Charles Dudley Warner—lasted from the end of the Civil War until the mid-1890s (22). Why "gilded" instead of, say, "golden"?

FOR WRITING

1. In a paragraph or two, give an example of a person or organization whose social activity supports (or refutes) Huffington's claim about the importance of empathy in today's economic and social climate.

2. Huffington comes to the conclusion that perhaps "a great wave of giving is coming" (22). Compose an argument of your own that supports (or refutes) this claim. Be sure to give specific examples of the activities and policies of particular people and organizations.

MIND AND MEDIA:
IS *GOOGLE* MAKING US STUPID?

❖◇

When Johannes Gutenberg (1398–1468) and his colleagues invented movable-type printing, one of the first books to be produced was an elegant edition of the *Holy Bible* (*Biblia Sacra*, 1455). When John Timothy Berners-Lee and his colleagues at the CERN laboratories invented the World Wide Web in the early 1990s, the first text to be uploaded to a website could not have been more different. It was apparently a promotional photo of the Cernettes, an all-female singing group. Of course, the scientists were probably not thinking of Gutenberg when they opened a portal into a new world of digitalized communication, but their landmark posting hints at fundamental differences between the two technologies. Reading a densely textured book requires time and reflection—and, some argue, fosters habits of in-depth thinking that have enriched human culture for centuries. In the last 25 years, however, everything has been speeding up. In seconds, we can now process snippets of text, images, and even sounds that once would have taken ages to locate in the great libraries of the world—if they could be found at all. Is the new technology making us more comprehensive but shallower thinkers? Or is the Internet our best hope for staying on top of an expanding universe of data and once-inaccessible knowledge?

In the following essays, **Steven Pinker**, **Nicholas Carr**, and **Andrea Lunsford** address these and other fundamentals questions about the effects of media and technology on human intelligence as we advance, retreat, or otherwise make the shift (if there is one) from Gutenberg to *Google*.

STEVEN PINKER

MIND OVER MASS MEDIA

Steven Pinker (b. 1954) is a professor of psychology at Harvard. While still a freshman at McGill University in Montreal, Pinker came to the conclusion that "language is the key to understanding the human mind," a claim he supports in numerous books, including *The Stuff of Thought: Language as a Window into Human Nature* (2007). In the following op-ed piece, written for the *New York Times* in 2010, Pinker counters the claims of media critics who argue that *PowerPoint, Google, Twitter* and other technologies are turning our brains to mush. Pinker concedes, however, that the new media, and especially social media, require us "to develop strategies of self-control, as we do with every other temptation in life."

❖⌄❖⌄❖⌄❖⌄❖⌄❖⌄❖⌄❖⌄❖⌄❖⌄❖⌄❖⌄❖⌄❖⌄❖⌄❖⌄❖⌄❖⌄❖⌄

N ew forms of media have always caused moral panics: the printing press, newspapers, paperbacks, and television were all once denounced as threats to their consumers' brainpower and moral fiber.

So too with electronic technologies. PowerPoint, we're told, is reducing discourse to bullet points. Search engines lower our intelligence, encouraging

1

2

us to skim on the surface of knowledge rather than dive to its depths. Twitter is shrinking our attention spans.

But such panics often fail basic reality checks. When comic books were accused of turning juveniles into delinquents in the 1950s, crime was falling to record lows, just as the denunciations of video games in the 1990s coincided with the great American crime decline. The decades of television, transistor radios, and rock videos were also decades in which I.Q. scores rose continuously. 3

For a reality check today, take the state of science, which demands high levels of brainwork and is measured by clear benchmarks of discovery. These days scientists are never far from their e-mail, rarely touch paper, and cannot lecture without PowerPoint. If electronic media were hazardous to intelligence, the quality of science would be plummeting. Yet discoveries are multiplying like fruit flies, and progress is dizzying. Other activities in the life of the mind, like philosophy, history, and cultural criticism, are likewise flourishing, as anyone who has lost a morning of work to the Web site *Arts & Letters Daily* can attest. 4

The logic of syllogistic arguments like this is outlined on p. 525.

Critics of new media sometimes use science itself to press their case, citing research that shows how "experience can change the brain." But cognitive neuroscientists roll their eyes at such talk. Yes, every time we learn a fact or skill the wiring of the brain changes; it's not as if the information is stored in the pancreas. But the existence of neural plasticity does not mean the brain is a blob of clay pounded into shape by experience. 5

Experience does not revamp the basic information-processing capacities of the brain. Speed-reading programs have long claimed to do just that, but the verdict was rendered by Woody Allen after he read *War and Peace*[1] in one sitting: "It was about Russia." Genuine multitasking, too, has been exposed as a myth, not just by laboratory studies but by the familiar sight of an S.U.V. undulating between lanes as the driver cuts deals on his cellphone. 6

Moreover, as the psychologists Christopher Chabris and Daniel Simons show in their new book *The Invisible Gorilla: And Other Ways Our Intuitions Deceive Us*, the effects of experience are highly specific to the experiences 7

---

1. Famously lengthy historical novel by Russian writer Leo Tolstoy (1869).

themselves. If you train people to do one thing (recognize shapes, solve math puzzles, find hidden words), they get better at doing that thing, but almost nothing else. Music doesn't make you better at math, conjugating Latin doesn't make you more logical, brain-training games don't make you smarter. Accomplished people don't bulk up their brains with intellectual calisthenics; they immerse themselves in their fields. Novelists read lots of novels, scientists read lots of science.

The effects of consuming electronic media are also likely to be far more limited than the panic implies. Media critics write as if the brain takes on the qualities of whatever it consumes, the informational equivalent of "you are what you eat." As with primitive peoples who believe that eating fierce animals will make them fierce, they assume that watching quick cuts in rock videos turns your mental life into quick cuts or that reading bullet points and Twitter postings turns your thoughts into bullet points and Twitter postings.

Yes, the constant arrival of information packets can be distracting or addictive, especially to people with attention deficit disorder. But distraction is not a new phenomenon. The solution is not to bemoan technology but to develop strategies of self-control, as we do with every other temptation in life. Turn off e-mail or Twitter when you work, put away your Blackberry at dinner time, ask your spouse to call you to bed at a designated hour.

And to encourage intellectual depth, don't rail at PowerPoint or Google. It's not as if habits of deep reflection, thorough research, and rigorous reasoning ever came naturally to people. They must be acquired in special institutions, which we call universities, and maintained with constant upkeep, which we call analysis, criticism, and debate. They are not granted by propping a heavy encyclopedia on your lap, nor are they taken away by efficient access to information on the Internet.

The new media have caught on for a reason. Knowledge is increasing exponentially; human brainpower and waking hours are not. Fortunately, the Internet and information technologies are helping us manage, search, and retrieve our collective intellectual output at different scales, from Twitter and previews to e-books and online encyclopedias. Far from making us stupid, these technologies are the only things that will keep us smart.

UNDERSTANDING THE ESSAY

. . . .

1. Why does Steven Pinker think that "critics of new media" are wrong when they ARGUE that these technologies are "making us stupid" (5, 11)? In his view, what effect *will* those media have? How convincing is his argument? Explain.

2. We do not naturally and automatically acquire "intellectual depth" and "habits of deep reflection," Pinker writes (10). According to Pinker, how and where—in what kinds of special institutions—*do* we develop these capacities?

3. Pinker often uses ANECDOTAL evidence, for instance when he refers to the "familiar sight" of an S.U.V. driver on a cell phone (6). How effective is this kind of evidence? Where does Pinker provide more scholarly proof, such as expert testimony and formal logical reasoning?

4. Explain the PUN in Pinker's reference to "the effects of consuming electronic media" (8).

5. The word *panic* appears several times in Pinker's essay (1, 3, 8). Does his argument warrant his use of the term, or is Pinker committing the logical fallacy (or strategy) of "begging the question" here? Explain.

6. Pinker compares critics of the new media to "primitive peoples who believe that eating fierce animals will make them fierce" (8). Is this a valid comparison? Why or why not? How and how well does Pinker use this ANALOGY to support his argument?

HAL AND ME

Nicholas Carr (b. 1959) is a writer whose work focuses on technology, business, and culture. A graduate of Dartmouth with an MA from Harvard in American Literature, Carr is the author of "Is Google Making Us Stupid?"—a widely read (and debated) essay that formed the cover article for the Ideas Issue of the *Atlantic* magazine in 2008. Basically, Carr's answer to the question posed in that article is affirmative, a position he develops more fully in *The Shallows: What the Internet Is Doing to Our Brains* (2010). In the following complete section from that book, Carr traces the scattering effect of "the Net" upon his own powers of concentration and reflection. This same "remapping of the neural circuitry," he argues, may be spreading to "society as a whole."

"Dave, stop. Stop, will you? Stop, Dave. Will you stop?" So the supercomputer HAL pleads with the implacable astronaut Dave Bowman in a famous and weirdly poignant scene toward the end of Stanley Kubrick's 2001: *A Space Odyssey.* Bowman, having nearly been sent to a deep-space death by the malfunctioning machine, is calmly, coldly disconnecting the memory circuits that control its artificial brain. "Dave, my mind is going," HAL says, forlornly. "I can feel it. I can feel it."

I can feel it too. Over the last few years I've had an uncomfortable sense that someone, or something, has been tinkering with my brain, remapping the neural circuitry, reprogramming the memory. My mind isn't going—so far as I can tell—but it's changing. I'm not thinking the way I used to think. I feel it most strongly when I'm reading. I used to find it easy to immerse myself in a book or a lengthy article. My mind would get caught up in the twists of the narrative or the turns of the argument, and I'd spend hours strolling through long stretches of prose. That's rarely the case anymore. Now my concentration starts to drift after a page or two. I get fidgety, lose the thread, begin looking for something else to do. I feel like I'm always dragging my wayward brain back to the text. The deep reading that used to come naturally has become a struggle.

I think I know what's going on. For well over a decade now, I've been spending a lot of time online, searching and surfing and sometimes adding to the great databases of the Internet. The Web's been a godsend to me as a writer. Research that once required days in the stacks or periodical rooms of libraries can now be done in minutes. A few Google searches, some quick clicks on hyperlinks, and I've got the telltale fact or the pithy quote I was after. I couldn't begin to tally the hours or the gallons of gasoline the Net has saved me. I do most of my banking and a lot of my shopping online. I use my browser to pay my bills, schedule my appointments, book flights and hotel rooms, renew my driver's license, send invitations and greeting cards. Even when I'm not working, I'm as likely as not to be foraging in the Web's data thickets—reading and writing emails, scanning headlines and blog posts, following *Facebook* updates, watching video streams, downloading music, or just tripping lightly from link to link to link.

The Net has become my all-purpose medium, the conduit for most of the information that flows through my eyes and ears and into my mind. The advantages of having immediate access to such an incredibly rich and easily searched store of data are many, and they've been widely described and duly applauded. "Google," says Heather Pringle, a writer with *Archaeology* magazine, "is an astonishing boon to humanity, gathering up and concentrating information and ideas that were once scattered so broadly around the world that hardly anyone could profit from them."[1] Observes *Wired's* Clive Thompson, "The perfect recall of silicon memory can be an enormous boon to thinking."[2]

The boons are real. But they come at a price. As McLuhan[3] suggested, media aren't just channels of information. They supply the stuff of thought, but they also shape the process of thought. And what the Net seems to be doing is chipping away my capacity for concentration and contemplation. Whether I'm online or not, my mind now expects to take in information the way the Net distributes it: in a swiftly moving stream of particles. Once I was a scuba diver in the sea of words. Now I zip along the surface like a guy on a Jet Ski.

Maybe I'm an aberration, an outlier. But it doesn't seem that way. When I mention my troubles with reading to friends, many say they're suffering from similar afflictions. The more they use the Web, the more they have to fight to stay focused on long pieces of writing. Some worry they're becoming chronic scatterbrains. Several of the bloggers I follow have also mentioned the phenomenon. Scott Karp, who used to work for a magazine and now writes a blog about online media, confesses that he has stopped reading books altogether. "I was a lit major in college, and used to be [a] voracious book reader," he writes. "What happened?" He speculates on the answer: "What if I do all my reading on the web not so much because the way I read has changed, i.e. I'm just seeking convenience, but because the way I THINK has changed?"[4]

Bruce Friedman, who blogs about the use of computers in medicine, has also described how the Internet is altering his mental habits. "I now have almost totally lost the ability to read and absorb a longish article on the web or in print," he says.[5]

1. Heather Pringle, "Is Google Making Archaeologists Smarter?," *Beyond Stone & Bone* blog (Archaeological Institute of America), February 27, 2009, http://archaeology.org/blog/?p=332.

2. Clive Thompson, "Your Outboard Brain Knows All," *Wired,* October 2007.

3. Marshall McLuhan (1911–1980), Canadian scholar and cultural critic who coined the famous phrase, "the medium is the message" [Editor's note; all other notes are the author's].

4. Scott Karp, "The Evolution from Linear Thought to Networked Thought," *Publishing 2.0* blog, February 9, 2008, http://publishing2.com/2008/02/09/the-evolution-from-linear -thought-to-networked-thought.

5. Bruce Friedman, "How Google Is Changing Our Information-Seeking Behavior," *Lab Soft News* blog, February 6, 2008, http://labsoftnews.type pad.com/lab_soft_news/2008/02 /how-google-is-c.html.

A pathologist on the faculty of the University of Michigan Medical School, Friedman elaborated on his comment in a telephone conversation with me. His thinking, he said, has taken on a "staccato" quality, reflecting the way he quickly scans short passages of text from many sources online. "I can't read *War and Peace* anymore," he admitted. "I've lost the ability to do that. Even a blog post of more than three or four paragraphs is too much to absorb. I skim it."

Philip Davis, a doctoral student in communication at Cornell who con-   8
tributes to the Society for Scholarly Publishing's blog, recalls a time back in the 1990s when he showed a friend how to use a Web browser. He says he was "astonished" and "even irritated" when the woman paused to read the text on the sites she stumbled upon. "You're not supposed to read web pages, just click on the hypertexted words!" he scolded her. Now, Davis writes, "I read a lot—or at least I should be reading a lot—only I don't. I skim. I scroll. I have very little patience for long, drawn-out, nuanced arguments, even though I accuse others of painting the world too simply."[6]

Karp, Friedman, and Davis—all well-educated men with a keenness for   9
writing—seem fairly sanguine about the decay of their faculties for reading and concentrating. All things considered, they say, the benefits they get from using the Net—quick access to loads of information, potent searching and filtering tools, an easy way to share their opinions with a small but interested audience—make up for the loss of their ability to sit still and turn the pages of a book or a magazine. Friedman told me, in an email, that he's "never been more creative" than he has been recently, and he attributes that "to my blog and the ability to review/scan 'tons' of information on the web." Karp has come to believe that reading lots of short, linked snippets online is a more efficient way to expand his mind than reading "250-page books," though, he says, "we can't yet recognize the superiority of this networked thinking process because we're measuring it against our old linear thought process."[7] Muses Davis, "The Internet may have made me a less patient reader, but I think that in many

The testimony of experts, p. 527, is a common form of evidence in argument.

6. Philip Davis, "Is Google Making Us Stupid? Nope!" *The Scholarly Kitchen* blog, June 16, 2008, http://scholarlykitchen.sspnet.org/2008/06/16/is-google-making-us-stupid-nope.

7. Scott Karp, "Connecting the Dots of the Web Revolution." *Publishing* 2.0 blog, June 17, 2008, http://publishing 2.com/2008/06/17/connecting-the-dots-of-the-web-revolution.

ways, it has made me smarter. More connections to documents, artifacts, and people means more external influences on my thinking and thus on my writing."[8] All three know they've sacrificed something important, but they wouldn't go back to the way things used to be.

For some people, the very idea of reading a book has come to seem old-fashioned, maybe even a little silly—like sewing your own shirts or butchering your own meat. "I don't read books," says Joe O'Shea, a former president of the student body at Florida State University and a 2008 recipient of a Rhodes Scholarship. "I go to Google, and I can absorb relevant information quickly." O'Shea, a philosophy major, doesn't see any reason to plow through chapters of text when it takes but a minute or two to cherry-pick the pertinent passages using Google Book Search. "Sitting down and going through a book from cover to cover doesn't make sense." he says. "It's not a good use of my time, as I can get all the information I need faster through the Web." As soon as you learn to be "a skilled hunter" online, he argues, books become superfluous.[9]

O'Shea seems more the rule than the exception. In 2008, a research and consulting outfit called nGenera released a study of the effects of Internet use on the young. The company interviewed some six thousand members of what it calls "Generation Net"—kids who have grown up using the Web. "Digital immersion," wrote the lead researcher," has even affected the way they absorb information. They don't necessarily read a page from left to right and from top to bottom. They might instead skip around, scanning for pertinent information of interest."[10] In a talk at a recent Phi Beta Kappa meeting, Duke University professor Katherine Hayles confessed, "I can't get my students to read whole books anymore."[11] Hayles teaches English; the students she's talking about are students of literature.

10

11

8. Davis, "Is Google Making Us Stupid? Nope!"

9. Don Tapscott, "How Digital Technology Has Changed the Brain," *Business-Week Online*, November 10, 2008, www.businessweek.com/technology/content/nov2008/tc2008117 –034517.htm.

10. Don Tapscott, "How to Teach and Manage 'Generation Net,'" *Business Week Online*, November 30, 2008, www.businessweek.com/technology/content/nov2008/tc20081130 -713563.htm.

11. Quoted in Naomi S. Baron, *Always On: Language in an Online and Mobile World* (Oxford: Oxford University Press, 2008), 204.

People use the Internet in all sorts of ways. Some are eager, even compul-   12
sive adopters of the latest technologies. They keep accounts with a dozen or
more online services and subscribe to scores of information feeds. They blog
and they tag, they text and they twitter. Others don't much care about being on
the cutting edge but nevertheless find themselves online most of the time, tapping away at their desktop, their laptop, or their mobile phone. The Net has
become essential to their work, school, or social lives, and often to all three. Still
others log on only a few times a day—to check their email, follow a story in the
news, research a topic of interest, or do some shopping. And there are, of course,
many people who don't use the Internet at all, either because they can't afford to
or because they don't want to. What's clear, though, is that for society as a whole
the Net has become, in just the twenty years since the software programmer
Tim Berners-Lee wrote the code for the World Wide Web, the communication
and information medium of choice. The scope of its use is unprecedented, even
by the standards of the mass media of the twentieth century. The scope of its
influence is equally broad. By choice or necessity, we've embraced the Net's
uniquely rapid-fire mode of collecting and dispensing information.

We seem to have arrived, as McLuhan said we would, at an important   13
juncture in our intellectual and cultural history, a moment of transition between
two very different modes of thinking. What we're trading away in return for the
riches of the Net—and only a curmudgeon would refuse to see the riches—is
what Karp calls "our old linear thought process." Calm, focused, undistracted,
the linear mind is being pushed aside by a new kind of mind that wants and
needs to take in and dole out information in short, disjointed, often overlapping
bursts—the faster, the better. John Battelle, a onetime magazine editor and journalism professor who now runs an online advertising syndicate, has described
the intellectual frisson he experiences when skittering across Web pages: "When
I am performing bricolage in real time over the course of hours, I am 'feeling' my
brain light up, I [am] 'feeling' like I'm getting smarter."[12] Most of us have experienced similar sensations while online. The feelings are intoxicating—so much
so that they can distract us from the Net's deeper cognitive consequences.

12. John Battelle, "Google: Making Nick Carr Stupid, but It's Made This Guy Smarter,"
John Battelle's Searchblog, June 10, 2008, http://battellemedia.com/archives/004494.php.

For the last five centuries, ever since Gutenberg's printing press made book reading a popular pursuit, the linear, literary mind has been at the center of art, science, and society. As supple as it is subtle, it's been the imaginative mind of the Renaissance, the rational mind of the Enlightenment, the inventive mind of the Industrial Revolution, even the subversive mind of Modernism. It may soon be yesterday's mind.

14

UNDERSTANDING THE ESSAY

1. For "society as a whole," says Nicholas Carr, the Internet has become, in just the last twenty years or so, "the communication and information medium of choice" (12). How valid is this assumption? Explain.

2. The Internet, says Carr, seems to be "chipping away" at his (and our) "capacity for concentration and contemplatation" (5). Why, in Carr's view, is "the Net" having this particular effect? What specific evidence does he offer? Is it sufficient to support this CLAIM?

3. If Carr believes that surfing the web is producing a shallow-minded society, why does he admit that the "boons" of Internet use "are real" (5)? Is this an effective, even a necessary strategy of ARGUMENT? Why or why not?

4. What *are* some of the major boons of surfing the web, according to Carr? Are they sufficient to compensate for the loss, experienced by Carr and others, "of the ability to sit still and turn the pages of a book or magazine" (9)? Why or why not?

5. Once he was a "scuba diver in the sea of words"; now, says Carr, he's skimming along the surface like "a guy on a Jet Ski" (5). Arguments by ANALOGY are only as strong as the COMPARISONS they're based on. How well does this comparison support Carr's argument? Explain.

6. In *2001: A Space Odyssey*, the Kubrick film to which Carr refers at the beginning of his essay, the astronaut Dave Bowman is deactivating the spaceship's computer system (HAL) because it has developed a mind of its own and has decided to send Bowman into deep space. What are some of the implications of this ALLUSION for Carr's general argument about "the Net"? Of his allusion to the work of media theorist Marshall McLuhan, who famously said, "the medium is the message"?

ANDREA LUNSFORD

OUR SEMI-LITERATE YOUTH?
NOT SO FAST

Andrea Lunsford (b. 1942) is a professor of English and director of the program in writing and rhetoric at Stanford University. After graduating from the University of Florida, Lunsford taught English at Colonial High School in Orlando before earning a PhD in rhetoric from the Ohio State University "Our Semi-Literate Youth? Not So Fast" reports on research by Lunsford and others about trends in undergraduate writing (and thinking) as a result of increased use of digital technologies. Based on their findings, Lunsford argues, writing and literacy should be redefined for the digital age; and teachers of writing, she implies, should reconsider how they teach.

⬧⬧⬧⬧⬧⬧⬧⬧⬧⬧⬧⬧⬧⬧⬧⬧⬧⬧⬧⬧⬧⬧⬧⬧⬧⬧⬧⬧⬧⬧

Two stories about young people, and especially college-age students, are circulating widely today. One script sees a generation of twitterers and texters, awash in self-indulgence and narcissistic twaddle, most of it riddled with errors. The other script doesn't diminish the effects of technology, but it presents young people as running a rat race that is fueled by the Internet and its toys, anxious kids who are inundated with mountains of indigestible information yet obsessed with making the grade, with success, with coming up with the "next big thing," but who lack the writing and speaking skills they need to do so.

No doubt there's a grain of truth in both these depictions. But the doom- 2
sayers who tell these stories are turning a blind eye on compelling alternative narratives. As one who has spent the last 30-plus years studying the writing of college students, I see a different picture. For those who think Google is making us stupid and Facebook is frying our brains, let me sketch that picture in briefly.

Anticipating the views of opponents, p. 529, can smooth the way for your own claims.

In 2001, I and my colleagues began a longitudinal study of writing at 3
Stanford, following a randomly selected group of 189 students from their first day on campus through one year beyond graduation; in fact, I am still in touch with a number of the students today. These students—about 12 percent of that year's class—submitted the writing they did for their classes and as much of their out-of-class writing as they wanted to an electronic database, along with their comments on those pieces of writing. Over the years, we collected nearly 15,000 pieces of student writing: lab reports, research essays, PowerPoint presentations, problem sets, honors theses, email and textings (in 11 languages), blogs and journals, poems, documentaries, even a full-length play entitled *Hip-Hopera*. While we are still coding these pieces of writing, several results emerged right away. First, these students were writing A LOT, both in class and out, though they were more interested in and committed to writing out of class, what we came to call "life writing," than they were in their school assignments. Second, they were increasingly aware of those to whom they were writing and adjusted their writing styles to suit the occasion and the audience. Third, they wanted their writing to count for something; as they said to us over and over, good writing to them was performative, the kind of writing that "made something happen in the world." Finally, they increasingly saw writing as collaborative, social, and participatory rather than solitary.

So yes, these students did plenty of emailing and texting; they were online 4
a good part of every day; they joined social networking sites enthusiastically. But rather than leading to a new illiteracy, these activities seemed to help them develop a range or *repertoire* of writing styles, tones, and formats along with a

range of abilities. Here's a student sending a text message to friends reporting on what she's doing on an internship in Bangladesh (she refers in the first few words to the fact that power has been going on and off ever since she arrived): "Next up: words stolen from before the power went out****~~~~~Whadda-ya-know, I am back in Dhaka from the villages of Mymensingh. I'm familiar enough with the villages now that it's harder to find things that really surprise me, though I keep looking ☺." In an informal message, this students feels free to use fragments ("Next up"), slang ("whadda-ya-know"), asterisks and tildas for emphasis, and a smiley.

Now look at a brief report she sends to the faculty adviser for her internship in Bangladesh: "In June of 2003, I traveled to Dhaka, Bangladesh for 9 weeks to intern for Grameen Bank. Grameen Bank is a micro-credit institution which seeks to alleviate poverty by providing access to financial capital. Grameen Bank provides small loans to poor rural women, who then use the capital to start small businesses and sustain income generating activities." Here the student is all business, using formal academic style to begin her first report. No slang, no use of special-effects markings: just the facts, ma'am. In the thousands of pieces of student writing we have examined, we see students moving with relative ease across levels of style (from the most informal to the most formal): these young people are for the most part aware of the context and audience for their writing—and they make the adjustments necessary to address them effectively.

Ah, you say, but these are students at Stanford—the crème de la crème. And I'll agree that these students were all very keen, very bright. But they were not all strong writers or communicators (though our study shows that they all improved significantly over the five years of the study) and they did not all come from privilege—in fact, a good number far from it. Still, they were part of what students on this campus call the "Stanford bubble." So let's look beyond that bubble to another study I conducted with researcher Karen Lunsford. About 18 months ago, we gathered a sample of first-year student writing from across all regions of the United States, from two-year and four-year schools, big schools and small schools, private and public. Replicating a study I'd conducted twenty-five years ago, we read a random sample of these student essays with a fine-tooth eye, noting every formal error in every piece of writing. And what did we find?

First, that the length of student writing has increased nearly three-fold in these 25 years, corroborating the fact that students today are writing more than ever before. Second, we found that while error patterns have changed in the last twenty-five years, the ratio of errors to number of words has remained stable not just for twenty-five years but for the last 100 years. In short, we found that students today certainly make errors—as all writers do—but that they are making no more errors than previous studies have documented. Different errors, yes— but more errors, no.

We found, for example, that spelling—the most prevalent error by over 300 percent some 25 years ago—now presents much less of a problem to writers. We can chalk up that change, of course, to spell-checkers, which do a good job overall—but still can't correct words that sound alike (to, too, two). But with technology, you win some and you lose some: the most frequent error in our recent study is "wrong word," and ironically a good number of these wrong words come from advice given by the sometimes-not-so-trusty spell-checkers. The student who seems from the context of the sentence to be trying to write "frantic," for example, apparently accepts the spell-checker's suggestion of "fanatic" instead. And finally, this recent study didn't turn up any significant interference from Internet lingo—no IMHOs, no LOLs, no 2nites, no smileys. Apparently, by the time many, many students get to college, they have a pretty good sense of what's appropriate: at the very least, they know the difference between a Facebook friend and a college professor.

7

In short, the research my colleagues and I have been doing supports what other researchers are reporting about digital technologies and learning. First, a lot of that learning (perhaps most of it) is taking place outside of class, in the literate activities (musical compositions, videos, photo collages, digital stories, comics, documentaries) young people are pursuing on their own. This is what Mimi Ito calls "kid-driven learning." Second, the participatory nature of digital media allows for more—not less—development of literacies, as Henry Jenkins argues compellingly.

8

If we look beyond the hand-wringing about young people and literacy today, beyond the view that paints them as either brain-damaged by technology or as cogs in the latest race to the top, we will see that the changes brought about

9

by the digital revolution are just that: changes. These changes alter the very grounds of literacy as the definition, nature, and scope of writing are all shifting away from the consumption of discourse to its production across a wide range of genres and media, away from individual "authors" to participatory and collaborative partners-in-production; away from a single static standard of correctness to a situated understanding of audience and context and purpose for writing. Luckily, young people are changing as well, moving swiftly to join in this expanded culture of writing. They face huge challenges, of course—challenges of access and of learning ever new ways with words (and images). What students need in facing these challenges is not derision or dismissal but solid and informed instruction. And that's where the real problem may lie—not with student semi-literacy but with that of their teachers.

WORKS CITED

Fishman, Jenn, Andrea A. Lunsford, Elizabeth McGregor, and Mark Otuteye. "Performing Writing, Performing Literacy." *College Composition and Communication* 57.2 (2005): 224–252. Print.

Ito, Mizuko, Heather Horst, Matteo Bittanti, danah boyd, Becky Herr-Stephenson, Patricia Lange, C.J. Pascoe, and Laura Robinson. *Living and Learning with New Media: Summary of Findings from the Digital Youth Project.* Cambridge: MIT Press, 2009. Print.

Ito, Mizuko, Sonja Baumer, Matteo Bittanti, danah boyd, Rachel Cody, Becky Herr-Stephenson, Heather Horst, and Patricia Lange. *Hanging Out, Messing Around, and Geeking Out: Kids Living and Learning with New Media.* Cambridge: MIT Press, 2009. Print.

Jenkins, Henry. *Confronting the Challenges of Participatory Culture: Media Education for the 21st Century.* Cambridge: MIT Press, 2009. Print.

———. *Convergence Culture: When Old and New Media Collide.* New York: NYU Press, 2008. Print.

Lunsford, Andrea A., and Karen J. Lunsford. "'Mistakes are a Fact of Life': A National Comparative Study." *College Composition and Communication* 59:4 (2008): 781–807. Print.

Rogers, Paul M. "The Development of Writers and Writing Abilities: A Longitudinal Study across and beyond the College-Span." Diss. University of California, Santa Barbara, 2008. Print.

UNDERSTANDING THE ESSAY

1. When Andrea Lunsford and her colleagues did a longitudinal study of undergraduate student writing at Sanford, she says, "several results emerged right away" (3). What were some of those preliminary results?

2. The students in Lunsford's study "did plenty of" emailing, texting, and other forms of online social networking and writing (4). These "activities," however, did not lead to "a new illiteracy," Lunsford argues (4). In her view, what did they lead to? Does Lunsford offer convincing evidence to support this part of her CLAIM? Point to specific EXAMPLES in her text.

3. How might the following words and phrases in Lunsford's text be said to confirm (or disprove) what she says about "a range . . . of styles, tones, and formats" as a mark of good writing: *longitudinal* (3), *crème de la crème* (6), *just the facts, ma'am* (5), *fine-tooth eye* (6), *you win some and you lose some* (7)?

4. "Ah, you say, but these are students at Stanford" (6). Is Lunsford wise to bring up this counterargument at this point in her ARGUMENT? Why or why not?

5. A significant portion of Lunsford's argument has to do with "errors" in student writing (6). What claim is she making here? How and how well does she support that claim? Point to specific details in her argument.

6. "In short," says Lunsford near the end of her argument, "the research my colleagues and I have done supports what other researchers are reporting about digital technologies and learning" (8). So what larger conclusion(s) about technology and literacy do Lunsford and colleagues come to? How and how effectively is this claim supported by her earlier, narrower conclusions about student writing at particular universities?

MIND AND MEDIA: IS *GOOGLE* MAKING US STUPID?

ANALYZING THE ARGUMENTS

. . . .

1. Among the three writers in this debate, which one(s) make the strongest argument that digital technologies are actually changing the way we think? What makes that (those) argument(s) particularly convincing?

2. In what ways might Nicholas Carr's "Hal and Me" be seen as an answer to Steven Pinker's "Mind over Mass Media"? Which argument do you find more convincing? Why?

3. Andrea Lunsford agrees with Pinker and Carr that digital technology may be changing how we think and write. How might her argument be seen to offer an alternative to their otherwise opposing points of view? Explain.

4. Whether or not you agree with their conclusions, which of these writers do you find most credible? Why? What strategies do they use to establish their credibility? For example, how well do they anticipate opposing arguments? Refer to particular passages.

FOR WRITING

. . . .

1. Choose a claim from one of these three arguments that you think could use more support. Write a paragraph providing additional evidence to support (or refute) that claim.

2. Write an argument that either supports or opposes the claim that sitting still and reading an entire book is no longer "worthwhile." Feel free to cite your own experience or that of your family or friends to support your argument.

3. Write a "modest proposal" suggesting that society should cease to use *Google* and other digital technology for an entire year. Be sure to cite the specific advantages of your proposal.

MONEYBALL:
ARE COLLEGE SPORTS
WORTH THE PRICE?

In 2011, the University of Miami Hurricanes ran into heavy weather: roughly half the football team was accused of accepting "gifts" for their services on the field. The case is pending before the National Collegiate Athletic Association (NCAA), the governing body of college sports. A year earlier, several star football players at Ohio State traded sports memorabilia for cash and tattoos. As a result, the school vacated the 2010 season and gave up scholarships under NCAA sanctions and the head coach resigned. Money and college sports: the scandals go back at least to 1947, when players on the City College of New York's basketball team began accepting bribes in exchange for point shaving. In the end, 32 players from seven schools were arrested. Perhaps such scandals could be avoided if college athletes were openly paid for their work like everyone else, including those rank-and-file professional athletes who make good salaries but attract fewer fans than the best college players. Should college athletes be paid what they're worth? How much is that? Or are the excesses of sportsbiz out of place in college? Should big-time college athletics be benched permanently?

In the following essays, **Michael Rosenberg**, **Joe Posnanski**, and **Laura Pappano** address—and argue how to resolve—these and other issues related to the long but turbulent marriage of money and college sports.

MICHAEL ROSENBERG

LET STARS GET PAID

Michael Rosenberg (b. 1954) is a sports writer and Michigan fan who worked for the *Detroit Free Press* for twelve years before joining the staff of *Sports Illustrated* in 2012. He is the author of *War as They Knew It: Woody Hayes, Bo Schembechler, and America in a Time of Unrest* (2008). In the following sports column (SI.com, July 26, 2011), Rosenberg argues that "corruption" in college sports can be reduced by changing the rules instead of simply punishing players who game the system for pay and other perks.

◇◇◇◇◇◇◇◇◇◇◇◇◇◇◇◇◇◇◇◇◇◇◇◇◇◇◇◇◇◇◇◇◇◇◇◇◇

E very Saturday in the fall, we pack college stadiums, raise the American flag, stand quietly as a marching band plays "The Star-Spangled Banner," and cheer for a sport that prohibits capitalism.

College athletes cannot be paid. Every American knows this. The concept is as entrenched in our bloodstreams as cholesterol. We have accepted it for so long, and gone along with the NCAA's[1] definition of right and wrong for so many years, that we don't even remember the reasons anymore.

1. The National Collegiate Athletic Association, the governing body of intercollegiate sports in the United States.

They can't be paid because they can't be paid, because they just can't, because it's not allowed, because if it were allowed, then they could be paid. And they can't. Because it's not allowed. Got it?

So when Cam Newton allegedly earns $180,000 playing college football to help repair his father's church, he is a villain. When Terrelle Pryor and A. J. Green sell memorabilia, they get suspended, even though their schools openly sell memorabilia.

When Robert Traylor, the poor son of a crack-addicted mother and absentee father, takes money from a booster, he gets exiled. When Reggie Bush accepts thousands of dollars from somebody who sees his pro potential, he has to return his Heisman Trophy.[2]

Former Auburn University quarterback Cam Newton, who now plays in the NFL.

Stanford quarterback Andrew Luck, who probably would have been the No. 1 pick in last April's NFL Draft,[3] turned down millions to return for his senior season. Given his worth, shouldn't he be able to make money while in college?

Look, cheating is wrong. The point here is not to excuse the cheaters. I hate cheating. The point is to redefine cheating.

The 2010–2011 NCAA manual says the "Principle of Amateurism" is important because college athletics are an "avocation" and . . . hang on, here comes the punchline: "student-athletes should be protected from exploitation by professional and commercial enterprise."

Really? When an athlete sells his jersey so he can pay rent, and the NCAA suspends him, is the NCAA really protecting him? Who is the NCAA kidding?

2. The most prestigious award in college football awarded annually to one player.

3. An annual event in which the teams of the National Football League (NFL) select former college football players for the upcoming season.

If major college sports did not exist, nobody would try to create them— 　10
not as we know them today. The entire enterprise is preposterous. If there were
no college sports, 100 school presidents would never issue the following press
release:

> We have decided to create sports teams to represent our universities.
> We will have to admit a lot of students with inferior academic records
> solely because they can play football or basketball, but hey, we're cool
> with that. Anyway, what matters here is that we can make billions of
> dollars doing this, and we're not going to let the players have anything
> beyond room, board, meals, and a few other sundries. Not only that,
> but we will not allow ANYBODY to give them money. We have decided
> money is bad for them. It . . . uh . . . corrupts! Yes. It corrupts. Now:
> Who wants to buy a personal-seat license?

We have a system where coaches are worth $5 million a year but star play- 　11
ers are worth $40,000—a structure completely incongruous with the rest of the
sports landscape.

It's time to start over. College sports have so many redeeming qualities— 　12
the sense of community, the thrill of competition, and goshdarnit, I'll even throw
"life lessons for young people" in there. Why are we so obsessed with restraining
the income of players? Who is winning here? What are we protecting?

That NCAA manual devotes 16 pages to amateurism. We can cut it down 　13
to one, with one principle: Athletes may not be paid directly with university funds.

That's it. One rule. There is your "amateurism." This way, universities can 　14
spend their booster donations, TV money, and sponsorship dollars subsidizing
facilities, staff, operating costs, and athletic scholarships. College athletics will
continue to thrive across dozens of sports.

But those who can cash in on their fame and success will be able to do it. If 　15
a wealthy South Carolina alum wants to give $50,000 a year to every Game-
cock, he can do it.

Is this fair? No, not really. If we wanted to be completely fair, then football 　16
and basketball players would not be forced to subsidize non-revenue athletes.

But this is a start. It's a way to keep what we love about college athletics without unduly penalizing athletes.

For more help with logical fallacies, see p. 526.

17 Some day, we will look back on this era of college sports the way we look back on Prohibition.[4] We'll see that there were some good intentions behind it, along with some misguided fears. The problem with amateurism in college sports is the same problem the nation had with Prohibition: It is impossible to enforce.

18 The simple fact is that college athletes want to get paid (who wouldn't?) and there are literally thousands of people out there who would like to pay them. Why are we stopping this? What is the big deal? What do you think would happen if your starting quarterback was allowed to take $100,000 from somebody who enjoyed watching him play? Would the Earth crash into the sun?

19 I once had a remarkably circular conversation with former NCAA president Myles Brand about the NCAA's amateurism rules. One of his chief arguments was this: "The fact is we don't pay students in other areas when they are engaged in activities as part of their education."

20 That may be (mostly) true. But colleges don't prevent their students from making additional money either. If a student at the University of Southern California School of Cinematic Arts is offered $2 million to direct a major-studio movie, that student would still be allowed to take his film classes. USC wouldn't say, "Hey, that's no good. Give us your money so we can pay a professor seven figures."

21 This is not about whether college athletes are "exploited." That argument is a canard. Yes, they get a free education, and get to eat free meals, and get tutors and great weightlifting facilities. So does Kobe Bryant. (Well, he did, until last month.)

22 With every booster scandal, we confirm what we already suspect: Many people are eager to pay these young men for their work, and the NCAA cabal won't allow it.

23 Should college athletes be paid? That's not really the question. No, the question is this: Should college athletes be allowed to be paid? Should they be allowed to take money for doing something perfectly legal?

---

4. Constitutional ban on the sale and consumption of alcohol in 1919; repealed in 1933.

Of course they should. In America in 2011, why are we even debating this?   24

Colleges have assigned themselves the role of Robin Hood: they take the   25
earnings of football and basketball players and give most of it to swimmers, soc-
cer players, and other not-so-popular athletes.

That's not terrible. But it is still wrong. And yet . . . well, progress comes   26
in small steps, and for now, I'm willing to let schools keep on doing that. Really.
Just loosen the rules so the most popular athletes can cash in on their fame and
success. Let them sign endorsement deals, take money from boosters, and get
free tattoos and meals.

Then the NCAA can stop slapping every hand that is out and focus its   27
energy and money on academic fraud and education standards for athletes.

The republic will survive. Fans will still watch the NCAA tournament.   28
Double-reverses will still be thrilling. Alabama will still hate Auburn. Everybody will still hate Duke. Let's do what's right and reexamine what we think is
wrong.

UNDERSTANDING THE ESSAY

1. Michael Rosenberg says he is not arguing that college athletes *should* be paid.
   What CLAIM *is* he making? Where does he state that claim most clearly and
   directly? What are some of the main reasons he gives to support it?

2. Beyond hoping to convince readers to accept the truth or accuracy of an author's
   claim, an ARGUMENT can also seek to convince readers to act in a certain way.
   What action does Rosenberg want his readers to take? Where does he spell
   out that part of his argument?

3. Rosenberg gives an excellent, if comic, example of circular reasoning in paragraph 3. What's faulty, in general, about such logic? About the specific reasoning, as Rosenberg sees it, of the NCAA president's defense of "amateurism rules" (19)? Explain.

4. Rosenberg refers to the NCAA as a *cabal* (22). What are the implications of
   this term, and why does he use it?

5. "Look, cheating is wrong. The point here is not to excuse cheaters. I hate
   cheating" (7). These words are not aimed at the reader's faculties of reason

but at his or her emotions and moral sense. Is this an effective strategy? Why or why not?

6. Rosenberg does not condone cheating in college sports, he says. Rather he wants "to redefine cheating" (7). How? Point to specific passages in the text.

7. Arguments often hinge on definitions of terms. When he says that cheating should be redefined, is Rosenberg adopting a good strategy of argument, or is he merely begging the question? Explain.

JOE POSNANSKI

COLLEGE ATHLETES
SHOULD NOT BE PAID

Joe Posnanski (b. 1967) is a sports journalist and former columnist for *Sports Illustrated* who now has his own *Joe Blog*. In addition to *The Soul of Baseball* (2007), which won a Casey award for the best baseball book of the year, he is the author of *Paterno* (2012), a biography of the late, controversial Penn State coach. A native of Cleveland, Posnanski is the type of sports enthusiast who, according to a colleague, "revels in sports for their own sake, but also eagerly plumbs them for metaphors for life." In "College Athletes Should Not Be Paid" (SI.com, July 28, 2011), Posnanski plumbs the "vital" relationship between colleges and their students and alumni—a connection, he argues, that "is at its strongest with sports."

◇∿

M y great good friend Michael Rosenberg has a wonderful knack of writing things that strike powerful disagreement inside me. It is one of his many gifts. This is not to say that I always, or even often, disagree with Michael. I don't. I think Michael's one of the best sportswriters in the country and we see things the same way the vast majority of the time. Maybe that's why when I *do* disagree with him—like I did with a Tiger Woods column he wrote a couple of

1

years ago or the let's pay the stars of college sports piece he wrote this week—it's a pretty strong emotion, the sort of emotion that pushes me to mumble to myself and to start a new file on my computer.

There is something I have wanted to say for a while about big-time col- 2
lege athletics, but it is one of those weird thoughts that is both blindingly obvious and strangely difficult to put into words. That's why I had never written it before. It was reading Michael's piece, and this sentence in particular— "If we wanted to be completely fair, then football and basketball players would not be forced to subsidize non-revenue athletes"—that opened the door. It has been a long time since I read a sentence I more strongly disagreed with.

And that led to the words that form the heart of this piece . . . words that, 3
I have to say, surprised me: "College athletics are *not* about the players."

You are more than welcome to stop reading now. 4

What is the question here? Let's talk about this for a second here before moving 5
to the big point. Most people frame the question like so: Should the See p. 524 for ways to state a claim so it is easier to defend. best college athletes in the most successful sports be paid for all the hard work they put in and for all the revenue they help generate at colleges across America?

When the question is framed like that, it's hard to see how there are two 6
sides to the argument: *of course* they should get paid. This is America.

But, really, that's not the question, is it? I hate to bring up this old bit, but 7
to get where we are going I must: Big-time athletes do get paid. They get free college tuition. We all used to believe that was worth something (parents of college aged kids know that it's worth something). They get room and board. At the kinds of schools we are talking about, they get incredible facilities to train, the best coaching available (how much does it cost just to send your child to one of these coach's *camps*?), public relations machines to help them build their brand, national exposure, free travel, the best doctors, direct access to the professional ranks, youthful fame that can open doors for the rest of their lives, priceless experiences, and so on. How much do you think parents would pay to send their son to play four years of basketball at Duke for Mike Krzyzewski? Is there a price tag you could put on that?

Mike Krzyzewski (Coach K) of Duke University instructs his players.

I'm not saying this to make any point except that the question has to be   8
asked the right way. The question is: Should big-time college athletes (in the
revenue-producing sports, of course) get paid *more* than they do now?

I have long thought: Yes. They should. I've never believed in amateur-   9
ism for amateurism's sake. I've never bought into the notion that by keeping
money away from players you are doing them favors. The arcane rules of the
NCAA[1] drive me mad, just like they drive Andy Staples and everyone else mad.
The occasional story that comes out about schools getting in trouble for paying
the plane fare to send a player home to his grandmother's funeral, or anything like
that, makes me so angry I wish the whole system was burned to the ground. I
have long wished they could at least give players a stipend or something.

1. The National Collegiate Athletic Association, the governing body of college sports.

But here is my problem: Every time I read another story about *why* star players should get paid more—and remember, we are almost always talking only about the stars, almost always talking about a few dozen players scattered across America—I come away feeling more and more like they should not. The biggest argument for paying the athletes comes down to this: College players (those stars especially) are the reason why these schools are generating so much money and so they deserve a much bigger piece of the pie. These sports are *about* them. 10

And you know what? I totally, completely, utterly, and thoroughly disagree with that. 11

Ask yourself this: What would happen if tomorrow every single player on the Auburn football team quit and re-formed as a professional team called the Birmingham Bandits. Who would go to their games? Anyone? How much would those talented young men get paid? 12

Ask yourself this: What would happen if all the ACC basketball schools dropped their players and replaced them with Division II[2] talent? Would North Carolina–Duke suddenly play in empty arenas? 13

Ask yourself this: Say the first, second, and third All-America Teams in college football tomorrow went into the NFL.[3] They just left. How many fewer fans would the college games draw? How many fewer people would watch Texas and Tennessee and Iowa? 14

Ask yourself this: Why do we care about college football? We know that the skill level in college football is vastly inferior to the skill level of NFL teams. Heck, many Heisman Trophy[4] winners are not even NFL prospects. Yet, by the millions, we watch. We cheer. We buy. We rejoice. We gripe. We wear. We eat. We live it. Many of us even argue that we *prefer* the quality and style of college to pro, we *like* watching those games more. But is it the quality and style we prefer or is it passion, youth, exuberance, and that we feel closer to the game? 15

---

2. When its three new members have fully joined, the Atlantic Coast Conference will consist of 15 major college athletic programs; Division II teams in the NCAA compete at an intermediate (and less expensive) level.

3. National Football League.

4. Awarded annually to the single most outstanding player in college football.

No, college athletics is not *about* the players. College athletics is FOR the $\quad$ 16
players, but that's a different thing, and that's a distinction we don't often make.
College football only works on this grand scale, I believe, because it's about
the colleges. The alumni connect to it. The people in the town connect to it. The
people in the state connect to it. People are proud of their connection to the
University of South Carolina and Clemson, they are inspired by Alabama and
Auburn, Penn State and Notre Dame and Stanford, they identify themselves
through Missouri and Wisconsin and Florida and Texas A&M. The players
matter because they chose those schools, they play for those schools, they win
for those schools, and they lose for those schools, too. Everyone, of course, wants
them to be the best players available, and some are willing to cheat the current
system to get those players. But soon the players move on, and the love affair continues, just as strong, just as vital. The *connection* is what drives college football.

Otherwise, without that connection, it's just football that isn't nearly as $\quad$ 17
well played as the NFL.

Big-time college football . . . big-time college basketball . . . these are about $\quad$ 18
the schools that play them. They are about the institutions, the campuses, the
landmarks, being young—the front of the jersey and not the back, as coaches
love to say. This connection—fan to college—is at its strongest with sports.
People might get irritated when the alumni fundraisers find them at their new
address (how do they always find me?). They might not want to send in money
to build a better library. But they'll buy sweatshirts, and they'll buy tickets, and
they'll travel to bowl games, and they'll pay for pay-per-view, and they'll take a
chartered bus to a subregional in Tulsa. This direct line to sports is how they
support—and how they love—their school.

So it seems obvious to me that the money from football—revenue-driving $\quad$ 19
basketball too—should go to offer more and better opportunities at those
colleges. That should be its singular purpose. The money from football—as
much of it as possible—should pay for talented young tennis players to go to
that school. It should pay to give opportunities to gifted swimmers, dedicated
runners, hard-working volleyball players, and so on. The point is not how many
people watch those athletes play, or how many people care about the sports they
play. The point is about opportunity and education and developing people and

creating a richer environment at the school. My friend Mechelle Voepel was just telling me about Caton Hill—have you heard of her? She played basketball at Oklahoma. She's now a flight surgeon in the Army, and she says basketball helped her get there. How many stories are there like that from softball and track and lacrosse and all the rest? If football is pulling in all this cash and is not offering those kinds of chances, if it is not making the colleges better places, then who needs it?

Michael in his piece does not say that the schools should pay the players—at least for now. No, he makes the argument that basically they should allow boosters to pay the players, and allow the players to take whatever money and benefits and endorsements they can get. I can only imagine a college sport where high school kids hire agents and send them from school to school to cut the best deal they can make with various car dealers, CEOs, and tattoo-parlor owners. I can only imagine how many people will take the money they normally give to the school and instead spend it to get a running back they can call their very own. Maybe they can have the players wear a little patch on their shoulders with the name of the booster who gave the player the money to come to the school. That touchdown was scored by Tommy Tutone and brought to you by Bob's Trucking. 20

But, even that doesn't bother me much. I'm all for the NCAA loosening up on the rules. No, it's the larger point. Schools are drowning *now*. I have good friends, both of them have good jobs, both of them have saved responsibly, and they have no idea how they can afford to send all three of their kids to college. No idea. And their kids are smart, they're getting some scholarship money, but the price is still overwhelming. Look around: Schools are slashing sports. They are raising tuition prices. They are cutting scholarships. Meanwhile college football and basketball—especially football—has become an arms race, with insane salaries being paid to coaches, and cathedrals built for weight training, and video equipment that the Pentagon would envy. 21

I'm not sure how you stop that. Maybe you can't stop it. Maybe you don't even want to stop it . . . that's a whole other topic. But paying the stars seems to be sending college football careening away from anything close to the point. College football is not popular because of the stars. College football is popular 22 because of that first word. Take away the college part, add in money, and you are left with professional minor league football and a developmental basketball league. See how many people go watch that.

UNDERSTANDING THE ESSAY

1. Joe Posnanski begins his essay by saying what a good friend Michael Rosenberg (author of the previous essay) is to him and what a great sportswriter he is. Is this a good strategy of ARGUMENT, given that Posnanski is about to attack his colleague's position? Explain.

2. Reframing the question at issue is a common tactic in debate. Posnanski adopts it when he asks, "What is the question here?" (5). What *was* the original question? How does Posnanski reframe it, and how does this change help (if it does help) to advance his argument?

3. "Ask yourself this"—with this phrase, Posnanski introduces several what-ifs (12–15). How accurate are his conclusions in each hypothetical case? How and how well do these what-ifs prove the point he is making here about the importance of college sponsorship?

4. Posnanski describes NCAA rules as *arcane* (9). Why might he choose this term rather than, say, *complicated* or *confusing*?

5. "I totally, completely, utterly and thoroughly disagree with that" (11). What point is Posnanski disagreeing with so absolutely and unequivocally here? What effect might he hope to have upon the audience by being so emphatic—and personal? Does the strategy work? Why or why not?

6. "No, college athletics is not *about* the players. College athletics is *for* the players, but that's a different thing, and that's a distinction that we don't often make" (16). What distinction is Posnanski making here? How well does he demonstrate that this distinction (and thus the conclusion of his entire argument) is valid? Explain.

LAURA PAPPANO

HOW BIG-TIME SPORTS ATE COLLEGE LIFE

Laura Pappano (b. 1962) is a journalist who writes about education, social issues, and gender (especially in sports). A graduate of Yale, she is the author of *Inside School Turnarounds* (2010) and co-author of *Playing with the Boys* (2008). The following selection (from the *New York Times*, January 20, 2012) examines how revenue-producing sports, especially football and basketball, have spilled over into all aspects of campus life, including academics. What can be done to turn back the tide? The best hope, Pappano argues on the basis of her extensive research and numerous interviews, lies in what many faculty members and academic administrators call "balance."

◇╲╱◇╲╱◇╲╱◇╲╱◇╲╱◇╲╱◇╲╱◇╲╱◇╲╱◇╲╱◇╲╱◇╲╱◇╲╱◇╲╱◇╲╱◇

It was a great day to be a Buckeye. Josh Samuels, a junior from Cincinnati, dates his decision to attend Ohio State to November 10, 2007, and the chill he felt when the band took the field during a football game against Illinois. "I looked over at my brother and I said, 'I'm going here. There is nowhere else I'd rather be.'" (Even though Illinois won, 28–21.)

Tim Collins, a junior who is president of Block O, the 2,500-member student fan organization, understands the rush. "It's not something I usually admit to, that I applied to Ohio State 60 percent for the sports. But the more I do tell that to people, they'll say it's a big reason why they came, too."

Ohio State boasts 17 members of the American Academy of Arts and Sciences, three Nobel laureates, eight Pulitzer Prize winners, 35 Guggenheim Fellows, and a MacArthur winner. But sports rule.

"It's not, 'Oh, yeah, Ohio State, that wonderful physics department.' It's football," said Gordon Aubrecht, an Ohio State physics professor.

Last month, Ohio State hired Urban Meyer to coach football for $4 million a year plus bonuses (playing in the B.C.S. National Championship game nets him an extra $250,000; a graduation rate over 80 percent would be worth $150,000).[1] He has personal use of a private jet.

Dr. Aubrecht says he doesn't have enough money in his own budget to cover attendance at conferences. "From a business perspective," he can see why Coach Meyer was hired, but he calls the package just more evidence that the "tail is wagging the dog."

Dr. Aubrecht is not just another cranky tenured professor. Hand-wringing seems to be universal these days over big-time sports, specifically football and men's basketball. Sounding much like his colleague, James J. Duderstadt, former president of the University of Michigan and author of "Intercollegiate Athletics and the American University," said this: "Nine of 10 people don't understand what you are saying when you talk about research universities. But you say 'Michigan' and they understand those striped helmets running under the banner."

For good or ill, big-time sports has become the public face of the university, the brand that admissions offices sell, a public-relations machine thanks to ESPN exposure. At the same time, it has not been a good year for college athletics. Child-abuse charges against a former Penn State assistant football coach brought down the program's legendary head coach and the university's president. Not long after, allegations of abuse came to light against an assistant basketball

---

1. The Bowl Championship Series (BCS) selects the ten teams that compete in the NCAA championship in Division I, the highest level of play.

coach at Syracuse University. Combine that with the scandals over boosters showering players with cash and perks at Ohio State and, allegedly, the University of Miami, and a glaring power gap becomes apparent between the programs and the institutions that house them.

"There is certainly a national conversation going on now that I can't ever recall taking place," said William E. Kirwan, chancellor of the University of Maryland system and codirector of the Knight Commission on Intercollegiate Athletics. "We've reached a point where big-time intercollegiate athletics is undermining the integrity of our institutions, diverting presidents and institutions from their main purpose." 9

The damage to reputation was clear in a November survey by Widmeyer Communications in which 83 percent of 1,000 respondents blamed the "culture of big money" in college sports for Penn State officials' failure to report suspected child abuse to local law enforcement; 40 percent said they would discourage their child from choosing a Division I institution "that places a strong emphasis on sports," and 72 percent said Division I sports has "too much influence over college life." 10

For tips on using statistics to support an argument, see p. 522.

Has big-time sports hijacked the American campus? The word today is "balance," and the worry is how to achieve it. 11

The explosion in televised games has spread sports fever well beyond traditional hotbeds like Alabama and Ole Miss. Classes are canceled to accommodate broadcast schedules, and new research suggests that fandom can affect academic performance. Campus life itself revolves around not just going to games but lining up and camping out to get into them. 12

"It's become so important on the college campus that it's one of the only ways the student body knows how to come together," said Allen Sack, president-elect of the Drake Group, a faculty network that lobbies for academic integrity in college sports. "In China and other parts of the world, there are no gigantic stadiums in the middle of campus. There is a laser focus on education as being the major thing. In the United States, we play football." 13

Dr. Sack, interim dean of the University of New Haven's college of business, was sipping orange juice at a coffee shop a few blocks from the Yale Bowl. It was a fitting place to meet, given that when the Ivy League was formed in 14

1954, presidents of the eight member colleges saw where football was headed and sought to stop it. The pact they made, according to a contemporaneous account in the *Harvard Crimson*, aimed to ensure that players would "enjoy the game as participants in a form of recreational competition rather than as professional performers in public spectacles."

There is nothing recreational about Division I football today, points out 15 Dr. Sack, who played for Notre Dame in the 1960s. Since then, athletic departments have kicked the roof off their budgets, looking more like independent franchises than university departments.

It is that point—"this commercial thing" in the middle of academia, as 16 Charles T. Clotfelter, a public policy professor at Duke, put it—that some believe has thrown the system out of kilter. In his recent book *Big-Time Sports in American Universities*, Dr. Clotfelter notes that between 1985 and 2010, average salaries at public universities rose 32 percent for full professors, 90 percent for presidents and 650 percent for football coaches.

The same trend is apparent in a 2010 Knight Commission report that 17 found the 10 highest-spending athletic departments spent a median of $98 million in 2009, compared with $69 million just four years earlier. Spending on high-profile sports grew at double to triple the pace of that on academics. For example, Big Ten colleges, including Penn State, spent a median of $111,620 per athlete on athletics and $18,406 per student on academics.

Division I football and basketball, of course, bring in millions of dollars a 18 year in ticket sales, booster donations, and cable deals. Penn State football is a money-maker: 2010 Department of Education figures show the team spending $19.5 million and bringing in almost $73 million, which helps support 29 varsity sports. Still, only about half of big-time programs end up in the black; many others have to draw from student fees or the general fund to cover expenses. And the gap between top programs and wannabes is only growing with colleges locked into an arms race to attract the best coaches and build the most luxurious venues in hopes of luring top athletes, and donations from happy alumni.

College sports doesn't just demand more and more money; it is demand- 19 ing more attention from fans.

Glen R. Waddell, associate professor of economics at the University of   20
Oregon, wanted to know how much. In a study published last month as part
of the National Bureau of Education Research working paper series, Oregon
researchers compared student grades with the performance of the Fighting
Ducks, winner of this year's Rose Bowl and a crowd pleaser in their Nike uniforms in crazy color combinations and mirrored helmets.

"Here is evidence that suggests that when your football team does well,   21
grades suffer," said Dr. Waddell, who compared transcripts of over 29,700 students from 1999 to 2007 against Oregon's win-loss record. For every three
games won, grade-point average for men dropped 0.02, widening the G.P.A.
gender gap by 9 percent. Women's grades didn't suffer. In a separate survey of
183 students, the success of the Ducks also seemed to cause slacking off: students reported studying less (24 percent of men, 9 percent of women), consuming more alcohol (28 percent, 20 percent), and partying more (47 percent, 28
percent).

While acknowledging a need for more research, Dr. Waddell believes the   22
results should give campus leaders pause: fandom can carry an academic price.
"No longer can it be the case where we skip right over that inconvenience," he
said.

Dr. Clotfelter, too, wanted to examine study habits. He tracked articles   23
downloaded from campus libraries during March Madness, the National Collegiate Athletic Association basketball tournament. Library patrons at universities with teams in the tournament viewed 6 percent fewer articles a day as long
as their team was in contention. When a team won an upset or close game,
article access fell 19 percent the day after the victory. Neither dip was made up
later with increased downloads.

"Big-time sports," Dr. Clotfelter said, "have a real effect on the way people   24
in universities behave."

* * *

Television has fed the popularity. The more professional big-time college   25
sports has become, the more nonathletes have been drawn in, said Murray
Sperber, author of *Beer and Circus: How Big-Time College Sports Has Crippled*

Undergraduate Education. "Media coverage gets into kids' heads," he said, "and by the time they are ready to choose a college, it becomes a much bigger factor than it was historically."

In the last ten years, the number of college football and basketball games on ESPN channels rose to 1,320 from 491. This doesn't include games shown by competitors: the Big 10 Network, Fox, CBS/Turner, Versus, and NBC. All that programming means big games scheduled during the week and television crews, gridlock, and tailgating on campus during the school day.

26

"How can you have a Wednesday night football game without shutting down the university for a day or two?" asked Dr. Sack of the Drake Group with a twinge of sarcasm. He's not exactly wrong, though. Last semester, the University of Central Florida canceled afternoon classes before the televised game against the University of Tulsa. Mississippi State canceled a day of classes before a Thursday night broadcast of a football game against Louisiana State, creating an online skirmish between Bulldog fans and a blogger who suggested parents should get their tuition back.

27

Even Boston College bowed, canceling afternoon classes because the football game against Florida State was on ESPN at 8 p.m. Janine Hanrahan, a Boston College senior, was so outraged at missing her political science class, "Immigration, Processes, and Policies," that she wrote an opinion piece headlined "B.C.'s Backwards Priorities" in the campus newspaper. "It was an indication that football was superseding academics," she explained. ("We are the national role model," a university spokesman, Jack Dunn, responded. "We are the school everyone calls to say, 'Where do you find the balance?'")

28

Universities make scheduling sacrifices not just for the lucrative contracts but also because few visuals build the brand better than an appearance on ESPN's road show "College GameDay." (In November, it had John L. Hennessey, president of Stanford, out on the Oval at daybreak working the crowd.) The school spirit conveyed by cheering thousands—there were 18,000 on Francis Quadrangle at the University of Missouri, Columbia, on October 23, 2010, for "GameDay"—is a selling point to students choosing colleges. When Missouri first started recruiting in Chicago a decade ago, few prospective students had ever heard the university's nickname, "Mizzou," according to the admis-

29

sions director, Barbara Rupp. "Now they know us by 'Mizzou,'" thanks in part to "GameDay." "I can't deny that," she said.

Universities play the sports card, encouraging students to think of themselves as fans. A Vanderbilt admissions blog last fall featured "My Vandy Fanatic Weekend" describing the thrill of attending a basketball game and football game back to back. "One of the things we hear in the admissions office is that students these days who are serious about academics are still interested in sports," said John Gaines, director of undergraduate admissions. Mr. Gaines slipped in that its academic competitor Washington University in St. Louis is only Division III. "We always make sure we throw in a few crowd shots of people wearing black and gold" during presentations. Imagine, he is saying, "calling yourself a Commodore."

Or calling yourself a Cornhusker. A few years ago, the "Big Red Welcome" for new University of Nebraska students began including a special treat: the chance to replicate the football team's famed "tunnel walk," jogging along the snaking red carpet below Memorial Stadium, then crashing through the double doors onto the field (though without the 86,000 fans).

When Kirk Kluver, assistant dean for admissions at Nebraska's College of Law, set up his information table at recruiting fairs last year, a student in Minnesota let him know he would "check out Nebraska now that you are part of the Big 10." He got the same reaction in Arizona. Mr. Kluver said applications last fall were up 20 percent, while law school applications nationally fell 10 percent.

Penn State's new president, Rodney Erickson, announced last month that he wanted to lower the football program's profile. How is unclear. A Penn State spokeswoman declined to make anyone available to discuss the future besides releasing a statement from Dr. Erickson about seeking "balance."

What would balance really look like?

Duke officials pride themselves in offering both an excellent education and a stellar sports program.

Six years ago this spring, Duke experienced its own national scandal when three lacrosse players were accused of rape by a stripper hired for a party at the "lacrosse house"—a bungalow since torn down. The charges were found to be false, but the episode prompted university leaders to think hard about the relationship between academics and athletics.

Kevin M. White, the athletic director, now reports directly to the president of Duke. It was part of structural changes to more healthily integrate athletics into university life, said James E. Coleman Jr., a law professor who is chairman of the faculty athletics council and was chairman of the committee that investigated the athletes' behavior. (Vanderbilt made an even stronger move in 2008, disbanding the athletics department and folding it into the student life division.) Sitting in his office on Duke's Durham, North Carolina, campus, Dr. Coleman set his lunch tray on a mountain of papers and explained the challenges. He calls sports "a public square for universities" but also acknowledges how rising commercialism comes with strings that "have become spider webs."

A 2008 report by the athletics department, "Unrivaled Ambition: A Strategic Plan for Duke Athletics," praises the K-Ville bonding experience and the "identity and cohesion," of the rivalry with U.N.C. as it describes in stressful language the facilities arms race, skyrocketing coach salaries, and the downside of television deals.

"We no longer determine at what time we will play our games, because they are scheduled by TV executives," it laments, going on to complain about away games at 9 p.m. "Students are required to board a flight at 2 a.m., arriving back at their dorms at 4 or 5 a.m., and then are expected to go to class, study, and otherwise act as if it were a normal school day." And: "our amateur student-athletes take the field with a corporate logo displayed on their uniform beside 'Duke.' "

"The key thing is to control the things you can control and make sure the athletic program doesn't trump the rest of the university, as it has in some places," Dr. Coleman said. "These presidents have to do more than pay lip service to this notion of balance between athletics and academics." He suggests that elevating academic standards for athletes is one way to assert university—not athletic department—control over programs.

He has also tried to foster rapport between faculty members and the athletic department. "The difficulty is having faculty understand athletics," he said. "Both sides need to cross lines. Otherwise, it becomes these two silos with no connection." Last month, Dr. Coleman hosted a lunch that brought together Mr. White, athletics staff members and professors on his committee. He's also revamping a program to match faculty members with coaches, and sends them sports-related articles to bone up on issues.

Pointed questions about oversight of its athletic program were raised at Penn State's faculty senate meeting last month, and faculty involvement is the subject of a national meeting of the Coalition on Intercollegiate Athletics at the University of Tulsa this weekend. John S. Nichols, the group cochairman and professor emeritus at Penn State, says professors typically ignore the many issues that swirl around sports and influence the classroom. His list includes decisions about recruiting and admissions, and even conference realignments. Starting in 2013, the Big East will stretch over seven states, meaning not just football and basketball players but all student athletes—and some fans—will be making longer trips to away games. Dr. Nichols says it is time to "put some checks in place" on uncontrolled growth of athletics "or consider a different model." 42

To be sure, efforts to rehabilitate major college sports are not new. Amid much debate, an NCAA plan to raise scholarship awards by $2,000 was being reviewed this month. Some have seen it as the athletes' due, for the money they bring in, and others as pay for play; some colleges have complained they can't afford it. 43

Many are skeptical that reining in college sports is even possible; the dollars are simply too attractive, the pressures from outside too great. Mr. White said that it was naïve "to think we will ever put the toothpaste back in the tube." He added, "There is an oversized, insatiable interest in sports, and college sports is part of that." 44

But some decisions are in university hands. 45

Despite Duke's ascent to basketball royalty, Cameron Indoor Stadium—built in 1940, renovated in the 1980s, and at 9,300 seats one of the smallest venues for a big-time program—still gives thousands of the best seats to students. At many large programs, courtside seats and luxury boxes go to boosters. But "outsiders with money," Dr. Coleman said, can make demands and change 46 the way the team fits in with a university. "We could easily double the size of our basketball stadium and sell it out," he said. "That will never happen. If it does, you will know Duke has gone over to the dark side."

UNDERSTANDING THE ESSAY

. . . .

1. Early in her ARGUMENT, Laura Pappano raises a key question in the ongoing national debate about college athletics: "Has big-time sports hijacked the American campus?" (11)? To what extent is this a RHETORICAL QUESTION, one that the author already has an answer to and is actually using to make a statement? Explain.

2. What are the implications of the word *hijacked* (11)? Why do you think Pappano chose this term instead of framing her question in more neutral language, such as *"come to play too large a part"* or even *"taken over"*? Point out other places in her essay where Pappano's word choice suggests what her own views might be.

3. A key word throughout Pappano's essay is *balance* (11, 28, 34). What do college and sports officials mean by the term? Why, according to Pappano, are they so concerned with balance?

4. "Balance" is an important concept in newspaper reporting as well as sports— and in argumentation. How balanced (showing both sides of the question) is Pappano's presentation of the issues she is writing about? How does she achieve (or fail to achieve) balance? Point to specific passages in her essay.

5. Although she cites specific examples of particular schools—and even of individual students—Pappano also uses other kinds of EVIDENCE, such as statistics and expert testimony, to frame and support the argument that the balance between college sports and academics needs to be redressed. Which pieces of evidence do you find most convincing? Do the pieces add up to sufficient proof? Why or why not?

6. What is Pappano's apparent PURPOSE in returning, at the end of her argument, to the EXAMPLE of big-time basketball at Duke? How and how well has she developed the Duke example to prepare readers for this conclusion?

MONEYBALL: ARE COLLEGE SPORTS WORTH THE PRICE?

ANALYZING THE ARGUMENTS

. . . .

1. Among the three writers in this debate, which one(s) make the strongest argument for the value (whether monetary or moral or both) of college sports? What makes that (those) arguments particularly convincing? Cite particular passages and pieces of evidence.

2. Joe Posnanski's "College Athletes Should Not Be Paid" is a direct response to Michael Rosenberg's "Let Stars Get Paid." Point out specific places where he confronts his opponent's views, and identify some of the strategies he draws on, such as using logic, appealing to the reader's emotions or sense of ethics, citing facts and figures, etc. Explain why you find those strategies to be especially effective here—or ineffective.

3. Whether or not you agree with their conclusions, which of these three writers do you find most credible? How do they establish their credibility? For example, which ones seem most OBJECTIVE, or best informed, or most committed to their subjects? Refer to particular passages in the texts.

FOR WRITING

. . . .

1. Choose a CLAIM from one of these three arguments that you think could use more support. Write a paragraph providing additional evidence to support (or refute) that claim.

2. Write an argument that either supports or opposes one of the following claims: (1) profits from big-time college sports help to pay for minor sports and academic programs; (2) the most vital connection between most alumni and their schools is the sports connection; (3) sports have eaten a big hole in college life. Be sure to back up your claim with copious evidence.

CHAPTER THIRTEEN
CLASSIC ESSAYS
AND SPEECHES

꠵꠵꠵꠵꠵꠵꠵꠵꠵꠵꠵꠵꠵꠵꠵꠵꠵꠵꠵꠵꠵꠵꠵꠵꠵꠵꠵꠵꠵꠵꠵꠵

T HE essays and speeches in this chapter are "classics"—timeless examples of good writing across the centuries. What makes them timeless? Jonathan Swift's "A Modest Proposal," for instance, is nearly 300 years old, and the speaker is a "projector," a word we don't even use anymore in the sense that Swift used it, for a person who is full of foolish projects. However, the moral and economic issues that Swift addresses are as timely today as they were in the eighteenth century. His greedy countrymen, Swift charges—not to mention English landlords and "a very knowing American of my acquaintance"—will do anything for money (9).

What Makes a Classic

This sense of relevance—the feeling that what the writer has to say applies directly to us and our time—is one measure of a "classic." We feel it with all the essays and speeches in this chapter, including the Declaration of Independence; Abraham Lincoln's Second Inaugural Address; Sojourner Truth's "Ain't I a Woman?"; Virginia Woolf's "The Death of the Moth"; and Martin Luther King Jr.'s "I Have a Dream."

In addition to their timeless themes, the works in this chapter are classics because the writer of each one has a brilliant command of language and of the fundamental forms and patterns of written or spoken discourse. By taking apart these great essays and speeches, you will find that they are constructed using the same basic strategies and techniques of writing you have been studying through-out this book. All the basic modes of writing are here—NARRATION, DESCRIP-TION, EXPOSITION, and ARGUMENT—but interwoven seamlessly to make a *text*, a written fabric of words with each strand worked carefully into the grand design.

Let's look more closely at Virginia Woolf's influential "The Death of the Moth" as an example of how a great writer combines the basic patterns of writ-ing into a unified whole. These patterns are all the more tightly woven because Woolf's essay not only makes connections, it is *about* the connectedness of all living things.

Mixing the Modes

As in Annie Dillard's essay on the same subject at the beginning of this book, the eponymous moth gives Woolf's essay a visual and thematic focal point. (*Epony-mous*, meaning "name-giving," is not a word you get to use every day.) Thus much of her essay is devoted to a detailed description of "the present specimen, with his narrow hay-coloured wings, fringed with a tassel" (1). The moth's little world is so limited that we wonder, at first, why Woolf is bothering to show it to us: "He flew vigorously to one corner" of the surrounding windowpane and, "after waiting there a second, flew across to the other. What remained for him," Woolf wonders, "but to fly to a third corner and then to a fourth?" (2).

This question is soon answered, and we discover that the physical SETTING Woolf describes here is the framework of a NARRATIVE. What remains for the moth is to die. Just when the NARRATOR, deeply absorbed in her book, has for-gotten the moth, it catches her attention again: "He was trying to resume his dancing, but seemed either so stiff or so awkward that he could only flutter to the bottom of the window-pane; and when he tried to fly across it he failed" (4).

At first, Woolf's narrator does not realize the significance of what she sees. "Being intent on other matters," she says, "I watched these futile attempts for a time without thinking, unconsciously waiting for him to resume his flight, as one waits for a machine, that has stopped momentarily, to start again without considering the reason for its failure" (4).

Here is the basic PLOT of Woolf's narrative: not the death of a moth but the writer's sympathetic *observation* of the creature's death—and her inability to stop it. The writer can only chronicle death; she cannot conquer it. "But, as I stretched out a pencil, meaning to help him to right himself," says the writer at her desk, "it came over me that the failure and awkwardness were the approach of death. I laid the pencil down again" (4). The real story here is in the writer's mind. To explain the significance of that story, Woolf draws on common techniques of exposition; in particular, she uses COMPARISON AND CONTRAST and DEFINITION.

The writer's window looks out onto the nearby fields and the rolling hills beyond. The earth is gleaming from the plough, and the birds are rising and falling "as if a vast net with thousands of black knots in it has been cast up into the air" (1). What could the frail moth possibly have to do with all this "vigour," the writer wonders, even as her celebrated description of the "net" of blackbirds captures the interconnectedness of life?

As the thought of connections rises in the writer's mind, she makes a direct comparison between the moth and the scene outside her window: "The same energy which inspired the rooks, the ploughmen, the horses, and even, it seemed, the lean bare-backed downs, sent the moth fluttering from side to side of his square of the window-pane" (2).

That energy is "pure life" (3). But what is life, essentially? Woolf can now answer this momentous question because she has made the connection between the moth and the scene outside her window: "It was as if someone had taken a tiny bead of pure life and decking it as lightly as possible with down and feathers, had set it dancing and zigzagging to show us the true nature of life" (3).

Life is to be defined, at bottom, as motion, animation, and when that motion ceases, that is death: "One could only watch the extraordinary efforts made by those tiny legs against an oncoming doom which could, had it chosen, have submerged an entire city, not merely a city, but masses of human beings; nothing, I knew, had any chance against death" (5). (This essay was written shortly before Woolf's suicide by drowning.)

Woolf's essay, then, is a description of the moth and the downs, a narrative about the woman watching them, and an exposition on the nature of life and death. It is also an argument. Having defined life, Woolf subtly makes the case for how it should be lived. If a mere moth, a "tiny bead of pure life," expends its little energy "dancing and zigzagging" to the fullest extent that its meager compass will allow (3), then the woman musing aloud to herself on this "pleasant morning, mid-September, mild, benignant, yet with a keener breath than that of the summer months" (1), should perhaps convince herself (and us) to do likewise.

To reduce Woolf's subtle essay to another moth-to-the-flame message about being inspired by life or making hay while the sun shines, however, would kill it. The meaning of a complex piece of writing is not to be extracted like pulling a thread from a tapestry. We can dissect a great essay into its constituent parts, but its meaning derives from the essay as a whole—from all the modes of writing working together. Keep this lesson in mind as you study the other fine specimens in this chapter.

THOMAS JEFFERSON

THE DECLARATION
OF INDEPENDENCE

Thomas Jefferson (1743–1826) was the third president of the United States. A lawyer by training, he was also a philosopher and man of letters. Charged with drafting the Declaration of Independence (1776), he was assisted by Benjamin Franklin, John Adams, and the Continental Congress at large. A model of the rational thinking of the Enlightenment, the Declaration is as much a timeless essay on tyranny and human rights as a legal document announcing the colonies' break with England. The version reprinted here is that published on the website of the United States National Archives, www.archives.gov.

When in the Course of human events, it becomes necessary for one people to dissolve the political bands which have connected them with another, and to assume among the powers of the earth, the separate and equal station to which the Laws of Nature and of Nature's God entitle them, a decent respect to the opinions of mankind requires that they should declare the causes which impel them to the separation.

1

We hold these truths to be self-evident, that all men are created equal, that they are endowed by their Creator with certain unalienable Rights, that among these are Life, Liberty and the pursuit of Happiness. That to secure these rights, Governments are instituted among Men, deriving their just powers from the consent of the governed. That whenever any Form of Government becomes destructive of these ends, it is the Right of the People to alter or to abolish it, and to institute new Government, laying its foundation on such principles and organizing its See p. 525 for arguing from general premises to a specific conclusion. powers in such form, as to them shall seem most likely to effect their Safety and Happiness. Prudence, indeed, will dictate that Governments long established should not be changed for light and transient causes; and accordingly all experience hath shewn, that mankind are more disposed to suffer, while evils are sufferable, than to right themselves by abolishing the forms to which they are accustomed. But when a long train of abuses and usurpations pursuing invariably the same Object evinces a design to reduce them under absolute Despotism, it is their right, it is their duty, to throw off such Government, and to provide new Guards for their future security. Such has been the patient sufferance of these Colonies; and such is now the necessity which constrains them to alter their former Systems of Government. The history of the present King of Great Britain[1] is a history of repeated injuries and usurpations, all having in direct object the establishment of absolute Tyranny over these States. To prove this, let Facts be submitted to a candid world.

2

He has refused his Assent to Laws, the most wholesome and necessary for the public good.

3

He has forbidden his Governors to pass Laws of immediate and pressing importance, unless suspended in their operation till his Assent should be obtained; and when so suspended, he has utterly neglected to attend to them.

4

He has refused to pass other Laws for the accommodation of large districts of people, unless those people would relinquish the right of Representation in the Legislature, a right inestimable to them and formidable to tyrants only.

5

---

1. George III (ruled 1760–1820).

He has called together legislative bodies at places unusual, uncomfortable, and distant from the depository of their public Records, for the sole purpose of fatiguing them into compliance with his measures. 6

He has dissolved Representative Houses repeatedly, for opposing with manly firmness his invasions on the rights of the people. 7

He has refused for a long time, after such dissolutions, to cause others to be elected; whereby the Legislative powers, incapable of Annihilation, have returned to the People at large for their exercise; the State remaining in the mean time exposed to all the dangers of invasion from without, and convulsions within. 8

He has endeavoured to prevent the population of these States; for that purpose obstructing the Laws of Naturalization of Foreigners; refusing to pass others to encourage their migration hither, and raising the conditions of new Appropriations of Lands. 9

He has obstructed the Administration of Justice, by refusing his Assent to Laws for establishing Judiciary powers. 10

He has made Judges dependent on his Will alone, for the tenure of their offices, and the amount and payment of their salaries. 11

He has erected a multitude of New Offices, and sent hither swarms of Officers to harass our people, and eat out their substance. 12

He has kept among us, in time of peace, Standing Armies without the Consent of our legislatures. 13

He has affected to render the Military independent of and superior to the Civil power. 14

He has combined with others to subject us to a jurisdiction foreign to our constitution, and unacknowledged by our laws; giving his Assent to their acts of pretended Legislation: 15

For Quartering large bodies of armed troops among us: 16

For protecting them, by a mock Trial, from punishment for any Murders which they should commit on the Inhabitants of these States: 17

For cutting off our Trade with all parts of the world: 18

For imposing Taxes on us without our Consent: 19

For depriving us in many cases, of the benefits of Trial by Jury: 20

For transporting us beyond the Seas to be tried for pretended offenses: 21

For abolishing the free System of English Laws in a neighbouring Prov-   22
ince, establishing therein an Arbitrary government, and enlarging its Boundaries so as to render it at once an example and fit instrument for introducing the
same absolute rule into these Colonies:

For taking away our Charters, abolishing our most valuable Laws, and   23
altering fundamentally the Forms of our Governments:

For suspending our own Legislatures, and declaring themselves invested   24
with power to legislate for us in all cases whatsoever.

He has abdicated Government here, by declaring us out of his Protection   25
and waging War against us.

He has plundered our seas, ravaged our Coasts, burnt our towns and   26
destroyed the lives of our people.

He is at this time transporting large Armies of foreign Mercenaries to   27
compleat the works of death, desolation and tyranny, already begun with circumstances of Cruelty & perfidy scarcely paralleled in the most barbarous ages,
and totally unworthy the Head of a civilized nation.

He has constrained our fellow Citizens taken Captive on the high Seas to   28
bear Arms against their Country, to become the executioners of their friends
and Brethren, or to fall themselves by their Hands.

He has excited domestic insurrections amongst us, and has endeavoured   29
to bring on the inhabitants of our frontiers, the merciless Indian Savages, whose
known rule of warfare, is an undistinguished destruction of all ages, sexes and
conditions.

In every stage of these Oppressions We have Petitioned for Redress in the   30
most humble terms: Our repeated Petitions have been answered only by repeated
injury. A Prince whose character is thus marked by every act which may define
a Tyrant, is unfit to be the ruler of a free people.

Nor have We been wanting in attentions to our British brethren. We have   31
warned them from time to time of attempts by their legislature to extend an
unwarrantable jurisdiction over us. We have reminded them of the circumstances of our emigration and settlement here. We have appealed to their native
justice and magnanimity, and we have conjured them by the ties of our com-

mon kindred to disavow these usurpations, which would inevitably interrupt our connections and correspondence. They too have been deaf to the voice of justice and of consanguinity. We must, therefore acquiesce in the necessity, which denounces our Separation, and hold them, as we hold the rest of mankind, Enemies in War, in Peace Friends.

We, therefore, the Representatives of the United States of America, in General Congress, Assembled, appealing to the Supreme Judge of the world for the rectitude of our intentions, do, in the Name, and by Authority of the good People of these Colonies, solemnly publish and declare, That these United Colonies are, and of Right ought to be Free and Independent States; that they are Absolved from all Allegiance to the British Crown, and that all political connection between them and the State of Great Britain, is and ought to be totally dissolved; and that as Free and Independent States, they have full Power to levy War, conclude Peace, contract Alliances, establish Commerce, and to do all other Acts and Things which Independent States may of right do. And for the support of this Declaration, with a firm reliance on the protection of divine Providence, we mutually pledge to each other our Lives, our Fortunes and our sacred Honor.

32

UNDERSTANDING THE ESSAY

. . . .

1. Thomas Jefferson's main PURPOSE in the Declaration of Independence is to declare the sovereignty of the United States. How and where does he use CAUSE AND EFFECT to help achieve this purpose?

2. How does Jefferson DEFINE what it means to be a tyrant? In what way does this definition help him achieve his main purpose?

3. Above all, the Declaration of Independence is a logical ARGUMENT. How and where does Jefferson use INDUCTION (reasoning from specific instances to a general conclusion) to make the point that King George is indeed a tyrant?

4. Once Jefferson reaches this conclusion about King George, he uses it as the minor (or narrower) premise of a DEDUCTIVE argument (from general principles to specific conclusions). The conclusion of that argument is that "these United Colonies are, and of Right ought to be Free and Independent States" (32). What is the major (or broader) premise of this deductive argument? Explain.

5. Jefferson refers to the British people as "our British brethren" (31). Why? What AUDIENCE does he have in mind here, and why would he need to convince them that his cause is just?

6. According to Jefferson and the other signers of the Declaration, what is the purpose of government, and where does a government get its authority? What form of government do they envision for the states, and how well does the Declaration make the case for this form of government? Explain.

JONATHAN SWIFT

A MODEST PROPOSAL

Jonathan Swift (1667–1745) was born in Ireland and educated at Trinity College, Dublin, where he was censured for breaking the rules of discipline, graduating only by "special grace." He was ordained as a clergyman in the Anglican Church in 1694 and became dean of St. Patrick's, Dublin, in 1713. Swift's satires in prose and verse, including *Gulliver's Travels* (1726), addressed three main issues: political relations between England and Ireland; Irish social questions; and matters of church doctrine. Swift's best-known essay was published in 1729 under the full title "A Modest Proposal For Preventing the Children of Poor People in Ireland, from being a Burden to Their Parents or Country, and For making them Beneficial to the Publick." Using irony as his weapon, Swift pours into the essay his deep contempt for materialism and for logic without compassion.

It is a melancholy object to those who walk through this great town[1] or travel in the country, when they see the streets, the roads, and cabin doors, crowded with beggars of the female sex, followed by three, four, or six children, all in rags and importuning every passenger for an alms. These mothers, instead of being able to work for their honest livelihood, are forced to employ all their time in strolling to beg sustenance for their helpless infants, who, as they grow up, either turn thieves for want of work, or leave their dear native country to fight for the Pretender in Spain, or sell themselves to the Barbadoes.[2]

I think it is agreed by all parties that this prodigious number of children in the arms, or on the backs, or at the heels of their mothers, and frequently of their fathers, is in the present deplorable state of the kingdom a very great additional grievance; and therefore whoever could find out a fair, cheap, and easy method of making these children sound, useful members of the commonwealth would deserve so well of the public as to have his statue set up for a preserver of the nation.

But my intention is very far from being confined to provide only for the children of professed beggars; it is of a much greater extent, and shall take in the whole number of infants at a certain age who are born of parents in effect as little able to support them as those who demand our charity in the streets.

As to my own part, having turned my thoughts for many years upon this important subject and maturely weighed the several schemes of other projectors,[3] I have always found them grossly mistaken in their computation. It is true, a child just dropped from its dam may be supported by her milk for a solar year, with little other nourishment; at most not above the value of two shillings,[4] which the mother may certainly get, or the value in scraps, by her lawful occupation of begging; and it is exactly at one year old that I propose to provide for them in such a manner as instead of being a charge upon their

1. Dublin, capital city of Ireland.
2. That is, sell themselves into indentured servitude to masters in Barbados, an island colony in the West Indies. The pretender to the throne of England was James Francis Edward Stuart (1688–1766), son of the deposed James II.
3. Men whose heads were full of foolish schemes or projects.
4. The British pound sterling was made up of twenty shillings; five shillings made a crown.

parents or the parish, or wanting food and raiment for the rest of their lives, they shall on the contrary contribute to the feeding, and partly to the clothing, of many thousands.

There is likewise another great advantage in my scheme, that it will prevent those voluntary abortions, and that horrid practice of women murdering their bastard children, alas, too frequent among us, sacrificing the poor innocent babes, I doubt, more to avoid the expense than the shame, which would move tears and pity in the most savage and inhuman breast.

The number of souls in this kingdom being usually reckoned one million and a half, of these I calculate there may be about two hundred thousand couple whose wives are breeders; from which number I subtract thirty thousand couples who are able to maintain their own children, although I apprehend there cannot be so many under the present distress of the kingdom; but this being granted, there will remain an hundred and seventy thousand breeders. I again subtract fifty thousand for those women who miscarry, or whose children die by accident or disease within the year. There only remain an hundred and twenty thousand children of poor parents annually born. The question therefore is, how this number shall be reared and provided for, which, as I have already said, under the present situation of affairs, is utterly impossible by all the methods hitherto proposed. For we can neither employ them in handicraft or agriculture; we neither build houses (I mean in the country) nor cultivate land. They can very seldom pick up a livelihood by stealing till they arrive at six years old, except where they are of towardly parts,[5] although I confess they learn the rudiments much earlier, during which time they can however be looked upon only as probationers, as I have been informed by a principal gentleman in the county of Cavan,[6] who protested to me that he never knew above one or two instances under the age of six, even in a part of the kingdom so renowned for the quickest proficiency in that art.

I am assured by our merchants that a boy or a girl before twelve years old is no salable commodity; and even when they come to this age they will not

5. Having natural ability.

6. A county in northeast Ireland.

yield above three pounds, or three pounds and half a crown at most on the Exchange; which cannot turn to account either to the parents or the kingdom, the charge of nutriment and rags having been at least four times that value.

I shall now therefore humbly propose my own thoughts, which I hope will not be liable to the least objection. 8

I have been assured by a very knowing American of my acquaintance in London, that a young healthy child well nursed is at a year old a most delicious, nourishing, and wholesome food, whether stewed, roasted, baked, or boiled; and I make no doubt that it will equally serve in a fricassee or a ragout. 9

I do therefore humbly offer it to public consideration that of the hundred and twenty thousand children, already computed, twenty thousand may be reserved for breed, whereof only one fourth part to be males, which is more than we allow to sheep, black cattle, or swine; and my reason is that these children are seldom the fruits of marriage, a circumstance not much regarded by our savages, therefore one male will be sufficient to serve four females. That the remaining hundred thousand may at a year old be offered in sale to the persons of quality and fortune through the kingdom, always advising the mother to let them suck plentifully in the last month, so as to render them plump and fat for a good table. A child will make two dishes at an entertainment for friends; and when the family dines alone, the fore or hind quarter will make a reasonable dish, and seasoned with a little pepper or salt will be very good boiled on the fourth day, especially in winter. 10

I have reckoned upon a medium that a child just born will weigh twelve pounds, and in a solar year if tolerably nursed increaseth to twenty-eight pounds. 11

I grant this food will be somewhat dear, and therefore very proper for landlords, who, as they have already devoured most of the parents, seem to have the best title to the children. 12

Infant's flesh will be in season throughout the year, but more plentiful in March, and a little before and after. For we are told by a grave author, an eminent French physician,[7] that fish being a prolific diet, there are more children 13

---

7. François Rabelais (1494?–1553), French satirist.

born in Roman Catholic countries about nine months after Lent than at any other season; therefore, reckoning a year after Lent, the markets will be more glutted than usual, because the number of popish infants is at least three to one in this kingdom; and therefore it will have one other collateral advantage, by lessening the number of Papists[8] among us.

I have already computed the charge of nursing a beggar's child (in which list I reckon all cottagers, laborers, and four fifths of the farmers) to be about two shillings per annum, rags included; and I believe no gentleman would repine to give ten shillings for the carcass of a good fat child, which, as I have said, will make four dishes of excellent nutritive meat, when he hath only some particular friend or his own family to dine with him. Thus the squire will learn to be a good landlord, and grow popular among the tenants; the mother will have eight shillings net profit, and be fit for work till she produces another child. 14

Those who are more thrifty (as I must confess the times require) may flay the carcass; the skin of which artificially[9] dressed will make admirable gloves for ladies, and summer boots for fine gentlemen. 15

As to our city of Dublin, shambles[10] may be appointed for this purpose in the most convenient parts of it, and butchers we may be assured will not be wanting; although I rather recommend buying the children alive, and dressing them hot from the knife as we do roasting pigs. 16

A very worthy person, a true lover of his country, and whose virtues I highly esteem, was lately pleased in discoursing on this matter to offer a refinement upon my scheme. He said that many gentlemen of this kingdom, having of late destroyed their deer, he conceived that the want of venison might be well supplied by the bodies of young lads and maidens, not exceeding fourteen years of age nor under twelve, so great a number of both sexes in every country being now ready to starve for want of work and service; and these to be disposed of by 17

---

8. Roman Catholics, called Papists because of their allegiance to the pope. Though Catholics made up the majority of the Irish population in this period, English Protestants controlled the government, and Catholics were subject to discrimination and oppressive policies.

9. Skillfully, artfully.

10. Slaughterhouses.

their parents, if alive, or otherwise by their nearest relations. But with due deference to so excellent a friend and so deserving a patriot, I cannot be altogether in his sentiments; for as to the males, my American acquaintance assured me from frequent experience that their flesh was generally tough and lean, like that of our schoolboys, by continual exercise, and their taste disagreeable; and to fatten them would not answer the charge. Then as to the females, it would, I think with humble submission, be a loss to the public, because they soon would become breeders themselves: and besides, it is not improbable that some scrupulous people might be apt to censure such a practice (although indeed very unjustly) as a little bordering upon cruelty; which, I confess, hath always been with me the strongest objection against any project, how well 'soever intended.

But in order to justify my friend, he confessed that this expedient was put into his head by the famous Psalmanazar, a native of the island Formosa,[11] who came from thence to London above twenty years ago, and in conversation told my friend that in his country when any young person happened to be put to death, the executioner sold the carcass to persons of quality as a prime dainty; and that in his time the body of a plump girl of fifteen, who was crucified for an attempt to poison the emperor, was sold to his Imperial Majesty's prime minister of state, and other great mandarins of the court, in joints from the gibbet,[12] at four hundred crowns. Neither indeed can I deny that if the same use were made of several plump young girls in this town, who without one single groat[13] to their fortunes cannot stir abroad without a chair, and appear at the playhouse and assemblies in foreign fineries which they never will pay for, the kingdom would not be the worse. 18

A single extended example may be sufficient to serve the purpose.

Some persons of a desponding spirit are in great concern about that vast number of poor people who are aged, diseased, or maimed, and I have been desired to employ my thoughts what course may be taken to ease the nation of so grievous an encumbrance. But I am not in the least pain upon that matter, 19

---

11. Former name of Taiwan. George Psalmanazar (1679?–1763), a Frenchman, fooled British society for several years by masquerading as a pagan Formosan.

12. A structure for hanging a felon.

13. A British coin of the time, worth the equivalent of four cents.

because it is very well known that they are every day dying and rotting by cold and famine, and filth and vermin, as fast as can be reasonably expected. And as to the younger laborers, they are now in almost as hopeful a condition. They cannot get work, and consequently pine away for want of nourishment to a degree that if at any time they are accidentally hired to common labor, they have not strength to perform it; and thus the country and themselves are happily delivered from the evils to come.

I have too long digressed, and therefore shall return to my subject. I think the advantages by the proposal which I have made are obvious and many, as well as of the highest importance. 20

For first, as I have already observed, it would greatly lessen the number of Papists, with whom we are yearly overrun, being the principal breeders of the nation as well as our most dangerous enemies; and who stay at home on purpose to deliver the kingdom to the Pretender, hoping to take their advantage by the absence of so many good Protestants, who have chosen rather to leave their country than stay at home and pay tithes against their conscience to an Episcopal curate.[14] 21

Secondly, the poorer tenants will have something valuable of their own, which by law may be made liable to distress, and help to pay their landlord's rent, their corn and cattle being already seized and money a thing unknown. 22

Thirdly, whereas the maintenance of an hundred thousand children, from two years old and upward, cannot be computed at less than ten shillings a piece per annum, the nation's stock will be thereby increased fifty thousand pounds per annum, besides the profit of a new dish introduced to the tables of all gentlemen of fortune in the kingdom who have any refinement in taste. And the money will circulate among ourselves, the goods being entirely of our own growth and manufacture. 23

Fourthly, the constant breeders, besides the gain of eight shillings sterling per annum by the sale of their children, will be rid of the charge of maintaining them after the first year. 24

14. Tithes are taxes or levys, traditionally 10 percent of one's income, paid to the church or other authority. Swift blamed much of Ireland's poverty upon large landowners who avoided church tithes by living (and spending their money) abroad.

Fifthly, this food would likewise bring great custom to taverns, where the   25
vintners will certainly be so prudent as to procure the best receipts for dressing
it to perfection, and consequently have their houses frequented by all the fine
gentlemen, who justly value themselves upon their knowledge in good eating;
and a skillful cook, who understands how to oblige his guests, will contrive to
make it as expensive as they please.

Sixthly, this would be a great inducement to marriage, which all wise   26
nations have either encouraged by rewards or enforced by laws and penalties. It
would increase the care and tenderness of mothers toward their children, when
they were sure of a settlement for life to the poor babes, provided in some sort
by the public, to their annual profit instead of expense. We should see an honest
emulation among the married women, which of them could bring the fattest
child to the market. Men would become as fond of their wifes during the time of
their pregnancy as they are now of their mares in foal, their cows in calf, or sows
when they are ready to farrow; nor offer to beat or kick them (as is too frequent
a practice) for fear of a miscarriage.

Many other advantages might be enumerated. For instance, the addition   27
of some thousand carcasses in our exportation of barreled beef, the propagation
of swine's flesh, and improvement in the art of making good bacon, so much
wanted among us by the great destruction of pigs, too frequent at our tables,
which are no way comparable in taste or magnificence to a well-grown, fat,
yearling child, which roasted whole will make a considerable figure at a lord
mayor's feast or any other public entertainment. But this and many others I
omit, being studious of brevity.

Supposing that one thousand families in this city would be constant   28
customers for infants' flesh, besides others who might have it at merry meet-
ings, particularly weddings and christenings, I compute that Dublin would
take off annually about twenty thousand carcasses, and the rest of the kingdom (where probably they will be sold somewhat cheaper) the remaining
eighty thousand.

I can think of no one objection that will possibly be raised against this   29
proposal, unless it should be urged that the number of people will be thereby
much lessened in the kingdom. This I freely own, and it was indeed one

principal design in offering it to the world. I desire the reader will observe, that I calculate my remedy for this one individual kingdom of Ireland and for no other that ever was, is, or I think ever can be upon earth. Therefore let no man talk to me of other expedients:[15] of taxing our absentees at five shillings a pound: of using neither clothes nor household furniture except what is of our own growth and manufacture: of utterly rejecting the materials and instruments that promote foreign luxury: of curing the expensiveness of pride, vanity, idleness, and gaming in our women: of introducing a vein of parsimony, prudence, and temperance: of learning to love our country, in the want of which we differ even from Laplanders and the inhabitants of Topinamboo:[16] of quitting our animosities and factions, nor acting any longer like the Jews, who were murdering one another at the very moment their city[17] was taken: of being a little cautious not to sell our country and conscience for nothing: of teaching landlords to have at least one degree of mercy toward their tenants: lastly, of putting a spirit of honesty, industry, and skill into our shopkeepers; who, if a resolution could now be taken to buy only our native goods, would immediately unite to cheat and exact upon us in the price, the measure, and the goodness, nor could ever yet be brought to make one fair proposal of just dealing, though often and earnestly invited to it.

Therefore I repeat, let no man talk to me of these and the like expedients, till he hath at least some glimpse of hope that there will ever be some hearty and sincere attempt to put them in practice. 30

But as to myself, having been wearied out for many years with offering vain, idle, visionary thoughts, and at length utterly despairing of success, I fortunately fell upon this proposal, which, as it is wholly new, so it hath something solid and real, of no expense and little trouble, full in our own power, and whereby we can incur no danger in disobliging England. For this kind of commodity will not bear exportation, the flesh being of too tender a consistence to 31

15. The following are all measures that Swift himself proposed in various pamphlets.

16. The British of Swift's time would have considered the inhabitants of Lapland (region in northern Europe) and Topinamboo (area in the jungles of Brazil) highly uncivilized.

17. Jerusalem, sacked by the Romans in 70 C.E.

admit a long continuance in salt, although perhaps I could name a country[18] which would be glad to eat up our whole nation without it.

After all, I am not so violently bent upon my own opinion as to reject any 32 offer proposed by wise men, which shall be found equally innocent, cheap, easy, and effectual. But before something of that kind shall be advanced in contradiction to my scheme, and offering a better, I desire the author or authors will be pleased maturely to consider two points. First, as things now stand, how they will be able to find food and raiment for an hundred thousand useless mouths and backs. And secondly, there being a round million of creatures in human figure throughout this kingdom, whose sole subsistence put into a common stock would leave them in debt two millions of pounds sterling, adding those who are beggars by profession to the bulk of farmers, cottagers, and laborers, with their wives and children who are beggars in effect; I desire those politicians who dislike my overture, and may perhaps be so bold to attempt an answer, that they will first ask the parents of these mortals whether they would not at this day think it a great happiness to have been sold for food at a year old in the manner I prescribe, and thereby have avoided such a perpetual scene of misfortunes as they have since gone through by the oppression of landlords, the impossibility of paying rent without money or trade, the want of common sustenance, with neither house nor clothes to cover them from the inclemencies of the weather, and the most inevitable prospect of entailing the like or greater miseries upon their breed forever.

I profess, in the sincerity of my heart, that I have not the least personal 33 interest in endeavoring to promote this necessary work, having no other motive than the public good of my country, by advancing our trade, providing for infants, relieving the poor, and giving some pleasure to the rich. I have no children by which I can propose to get a single penny; the youngest being nine years old, and my wife past childbearing.

18. England.

UNDERSTANDING THE ESSAY

. . . .

1. Jonathan Swift's essay is celebrated for its IRONY, which is sometimes misdefined as saying the opposite of what is meant. But Swift is not really arguing that the people of Ireland should not eat children. What is he ARGUING? (Clue: see paragraph 29.) How would you define irony based on this example?

2. SATIRE is writing that exposes vice and wrongdoing to ridicule for the purpose of correcting them. Who are the wrongdoers addressed in Swift's great satire?

3. Swift's projector offers what he considers a serious solution to a serious problem. How would you describe the projector's personality and TONE of voice? How does using the persona of the projector contribute to Swift's irony throughout the essay? Give specific examples from the text.

4. In "A Modest Proposal," the projector uses both PROCESS ANALYSIS (how to solve Ireland's economic woes) and CAUSE AND EFFECT (the causes of Ireland's poverty and moral condition; the effects of the proposed "improvements"). How do these two modes of exposition work together to support the projector's logical argument?

5. Swift's persona is the soul of reason, yet what he proposes is so horrible and bizarre that any reader would reject it. Why do you think Swift resorts to the METAPHOR of cannibalism? How does it help him to critique arguments that depend on pure reason, even when the situations they address are truly desperate?

ABRAHAM LINCOLN

SECOND INAUGURAL ADDRESS

Abraham Lincoln (1809–1865) was the sixteenth president of the United States. Largely self-taught, Lincoln studied law as a young man and spent eight years in the Illinois state legislature before being elected president in 1860. By the time Lincoln took office, seven states had seceded from the Union, and his first inaugural address was a conciliatory speech calling for national unity. Four years later, slavery had been abolished and the Civil War was drawing to a close. Lincoln's Second Inaugural Address was delivered on March 4, 1865; several weeks after delivering these words, he was assassinated.

❖⌄◇⌃◇⌄◇⌃◇⌄◇⌃◇⌄◇⌃◇⌄◇⌃◇⌄◇⌃◇⌄◇⌃◇⌄◇⌃◇⌄◇⌃◇⌄◇⌃◇⌄◇⌃◇⌄◇⌃◇⌄❖

A t this second appearing to take the oath of the presidential office, there is   1
less occasion for an extended address than there was at the first. Then a
statement, somewhat in detail, of a course to be pursued, seemed fitting and
proper. Now, at the expiration of four years, during which public declarations
have been constantly called forth on every point and phase of the great contest
which still absorbs the attention, and engrosses the energies of the nation, little
that is new could be presented. The progress of our arms, upon which all else
chiefly depends, is as well known to the public as to myself; and it is, I trust,

reasonably satisfactory and encouraging to all. With high hope for the future, no prediction in regard to it is ventured.

On the occasion corresponding to this four years ago, all thoughts were anxiously directed to an impending civil war. All dreaded it—all sought to avert it. While the inaugural address was being delivered from this place, devoted altogether to *saving* the Union without war, insurgent agents were in the city seeking to *destroy* it without war—seeking to dissolve the Union, and divide effects, by negotiation.[1] Both parties deprecated war; but one of them would *make* war rather than let the nation survive; and the other would *accept* war rather than let it perish. And the war came.

One-eighth of the whole population were colored slaves, not distributed generally over the Union, but localized in the Southern part of it. These slaves constituted a peculiar and powerful interest. All knew that this interest was, somehow, the cause of the war. To strengthen, perpetuate, and extend this interest was the object for which the insurgents would rend the Union, even by war; while the government claimed no right to do more than to restrict the territorial enlargement of it. Neither party expected for the war, the magnitude, or the duration, which it has already attained. Neither anticipated that the *cause* of the conflict might cease with, or even before, the conflict itself should cease. Each looked for an easier triumph, and a result less fundamental and astounding. Both read the same Bible, and pray to the same God; and each invokes His aid against the other. It may seem strange that any men should dare to ask a just God's assistance in wringing their bread from the sweat of other men's faces; but let us judge not that we be not judged.[2] The prayers of both could not be answered; that of neither has been answered fully. The Almighty has His own purposes. "Woe unto the world because of offenses! for it must needs be that offenses

Page 477 suggests when to weave a cause-and-effect analysis into an argument.

---

1. Prior to the start of the Civil War, representatives from the slave-holding states attempted to convince the federal government to allow them to secede and form their own union.

2. "Let us judge not" alludes to Jesus' Sermon on the Mount ("Judge not, that ye be not judged") in Matthew 7:1; "wringing their bread from the sweat of other men's faces" alludes to God's curse on Adam ("In the sweat of thy face shalt thou eat bread") in Genesis 3:19.

come; but woe to that man by whom the offense cometh!"[3] If we shall suppose that American slavery is one of those offenses which, in the providence of God, must needs come, but which, having continued through His appointed time, He now wills to remove, and that He gives to both North and South, this terrible war, as the woe due to those by whom the offense came, shall we discern therein any departure from those divine attributes which the believers in a Living God always ascribe to Him? Fondly do we hope—fervently do we pray—that this mighty scourge of war may speedily pass away. Yet, if God wills that it continue, until all the wealth piled by the bondman's two hundred and fifty years of unrequited toil shall be sunk, and until every drop of blood drawn with the lash, shall be paid by another drawn with the sword, as was said three thousand years ago, so still it must be said, "the judgments of the Lord are true and righteous altogether."[4]

With malice toward none; with charity for all; with firmness in the right, as God gives us to see the right, let us strive on to finish the work we are in; to bind up the nation's wounds; to care for him who shall have borne the battle, and for his widow, and his orphan—to do all which may achieve and cherish a just, and a lasting peace, among ourselves, and with all nations.   4

UNDERSTANDING THE ESSAY

1. Compared to the inaugural speeches of most presidents, Abraham Lincoln's Second Inaugural Address is remarkably short. Why? What is the main PURPOSE of his speech, and what knowledge (and sentiment) does he assume on the part of his AUDIENCE in order to accomplish that purpose in so few words?

2. Lincoln calls for action "with malice toward none; with charity for all," including the people of the vanquished Southern states (4). Unlike his first inaugural address, this second one is delivered from a position of strength. How and where, then, does the author counterbalance conciliatory language like this with "firmness" (4)?

3. From Matthew 18:7, Jesus' speech to his disciples.
4. From Psalms 19:9.

3. As he contemplates the opposing sides in the war, Lincoln reasons that "[n]either anticipated that the *cause* of the conflict might cease with, or even before, the conflict itself should cease" (3). If the still-continuing conflict is the effect, what is the great *cause* to which Lincoln refers? For what purpose does Lincoln use CAUSE AND EFFECT in this speech? What point is he making here?

4. Toward the end of paragraph 3 ("If we shall suppose . . ."), Lincoln uses logical reasoning to make the ARGUMENT that the Civil War and all its woes are, in some measure, the will of God. How valid is his reasoning here? Explain.

5. Compare and contrast Lincoln's Second Inaugural Address with Johnson C. Montgomery's "The Island of Plenty" (Chapter 12) as appeals to their audiences' sense of right and wrong in time of crisis. Compare the strategies each writer uses to lay out the challenges they see ahead and to motivate their audiences to meet them. Which man comes across as the more credible speaker? Explain why by pointing to specific passages in the texts.

SOJOURNER TRUTH

AIN'T I A WOMAN?

Sojourner Truth (c. 1797–1883) is the name assumed by Isabella Baumfree, who was born into slavery in Hurley, New York, and legally freed in 1827. Unable to read or write, Truth nonetheless knew both English and Dutch (her first language) and became a celebrated speaker in the causes of both abolition and women's rights. Although the phrase does not appear in the first recorded version, "Ain't I a Woman?" is the title usually given to a brief extemporaneous speech that Truth delivered at the Women's Convention in Akron, Ohio, in 1851. The version reprinted here derives from the second published version, that of abolitionist writer and speaker Frances Dana Gage, in the *National Anti-Slavery Standard* on May 2, 1863. The speech is something of a collaboration because—in addition to assigning a black Southern dialect to the speaker—Gage added the title phrase and many specific details into Truth's plea for equal rights for women and blacks.

Well, children, where there is so much racket there must be something out of kilter. I think that 'twixt the negroes of the South and the women at the North, all talking about rights, the white men will be in a fix pretty soon. But what's all this here talking about?   1

That man over there says that women need to be helped into carriages, and lifted over ditches, and to have the best place everywhere. Nobody ever helps me into carriages, or over mud-puddles, or gives me any best place! And ain't I a woman? Look at me! Look at my arm! I have ploughed and planted, and gathered into barns, and no man could head me! And ain't I a woman? I could work as much and eat as much as a man—when I could get it—and bear the lash as well! And ain't I a woman? I have borne thirteen children, and seen most all sold off to slavery, and when I cried out with my mother's grief, none but Jesus heard me! And ain't I a woman?

Making a point with personal experience is discussed on p. 523.

Then they talk about this thing in the head; what's this they call it? [member of audience whispers, "intellect"] That's it, honey. What's that got to do with women's rights or negroes' rights? If my cup won't hold but a pint, and yours holds a quart, wouldn't you be mean not to let me have my little half measure full?

Then that little man in black there, he says women can't have as much rights as men, 'cause Christ wasn't a woman! Where did your Christ come from? Where did your Christ come from? From God and a woman! Man had nothing to do with Him.

If the first woman God ever made was strong enough to turn the world upside down all alone, these women together ought to be able to turn it back, and get it right side up again! And now they is asking to do it, the men better let them.

Obliged to you for hearing me, and now old Sojourner ain't got nothing more to say.

UNDERSTANDING THE ESSAY

. . . .

1. What "racket" is Truth referring to in the opening paragraph of her speech? What is "out of kilter" in her view and that of the other women who attended the 1851 Women's Convention in Ohio (1)? What solution to this imbalance do they propose?

2. What EVIDENCE does Truth offer to support her CLAIM that women are the equal of men? How sufficient is that evidence to prove her point? Explain.

3. If women want to set the world right again, Truth, argues, "the men better let them" (5). Does this part of her ARGUMENT appeal mostly to the listener's intellect ("this thing in the head"), emotions, or sense of ethics (3)?

4. Why does Truth address her AUDIENCE as "children" (1)? Is this an effective strategy? Why or why not?

5. What is Truth's point in drawing an ANALOGY between "these women" and Eve (5)? Explain.

6. "Ain't I a woman?" is clearly a RHETORICAL QUESTION. What is the effect of repeating it four times in this short speech?

VIRGINIA WOOLF

THE DEATH OF THE MOTH

Virginia Woolf (1882–1941) was a distinguished novelist and essayist, the center of the "Bloomsbury Group" of writers and artists that flourished in London from about 1907 to 1930. Suffering from recurrent depression, she drowned herself in the river Ouse near her home at Rodmell, England. *The Voyage Out* (1915), *Mrs. Dalloway* (1925), *To the Lighthouse* (1927), *Orlando* (1928), and *The Waves* (1931) are among her works that helped to alter the course of the novel in English. Today she is recognized as a psychological novelist especially gifted at exploring the minds of her female characters. "The Death of the Moth" is the title essay of a collection published in 1942, soon after her suicide. It is a personal narrative in which she depicts herself at her desk, being distracted by a moth that expires on her windowsill. This "tiny bead of pure life" causes her to reflect on the life force infusing the natural world beyond her study (3).

Moths that fly by day are not properly to be called moths; they do not excite that pleasant sense of dark autumn nights and ivy-blossom which the commonest yellow underwing asleep in the shadow of the curtain never fails to rouse in us. They are hybrid creatures, neither gay like butterflies nor sombre like their own species. Nevertheless the present specimen, with his narrow hay-coloured wings, fringed with a tassel of the same colour, seemed to be content with life. It was a pleasant morning, mid-September, mild, benignant, yet with a keener breath than that of the summer months. The plough was already scoring the field opposite the window, and where the share had been, the earth was pressed flat and gleamed with moisture. Such vigour came rolling in from the fields and the down beyond that it was difficult to keep the eyes strictly turned upon the book. The rooks too were keeping one of their annual festivities; soaring round the tree-tops until it looked as if a vast net with thousands of black knots in it has been cast up into the air; which, after a few moments sank slowly down upon the trees until every twig seemed to have a knot at the end of it. Then, suddenly, the net would be thrown into the air again in a wider circle this time, with the utmost clamour and vociferation, as though to be thrown into the air and settle slowly down upon the tree-tops were a tremendously exciting experience.

The same energy which inspired the rooks, the ploughmen, the horses, and even, it seemed, the lean bare-backed downs, sent the moth fluttering from side to side of his square of the window-pane. One could not help watching him. One was, indeed, conscious of a queer feeling of pity for him. The possibilities of pleasure seemed that morning so enormous and so various that to have only a moth's part in life, and a day moth's at that, appeared a hard fate, and his zest in enjoying his meagre opportunities to the full, pathetic. He flew vigorously to one corner of his compartment, and, after waiting there a second, flew across to the other. What remained for him but to fly to a third corner and then to a fourth? That was all he could do, in spite of the size of the downs, the width of the sky, the far-off smoke of houses, and the romantic voice, now and then, of a steamer out at sea. What he could do he did. Watching him, it seemed as if a fiber, very thin but pure, of the enormous energy of the world had been thrust into his frail and diminutive body. As often as he crossed the pane, I could fancy that a thread of vital light became visible. He was little or nothing but life.

2

For artfully working comparisons into a text, see p. 361.

Yet, because he was so small, and so simple a form of the energy that was rolling in at the open window and driving its way through so many narrow and intricate corridors in my own brain and in those of other human beings, there

3

was something marvelous as well as pathetic about him. It was as if someone had taken a tiny bead of pure life and decking it as lightly as possible with down and feathers, had set it dancing and zigzagging to show us the true nature of life. Thus displayed one could not get over the strangeness of it. One is apt to forget all about life, seeing it humped and bossed and garnished and cumbered so that it has to move with the greatest circumspection and dignity. Again, the thought of all that life might have been had he been born in any other shape caused one to view his simple activities with a kind of pity.

After a time, tired by his dancing apparently, he settled on the window ledge in the sun, and the queer spectacle being at an end, I forgot about him. Then, looking up, my eye was caught by him. He was trying to resume his dancing, but seemed either so stiff or so awkward that he could only flutter to the bottom of the window-pane; and when he tried to fly across it he failed. Being intent on other matters I watched these futile attempts for a time without thinking, unconsciously waiting for him to resume his flight, as one waits for a machine, that has stopped momentarily, to start again without considering the reason for its failure. After perhaps a seventh attempt he slipped from the wooden ledge and fell, fluttering his wings, on to his back on the window-sill. The helplessness of his attitude roused me. It flashed upon me that he was in difficulties; he could no longer raise himself; his legs struggled vainly. But, as I stretched out a pencil, meaning to help him to right himself, it came over me that the failure and awkwardness were the approach of death. I laid the pencil down again.

The legs agitated themselves once more. I looked as if for the enemy against which he struggled. I looked out of doors. What had happened there? Presumably it was midday, and work in the fields had stopped. Stillness and quiet had replaced the previous animation. The birds had taken themselves off to feed in the brooks. The horses stood still. Yet the power was there all the same, massed outside indifferent, impersonal, not attending to anything in par-ticular. Somehow it was opposed to the little hay-coloured moth. It was useless to try to do anything. One could only watch the extraordinary efforts made by those tiny legs against an oncoming doom which could, had it chosen, have sub-merged an entire city, not merely a city, but masses of human beings; nothing, I knew, had any chance against death. Nevertheless after a pause of exhaustion the legs fluttered again. It was superb this last protest, and so frantic that he succeeded at last in righting himself. One's sympathies, of course, were all on the side of life. Also, when there was nobody to care or to know, this gigantic effort on the part of an insignificant little moth, against a power of such magnitude, to retain what no one else valued or desired to keep, moved one strangely. Again, somehow, one saw life, a pure bead. I lifted the pencil again, useless though I knew it to be. But even as I did so, the unmistakable tokens of death showed themselves. The body relaxed, and instantly grew stiff. The struggle was over. The insignificant little creature now knew death. As I looked at the dead moth, this minute wayside triumph of so great a force over so mean an antagonist filled me with wonder. Just as life had been strange a few minutes before, so death was now as strange. The moth having righted himself now lay most decently and uncomplainingly composed. O yes, he seemed to say, death is stronger than I am.

UNDERSTANDING THE ESSAY

1. In this personal NARRATIVE, Virginia Woolf presents herself with pencil in hand, perhaps sitting alone in her study or workroom reading and writing. Why are there no other people in the room? What is the significance of Woolf's keeping a window open to the world outside?

2. Woolf DESCRIBES the moth in considerable detail. Why do you think she tells us so little about what she herself and her room look like? What does this CONTRAST achieve in the essay?

3. Woolf seems to have trouble concentrating on her work. Why? How does she show us that this is the case?

4. How would you describe Woolf's general state of mind in the essay? How does it compare with the "vigour" of the scene outside (1)? What is the significance of her finding both life and death to be "strange" (5)?

5. Published posthumously in 1942, "The Death of the Moth" was written shortly before Woolf experienced a mental breakdown and committed suicide. Are these facts relevant to a reading of the essay? Why or why not?

MARTIN LUTHER KING JR.

I HAVE A DREAM

Martin Luther King Jr. (1929–1968) was a clergyman and civil rights activist known for his doctrine of nonviolent protest. A graduate of Morehouse College and Crozer Theological Seminary, he was awarded a PhD in theology from Boston University in 1955. That same year, as a member of the executive committee of the NAACP, King led a boycott of the segregated bus system in Montgomery, Alabama. The boycott resulted in a Supreme Court ruling banning racial segregation on the city's buses. After this landmark case, King spoke and demonstrated tirelessly in the cause of civil rights. His efforts culminated in the peaceful march on Washington, D.C., in 1963 of more than a quarter of a million protesters, to whom he delivered his "I Have a Dream" address from the steps of the Lincoln Memorial. The next year King received the Nobel Peace Prize. He was assassinated on April 4, 1968, in Memphis, Tennessee.

Five score years ago, a great American, in whose symbolic shadow we stand, signed the Emancipation Proclamation.[1] This momentous decree came as a great beacon light of hope to millions of Negro slaves who had been seared in the flames of withering injustice. It came as a joyous daybreak to end the long night of captivity.

But one hundred years later, we must face the tragic fact that the Negro is still not free. One hundred years later, the life of the Negro is still sadly crippled by the manacles of segregation and the chains of discrimination. One hundred years later, the Negro lives on a lonely island of poverty in the midst of a vast ocean of material prosperity. One hundred years later, the Negro is still languishing in the corners of American society and finds himself an exile in his own land. So we have come here today to dramatize an appalling condition.

In a sense we have come to our nation's capital to cash a check. When the architects of our republic wrote the magnificent words of the Constitution and the Declaration of Independence, they were signing a promissory note to which every American was to fall heir. This note was a promise that all men would be guaranteed the inalienable rights of life, liberty, and the pursuit of happiness.

It is obvious today that America has defaulted on this promissory note insofar as her citizens of color are concerned. Instead of honoring this sacred obligation, America has given the Negro people a bad check which has come back marked "insufficient funds." But we refuse to believe that the bank of justice is bankrupt. We refuse to believe that there are insufficient funds in the great vaults of opportunity of this nation. So we have come to cash this check—a check that will give us upon demand the riches of freedom and the security of justice. We have also come to this hallowed spot to remind America of the fierce urgency of *now*. This is no time to engage in the luxury of cooling off or to take the tranquilizing drug of gradualism. *Now* is the time to rise from the dark and desolate valley of segregation to the sunlit path of racial justice. *Now* is the time to open the doors of opportunity to all of God's children. *Now* is the time

1. In 1863, President Abraham Lincoln signed a decree declaring that "all persons held as slaves within any States . . . shall be then, thenceforward, and forever free."

to lift our nation from the quicksands of racial injustice to the solid rock of brotherhood.

It would be fatal for the nation to overlook the urgency of the moment and to underestimate the determination of the Negro. This sweltering summer of the Negro's legitimate discontent will not pass until there is an invigorating autumn of freedom and equality. Nineteen sixty-three is not an end, but a beginning. Those who hope that the Negro needed to blow off steam and will now be content will have a rude awakening if the nation returns to business as usual. There will be neither rest nor tranquility in America until the Negro is granted his citizenship rights. The whirlwinds of revolt will continue to shake the foundations of our nation until the bright day of justice emerges.

But there is something that I must say to my people who stand on the warm threshold which leads into the palace of justice. In the process of gaining our rightful place we must not be guilty of wrongful deeds. Let us not seek to satisfy our thirst for freedom by drinking from the cup of bitterness and hatred.

See p. 529 for anticipating objections to an argument.

We must forever conduct our struggle on the high plane of dignity and discipline. We must not allow our creative protest to degenerate into physical violence. Again and again we must rise to the majestic heights of meeting physical force with soul force. The marvelous new militancy which has engulfed the Negro community must not lead us to distrust of all white people, for many of our white brothers, as evidenced by their presence here today, have come to realize that their destiny is tied up with our destiny and their freedom is inextricably bound to our freedom. We cannot walk alone.

And as we walk, we must make the pledge that we shall march ahead. We cannot turn back. There are those who are asking the devotees of civil rights, "When will you be satisfied?" We can never be satisfied as long as our bodies, heavy with the fatigue of travel, cannot gain lodging in the motels of the highways and the hotels of the cities. We cannot be satisfied as long as the Negro's basic mobility is from a smaller ghetto to a larger one. We can never be satisfied as long as a Negro in Mississippi cannot vote and a Negro in New York believes he has nothing for which to vote. No, no, we are not satisfied, and we will not be satisfied until justice rolls down like waters and righteousness like a mighty stream.

I am not unmindful that some of you have come here out of great trials   9
and tribulations. Some of you have come fresh from narrow cells. Some of you
have come from areas where your quest for freedom left you battered by the
storms of persecution and staggered by the winds of police brutality. You have
been the veterans of creative suffering. Continue to work with the faith that
unearned suffering is redemptive.

Go back to Mississippi, go back to Alabama, go back to Georgia, go back   10
to Louisiana, go back to the slums and ghettos of our northern cities, knowing
that somehow this situation can and will be changed. Let us not wallow in the
valley of despair.

I say to you today, my friends, that in spite of the difficulties and frustra-   11
tions of the moment, I still have a dream. It is a dream deeply rooted in the
American dream.

I have a dream that one day this nation will rise up and live out the true   12
meaning of its creed: "We hold these truths to be self-evident: that all men are
created equal."

I have a dream that one day on the red hills of Georgia the sons of former   13
slaves and the sons of former slaveowners will be able to sit down together at a
table of brotherhood.

I have a dream that one day even the state of Mississippi, a desert state,   14
sweltering with the heat of injustice and oppression, will be transformed into an
oasis of freedom and justice.

I have a dream that my four children will one day live in a nation where   15
they will not be judged by the color of their skin but by the content of their
character.

I have a dream today.   16

I have a dream that one day the state of Alabama, whose governor's lips   17
are presently dripping with the words of interposition and nullification,[2] will be
transformed into a situation where little black boys and black girls will be able

2. George Wallace (1919–1998), four-time governor of Alabama, was a fierce opponent of
the civil rights movement. In 1963 he defied U.S. law and mounted a campaign against the
integration of Alabama public schools.

to join hands with little white boys and white girls and walk together as sisters and brothers.

I have a dream today.

I have a dream that one day every valley shall be exalted, every hill and mountain shall be made low, the rough places will be made plain, and the crooked places will be made straight, and the glory of the Lord shall be revealed, and all flesh shall see it together.[3]

This is our hope. This is the faith with which I return to the South. With this faith we will be able to hew out of the mountain of despair a stone of hope. With this faith we will be able to transform the jangling discords of our nation into a beautiful symphony of brotherhood. With this faith we will be able to work together, to pray together, to struggle together, to go to jail together, to stand up for freedom together, knowing that we will be free one day.

This will be the day when all of God's children will be able to sing with a new meaning, "My country, 'tis of thee, sweet land of liberty, of thee I sing. Land where my fathers died, land of the pilgrim's pride, from every mountainside, let freedom ring."

And if America is to be a great nation this must become true. So let freedom ring from the prodigious hilltops of New Hampshire. Let freedom ring from the mighty mountains of New York. Let freedom ring from the heightening Alleghenies of Pennsylvania!

Let freedom ring from the snowcapped Rockies of Colorado!

Let freedom ring from the curvaceous peaks of California!

But not only that; let freedom ring from Stone Mountain of Georgia![4]

Let freedom ring from Lookout Mountain of Tennessee![5]

Let freedom ring from every hill and every molehill of Mississippi. From every mountainside, let freedom ring.

---

3. King is quoting a famous passage from the book of Isaiah (40:4–5).

4. The figures of three leaders of the Confederacy are carved onto the face of Stone Mountain, near Atlanta.

5. Site of a major battle during the Civil War in 1863.

When we let freedom ring, when we let it ring from every village and   28
every hamlet, from every state and every city, we will be able to speed up that
day when all of God's children, black men and white men, Jews and Gentiles,
Protestants and Catholics, will be able to join hands and sing in the words of the
old Negro spiritual, "Free at last! free at last! thank God Almighty, we are free
at last!"

UNDERSTANDING THE SPEECH

1. Speaking in 1963, a hundred years after slavery was abolished by President Lincoln's Emancipation Proclamation, Martin Luther King Jr. tells his vast AUDIENCE that African Americans still are "not free" (2). Why not? How and where does he DESCRIBE this "appalling condition" (2)?

2. King uses his description of segregation as the basis for an ARGUMENT. What is the central CLAIM of that argument? What does King ask his audience to do about the situation he describes?

3. What does King mean by "the tranquilizing drug of gradualism"(4)? Why does he warn his audience to resist it?

4. King does not describe his "dream" until almost midway through his speech (11). Why? How does the first half of King's address help to prepare his audience for the vision of the future he presents in the second half?

5. In King's vision, the oppressed do not rise up and crush their oppressors. Why not? How do the details by which he DEFINES his dream fit in with what King tells his audience in paragraphs 6–7 and with his general philosophy of nonviolence?

6. King relies heavily on FIGURES OF SPEECH throughout his address, particularly METAPHOR: the nation has given its black citizens a "bad check" (4); racial injustice is "quicksands" (4); brotherhood is a "table" (13); freedom is a bell that rings from the "hilltops" (22). Choose several of these figures that you find particularly effective, and explain how they help King to COMPARE AND CONTRAST the "appalling condition" of the past and present with his brighter vision for the future.

USING SOURCES IN YOUR WRITING

W HATEVER your purpose, academic research requires "poking and pry- ing" into sources of information that go well beyond your own immedi- ate knowledge of a subject. If you're examining the student loan controversy of 2007, for example, you'll consult news stories and blog commentary published at that time. Or if you're analyzing a poem by Rita Dove, you'll study Dove's other poetry and read critical interpretations of her work in literary journals. This appendix shows how to find reliable sources, use what you learn in your own writing, and document your sources accurately.

FINDING AND EVALUATING SOURCES

As you do your research, you will encounter a wide range of potential sources— print and online, general and specialized, published and firsthand. You'll need to evaluate these sources carefully, choose the ones that best support your the- sis, and decide how to incorporate each source into your own paper.

Finding Appropriate Sources

The kinds of sources you turn to will depend on your topic. If you're doing research on a literary or historical topic, you might consult scholarly books and articles and standard reference works such as *The Dictionary of American Bio- graphy* or the *Literary History of the United States*. If your research is aimed at a current issue, you would likely consult newspapers and other periodicals, websites, and recent books.

Check your assignment to see if you are required to use primary or secondary sources—or both. PRIMARY SOURCES are original works, such as historical documents, literary works, eyewitness accounts, diaries, letters, and lab studies, as well as any original field research you do. SECONDARY SOURCES include books and articles, reviews, biographies, and other works that interpret or discuss primary sources. For example, novels and poems are primary sources; articles interpreting them are secondary sources.

Whether a work is considered primary or secondary often depends on your topic and purpose. If you're analyzing a poem, a critic's article analyzing the poem is a secondary source—but if you're investigating the critic's work, the article would be a primary source.

LIBRARY-BASED SOURCES

When you conduct academic research, it is often better to start with your library's website rather than with a commercial search engine such as *Google*. Library websites provide access to a range of well-organized resources, including scholarly databases through which you can access authoritative articles that have been screened by librarians or specialists in a particular field. In general, there are three kinds of sources you'll want to consult: reference works, books, and periodicals.

- *Reference works.* The reference section of your school's library is the place to find encyclopedias, dictionaries, atlases, almanacs, bibliographies, and other reference works. Remember, though, that reference works are only a starting point, a place where you can get an overview of your topic or basic facts about it. Some reference works are *general*, such as *The New Encyclopaedia Britannica* or the *Statistical Abstract of the United States*. Others are *specialized*, providing in-depth information on a single field or topic.

- *Books.* The library catalog is your main source for finding books. Most catalogs are computerized and can be accessed through the library's website. You can search by author, title, subject, or keyword. When you click on a specific source, you'll find more bibliographic data about author, title, and publication; the call number (which identifies the book's location on the library's shelves); related subject headings (which may lead to other useful materials in the library)—and more.

- *Periodicals.* To find journal and magazine articles, you will need to search periodical indexes and databases. Indexes (such as the *New York Times Index*) provide listings of articles organized by topics; databases (such as LexisNexis) provide the full texts. Although some databases are available for free, many can be accessed by subscription through your library.

WEB-BASED SOURCES

The Web offers countless sites sponsored by governments, educational institutions, organizations, businesses, and individuals. Because it is so vast and dynamic, however, finding useful information can be a challenge. There are several ways to search the Web:

- *Keyword searches. Google, Bing, Ask.com, Yahoo!, AltaVista,* and *Lycos* all scan the Web looking for the keywords you specify.

- *Metasearches. Copernic Agent, SurfWax,* and *Dogpile* let you use several search engines simultaneously.

- *Academic searches.* For peer-reviewed academic writing in many disciplines, try *Google Scholar;* or use *Scirus* for scientific, technical, and medical documents.

Although many websites provide authoritative information, keep in mind that Web content varies greatly in its stability and reliability: what you see on a site today may be different (or gone) tomorrow. So save or make copies of pages you plan to use, and carefully evaluate what you find. Here are just a few of the many resources available on the Web.

- *Indexes, databases, and directories.* Information put together by specialists and grouped by topics can be especially helpful. You may want to consult *Librarians' Internet Index* (an annotated subject directory of more than 20,000 websites selected by librarians); *Infomine* (a huge collection of databases, mailing lists, catalogs, articles, directories, and more); or *The*

World Wide Web Virtual Library (a catalog of websites on numerous subjects, compiled by experts).

- *News sites.* Many newspapers, magazines, and radio and TV stations have websites that provide both up-to-the-minute information and also archives of older news articles. Through *Google News* and *NewsLink,* for example, you can access current news worldwide, whereas *Google News Archive Search* has files going back to the 1700s.

- *Government sites.* Many government agencies and departments maintain websites where you can find government reports, statistics, legislative information, and other resources. *USA.gov* offers information, services, and other resources from the U.S. government.

- *Digital archives.* These sites collect and organize materials from the past—including drawings, maps, recordings, speeches, and historic documents—often focusing on a particular subject or country. For example, the National Archives and Records Administration and the Library of Congress both archive items relevant to the culture and history of the United States.

- *Discussion lists and forums.* Online mailing lists, newsgroups, discussion groups, and forums let members post and receive messages from other members. To join a discussion with people who are knowledgeable about your topic, try searching for your topic—for example, for "E. B. White discussion forum." Or consult a site such as *Google Groups.*

SEARCHING ELECTRONICALLY

When you search for subjects on the Web or in library catalogs, indexes, or databases, you'll want to come up with keywords that will lead to the information you need. Specific commands vary among search engines and databases, but most search engines now offer "Advanced Search" options that allow you to narrow your search by typing keywords into text boxes labeled as follows:

- All of these words
- The exact phrase
- Any of these words
- None of these words

In addition, you may filter the results to include only full-text articles (articles that are available in full online); only certain domains (such as *.edu,* for educational sites; *.gov,* for government sites; or *.org,* for nonprofit sites); and, in library databases, only scholarly, peer-reviewed sites. Type quotation marks around words to search for an exact phrase: "Twitter revolution" or "Neil Gaiman."

Some databases may require you to limit searches through the use of various symbols or Boolean operators (AND, OR, NOT). See the Advanced Search instructions for help with such symbols, which may be called *field tags.*

If a search turns up too many sources, be more specific (*homeopathy* instead of *medicine*). If your original keywords don't generate good results, try synonyms (*home remedy* instead of *folk medicine*). Keep in mind that searching requires flexibility, both in the words you use and the methods you try.

Evaluating Sources

Searching the *Health Source* database for information on the incidence of meningitis among college students, you find seventeen articles. An "exact words" *Google* search yields thirty-seven. How do you decide which sources to read? The following questions can help you select reliable and useful sources.

- *Is the source relevant?* Look at the title and at any introductory material to see what it covers. Does the source appear to relate directly to your purpose? What will it add to your work?

- *What are the author's credentials?* Has the author written other works on this subject? Is he or she known for taking a particular position on it? If the author's credentials are not stated, you might do a Web search to see what else you can learn about him or her.

- *What is the stance?* Does the source cover various points of view or advocate only one perspective? Does its title suggest a certain slant? If you're evaluating a website, check to see whether it includes links to sites expressing other perspectives.

- *Who is the publisher?* Books published by university presses and articles in scholarly journals are peer-reviewed by experts in the field before they are published. Those produced for a general audience do not always undergo such rigorous review and factchecking. At well-established publishing houses, however, submissions are usually vetted by experienced editors or even editorial boards.

- *If the source is a website, who is the sponsor?* Is the site maintained by an organization, interest group, government agency, or individual? If the site doesn't give this information on its homepage, look for clues in the URL domain: *.edu* is used mostly by colleges and universities, *.gov* by government agencies, *.org* by nonprofit organizations, *.mil* by the military, and *.com* by commercial organizations. Be aware that the sponsor may have an agenda—to argue a position, present biased information, or sell a product— and that text on the site does not necessarily undergo rigorous review or factchecking.

- *What is the level of the material?* Texts written for a general audience might be easier to understand but may not be authoritative enough for academic work. Scholarly texts will be more authoritative but may be harder to comprehend.

- *How current is the source?* Check to see when books and articles were published and when websites were last updated. (If a site lists no date, see if links to other sites still work; if not, the site is probably too dated to use.) A recent publication date or updating, however, does not necessarily mean the source is better—some topics require current information whereas others call for older sources.

- *Does the source include other useful information?* Is there a bibliography that might lead you to additional materials? How current or authoritative are the sources it cites?

Taking Notes

When you find material that will be useful to your argument, take careful notes.

- *Use index cards, a computer file, or a notebook,* labeling each entry with information that will allow you to keep track of where it comes from—

author, title, the pages or the URL, and (for online sources) the date of access.

- *Take notes in your own words and use your own sentence patterns.* If you make a note that is a detailed paraphrase, label it as such so that you'll know to provide appropriate documentation if you use it.

- *If you find wording that you'd like to quote,* be sure to enclose the exact words in quotation marks to distinguish your source's words from your own words.

- *Label each note with a subject heading* so you can organize your notes easily when constructing an outline for your paper.

INCORPORATING SOURCE MATERIALS INTO YOUR TEXT

There are many ways to incorporate source materials into your own text. Three of the most common are quoting, paraphrasing, or summarizing. Let's look at the differences among these three forms of reference, and then consider when to use each one and how to work these references into your text.

Quoting

When you quote someone else's words, you reproduce his or her language exactly, in quotation marks—though you can add your own words in brackets or omit unnecessary words in the original by using ellipsis marks (. . .). This example from Mary Roach's "How to Know If You Are Dead" uses all of these conventions:

> In her analysis of the life-saving role of human cadavers, Mary Roach notes that "a gurney with a [newly deceased] cadaver commands no urgency. It is wheeled by a single person, . . . like a shopping cart" (167).

Paraphrasing

When you paraphrase, you restate information from a source in your own words, using your own sentence structures. Because a paraphrase includes all the main points of the source, it is usually about the same length as the original.

Here is a paragraph from Diane Ackerman's essay "Why Leaves Turn Color in the Fall," followed by two sample paraphrases. The first demonstrates some of the challenges of paraphrasing.

ORIGINAL SOURCE

Where do the colors come from? Sunlight rules most living things with its golden edicts. When the days begin to shorten, soon after the summer solstice on June 21, a tree reconsiders its leaves. All summer it feeds them so they can process sunlight, but in the dog days of summer the tree begins pulling nutrients back into its trunk and roots, pares down, and gradually chokes off its leaves. A corky layer of cells forms at the leaves' slender petioles, then scars over. Undernourished, the leaves stop producing the pigment chlorophyll, and photosynthesis ceases. Animals can migrate, hibernate, or store food to prepare for winter. But where can a tree go? It survives by dropping its leaves, and by the end of autumn only a few fragile threads of fluid-carrying xylem hold leaves to their stems.

UNACCEPTABLE PARAPHRASE

Ackerman tells us where the colors of leaves come from. The amount of sunlight is the trigger, as is true for most living things. At the end of June, as daylight lessens, a tree begins to treat its leaves differently. It feeds them all summer so they can turn sunlight into food, but in August a tree begins to redirect its food into its trunk and roots, gradually choking the leaves. A corky group of cells develops at the petioles, and a scar forms. By autumn, the leaves don't have enough food, so they stop producing chlorophyll, and photosynthesis also stops. Although animals are able to migrate, hibernate, or stow food for the winter, a tree cannot go anywhere. It survives only by dropping its leaves, and by the time winter comes only a few leaves remain on their stems (257).

This first paraphrase borrows too much of the language of the original or changes it only slightly. It also follows the original sentence structure too closely. The following paraphrase avoids both of these pitfalls.

ACCEPTABLE PARAPHRASE

Ackerman explains why leaves change color. Diminishing sunlight is the main instigator. A tree nourishes its leaves—and encourages photosynthesis—for most of the summer. By August, however, as daylight continues to lessen, a tree starts to reroute its food to the roots and trunk, a process that saves the tree but eventually kills the leaves. In autumn, because the leaves are almost starving, they can neither manufacture chlorophyll to stay green nor carry out photosynthesis. By this time, the base of the petiole, or leaf's stem, has hardened, in preparation for the final drop. Unlike animals, who have many ways to get ready for winter—hiding food ahead of time, moving to a warm climate, sleeping through winter—a tree is immobile. It can make it through the winter only by losing its leaves (257).

Summarizing

Unlike a paraphrase, a summary does not present all the details in the original source, so it is generally as brief as possible. Summaries may boil down an entire book or essay into a single sentence, or they may take a paragraph or more to present the main ideas. Here, for example, is a summary of the Ackerman paragraph:

In late summer and fall, Ackerman explains, trees put most of their food into their roots and trunk, which causes leaves to change color and die but enables trees to live through the winter (257).

Deciding Whether to Quote, Paraphrase, or Summarize

Follow these rules of thumb to determine whether you should quote a source directly, paraphrase it in detail, or merely summarize the main points.

- *Quote* a text when the exact wording is critical to making your point (or that of an authority you wish to cite), or when the wording itself is part of what you're analyzing.

- *Paraphrase* when the meaning of a text is important to your argument but the original language is not essential, or when you're clarifying or interpreting the ideas (not the words) in the text.

- *Summarize* when the main points of the text are important to your argument but the details can be left out in the interest of conciseness.

Using Signal Phrases

When you quote, paraphrase, or summarize a source, identify your source clearly and use a signal phrase ("she says," "he thinks") to distinguish the words and ideas of your source from your own. Consider this example:

> Professor and textbook author Elaine Tyler May claims that many high-school history textbooks are too bland to interest young readers (531).

This sentence summarizes a general position about the effectiveness of certain textbooks ("too bland"), and it attributes that view to a particular authority (Elaine Tyler May), citing her credentials (professor, textbook author) for speaking as an authority on the subject. By using the signal phrase "claims that," the sentence also distinguishes the words and ideas of the source from those of the writers.

The verb you use in a signal phrase can be neutral (*says* or *thinks*), or it can indicate your (or your source's) stance toward the subject. In this case, the use of the verb *claims* suggests that what the source says is arguable (or that the writer of the sentence believes it is). The signal verb you choose can influence your reader's understanding of the sentence and of your attitude toward what it says.

ACKNOWLEDGING SOURCES AND AVOIDING PLAGIARISM

As a writer, you must acknowledge any words and ideas that come from others. There are numerous reasons for doing so: to give credit where credit is due, to recognize the various authorities and many perspectives you have considered, to show readers where they can find your sources, and to situate your own arguments in the ongoing academic conversation. Using other people's words and ideas without acknowledgment is plagiarism, a serious academic and ethical offense.

MATERIAL THAT DOESN'T HAVE TO BE ACKNOWLEDGED

- Facts that are common knowledge, such as the name of the current president of the United States
- Well-known statements accompanied by a signal phrase: "As John F. Kennedy said, 'Ask not what your country can do for you; ask what you can do for your country.'"

MATERIAL THAT REQUIRES ACKNOWLEDGMENT

- Direct quotations, paraphrases, and summaries
- Arguable statements and any information that is not commonly known (statistics and other data)
- Personal or professional opinions and assertions of others
- Visuals that you did not create yourself (charts, photographs, and so on)
- Collaborative help you received from others

Plagiarism is (1) using another writer's exact words without quotation marks, (2) using another writer's words or ideas without in-text citation or other documentation, (3) paraphrasing or summarizing someone else's ideas using language or sentence structure that is close to the original. The following practices will help you avoid plagiarizing:

- *Take careful notes,* clearly labeling quotations and using your own phrasing and sentence structure in paraphrases and summaries.

- *Check all paraphrases and summaries* to be sure they are stated in *your* words and sentence structures—and that you put quotation marks around any of the source's original phrasing.

- *Know what sources you must document,* and identify them both in the text and in a works-cited list.

- *Check to see that all quotations are documented;* it is not enough just to include quotation marks or indent a block quotation.

- *Be especially careful with online material*—copying source material directly into a document you are writing invites plagiarism. Like other sources, information from the Web must be acknowledged.

- *Recognize that plagiarism has consequences.* A scholar's work will be discredited if it too closely resembles the work of another scholar. Journalists who plagiarize lose their jobs, and students routinely fail courses or are dismissed from school when they are caught cheating—all too often by submitting essays that they have purchased from online "research" sites.

So, don't take the chance. If you're having trouble with an assignment, ask your instructor for assistance. Or visit your school's writing center. Writing centers can help with advice on all aspects of your writing, including acknowledging sources and avoiding plagiarism.

DOCUMENTATION

Taken collectively, all the information you provide about sources is your *documentation.* Many organizations and publishers—for example, the American Psychological Association (APA), the University of Chicago Press, and the Council of Science Editors (CSE)—have their own documentation styles. The focus here is on the documentation system of the Modern Language Association (MLA) because it is one of the most common systems used in college courses, especially in the liberal arts.

The MLA's documentation system has two basic parts (1) brief in-text references for quotations, paraphrases, or summaries and (2) more detailed information for each in-text reference in a list of works cited at the end of the text. MLA style requires that each item in your works-cited list include the following information: author, editor, or organization; title of work; place of publication; publisher; date of publication; medium of publication; and, for online sources, date when you accessed the source. Here is an example of how the two parts work together. Note that you can identify the author either in a signal phrase or in parentheses:

See pp. 672–79 for a sample paper with MLA-style citations.

IN-TEXT CITATIONS (WITH AND WITHOUT SIGNAL PHRASE)

As Lester Faigley puts it, "The world has become a bazaar from which to shop for an individual 'lifestyle'" (12).

As one observer suggests, "The world has become a bazaar from which to shop for an individual 'lifestyle'" (Faigley 12).

CORRESPONDING WORKS-CITED REFERENCE

Faigley, Lester. *Fragments of Rationality: Postmodernity and the Subject of Composition.* Pittsburgh: U of Pittsburgh P, 1992. Print.

MLA IN-TEXT DOCUMENTATION

1. Author in signal phrase 654
2. Author in parentheses 654
3. After a block quotation 654
4. Two or more authors 655
5. Organization as author 655
6. Author unknown 656
7. Literary works 656
8. Works cited together 656
9. Source in another source 657
10. Work without page numbers 657
11. An entire work 657

Brief documentation in your text makes clear to your reader what you took from a source and where within the source you found the information. As you cite each source, you will need to decide whether or not to name the author in a signal phrase—"as Toni Morrison writes"—or in parentheses—"(Morrison 24)." For either style of reference, try to put the parenthetical citation at the end of the sentence or as close as possible to the material you've cited without awkwardly interrupting the sentence. When citing a direct quotation (as in no. 1), note that the parenthetical reference comes after the closing quotation marks but before the period at the end of the sentence.

1. AUTHOR NAMED IN A SIGNAL PHRASE

If you mention the author in a signal phrase, put only the page number(s) in parentheses. Do not write *page* or *p*.

> McCullough describes John Adams as having "the hands of a man accustomed to pruning his own trees, cutting his own hay, and splitting his own firewood" (18).

2. AUTHOR NAMED IN PARENTHESES

If you do not mention the author in a signal phrase, put his or her last name in parentheses along with the page number(s). Do not use punctuation between the name and the page number(s).

> One biographer describes John Adams as someone who was not a stranger to manual labor (McCullough 18).

3. AFTER A BLOCK QUOTATION

When quoting more than three lines of poetry, more than four lines of prose, or dialogue between two or more characters from a drama, set off the quotation from the rest of your text, indenting it one inch (or ten spaces) from the left margin. Do not use quotation marks, and place any parenthetical documentation *after* the final punctuation.

In *Eastward to Tartary*, Kaplan captures ancient and contemporary Antioch:

> At the height of its glory in the Roman-Byzantine age, when it had an amphitheater, public baths, aqueducts, and sewage pipes, half a million people lived in Antioch. Today the population is only 125,000. With sour relations between Turkey and Syria, and unstable politics throughout the Middle East, Antioch is now a backwater—seedy and tumbledown, with relatively few tourists. I found it altogether charming. (123)

4. TWO OR MORE AUTHORS

For a work by two or three authors, name all the authors, either in a signal phrase or in parentheses.

> Carlson and Ventura's stated goal is to introduce Julio Cortázar, Marjorie Agosín, and other Latin American writers to an audience of English-speaking adolescents (5).

For a work with four or more authors, you can mention all their names *or* just the name of the first author followed by *et al.*, which means "and others."

> One popular survey of American literature breaks the contents into sixteen thematic groupings (Anderson, Brinnin, Leggett, Arpin, and Toth 19–24).
>
> One popular survey of American literature breaks the contents into sixteen thematic groupings (Anderson et al. 19–24).

5. ORGANIZATION OR GOVERNMENT AS AUTHOR

Cite the organization either in a signal phrase or in parentheses. It's acceptable to shorten long names.

The U.S. government can be direct when it wants to be. For example, it sternly warns, "If you are overpaid, we will recover any payments not due you" (Social Security Administration 12).

6. AUTHOR UNKNOWN

If you can't determine an author, use the work's title or a shortened version of the title in the parentheses.

> A powerful editorial in last week's paper asserts that healthy liver donor Mike Hurewitz died because of "frightening" faulty postoperative care ("Every Patient's Nightmare").

7. LITERARY WORKS

When referring to literary works that are available in many different editions, you need to cite additional information so that readers of any edition can locate the text you are citing.

Novels: Give the page and chapter number of the edition you are using.

> In *Pride and Prejudice,* Mrs. Bennett shows no warmth toward Jane and Elizabeth when they return from Netherfield (105; ch. 12).

Verse plays: Give the act, scene, and line numbers; separate them with periods.

> Macbeth develops the vision theme when he addresses the Ghost with "Thou hast no speculation in those eyes / Which thou dost glare with" (3.3.96–97).

Poems: Give the part and line numbers (separated by periods). If a poem has only line numbers, use the word *line(s)* in the first reference.

> The mere in *Beowulf* is described as "not a pleasant place!" (line 1372). Later, it is called "the awful place" (1378).

8. TWO OR MORE WORKS CITED TOGETHER

If you cite the works in the same parentheses, separate the references with a semicolon.

Critics have looked at both *Pride and Prejudice* and *Frankenstein* from a cultural perspective (Tanner 7; Smith viii).

9. SOURCE QUOTED IN ANOTHER SOURCE

When you are quoting text that you found quoted in another source, use the abbreviation *qtd. in* in the parenthetical reference.

> Charlotte Brontë wrote to G. H. Lewes: "Why do you like Miss Austen so very much? I am puzzled on that point" (qtd. in Tanner 7).

10. WORK WITHOUT PAGE NUMBERS

For works without page numbers, including many online sources, identify the source using the author or other information either in a signal phrase or in parentheses. If the source has paragraph or section numbers, use them with the abbreviations *par.* or *sec.*

> Studies reported in *Scientific American* and elsewhere show that music training helps children to be better at multitasking later in life ("Hearing the Music," par. 2).

11. AN ENTIRE WORK

If you refer to an entire work rather than a part of it, there's no need to include page numbers.

> At least one observer considers Turkey and Central Asia to be explosive (Kaplan).

MLA LIST OF WORKS CITED

BOOKS

1. One author 660
2. Multiple books by an author 660
3. Two or three authors 660
4. Four or more authors 660
5. Organization as author 661
6. Anthology 661
7. Work(s) in an anthology 661

8. Author and editor 661
9. Translation 662
10. Introduction or afterword 662
11. Multivolume work 662
12. Subsequent edition 662
13. Reference-book article 662

PERIODICALS

14. Journal article 663
15. Magazine article 663
16. Newspaper article 664

17. Unsigned article 664
18. Editorial 664
19. Book review 664

ONLINE SOURCES

20. Entire website 665
21. Work from a website 666
22. Online book 666
23. Online journal article 666
24. Online magazine article 666
25. Article in a database 667
26. Online newspaper article 667

27. Online editorial 667
28. Blog entry 667
29. Email correspondence 667
30. Online forum posting 667
31. Online reference article 668
32. Podcast 668

OTHER KINDS OF SOURCES

33. Art 668
34. Cartoon 668
35. CD-ROM or DVD-ROM 669
36. Film, DVD, or video clip 669
37. Interview 669
38. Letter 669

39. Map 670
40. Musical score 670
41. Sound recording 670
42. TV or radio program 670
43. Digital file 670

SOURCES NOT COVERED BY MLA 671
SAMPLE PAPER 671

A works-cited list provides full bibliographic information for every source cited in your text. Here's some general advice to help you format your list:

- Start the list on a new page.
- Center the title (Works Cited) one inch from the top of the page.
- Double-space the whole list.
- Begin each entry flush with the left-hand margin and indent subsequent lines one-half inch or five spaces.
- Alphabetize entries by the author's last name. If a work has no identifiable author, use the first major word of the title (disregard *A, An, The*).
- If you cite more than one work by a single author, list them all alphabetically by title, and use three hyphens in place of the author's name after the first entry (see no. 3 for an example).

Books

For most books, you'll need to list the author; the title and any subtitle; and the place of publication, publisher, date, and the medium—*Print*. A few details to note when citing books:

- *Authors*: List the primary author last-name-first, and include any middle name or initial after the first name.
- *Titles*: Capitalize all principal words in titles and subtitles, including short verbs such as *is* and *are*. Do not capitalize *a, an, the, to,* or any preposition or conjunction unless they begin a title or subtitle. Italicize book titles, but place quotation marks around works within books.
- *Publication place and publisher*: If there's more than one city listed on the title page, use only the first. Use a shortened form of the publisher's name (Norton for W. W. Norton & Company; Princeton UP for Princeton University Press).
- *Dates*: If more than one year is given, use the most recent one.

1. ONE AUTHOR

Miller, Susan. *Assuming the Positions: Cultural Pedagogy and the Politics of Commonplace Writing*. Pittsburgh: U of Pittsburgh P, 1998. Print.

2. TWO OR MORE WORKS BY THE SAME AUTHOR(S)

Give the author's name in the first entry, and then use three hyphens in the author slot for each of the subsequent works, listing them alphabetically by the first important word of each title.

Kaplan, Robert D. *The Coming Anarchy: Shattering the Dreams of the Post Cold War*. New York: Vintage, 2001. Print.

———. *Eastward to Tartary: Travels in the Balkans, the Middle East, and the Caucasus*. New York: Vintage, 2001. Print.

3. TWO OR THREE AUTHORS

Follow the order of names on the book's title page. List the second and third authors first-name-first.

Malless, Stanley, and Jeffrey McQuain. *Coined by God: Words and Phrases That First Appear in the English Translations of the Bible*. New York: Norton, 2003. Print.

Sebranek, Patrick, Verne Meyer, and Dave Kemper. *Writers INC: A Guide to Writing, Thinking, and Learning*. Burlington: Write Source, 1990. Print.

4. FOUR OR MORE AUTHORS

You may give each author's name or the name of the first author only, followed by *et al.* (Latin for "and others").

Anderson, Robert, et al. *Elements of Literature: Literature of the United States*. Austin: Holt, 1993. Print.

5. ORGANIZATION OR GOVERNMENT AS AUTHOR

> Diagram Group. *The Macmillan Visual Desk Reference.* New York: Macmillan, 1993. Print.

For a government publication, give the name of the government first, followed by the names of any department and agency.

> United States. Dept. of Health and Human Services. Natl. Inst. of Mental Health. *Autism Spectrum Disorders.* Washington: GPO, 2004. Print.

6. ANTHOLOGY

Use this model only when you are citing the whole anthology or the contributions of the editor(s).

> Kitchen, Judith, and Mary Paumier Jones, eds. *In Short: A Collection of Brief Creative Nonfiction.* New York: Norton, 1996. Print.

7. WORK(S) IN AN ANTHOLOGY

Give the inclusive page numbers of the selection you are citing.

> Achebe, Chinua. "Uncle Ben's Choice." *The Seagull Reader: Literature.* Ed. Joseph Kelly. New York: Norton, 2005. 23–27. Print.

To document two or more selections from one anthology, list each selection by author and title, followed by the editors' names and the pages of the selection. In addition, include in your works-cited list an entry for the anthology itself (no. 6).

> Hiestand, Emily. "Afternoon Tea." Kitchen and Jones 65–67.

> Ozick, Cynthia. "The Shock of Teapots." Kitchen and Jones 68–71.

8. AUTHOR AND EDITOR

Start with the author if you've cited the text itself.

> Austen, Jane. *Emma.* Ed. Stephen M. Parrish. New York: Norton, 2000. Print.

Start with the editor if you've cited his or her contribution.

> Parrish, Stephen M., ed. *Emma*. By Jane Austen. New York: Norton, 2000. Print.

9. TRANSLATION

> Dostoevsky, Fyodor. *Crime and Punishment*. Trans. Richard Pevear and Larissa Volokhonsky. New York: Vintage, 1993. Print.

10. FOREWORD, INTRODUCTION, PREFACE, OR AFTERWORD

> Tanner, Tony. Introduction. *Pride and Prejudice*. By Jane Austen. London: Penguin, 1972. 7–46. Print.

11. MULTIVOLUME WORK

If you cite all the volumes, give the number of volumes after the title.

> Sandburg, Carl. *Abraham Lincoln: The War Years*. 4 vols. New York: Harcourt, 1939. Print.

If you cite only one volume, give the volume number after the title.

> Sandburg, Carl. *Abraham Lincoln: The War Years*. Vol. 2. New York: Harcourt, 1939. Print.

12. EDITION OTHER THAN THE FIRST

> Gibaldi, Joseph. *MLA Handbook for Writers of Research Papers*. 6th ed. New York: MLA, 2003. Print.

13. ARTICLE IN A REFERENCE BOOK

Provide the author's name if the article is signed. If a reference book is well known, give only the edition and the year of publication.

> "Iraq." *The New Encyclopaedia Brittanica*. 15th ed. 2007. Print.

If a reference book is less familiar, give complete publication information.

Benton-Cohen, Katherine. "Women in the Reform and Progressive Era." *A History of Women in the United States.* Ed. Doris Weatherford. 4 vols. Danbury, CT: Grolier, 2004. Print.

Periodicals

For most articles, you'll need to list the author, the article title and any subtitle, the periodical title, any volume and issue number, the date, inclusive page numbers, and the medium—*Print.* A few details to note when citing periodicals:

- *Authors*: Format authors as you would for a book.
- *Titles*: Capitalize titles and subtitles as you would for a book. Omit any initial *A, An,* or *The.* Italicize periodical titles; place article titles within quotation marks.
- *Dates*: Abbreviate the names of months except for May, June, and July: Jan., Feb., Mar., Apr., Aug., Sept., Oct., Nov., Dec. Journals paginated by both volume and issue need only the year (in parentheses).
- *Pages*: If an article does not fall on consecutive pages, give the first page with a plus sign (55+).

14. ARTICLE IN A JOURNAL

Bartley, William. "Imagining the Future in *The Awakening*." *College English* 62.6 (2000): 719–46. Print.

For journals that do not have volume numbers, give the issue number after the title, followed by the year of publication and inclusive page numbers.

Flynn, Kevin. "The Railway in Canadian Poetry." *Canadian Literature* 174 (2002): 70–95. Print.

15. ARTICLE IN A MAGAZINE

Cloud, John. "Should SATs Matter?" *Time* 12 Mar. 2001: 62+. Print.

For a monthly magazine, include only the month and year.

> Fellman, Bruce. "Leading the Libraries." *Yale Alumni Magazine* Feb.
> 2002: 26–31. Print.

16. ARTICLE IN A DAILY NEWSPAPER

> Springer, Shira. "Celtics Reserves Are Whizzes vs. Wizards." *Boston Globe*
> 14 Mar. 2005: D4+. Print.

If you are documenting a particular edition of a newspaper, specify the edition (*late ed., natl. ed.,* and so on) after the date.

> Margulius, David L. "Smarter Call Centers: At Your Service?" *New York
> Times* 14 Mar. 2002, late ed.: G1+. Print.

17. UNSIGNED ARTICLE

> "Coal Mine Inspections Fall Short." *Atlanta Journal-Constitution* 18
> Nov. 2007: A7. Print.

18. EDITORIAL OR LETTER TO THE EDITOR

> "Gas, Cigarettes Are Safe to Tax." Editorial. *Lakeville Journal* 17 Feb.
> 2005: A10. Print.

> Festa, Roger. "Social Security: Another Phony Crisis." Letter. *Lakeville
> Journal* 17 Feb. 2005: A10. Print.

19. BOOK REVIEW

> Frank, Jeffrey. "Body Count." Rev. of *The Exception*, by Christian Jun-
> gersen. *New Yorker* 30 July 2007: 86–87. Print.

Online Sources

Not every online source gives you all the data that the MLA would like to see in a works-cited entry. Ideally, you'll be able to list the author's name, the title, information about print publication (if applicable), information about electronic publication (title of site, editor, date of first electronic publication and/or most recent revision, name of publisher or sponsoring institution), the publication medium, date of access, and, if necessary, a URL. Here are a few details to note when citing online sources:

- *Authors or editors and title*: Format authors and titles as you would for a print book or periodical.

- *Publisher*: If the name of the publisher or sponsoring institution is unavailable, use *N.p.*

- *Dates*: Abbreviate the months as you would for a print periodical. Although MLA asks for the date when materials were first posted or most recently updated, you won't always be able to find that information; if it's unavailable, use *n.d.* Be sure to include the date on which you accessed the source.

- *Pages*: If the citation calls for page numbers but the source is unpaginated, use *n. pag.* in place of page numbers.

- *Medium*: Indicate the medium—Web, email, PDF, MP3, jpeg, and so on.

- *URL*: MLA assumes that readers can locate most sources on the Web by searching for the author, title, or other identifying information, so they don't require a URL for most online sources. When readers cannot locate the source without a URL, give the address of the website in angle brackets. When a URL won't fit on one line, break it only after a slash (and do not add a hyphen). If a URL is very long, consider using the one from the site's homepage or search page instead.

20. ENTIRE WEBSITE OR PERSONAL WEBSITE

Zalta, Edward N., ed. *Stanford Encyclopedia of Philosophy*. Metaphysics Research Lab, Center for the Study of Language and Information, Stanford U, 2007. Web. 14 Nov. 2010.

Nunberg, Geoffrey. Home page. School of Information, U of California, Berkeley, 2009. Web. 3 Apr. 2009.

21. WORK FROM A WEBSITE

Buff, Rachel Ida. "Becoming American." *Immigration History Research Center*. U of Minnesota, 24 Mar. 2008. Web. 4 Apr. 2008.

22. ONLINE BOOK OR PART OF A BOOK

Cite a book you access online as you would a print book, adding the name of the site or database, the medium, and the date of access. (See next page for examples.)

Anderson, Sherwood. *Winesburg, Ohio.* New York: B. W. Huebsch, 1919. *Bartleby.com.* Web. 7 Apr. 2008.

If you are citing a part of a book, put the part in quotation marks before the book title. If the online book is paginated, give the pages; if not, use *N. pag.*

Anderson, Sherwood. "The Philosopher." *Winesburg, Ohio.* New York: B. W. Huebsch, 1919. N. pag. *Bartleby.com.* Web. 7 Apr. 2008.

To cite a book you've downloaded onto a Kindle, Nook, or other digital device, follow the setup for a print book, but indicate the ebook format at the end of your citation.

Larson, Erik. *The Devil in the White City: Murder, Mayhem, and Madness at the Fair That Changed America.* New York: Vintage, 2004. Kindle.

23. ARTICLE IN AN ONLINE JOURNAL

If a journal does not number pages or if it numbers each article separately, use *n. pag.* in place of page numbers.

Moore, Greggory. "The Process of Life in *2001: A Space Odyssey*." *Images: A Journal of Film and Popular Culture* 9 (2000): n. pag. Web. 12 May 2009.

24. ARTICLE IN AN ONLINE MAGAZINE

Landsburg, Steven E. "Putting All Your Potatoes in One Basket: The Economic Lessons of the Great Famine." *Slate.* Slate, 13 Mar. 2001. Web. 8 Dec. 2007.

25. ARTICLE ACCESSED THROUGH DATABASE

For articles accessed through a library's subscription services, such as InfoTrac and EBSCOhost, cite the publication information for the source, followed by the name of the database.

> Bowman, James. "Moody Blues." *American Spectator* June 1999: 64–65. *Academic Search Premier.* Web. 15 Mar. 2005.

26. ARTICLE IN AN ONLINE NEWSPAPER

> Mitchell, Dan. "Being Skeptical of Green." *New York Times.* New York Times, 24 Nov. 2007. Web. 26 Nov. 2007.

27. ONLINE EDITORIAL

> "Outsourcing Your Life." Editorial. *ChicagoTribune.com.* Chicago Tribune, 24 Nov. 2004. Web. 3 Jan. 2008.

28. BLOG ENTRY

If the entry has no title, use "Blog entry" (without quotation marks). Cite a whole blog as you would a personal website (no. 20). If the publisher or sponsor is unavailable, use *N.p.*

> Gladwell, Malcolm. "Underdogs." N.p., 13 May 2009. Web. 11 Aug. 2011.

29. EMAIL CORRESPONDENCE

> Smith, William. "Teaching Grammar—Some Thoughts." Message to the author. 15 Feb. 2008. Email.

30. POSTING TO AN ELECTRONIC FORUM

> Mintz, Stephen H. "Manumission During the Revolution." H-Net List on Slavery. Michigan State U, 14 Sept. 2006. Web. 18 Apr. 2009.

31. ARTICLE IN AN ONLINE REFERENCE WORK OR WIKI

"Dubai." *MSN Encarta.* Microsoft Corporation, 2008. Web. 20 June 2008.

For a wiki, cite the date of the last modification or update as the publication date.

"Pi." *Wikipedia.* Wikimedia Fundation, 6 Aug. 2011. Web. 11 Aug. 2011.

32. PODCAST

Blumberg, Alex, and Adam Davidson. "The Giant Pool of Money."
   Host Ira Glass. *This American Life.* Chicago Public Radio, 9 May
   2008. Web. 18 Sept. 2008.

Other Kinds of Sources

Many of the sources in this section can be found online. If there is no Web model here, start with the guidelines most appropriate for the source you need to cite, omit the original medium, and end your citation with the title of the website, italicized; the medium (Web); and the day, month, and year of access.

33. ART (PRINT AND ONLINE)

Van Gogh, Vincent. *The Potato Eaters.* 1885. Oil on canvas. Van Gogh
   Museum, Amsterdam.

Warhol, Andy. *Self-Portrait.* 1979. Polaroid Polacolor print. J. Paul
   Getty Museum, Los Angeles. *The Getty.* Web. 5 Jan. 2008.

34. CARTOON OR COMIC STRIP (PRINT AND ONLINE)

Chast, Roz. "The Three Wise Men of Thanksgiving." Cartoon. *New
   Yorker* 1 Dec. 2003: 174. Print.

Adams, Scott. "Dilbert." Comic strip. *Dilbert.com.* United Features
   Syndicate, 9 Nov. 2007. Web. 26 Nov. 2007.

35. CD-ROM OR DVD-ROM

Cite like a book, but indicate any pertinent information about the edition or version.

> *Othello*. Princeton: Films for the Humanities and Sciences, 1998. CD-ROM.

36. FILM, DVD, OR VIDEO CLIP

> *Super 8*. Dir. J. J. Abrams. Perf. Joel Courtney, Kyle Chandler, and Elle Fanning. Paramount, 2011. Film.

To cite a particular person's work, start with that name.

> Cody, Diablo, scr. *Juno*. Dir. Jason Reitman. Perf. Ellen Page, Michael Cera, Jennifer Garner, and Jason Bateman. Fox Searchlight, 2007. DVD.

Cite a video clip from YouTube or a similar site as you would a short work from a website.

> PivotMasterDX, dir. "Storaged." *YouTube*. YouTube, 29 Apr. 2009. Web. 11 Aug. 2011.

37. BROADCAST, PUBLISHED, AND PERSONAL INTERVIEW

> Gates, Henry Louis, Jr. Interview. *Fresh Air*. NPR. WNYC, New York. 9 Apr. 2002. Radio.

> Brzezinski, Zbigniew. "Against the Neocons." *American Prospect* Mar. 2005: 26–27. Print.

> Berra, Yogi. Personal interview. 17 June 2001.

38. PUBLISHED LETTER

> White, E. B. Letter to Carol Angell. 28 May 1970. *Letters of E. B. White*. Ed. Dorothy Lobarno Guth. New York: Harper, 1976. 600. Print.

39. MAP (PRINT AND ONLINE)

Toscana. Map. Milan: Touring Club Italiano, 1987. Print.

"Austin, TX." Map. *Google Maps*. Google, 11 Aug. 2011. Web. 11 Aug. 2011.

40. MUSICAL SCORE

Beethoven, Ludwig van. *String Quartet No. 13 in B Flat, Op. 130*. 1825. New York: Dover, 1970. Print.

41. SOUND RECORDING (WITH ONLINE VERSION)

Whether you list the composer, conductor, or performer first depends on where you want to place the emphasis.

Beethoven, Ludwig van. *Missa Solemnis*. Perf. Westminster Choir and New York Philharmonic. Cond. Leonard Bernstein. Sony, 1992. CD.

The Beatles. "Can't Buy Me Love." *A Hard Day's Night*. United Artists, 1964. MP3 file.

Davis, Miles. "So What." *Birth of the Cool*. Columbia, 1959. *Miles Davis*. Web. 14 Feb. 2009.

42. TELEVISION OR RADIO PROGRAM (WITH ONLINE VERSION)

"Stirred." *The West Wing*. Writ. Aaron Sorkin, Dir. Jeremy Kagan. Perf. Martin Sheen. NBC. WPTV, West Palm Beach, 3 Apr. 2002. Television.

"Bush's War." *Frontline*. Writ. and Dir. Michael Kirk. *PBS.org*. PBS, 24 Mar. 2008. Web. 10 Apr. 2009.

43. MP3, JPEG, PDF, OR OTHER DIGITAL FILE

For downloaded songs, photographs, PDFs, and other documents stored on your computer or another digital device, follow the guidelines for the type of work you are citing (art, journal article, and so on) and give the file type as the medium. (See next page for examples.)

> Talking Heads. "Burning Down the House." *Speaking in Tongues.* Sire, 1983. Digital file.
>
> Taylor, Aaron. "Twilight of the Idols: Performance, Melodramatic Villainy, and *Sunset Boulevard.*" *Journal of Film and Video* 59 (2007): 13–31. PDF file.

Citing Sources Not Covered by MLA

To cite a source that isn't covered by the MLA guidelines, look for models similar to the source you're citing. Give any information readers will need in order to find the source themselves—author, title, subtitle; publisher and/or sponsor; medium; dates; and any other pertinent information. You might want to try out the citation yourself, to be sure it will lead others to your source.

SAMPLE STUDENT RESEARCH PAPER

Dylan Borchers wrote the following research paper for a first-year writing class. He used MLA style for his essay, but documentation styles vary from discipline to discipline, so ask your instructor if you're not sure which style you should use.

Dylan Borchers

Professor Bullock

English 102, Section 4

31 March 2009

Against the Odds:

Harry S. Truman and the Election of 1948

"Thomas E. Dewey's Election as President Is a Foregone Conclusion," read a headline in the *New York Times* during the presidential election race between incumbent Democrat Harry S. Truman and his Republican challenger, Thomas E. Dewey. Earlier, *Life* magazine had put Dewey on its cover with the caption "The Next President of the United States" (qtd. in "1948 Truman-Dewey Election"). In a *Newsweek* survey of fifty prominent political writers, each one predicted Truman's defeat, and *Time* correspondents declared that Dewey would carry 39 of the 48 states (Donaldson 210). Nearly every major media outlet across the United States endorsed Dewey and lambasted Truman. As historian Robert H. Ferrell observes, even Truman's wife, Bess, thought he would be beaten (270).

The results of an election are not so easily predicted, as the famous photograph on page 2 shows. Not only did Truman win the election, but he won by a significant margin, with 303 electoral votes and 24,179,259 popular votes, compared to Dewey's 189 electoral votes and 21,991,291 popular votes (Donaldson 204–07). In fact, many historians and political analysts argue that Truman would have won by an even greater margin had third-party Progressive candidate Henry A. Wallace not split the Democratic vote in New York State

Fig. 1. President Harry S. Truman holds up an Election Day edition of the *Chicago Daily Tribune*, which mistakenly announced "Dewey Defeats Truman." St. Louis, 4 Nov. 1948 (Rollins).

and Dixiecrat Strom Thurmond not won four states in the South (McCullough 711). Although Truman's defeat was heavily predicted, those predictions themselves, Dewey's passiveness as a campaigner, and Truman's zeal turned the tide for a Truman victory.

 In the months preceding the election, public opinion polls predicted that Dewey would win by a large margin. Pollster Elmo Roper stopped polling in September, believing there was no reason to continue, given a seemingly inevitable Dewey landslide. Although the margin narrowed as the election drew near, the other pollsters predicted a Dewey win by at least 5 percent (Donaldson 209). Many historians believe that these predictions aided the president in the long run. First, surveys showing Dewey in the lead may have prompted some of Dewey's supporters to feel overconfident about their candidate's chances and therefore to stay home from the polls on Election Day. Second, these same surveys may have energized Democrats to mount late get-out-the-vote efforts ("1948 Truman-Dewey Election"). Other analysts believe that the overwhelming predictions of a Truman loss also kept at home some Democrats who approved of Truman's policies but saw a Truman loss as inevitable. According to political analyst Samuel Lubell, those Democrats may have saved Dewey from an even greater defeat (Hamby, *Man of the People* 465). Whatever the impact on the voters, the polling numbers had a decided effect on Dewey.

Historians and political analysts alike cite Dewey's overly cautious campaign as one of the main reasons Truman was able to achieve victory. Dewey firmly believed in public opinion polls. With all indications pointing to an easy victory, Dewey and his staff believed that all he had to do was bide his time and make no foolish mistakes. Dewey himself said, "When you're leading, don't talk" (qtd. in McCullough 672). Each of Dewey's speeches was well-crafted and well-rehearsed. As the leader in the race, he kept his remarks faultlessly positive, with the result that he failed to deliver a solid message or even mention Truman or any of Truman's policies. Eventually, Dewey began to be perceived as aloof and stuffy. One observer compared him to the plastic groom on top of a wedding cake (Hamby, "Harry S. Truman"), and others noted his stiff, cold demeanor (McCullough 671–74).

As his campaign continued, observers noted that Dewey seemed uncomfortable in crowds, unable to connect with

---

If you quote text that's quoted in another source, cite that source in a parenthetical reference

If you cite two or more works closely together, give a parenthetical citation for each one

ordinary people. And he made a number of blunders. One
took place at a train stop when the candidate, commenting on
the number of children in the crowd, said he was glad they
had been let out of school for his arrival. Unfortunately for
Dewey, it was a Saturday ("1948: The Great Truman Surprise"). Such gaffes gave voters the feeling that Dewey was out
of touch with the public.

Again and again through the autumn of 1948, Dewey's
campaign speeches failed to address the issues, with the
candidate declaring that he did not want to "get down in the
gutter" (qtd. in McCullough 701). When told by fellow
Republicans that he was losing ground, Dewey insisted that
his campaign not alter its course. Even *Time* magazine,
though it endorsed and praised him, conceded that his
speeches were dull (McCullough 696). According to historian
Zachary Karabell, they were "notable only for taking place,
not for any specific message" (244). Dewey's numbers in the
polls slipped in the weeks before the election, but he still held
a comfortable lead over Truman. It would take Truman's
famous whistle-stop campaign to make the difference.

Few candidates in U.S. history have campaigned for the
presidency with more passion and faith than Harry Truman.
In the autumn of 1948, he wrote to his sister, "It will be the
greatest campaign any President ever made. Win, lose, or
draw, people will know where I stand" (91). For thirty-three
days, Truman traveled the nation, giving hundreds of
speeches from the back of the *Ferdinand Magellan* railroad
car. In the same letter, he described the pace: "We made
about 140 stops and I spoke over 147 times, shook hands with

at least 30,000 and am in good condition to start out again tomorrow for Wilmington, Philadelphia, Jersey City, Newark, Albany and Buffalo" (91). McCullough writes of Truman's campaign:

> No President in history had ever gone so far in quest of support from the people, or with less cause for the effort, to judge by informed opinion. . . . As a test of his skills and judgment as a professional politician, not to say his stamina and disposition at age sixty-four, it would be like no other experience in his long, often difficult career, as he himself understood perfectly. More than any other event in his public life, or in his presidency thus far, it would reveal the kind of man he was. (655)

He spoke in large cities and small towns, defending his policies and attacking Republicans. As a former farmer and relatively late bloomer, Truman was able to connect with the public. He developed an energetic style, usually speaking from notes rather than from a prepared speech, and often mingled with the crowds that met his train. These crowds grew larger as the campaign progressed. In Chicago, over half a million people lined the streets as he passed, and in St. Paul the crowd numbered over 25,000. When Dewey entered St. Paul two days later, he was greeted by only 7,000 supporters ("1948 Truman-Dewey Election"). Reporters brushed off the large crowds as mere curiosity seekers wanting to see a president (McCullough 682). Yet Truman persisted, even if he often seemed to be the only one who thought he could win. By going directly to the American people and connecting with them, Truman built the momentum needed to surpass Dewey and win the election.

The legacy and lessons of Truman's whistle-stop campaign continue to be studied by political analysts, and politicians today often mimic his campaign methods by scheduling multiple visits to key states, as Truman did. He visited California, Illinois, and Ohio 48 times, compared with 6 visits to those states by Dewey. Political scientist Thomas M. Holbrook concludes that his strategic campaigning in those states and others gave Truman the electoral votes he needed to win (61, 65).

The 1948 election also had an effect on pollsters, who, as Elmo Roper admitted, "couldn't have been more wrong" (qtd. in Karabell 255). *Life* magazine's editors concluded that pollsters as well as reporters and commentators were too convinced of a Dewey victory to analyze the polls seriously, especially the opinions of undecided voters (Karabell 256). Pollsters assumed that undecided voters would vote in the same proportion as decided voters—and that turned out to be a false assumption (Karabell 258). In fact, the lopsidedness of the polls might have led voters who supported Truman to call themselves undecided out of an unwillingness to associate themselves with the losing side, further skewing the polls' results (McDonald, Glynn, Kim, and Ostman 152). Such errors led pollsters to change their methods significantly after the 1948 election.

In a work by four or more authors, either cite them all or name the first one followed by "et al."

After the election, many political analysts, journalists, and historians concluded that the Truman upset was in fact a victory for the American people, who, the *New Republic* noted, "couldn't be ticketed by the polls, knew its own mind and had picked the rather unlikely but courageous figure of Truman to carry its banner" (qtd. in McCullough 715). How "unlikely" is unclear, however; Truman biographer Alonzo Hamby notes that "polls of scholars consistently rank Truman among the top eight presidents in American history" (*Man of the People* 641). But despite Truman's high standing, and despite the fact that the whistle-stop campaign is now part of our political landscape, politicians have increasingly imitated the style of the Dewey campaign, with its "packaged candidate who ran so as not to lose, who steered clear of controversy, and who made a good show of appearing presidential" (Karabell 266). The election of 1948 shows that voters are not necessarily swayed by polls, but it may have presaged the packaging of candidates by public relations experts, to the detriment of public debate on the issues in future presidential elections.

Works Cited

Donaldson, Gary A. *Truman Defeats Dewey*. Lexington: UP of
Kentucky, 1999. Print.

Ferrell, Robert H. *Harry S. Truman: A Life*. Columbia: U of
Missouri P, 1994. Print.

Hamby, Alonzo L., ed. "Harry S. Truman (1945–1953)." *Ameri-
canPresident.org*. Miller Center of Public Affairs, U of
Virginia, 11 Dec. 2003. Web. 17 Mar. 2009.

——. *Man of the People: A Life of Harry S. Truman*. New
York: Oxford UP, 1995. Print.

Holbrook, Thomas M. "Did the Whistle-Stop Campaign Matter?" *PS: Political Science and Politics* 35.1 (2002): 59–66.
Print.

Karabell, Zachary. *The Last Campaign: How Harry Truman Won
the 1948 Election*. New York: Knopf, 2000. Print.

McCullough, David. *Truman*. New York: Simon & Schuster,
1992. Print.

McDonald, Daniel G., Carroll J. Glynn, Sei-Hill Kim, and Ron-
ald E. Ostman. "The Spiral of Silence in the 1948 Presidential Election." *Communication Research* 28.2 (2001):
139–55. Print.

"1948: The Great Truman Surprise." *Media and Politics Online
Projects: Media Coverage of Presidential Campaigns*. Dept.
of Political Science and International Affairs, Kennesaw
State U, 29 Oct. 2003. Web. 20 Mar. 2009.

"1948 Truman-Dewey Election." *Electronic Government Project:
Eagleton Digital Archive of American Politics*. Eagleton
Inst. of Politics, Rutgers, State U of New Jersey, 2004.
Web. 19 Mar. 2009.

Center the
heading

Alphabetize the
list by authors' last
names or by title
for works with no
author

Begin each entry
at the left margin;
indent subsequent
lines $\frac{1}{2}$ inch or five
spaces

If you cite more
than one work by
a single author,
list them alpha-
betically by title,
and use three
hyphens in place
of the author's
name

Rollins, Byron. Untitled photograph. "The First 150 Years: 1948." *AP History*. Associated Press, n.d. Web. 23 Mar. 2009.

Truman, Harry S. "Campaigning, Letter, October 5, 1948." *Harry S. Truman*. Ed. Robert H. Ferrell. Washington: CQ P, 2003. 91. Print.

Check to be sure that every source you use is in the works-cited list

PERMISSIONS
ACKNOWLEDGMENTS

Heidi Julavits: "The Kyoto Treat," *New York Times Magazine,* January 1, 2006. © 2006, The New York Times. Reprinted by permission.

Jon Katz: "How Boys Become Men," originally appeared in *Glamour,* January 1993. Reprinted by permission of SLL/Sterling Lord Literistic, Inc. Copyright by Jon Katz.

Martin Luther King Jr.: "I Have a Dream." Reprinted by arrangement with The Heirs to the Estate of Martin Luther King Jr., c/o Writers House as agent for the proprietor, New York, NY. Copyright © 1963 Dr. Martin Luther King Jr.; copyright renewed 1991 Coretta Scott King.

Barbara Kingsolver: Excerpt from "In Case You Ever Want to Go Home Again" (pp. 39–43) from *High Tide in Tucson: Essays From Now or Never* by Barbara Kingsolver. Copyright © 1995 by Barbara Kingsolver. Reprinted by permission of HarperCollins Publishers.

Geeta Kothari: "If You Are What You Eat, Then What Am I?" Originally published in *The Kenyon Review* (Winter 1999). Reprinted with the permission of the author.

Richard Lederer: "English Is a Crazy Language." Reprinted with the permission of Atria Books, a Division of Simon & Schuster, Inc., from *Crazy English: The Ultimate Joy Ride Through Our Language* by Richard Lederer. Copyright © 1989 by Richard Lederer.

Yiyun Li: "Orange Crush," *New York Times Magazine,* January 22, 2006. © 2006, The New York Times. Reprinted by permission of the author.

Andrea Lunsford: "Our Semi-Literate Youth? Not So Fast," by Andrea Lunsford. Reprinted by permission of the author.

Robert Lustig, Laura Schmidt, Claire Brindis: "The Truth about Toxic Sugar," by Robert Lustig, Laura Schmidt, Claire Brindis from *Nature,* February 2, 2012. Copyright © 2012 Nature Publishing Group. Reprinted with permission.

Myriam Marquez: "Why and When We Speak Spanish in Public," *Orlando Sentinel*, July 15, 1999. Used with permission of the Orlando Sentinel, copyright © 1999.

Cherokee Paul McDonald: "A View from a Bridge." Reprinted by permission of the author and Jay Garon-Brooke Associates, Inc.

Erin McKean: "Redefining Definition," by Erin McKean from *The New York Times*, 12/20/2000. © 2000 The New York Times. All rights reserved. Used by permission and protected by the Copyright Laws of the United States. The printing, copying, redistribution, or retransmission of the Material without express written permission is prohibited.

Mary Mebane: "Chapter 18 (The Back of the Bus)," from *Mary* by Mary Mebane, copyright © 1981 by Mary Elizabeth Mebane. Used by permission of Viking Penguin, a division of Penguin Group (USA) Inc.

Johnson C. Montgomery: "Island of Plenty." First appeared in *Newsweek* magazine. Reprinted by permission of Nancy Montgomery Moyer.

Marissa Nuñez: "Climbing the Golden Arches," from *Starting with 'I': Personal Essays by Teenagers*. Copyright © 1997 by Youth Communication ® / New York Center, Inc. Reprinted by permission of Persea Books, Inc. (New York).

The Onion: "All Seven Deadly Sins Committed At Church Bake Sale," *The Onion*, Dec. 12, 2001, pp. 37–45. Reprinted with permission of *The Onion*. Copyright © 2001, by Onion, Inc. www.theonion.com.

Laura Pappano: "How Big Time Sports Ate College Life," by Laura Pappano. From *The New York Times*, 1/20/2012. © 2012 The New York Times. All rights reserved. Used by permission and protected by the Copyright Laws of the United States. The printing, copying, redistribution, or retransmission of the Material without express written permission is prohibited.

Adam Penenberg and Marc Berry: "The Pizza Plot" by Adam Penenberg and Marc Berry. Originally printed in *The New York Times*, 12/3/2000. Reprinted with permission of the author.

IMAGES

R. Lee Institute for Health Policy Studies, USCF. p. 304: Lynda Barry, Used with Permission by Drawn & Quarterly. p. 305: Courtesy of Jessica Walden. p. 309: Marie Read. p. 316: Larry D. Moore/Wikimedia. p. 322: AP/Wide World Photo. p. 327: Courtesy of Jeffrey Skinner. p. 329: Mick Stevens. p. 333: Courtesy of Philip Weiss. p. 363: Courtesy of Junenoire Photography. p. 364: Courtesy of Dan Treadway. p. 368: Photo by Mark Ostow. p. 373: Hank Walker/ Time Life Pictures/Getty Images. p. 377: Time Life Pictures/Getty Images. p. 378: Time Life Pictures/Getty Images. p. 382: Colin McPherson/Corbis. p. 383: Stan Tess/Alamy. p. 385: Patrick Batchelder/Alamy. p. 390: Used by permission of Gary Soto. p. 397: Jocelyn Augustino/Redux. p. 406: Fred R. Conrad/The New York Times/Redux. p. 407: Jeff Miller/U of Wisconsin-Madison. p. 421: Courtesy of Douglas Ray. p. 422: Courtesy of Lawrence Collerd. p. 427: Larry Marano/Getty Images. p. 436: Courtesy of Tanya Maria Barrientos. p. 442: Photo by Jean Grace. p. 449: Courtesy of Erin McKean/Wikimedia. p. 454: Courtesy of Jack Horner/Museum of the Rockies. p. 459: Courtesy of Mike Rose. p. 462: Courtesy of Mike Rose. p. 463: Corbis. p. 466: Courtesy of Mike Rose. p. 481: Courtesy of World Wildlife Federation/Euro RSCG Finland. p. 482: Courtesy of Elisa Gonzales. p. 487: Photo by Jacqueline Salmon. p. 489: New York World-Telegram and the Sun Newspaper Photograph Collection, Library of Congress. p. 499: Marc Brasz/Corbis. p. 506: Patrick Farrell/Miami Herald. p. 510: Joyce Ravid. p. 533: Courtesy of Marilyn Moller. p. 545: Courtesy of Mark D. White. p. 545: Courtesy of Robert Arp. p. 550: David Shankbone/ Wikimedia. p. 559: z91/Press/Newscom. p. 563: Joanie Simon. p. 578: Sports Illustrated. p. 579: Gary C. Caskey/UPI/Landov. p. 584: Erick W. Rasco/ Sports Illustrated/Getty Images. p. 586: ZUMA Press, Inc./Alamy. p. 591: Photo by Donavan Lynch. p. 606: The Granger Collection. p. 612: The Granger Collection. p. 623: Alexander Helser/FPG/Archive Photos/Getty Images. p. 627: The Granger Collection. p. 630: Time Life Pictures/Mansell/Time Life Pictures/Getty Images. p. 634: Lee Lockwood/Time Life Pictures/Getty Images.

GLOSSARY / INDEX

A

ABSTRACT, 39, 59, 65, 185, 191 General, having to do with essences and ideas: Liberty, truth, and beauty are abstract concepts. Most writers depend upon abstractions to some degree; however, abstractions that are not fleshed out with vivid particulars are unlikely to hold a reader's interest. See also CONCRETE.

Addison, Liz 534

Ain't I a Woman? (Truth), 627

All Seven Deadly Sins Committed at Church Bake Sale (The Onion), 200

ALLUSION A passing reference, especially to a work of literature. When feminist Lindsy Van Gelder put forth the "modest proposal" that words of feminine gender be used whenever English traditionally uses masculine words, she had in mind Jonathan Swift's essay by that title (reprinted here in Chapter 13). This single brief reference carries the weight of Swift's entire essay behind it, humorously implying that the idea being advanced is about as modest as Swift's tongue-in-cheek proposal that Ireland eat its children as a ready food supply for a poor country. Allusions, therefore, are an efficient means of enlarging the scope and implications of a statement. They work best, of course, when they refer to works most readers are likely to know.

This Glossary/Index defines key terms and concepts and directs you to pages in the book where they are used or discussed. Terms set in SMALL CAPITAL LETTERS are defined elsewhere in the glossary / index.

ANALOGY, 527, 548 A COMPARISON that explains aspects of something unfamiliar by likening it to something that is more familiar. In EXPOSITORY writing, analogies are used as aids to explanation and as organizing devices. In a PERSUASIVE essay, a writer may argue that what is true in one case is also true in the similar case that he or she is advancing. An ARGUMENT "by analogy" is only as strong as the terms of the analogy are close.

ANECDOTE, 523, 125, 127, 187 A brief NARRATIVE or humorous story, often told for the purpose of EXEMPLIFYING or explaining a larger point. Anecdotal evidence is proof based on such stories rather than on rigorous statistical or scientific inquiry.

ARGUMENT, 17, 19, 33, 517–32 An argument makes a case or proves a point. It seeks to convince someone to act in a certain way or to believe in the truth or validity of a statement or CLAIM. According to traditional definitions of argumentation and persuasion, a writer can convince a reader in one of three ways: by appealing to reason, by appealing to the reader's emotions, or by appealing to the reader's sense of ethics.

Arp, Robert, 545

Ashen Guy: Lower Broadway, September 11, 2001, The (Beller), 149

AUDIENCE, 25, 64, 127, 188, 241, 298, 357, 416, 474–76, 521 The people to whom a piece of writing is addressed. Writers are more likely to achieve their purpose in writing if they keep the needs and expectations of their audience in mind throughout the writing process when making choices about topics, DICTION, support, and so on. For example, an essay written for athletes that attacks the use of performance-enhancing drugs in sports might emphasize the hazards of taking steroids. On the other hand, an essay with the same PURPOSE but written for an audience of sports fans might focus more on the value of fair play and of having heroes who are drug-free.

B

Back of the Bus, The (Mebane), 167
Barker, Carrie, 135
Barrientos, Tanya Maria, 436
Barry, Dave, 427
Barry, Lynda, 177
Beller, Thomas, 149
Berry, Marc, 342
Blue-Collar Brilliance (Rose), 459
Bracken County, Northern Kentucky (Welte), 72
Buffett, Warren, 274
But Two Negatives Equal a Positive (Barker), 135
Brindis, Claire, 284
Brooks, David, 279

C

Carr, Nicholas, 563
Catton, Bruce, 373

CAUSAL CHAIN A series of circumstances or events in which one circumstance or event CAUSES another, which in turn causes another and so on—all leading to an ultimate EFFECT. A row of dominoes on end is a classic example: The fall of one domino causes another to tip over, which in turn pushes over another domino, until the entire row has toppled.

CAUSE AND EFFECT, 33, 471–80 A strategy of EXPOSITION. Cause and effect essays analyze why an event occurred and/or trace its consequences. See the introduction to Chapter 11 for further discussion of this strategy.

Chapels (Iyer), 382
Chasing Loons (Walden), 305
City of Big Shoulders (Collerd), 422

CLAIM, 518, 521–28 The main point that an ARGUMENT is intended to prove or support; a statement that is debatable, that rational people can disagree with.

CLASSIFICATION, 32, 238–45 A strategy of EXPOSITION that puts people or things into categories based on their distinguishing characteristics. Strictly speaking, classification assigns individuals to categories (*This coin is an Indian-Head penny*), and division separates individuals in a group according to a given trait or traits (*Put the pennies in a box, the nickels in this one, and give me the quarters and half dollars*). Classification is a mode of organizing an essay as well as a means of obtaining knowledge. See Chapter 7 for further discussion of this strategy.

CLICHÉ A tired expression that has lost its original power to surprise because of overuse: *We'll have to go back to the drawing board. The quarterback turned the tables and saved the day.*

CLIMAX, 123–24, 129 An aspect of PLOT in NARRATIVE writing. The climax is the moment when the action of a narrative is most intense—the culmination, after which the dramatic tension is released.

Climbing the Golden Arches (Nuñez), 493
Cohen, Roger, 406
College Athletes Should Not Be Paid (Posnanski), 584
Color of Success, The (Watts), 247
Collerd, Lawrence, 422

COMPARISON AND CONTRAST, 32, 353–62 A strategy of EXPOSITORY writing that explores the similarities and differences between two persons, places, things, or ideas. See Chapter 9 for a more detailed explanation.

CONCRETE, 39, 59, 65, 185, 191 Definite, particular, capable of being perceived directly. Opposed to ABSTRACT. *Rose, Mississippi, pinch* are more concrete words than *flower, river, touch. Five-miles-per-hour* is a more concrete idea than *slowness.* It is good practice to make your essays as concrete as possible, even when you are writing on a general topic. If you are DEFINING an ideal wife or husband, cite specific wives or husbands you have known or heard about.

CONNOTATIONS   The implied meaning of a word; its overtones and associations over and above its literal meaning. The strict meaning of *home*, for example, is "the place where ones lives"; but the word connotes comfort, security, and love.

Crenshaw, Paul, 79

D

Death of the Moth, The (Woolf), 630
Declaration of Independence,
   The (Jefferson), 606

DEDUCTION, 517, 525   A form of logical reasoning that proceeds from general premises to specific conclusions. See also SYLLOGISM.

DEFINITION, 32, 412–20   A basic strategy of EXPOSITORY writing. Definitions give the essential meaning of something. *Extended* definitions enlarge on that basic meaning by analyzing the qualities, recalling the history, explaining the purpose, or giving SYNONYMS of whatever is being defined. See the introduction to Chapter 10 for further discussion of this strategy.

DESCRIPTION, 17, 31, 48, 59–70   One of four MODES OF WRITING. Description appeals to the senses: it tells how something looks, feels, sounds, smells, or tastes. An *objective* description focuses on verifiable facts and the observable physical details of a subject, whereas a *subjective* description conveys the writer's thoughts and feelings about a subject, in addition to its physical characteristics. See the introduction to Chapter 4 for further discussion of the descriptive mode.

DIALOGUE, 125, 131   Direct speech, especially between two or more speakers in a NARRATIVE, quoted word for word.

DICTION   Word choice. Mark Twain was talking about diction when he said that the dif-

ference between the almost right word and the right word is the difference "between the lightning bug and the lightning." *Standard* diction is defined by dictionaries and other authorities as the language taught in schools and used in the national media. *Nonstandard* diction includes words like *ain't* that are generally not used in formal writing. *Slang* includes figurative language of a group (*moll, gat, heist*) or fashionable, coined words (*bonkers, weirdo*) and extended meanings (*dough* for money; *garbage* for nonsense). Slang words often pass quickly into the standard language or just as quickly fade away. *Colloquial diction* is the language of informal speech or writing: *I'm crazy about you, Virginia. Regional* language is that spoken in certain geographic areas—for example, *remuda*, a word for a herd of riding horses, is used in the Southwest. *Obsolete* language includes terms like *pantaloons* and *palfrey* (saddle horse) that were once standard but are no longer used.

Dillard, Annie, 2

DIVISION   *See* CLASSIFICATION.

Dollar Store Economy, The (Hitt), 262

DOMINANT IMPRESSION, 61–67   In DESCRIPTIVE writing, the main impression of a subject that a writer creates through the use of carefully selected details.

Doyle, Brian, 85

E

Empathy (Huffington), 550
English Is a Crazy Language (Lederer), 216

ETYMOLOGY, 414–15, 419   A word's history or the practice of tracing such histories. The modern English word *march*, for example, is derived from the French *marcher* ("to walk"), which in turn is derived from the Latin word *marcus* ("a hammer"). The etymological definition of *march* is thus "to walk with a measured tread, like the rhythmic pounding of a hammer." In most dictionaries, the derivation, or etymology, of a word is explained in parentheses or brackets before the first definition is given.

EVIDENCE, 25, 30, 34–35, 517, 522   Proof; the facts and figures, examples, expert testimony, personal experience, and other support that a writer provides in order to make a point.

EXAMPLE, 31, 184–92   A specific instance of a general group or idea. Among "things that have given males a bad name," for example, humorist Dave Barry cites "violent crime, war, spitting, and ice hockey." See the introduction to Chapter 6 for more on using examples in writing.

EXPOSITION, 17   One of the four MODES OF WRITING. Expository writing is informative writing. It explains or gives directions. All the items in this glossary are written in the expository mode; and most of the practical prose that you write in the coming years will be—e.g., papers and examinations, job applications, business reports, insurance claims, your last will and testament.

Extraordinary Characteristics of Dyslexia, The (Horner), 454

F

Family History (Gonzales), 482

FIGURES OF SPEECH, 20, 67   Colorful words and phrases used in a nonliteral sense. Some common figures of speech: *Simile:* A stated comparison, usually with *like* or *as: He stood like a rock. Metaphor:* A comparison that equates two objects without the use of a stated connecting word: *Throughout the battle, Sergeant Phillips was a rock. Metonymy:* The use of one word or name in place or another commonly associated with it: *The White House* [for the president] *awarded the sergeant a medal. Personification:* The assignment of human traits to nonhuman objects: *The very walls have ears. Hyperbole:* Conscious exaggeration: *The mountain reached to the sky. Understatement:* The opposite of hyperbole, a conscious playing down: *After forty days of climbing the mountain,*

we felt that we had made a start. Rhetorical Question: A question to which the author expects no answer or that he answers himself: *Why climb the mountain? Because it is there.*

FLASHBACK   The NARRATIVE technique of interrupting the main PLOT of a story to show the reader an incident that occurred earlier in time.

FLASH-FORWARD   The NARRATIVE technique of interrupting the main PLOT of a story to show the reader an incident that occurs at some time in the future.

Football vs. Asian Studies (Treadway), 364

G

Gates, Henry Louis, Jr. , 499
Gender in the Classroom (Tannen), 397
Giant Step, A (Gates), 499
Gonzales, Elisa, 482
Goodman, Allegra, 322
Grant and Lee: A Study in Contrasts (Catton), 373
Guys vs. Men (Barry), 427

H

Hal and Me (Carr), 563
Happy Meals and Old Spice Guy (Weiss), 222
Harmony and the Dream (Brooks), 279
Hitt, Jack, 262
Hodgman, Ann, 106
Holy the Firm, From (Dillard), 3
Homeward Bound (Wu), 206
Hood, Ann, 510
Horner, Jack, 454
Horton, Alex, 211
How Big-Time Sports Ate College Life (Pappano), 591
How Boys Become Men (Katz), 316
How I Wrote the Moth Essay—and Why (Dillard), 8
How to Get Out of a Locked Trunk (Weiss), 333
Huffington, Arianna, 550

HYPERBOLE   Exaggeration. See FIGURES OF SPEECH.

I

I Have a Dream (King), 634
If You Are What You Eat, Then What Am I?
(Kothari), 442
In Case You Ever Want to Go Home Again
(Kingsolver), 143

INDUCTION, 517, 525 A form of logical reasoning that proceeds from specific examples to general principles. As a rule, an inductive ARGUMENT is only as valid as its examples are representative. See the introduction to Chapter 12.

IRONY, 320, 612 A statement that implies something other than what the words generally mean. For example, when Russell Baker writes that New Yorkers find Toronto "hopelessly bogged down in civilization," what he implies is that New Yorkers define "civilization" in an uncivilized way. Irony of situation, as opposed to verbal irony, occurs when events turn out differently than expected. It was ironic that Hitler, with his dream of world domination, committed suicide in the end.

Island of Plenty, The (Montgomery), 539
Iyer, Pico, 382

J

Jacoby, Jeff, 368
Jefferson, Thomas, 606
Joyas Voladoras (Doyle), 85
Julavits, Heidi, 155

K

Katz, Jon, 316
King, Martin Luther, Jr. , 634
King, Kennedy, and the Power of Words
(Wendel), 487
Kingsolver, Barbara, 143
Kothari, Geeta, 442

L

Laugh, Kookaburra (Sedaris), 227
Lederer, Richard, 216
Let Stars Get Paid (Rosenberg), 578
Li, Yiyun, 161

Like Mexicans (Soto), 390
Lincoln, Abraham, 623

LOGICAL FALLACY, 473, 526–28 An error in logical reasoning. Common logical fallacies include reasoning *past hoc; ergo propter hoc, non sequiturs*; begging the question; arguing *ad hominem*; and false ANALOGIES. See the introduction to Chapter 12 for further discussion of logical fallacies.

Long Beautiful Hair (Hood), 510
Lunsford, Andrea, 570
Lustig, Robert, 284

M

Marquez, Myriam, 506
McDonald, Cherokee Paul, 90
McKean, Erin, 449
Meaning of Life, The (Cohen), 406
Mebane, Mary, 167

METAPHOR, 67 A direct COMPARISON that identifies one thing with another. See FIGURES OF SPEECH.

Metal Memorials (Horton), 211

METONYMY A form of verbal association. See FIGURES OF SPEECH.

Mind Over Mass Media (Pinker), 559
Miss Dennis School of Writing,
The (Steinbach), 96

MODES OF WRITING, 16, 31–34, 37, 48–54 Basic patterns of writing, including DESCRIPTION, NARRATION, EXPOSITION, and ARGUMENTATION. Description is explained in detail in Chapter 4; narration, in Chapter 5; exposition, in Chapters 6–11; and argumentation, in Chapter 12.

Modest Proposal, A (Swift), 612
Montgomery, Johnson C., 539
Mother Tongue (Tan), 253

N

NARRATION, 17, 31, 123–33 One of the four MODES OF WRITING. An account of actions and events that happen to someone or something in a particular place and time. Because narration is essentially storytelling, it is often used in fiction; however, it is also an important element in almost all writing and speaking. The opening of Lincoln's *Gettysburg Address*, for example, is in the narrative mode: "Fourscore and seven years ago our fathers brought forth on this continent a new nation . . ."

NARRATOR, 68, 123–25, 130–31 In a NARRATIVE, the person who is telling the story. The narrator can participate directly in the events of the story—or serve mainly as an observer reporting on those events.

No Wonder They Call Me a Bitch
        (Hodgman), 106
Nuñez, Marissa, 493

O

Once More to the Lake (White), 114
Onion, The, 200

ONOMATOPOEIA The use of words that sound like what they refer to: *What's the buzz?* or *The cat purred, the dog barked, and the clock ticked.*

Orange Crush (Li), 161
Our Semi-Literate Youth? Not So Fast
        (Lunsford), 570

OXYMORON An apparent contradiction or bringing together of opposites for RHETORICAL or humorous effect, as in *eloquent silence, mournful optimist,* or (some would say) *military intelligence, civic organization.*

P

Pappano, Laura, 591
Penenberg, Adam, 342

PERSONIFICATION, 61, 68 Assigning human characteristics to inanimate objects or ideas: *Death lurked around the corner.* See FIGURES OF SPEECH.

PERSUASION The art of moving an AUDIENCE to action or belief. According to traditional definitions, a writer can persuade a reader in one of three ways: by appealing to the reader's reason, emotions, or sense of ethics.

Pinker, Steven, 559
Pizza Plot, The (Penenberg and Berry), 342

PLOT, 18, 123, 297, 604 The sequence of events in a story arranged in such a way as to have a beginning, middle, and end.

POINT OF VIEW, 61, 123, 130–31 The perspective from which a story is told or an account given. Point of view is often described according to the grammatical person of a NARRATIVE. An "I" narrative, for example, is told from the "first-person" point of view. A narrative that refers to "he" or "she" is told from the "third-person" point of view. If the speaker of a third-person narrative seems to know everything about his or her subject, including people's thoughts, the point of view is "omniscient"; if the speaker's knowledge is incomplete, the point of view is third-person "limited."

Posnanski, Joe, 584

PROCESS ANALYSIS, 292–303 A form of EXPOSITORY writing that breaks a process into its component operations or that gives directions. Most "how to" essays are essays in process analysis: how to write an essay; how to operate a fork lift; how to avoid a shark bite. Process analyses are usually divided into stages or steps arranged in chronological order. They differ from NARRATIVES in that they tell how something functions rather than what happens to something or someone. See the introduction to Chapter 8 for further discussion of this expository strategy.

PUN A play on words, usually involving different words that sound alike, or different meanings of the same word: *The undertaker was a grave man.*

PURPOSE, 24–25, 64, 127, 188, 241, 298, 357, 416, 475, 521 A writer's goal, or reason for writing. For example, the purpose may be to *inform* readers by explaining an important subject, such as climate change; to *persuade* readers to act, such as to combat climate change by buying more fuel-efficient cars; to *entertain* readers, such as by telling them a heart-warming story of an animal that successfully adapted to the loss of its natural habitat; or simply to *express* the writer's feelings, for example, his or her indignation about environmental damage or waste.

R

Redefining Definition (McKean), 449

RHETORIC, 491 The art of using language effectively in speech and in writing. The term originally belonged to oratory, and it implies the presence of both a speaker (or writer) and a listener (or reader). This book is a collection of the rhetorical techniques and strategies that some successful writers have found helpful for communicating effectively with an audience.

RHETORICAL QUESTION, 192 A question that is really a statement. See FIGURES OF SPEECH.

Rose, Mike, 459
Rosenberg, Michael, 578

S

Sanctuary of School, The (Barry), 177

SATIRE, 204, 612, 622 A form of writing that attacks a person or practice in hopes of improving either. For example, in "A Modest Proposal" (Chapter 13), Jonathan Swift satirizes the materialism that had reduced his native Ireland to extreme poverty. His intent was to point out the greed of many of his countrymen and thereby shame them all into looking out for the public welfare. This desire to correct vices and follies distinguishes *satire* from *sarcasm*, which is intended primarily to wound. See also IRONY.

Schmidt, Laura, 284
Se Habla Español (Barrientos), 436
Second Inaugural Address (Lincoln), 623
Sedaris, David, 227

SETTING, 123, 603 The physical place or scene in which an action or event occurs, especially important in NARRATIVE and DESCRIPTIVE writing.

Should Batman Kill the Joker? (White and Arp), 545

SIMILE, 61, 67 A COMPARISON that likens one thing to another, usually with *like* or *as*. See FIGURES OF SPEECH.

Skinner, Jeffrey, 327
Soto, Gary, 390
So, You Want to Be a Writer? Here's How. (Goodman), 322
Some Stepping-Stones to Writing Poetry (Skinner), 327
Steinbach, Alice, 96
Stop Coddling the Super-Rich (Buffett), 274
Storm Country (Crenshaw), 79
Swift, Jonathan, 612

SYLLOGISM, 525, 543 The basic form of DEDUCTIVE reasoning, in which a conclusion is drawn from a major (or wider) premise or assumption and a minor (or narrower) premise. For example, *Major premise*: All men are mortal. *Minor premise*: Socrates is a man. *Conclusion*: Socrates is mortal.

SYNONYM, 414, 419 A word or phrase that has essentially the same meaning as that of another word or phrase: for example, *make do* or *get by* for *cope*.

T

Tan, Amy, 253
Tannen, Deborah, 397
Technologically Challenged Life, My (Wunderlich), 194

THESIS, 30–31, 34, 36, 66, 129, 190, 244 The main point that a paragraph or an essay is intended to make or prove. A *thesis statement* is a direct statement of that point.

TONE, 21, 22, 529 An author's attitude toward his or her subject or audience: sympathy, longing, amusement, shock, sarcasm—the range is endless. When analyzing the tone of a passage, consider what quality of voice you would use in reading it aloud.

TOPIC SENTENCE, 37, 44–46 A sentence, often at the beginning of a paragraph, that states the paragraph's main point. The details in the rest of the paragraph should support the topic sentence.

Toxic Truth about Sugar, The (Lustig, Schmidt, and Brindis), 284

TRANSITIONS, 46–48 Connecting words or phrases—such as *next, by contrast, nevertheless, therefore, on the other hand*—that link sentences, paragraphs, and ideas in a piece of writing.

Treadway, Dan, 364
Truth, Sojourner, 627
Turning Japanese (Julavits), 155
Two Years Are Better Than Four (Addison), 534

U

UNDERSTATEMENT, 112 A verbal playing down or softening for humorous or ironic effect. See FIGURES OF SPEECH.

V

VANTAGE POINT, 68 In a DESCRIPTION, the physical perspective from which a subject is described. See the introduction to Chapter 4 for further discussion of vantage point.

View from a Bridge, A (McDonald), 90

W

Walden, Jessica, 305
Watching Oprah from Behind the Veil (Jacoby), 368
Watts, Eric A., 247
Weiss, Philip, 333
Weiss, Joanna, 222
Welte, Grace, 72
Wendel, Tim, 487
White, E. B., 114
White, Mark D., 545
Why and When We Speak Spanish in Public (Marquez), 506
Woolf, Virginia, 630
Wu, Janet, 206
Wunderlich, Monica, 194